MANAGERIAL ECONOMICS

MANAGERIAL ECONOMICS

text and cases

by

Erwin Esser Nemmers, Ph.D., S.J.D., C.P.A.

Associate Professor of Business Administration

Graduate School of Business Administration

Northwestern University

John Wiley & Sons, Inc.

New York · London

Inscribed to my brother,
Frederic Esser Nemmers,
Mathematician

Preface

This book is intended both as a complement to and a substitute for the traditional intermediate course in economic theory. Our academic program today is such that the typical college graduate with a major in economics is, unfortunately, ill-equipped to go into business after graduation. I believe this need not be. It seems likely that in the future the area which (for want of a better term) is today called managerial economics will come to be a second course in economics at least coordinate with the traditional intermediate theory course. Or, it may be that the traditional intermediate theory course will eventually include managerial economics. This book seeks to implement such a development. If managerial economics is to become part of the kit of the college major in economics and part of the graduate program in business, no better mode of exposition can be employed than case material, since the heart of managerial economics is decision making. Whatever may be the advantages of the "case method" in other fields of study, this material is absolutely essential to the study of managerial economics. I do not subscribe to the proposition that the student should be taught only micro-economic theory in a form which is not applicable in real life.

It is common in the preface of a textbook for the author to state that he is not addressing his remarks to colleagues or experts. I repeat this statement since it is particularly applicable to this book. Unless we are prepared to have a volume several times the length of this one, a selection must be made of the major areas to be included and even within any included area a selection must be made as to what will be omitted and what the emphasis will be on the aspects that are included. I can illustrate this quickly. In the section on pricing, we have included "target pricing" (that is, pricing towards a rate of return) and excluded the traditional average-cost pricing versus marginal-cost pricing discussion. I have done so for two reasons: (1) the student is much more likely to have previously explored the traditional discussion and (2) the average versus marginal conflict is covered at other points in the book (for example, in Case VI-5).

As an example of emphasis, my discussion of the graphic method of fitting additive and multiplicative predicting equations (in Part I) is about as long in pages as the balance of the pages on forecasting. This emphasis results from my experience with this topic in the classroom.

I assume that the student reader of this book has had only the first course in economics (usually taken in the sophomore year), a very elementary knowledge of accounting, and the first course in statistics.

The graphic method (as contrasted with the "mathematical" approach) permeates my approach. I have found from classroom experience that a much larger percentage of students feel "at home" with the graphic method. This, no doubt, is a consequence of the heavy emphasis on the graphic method to be found in almost all current books covering principles of economics.

The thread of capital budgeting runs through the entire book. Capital budgeting presupposes forecasting (Part I), and that is where we start. Both revenues (Part II) and outlays (Part III) must be forecast and analyzed. Pricing is towards a target rate of return (Part IV), and this may be constrained by regulation (Part V), which must be considered in the investment decision (Part VI).

I am indebted to my students in the Graduate School of Business Administration at Northwestern University not only for the classroom testing of the Case materials, but also for the very development of the basic materials for many of the situations as is appropriately acknowledged in the "industry cases." For specific situations drawn from the experience of individual companies, I am indebted to my industrial friends who have graciously admitted me into their confidence. I am indebted to Mr. J. C. Gregory of the Atlantic Refining Company for permission to include his work (Gregory's Interest Tables, pages 394–408), which is widely used by companies in practice. I am also indebted to the many copyright holders who have permitted use of their materials.

My work on this book has benefited greatly from the reading of the manuscript by Professor Myron Umbreit, Professor and Chairman of the Department of Business Economics, and Professor Donald P. Jacobs, Associate Professor of Finance, both of Northwestern University. Acknowledgment is also made to Frederic Esser Nemmers, mathematician, General Motors Corporation, for discussions of certain aspects of the manuscript. This work was begun while I was a Ford Foundation Faculty Research fellow at the University of Wisconsin and has been favored by the encouragement and released time given by Dean Richard Donham of Northwestern University.

My thanks also to the following ladies for typing services: Marian Bennett, Patricia Engelbrecht, Joan Kalisiak, Gretel Murphy, Myrtle Schultz, Eileen Velen, and Beverly Zwierzykowski.

ERWIN ESSER NEMMERS

Evanston, Illinois
February, 1962

Contents

xi

part I
Forecasting techniques

Good forecasting is vital to modern business; everyone forecasts, whether explicitly or implicitly. Perhaps the greatest single aspect which makes forecasting so important to the modern businessman is change or instability in the patterns that can be expected in the future operations of a business. Not very many years ago the businessman could foretell with considerable accuracy what products would be bought in the immediate future, what processes would be used to make them, and to a considerable degree who would supply these products to the market. To the extent that changes were occurring in any of these products, processes, or suppliers, the rate of change was generally slow enough to permit the businessman to adjust his activities without engaging in formal analysis. In consequence, he simply assumed the present situation would continue.

In recent years, particularly because of the development of communication and transportation facilities, this rate of change has accelerated. The problem of adjustment has also grown because of the increased complexity of products and processes and the greater adaptability and flexibility of competing producers in adding or dropping products or processes.

Unless some foreknowledge is available of events that are likely to transpire, the probability that the businessman is doing the right thing by continuing to do what he presently is doing is greatly reduced by these recent developments. In other words, every businessman must consider the impact of future conditions[1] on his business and must be prepared to adjust his activities to changing conditions.

[1] The word "conditions" is ambiguous. In the present frame of reference, "conditions" refers to changes in the future *values* of independent variables rather than a change in the fundamental structure or relationship of those variables.

1

CRITERIA IN CHOOSING FORECASTING METHODS

The problem of selecting a forecasting method to achieve this goal is itself an economic problem, that is, the results achievable by a forecasting method must be weighed against the costs of the method. Cost versus results, then, is the first criterion to be considered. But the results that can be achieved by a forecasting method are difficult to estimate before the cost of making the forecast has been expended. Hence the choice among available forecasting methods must be made on a priori grounds as to which method is likely to give the best results.

Second, forecasts are only as good as the degree of confidence placed in them by those who are charged with decision making and forward planning. Thus not only is it a question of results *achievable* with the forecasting method but also of results *achieved.* In part this is the problem of educating the people who will use the forecast, but there are limits to how much education is possible if the method of forecasting is so complex that the men making the decisions do not fully understand the forecasting methods, assumptions, and probabilities.

Third, the forecasting method must produce an improvement over existing practices in the accuracy of estimating the future. One of the most difficult aspects of forecasting is the determination of turning points in the cycle. For example, mere projection of an existing trend will never establish a turning point, but it may be substantially "right" between turning points.

Fourth, the longer the "lead" the forecast has before the event, the greater its value. A somewhat less accurate forecast which can be made earlier in point of time may be more valuable than a more accurate forecast which becomes available later in time. Moreover, once a basis for a forecast is found that has a sufficient "lead," further costs incurred to make it available sooner may not be warranted.

SHORT-RUN AND LONG-RUN FORECASTING

It would be arbitrary to attempt to classify forecasts according to the number of years over which the forecast extends. But if the forecast is for a short period, such as a year, the seasonal pattern of the business is frequently of major importance. Hence it is necessary to apply a seasonal index to the current level of activity even if such a simple type of forecast as projecting the present trend is used.

Furthermore, short-run forecasts may rely upon variables that are different from those of long-run forecasts. This is particularly true of forecasts for an individual company where the present status of inventories and the capacity of competitors to produce loom large. On the other hand, in long-run forecasts such conditions may prove temporary and less important than such factors as population changes or age group patterns or changes in consumption patterns of products such as beer, farm products, etc. For example, a manufacturer of baby food finds the demand for his product decreasing if the birth rate declines; "suburbia" living vitally affects the construction and house fabrication fields.

TYPES OF FORECASTING METHODS

The classification of forecasting methods is arbitrary, since any grouping will involve overlapping. Common types of forecasting may be classified under four main headings: the *projection of the present trend, opinion surveys, economic indicators,* and *model building.*

Projecting the Present Series

The projection of the present series can be achieved in a number of ways. A trend line can be fitted through the series either visually or by more refined techniques such as the familiar line of least squares presented in elementary statistics. This trend line is then extrapolated into the future. The projection of the existing series by a trend line will not, of course, indicate any turning point. If the situation involves a series which is slow to change and typically has moved in only one direction, such as population, then this method may be satisfactory. This is particularly true if consideration is given to the small expense in preparing it.

Essentially the same assumptions are involved in other types of projection which consider only the most recent data rather than a trend fitted to data over a long period of time. For example, the last two or three values of a series might be considered as setting the pattern. This is the basis of a weather forecast. Thus, the forecast for a year might be prepared on the basis of the most recent 2 or 3 months seasonally adjusted and then a seasonal index applied to this base in order to establish the forecast for the next year. This method cannot predict turning points, but between turning points it may yield highly reliable results. If the turning points develop slowly, the errors of forecast will be smaller for a given time period than if the turning points develop quickly. Also, if the turning points are spaced at long time intervals from each other, the forecast will have long periods of reliable results.

A third form of this same method involves the removal of trend and seasonal from the data, leaving the cyclical and irregular effects. A cycle can then be established from this remainder, and the forecast will include turning points. This method is covered in elementary statistics books with the familiar mnemonic notation, $O = TSCI$, where O is the original data, T the trend, S the seasonal index, C the cyclical index, and I the irregular residual. The multiplicative equation is the most common form. Trend may be established by fitting a least-squares line to the original data. The trend values are then divided out ($TSCI/T$). A seasonal index is established for the remainder and the seasonal effect divided out (SCI/S). A cycle is then fitted to this remainder. Less frequently, trend and seasonal values are *subtracted* out where the relationship is assumed to be additive. Thus $O = T + S + C + I$, the detrending process is $(T + S + C + I) - T$, and the deseasonalizing is $(S + C + I) - S$.

Thus, to illustrate with a very simple case, we assume a situation in which the actual data are:

Year	Sales in Millions
1950	$100
1951	106
1952	110
1953	108
1954	107
1955	115
1956	120
1957	126
1958	120
1959	122

A straight line of least squares fitted [2] to the data establishes the trend as Y (sales in millions) $= 101.97 + 2.54X$ (with X measured in years and origin at 1950).

The trend values computed from the equation of this line of least squares are shown in Table I-1, together with the residuals after the removal of the trend from the actual data by both the division and the subtraction methods.

In a similar manner, after a seasonal index has been computed for the data in columns 3 and 4, but with monthly figures rather than

[2] The method of fitting a line of least squares is explained in any elementary statistics book. A line of least squares fitted to a series of observations minimizes the sum of the squares of the deviations of the observations from the line.

TABLE I-1

**Hypothetical Original Annual Sales Data with Trend Removed
by Division and Subtraction**

	(1)	(2)	(3)	(4)
			Seasonal, Cyclical, and Irregular	Seasonal, Cyclical, and
	Sales in Millions	Trend Value	Residual After	Irregular Residual After
	(*TSCI* or	Computed from	Trend Divided Out	Trend Subtracted Out
Year	$T + S + C + I$)	$Y = 101.97 + 2.54X$	(*TSCI/T*)	$[(T + S + C + I) - T]$
1950	100	101.97	0.9807	−1.97
1951	106	104.51	1.0143	1.49
1952	110	107.05	1.0276	2.95
1953	108	109.59	0.9855	−1.59
1954	107	112.13	0.9542	−5.13
1955	115	114.67	1.0029	0.33
1956	120	117.21	1.0239	2.79
1957	126	119.75	1.0522	6.25
1958	120	122.29	0.9813	−2.29
1959	122	124.83	0.9773	−2.83

annual,[3] the seasonal value established by the seasonal index will be divided out (or subtracted out) of the residual containing the seasonal, cyclical, and irregular values shown in columns 3 and 4. Instead of the simplified annual data we have employed, monthly data will be used, both to establish the trend and then after dividing out (or subtracting out) the monthly trend value to get a residual (which includes seasonal, cyclical, and irregular effects), a seasonal index will be established using these residual values. Then, in turn, the seasonal effect will be eliminated by dividing the residual by the seasonal index (or subtracting from the residual the difference between the residual and the value established by the seasonal index). The figure remaining after this adjustment for the seasonal effect will then include the cyclical and irregular effects.

Then a sine curve, for example, may be fitted to the remaining data to establish the cycle. Or another function rather than a sine curve may be suggested by the remaining data.

We have proceeded far enough to see that a number of assumptions have been made. First, we have assumed that the order of removal of the effects should be first trend, then seasonal, and then cyclical. The resulting values would be affected if the order of removal were changed. Second, we have assumed that the effects are independent of

---

[3] Annual data were used rather than monthly data in this illustration of the removal of trend in order to reduce the number of observations for the 10-year period from 120 to 10.

each other, that is, that the factors determining trend are not the same as (or related to) the factors determining the cycle, for example. Third, we have assumed that trend is linear (or whatever function is fitted) and that the cycle is regular, namely, that each swing of the cycle follows the pattern of the preceding swing, that the distance between the peaks of the cycle is constant, etc.

This third form of projection from past data attempts to get at whatever cycle is in the data, but the methods of removing trend and seasonal values have been criticized on the ground that these very methods of computing induce cycles into the data when the data actually do not have such cycles. This would be particularly true when, for example, a moving average has been used.[4]

An even more discouraging aspect of this third form of projection is that it assumes that trend and cycle can be separated from each other. Both may be the result of the same set of factors. Even more of a problem is the possibility that the irregular (or random) movements may outweigh the regular (trend and/or cyclical) movements. The shorter the time periods involved, the greater the likelihood that random outweighs regular. This follows for the same reason that the smaller the sample, the greater the likelihood that the individual values are not representative of the distribution in the universe even though a larger sample has a higher probability of containing extreme values.

Opinion Surveys

Opinion surveys rest upon the assumption that future conduct depends in part on what people presently believe or presently plan for the future. To the extent that present plans are only a partial basis for future conduct and to the extent that *expected* conditions which form the groundwork for the plan *change* and hence produce changes in future conduct, the survey will be inaccurate as a forecasting tool.

Surveys of this type can be classified into *individual company studies, industry-wide studies,* and *economy-wide studies.*

The Individual Company Survey

An individual company may conduct a survey of its actual and contemplated customers either on a sample basis or by attempting to reach all in its universe. This method is exposed to several sources of error peculiar to the individual company. Where customers have alternative sources of supply they may tell the poll taker what their total future requirements are expected to be rather than the orders

---

[4] Eugene Slutsky, "The Summation of Random Causes as the Source of Cyclic Processes," *Econometrica,* vol. 5 (1936–37), pp. 105–146.

expected to be placed against the surveying company. In addition, the current (or immediate past or expected future) situation with regard to whether the market is expected to be a sellers' or a buyers' market will influence the customers' answers to the survey. In an expected shortage situation, the customer may give statements increasing his future requirements on the assumption that the cutback by rationing on the part of the supplier will give him just about the quantity he actually wants.

Instead of polling the customers, the company may poll its sales force, starting at the customer level and combining and re-evaluating by regions or divisions. But a sales force is usually assigned goals or quotas, which are often somewhat inflated to induce effort. The sales force can quickly adopt these targets as forecasts. A survey of the sales force as a basis for forecasting typically is either overoptimistic or overpessimistic in its general level, although frequently much more accurate in establishing monthly or quarterly deviations from the general level.

Another way a company can make its own survey is by polling its department heads. A company employs this method particularly when the limiting factor is not the availability of sales but a bottleneck in some functional area such as inability to produce all that can be sold or inability to finance sales or some similar limitation.

One particular area of individual company sales forecasting that has been developed more than any other area is the new product situation. Here sampling is used extensively. This process may involve intensive study of a small but carefully stratified group, or it may be the controlled type in which two markets thought to be identical and free of intermarket movement are tested with the same or different products to measure the difference in response to the same or different products.

Industry-Wide Surveys

Unless we classify surveys of capital investment programs under this heading, little has been done on industry-wide surveys as a basis for forecasting. Some trade associations perform annual surveys and issue annual forecasts on the basis of polls, however. For example, the Edison Electric Institute, working with the trade journal *Electrical World*, conducts surveys of the plans of the electric power utilities and translates these plans into specific forecasts for generating, transmission, and distribution expenditures for both equipment and its installation.

The Survey Research Center of the University of Michigan has done considerable survey work in the field of consumer finance particularly with reference to consumer durables (such as automobiles and household appliances) and housing.[5] To date the results of this program have not been as promising as the model building procedure to be discussed later but are effective when used with a model. On re-interviews (within the period of the plans that were the subject of the initial interviews) many people cannot even remember that they were interviewed previously, much less what were the expectations they stated at the time of the interview. Model building which seeks the basic demand determinants for a particular good in such factors as incomes, age groups, price, replacement time (average age), population, and temperature has been able to predict what people will do more accurately than opinion surveys. This suggests that many buyers do not recognize the factors which determine their own decisions. Thus instead of recognizing that a decline in income is responsible for a deferred purchase, the individual may rationalize the decision by stating he dislikes the new model.

Economy-Wide Surveys

In the area of economy-wide surveys, the poll seeks a basis for forecasting broad economic categories such as business investment and expenditures, inventory movements, or even general economic conditions.

Two prominent illustrations are the McGraw-Hill and the Department of Commerce-Securities and Exchange Commission[6] annual surveys of planned business investment. The Department of Commerce-Securities and Exchange Commission also has a quarterly survey. The McGraw-Hill survey covers less than 500 companies, but these account for 60 per cent of the investment by the major capital using industries. The government surveys cover 2,500 companies. These surveys have proven reasonably accurate with the exception of the effects of such unpredictable events as the Korean War. The accuracy of the government survey is shown in Figure I-1, giving the results of 10 years of the survey against the actual facts as they developed. One particular reason why surveys of planned investment during the next year are likely to prove accurate is that investment decisions once made are not as easily reversed as production decisions. The execution

---

[5] The results of these surveys have appeared in the issues of the *Federal Reserve Bulletin*. For examples of case studies in forecasting, see Oscar Goodman, *Sales Forecasting* (Madison, Wis.: Bureau of Business Research, University of Wisconsin, 1954).

[6] The McGraw-Hill annual study appears in *Business Week*. The Department of Commerce–Securities and Exchange Commission annual survey is published in the *Survey of Current Business*. Mention should also be made of the annual survey by the National Industrial Conference Board appearing in *Newsweek*.

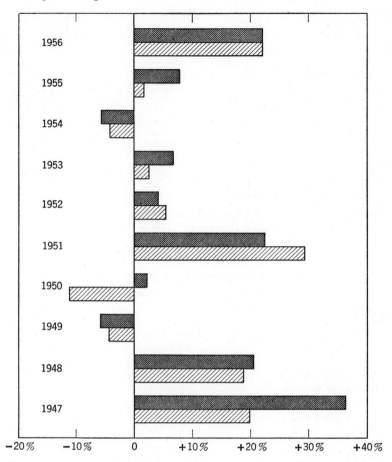

Figure I-1. Comparison of government forecast (cross-hatch bars) and actual (solid black bars) per cent change in business investment over previous year. (From *Survey of Current Business,* January 1957, p. 16.)

of such decisions typically requires a long period of time. Thus if such a survey of business investment plans were undertaken for a 5-year period rather than for a 1-year period, the accuracy would decrease and would approach that of an annual survey of consumer expenditures.

The importance of these surveys of business investment plans to forecasting in the capital goods producing industries is obvious. Moreover, the survey of business investment plans is also extremely important for forecasting the national income or gross national product because the relative amplitude of the change in business investment from year to year is much greater than that of the change in consumer expenditures, for example. Investment decisions are more volatile and hence, harder to predict.

Economic Indicators

Another approach to forecasting that has received extensive attention is the use of economic indicators. This approach can be broadly classified as involving (1) the lead-lag technique and (2) the diffusion index and the pressure index.

Lead-Lag Technique

In the lead-lag technique, an economic series is sought which consistently leads the series whose forecast is being undertaken. The outstanding work in this area has been that of G. H. Moore and the National Bureau of Economic Research.[7] The "lead" which the indicating series has will vary with the stage of the business cycle. Typically, the leading series has one lead time during periods of revival and another and different lead time during periods of recession.

For example, Moore found the average lead time of indicators as follows:

Indicator	Lead at Peak of Cycle	Lead at Trough of Cycle
Pig iron production	2.0 months	3.0 months
Average hours worked per week	3.8 months	2.6 months
Business failures and liabilities	10.5 months	7.5 months
Bureau of Labor Statistics index of wholesale prices	2.6 months	3.2 months

Moore's work is particularly directed at forecasting the business cycle. However, the same technique is often applicable to a particular industry and often with a greater degree of accuracy than the survey technique. Difficulty arises in forecasting for those industries which are themselves leaders of the general business cycle, such as the construc-

[7] G. H. Moore, *Statistical Indicators of Cyclical Revivals and Recessions,* Occasional Paper 31 (New York: National Bureau of Economic Research, 1950) and *Business Cycle Indicators,* 2 vols. (New York: National Bureau of Economic Research, 1961). Another important contribution is Julius Shiskin, *Signals of Recession and Recovery,* Occasional Paper 77 (New York: National Bureau of Economic Research, 1961). The Bureau of Census, Department of Commerce began the monthly publication, *Business Cycle Developments,* in October, 1961. Mention must also be made of the older monthly publication by the Joint Economic Committee, *Economic Indicators.*

tion industry, unless one is prepared to assume that the leader of a cycle bears a set relation to a series lagging in the prior cycle. Since these industries are typically capital goods producing, the other survey techniques already discussed are usually more fruitful than an effort to use indicators.

It is particularly helpful in the lead-lag technique, to employ several indicators. In this way, "confirmation" of the movement of one indicator can be sought from the others. Since no indicator performs with perfect reliability, "random" movements of one indicator can be detected in this way.

Lag indicators are as important as lead indicators. "Confirmation" of a turning point indicated by a lead indicator can be sought from the lag indicator. For example, suppose that we have a lead indicator such as residential housing starts which leads by a year the series we are investigating, say, distribution transformers. Suppose that the lead indicator has been going up for two years. Suppose further that a lag indicator such as power sales has correlated well with the series of distribution transformer sales by a lag of 6 months. Then, when residential housing starts begin a downward movement, the lag indicator may "confirm" this movement when it starts down.

Diffusion and Pressure Index Techniques

Closely allied to the lead-lag technique is the diffusion index technique, also developed by Moore, and the pressure index technique. There are actually two separate concepts involved. The first may be called the diffusion index and measures the time spread of the movement among indicators as first one indicator, for example, moves up, then others, but at varying intervals of time. Thus, in Figure I-2, we have a diffusion index showing the path of the percentage of eight leading series that are expanding from 1947 through 1954. In general, as the percentage of indicators rising reaches 25 per cent, the trough is indicated and as the percentage reaches 75 per cent, a peak is indicated. Note that in Figure I-2, leading indicators were used and hence the diffusion index is in *advance* of the cycle. Thus the diffusion index may be taken as indicating the turning point with greater reliability than would any one of the component series individually.

Another separate proposition is the pressure index concept. In addition to what has already been stated about the diffusion index, it may be taken as an hypothesis that the diffusion index should also be considered as a pressure index. This is the proposition that, much like Newton's law that every action has an equal and opposite reaction, the diffusion index is to be taken as establishing the amplitude of the current deviation as a measure of the pressure being built up for a

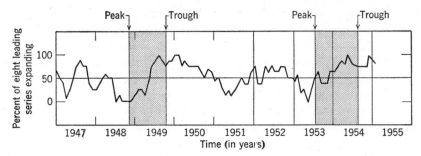

Figure I-2. Diffusion index of Business Indicators, 1947–1955. The eight leading series used are: the liabilities of business failures, industrial stock prices, new orders of durable goods manufacturers, residential construction contracts, commercial and industrial construction contracts, average work week in manufacturing, number of new incorporations, and basic prices. All series except the second and the last are seasonally adjusted. The index is computed from directions of change in centered moving averages applied to each seasonally adjusted indicator; the number of rising indicators is taken as a percentage of the total number in the group. Shaded areas represent business cycle contractions (November 1948 through October 1949 and July 1953 through August 1954); unshaded areas represent expansions. (*Source:* National Bureau of Economic Research as presented by G. H. Moore in an address in Chicago.)

future deviation in the opposite direction which will depart as much from the reference point (and in the opposite direction) as the present deviation.

A diffusion index may be recognized as a measure of the turning points and as a measure of the degree of certainty as to the direction of the business cycle without becoming involved with the hypothesis that the pressure being built up will produce an opposite movement of equal intensity.

In current industry forecasting, various types of pressure indices have been devised. One important pressure index being used is the ratio of (*a*) the raw material inventory available to an industry to (*b*) new orders for finished goods making heavy use of that raw material. This pressure index can be employed to predict the price of the raw material. In this case, close attention must be given to the ability of the raw material producers to alter the flow of the raw material quickly since the pressure will disappear if the supplying industry can speedily alter its rate of production.

Model Building

The last type of forecasting technique to be discussed is model building, a part of the area called econometrics which may be defined as the science of establishing the mathematical or statistical relationship existing between a number of economic variables. A model or hypothesis as to the assumed relationships between the economic variables is constructed. Then economic measurements are applied to each variable and the degree of relationship is determined. In the case of forecasting, model building seeks the basic demand determinants for the product, such as income and price of the good. Once the relevant demand determinants are identified, the precise relationship of each determinant to the demand for the product is investigated.

The lead-lag technique already discussed can be considered as a very simple model, namely, that the two variables (the indicating series and the series being forecast) are unit for unit related with a fixed time gap (or a time gap that varies in a consistent pattern). However, instead of a theory of such a simple relationship which may have a large margin of error, we may hypothesize either (1) that the relationship involves not just two variables, but three or more; or (2) that the relationship is not unit for unit but follows, for example, an accumulative pattern such that as there is a change of one unit in the leading series there is a change of more than one unit (or less) in the series being forecast.

At the outset it is important to establish certain points clearly. The method of proceeding makes extensive use of the concept of probability. Thus on the basis of a finite sample of information we attempt to infer the relationship which is most likely to exist in the entire population or universe. In order to proceed in this manner it is helpful if each observation or value in a series be independent of other values in the same series. This is an important condition and is usually described by the term "random" or "stochastic." In dealing with a company's sales history over time, the values for each year's sales may not be entirely independent of the preceding year's sales. To the extent that this independence is missing the use of techniques of analysis assuming independence will result in error, and it will be necessary to use techniques which deal with the situation where such independence is missing.[8]

A corollary of this concept of probability and independence is the notion that any forecast or estimate of a single future value is the prediction of that value which is most likely to develop.

As this point it should be noted that when we state the variables are independent, we actually mean that the relationship is no more than "one way." Thus the "lead" variable may or may not exert causation on the following variables, but not vice versa.

[8] The matter of testing for independence in variables will be discussed later in this part beginning at the heading "Multicollinearity."

Reverting to the initial situation (in which no interrelation is assumed), we could then say that we start from the situation in which one variable is dependent on another such that: $Y = f(X)$. This is, of course, read as "Y is a function of X." Thus Y, the number of housing starts per year, might be a function of (that is, have a stable relation to) X where X is the number of households formed.

We could then analyze the situation by the use of a least-squares line. Our purpose is to establish the most probable relation between two variables. The equation of the line of least squares will establish the values (or weights) which are to be applied to X (the independent variable whose values are known) in order to give the most likely value for Y (the dependent variable whose values will be predicted by the equation).

If the relationship is linear, the equation will take the form, $Y = a + bX$, in which a and b are constants with a being the "Y intercept" or the value of Y when X is zero, and b being the slope of the line ($\Delta Y/\Delta X$, or the change in Y that is associated with a given change in X).

Thus if the equation is $Y = 0.2 + X$ and Y is in terms of hundreds of thousands of new housing starts and X is in terms of hundreds of thousands of new households formed and if we know (or expect) that in a given year 400,000 new households will be formed, then we expect (from substituting 4 for X in the equation) that 420,000 new housing starts will be undertaken.

If the relationship is curvilinear, the most common type for business data is parabolic and the equation is $Y = a + bX + cX^2$ with c, the constant, related to the curvature of the curve, and a the Y intercept (as in the case of a straight line) and b the slope (as in the case of a straight line) except that it is the slope at the Y intercept.

These equations are known as "predicting equations," since if the value of X is given the most likely value of Y can be predicted by substituting the value of X in the equation.

In connection with the predicting equation, we can apply the standard error estimate[9] as a measure of the margin of error in our

---

[9] The standard error of estimate (also called the root mean square) is:

$$Sy = \sqrt{(Y - Y_c)^2/N - M}$$

where Y is the actual value of an item in the series and Y_c is the value computed by substituting the X value of that item in the equation of the line of least squares. N is the number of items. Adjustment is required to deal with the matter of degrees of freedom as more explanatory variables are added where the series includes less than about sixty observations. This is recognized by M, the number forecast. The standard error of estimate establishes the range (either side of the line of least squares) within which there is a 67 per cent probability that any actual observation of Y will fall.[10] Double the standard error of estimate increases this probability to about 95 per cent and triple the standard error to about 99 per cent.

When we are concerned with a relationship such that the predicted variable depends on two or more variables, we are involved with multiple correlation.

GRAPHIC MULTIPLE CORRELATION[11]

Multiple correlation can be conveniently dealt with graphically rather than by the standard method available in statistics books. The graphic method has two advantages: it saves in time of computation if computing machinery is not available, and it is a procedure which is more meaningful to those who are less mathematically inclined.[12]

A simple illustration, followed step by step, should clarify matters

---

of constants in the equation, that is, the number of a and b terms. It should be remembered that the correction for the degrees of freedom assumes that the sample is random. There frequently is serious question whether this condition exists but economists cavalierly assume it does.

[10] Assuming that the values of Y are normally distributed.

[11] This short section reflects much of the thinking found in Wilfred Malenbaum and John D. Black, "The Use of the Short-Cut Graphic Method of Multiple Correlation," *Quarterly Journal of Economics*, vol. 52 (1937–1938), pp. 66–112.

[12] A classic statement of the advantages of graphic multiple correlation is set forth by Joel Dean in his *Managerial Economics* (Englewood Cliffs, N.J.: Prentice-Hall, 1951) at p. 172: "Although multiple correlation is itself an involved and expensive operation, the principle can be used on a more modest scale by graphic correlation, which gives fairly good approximations and is accessible to anyone with paper, pencil and *an eye for curves*. One virtue of the graphic method is that it needs no algebraic form, and the analyst has a free hand to choose the shape of the functions. He is liberated from the simple types of formulas that must be used in full correlation analysis, which are a travesty of the vast and intricate (if not impersonal) forces of the marketplace. But this virtue is also a peril, because there is usually a temptation to let the curve wiggle at will so long as it follows the dot and thus pick up many accidental historical variations as significant relations."

Because from classroom experience we have found that it takes a good deal more than "an eye for curves" for most students to do graphic multiple correlation we have set down in the following pages the details for the steps used for graphic multiple correlation in both the additive and multiplicative forms. It should be added that Dean's statement in the above quotation about the expense of multiple correlation antedates today's widespread availability of computing machinery.

considerably even for those with a minimum of statistical and mathematical background.

We will illustrate the graphic procedure for establishing a predicting equation in two forms: the additive and the multiplicative. The additive equation follows the general form:

$$Y = a + bX + cZ + \cdots + mR$$

In this case Y, the variable being predicted, is stated as determined by a, a constant, plus the product of b, a constant, times the value of X (the first independent variable) plus the product of c, a constant, times the value of Z (the second variable). If there are more than two independent variables, the process continues.

The multiplicative equation follows the general form:

$$Y = aX^bZ^c \cdots R^m$$

In this case Y, the variable being predicted, is stated as determined by the product of a, a constant, times X (the first independent variable) raised to the power b and times Z (the second independent variable) raised to the power c. If there are more than two independent variables, the process continues.

In the following illustration, the data of the first three columns of Table I-2 will be analyzed graphically, first to establish an additive form of predicting equation and then to establish a multiplicative form.

The Predicting Equation in Additive Form

Table I-2 presents data for a 10-year period on the sales pattern of the residential central air conditioning industry (Y) together with two independent variables, new housing starts, (X), and per capita income of the total population in constant dollars, (Z). The problem is to establish the likelihood that these two variables have a relationship to the sales of the industry. We are thus examining the hypothesis that $Y = f(X, Z)$, namely that Y is a function of X and Z.

In this case we are using hypothetical historical data. However, cross-sectional data or data developed from controlled experiments can be handled in the same way. Historical data are readings taken at different intervals over a period of time. We are assuming each value of Y is independent of other values of Y in the series. Cross-sectional data, on the other hand, consider variations in consumption by individuals or families or geographical areas at the *same* point in time but separated by differences in geography, income or some other variable.

Both residential air conditioning sales (Y) and new housing starts

TABLE I-2

The Predicting Equation in Additive Form*

	(1) Residential Central Air Conditioning Sales in Thousands of Units Y	(2) New Housing Starts in tens of Thousands of Units X	(3) Income Per Capita in Tens of Constant Dollars Z	(4) Sales Estimated from Line in Chart I-1 $Y_x = 62 + 0.52X$	(5) Deviation of Actual Sales from Estimated Sales in Chart I, = 1 Column 1 minus 4. Plotted in Chart I-3 against Income	(6) Estimated Sales with Income Held Constant: $Y - (-30 + 0.26Z)$ Plotted in Chart I-4 against X	(7) Sales Estimated from Housing Starts and Income $Y = 40 + 0.44X + 0.26Z$ Chart I-5	(8) Actual Sales Less Estimated Sales Column 1 minus 7
Year 1	139	144	140	137	2	132.6	139.8	−0.8
Year 2	93	88	50	108	−15	110.0	91.7	1.3
Year 3	112	98	122	113	−1	110.3	114.8	−2.8
Year 4	111	83	120	105	6	109.8	107.7	3.3
Year 5	122	83	175	105	17	106.5	122.0	0.0
Year 6	133	133	138	131	2	127.1	134.4	−1.4
Year 7	128	111	126	120	8	125.2	121.6	6.4
Year 8	104	86	100	107	−3	108.0	103.8	0.2
Year 9	121	107	130	118	3	117.2	120.9	−0.1
Year 10	120	136	75	133	−13	130.5	119.3	0.7
Total:	1183	1069	1176		6			+7.0
Arithmetic mean:	118	107	117.6		0.6	118.0		

* The data in this table are hypothetical. Columns 1, 2, and 3 state the given data. Columns 4 through 8 are computed from columns 1, 2, and 3.

are expressed in *physical* units. However, income (Z) is expressed in *monetary* units. In order to eliminate the effect of changes in the price level, income (Z) has already been adjusted by a price index.[13] This adjustment makes monetary units comparable with physical units.

The income data have further been adjusted to a per capita basis to allow for changes in population. This adjustment might be questioned. Why should not units of sales (Y) and units of new housing starts (X) be likewise so adjusted? Here we are *supposing* that population changes affect units of sales of central air conditioning, new housing starts, and income in different ways. If population changes affect each of the three variables (air conditioning sales, new housing starts and income) in the same way, we would have used total income rather than per capita income.

Our supposition may be in error and it may be that income per family or even total income of individuals will give us a better relationship than per capita income. One approach is to use each (per capita income, income per family and total income) in turn and select the one which gives the highest correlation coefficient and the lowest standard error of the coefficient of each term in the regression equation.

Columns 1, 2 and 3 of Table I-2 give us the three series we are examining. Columns 4 through 8 are computed from these series.

Explanation of Chart I-1

In graphic multiple correlation we use scatter diagrams such as those in Charts I-1, I-2, I-3, and I-4. Chart I-1 shows the data of columns 1 and 2 of Table I-2 plotted on a scatter diagram with air conditioner sales (Y) on the vertical axis and new housing starts (X) on the horizontal axis. Each point is labeled with the applicable year to facilitate our computation. The arithmetic mean of each series appears at the foot of columns 1, 2, and 3. The arithmetic mean of the sales series and new housing starts series is then plotted as a single point and indicated by an X on the scatter diagram.

A regression line is now passed visually through the points in Chart I-1. The line, if straight, must go through the arithmetic means indicated by X on the graph. The slope of the line should be such that approximately the same number of plotted points are above and below this line with due regard to the fact that plotted points further from the line are to be given greater weight than plotted points closer to the line (because squaring of each deviation from the line is involved).

[13] This adjustment involves dividing the income figure of each year in current dollars by the price index of that year. When this is done, the series will be in constant dollars of the same purchasing power as the dollars of the base year of the index.

CHART I-1

Regression of Y (Air Conditioner Sales) on X (New Houses Started), Using a Straight Line—Column 1 of Table I-2 against Column 2 of Table I-2 (Equation: $Y_x = 62 + 0.52X$)

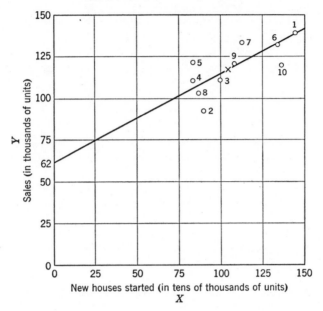

The purpose is to approximate that line of least squares that would minimize the sum of the squares of the vertical deviations of the plotted points from the line.

In this process we are assuming that the differences in the Y value are associated only with the differences in the X values. In statistical terms, we are assuming that the influence of Z is being held statistically constant. Since this is not so, we are getting only an approximation. The error involved in so doing is partially corrected in the next step when a line is passed through the Y deviations plotted against the Z values. In this step X is being held statistically constant. The remaining error will be further reduced when, in Chart I-4 we return to the procedure of Chart I-1 but with Z held statistically constant. Two lines of least squares exist: one minimizing the sum of the squares of the vertical deviations of the plotted points from the line and the other minimizing the sum of the squares of the horizontal deviations of the plotted points. The line in Chart I-1 minimizes the sum of the squares of the vertical deviations.

The equation of the regression line in Chart I-1 can easily be

CHART I-2

Regression of Y (Air Conditioner Sales) on X (New Houses Started), Using a Parabola—Column 1 of Table I-2 Against Column 2 of Table I-2 (Equation: $Y = 130 + 0.46X_1 + 0.005X_1^2$)

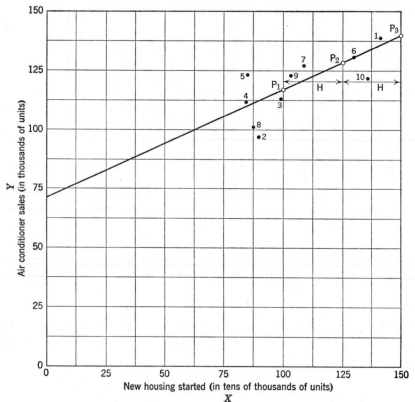

established. The general form of the equation of a straight line is $Y = a + bX$, in which a is the Y intercept (value of Y when X is zero) and b is the slope of the line. The Y intercept is approximately 62 and the slope of the line (change in Y associated with change in X) is about 0.52. Hence the equation is $Y = 62 + 0.52X$. We designate Y in this equation as Y_x, because the equation shows the relation of Y to X only. If this had been the case of Y being the air conditioner sales in units and X the price per unit, then the points would have been such that the line would have had a negative slope.

Explanation of Chart I-2

Although in Chart I-1 we have shown a straight line as the most appropriate fit, a curved line can be used when the plotted points so indicate. A curved line would not, however, pass through the arithmetic means. Some difficulty may be experienced in establishing the equation for the curved line. However, the most usual curved line is a parabola and the equation of a parabola can be readily approximated. The general form of a parabola is $Y = a + bX + cX^2$. Take three points on a visually fitted parabola such that the *horizontal* distances are equal between points 1 and 2 and between points 2 and 3. This has been done in Chart I-2. Then, labeling the points from left to right (P_1, P_2, and P_3), we can get the "a" value for the general form of parabola equation as the vertical reading of point 2 (here 130). This is the Y intercept transformed. By "transformed," we mean we will proceed as if the Y-axis passed through point 2. This is where $X = 125$. The "b" value is the vertical reading of point 3 less the vertical reading of point 1 divided by the horizontal distance from point 1 to point 3. On Chart I-2 this is $(140 - 117)/50 = 0.46$. The "c" value is the vertical reading of point 1 plus the vertical reading of point 3, and from this sum deduct double the vertical reading of point 2 and divide this difference by double the square of the horizontal distance from point 1 to point 2.[14] On Chart I-2 this is $[(117 + 140) - (2 \times 125)]/2(25)^2 = 0.005$. To summarize, the equation of the curve by this estimate is $Y = 130 + 0.46X_1 + 0.005X_1^2$.[15] Note that we have used X_1 in the equation since the X values must be adjusted by deducting 125 from each X value because of the transformation of the Y-axis from $X = 0$ to $X = 125$. Furthermore, the a value in the transformed equation is 130, rather than the 70 value of a in the untransformed equation, as appears in Chart I-2. The equation of the curve, fitted by least squares, is $Y = 70.8 + 0.44X + 0.00004X^2$.

The regression line (as in Chart I-1) then is the average relation between sales of residential central air conditioning units (Y) and new

---

[14] In equation form: $a = P_2$ (the transformed Y intercept)

$$b = \frac{P_3 - P_1}{2H}$$

$$c = [P_1 + P_3 - 2P_2]/2H^2$$

Where P indicates the vertical reading of each point identified in the text above and H indicates the horizontal distance from P_1 to P_2.

[15] In the case of a parabola, it is extremely dangerous to extrapolate the curve outside the range of the data except for short distances. This particular parabola has only slight curvature, and the visual fit might have erred by employing too much curvature. The data of Table I-2 are being employed for several fittings: first for the straight lines of Charts I-1, I-3, and I-4 and later for the logarithmic straight lines in Charts I-6 and I-7, as well as for the parabola just discussed. In a case where the parabola is more appropriate, the curvature will be easier to identify than in the present illustration.

CHART I-3

Regression of Unexplained Air Conditioner Sales Deviations (From Regression Line in Chart I-1) on Z (Per Capita Income)—Column 5 of Table I-2 Against Column 3 of Table I-2 (Equation: $Y_z = -30 + 0.26Z$)

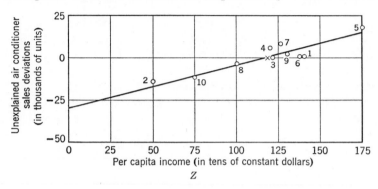

housing starts (X). This average relationship is recorded in column 4 of Table I-2 and is established either by reading from the line the Y values that go with each X value or by setting each X value in the equation and solving for Y. The deviations of the plotted points from the line show the extent to which housing starts do not explain the sales of residential air conditioning units. These deviations of the plotted points of Chart I-1 from the regression line (such deviations being measured vertically and with a plus sign if they are above the regression line and a minus sign if they are below the regression line) are attributable to income variations and other unknown variables (including mere random variations and errors in the data, etc.). These deviations are recorded in column 5 of Table I-2, and may be computed by vertical readings of Chart I-1 from each point to the regression line or simply by substracting the value in column 4 from the value in column 1 of Table I-2.

Explanation of Chart I-3

These (as yet) unexplained deviations of column 5 (Table I-2) are now to be examined for the relationship that income has to sales. This is done in Chart I-3, where the (as yet) unexplained deviations of sales from the regression line of Chart I-1 are scaled on the vertical axis, and income per capita in constant dollars (Z) is scaled on the horizontal axis. The points determined by income (column 3 of Table I-2) and these (as yet) unexplained deviations (column 5 of Table I-2) are now plotted and each point identified with its year. The arithmetic mean of the deviations is taken to be zero,[16] and this is plotted as a point with the arithmetic mean of the income series ($117.6) and marked with an X as in Chart I-3.

Again a regression line is passed through the points in Chart I-3, just as in the case of Chart I-1. Again the line (if a straight line) must go through the arithmetic means indicated by X on the graph. And again, the slope of the line should be such that approximately the same number of plotted points are above and below the line with due regard to the fact that plotted points further from the line are to be given greater weight than plotted points closer to the line.

As with the line in Chart I-1, the equation of the line in Chart I-3 can be established as $Y_z = -30 + 0.26Z$ with the Y intercept as -30, and the slope of the line 0.26. Again, we designate Y in this equation as Y_z, because the equation shows the relation of Y deviations of the first equation to Z.

The regression line in Chart I-3 shows the relation between sales of residential central air conditioning units and per capita income in constant dollars after allowance is made for the first estimate of the effect of new housing starts on such sales.

Again, the regression line of Chart I-3 might be a curved rather than a straight line. In this case all the remarks already made about the curved line in Chart I-2 apply.

Column 6 records the estimate of sales with income held constant. Thus column 6 is the adjusted value determined by adjusting the Y value of column 1 for the influence of income which was established in Chart I-3 as $-30 + 0.26Z$.

Explanation of Chart I-4

The adjusted Y values of column 6 of Table I-2 are then plotted in Chart I-4 against the X values of column 2 (new housing starts) to get the relationship of sales (Y) to new housing starts (X) when income (Z) is held constant. The regression line of Chart I-4 establishes this relationship as $Y_x = 70 + 0.44X$.

The question may occur to the reader that the analysis is influenced by which independent variable $(X$ or $Z)$ is taken first. We took X first, but the answer would be about the same for X if Z had been analyzed first. It is customary, however, to examine first the more significant variable. Which is the more significant can quickly be

---

[16] In Table I-2, this mean is actually 0.6, but this is because of the inaccuracies of reading off of Chart I-1 and the inaccuracy in determining the right regression line. If the value of this mean turns out to be large, it means that the regression line used is in large error as to its slope.

CHART I-4

Adjustment of Error in Chart I—Column 6 of Table I-2 Against Column 2 of Table I-2

(Equation: $Y_x = 70 + 0.44X$)

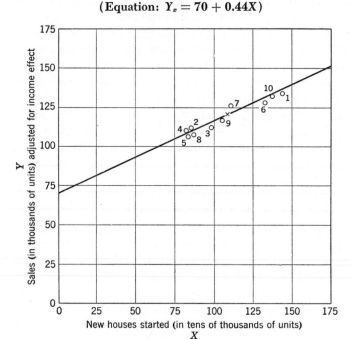

determined by making two scatter diagrams the same as Chart I-1 (one for X and Y, and one for Z and Y). That diagram on which the plotted points show a pattern more clearly conforming to a straight line or curve indicates which independent variable (X or Z) is more significant.

Explanation of Chart I-5

We are now ready to make a forecast. Column 7 in Table I-2 records the air conditioner sales as determined by the average relationship of such sales to new housing starts combined with per capita income in constant dollars as estimated from the predicting equation which we can now state. This equation is established by combining the terms of the equations of Charts I-3 and I-4:

$$Y_x = 70 + 0.44X \qquad \text{(Equation of Chart I-4)}$$
$$Y_z = -30 + 0.26Z \qquad \text{(Equation of Chart I-3)}$$
$$Y = 40 + 0.44X + 0.26Z \qquad \text{(Combined)}$$

The sizes of the coefficients of the independent variables tell us the relative importance of changes in the variables, provided the units of the independent variables are of the same order of magnitude (which is true here). Thus in the present case, changes in units of X (new housing starts) are more important than changes in units of Z (income).

By substituting the X and Z values of any year in the equation $Y = 40 + 0.44X + 0.26Z$, we get the Y value shown in column 7 of Table I-2.

Chart I-5 plots the air conditioner sales as predicted by this equation (and as computed in column 7 of Table I-2) alongside the actual sales (from column 1).

Then, to forecast for any future years, we simply substitute the X and Z values of such years in the equation to get the predicted Y value. Thus if, in a future year, we expect new housing starts to be 1.5

CHART I-5

Actual (Solid Line) and Estimated (Broken Line) Air Conditioner Sales for 10 Years—Columns 1 and 7, Respectively, of Table I-2 (Equation: $Y = 40 + 0.44X + 0.26Z$)

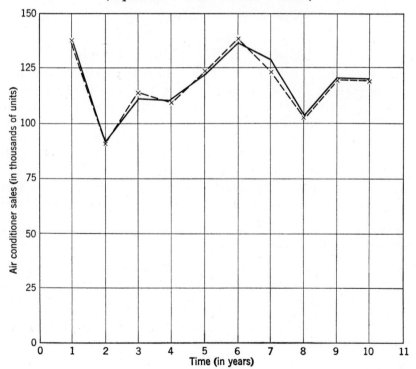

million and per capita income in constant dollars to be $1,500, the forecast for sales (from substituting in the predicting equation) is 145,000 units.[17]

Column 8 in Table I-2 shows the deviation of actual residential air conditioning sales (column 1) from the sales figures as estimated (column 7) from the relationships we have established of such sales to new housing starts and per capita income in constant dollars. This deviation is the unexplained variation finally remaining. The coefficient of multiple determination (R^2) enables us to measure just how much the explained and unexplained variation is. The standard formula for the explained variation is:[18]

$$R^2 = 1 - \left[\frac{\Sigma(d^2)}{\Sigma(Y^2) - (\Sigma Y/N)^2 N} \right] \cdot \left[\frac{N-1}{N-M} \right]$$

where Σ = the sum of
  d = the deviation of the actual sales from the estimated (column 8)
  N = number of observations
  Y = the actual sales
  M = the number of constants in the multiple regression equation

In our case substituting yields:

$$R^2 = 1 - \left[\frac{64.5}{141,649 - [(1183/10)^2]10} \right] \cdot \left[\frac{10-1}{10-3} \right] = 0.951$$

In this instance data was used for a 10-year period. The use of a 20-year period is preferred since the error from the size of the sample is thereby considerably reduced. However, there often are situations (as with new products and industries) where the entire history does not extend over 10 years. Or there are situations in which the economic or technological changes over a twenty year period (as they apply to the problem being investigated) are so severe[19] that the error of a sample involving a smaller number of years is likely to be less than the error introduced by assuming *ceteris paribus* (other things being

---

[17] The estimate is, of course, subject to a standard error of estimate, which is 3.05 thousand in the present case, namely:

$$\sqrt{\Sigma(\text{deviations in column 8 of Table I-2})^2/10 - 3}$$

[18] For a more complete presentation of the computation of the coefficient of multiple determination, see Mordecai Ezekiel and Karl A. Fox, *Methods of Correlation and Regression Analysis*, 3rd ed. (New York: Wiley, 1959).

[19] For example, a radical shift in demand for the product being analyzed with the shift originating in a major change of tastes.

equal) about the impact of the variables not included in the study, such as product change.

The entire preceding graphic fit of the three variables was done first and then the result checked for accuracy by using an IBM-650 computer. The results are:

Graphically fitted equation: $Y = 40 + 0.44X + 0.26Z$ with standard error of estimate of 3.1.

IBM-650 computed equation:[20] $Y = 43.9 + 0.42X + 0.25Z$ with standard error of estimate of 2.4.

The Predicting Equation in Multiplicative Form

In Table I-3 we have for convenience restated the assumed data of the first three columns of Table I-2.

In developing a predicting equation in multiplicative form, the process used in establishing a predicting equation in additive form is largely repeated except that a graph of logarithmic paper on both axes is used rather than a graph of arithmetic paper.[21] As will be explained in Part II, elasticity may be determined directly as the slope of a straight line fitted to data plotted on logarithmic paper. Hence when a predicting equation is in the multiplicative form, the exponent of each independent variable will be its elasticity. Thus in the case of the data in Table I-3, if the multiplicative predicting equation is established as

$$Y = 5.5X^{0.433}Z^{0.221}$$

a change of 1 per cent in X is associated with a change of 0.433 per cent in Y and a change of 1 per cent in Z is associated with a change of 0.221 per cent in Y. The establishment of these elasticities is one of the chief reasons for analyzing the data in terms of a multiplicative predicting equation rather than an additive predictive equation.

The Use of Double Logarithmic Paper

By using double logarithmic paper instead of arithmetic paper, we can plot the points directly with the same effect as if logarithms of the points had been plotted on arithmetic paper. In the case of the general form of the equation we seek to fit, namely, $Y = aX^bZ^c$, the equation can be stated in logarithmic form, as $\log Y = \log a + b \log X + c \log Z$. If we would proceed to duplicate the process of the fitting of the additive predicting equation demonstrated above with Table

---

[20] Using program developed by Northwestern University Computing Center.

[21] Instead of using paper that is scaled logarithmically, one may also use paper scaled arithmetically, and plot the points in logarithms rather than natural numbers.

TABLE I-3

Data and Computations to Fit Multiplicative Equation $Y = aX^bZ^c$

Year	(1) Y*	(2) X†	(3) Z‡	(4) $X^{0.645}$	(5) $\dfrac{Y}{X^{0.645}}$	(6) $Z^{0.289}$	(7) $\dfrac{Y}{Z^{0.289}}$	(8) $X^{0.433}$	(9) $\dfrac{Y}{X^{0.433}}$	(10) $Z^{0.221}$	(11) Y Computed 5.5 times column (8)·(10)	(12) Y Actual minus Y Computed, column 1 minus column 11
1	139	144	140	24.6	5.65	4.17	33.3	8.60	16.15	16.4	141	−2
2	93	88	50	17.9	5.20	3.10	30.0	6.97	13.33	13.1	91.3	2
3	112	98	122	19.2	5.83	4.01	27.9	7.29	15.37	15.9	115.9	−4
4	111	83	120	17.3	6.42	4.00	27.7	6.78	16.37	15.8	107.1	4
5	122	83	175	17.3	7.05	4.45	27.4	6.78	18.00	17.1	115.8	6
6	133	133	138	23.5	5.66	4.16	31.9	8.32	15.97	16.4	136.5	−3
7	128	111	126	20.9	6.12	4.05	31.5	7.72	16.56	16.0	123.5	4
8	104	86	100	17.6	5.91	3.78	27.5	6.89	15.08	15.25	105.1	−1
9	121	107	130	20.4	5.93	4.08	29.6	7.59	15.93	16.1	122.1	−1
10	120	136	75	23.8	5.04	3.48	34.4	8.41	14.25	14.25	119.9	0
Total												+5

* Residential air conditioning sales in thousands of units.
† New housing starts in tens of thousands of units.
‡ Income per capita in tens of constant dollars.

I-2 and Charts I-1, I-3, and I-4 in all respects except that we use double logarithmic paper instead of arthmetic paper, we would develop equations of the form

$$Y_x = aX^b$$
$$Y_s = dZ^c$$

and combining them will yield

$$Y = aX^b + dX^c$$

This, however, is not the form of equation we desire because of the presence of the plus sign between the two terms whereas we seek a multiplication sign at that point.

To overcome this problem, we will make one change in the process of graphic fitting used in the case of the additive predicting equation (in addition to substituting double logarithmic paper for arithmetic paper). This change will be to divide out (rather than to subtract out as in Table I-2, column 5) the average relationship between Y (the dependent variable) and X (the first independent variable) when proceeding to determine the relationship between Y (with the average effect of X removed) and Z. Consequently, when combining the average relations of Y (with the average effect of Z removed) and X with Y (with the average relation of X removed) and Z, we will multiply rather than add as was done in Table I-2, column 7. This will yield an equation in the form $Y = aX^bZ^c$. The coefficient a will be established separately.

Graphic Fitting of Multiplicative Predicting Equation $Y = aX^bZ^c$ [22]

Columns 1, 2, and 3 of Table I-3 set forth the same data as appear in columns 1, 2, and 3 of Table I-2.

In part A of Chart I-6, the data of columns 1 and 2 of Table I-3 (Y and X) are plotted against each other. Then a *trial* straight line is visually run through the plotted points. The slope of this line ($\Delta Y/\Delta X$) is 0.645. This slope is established through the use of a metric ruler scaled in millimeters. The vertical segment shown by the brackets is 24.4 millimeters, and the horizontal segment is 37.9 millimeters. The slope could also be obtained by dividing the vertical distance as read from the Y-axis (179–100), by the horizontal distance as read from the X-axis (200–80). In column 4 of Table I-3, the X values of column 2 are raised to the power of 0.645 (by taking the anti-log of the product of 0.645 times the log of each X value in column 2). In column 5 of Table I-3, the Y values of column 1 are divided by the

[22] I am pleased to acknowledge the assistance of Mr. R. C. Hannenberg, M.B.A. (Northwestern) in preparing this section.

CHART I-6

Part A: First Trial Relationship of Y and X as Set Forth in Table I-3—Column 1 versus Column 2 (Calculation of Slope: 24.4/37.9 = 0.645)

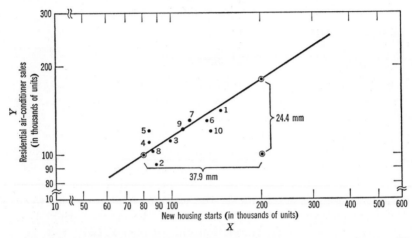

Part B: First Trial Relationship of $Y/X^{0.645}$ Against Z as Set Forth in Table I-3—Column 5 versus Column 3 (Calculation of Slope: 13/45 = 0.289)

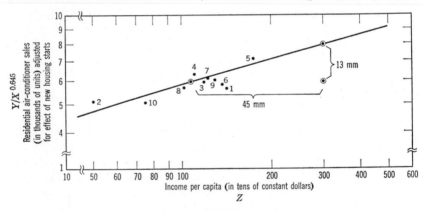

$X^{0.645}$ values of column 4. Thus column 5 shows Y with the average effect of X removed, assuming that the average relation is correctly shown when the power of X is 0.645.

In part B of Chart I-6, the data of columns 3 and 5 (Z and $Y/X^{0.645}$) are plotted against each other. A straight line is visually run through the plotted points. The slope of this line is 0.289. This straight line indicates the average relationship of Y (with the effect of X removed) and Z.

In column 6 of Table I-3, Z is raised to the 0.289 power (by taking the anti-log of the product of 0.289 times the log of each Z value of column 3). In column 7, the Y values of column 1 are divided by the values just established in column 6. After this step, the values in column 7 are the Y values with the average effect of Z removed.

We are now ready to make the final fitting. In part A of Chart I-7, the values of column 7 (Y with the average effect of Z removed) are plotted against the X values of column 2 and a straight line fitted visually. The slope of this line is 0.433 and indicates the true relationship of Y and X (with the effect of Z already removed from Y).

Then, in column 9, we remove the average effect of X from Y by dividing Y (column 1) by $X^{0.433}$ as shown in column 8 (these are the X values of column 2, which we raised to the power of 0.433 by taking the anti-log of the product of 0.433 times the log of each X value in column 2).

Then in part B of Chart I-7, the values of column 9 (Y with the average effect of X removed) are plotted against Z (column 3), and a straight line is fitted visually. The slope of this straight line is 0.221 and indicates the average relation of Y (with the effect of X removed) to Z.

At this point we can state the relationship of Y to X and Z as $Y = aX^{0.433}Z^{0.221}$ except that the a value of the product of the intercepts of the two straight lines on Chart I-7 remains to be determined. This value a in the equation $Y/X^{0.433} = aZ^{0.221}$ (lower part of Chart I-7) can be established by simple substitution for $Y/X^{0.433}$ and Z, and solving to get the average value of the unknown a.

Thus (in part B of Chart I-7), by taking at random three vertical values of $Y/X^{0.433}$ (20, 14.5, and 10) and reading from the line the associated horizontal values of Z (350, 80, and 15), we can substitute in the equation $Y/X^{0.433} = aZ^{0.221}$ as follows:

$$20 \ \ = a(350)^{0.221} \text{ and solving, } a = 5.48$$
$$14.5 = a(\ 80)^{0.221} \text{ and solving, } a = 5.51$$
$$10 \ \ = a(\ 15)^{0.221} \text{ and solving, } a = 5.50$$

Taking the average value of a as 5.5, we now have the multiplicative predicting equation

$$Y = 5.5X^{0.433}Z^{0.221}$$

Substituting the values of X (column 2) and Z (column 3) in this equation, we get the values of column 11, which are the estimates of Y to be compared with the actual values of Y in column 1. For computation, this substitution in the predicting equation is simply 5.5 times the product of column 8 times column 10.

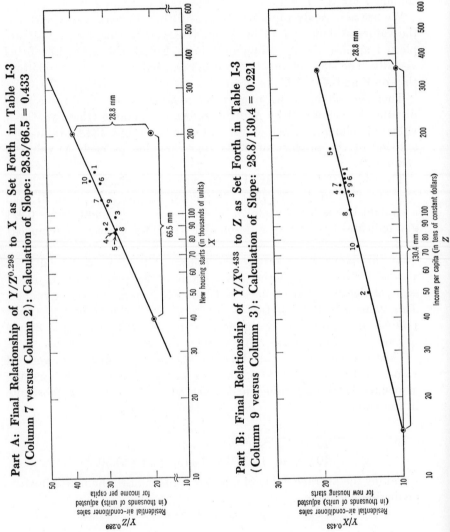

CHART I-7

Part A: Final Relationship of $Y/Z^{0.298}$ to X as Set Forth in Table I-3
(Column 7 versus Column 2): Calculation of Slope: $28.8/66.5 = 0.433$

Part B: Final Relationship of $Y/X^{0.433}$ to Z as Set Forth in Table I-3
(Column 9 versus Column 3): Calculation of Slope: $28.8/130.4 = 0.221$

Column 12 shows the differences between actual and computed sales (columns 1 and 11). R^2 is 0.939 for the multiplicative predicting equation. These differences between actual and computed sales can be compared with column 8 of Table I-2 which shows the differences between actual Y and computed Y in the case of the additive predicting equation for the same data, $Y = 40 + 0.44X + 0.26Z$. This comparison shows the two forms of equation yield quite similar results in our case.

This illustrates the difficulty that can be encountered in selecting the correct form of curve to be fitted when the number of observations (here 10) is small. In the present situation the fitting of an arithmetic straight line and a logarithmic straight line gives equally good fits. It is clear that which of this two lines is used for extrapolation will significantly affect the forecast particularly as the extrapolation proceeds farther from the range of observations. If the data had been a series of twenty rather than ten values, the difficulty in selecting the appropriate type of line to fit would be reduced. However, over a period of 20 years, radical changes, such as changes of taste, may occur and it may be the lesser of two evils to use a period of 10 years rather than nonhomogeneous data over 20 years.

If the orders of magnitude of X and Z are about the same (both about 100, for example, as here), comparison can also be made of the significance of X and Z individually by comparing the ratio of the two coefficients of X and Z in the additive equation (0.44/0.26) with the ratio of the two exponents of X and Z in the multiplicative equation (0.433/0.221).

The entire preceding graphic fit of the three variables in a multiplicative form was done first and then the result checked for accuracy by using an IBM-650 computer. The results are:

Graphically fitted equation: $Y = 5.5X^{0.433}Z^{0.221}$ with standard error of estimate of 3.6.

IBM-650 computed equation:[23] $Y = 7.4X^{0.370}Z^{0.221}$ with standard error of estimate of 2.66.

Graphic Multiple Correlation Involving More Than Three Variables[24]

If the proposed study involves more than three variables, the graphic multiple correlation method is still usable. Thus in the example we have used above of the residential air conditioning industry, we would simply take the remaining unexplained variation (column 8 of Table

[23] Using program developed by Northwestern University Computing Center.

[24] One of the more widely known illustrations of graphic analysis involving more than three variables is the case of the California Clingstone Peach Industry in Malcolm NcNair and Richard S. Meriam, *Problems in Business Economics* (New York: McGraw-Hill, 1941), pp. 102–111.

I-2) and the third independent variable (say average square foot per residence) and plot these against each other as was done in Chart I-3 in order to establish the average relation (regression line) between these two and then return for correction of the line in Chart I-1. This can, of course, be done in similar manner for additional variables. We are involved, however, with a change in the degrees of freedom as we keep adding explanatory independent variables. Failure to correct for this will produce an artificially high degree of correlation in the calculations.

MULTICOLLINEARITY [25]

Very often in the case of economic series, the relationship existing among the explanatory or independent variables is such that not only is Y (the dependent variable) related to each of X and Z (independent variables), but X and Z are related to each other in a linear fashion. This relationship is called multicollinearity. When multicollinearity is present, the multiple regression equation correctly predicts Y when the effects of changes in both X and Z are considered. But we are left with the problem of determining the *separate* influences of each of the independent variables on the dependent variable. Thus Y, the consumption of a particular good, may be influenced by both X, the gross national product and Z, the amount of savings. There is, however, a relationship between gross national product (X) and the amount of savings (Z) as well as between Y and X and between Y and Z. It was pointed out earlier that when a multiplicative equation, such as $Y = aX^bZ^c$, is fitted, the exponents of X (b) and Z (c) are elasticities.

However, this statement is based upon the assumption that X and Z are not interrelated. Hence a method for dealing with multicollinearity is essential. Partial correlation is the usual statistical technique by which the influence of X on Y can be determined when Z is held constant. Similarly for the influence of Z on Y while X is constant. Partial correlation may be of little assistance in certain cases, such as when multicollinearity is extreme. The multicollinearity, unless it is extreme, will not affect the character of the estimates of the coefficients of the independent variables. As long as it can be assumed that the residuals of the correlation (the variation unexplained by the regression equation) are independent of (not related in a systematic manner to) the

[25] For an introduction to the collinearity problem, see E. F. Beach, *Economic Models: An Exposition* (New York: Wiley, 1957), pp. 171–175, 182–184. The classical treatment is found in Ragnar Frisch, *Statistical Confluence Analysis* (Oslo: Universitetets Konomiske Institutt, 1934).

independent variables, then the estimates of the coefficients of the independent variables are the best and unbiased even though there may be correlation between the independent variables. Difficulty arises only if there are exact linear relations among the independent variables.

To repeat, even when there is multicollinearity, the multiple regression equation remains valid; that is, the predicting of Y on the basis of X *and* Z is not invalidated by the existence of a relationship between X and Z. Only the effort to state *separately* the influences of X on Y and of Z on Y may be invalidated.

Testing for Multicollinearity

A geometric technique is available for judging whether multicollinearity exists in a regression equation. The Y and X values are plotted against each other on a graph and a trend line is fitted to the Y and X observations. Then the Y and Z values are plotted against each other on a second graph and a trend line is fitted to the Y and Z observations. Then the vertical *deviations* of the points on the Y versus X map (from the trend line of the Y versus X map) are plotted on a third graph against the vertical *deviations* of the points on the Y vs. Z map (from the trend line of the Y vs. Z map), *using* the Y value which is common to the X deviation and the Z deviation as the basis for plotting. This is clarified by the illustrative data in Table I-4, which are plotted in Chart I-8.

TABLE I-4

Summary of Hypothetical Deviations of Y from a Trend Line of Y versus X and of Y from a Trend Line of Y versus Z

Observed Y Value	Deviation of Observed Y Value from Trend Line on the Y Versus X Map	Deviation of Observed Y Value from Trend Line on the Y Versus Z Map
100	6	−4
120	−4	8
130	−2	−1
140	3	6
etc.		

Chart I-8 shows there is no pattern among the few instances of Table I-4.

If a linear pattern appears on the third map, there is multicollinearity and the separate effects of X on Y and of Z on Y cannot be

CHART I-8

Testing for Multicollinearity—Plotting Against Each Other the Deviations
of the Dependent Variable From the Trend Lines Fitted Separately to Two
Independent Variables

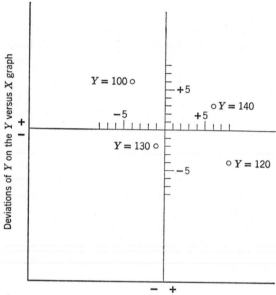

Deviations of Y on the Y versus Z graph

Source: Table I-4.

established by correlation techniques. The stronger the pattern, the
stronger the multicollinearity. The precise degree of correlation between the two sets of deviations can be determined by the usual correlation computation. In this situation either Y or Z is discarded and
another explanatory variable is sought. Whether X or Z is to be discarded would be decided by which of the two has the smallest correlation with Y when considered separately.

Dealing with Multicollinearity

The present state of statistical development offers little help in
dealing with multicollinearity except to discard one or the other of
the variables Y or Z. But the simultaneous equation method can be
used in the situation of multicollinearity. The Cowles Foundation for
Research in Economics has been an advocate of the use of simultaneous

equations[26] when multicollinearity exists among the endogenous variables, namely, those variables that are explained by the model or system since these variables both determine other variables in the model and are determined by them. As was previously explained, multicollinearity among the exogenous variables, namely, those variables known or determined outside the model will not, unless the multicollinearity is extreme, affect the estimates made by least-squares methods.

Under the simultaneous equation method, a number of equations are established with each equation stating a particular relationship of the variables. The solution of the system (in which there are as many equations as there are unknowns) will give a result which takes account of the intercorrelation between the independent and dependent variables as well as between the independent variables themselves. By the usual addition-subtraction method for simultaneous equations, we eliminate all but one of the independent variables, and the dependent variable then appears as a function of the single remaining independent variable. Determinants can also be used to solve the system.

AUTOCORRELATION

Very often in the case of economic time series, one value of a variable is related to (not independent of) the value of the same variable at an earlier point in time. Thus the price in one month may be correlated to the price of the prior month. This is called autocorrelation.[27]

The fact that there is a secular trend over time in an economic series introduces autocorrelation into the series. Similarly a regular seasonal pattern involves autocorrelation.

No graphic method of testing for autocorrelation is available.[28]

[26] See, for example, E. G. Bennion, "The Cowles Commission's Simultaneous Equation Approach: A Simplified Explanation," *Review of Economics and Statistics,* vol. 34 (1952), pp. 49–56.

[27] Sometimes the term "serial correlation" is used for this situation. However, it is better to reserve the term "serial correlation" to describe the relation of lead (or lag) between two *different* time series.

[28] The several statistical tests for autocorrelation require a large sample. But since economic time series usually involve a relatively small number of observations, the usefulness of these statistical tests is limited. For a statistical method of testing for autocorrelation, see B. I. Hart, "Significance Levels for the Ratio of the Mean Square Successive Differences to the Variance," *Annals of Mathematical Statistics,* vol. 13 (1942), pp. 445ff. Hart, using the Von Neumann ratio

The main concern of the economist with autocorrelation is that it seriously affects the tests of significance.

The most common way to remove autocorrelation is to eliminate the trend from each of the series of dependent and independent variables and then to proceed with the differences of the observed values of the series from the trend values. These differences (of the Y, X and Z series, for example) may then be analyzed by the methods of multiple correlation which we have already explained.

Instead of the mechanics of trend elimination, we can achieve the same result by introducing time into the regression equation as an explicit term. For example,

$$Y = a + bX + cZ + dT$$

with T having a defined origin and measured in appropriate time units from that origin.

Another method of dealing with autocorrelation is the method of first differences, namely, to use the differences between two successive values of a series at two successive points in time.[29] Thus, for example, the *change* in price of a good from point 1 in time to point 2 in time may be treated as the dependent variable to be analyzed against the change in income from point 1 in time to point 2 in time as the independent variable and the change in population from point 1 in time to point 2 in time as the second independent variable.

APPLICABILITY OF TECHNIQUES DISCUSSED IN THIS PART TO OTHER ECONOMIC PROBLEMS

While the techniques discussed in this part have been framed in a context leading to the discussion of the forecasting of sales, it should be clear that they can be employed in a wide range of economic prob-

---

establishes a statistic, k, which is defined as the ratio, m^2/σ^2, where σ^2 is the variance of the variable whose autocorrelation is being examined and m^2 is the sum of the squares of the successive differences in the values of the variable divided by the number of observations of the variable less one. The resulting value of k is then compared to a table setting confidence limits for k (based on the number of observations of the variable). If the value of k falls within these limits, autocorrelation exists. Another approach to testing for autocorrelation is to examine the regression residuals (the error term, or variation unexplained by the equation fitted by least squares). This method, commonly called the Durbin-Watson test, is explained in J. Durbin and G. S. Watson, "Testing for Serial Correlation in Least Squares Regression I," *Biometrika*, vol. 37 (1950), pp. 409–421, and Part II in *ibid.*, vol. 38 (1951), pp. 159–178.

[29] An illustration of this method appears later, in Part IV—Pricing Analysis, under the heading "Shoe-Pricing Analysis."

lems. Thus graphic multiple correlation is employed later, in Part III, in dealing with the production function and the optimum allocation of resources in production.

EXERCISE

Fit graphically an equation of the form $Y = aX^b Z^c$ to the data of Table III-4 in Part III. (Hint: We are seeking the slope of the logarithmic line, so do not run one line through the fifteen points on each graph.)

CASE I-1. SUNBURST CORPORATION *
Forecasting—Short-Term—Using an Indicator

Sunburst Corporation, formed in 1947, was engaged in the manufacture of distribution transformers. Mr. Ross had the problem in 1959 of preparing the company's forecast of industry sales for 1960.

A distribution transformer takes electric power† and steps it down to 110 and 220 volts for residential, commercial or industrial use. A complete standard line of distribution transformers involves some 1,200 to 1,500 models, ranging in price, on terms of net 30 days, from somewhat under $200 to several thousand dollars per unit. In addition, the number of "special" types to meet a particular customer's needs is practically limitless.

More than half the American sales in this field are by General Electric and Westinghouse. Line Material which has since become a division of McGraw Edison Co., and Allis Chalmers Co. sell significant percentages of the market. Some twenty other producers share the last quarter of the market. Of these twenty the largest are Wagner Electric Co., Moloney Electric Co., Kuhlman Electric Co., and Standard Transformer Co. All of these transformer manufacturers are engaged in the manufacture of other products for the electrical market such as motors, fuses, and cutouts. In addition, these manufacturers make transmission as well as distribution transformers. Transmission transformers experience greater fluctuations in demand than distribution transformers and consequently frequent "white sales" result. Sunburst limited itself to distribution transformers.

Sunburst was the first transformer company established in the United States since the 1920's, although transformer repair shops, which may engage in a small amount of manufacturing, come and go. By 1959, Sunburst had risen to become seventh in the nation in volume of distribution transformers.

Purchasers of distribution transformers can be classified into four categories: privately owned electric utilities, municipally owned electric utilities, rural electric cooperatives and public utility districts, and

* With the assistance of John Bonge, M.B.A. (Northwestern).

† A distribution transformer *receives electric* power from systems of 2,400, 4,000, 4,800, 7,200, 7,620, or 14,400 volts. High-tension lines are stepped down to these six voltages by substation or transmission transformers. Distribution transformers come in standard *capacity* sizes of 1½KVA, 3KVA, 5KVA, 7½KVA, 10KVA, 15KVA, 25KVA, 37½KVA, 50KVA, 75KVA, 100KVA, 167KVA, 250KVA, 333KVA, and 500KVA. Distribution transformers come in various types to handle differences in taps, protective equipment, devices, etc.

CASE I-1. TABLE I

Growth in Electric Power Industry in the U.S.

Kilowatt hours generated in millions by producers

Year	Total	By Privately Owned	By Cooperatives (REA)	By Municipally Owned	By Federal Projects	By State Owned and Public Utility Districts
1930	91,112	86,109	incl. in state and public utility districts	4,020	465	518
1935	95,287	89,330		4,670	555	732
1940	141,837	125,411		6,667	8,583	1,176
1945	222,486	180,926		10,414	28,000	3,146
1946	223,178	181,020		11,600	26,960	3,598
1947	255,739	208,106	404	13,246	29,877	4,106
1948	282,698	228,231	650	13,961	35,373	4,483
1949	291,100	233,112	764	14,243	38,102	4,879
1950	329,141	266,860	986	16,101	40,387	4,807
1951	370,673	301,845	1,264	18,504	44,120	4,940
1952	399,224	322,126	1,526	17,490	52,492	5,590
1953	442,665	354,272	1,897	21,625	58,064	6,807
1954	471,686	370,970	2,476	23,505	67,804	6,931
1955	547,038	420,869	3,044	25,852	89,064	8,209
1956	600,592	458,954	3,398	28,000	100,710	9,530
1957	631,380	488,828	3,030	27,851	109,177	10,509
1958	644,760	490,305	3,285	28,352	110,438	12,256
1959	710,006	544,234	4,404	34,618	109,052	17,698

Source: *Electric Utility Industry in U.S. Statistical Bulletin for 1956* (New York: Edison Electric Institute, 1960) Table 9, p. 14.
Note: Public utility districts are publicly owned operations peculiar to the Pacific Northwest. Cooperatives are distorted in their relative position because they buy most of their power. Table II where their KWH sales are shown gives a more proportioned picture.

industrial companies. A measure of their relative purchases is indicated by the percentages of total electricity generated as shown in Table I. The growth of cooperatives is depicted in Table II, because

CASE I-1. TABLE II

REA Cooperatives (Active Borrowers Only)

Construction loans, KWH sold, and per cent of farms electrified in U.S.

Year	(a) REA Loans Approved	(b) KWH Sold (in Thousands)	(c) Per Cent Farms Electrified
1935	—	—	10.9
1937	—	—	16.8
1938	—	—	19.1
1939	$ 86,798,000	—	22.1
1940	83,409,000	311,479	27.1
1941	82,534,000	724,385	34.9
1942	26,479,000	1,150,536	40.3
1943	13,274,000	1,572,466	—
1944	43,958,000	1,749,509	—
1945	149,255,000	1,950,729	52.9
1946	291,055,000	2,243,837	61.0
1947	232,518,000	3,056,100	—
1948	384,397,000	4,252,091	68.6
1949	424,355,246	5,564,323	78.2
1950	312,357,000	6,883,939	78.3
1951	172,807,000	8,567,462	84.0
1952	184,503,000	10,127,863	88.1
1953	144,649,000	11,804,174	90.8
1954	171,485,000	13,829,131	—
1955	180,096,000	15,738,772	—
1956	189,804,800	17,077,279	94.2
1957	300,461,514	19,039,217	94.8
1958	213,802,000	20,513,355	95.4
1959	177,292,000	23,561,939	96.0
1960	220,108,000	26,225,296	96.5

Sources: (a) and (b): *Annual Statistical Report, Rural Electrification Administration* (Washington; Dept. of Agriculture) various years; (c) *Annual Report of Administrator. Rural Electrification Administration* (Washington: Dept. of Agriculture) and *Statistical Abstract of the U.S.*, various years.

Note: Of a total of $2,778,136,000 in REA loans from 1935 through 1953, $2,251,886,000 was for distribution systems. However, by 1960, only 59 per cent of the loans was for distribution.

their situation is distorted in Table I since the cooperatives buy almost all their power rather than generate it. Industrial company purchases of transformers for their own premises are less than 1 per cent of the total. Distribution transformers are calculated by rule of thumb as about 15 per cent in dollars of total distribution purchases by utilities.

The following table shows the prior record of the industry in buying distribution transformers based on (a) the total of distribution expenditures as they appear in *Electrical World,* and (b) the application of a rule-of-thumb 15 per cent of distribution expenditures for transformers. Some basis for further small adjustments was available to Mr. Ross and the final result arrived at by him is as follows:

ESTIMATED U.S. DISTRIBUTION TRANSFORMER SALES, 1950–59
(In Millions)

1950	$188	1955	$222
1951	230	1956	250
1952	167	1957	235
1953	183	1958	205
1954	178	1959	240

Table III shows the total distribution expenditures for privately owned utilities only and likewise the data on per capita consumption of electric power in the United States.

If one wants to consider the above data on the sales of distribution transformers in terms of constant dollars, the following price index is available.

WHOLESALE PRICE INDEX, 1950–59
Machinery and Motive Products Series, Base 1947–1949 = 100

1950	118.9	1955	128.4
1951	119.0	1956	137.8
1952	121.5	1957	146.1
1953	123.0	1958	150.1
1954	124.6	1959	153.0

Source: Department of Commerce, *Survey of Current Business.*

There was a belief in the distribution transformer industry that new housing starts (nonfarm residential) somehow had a strong bearing on the sale of distribution transformers. Housing is normally in the process of construction for a considerable period of time with the exception of prefabricated houses.

CASE I-1. TABLE III

Growth in Electric Power Industry in the U.S.

Year	Distribution Expenditures in Millions by Privately Owned Utilities	KWH in Millions Generated and Imported	Estimated Population	Per Capita KWH
1940	$ 225	182,021	131,954,000	1,380
1945	160	273,817	132,481,000	2,067
1946	345	272,000	140,054,000	1,942
1947	560	309,315	143,446,000	2,156
1948	750	338,353	146,093,000	2,316
1949	835	346,654	148,665,000	2,332
1950	785	390,460	151,228,000	2,582
1951	810	435,545	151,383,000	2,840
1952	879	465,324	155,767,000	2,987
1953	938	516,177	158,320,000	3,260
1954	993	546,985	161,183,000	3,394
1955	1,093	633,078	164,303,000	3,853
1956	1,274	689,352	167,259,000	4,121
1957	1,270	719,957	170,293,000	4,228
1958	1,125	728,070	173,232,800	4,203
1959	1,163	798,858	176,511,000	4,526
1960	—	844,985	179,977,000	4,695

Source: Electric Utility Industry in U.S., Statistical Bulletin for 1960 (New York: Edison Electric Institute) Table 8 and Table 49.

The following table shows the data on housing starts.

NONFARM RESIDENTIAL HOUSING STARTS IN U.S.
(In Millions of Units)

1950	1.396	1955	1.329
1951	1.091	1956	1.118
1952	1.127	1957	1.039
1953	1.194	1958	1.209
1954	1.220	1959	1.350

Source: Joint Economic Committee: Economic Indicators.

Prepare a forecast of distribution transformer sales for 1960.

CASE I-2. HEVY-TRUCK COMPANY

Forecasting—Long and Short-Term Forecast of Producer's Good

In 1958, the Hevy-Truck Co. found itself plagued with planning difficulties stemming from the difficulty in forecasting future shipments with reasonable accuracy.

Hevy-Truck made truck-tractors in the 19,500 pound (gross vehicle weight) and over class. Hevy-Truck knew that it was being aided by several movements under way in the transportation area. For the preceding 10 years, trucking had been increasing its share of freight movement primarily at the expense of the railroads. The data in Table I show this. But, total freight movement had not been keeping pace with the growth of the economy (see column 7 of Table II). However, the net balance was in favor of truck freight growth exceeding the growth of the economy (see column 10 of Table II).

In connection with Tables I and II, the concept of national income originating in the various transportation areas is used rather than tonnage figures on the ground that *ability and need* to buy truck equipment is the issue. Characteristically less remunerative freight involves heavier tonnages.

Another phenomenon observed was the increasing importance of large (over 19,500 GVW) trucks in moving truck freight. This is shown in Table III. Trucks have an average life of 6 to 7 years which has been rising over the prior 10 years. However, as high as 10 per cent of trucks at any one time are 12 years old and older. The ten year period 1946 through 1956 (Table III) indicates that sales of over 19,500 GVW trucks have been increasing at an average of 8,600 units per year. This has been computed from the slope of a straight line least-squares fit. Hevy-Truck's sales figures over the same period and computed in the same way show a much faster rate of growth than the industry figure.

The problem of Hevy-Truck was to arrive at both a short-run forecast and a long-run forecast.

Hevy-Truck had applied considerable effort to the forecasting problem. One approach was to study the large purchasers of their trucks. This led to difficulty, however, in that the prospective buyer in a competitive area such as trucks would tell each of several producers that he contemplated buying a given number of trucks 4 to 6 months hence. The result was an over-optimistic forecast. In some cases the purchaser would introduce his own ideas of the delivery that could be expected

CASE I-2. TABLE I
National Income Originating in Freight by Type of Carrier

Year	(1) Calculated National Income Originating in Freight (in Millions)	(2) National Income Originating in Highway Freight (in Millions)	(3) (2) as Per Cent of (1)	(4) National Income Originating with Railroad (in Millions)	(5) (4) as Per Cent of (1)	(6) National Income Originating with Water Carriers (in Millions)	(7) (6) as Per Cent of (1)	(8) Calculated Air Freight (in Millions)	(9) (8) as Per Cent of (1)	(10) National Income Originating in Pipelines (in Millions)	(11) (10) as Per Cent of (1)	(12) National Income Originating in Allied Service (in Millions)	(13) (12) as Per Cent of (1)
1946	$8,637	$1,699	19.67%	$5,466	63.28%	$823	9.53%	$217	2.5%	$126	1.5%	$502	5.8%
1947	9,886	1,993	20.16	6,294	63.67	814	8.23	243	2.4	151	1.5	610	6.2
1948	10,991	2,272	20.67	7,104	64.63	810	7.37	306	2.8	192	1.7	582	5.2
1949	10,304	2,377	23.07	6,369	61.81	750	7.20	349	3.4	202	2.0	571	5.5
1950	11,541	2,780	24.09	7,109	61.60	746	6.46	432	3.7	255	2.2	608	5.3
1951	12,966	3,128	24.12	7,792	60.10	966	7.45	540	4.2	281	2.2	745	5.7
1952	13,382	3,415	25.52	7,900	59.03	931	6.96	678	4.7	292	2.2	781	5.8
1953	13,697	3,807	27.79	7,717	56.34	1,000	7.30	688	5.0	300	2.2	804	5.9
1954	12,454	3,881	31.16	6,553	52.62	853	6.84	730	5.9	286	2.3	808	6.5
1955	13,526	4,397	32.51	6,912	51.10	930	6.88	833	6.2	308	2.3	896	6.6
1956	14,441	4,801	33.25	7,254	50.23	993	8.33	945	6.6	328	2.3	970	6.7

Source: Economic Almanac (New York: Crowell, 1958), p. 105ff.

CASE I-2. TABLE II

National Income and Segment Originating in Highway Freight

Year	(1) National Income Originating in Transportation* (in Millions)	(2) Deduct Local and Highway Passenger Part* (in Millions)	(3) Deduct Air Passenger Part† (in Millions)	(4) Total Deduction (2) + (3) (in Millions)	(5) Calculated National Income Originating in Freight Transportation (in Millions)	(6) National Income (in Billions)	(7) (5) as Per Cent of (6)	(8) National Income Originating in Highway Freight (in Millions)	(9) (8) as Per Cent of (5)	(10) (8) as Per Cent of (6)
1946	$10,245	$1,412	$195.3	$1,608	$ 8,637	$179.6	4.81%	$1,699	19.67%	0.94%
1947	11,498	1,393	218.7	1,612	9,886	197.2	5.01	1,993	20.16	1.01
1948	12,644	1,378	275.4	1,653	10,991	221.6	4.96	2,272	20.67	1.03
1949	11,969	1,351	314.1	1,665	10,304	216.2	4.77	2,377	23.07	1.10
1950	13,266	1,336	388.8	1,725	11,541	240.0	4.81	2,780	24.09	1.16
1951	14,884	1,432	486.0	1,918	12,965	277.0	4.68	3,128	24.12	1.13
1952	15,399	1,452	565.2	2,017	13,382	290.2	4.61	3,415	25.52	1.18
1953	15,775	1,459	619.2	2,078	13,697	302.1	4.53	3,807	27.79	1.26
1954	14,493	1,382	657.0	2,039	12,454	299.0	4.16	3,881	31.16	1.30
1955	15,652	1,376	747.7	2,126	13,526	324.1	4.17	4,397	32.51	1.36
1956	16,713	1,422	850.5	2,272	14,441	343.6	4.20	4,801	33.25	1.40

Source: Department of Commerce as reported in Economic Almanac (New York: Crowell, 1958), p. 105ff.

* Includes allied transportation services aggregating about 6 per cent of total transportation income.

† Estimated at 90 per cent of total air, the ratio of passenger and freight revenues. This is conservative because air passenger is known to be much more profitable than air freight.

No deduction for rail passengers because passengers are less than 10 per cent of rail revenues and passenger hauling on rails is known to be at best breakeven income-wise.

Note: Comparing these calculations (which exclude passenger transportation) with the earlier figures does not affect the rate of charge in columns 7 and 9 although the absolute percentages are altered.

CASE I-2. TABLE III

Number of Trucks Sold Total and Over 19,500 GVW

Year	Total Trucks Sold, in Thousands	Total Trucks Sold Over 19,500 GVW, in Thousands
1946	931	40
1947	1,220	69
1948	1,364	71
1949	1,129	41
1950	1,332	76
1951	1,417	123
1952	1,213	152
1953	1,202	127
1954	1,038	86
1955	1,245	108
1956	1,100	138
	Average Annual Increase	Average Annual Increase*
	0	8.6

Source: Motor Truck Facts (Detroit: Automobile Manufacturers Association, annual).

* Average annual increase computed from line of least squares: $Y = 56 + 8.6X$ with Y in thousands of trucks and X in years, origin 1946.

in 4 to 6 months. If present conditions involved easy delivery, the customer would be inclined to underestimate his requirements particularly if general activity was reducing the work-load on his equipment. The result was an unduly pessimistic forecast.

Another approach Hevy-Truck took was to search for economic indicators which might lead truck purchases. The difficulty is that a substantial part of trucking is tied, for example, to construction activity and construction data lead other economic series. If economic indicators or determinants could be found, then multiple correlation analysis would form a basis for predictions for the industry as a whole. This would leave the problem of how to forecast Hevy-Truck's position in the industry.

An economist proposed to Hevy-Truck that a more naive approach might be more fruitful. He made this proposal on the basis of the margins of error which Hevy-Truck found "liveable." Hevy-Truck considered a forecast with a margin of error of ±10 per cent would be a vast improvement over its existing forecast results, particularly for short-run forecasts.

The economist examined the monthly record of shipments by Hevy-Truck shown in Table IV. He knew that all businesses have a seasonal

CASE I-2. TABLE IV

Monthly Shipments of Hevy-Truck Company in Units Each Year

Month	1953	1954	1955	1956	1957
January	1353	915	1323	2032	2648
February	1523	1013	1504	2419	2461
March	1477	1336	1686	2638	2468
April	1178	1191	2013	2800	2337
May	1181	1203	2020	3155	2549
June	1456	829	1431	2228	2310
July	805	1033	1550	2394	1612
August	1160	1232	1519	3094	2318
September	1017	1310	1838	2517	2359
October	1022	1286	1928	2772	2397
November	976	1292	1910	2396	2100
December	824	1386	1966	2665	2226

pattern, some more clearly defined than others. At first glance, the Hevy-Truck shipment record appears to have no particular seasonal consistency. Individual events, however, occurring with a certain regularity every few months could mask a seasonal, particularly when one of these events might push sales up and another push sales down. The over-all average annual growth rate complicates matters.

The economist decided to experiment with the link-relative method of computing a seasonal index. With a seasonal index hitched to an appropriate moving base, the economist might attempt a 12-month forecast every month. The link-relative method is best adapted to growth situations. Tables V and VI show the calculation of the seasonal index by this method, using the most recent 5-year shipment record and taking the median 3-year link-relative for computation.

Armed with the seasonal index the economist debated about the base to be used. The average of the most recent three month actual shipments seasonally adjusted was used to arrive at a base figure which could be taken as 100. Then the application of the seasonal

Case I-2. TABLE V

Hevy-Truck Seasonal Index Calculation (Link-Relative Method)

Month	1953 Actual Units Shipped*	1953 As Per Cent of Prior Month	1954 Actual Units Shipped*	1954 As Per Cent of Prior Month	1955 Actual Units Shipped*	1955 As Per Cent of Prior Month	1956 Actual Units Shipped*	1956 As Per Cent of Prior Month	1957 Actual Units Shipped*	1957 As Per Cent of Prior Month
January	1353	(100.0)†‡	915	111.0	1323	95.5	2032	(103.4)	2648	(99.4)
February	1523	(112.6)	1013	(110.7)	1504	(113.7)	2419	119.0	2461	92.9
March	1477	96.9	1336	113.2	1686	(112.1)	2638	(109.1)	2468	(100.3)
April	1178	79.8	1191	(89.2)	2013	119.4	2800	(106.1)	2337	(94.7)
May	1181	100.2	1203	(101.1)	2020	(100.3)	3155	112.7	2549	(109.1)
June	1456	112.3	829	68.9	1431	(70.9)	2228	(70.6)	2310	(90.6)
July	805	55.3	1033	124.6	1550	(108.3)	2394	(107.5)	1612	(69.8)
August	1160	144.1	1232	(119.3)	1519	98.0	3094	(129.2)	2318	(143.9)
September	1017	(87.6)	1310	(110.6)	1838	121.1	2517	81.4	2359	(101.7)
October	1022	(100.5)	1286	98.2	1928	(104.9)	2772	110.1	2397	(101.6)
November	976	(95.6)	1292	100.4	1910	(99.1)	2396	86.5	2100	(87.6)
December	824	84.4	1386	(107.3)	1966	(102.9)	2665	111.2	2226	(106.0)

* Actual shipments per month from Table IV.
† The median three link-relatives of the five for each month are marked in parentheses.
‡ December 1952 shipments: 1353.

CASE I-2. TABLE VI

Seasonal Index Computation of Hevy-Truck Company (Link-Relative Method) Median of 5 Years: 1953–1957

Month	Average of Median 3 (See Table V for Median 3)	(1) Typical Link-Relative	(2) Welded Link-Relative	(3) Corrected Link-Relative	(4) Seasonal Index
January	(302.8)/3 =	100.9	100.0	100.0/102.25 =	97.8
February	(337.0)/3 =	112.3	112.3 −1.6 =	110.7/102.25 =	108.3
March	(321.5)/3 =	107.2	120.4 −3.2 =	117.2 etc.	114.6
April	(290.0)/3 =	96.7	116.4 etc.	111.6	109.1
May	(310.5)/3 =	103.5	120.5	114.1	111.6
June	(232.1)/3 =	77.4	93.3	85.3	83.4
July	(285.6)/3 =	95.2	88.8	79.2	77.5
August	(392.4)/3 =	130.8	116.2	105.0	102.7
September	(299.9)/3 =	100.0	116.2	103.4	101.1
October	(307.0)/3 =	102.3	118.9	104.5	102.2
November	(282.3)/3 =	94.1	111.9	95.9	93.8
December	(316.2)/3 =	105.4	117.9	100.3	98.1
Total				1,227.2	
Average Month				102.25	
January		100.9	119.0		

Annual Drift 19.0
Monthly Drift 1.6

Notes: Column 2 applies the link-relative of each month to January as the base. Column 3 is column 2 minus the cumulative monthly drift of 1.6 for each month removed from January. The figure 119 is the succeeding January computed by multiplying December's 117.9 by January's 100.9. If drift is zero, this result is 100. Column 4 is column 3 divided by 102.25 to put the year on a 1,200 basis, namely, to express each month as a percentage of the average month.

index for each month to this base yielded the forecast. Table VII shows the forecast tested against actual and the deviation (both in units and percentage) of the forecast from the actual.

The average of the most recent three month actual shipments was arrived at for use as a base upon the following logic. The most recent months would reflect the swing in general business conditions and, with a minimum of delay, would project them into the forecast. A 3-month average would have the advantage of leveling the effect of any unusual month in the base. A 2-month average would not do as much of this leveling of an unusual month. A 4-month average would minimize the emphasis given to the most recent trend as reflected in the most recent 3 months.

In applying this forecasting method to the 12-month cycle, the economist noticed the typically larger than normal error in the June and July forecasts. Upon investigation this was accounted for by the vacation phenomena, not only the vacations of Hevy-Truck employees but of the employees of Hevy-Truck's purchasers. The economist proposed

Case I-2. TABLE VII
Twelve-Month Forecasts of Hevy-Truck Company Back Tested

Testing 1956—January 1 Forecast

Base Computation:

```
1928  October  1955 actual
1910  November 1955   "
1966  December 1955   "
3)5804 = 1935 average which is
seasonally adjusted as:
1935 ÷ (102.2 + 93.8 + 98.1)/3 =
1935/98.0 = 1977 (base)
```

Month	Actual	Forecast	Deviation	Deviation Per Cent
January	2032	1977·97.8 = 1933	−99	− 5.0
February	2419	1977·108.3 = 2141	−278	−11.8
March	2638	2265	−373	−14.4
April	2800	2157	−643	−23.8
May	3155	2213	−942	−29.8
June	2228	1648	−580 ⎫ = −1,442/2 = −721	
July	2394	1532	−862 ⎭	−32.0
August	3094	2030	−1064	−34.6
September	2517	1998	−519	−20.8
October	2772	2020	−752	−27.3

Testing 1956—April 1 Forecast

```
2032
2419
2638
3)7089 = 2363
2363 ÷ (97.8 + 108.3 + 114.6)/3 =
2363/106.9 = 2210
```

Month	Actual	Forecast	Deviation	Deviation Per Cent
April	2800	2410	−390	−13.9
May	3155	2466	−689	−21.8
June	2228	1842	−386 ⎫ = −1068/2 = −534	
July	2394	1712	−682 ⎭	−20.1
August	3094	2269	−825	−26.6
September	2517	2234	−283	−11.2
October	2772	2259	−513	−18.0
November	2396	2073	−323	−13.0
December	2665	2167	−498	−18.6
January	2648	2161	−487	−18.4

Testing 1956—May 1 Forecast

```
2419
2638
2800
3)7857 = 2618
2618 ÷ (108.3 + 114.6 + 109.1)/3 =
2618/110.7 = 2366
```

Month	Actual	Forecast	Deviation	Deviation Per Cent
May	3155	2644	−511	−16.3
June	2228	1973	−252 ⎫ = −813/2 = −456	
July	2394	1833	−561 ⎭	−18.0
August	3094	2429	−665	−21.5
September	2517	2391	−126	− 5.0
October	2772	2418	−354	−12.8
November	2396	2220	−176	− 7.4
December	2665	2321	−344	−12.9
January	2648	2313	−335	−12.7
February	2461	2562	+101	+ 4.1

Testing 1956—August 1 Forecast

```
3155 (Has June and July in Base)
2228
2394
3)7777 = 2592
2592 ÷ (111.6 + 83.4 + 77.5)/3 =
2592/90.8 = 2854
```

Month	Actual	Forecast	Deviation	Deviation Per Cent
August	3094	2931	−163	− 5.2
September	2517	2885	+368	+14.6
October	2772	2916	+144	+ 5.2
November	2396	2678	+282	+11.9
December	2665	2800	+135	+ 5.1
January	2648	2791	+143	+ 5.4
February	2461	3090	+629	+25.6
March	2468	3270	+802	+32.5
April	2337	3113	+776	+33.2
May	2549	3184	+635	+24.9
June	2310	2380	+70 ⎫ = 669/2 = +335	
July	1612	2211	+599 ⎭	+14.0

Testing 1957—January 1 Forecast

```
2772
2396
2665
3)7833 = 2611
2611 + (102.2 + 93.8 + 98.1)/3 =
2611/98.0 = 2664
```

Month	Forecast	Actual	Difference	%
January	2648	2604	− 44	− 2.0
February	2461	2884	+423	+16.8
March	2468	3052	+584	+23.3
April	2337	2906	+569	+24.9
May	2549	2972	+423	+16.2
June	2310	2221	− 89 ⎫	
July	1612	2064	+452 ⎭ = ±363/2 = +182	+ 9.0
August	2318	2735	+417	+17.7
September	2359	2693	+334	+13.8
October	2397	2722	+325	+13.2

Testing 1957—April 1 Forecast

```
2648
2461
2468
3)7577 = 2526
2526 + (97.8 + 108.3 + 114.6)/3 =
2526/106.9 = 2364
```

Month	Forecast	Actual	Difference	%
April	2337	2578	+241	−10.3
May	2549	2637	+ 88	+ 3.4
June	2310	1971	−339 ⎫	
July	1612	1831	+219 ⎭ = −120/2 = −60	3.0
August	2318	2427	+109	+ 4.6
September	2359	2389	+ 30	+ 1.2
October	2397	2415	+ 18	Less than 1%
November	2100	2218	+118	+ 5.6
December	2226	2318	+ 92	+ 4.1

Testing 1958—January 1 Forecast

```
2397
2100
2226
3)6723 = 2241
2241 + (102.2 + 93.8 + 98.8)/3 =
2241/98.3 = 2279 base
```

Month	Forecast	Actual	Difference	%
January	2536	2229	− 307	−12.1
February	2577	2468	− 109	− 4.2
March	2693	2612	− 81	− 3.0
April	2534	2486	− 48	− 1.9
May	2817	2543	− 274	− 9.7
June	2953	1900	−1053 ⎫	
July	1890	1766	− 124 ⎭ = −1177/2 = −529	−25.6
August	2174	2340	+ 166	+ 7.7

Testing 1958—April 1 Forecast

```
2536
2577
2693
3)7806 = 2602
2602 + (97.8 + 108.3 + 114.6)/3 =
2602/106.9 = 2434
```

Month	Forecast	Actual	Difference	%
April	2534	2655	+121	+ 4.8
May	2817	2717	−100	+ 3.6
June	2953	2030	−923 ⎫	
July	1890	1886	− 4 ⎭ = −927/2 = −463	−19.1
August	2174	2500	+326	+15.0
September	2269	2461	+192	+ 8.4
October	2533	2487	− 46	− 1.8
November		2283		
December		2388		

Testing 1958-59—June 1 Forecast

```
2693
2534
2817
3)8044 = 2681
2681 + (114.6 + 109.1 + 111.6)/3 =
2681/111.8 = 2398
```

Month	Forecast	Actual	Difference	%
June	2953	2000	−953 ⎫	
July	1890	1857	− 33 ⎭ = −986/2 = −493	−11.0
August	2174	2462	+288	+13.2
September	2269	2424	+155	+ 6.8
October	2533	2451	− 82	− 3.2
November		2249		
December		2352		

dealing with this by using a special 60-day month for this June-July period. Likewise he proposed excluding June-July from the base. Thus the monthly forecasts would cease with the forecast of June 1 and resume with the forecast of November 1 with the June 1 forecast covering the interim. Thus there would be 8 monthly forecasts in a year.

The economist noted that comparing the various forecasts, the margin of error for the forecast of months 6 to 12 months out would tend to decrease in the future, as these months came to be only 3 to 6 months out.

The economist was aware that there were theoretical objections to his procedure. He knew that his method was simply a horizontal projection of the average of the most recent three months with a seasonal index then applied. He knew he could compute the trend and incorporate this on a monthly basis before applying the seasonal index. But this would not result in predicting turning points. For example, the turning points of cyclical swings would cause trouble. Thus:

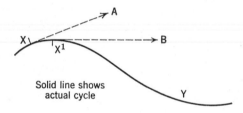

at point X, the method just outlined would be likely to project the future along the line to A whereas the actual line was going down. This method, however, should quickly correct itself to project to B. However, between points X^1 and Y the method should be "on target."

Because of this problem, the economist deliberately chose the 1956–58 period (with its recession) for testing. Table VII shows the results. If the period 1955–56 is used for testing the margin of error is lower.

Another problem is that *part* of the testing is done against a period whose data themselves formed part of the calculating process. However, if 1957 were excluded from the seasonal index determination and the testing done against 1957 data, the result would not be significantly affected.

Another problem is that the very great difficulties of Hevy-Truck in making forecasts had resulted in irregularities that have distorted the monthly data. For example, a serious underestimate of the future (of the order of 50 per cent) had led to the jamming of shipments near the month's end. In short, if a forecast is nearer to the fact to begin with, it is more likely that it will come true.

Evaluate this method.

How would you prepare Hevy-Truck's long-term forecast?

What would you do about developing a multiple correlation (graphic) method of forecasting for this case?

CASE I-3. OUTBOARD MOTORS*

Forecasting—Long-Term Forecast—Consumer Durable Goods

In its publication, *The Outboard Boating Industry and Its Market*, the Outboard Industry Association's 1959 Annual Conference sets forth the following forecast:

One widely used and accepted method of market forecasting is to first determine the economic index or economic data series which most closely follows your industry. The next step is to determine the exact relationship

CASE I-3. CHART I

Forecast of Motor Sales by Units, 1958–1970, Based on Trend of Personal Savings (Curve A = Estimated Motor Sales Increase Over 1958, Based on Trend of Personal Savings: Unit Shipment Increase—1,256,000; Percentage Increase—249; Curve B = Estimated Motor Sales from Household Purchasing Trend; Curve C = Estimated Motor Sales from Consumer Expenditures Trend)

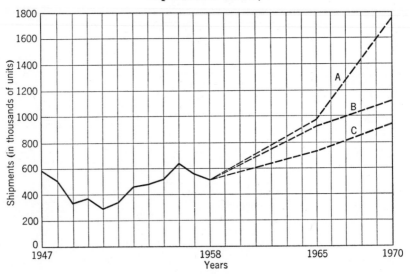

Source: Booz, Allen, and Hamilton, Consultants. Used by permission.

of this index or series to your industry; then on the basis of this established relationship (and with the future extension of the economic index or series available), to forecast the industry growth expected. Forecasts are generally

* With the assistance of Ben F. Hill, M.B.A. (Northwestern).

Case I-3. CHART II

Combined and Integrated Forecast of Motor Sales, 1958–1970, by Units (Estimated Increase over 1958: Unit Shipments—Minimum, 546,000; Maximum, 734,000; *Expected*, 679,000; Percentage—Minimum, 108; Maximum, 146; *Expected*, 135; Curve A = Expected; Curve B = Maximum; Curve C = Minimum)

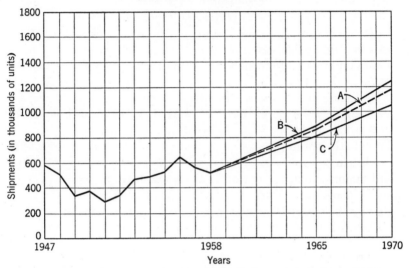

Source: Booz, Allen, and Hamilton, Consultants. Used by permission.

more accurate for the near future and tend to vary from the mark as you move into the future. Thus, the usual practice is to forecast in terms of a range which widens out as you move into the future.

More than one hundred indexes were examined to determine those most closely approximating the outboard industry. Three were chosen which appear to be most closely correlated.* These are patterns of consumer expenditures, household purchasing trends, and personal savings. Each of these was used to forecast first the unit motor sales of the industry. Forecasting with consumer expenditures as a base shows a prospective growth of unit motor sales of 83 per cent above 1958 levels by 1970. Using household purchasing trends, the industry motor forecast comes out at an increase of 122 per cent. Using personal savings, the increase is 249 per cent. Thus, one moves from a very conservative to a liberal forecast by utilizing the three economic series having most forecasting pertinence for the industry. These results are shown in Chart I.

To assure greater pertinence for the forecast, and using these three individual forecasts as a base, a combined and integrated forecast of motor sales was made. This is shown in Chart II. It will be noted that this results in

* The period used was apparently 1947–1958. Cf. Edwin R. Hodge, Jr., *A Study of the Outboard Motor Industry* (Bloomington, Ind.: Indiana University, 1951).

anticipated industry sales for 1970 ranging from 108 to 146 per cent above 1958 levels. The central tendency between these levels would indicate motor industry unit sales almost double the 1958 level.*

Returning from this conference, Mr. Har D. Head, the economist for one of the major outboard motor producers, felt disturbed by what he thought was undue optimism exhibited in this forecast. Preliminary to preparing his own forecast, Mr. Har D. Head gathered some data.

First, there was the sales record of the outboard motor industry shown in Table I. The equation of a trend line by least squares through the data on units sold for the years 1946 through 1958 is $Y = (436,900) (1.025)^x$, origin 1952 with x in 1-year units. The equation of a trend line by least squares through the data of annual dollar sales *adjusted by consumer price index* for the years 1946 through 1958 is $Y = (\$91,300,000) (1.112)^x$, origin 1952 with x in 1-year units.

Despite the optimistic demand situation indicated by this record Mr. Head began to explore the situation by examining two aspects of outboard motor demand. The first of these was whether the trend toward higher horsepower motors was likely to continue. This trend was suggested by the marked differences in annual rate of growth in number of units sold when compared to the annual rate of growth in sales dollars,

---

* For convenience in checking the statements the following data are set forth (the series "household purchasing trends" being unidentified):

Year	(1) Personal Consumption Expenditures	(2) Personal Savings	(3) Consumer Price Index
	In Billions of Current Dollars		1947–1949 = 100
1947	$165.4	$ 4.7	95.5
1948	178.3	11.0	102.8
1949	181.2	8.5	101.8
1950	195.0	12.6	102.8
1951	209.8	17.7	111.0
1952	219.8	18.9	113.5
1953	232.6	19.8	114.4
1954	238.0	18.9	114.8
1955	256.9	17.5	114.5
1956	269.9	23.0	116.2
1957	285.2	23.6	120.2
1958	293.2	24.4	123.5
1959	313.8	23.4	124.6
1960	328.2	26.0	126.4

Sources: Columns 1 and 2: *Economic Report of the President,* 1961, Table C-13; Column 3: *Economic Report of the President,* 1961, Table C-38.

Case I-3. TABLE I

Outboard Motor Sales, 1919–1960

Dollar Sales (in Millions)

Year(s)	Units Sold (in Thousands)	Average HP of New Units	Current Dollars	Adjusted by Consumer Price Index	Average Unit Price of New Units in Current Dollars
1919–30	357				
1931–33	41				
1934	23				
1935	41				
1936	50				
1937	100				
1938	100				
1939	120				
1940	130				
1941	170	3.6			
1942–45	(No Production During Second World War)				
1946	398	4.2	$ 48	$ 58	$120
1947	584	4.7	78	82	134
1948	499	5.2	73	71	145
1949	329	6.4	55	54	168
1950	367	6.9	63	61	171
1951	284	8.9	63	57	220
1952	337	8.4	70	62	208
1953	463	9.0	104	91	224
1954	479	10.3	116	101	243
1955	515	12.9	153	134	297
1956	642	14.2	213	183	332
1957	550	16.2	204	170	370
1958	504	20.7	234	190	466
1959	540	23.7	255	205	472
1960	508	27.4	243	192	478

Sources: 1934–1941 from *The Outboard Market, 1958*, Annual Market Research Notebook (Outboard Boating Club of America), p. 48; other years from *Boating* (Chicago: National Association of Engine and Boat Manufacturers, annual). Also, U.S. Department of Commerce, Bureau of the Census, Series, M31L, *Facts for Industry*. Consumer price index used is Bureau of Labor Statistics, *Bull. No. 1256*, U.S. City average of all items, base, 1947–1949.

considering sales dollars in constant dollars. One of the distinguishing features of an outboard motor in contrast to an inboard motor is the greater "utility" of the former in terms of its detachability with the consequent greater ease and lower cost in repairs. The economist speculated that somewhere in the horsepower range the advantage might shift to inboard motors.

A second aspect that disturbed Mr. Head was the question of the average life of an outboard motor. He was aware that in the case of consumer durable goods the rate of replacement was almost always an important question.

Accordingly Mr. Head developed the following information bearing

Case I-3. TABLE II

Outboard Motors in Use by Years, 1948–1960

Columns 1 Through 5 in Thousands of Units

Year	(1) Total in Use During Preceding Year	(2) Sold During Year Shown	(3) Total of Columns 1 and 2	(4) Total in Use During Year Shown	(5) Subtraction of (4) from (3) = Out of Use for Year	(6) Per Cent: Column 5 of 1	(7) Per Cent: Column 5 of 2
1948	1,857	499	2,356	2,321	35	1.9	7.0
1949	2,321	329	2,650	2,643	7	0.3	2.1
1950	2,643	367	3,010	2,811	199	7.5	54.4
1951	2,811	284	3,095	3,010	85	3.0	29.9
1952	3,010	337	3,347	3,219	128	4.3	38.0
1953	3,219	463	3,682	3,419	263	8.2	57.0
1954	3,419	479	3,898	3,740	158	4.6	33.0
1955	3,740	515	4,255	4,210	45	1.2	8.7
1956	4,210	642	4,852	4,740	112	2.7	17.5
1957	4,740	550	5,290	5,140	150	3.2	27.2
1958	5,140	504	5,644	5,485	159	3.1	31.6
1959	5,485	540	6,025	5,845	180	3.3	33.3
1960	5,845	508	6,353	6,050	303	5.2	59.6
						3.6*	

Source: columns 1 and 3: Boating 1960 (Chicago: National Association of Engine and Boat Manufacturers), p. 75; column 2: Table 1 of this case.

* Average unweighted arithmetic.

TABLE III

Manufacturers' Shipments Outboard Engines by Horsepower Rating for Selected Year (in Units)

Horsepower	1957	1956	1955	1954	1953	1952	1951 (Revised)	1950 (Revised)	1947
0.0– 2.9	52,634	50,689	11,695	21,932	8,378	50,019	14,850	18,871	83,951
3.0– 3.9			38,789	51,406	69,112		12,947	42,226	110,368
4.0– 4.9		104,400					10,510	18,038	
5.0– 5.9		1,441	95,735	110,043	113,222	95,345	91,334	116,658	247,696
6.0– 6.9				19,470					
7.0– 7.9								21,363	99,514
8.0– 8.9		88,577	72,424	81,081	90,443	90,156	71,036	53,127	
9.0– 9.9	137,169								
10.0–10.9			47,671	50,746	44,140	26,513		29,915	
11.0–11.9									
12.0–12.9		76,619	24,543					25,319	
13.0–13.9									
14.0–14.9	74,030								
15.0–15.9	111,236								
35.0 and up	174,457	319,761	223,871	144,672	138,060	75,386	91,020	41,656	42,929
TOTAL	549,976	641,527	514,728	479,350	463,335	337,419	291,697	367,173	584,458
Per Cent Change from Preceding Year Shown	–19%	25%	7%	3%	37%	15%	–20%	–36%	

Source: U.S. Dept. of Commerce, Bureau of the Census, Series M31L, *Facts for Industry.*

on average life of outboard motors. No direct information was available on this subject other than annual surveys as to the total number of outboard motors in use each year. Hence he constructed Table II.

Although the average annual rate of discards as a percentage of outboard motors in use each year was 3.6 per cent, the economist was aware he could not conclude that the average life of outboard motors was 28 years (100/3.6). The average life could only be established accurately by data as to the history of each year's sales. However, because the average annual number of new units sold had been relatively stable from 1946 through 1958, he felt safe in concluding that the average life was very probably over 20 years. In 1960, the ratio of new motors sold to used motors was five to three.

Turning to the question of the increasing horsepower of new units sold, the economist again found problems with the available data. The *Facts for Industry Series* (title now changed to *Current Industrial Facts*) of the Department of Commerce had been changing the classification of the data through the years (as so often happens). Table III summarizes data from this source.

On the other hand, industry sources yielded figures (Table IV) of

CASE I-3. TABLE IV

Estimated Sales of New Outboard Motors, by Horsepower Grouping

Year	Total Units Sold	0 to 6.9 hp	7.0 to 14.9 hp	Over 15 hp
1947	584,000	508,000	64,000	12,000
1948	499,000	404,000	80,000	15,000
1949	329,000	220,000	92,000	17,000
1950	367,000	224,000	110,000	33,000
1951	284,000	134,000	105,000	45,000
1952	337,000	175,000	111,000	51,000
1953	463,000	213,000	153,000	97,000
1954	479,000	201,000	163,000	115,000
1955	515,000	160,000	165,000	190,000
1956	642,000	173,000	225,000	244,000
1957	550,000	121,000	148,000	281,000
1958	504,000	86,000	126,000	292,000
1959	540,000	92,000	113,000	335,000
1960	508,000	83,000	79,000	346,000

Source: Boating, 1961 (Chicago: National Association of Engine and Boat Manufacturers).

Note: Unit figures are approximate, being obtained by multiplying percentage figures given in the source to total estimated new motors sold, and rounding.

CASE I-3. CHART III

Estimated Unit Sales of New Outboard Motors Sold by Horsepower Groups (Key: Cross-Hatched Portions = 15.0 Horsepower and Above; Dotted Portions = 7 to 14.9 Horsepower; Checked Portions = 0 to 6.9 Horsepower)

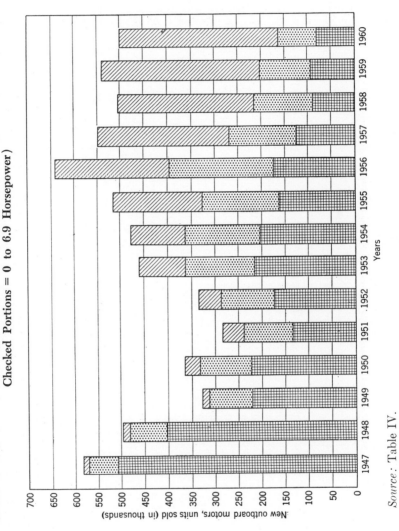

Source: Table IV.

Case I-3. TABLE V

Selected Information on Outboard Motors Available in Major Brands

Year	MERCURY Horsepower Available			JOHNSON and/or EVINRUDE* Horsepower Available			SCOTT-ATTWATER Horsepower Available		
	Minimum	Maximum		Minimum	Maximum		Minimum	Maximum	
1948	3.6	10.0	(3)	2.5	22.0	(5)	3.6	7.5	(2)
1949	3.5	10.0	(4)	2.5	22.0	(5)	3.6	7.5	(4)
1950	3.5	25.0	(5)	2.5	22.0	(5)	3.3	16.0	(5)
1951	3.5	25.0	(5)	2.5	25.0	(4)	3.6	16.0	(6)
1952	3.5	25.0	(5)	3.0	25.0	(4)	3.6	16.0	(5)
1953	5.0	25.0	(5)	3.0	25.0	(4)	3.6	16.0	(5)
1954	5.0	40.0	(5)	3.0	25.0	(4)	3.6	16.0	(5)
1955	5.0	40.0	(7)	3.0	25.0	(6)	3.6	30.0	(6)
1956	5.9	40.0	(5)	3.0	30.0	(6)	3.6	33.0	(6)
1957	6.0	60.0	(6)	3.0	35.0	(7)	3.6	40.0	(6)
1958	6.0	70.0	(9)	3.0	50.0	(6)	3.6	60.0	(8)
1959	6.0	70.0	(9)	3.0	50.0	(6)	3.6	60.0	(7)
1960				3.0	75.0	(6)	3.6	60.0	(6)

Sources: 1948–1958: *Outboard Dealer Trade-in Guide*, 1959 ed. (Chicago: Abos Publishing Co., 1959), *Sports Afield Boating Magazine*, pages 94, 95, 1959 Spring Ed.; 1960: 1960 brand catalog of company indicated.

* Not applicable to Evinrude prior to 1952. Evinrude motors were available in horsepowers up to 33.4 in 1948, 50.0 in 1949, 33.4 in 1950, and 25.0 in 1951.

The brands shown accounted for at least 75 per cent of total new outboard motors sold during the period shown.

The figures in parentheses indicate the number of motors of different horsepower available for the year, but not the number of models, since more than one model often appears in a horsepower class.

consistently classified data by horsepower grouping but with less refinement of the classification. Data for the year 1951 have been revised by the Department of Commerce but not by the industry in its series.* There are discrepancies between Tables III and IV. Thus in 1956, Table III shows 156,530 units sold in the 0- to 6.9-hp class, but Table IV shows 173,000 units. This is not an unusual situation in industrial statistics.

Chart III presents the data of Table IV in bar form and reveals the successive displacement of under 7-hp outboard motors by the 7- to 15-hp class and displacement of the 7- to 15-hp class by the class of 15 hp and up. The question remains whether another such replacement cycle is possible or whether the attempt to increase the size of outboard motors in horsepower will play into the hands of inboard motors. Table V shows the horsepower sizes available from the leading producers from 1948 to 1960.

Tables VI and VII set forth additional information showing the

CASE I-3. TABLE VI

Selected Information Regarding Outboard Motor Dollar Sales and Horsepower Trends

	(1)	(2)	(3)		(4)
		Adjusted New	New Motors Sold		Estimated
	New Outboard	Outboard	Average		Current Dollar
	Motor Sales	Motor Sales			Cost per
Year	(millions)	(millions)	Price	Horsepower	hp Unit
1946	$ 48	$ 58	$120	4.2	$28.60
1947	78	82	134	4.7	28.60
1948	73	71	145	5.2	28.00
1949	55	54	168	6.4	26.20
1950	63	61	171	6.9	24.80
1951	63	61	220	8.9	24.80
1952	70	62	208	8.4	24.80
1953	104	91	224	9.0	24.90
1954	116	101	243	10.3	23.60
1955	153	134	297	12.9	23.00
1956	213	183	332	14.2	23.40
1957	204	170	370	16.3	22.70
1958	234	190	466	20.7	23.20
1959	255	205	469	23.7	19.80
1960	243	192	478	27.4	17.50

Sources: Columns 1 and 3: *Boating, 1961* (Chicago, National Association of Engine and Boat Manufacturers); column 2: U.S. Department of Labor, Bureau of Labor Statistics, *Bull. No. 1256, Consumer Price Index,* United States city average, indexes of all items, annual average, pp. 39, 40, 41 (1947–1949 = 100) used to adjust motor sales of column 1; column 4: price in column 3 divided by horsepower in column 3, rounded. The *Consumer Price Index* for 1947 to 1960 (base 1947–1949 = 100) is set forth in a footnote at the beginning of this Case.

* In this industry, shipments and units produced are used interchangeably.

CASE I-3. TABLE VII

Price Changes for a Johnson Motor of the 5 to 6 Horsepower Class

		(1)	(2)	(3)
			Consumer	Constant
		Johnson	Price	Dollar
Year	Horsepower	F.O.B. Price	Index	Price (rounded)
1948	5.0	$160.00	102.8	$156
1949	5.0	170.00	101.8	167
1950	5.0	170.00	102.8	165
1951	5.0	187.50	111.0	169
1952	5.0	187.50	113.5	165
1953	5.0	187.50	114.4	164
1954	5.5	210.00	114.8	183
1955	5.5	210.00	114.5	183
1956	5.5	216.00	116.2	186
1957	5.5	230.00	120.2	191
1958	5.5	230.00	123.5	186

Source: Column 1: *Outboard Dealer Trade-In Guide, 1959* (Chicago: Abos Publishing Co.), pp. 26, 27, 28; column 2: U.S. Department of Labor, Bureau of Labor Statistics, *Bull. No. 1256, Consumer Price Index*, United States city average, indexes of all items, annual averages, pp. 39, 40, 41 (1947–1949 equals 100); column 3: column 1 divided by column 2.

growth in horsepower of new motors sold since 1946 and the average price of new motors and a typical motor, the 5 hp.

The sale of new boat trailers and motors over 15 hp show remarkably similar rates of growth as seen in Tables IV and VIII and Chart IV.

Outboard boating had shown a sharp rise in the recreational area in the decade from 1947 to 1958.

	Per Cent Increase in Sales 1947–1958
Outboard boating	430%
Fishing supplies	26
Golf equipment	43
Baseball equipment	30
Bowling supplies	216
Pianos	38
Organs	210

Source: The Outboard Boating Industry and Its Market, 1959 (Chicago: Outboard Industry Associations).

CASE I-3. CHART IV

**Relative Growth of New Boat Trailers (Curve A) and of New Outboard
Motors over 15 Horsepower (Curve B)**

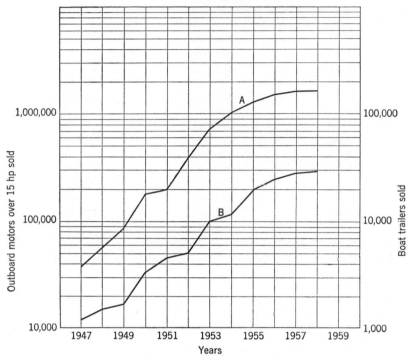

Source: Tables IV and VIII.

The national average of households with outboard motors was 9
per cent in 1958, but there is considerable variation by regions in the
number of households possessing outboard motors and boats as appears
in the sample of 1958 shown in Tables IX and X.

Tables X and XI reveal the importance of income and occupation
as factors in outboard motor sales.

The purposes (motivation) of outboard motor buyers are shown in
Table XII.

While he was assembling the above data, Mr. Head came across an
econometric study* in which outboard motor sales were related to
personal consumption expenditures, nonfarm residential construction,
personal savings lagged two years and disposable personal income.

* Made available by Richard Kyndberg, M.B.A. (Northwestern).

Case I-3. TABLE VIII

Unit Sales of New Outboard Boats and Boat Trailers for Selected Years

Year	Outboard Boats Sold	Boat Trailers Sold
1947	143,000	3,790
1948	198,000	5,700
1949	171,000	8,285
1950	131,000	18,390
1951	154,000	20,360
1952	164,000	39,220
1953	231,000	72,000
1954	223,000	103,000
1955	258,000	129,000
1956	302,000	151,000
1957	320,000	165,000
1958	316,000	168,000
1959	329,000	175,000
1960	300,000	160,000

Source: Boating, 1960 (Chicago: National Association of Engine and Boat Manufacturers).

By multiple correlation the following equation had been established for the data shown in Table XIII using Bimed Program 6 of the Medical School of the University of California at Los Angeles on the IBM-7090 machine:

$$Y = 236.67 + 4.985X, - 2.299X_2 + 1.9X_3 - 3.19X_4$$

R^2 for this equation is 0.943 with a standard error of estimate of 21.795.

$$Y = -235.726 + 4.859X_1 - 2.197X_2 + 1.939X_3 - 3.080X_4$$
$$\quad\quad\quad (2.481) \quad\quad (4.603) \quad\quad (0.800) \quad\quad (2.132)$$

The numbers in parentheses under the equation indicate the standard error of each of the coefficients of the independent variables above them.

The coefficients of partial correlation are as follows: R for the regression of Y on X_1 (holding the other independent variables statistically constant) is 0.527. Similarly, R^2 for the regression of Y on X_2 is −0.149, R for the regression of Y on X_3 is 0.608, and R for Y on X_4 is −0.416.

With this data before him, Mr. Head pondered how he should prepare an industry forecast since he considered the projections shown in Charts I and II to be entirely too mechanical and arbitrary.

Case I-3. TABLE IX

Per Cent of Households with Outboard Motors and Boats in Selected Metropolitan Areas

Cities	1958 With Outboard Motors	1958 With Outboard Boats	1959 With Outboard Motors	1960 With Outboard Motors
St. Paul	35	12	35	35
Duluth-Superior	27	15	26	30
Milwaukee	19	9	19	19
Seattle	18	12	19	20
Portland, Ore.	11	7	12	13
Sacramento	11	8	11	12
Columbus, Ohio	8	5	10	10
Chicago	8	3	8	8
Indianapolis	7	4	7	8
San Jose	7	4	8	9
Omaha	7	3	7	8
Phoenix	7	5	7	8
Salt Lake City	7	5	7	8
Wichita	5	4	5	6
Washington, D.C.	5	3	NA	NA
Cincinnati	5	3	NA	NA
Newark	4	3	NA	3
Denver	4	4	NA	5

Source: *The Outboard Boating Industry and Its Market, 1959.* (Chicago: Outboard Industry Association) and *Consolidated Consumer Analysis, 1960.*

CASE I-3. TABLE X

State Breakdown of Outboard Motor Purchases, Effective Buying Power and Population

	Per Cent of Motor Purchases			Per Cent of Buying Power		Per Cent of Estimated Population	
	56–57	57–58	1960	1957	1958	1957	1958
New York	9.41	8.82	9.37	11.01	11.71	9.69	9.54
California	6.92	7.11	9.93	9.90	10.12	8.18	8.30
Michigan	7.26	6.69	5.80	4.76	4.84	4.41	4.52
Illinois	6.00	5.55	4.72	6.89	6.78	5.62	5.61
Texas	5.36	5.10	5.37	4.93	4.79	5.44	5.44
Ohio	5.69	4.94	4.17	6.03	5.97	5.36	5.43
Florida	4.84	4.94	5.31	2.06	2.17	2.33	2.41
Minnesota	4.31	4.61	3.64	1.78	1.80	1.92	1.93
Wisconsin	3.96	3.94	3.66	2.18	2.14	2.21	2.22
Washington	3.33	3.60	3.44	1.76	1.70	1.58	1.60
New Jersey	2.94	2.95	2.97	4.17	4.01	3.28	3.29
Massachusetts	2.94	2.90	3.15	3.20	3.15	2.92	2.88
Pennsylvania	3.24	2.86	2.90	6.86	6.77	6.59	6.57
Indiana	2.91	2.75	2.48	2.74	2.70	2.61	2.62
Missouri	2.60	2.64	3.03	2.42	2.44	2.53	2.49
Louisiana	2.32	2.34	2.36	1.36	1.38	1.79	1.80
Iowa	1.78	1.88	1.63	1.50	1.40	1.59	1.58
Tennessee	1.75	1.84	1.97	1.49	1.43	2.05	2.03
Maryland	1.40	1.66	1.73	1.64	1.81	1.70	1.72
Connecticut	1.59	1.65	1.59	1.81	1.85	1.37	1.37
Oregon	1.37	1.65	1.91	1.00	0.96	1.04	1.04
Alabama	1.41	1.53	1.67	1.24	1.26	1.86	1.85
Oklahoma	1.52	1.49	1.28	1.13	1.08	1.34	1.31
Georgia	1.48	1.47	1.63	1.69	1.65	2.22	2.21
North Carolina	1.14	1.47	1.38	1.79	1.83	2.61	2.61
Virginia	1.45	1.39	1.48	1.91	1.89	2.21	2.23
Kansas	1.01	1.14	1.18	1.17	1.09	1.25	1.24
Maine	0.95	1.07	1.24	0.47	0.47	0.54	0.53
Kentucky	0.98	1.04	1.14	1.27	1.26	1.80	1.77
South Carolina	0.92	1.01	0.99	0.87	0.84	1.39	1.37
Arkansas	0.92	0.95	1.20	0.67	0.61	1.07	1.03
Mississippi	0.53	0.62	0.71	0.70	0.64	1.27	1.24
Nebraska	0.48	0.58	0.75	0.83	0.70	0.83	0.82
New Hampshire	0.51	0.56	0.63	0.31	0.31	0.33	0.33
Rhode Island	0.52	0.49	0.53	0.53	0.48	0.49	0.49
Utah	0.36	0.48	0.43	0.42	0.42	0.49	0.50
Colorado	0.38	0.47	0.63	0.89	0.93	0.96	0.97
Dist. of Columbia	0.45	0.44	0.36	0.69	0.64	0.51	0.49
West Virginia	0.37	0.43	0.26	0.90	0.90	1.16	1.15
Idaho	0.35	0.42	0.41	0.30	0.32	0.37	0.37
South Dakota	0.33	0.42	0.39	0.32	0.30	0.40	0.40
North Dakota	0.39	0.38	0.35	0.30	0.28	0.38	0.37
Montana	0.32	0.36	0.33	0.38	0.37	0.38	0.38
Delaware	0.30	0.35	0.28	0.26	0.29	0.24	0.24
Arizona	0.36	0.27	0.59	0.56	0.59	0.65	0.67
Vermont	0.27	0.26	0.34	0.19	0.19	0.22	0.22
New Mexico	0.19	0.19	0.28	0.41	0.39	0.50	0.50
Nevada	0.11	0.17	0.24	0.19	0.17	0.15	0.15
Wyoming	0.10	0.13	0.20	0.19	0.19	0.19	0.19
TOTAL	100.00%	100.00%	100.00%	100.00%	100.00%	100.00%	100.00%

Sources: The Outboard Market, 1958 (Chicago: Outboard Boating Club of America) and *The Boating Industry, 1960* (Chicago: National Association of Engine and Boat Manufacturers).

TABLE XI

Occupations of Outboard Motor Purchasers in 1960.*

	Per Cent of Employed Buyers					Per Cent Census Distribution of Employed Males	
	1956	1957	1958	1959	1960	1950	1960
Professional	11.6	13.5	13.2	14.9	16.4	7.3	10.7
Managers and proprietors	10.6	13.2	12.8	14.8	16.1	10.7	13.4
Clerical and sales	15.8	15.7	16.6	16.7	15.0	12.8	13.3
Skilled workers	39.2	34.5	32.0	29.6	28.6	18.6	18.9
Semi-skilled	10.1	9.7	13.9	11.2	10.8	20.0	19.5
Farmers, farm labor	4.2	4.5	4.0	4.0	3.6	15.1	9.5
Service workers	7.2	7.6	6.6	7.1	7.6	6.1	6.7
Factory labor	1.3	1.3	0.9	1.7	1.9	9.2	8.0
	100.0%	100.0%	100.0%	100.0%	100.0%	100.0%	100.0%

Source: Boating, 1960 (Chicago: National Association of Engine and Boat Manufacturers).
* In addition 7 per cent of purchasers were retired, students, etc.

CASE I-3. TABLE XII

Motivation for Buying Outboard Motors and Boats

	Per Cent of First Choice				Per Cent of All Choices			
	1955	1956	1957	1958	1955	1956	1957	1958
Uses of Motor Purchasers								
Hunting	8.7	8.9	8.7	3.7	7.3	7.5	7.4	6.7
Fishing	76.8	72.2	67.6	68.3	65.5	62.2	48.5	45.0
Racing	0.6	0.7	0.6	0.7	1.0	1.2	1.2	1.2
Cruising	11.9	14.8	17.5	19.5	18.6	20.4	28.0	28.8
Skiing	1.6	3.0	5.2	7.3	7.1	8.3	14.4	17.7
Rental	0.1	0.1	0.1	0.1	0.1	0.1	0.2	0.2
Commercial	0.3	0.3	0.3	0.4	0.4	0.3	0.3	0.4
Total	100.0%	100.0%	100.0%	100.0%	100.0%	100.0%	100.0%	100.0%
Uses of Boat Purchasers								
Hunting	8.8	8.4	8.4	5.0	7.2	6.7	6.7	6.5
Fishing	68.9	63.8	63.9	67.0	54.5	47.3	48.2	47.5
Racing	0.9	1.2	0.6	0.6	1.4	1.5	1.2	0.8
Cruising	18.4	21.2	17.5	20.9	27.1	29.7	28.0	27.5
Skiing	2.1	4.9	5.2	5.6	8.8	14.2	14.4	17.0
Rental	0.6	0.2	0.1	0.4	0.6	0.3	0.2	0.3
Commercial	0.3	0.3	0.3	0.5	0.4	0.3	0.3	0.4
Total	100.0%	100.0%	100.0%	100.0%	100.0%	100.0%	100.0%	100.0%

		1958	1959	1960
Cruising	Per cent of all uses mentioned	28.8	28.0	28.0
	Per cent of buyers mentioning	51.8	49.8	48.4
Fishing	Per cent of all uses mentioned	45.0	42.1	41.5
	Per cent of buyers mentioning	81.2	75.2	71.7
Hunting	Per cent of all uses mentioned	6.7	6.9	4.2
	Per cent of buyers mentioning	12.2	12.3	7.3
Skiing	Per cent of all uses mentioned	17.7	19.6	22.0
	Per cent of buyers mentioning	31.9	34.8	38.0
All other	Per cent of all uses mentioned	1.8	3.4	4.3
	Per cent of buyers mentioning	4.9	5.7	7.4

Source: The Outboard Market, 1959 and *1961* (Chicago: Outboard Boating Club of America).

CASE I-3. TABLE XIII

Outboard Motor Sales and Proposed Determinant Series

Year	Y Outboard Motor Sales in Millions (1)	X₁ Personal Consumption Expenditures in Billions (2)	X₂ NonFarm Residential Construction in Billions (3)	X₃ Personal Savings in Billions: 2-year lag (4)	X₄ Disposable Personal Income in Billions (5)	Yc Using Equation Stated in Text (6)	Y – Yc Column 1 minus Column 6 (7)
1944	—	—	—	$36.9	—		
1945	—	—	—	28.7	—		
1946	$ 48	$147.1	$ 4.8	13.5	$160.6	45	3
1947	78	165.4	7.5	4.7	170.1	83	−5
1948	73	178.3	10.1	11.0	189.3	50	23
1949	55	181.2	9.6	8.5	189.7	50	5
1950	63	195.0	14.1	12.6	207.7	62	1
1951	63	209.8	12.5	17.7	227.5	72	−9
1952	70	219.8	12.8	18.9	238.7	93	−23
1953	104	232.6	13.8	19.8	252.5	121	−17
1954	116	238.0	15.4	18.9	256.9	132	−16
1955	153	256.9	18.7	17.5	274.4	165	−12
1956	213	269.9	17.7	23.0	292.9	171	42
1957	204	285.2	17.0	23.6	308 8	195	9
1958	234	293.5	18.0	24.4	317.9	216	18
1959	255	313.8	22.3	23.4	337.3	247	8
1960	243	328.2	21.1	26.0	354.2	269	−26

Sources: column 1: Boating, 1960 (Chicago: National Association of Engine and Boat Manufacturers), columns 2, 3, 4, and 5: Economic Report of the President, 1961, Tables C-13 and C-31.

part II

Demand analysis and forecasting sales

In a real sense the separation of forecasting sales from demand analysis is arbitrary. A "complete" forecast should be based on a thorough demand analysis, although this does not imply that demand analysis is useful only in forecasting. At the very least, the forecast which rests heavily on a few carefully analyzed variables will be protected by an awareness of those factors being assumed constant if a broader demand analysis is completed. These factors being assumed constant (in their relationship to the product whose demand we are analyzing) may, with the passage of time, become much more significantly variable.

If a full demand analysis supports the forecast, the likelihood that changes in the constant factors will be detected earlier is greater than if the forecast is not buttressed by a demand analysis. For example, the predicting equation through random or offsetting errors may conceal for a period of time the movement of a factor which has appeared to be constant. On the other hand, if that factor were under continuous independent observation, its movement would have been detected earlier.

ELASTICITY OF DEMAND DEFINED

One of the most important concepts in demand analysis is elasticity, which is the sensitivity of change in the quantity of a product demanded to a change in a variable. The principal variables involved when demand elasticity is discussed are the price of that good (in the case of price elasticity), income (in the case of income elasticity) and the price of a substitute-product (in the case of substitute-product elasticity which is usually called cross elasticity).

More precisely, elasticity is the *relative* change in quantity demanded divided by the *relative* change in the variable (price, income or price of the other good). Hence the *units* in which quantity, price, etc. are stated are irrelevant since relative change is not affected by the units. A change of 10 per cent in quantity is a 10 per cent change whether measured in ounces, pounds or tons.

Elasticity of demand (E) is numerically measured as the ratio of the relative change in quantity of the product demanded to the relative change in the variable. Thus *price* elasticity of demand (E_p) is

$$E_p = \frac{\Delta Q/Q_1}{\Delta P/P_1}$$

where Δ indicates a small change in quantity (ΔQ) and a small change in price (ΔP). The subscript 1 indicates the quantity (and price) before the change. To avoid the use of the symbol Δ, we can state this[1]

$$E_p = \frac{(Q_1 - Q_2)/Q_1}{(P_1 - P_2)/P_1}$$

where the subscript 1 indicates the quantity demanded (and price) before the change in price and the subscript 2 indicates the quantity demanded (and price) after the change in price.

In the case of price elasticity of demand, E_p will have a negative sign.

Elasticity is commonly stated in the form of 1 per cent change. Thus if the price elasticity of demand is -1.5, a 1 per cent change in price will be accompanied by a 1.5 per cent change in quantity demanded (in the opposite direction).

---

[1] Various textbooks in economics give a number of alternative ways of stating this. The formula we have given is the arc elasticity of demand since it is the average over a short range. There is also point elasticity of demand which employs the rate of change at a point $\dfrac{dq}{q}$ and $\dfrac{dp}{p}$ rather than the average over a short distance. Because of the margin of error involved in economic data, the arc elasticity is adequate. Sometimes $(Q_1 + Q_2)$ and $(P_1 + P_2)$ are used in place of Q_1 and P_1 in the denominator. This uses an average of the quantity (and price) before and after the change instead of only the quantity (and price) before the change. *De gustibus non est disputandum.*

Point elasticity $[(dq/dp)(p/q)]$ uses the first derivative. If the demand equation were $q = 200 - 6p$, then we can readily compute the elasticity at a specific price, say 4. Substituting 4 for p in the demand equation, we get $q = 176$. Since $dq/dp = -6$, the elasticity at $p = 4$ is $-6(4/176) = -0.136$.

Elasticity, as thus defined, can vary from 0 to ∞ with 1 as a dividing point. Elasticities of 0 to 1 are referred to as relatively inelastic with the limit being an elasticity of zero for a vertical demand curve when quantity demanded is scaled on the X axis and price on the Y axis. Elasticities of 1 to ∞ are referred to as relatively elastic with the limit of infinite elasticity for a horizontal line when quantity demanded is scaled on the X axis and price on the Y axis. Unit elasticity, or price elasticity of 1, is a dividing line between elastic and inelastic and means that each relative change in price is offset by a relative change in quantity demanded so that *total* sales dollars (price times quantity) remain constant. A price elasticity less than 1 means that each change in price is not fully compensated by a change in quantity and thus as price decreases *total* sales dollars shrink. A price elasticity greater than 1 means that each change in price is more than compensated by a change in quantity and thus as price decreases *total* sales dollars increase.

Because elasticity involves not only the slope of the curve ($\Delta P/\Delta Q$) but also the absolute values of P and Q, the elasticity will be different for every point on a curve except (1) if the curve is a rectangular hyperbola in which case the elasticity is one throughout; (2) if the curve is horizontal in which case the elasticity is infinite throughout; and (3) if the curve is vertical in which case the elasticity is zero throughout.

Income elasticity of demand (E_i) is defined as:

$$E_i = \frac{\Delta Q/Q}{\Delta I/I}$$

where Δ indicates a small change in quantity demanded (ΔQ) and a small change in income (ΔI). If we want to avoid the use of the symbol Δ, this can be stated:

$$E_i = \frac{(Q_1 - Q_2)/Q_1}{(I_1 - I_2)/I_1}$$

where subscript 1 indicates the quantity demanded (and income) before the change in income and the subscript 2 indicates the quantity demanded (and income) after the change in income.

In the case of income elasticity of demand, E_i will have a positive sign when the good is superior and a negative sign when the good is inferior.

Cross (price) elasticity (E_c) is defined as:

$$E_c = \frac{\Delta Q_A/Q_{A1}}{\Delta P_B/P_{B1}}$$

where ΔQ_A indicates a small change in quantity demanded of product A and ΔP_B indicates a small change in price of product B. Beef and pork are traditionally referred to as examples of products having a high cross elasticity.

Cross (price) elasticity can also be stated as follows if we wish to avoid the use of the symbol Δ:

$$E_c = \frac{(Q_{A1} - Q_{A2})/Q_{A1}}{(P_{B1} - P_{B2})/P_{B1}}$$

where the subscript 1 indicates the quantity of product A demanded (and price of product B) before the change in price of product B, and the subscript 2 indicates the quantity of product A demanded (and price of product B) after the change in price of product B.

If the two goods are substitutes for each other, the cross elasticity will be positive and the greater the numerical value of the cross elasticity, the greater the degree of substitutability. If the two goods are complementary, the cross elasticity will be negative. The cross elasticity will also be negative if the income effect of a change in price outweighs the substitution effect.

Income and substitution effects of a price change are explained as follows. When the price of a good changes (declines, for example), the consumer (or producer) can obtain the prior quantity demanded with less income. The unused income will be applied in part (or as a limit, in total) to increasing the quantity taken of the good. This is the income effect.

The price change (decline, in our case) will also result in a greater quantity demanded because the lower price encourages substitution of more of the good whose price has declined in place of part of the quantity demanded of the near-substitute good. This is the substitution effect.

This is more precisely shown graphically in Figure II-1. Curve 1 shows all combinations of the two goods, X and Y, which are equally satisfying to a consumer. This is called an indifference curve since by definition all points on it are equally satisfying combinations. In the case of a production situation, curve 1 would represent all combinations of resources (say labor and machines) that could be used to turn out a given volume of output. Then the curve is called an isoquant.

Curve 2 is like curve 1 except that it represents a higher level of satisfaction (or output). The degree of curvature of curves 1 and 2 is dependent on the degree of substitutability of goods X and Y for each other. Thus a straight line (no curvature) would represent perfect substitutes

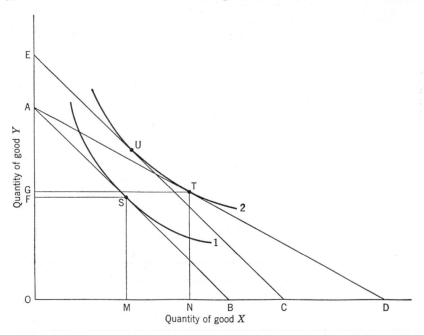

Figure II-1. Illustration of substitution and income effect.

The line AB is a price line and shows all the combinations of goods X and Y that can be bought for the same total expenditure so long as the prices of goods X and Y stay fixed. The line AD represents a fall (for all quantities) of the price of good X in the market place relative to the price of good Y which we assume has not changed.

The point of tangency, S (of curve 1 and the line AB) shows the quantities of goods X and Y that will be bought when the prices are as shown by the line AB and the preferences in consumption (or use in production) are as shown by curve 1. Thus OM units of good X and OF units of good Y will be taken when the price is as shown by AB and income is at that level.

The point of tangency, T (of curve 2, and the line AD) shows the quantities of goods X and Y that will be bought after the fall in the price of X that we have posited. Thus ON units of good X and OG units of good Y will be taken. As a result of the drop in price of good X, an increase in the consumption of both goods X and Y has occurred, namely of good X from OM to ON and of good Y from OF to OG. The income "released" by the drop in the price of good X has made possible the attainment of curve 2 which represents higher satisfaction (or output).

The price line EC is parallel to the price line AB and shows the same price relationship of goods X and Y to each other as is shown by the price line AB (as would any line parallel to AB). The line EC is so drawn as to be tangent to curve 2.

The consumer (producer) would as a result of the price change just posited, move from point S on Curve 1 to point T on Curve 2. This move involves two steps. First, we have the movement from S to U (the point of tangency of Curve 2 and the old price line EC). This movement is due to the increase in real income caused by the decrease in the price of good X and is described as the "income effect." The second movement is from point U on Curve 2 to point T on Curve 2 and is the adjustment between goods Y and X due to the change in their relative prices (as indicated by the price line AD replacing the price line AB after the cut in the price of good X). This is the "substitution effect" favoring good X.

The "income effect" may be positive or negative as to the change in the quantity of good X following an increase of income. There would be a negative change in the case of an "inferior" good such as potatoes, whose consumption is decreased by many people as their income increases. But the "substitution effect" always favors X. In general, the "substitution effect" outweighs the "income effect" even when the good is inferior.

ELASTICITY OF SUBSTITUTION

There is another measure of product substitution by buyers in the market besides the cross elasticity of demand which we have already discussed. That is the elasticity of substitution which is defined as:

$$E_s = \frac{\text{per cent change in ratio } \dfrac{\text{quantity demanded of } A}{\text{quantity demanded of } B}}{\text{per cent change in ratio } \dfrac{\text{price of } A}{\text{price of } B}}$$

This is particularly used in analyzing the production problem where A and B are factors used in production rather than final products bought by a consumer.

SHARE ELASTICITY

Following closely upon the heels of the concept of cross elasticity is the notion of share elasticity referring to the relationship of the percentage of a market that a particular producer has to the price differential between that producer's price schedule and the price schedules of his competitors. This concept is difficult to apply in most cases since the concept of a price differential between one producer's price schedule and that of his competitors involves the establishment of the price differential throughout the entire range of prices in a price schedule. However, where pricing of the producer and his competitors follows a systematic pattern over such a range, one may be able to quantify the concept.

While cross elasticity relates absolute sales differences of one product to price changes of competing products, share elasticity relates the market share of one producer as a percentage to the price changes of his competitors as a percentage.

SIGNIFICANCE OF ELASTICITY OF DEMAND

The three types of elasticity of demand (price, income and cross) are significant in forecasting because over periods of time, one or more of them may be constant. Thus in a forecast in which the quantity demanded of a particular product is found to depend heavily on two variables (say temperature and population), *all* of the types of elasticity may be assumed constant.

Classical economists of the nineteenth century (beginning with J. S. Mill) dealt particularly with the relationship of price of a product and quantity demanded of the product. This relationship is still the cornerstone of many elementary economics texts and courses. The reason why the nineteenth century economists considered this relationship important lies in the conditions of that society. Classical economists, with considerable validity, could assume as relatively constant the major variables whose rapid changes are so significant today, namely, *income, technology (particularly as to the possibility of new and substitute products), tastes, the prices of other goods, and other equally important variables.*

Tastes were more stable in the society of the nineteenth century partly because of the comparative lack of communication between countries, because of the local character of markets, because of the limited use of the efficiencies of larger scale production, and the lack of standardization (in parts, tolerances, etc.). The other variables were similarly more stable in large degree. They were changing but at a much slower rate than today. It is true that population grew rapidly and that the Industrial Revolution occurred in the nineteenth century but change was at a slower rate. Some may be inclined to dispute this interpretation of economic history but the author rests on his extensive industrial experience.

With other variables constant and price and quantity demanded the variables under examination, the importance of price elasticity is heightened. This points up the basic distinction between a situation in which investigation deals with points on the *same* demand curve (such as price elasticity involves) and the situation in which the demand curve itself has moved. For example, shifts of the demand curve (price-quantity demanded relationship) are involved when tastes change, when new products that are close substitutes are introduced and when incomes change (unless the income elasticity of demand is zero).

In addition to the greater constancy of variables (other than price and quantity demanded of the product) in the nineteenth century, products bought by consumers at that time were proportionately much more of what is today classified as consumer goods and much less semi-durable or durable consumer goods. The matter of consumers' inventories of goods and the average age of durable goods was not then as important.

However, the perpetuation of this nineteenth-century thinking in modern elementary textbooks cannot be easily justified. The change in the prices of all other goods (which can be treated as the purchasing power of money) and the change in population are dealt with in elementary textbooks through adjustment of price-quantity demanded data to per capita (population adjustment) and constant dollar (price of other goods) terms.

Hence, in the modern economy it is particularly important to analyze income elasticity of demand and cross elasticity of demand to detect any changes which may occur in these variables. The study of these elasticities together with price elasticity of demand should disclose any shift in tastes, for example.

To the extent that changes in tastes are effected through advertising as a dominant factor, a predicting equation will incorporate advertising as a significant variable.

DIFFICULTIES IN ESTABLISHING ELASTICITIES

Examination of some of the difficulties which confront us when we attempt to approximate elasticity (whether price elasticity, income elasticity or the elasticity of some other variable) will bring out that demand analysis ranges far and wide. It is easy to *say* that other things are being assumed constant when we are investigating historical data such as the relation of quantity sold and prices. But such a statement must be supported by evidence that is at least approximately true, if the results of making the assumption are to be useful.

To get the price-demand schedule for a single product for an individual firm is a major target. However, this involves treating the data as homogeneous, namely, assuming, for example, that the product itself stays constant, that the incomes, expectations and preferences of the buyers stay constant and that the relation of the prices of other and competing sellers stay constant with reference to our price. In addition to this, prices of our product must be moved back and forth while the market conditions just described remain stable. This seldom happens.

There is, however, one category of products particularly meeting the conditions of homogeneity we have just described and this is agricultural products. The classical work in this area is by Schultz[2] who used quite simple assumed relationships such as $x = a + by + ct$ where x is per capita consumption of the product, y is the deflated price, t is time removed from the base year, and a, b, and c are constants established by multiple correlation. Fitting such a relationship, Schultz used data for the period 1915 to 1929 and found the following price elasticities of demand for agricultural products with a typical R^2 of 0.9:

Sugar	−0.31	Potatoes	−0.31
Corn	−0.49	Oats	−0.56
Cotton	−0.12	Barley	−0.39
Hay	−0.43	Rye	−2.44

These results obtained during a period when there was no governmental intervention in the production and marketing process. In the case of wheat where there was primarily a world market rather than a national market, Schultz found the stability of the price-quantity relationship was lower (that is, R^2 was lower). We would thus expect the stability of the agricultural price elasticities to be no longer as great since the introduction of programs such as the food stamp, school lunch and other governmental activities affecting private demand.

There are areas in which conditions approximate the agricultural

[2] Henry Schultz, *Theory and Measurement of Demand* (Chicago: University of Chicago Press, 1938). The elasticities following in our text are established for sugar on p. 205 of Schultz, for corn on p. 257, for cotton on p. 305, for hay on p. 343, for potatoes on p. 425, for oats on p. 457, for barley on p. 473, and for rye on p. 491.

situation. Where price changes occur over very short periods of time (as in retailing), the other variables are not likely to move significantly. Where price is the dominant variable in sales because price comparisons are frequently made (as in retailing), and where style changes are slow (as in staple products) and where product differentiation is difficult and where income is held constant, we can expect to be able to determine price elasticity more accurately.

GRAPHIC MEASUREMENT OF ELASTICITY

We have set forth above the formulae for price, income and cross elasticities of demand. Rather than perform the computations indicated by the formulae, the elasticities can be determined graphically. Thus the data as to price and quantity demanded (or income and quantity demanded or price of product A and quantity demanded of product B) can be handled in either one of two ways.

1. The data can be plotted on double logarithmic paper.
2. What is the same thing, the logarithms of the data can be plotted on arithmetic paper.

Elasticity can then be measured directly as the slope of the line $(\Delta Y/\Delta X)$ *if* quantity demanded is plotted on the *vertical* axis and price (or income of the other product) is plotted on the *horizontal* axis.

Since economists traditionally plot quantity demanded on the horizontal axis and price on the vertical axis, it follows that price elasticity will be the reciprocal of the slope if the logarithms of the data are plotted in the traditional manner.[3]

Likewise, in the case of variables other than price, the logarithm of quantity may be graphed vertically. Then elasticity is the slope rather than the reciprocal of the slope.

It should be remembered that in determining the elasticity of one variable (such as price), all other variables (such as income) are held constant. Thus historical prices and quantities cannot simply be plotted against each other on logarithmic paper without adjusting the data, e.g., adjusting price with a price index for changes in the price level.

---

[3] Thus on the double log paper, with quantity demanded on the horizontal axis and price (income or price of the other good) on the vertical axis, elasticity is $\Delta X/\Delta Y$ or the reciprocal of the slope of the line $(\Delta Y/\Delta X)$ contrasted with the case when quantity demanded is plotted on the vertical axis and the other variable on the horizontal axis.

RELATIONSHIP OF ELASTICITY TO AN EQUATION IN MULTIPLICATIVE FORM

Predicting equations may be stated in an additive form such as:

$$Y = f(X + Z)$$

Or, predicting equations may be stated in multiplicative form such as:

$$Y = f(X \cdot Z)$$

When the equation is in multiplicative (or hyperbolic) form, the exponents of the independent variables are elasticities and are constant for all points on the curve. Thus in the equation, $Y = f(X \cdot Z)$ we have a situation in which the exponents of X and of Z are one. Then a 1 per cent change in X will be associated with a 1 per cent change in Y and a 1 per cent change in Z will be associated with a 1 per cent change in Y.[4] If the equation were $Y = X^{0.4}Z^{0.3}$, then a 1 per cent change in X would be associated with an 0.4 per cent change in Y and a 1 per cent change in Z with an 0.3 per cent change in Y.[5]

In the special case where the sum of the exponents of the independent variables is one, we have a linear and homogeneous function. Thus $Y = L^{0.75}C^{0.25}$.[6] This type of equation has particular significance (to be discussed in Part III) in considering production and costs. The special characteristic of this equation is that a 1 per cent change on one side of the equation is associated with a 1 per cent change on the other

[4] This is on the assumption that the independent variables X and Z are independent of each other and not themselves correlated. Cf. H. Wold and L. Jureen, *Demand Analysis* (New York: Wiley, 1953), Chapter 2.

[5] When elasticities are determined by this method, a least-squares bias can result either from errors in measuring the variables which are being considered as independent in the multiple correlation or from movements or shifts in the functions that are being estimated. If the errors involved in measuring the independent variables are random (not correlated with the true values of the independent variables nor with each other) they will tend to introduce a downward bias in the coefficients of the equation. Thus when quantity is the dependent variable, the price or income elasticity taken from the equation will tend to be underestimated. But when price in the dependent variable, price elasticity will tend to be overestimated since the estimated elasticity will be based on the reciprocal of the coefficient in the equation. Cf. A. C. Harberger, *The Demand for Durable Goods* (University of Chicago Press, 1960), p. 7f.

[6] This is the form of the famous Cobb-Douglas function, reported in C. W. Cobb and P. H. Douglas, "A Theory of Production," *American Economic Review*, vol. 18 supp. pp. 139f (1928) and expanded in later articles in the *Quarterly Journal of Economics* and *Journal of Political Economy*.

A function is homogeneous and linear when multiplication of each of the independent variables by a constant multiplies the dependent variable by the constant.

side of the equation. The exponents continued to state elasticities of the independent variables. Thus in the equation, a 1 per cent change in L is associated with an 0.75 per cent change in Y.

In the case of an equation in additive form—for example, $Y = f(X + Z)$—not only will the elasticity will be different for different points on the price-quantity curve, but if Y is quantity demanded and X is price and Z is income, then price elasticity will also change as income changes. In this situation, elasticity can be obtained by taking the partial derivative of the function with respect to X for any given values of X and Z.[7]

VERIFYING CERTAIN VARIABLES IN THE STUDY OF ELASTICITY

Thus in demand analysis if a predicting equation is developed which does not incorporate price as an independent variable because this variable was found not significant in the past period over which the equation was established, a separate check on this variable can be undertaken through periodic examination of price elasticity to make certain that no change has occurred. Similarly for income and cross elasticities.

SATURATION

One aspect that should receive attention in connection with any forecast or demand analysis is saturation. Too often this is either (a) ignored, or (b) assumed to be adequately considered when the specific determinants of quantity demanded are analyzed, such as price or income.

Thus, if graphic multiple correlation is being used, and if, for example, the demand for soft drinks is being analyzed, we might discover that total soft drink consumption is heavily correlated with temperature variations, with population and with income. A forecast might be made projecting a total consumption of soft drinks which on a per capita basis would exceed the average per capita human intake of liquids of about 40 ounces a day.

The forecaster must, therefore, devote particular attention to establishing a limit or saturation point. At any one time there is such a saturation point but the point may change through time. Thus when people think in terms of a one-car family we have one saturation point

---

[7] Thus if the values (parameters) of the function are $q = 100 - 0.7p^2 + 0.5y$, price elasticity is $\partial q/\partial p \cdot p/q = -1.4p^2/q$. Similarly, income elasticity is $\partial q/\partial y \cdot y/q = 0.5y/q$.

but when the two-car family becomes common, we may speak of a new saturation point.

We might measure saturation as simply the ratio of the existing stock (or buyers) to the maximum level of ownership (or buyers). Thus, if there are presently 50 million households and 48 million have refrigeration, the market may be said to be 96 per cent saturated.

It may be, for example, that household furniture expenditures may continue to expand with personal disposable income at approximately the ratio of the last ten years. However, as each household builds up an "inventory" of currently styled furniture, the question arises whether this ratio of household furniture expenditures to personal disposable income will not decline. To maintain the ratio would require that the average age of household furniture would have to drop. To be sure, the ratio could be maintained for a considerable period with the same average age though progressive increases in the value of each piece of furniture, or an increase in the "inventory" of furniture that each household wants or some similar basis.

What we are trying to say then, is that there may be factors existing in the demand situation which are presently constant (or "dormant"), but which may become variable (or "active") at some point of time in the future.

An Illustration of Saturation

We can illustrate the matter of saturation as well as the shift in demand determinants over time by examining the situation of chemical fertilizers.[8] Mehring, using data for the period 1910 to 1943, found that fertilizer expenditures could be predicted from the equation:

$$X_0 = 0.03293Y_{-1} + 0.01766Y_0 + 1.159\ P_{-1} - 18.844$$

where X_0 = fertilizer expenditures in a given year in millions of current dollars

Y_{-1} = crop income of farmers from crops in the prior year plus government payments received in millions of current dollars

Y_0 = crop income of farmers from crops in the given year plus government payments received in millions of current dollars

P_{-1} = the percentage of total cash income of farmers in the previous year remaining after production costs

The equation was quite satisfactory until 1949, except that from 1944 to 1949 farm income grew faster than available chemical fertilizer, and it took some years for supply to catch up.

[8] The following data is drawn from the Chemical Fertilizer Case at the end of this Part. The following equation has been corrected to remove an error in the original, as noted on p. 155.

Beginning with 1949, the equation lost its accuracy although it was several years before the industry recognized that the deviations between the forecast of the equation and actual data were something more than random.

After considerable work by economists in many parts of the nation, Professor King, in 1959, established a new equation, using data for the period 1911 to 1957:

$$Y_t = -55 + 1.0662Y_{t-1} - 3.504C + 4.801T - 3.220P + 5.659S$$

where Y_t = predicted nutrient consumption in thousands of tons of plant nutrient

Y_{t-1} = nutrient consumption in the prior year in thousands of tons

C = percentage change in corn acreage planted in millions of acres

T = percentage change in tobacco acreage planted in millions of acres

P = change in price of nutrient unit stated as an index number, 1912 = 100

S = percentage change in cash sales of crops from prior year in billions of current dollars

This equation explains 99.3 per cent of the annual variation in nutrient consumption from 1911 to 1957.

At the outset it should be noted that Mehring predicted fertilizer expenditures in money terms but King predicts nutrient consumption in physical terms. Fertilizer tons differ from nutrient tons in that the former includes "filler" such as sand and the latter only the usable chemicals in the fertilizer. The percentage of "filler" has been decreasing.

From 1953 to 1958 inclusive, annual per capita nutrient consumption has been highly stable, varying between 36.2 and 37.6 tons of nutrient per 1,000 people although from 1940 to 1952 this figure had grown steadily from 14.4 to 34.1. Fertilizer consumption appears to have saturated on a per capita basis as long as present food patterns of the people continue unchanged.

It would appear to be likely that there is a high degree of correlation between the independent variables used by Mehring and those used by King. This would go a long way towards explaining why two different equations might cover a common period (1911 to 1949) successfully, and yet one equation (Mehring) fails badly for the next period (1949 to 1958) while the other (King) satisfies that period.

However, this situation suggests two propositions:

1. That no amount of "back testing" is fully adequate support for a predicting equation.

2. That the more complicated and "artificially" related the terms of an equation, the more skeptical one can be about its use regardless of the excellence of its "back testing."

The first proposition rests upon the argument that it is quite possible to improve the coefficient of determination (for a regression line applied to a limited number of observations) by manipulating the independent variables until the fit is improved.

For example, in the case of the Mehring equation, the introduction into the equation of the current year's cash income is suspect. The fertilizer expenditure (X_0) is made before the cash income of the same year (Y_0). This cash income might be used as an index of the *expected* cash income of that year but such use would require further evidence because of the notorious inability of farmers (in the Mehring period) to estimate their incomes.

The second proposition is in part related to the first. Unless consideration is given to the fact that for each additional independent variable introduced a degree of freedom is lost, an artificially high correlation will result as variables are added.[9]

To say that the variables being added are "artificially" related is, of course, begging the question on our part. This matter is better illustrated in our section below on predicting equations.

DEMAND DETERMINANTS CAN FREQUENTLY BE ANTICIPATED FROM THE PRODUCT GROUP

It is of value in analyzing demand for a product for the first time to examine in the first instance those demand determinants which have been found in prior studies to be frequently significant with respect to the *broad product category* into which the product whose demand is being analyzed falls.

For this purpose products are frequently classified as:

> Consumers' nondurable goods
> Consumers' durable goods
> Producers' goods

[9] The use of ordinary tests of significance in the type of analysis we are examining can be challenged. Traditional statistical tests assume that the independent variables are random variables and normally (or at least independently) distributed. But as was brought out at the close of Part I above, there is mutual dependence between successive observations in an economic series.

Roos[10] uses a more refined classification:

Consumers' perishable goods
Consumers' semidurable goods
Consumers' durable goods
Capital goods
Construction materials
Fuels
Raw materials and supplies.

It is apparent that the Roos breakdown of producers' goods is valid since raw materials, for example, reflect volume of production while capital goods purchases are an investment decision and may be quite independent of the current production. The Roos classification reflects the long experience of the Econometric Institute with demand analysis and the demand determinants which seem to be indicated for each group.

Demand for Consumer Nondurable or Semidurable Goods

Purchases of consumer nondurable and semidurable goods frequently are significantly determined by:

1. Population and its characteristics;
2. Secular per capita consumption trend of the product;
3. Price (of the product and of substitutes) ;
4. Discretionary income and buying power.

The fact that consumer nondurable and semidurable goods are frequently related to population changes and characteristics calls for close attention to the fact that total population changes but at different rates of change in different time periods.[11]

Population characteristics, such as age groups, are clearly involved

---

[10] Charles Roos, *Dynamics of Economic Growth* (New York: Econometric Institute, 1957), pp. 108ff.

[11] Population forecasts prepared by the Bureau of the Census are available in *Statistical Abstract of the United States*. Four basic forecasts are made, each with different assumptions regarding future birth rates, etc. Forecasts of gross national product, consumer expenditures, new construction activity and many other economic series which may be employed in preparing the forecast for a particular industry or a particular product can be found in Bonnar Brown and M. Janet Hansen, *Production Trends in the United States Through 1975* (Menlo Park, California: Stanford Research Institute, 1957) and Economic Forecasting Operation, Marketing Services, General Electric Co.: *20-Year Economic Forecast, 1960–80* (Schenectady, N.Y.: General Electric Co., 1950). Other forecasts of such series are found in the periodicals *Fortune* and *Electrical World* and in occasional publications by the Econometric Institute (New York) and National Planning Association (Washington, D.C.).

in the demand for some products. Thus an increase in the birth rate
will lead to a relative increase in products used by children, such as
toys. Or an increase in the 18- to 30-year-old group leads to an increase
in the demand for beer.

Population characteristics which are of importance in some products
include male-female ratios, urban-rural ratios, geographic movements
(North-South, East-West), etc.

The dramatic growth of the American economy in the 1950's rested
in part on the changed population characteristics of that decade. It
would be a serious mistake to project such rates of change into the
decade of the 'sixties. In fact, the demographic aspect of economic
growth in the 'sixties appears to be less favorable than it was in the
1950's.

We will summarize briefly a few of these demographic aspects. The
population of the United States increased 14.9 per cent in the 1940's
and 18.5 per cent in the 1950's. The four basic forecasts of the Census
Bureau show the lowest estimate for the 1960's at 12.9 per cent and the
highest at 22.4 per cent but with the median less than for the 1950's.
The birthrate, which peaked in 1947 at 26.6 births per thousand population compared to a low of 18.4 in 1933, stood above 25 per thousand
until 1956, but dropped to 24.3 in 1958, to 24.1 in 1959 and to 23.6 in
1960.

There had been (1) a marked increase between 1940 and 1960 in
the proportion of women marrying, (2) a marked decrease in the average age at marriage, and (3) a marked decrease in the average "com-
pletion time" of family formation. The marriage situation is summarized in Table II-1. This movement appears to have reached its limit.
In fact, the acceleration of marriage age and family formation "com-
pletion time" in the 1950's may easily have "borrowed" children from
the 1960's.

The age group pattern shifted drastically in the 1950's. Thus the
percentage increase in the 0- to 9-year age group was 32 per cent from
1950 to 1960 and 37 per cent for the 10- to 19-year age group. These
rates will be nearer to zero and 5 per cent, respectively, in the 1960's.
On the other hand, the age group from 20 to 34 actually declined in
the 1950's as a result of depression birth rates. The 20- to 24-year
group will see a 60 per cent increase in the 1960's and the 25 to 34
age group will increase 10 per cent in the 1960's compared to a 4 per
cent increase in the 1950's.

Without completing the cycle of age groups, it is apparent that these
changes in rates of growth for population age groups will seriously
affect (downwards) the demand for infants' wear, toys, baby foods

and even for new early elementary school teachers and (upward) the demand for radios, clothes and apartments (the initial marital abode).

For our present purposes, the important point is that the age group factor must be treated as a variable in analyzing the demand for many types of goods and not as a constant or as a variable that will operate in the 1960's as it did in the 1950's. The last is the assumption made in a simple extrapolation. Similarly, other demographic aspects may require recognition as variables.

Consumer nondurables typically have a per capita secular trend which is basic to their demand analysis. Thus the increase in newsprint follows a rising educational level of the population plus increased leisure time. Or, a line of least squares fitted to *total* consumer nondurables shows a trend over several decades of an increase of 0.35 per cent per year per capita but in recent years this has been arrested since the younger population does not consume as much as the average of the population and the younger age group has increased faster than total population.

Price as a determinant of the volume of consumer nondurables is sometimes more important through cross-elasticity (involving substitute products) than it is directly in terms of price elasticity. Direct price elasticity can be expected to be more important with respect to those consumer nondurables which are capable of storage and free from style-change risks.

Discretionary income and buying power[12] can be expected to be determinants of the demand for many consumer nondurables, particularly those which are true luxuries.[13] To the extent that a product has

---

[12] Discretionary income is disposable personal income (personal income after income tax, but including transfer payments such as social security, unemployment compensation, and Veterans' Administration payments) less long-term (installment and fixed) committments payable within the period and necessary living costs at a minimum. Discretionary buying power brings into consideration (besides discretionary income): cash balances on hand, new consumer credit, and perhaps the stock of near liquid assets. A series for discretionary income from 1939 to 1959 can be found in National Industrial Conference Board, *Technical Paper # 6* (1958) and supplements. This series starts with the Department of Commerce figure for disposable personal income, and subtracts (a) imputed income, such as the rental value of owner-occupied residences, and income in kind, (b) fixed payments such as installment debt, mortgage debt, and rent of tenants, and (c) minimum expenditures for food, clothing, medical costs, home utilities, and local transportation.

[13] It must always be remembered that the economist uses "luxury" in a sense quite different from that of a layman. To an economist, a luxury is a product with high income elasticity of demand and possibly high price elasticity of the industry's demand curve (as opposed to the demand curve as seen by the in-

a neutral income elasticity of demand, the effect of a rising personal income will be reflected more in the secular trend.

Demand for Consumer Durables

Purchases of consumer durable goods differ significantly as to demand determinants from the determinants of consumer nondurable goods. The difference follows directly from the difference in durability.

Thus quantity demanded of consumer durables frequently is partially determined by:

1. The number of households;
2. Disposable income and discretionary income;
3. Credit terms;
4. Price (of the product or substitutes);
5. Existing stock of such goods;
6. Average age or durability of such stock.

To the extent that the consumer durable is used "by the household" rather than on an individual basis, it is clear that total household figures (and changes therein) are more important than total population figures (and changes therein). Household formation changes are somewhat independent of population changes (which, of course, depend on birth and death rates). In particular, changes in the number of households at any one time can move in the opposite direction from population changes. Thus as the small age group born in the late 1930's goes through the marriage period, the rate of new household formation goes down while population is still rising from the increased birth rate of the postwar period of World War II. The few consumer durables (for example, electric shavers) that are used individually could be expected to depend more on population than households.

Disposable income and discretionary income can be expected to be determinants of the quantity demanded in the case of consumer durables due to the relatively large price per unit (relative to incomes) and due to durability and hence postponability in the case of replacements. Particularly because of the "prestige" element as to new types of consumer durables and as to replacements of older types, changes in disposable income can be expected to have an effect independent of credit terms.

---

dividual producer). The economist's definition carries none of the connotation that the word luxury has for the layman, namely, implications that the product is *morally* unnecessary or *traditionally* not part of the minimum standard of living. Thus to an economist, hard liquor in the demand of an alcoholic is furthest possibly removed from being a luxury.

Changes in credit terms have an effect on demand for consumer durables. This is evidenced by the use of the regulation of installment credit by the Federal Reserve Board to deal with inflation and deflation. However, an index of credit terms may be difficult to develop.

On the demand side, the importance of price in the case of consumer durables rests heavily on the element of postponability. On the supply side, mass production and the ensuing large reduction of costs per unit is similarly of great importance in the case of consumers durables.

Since the size of existing stock is likely to have a significant relation to the demand for new purchases, the demand by new owners is separated for analysis from the demand of existing owners for replacements. Once saturation is achieved, new-owner demand may become almost zero and the demand depend almost entirely on replacements. Replacement demand often depends heavily on the age of the existing stock and on income because of the possibility of postponability.

Thus in some cases, demand for consumer durables when divided between new-owner demand and replacement demand may find different determinants acting on the two segments, or the same determinants but with quantitatively different pressures. Hence, age of existing stock may be dominant in the replacement demand of durables where new-owner demand is zero because of full saturation *and* the demand for the product has become income inelastic.

Demand for Capital Goods

Quantity demanded in the case of capital goods frequently is significantly determined by:

1. Profit (and tax) picture of the industry buying;
2. Depreciation and obsolescence situation;
3. Margin of unused capacity;
4. Prices of the good produced by the equipment;
5. Price of the equipment (or unit labor costs);
6. Long-term interest rate.

Situations 1, 3, and 4 can sometimes be reduced to one term, since, if an industry has over-capacity, its profits (and depreciation recovered) are likely to be low or negative and the prices of the goods produced by the equipment are low. This implies that the demand for capital goods will be constructed by segments with each segment being a different industry (or group of industries) using that capital good.

In the case of the demand for a particular capital good, the substitution effect between men and machines may be quite significant so that as unit labor costs rise (as when the wage rate increases or labor productivity falls) the demand for the capital good increases.

Price of the equipment is most likely to enter through postponability and therefore, average age of the existing stock, or through the substitution effect of unit labor costs.

This leaves the long term interest rate. We would expect, *ceteris paribus,* that a rise in the long term interest rate has a depressing effect on the purchase of capital goods. However, particularly at certain points in the business cycle the rate of return for debt and the rate of return for equity move in opposite directions. While the economist often means the cost of money, whether debt or equity, when he refers to the long term interest rate, even in this sense changes in the long term cost of money may be of minimum effect. In many industries, differences in the cost of money are a very small part of total costs and are overshadowed in importance by doubts as to feasibility of new fixed asset commitments. In such cases, differences in cost of money lead to different decisions only when there is considerable agreement as to the feasibility of the contemplated program. However, to illustrate the importance of the interest rate in certain industries such as steel and mining, the electric power industry has as high as 95 per cent of its assets in capital equipment, and capital charges (depreciation, interest and dividends) are as high as 30 per cent of total costs. The impact of a shift in the cost of money from 4 to 6 per cent, or vice versa, is clear, particularly if postponement is possible.

The demand analysis of capital goods can be placed in a larger framework than simply the relationship to the six variables we have listed above. First, the analysis examines the demand for the products made by the industry buying capital goods. The pattern of this demand when compared to existing facilities and their capacity establishes the actual margin of excess capacity (positive, negative or zero) present in the industry buying the capital goods whose demand we are investigating. The relation of this excess capacity to the future demand for that industry's product is considered next.

If the productivity of the capital good is constant (or if we adjust for varying productivity), the "needs" of the industry using that capital good are determinable.

The "ability" of the industry to buy can be gauged from its profit picture. Retained profits and depreciation charges are not the only sources of funds for buying, but they correlate closely with the ability to get additional new funds, either debt or equity.

Demand for Housing and Construction

Largely because of inadequate statistics over past years,[14] housing demand analysis is handicapped. However, the impact of the change in marital status indicated by Table II-1 is obvious.

TABLE II-1

Percentage of U.S. Population with Single Status, by Age Groups, 1940 to 1960

Age Group	1940	1950	1955	1960
18–19	87%	80%	78%	80%
20–24	60	43	43	41
25–34	24	14	14	13
35–44	12	9	9	8

Source: Department of Commerce: *U.S. Census of Population* and *Current Population Reports,* Series P-20, No. 105.

Added to this is the "doubling up" rate which was 6.8 per cent in 1942 and rose to 8.6 per cent in 1947 but fell to 4.8 per cent in 1953.

In the general area of construction (other than housing) similar difficulties arise because of inadequate statistics and their classification.

EXAMINATION OF SOME PREDICTING EQUATIONS DEVELOPED BY MULTIPLE CORRELATION

An examination of the empirical results obtained from predicting equations which have been developed for several commodities should provide a yardstick by which to evaluate this tool of economic analysis.

In making our selection of illustrations, we have been guided by several purposes. We have deliberately chosen predicting equations that were developed a number of years ago. It is one thing to fit an equation to historical data so as to minimize the deviations of the actual data from the statistics computed from the equation. It is quite

[14] Charles Roos, *Dynamics of Economic Growth* (New York: Econometric Institute, 1957), p. 201ff points out that the Bureau of Census reports 46 million housing units in 1950 and 37.3 for 1940 or an increase of 8.7 million in the decade. But the Bureau of Labor Statistics shows 5.7 million new nonfarm housing units built in the decade and the Department of Agriculture shows 0.9 million new farm housing units. Demolitions of 0.9 million in the decade do not reconcile the figures. Conversions, trailers, temporary housing and other aspects must be brought into the picture.

a different matter to apply that equation to predicting the future. It is a peculiarity of much of the published work in the area of predicting equations that it is concerned with the fitting of historical data, or "back casting" as it is called. Very little is published as to the actual dependability of predicting equations when applied to the future. It appears to be too easy to shrug one's shoulders and say the variables changed whenever a predicting equation yields poor results as to the future. Then the old equation is discarded and work starts on a new equation which will fit the recent data and the older data with a greater degree of dependability than the old equation. This is not unlike the problem of the sinner who asks forgiveness and then goes right back to sinning.

Another purpose in selecting the predicting equations to be examined has been to choose materials that are widely and publicly available so that the reader can experiment further if so inclined. Still another purpose in selecting consumers' durables as the subject of the predicting equations has been that this area is generally considered more difficult for a number of reasons, some of which were explored earlier, and some of which will be dealt with directly.

Equations Predicting Total Autos in Use

The *Survey of Current Business* in 1952 published an estimating equation[15] prepared by the Office of Business Economics of the Department of Commerce for automobiles. The equation is:

$$Y = 0.00009058 X_1^{1.069} X_2^{0.439}$$

in which Y = total private passenger car registration in thousands,[16]
X_1 = number of households in millions,
X_2 = disposable personal income in billions of 1939 dollars.

When this equation is fitted to data for 1925 through 1940, $R^2 = 0.96$.

As already noted, the multiplicative form of the equation has the advantage that the exponents of the independent variables directly state the elasticities if we can assume that there is no correlation between the independent variables. For example, the exponent 1.069 with the number of households in millions tells us that for each increase of 1 per cent in the number of households in millions, there is a 1.069

---

[15] April 1952, pp. 19–24.

[16] Actually this unit is stated in the *Survey of Current Business* to be in millions. Correspondence with Mr. L. Jay Atkinson of the Office of Business Economics who did the study reveals that the working papers have been destroyed. However, experimentation quickly discloses there is a simple error in units.

per cent increase in the number of total private passenger car registrations in thousands.

The logic behind the choice of these two variables as likely determinants of total passenger autos in use is quite clear. The use of households as a determinant rests on the hypothesis that in the case of the great number of existing passenger car owners, passenger cars are used on the basis of one per household. The choice of disposable personal income as the other determinant rests on the hypothesis that disposable personal income affects autos in use through raising some households to the threshold of being able to afford a car or two cars. The size of the exponents which developed for number of households (1.069) and disposable personal income (0.439) indicates that an increase of one per cent in millions of households had more than twice the effect on new car purchases as did an increase of one per cent in billions of constant dollars of disposable personal income during the period 1925 to 1940.

Other facts which have a bearing on the number of autos in use, namely, average age of cars at scrappage, credit terms available to new car purchasers, the relative price of cars, etc. are assumed, (a) constant, (b) self-cancelling, or (c) properly measured by the number of

CHART II-1

Annual Total Private Passenger Car Registrations for 1925 through 1951, Actual (Solid Line) and Predicted (Broken Line) from Equation:
$$Y = 0.00009058X_1^{1.069} X_2^{0.439}$$

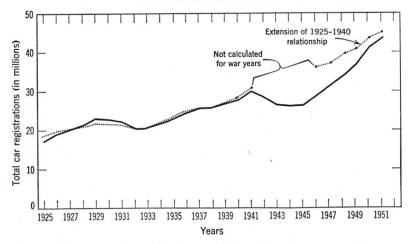

Source: Survey of Current Business (April 1952), p. 20.

households or disposable personal income or some combination of these two.

It is to be noted that the trend was not removed from any of the series. This vitiates the strict significance of R^2 since the degree of association is made artificially high by including the extent to which the trends of the series are parallel. However, when the purpose of the equation is predicting, the including of the association between variables is desirable.

The *Survey of Current Business* notes with respect to the data for 1946 through 1951 that it took six years after World War II for the car market to catch up because of the fact that new civilian cars were not available from 1942 through 1945. Hence the estimates for the period 1946 through 1951 are high, but the gap between actual total car registrations and those computed from the equation (which is based on 1925-to-1940 experience) closes each year from 1946 to 1951.

CHART II-2

Annual Total Private Passenger Car Registrations for 1946 to 1958, Actual (Solid Line) and Predicted (Broken Line) from the Equation: $Y = 0.00009058X_1^{1.069} X_2^{0.439}$

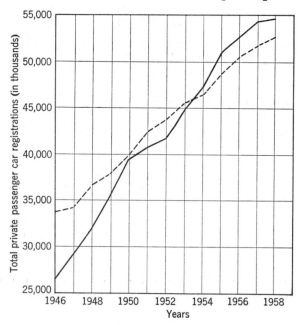

Source: Table II-2.

CHART II-3

Annual Total Private Passenger Car Registrations for 1946 to 1958, Actual and Predicted from the Equation: $Y = 0.00009058X_1^{1.069} X_2^{0.439}$

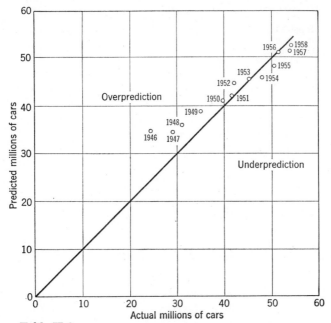

Source: Table II-2.

This is shown in Chart II-1 published in 1952 by the Survey of Current Business.

When this equation is used to compute the expected total private passenger car registrations for the period 1946 to 1958, the results are as shown in Table II-2 and in Charts II-2 and II-3.

In projecting a regression line beyond the 1925-to-1940 period whose data were used in establishing the equation, we cannot develop an R^2 in order to evaluate the performance of the equation.[17] To evaluate the performance of the predicting equation, we can examine the difference column in Table II-2 for a rough estimate or inspect Chart II-1 visually observing the deviations of actual from computed values in the period from which the equation was drawn and contrasting this performance with the deviations in the predicted period shown in Chart II-2.

---

[17] The regression line will not pass through the arithmetic mean of the new data and hence the algebraic sum of the deviations of actual data from computed points will not sum to zero.

TABLE II-2

Total Private Passenger Car Registrations for 1946 to 1958, Actual and Predicted from Equation: $Y = 0.00009058X_1^{1.069} X_2^{0.439}$

Year	X_1 Number of Households in Millions (1)	X_2 Disposable Personal Income in Billions of 1939 Dollars (2)	Total Private Passenger Car Registrations in Thousands Y-computed (3)	Total Private Passenger Car Registrations in Thousands Y-actual (4)	Difference $Y_c - Y_a$ (5)
1945	37.5	104.2	—	—	—
1946	38.2	103.3	33,950	26,464	7,486
1947	39.1	98.9	34,250	29,154	5,096
1948	40.7	104.1	36,562	31,789	4,773
1949	42.1	105.2	37,938	35,407	2,531
1950	43.6	113.7	40,910	39,419	1,491
1951	44.7	116.6	42,476	40,768	1,708
1952	45.5	119.8	43,811	41,788	2,023
1953	46.3	125.5	45,549	45,061	488
1954	46.9	126.4	46,300	47,106	−806
1955	47.8	134.4	48,571	51,028	−2,457
1956	48.8	139.9	50,526	52,671	−2,145
1957	49.5	142.7	51,757	54,344	−2,587
1958	50.4	141.8	52,617	54,775	−2,158

Sources: column 1: *Statistical Abstract of U.S.;* column 2: *Economic Report of President, 1959,* deflated by implicit deflator, personal consumption expenditures; column 4: R. L. Polk and Co.

If a more precise comparison is desired, the performance of the predicting equation can be contrasted with the results of a naive model, or with a series of naive models. Such a naive model might be, for example, one assuming that the annual increment of cars in use would be a constant annual increment as established by a least squares fit for 1925 to 1940. Then the sum of the squares of the deviations of the actual data from the regression line would be computed for the naive model and the same figure calculated for the predicting equation. These two sums may then be compared directly.

The equation of the suggested naive model for 1925 to 1940 is $Y = 23,572 + 404.9X$ [18] with Y the number of car registrations in thousands and X in years and centered at the midpoint of 1936 to 1937. Using this equation, the forecast for 1946 to 1958 would be as shown in Table II-3.

[18] Fitted by the method of semi-averages to the actual total private passenger car registrations in thousands:

1925	17,486	1929	22,500	1933	19,300	1937	25,331
1926	18,915	1930	22,345	1934	20,726	1938	24,455
1927	19,410	1931	21,484	1935	22,015	1939	25,745
1928	20,674	1932	19,752	1936	23,846	1940	27,158

Source: R. L. Polk and Co.

TABLE II-3

Total Private Passenger Car Registrations, Actual and Computed from Equation $Y = 23,572 + 404.9X$ (with X in Years and Origin at Midpoint 1936 to 1937) Compared with Results of Forecast in Table II-2

Year	Total Private Passenger Car Registrations in Thousands		Difference $Yc - Ya$ (3)	Difference Squared (4)	Difference from Table II-2 Squared (5)
	Y (computed) (1)	Y (actual) (2)			
1946	27,418	26,464	954	910,116	56,040,196
1947	27,823	29,154	−1331	1,771,561	25,969,216
1948	28,228	31,789	−3561	12,680,721	22,781,529
1949	28,633	35,407	−6774	45,887,076	6,405,961
1950	29,038	39,419	−10381	107,765,161	2,223,081
1951	29,443	40,768	−11325	128,255,625	2,917,264
1952	29,848	41,788	−11940	142,563,600	4,092,529
1953	30,253	45,061	−14808	219,276,864	238,144
1954	30,658	47,106	−16448	270,536,704	649,636
1955	31,063	51,028	−19965	398,601,225	6,036,849
1956	31,468	52,671	−21203	449,567,209	4,601,025
1957	31,873	54,344	−22471	504,945,841	6,692,569
1958	32,278	54,775	−22497	506,115,009	4,656,964
				2,788,876,712	143,304,963

Source: column 2: R. L. Polk and Co.

Note that when this forecast was made, cars were assumed to increase at 404.9 thousand per year during the war years.

It is apparent that the predicting equation substantially outperforms this particular naive model.

It is likewise apparent from Charts II-1 and II-2 that the predicting equation does not perform as well for the period 1946 to 1958 as it does for the period 1925 to 1940. There are two dominant reasons for this. First, all variables (other than the number of households and disposable personal income) affecting total passenger car registrations are assumed to exert the same effect in 1946 to 1958 as they did in 1925 to 1940. But this assumption is not true (e.g., the impact of wartime non-availability of private passenger cars). Second, the two variables dealt with in the predicting equation, namely, number of households and disposable personal income, are assumed to bear the same relationship to total private passenger car registration in 1946 to 1958 as these two variables bore in 1925 to 1940. This may or may not be true. We can only say "may or may not be true" because it is possible that the greater deviation in 1946 to 1958 is due entirely to other variables rather than to a change in the relationship of number of cars in use to the number of households and disposable personal income.

Although it should be rather obvious, the problem of homogeneity in data must be emphasized. Taking the total of all cars and handling this figure as has been done in the Department of Commerce study is to assume that each car is equal to every other car, not only at any one point in time but at each point in time. Thus a 1925 car is assumed identical with a 1940 car and the lowest price Ford equal to a Cadillac. This difficulty is much more vexing in the case of consumer durable goods than in the case of soft goods. To deal with this problem, some investigators have attempted adjustments. But in such a case the question is whether more error is removed than introduced. A 10-cubic-foot refrigerator is not a 4-cubic-foot refrigerator. Should the series be collected in terms of 4-cubic-foot units and the 10-cubic-foot units be included as the equivalent of 2.5 4-cubic-foot units?

Another vexing problem is with respect to prices of consumer durables. What are readily available are the suggested list prices for the models of the consumer durable good. But it takes little experience to realize that there is a serious year-to-year fluctuation in the margin that separates the suggested list price of a consumer durable from the actual price at which sales are being made in a given year. Thus immediately after World War II, sales of consumer durables were actually taking place at prices well above the suggested list price but today such sales are taking place at prices below the suggested list price. This, of course, does not mention the varying trade-in allowances involved. Some investigators in attempting to deal with this problem have used advertised newspaper prices instead of suggested list prices. Others have used the prices in Sears Roebuck catalogs on the ground that not only are these actual prices which avoid the trade-in problem since Sears does not deal in trade-ins but they constitute good average price figures over a period of time since Sears holds a price between catalogs whereas newspaper prices may represent the downward-biased "bargain-sale" prices.

Another problem is the determination of a price series to use. In the next Department of Commerce study to be discussed, the average retail price of cars is used. This price series was based on the average of the "low-priced three" (Ford, Chevrolet, and Plymouth) in their medium price line on the ground that this group constitutes the great bulk of cars and other models are priced at rather fixed differentials from this group.

Predicting Annual New Car Registrations

There also appeared in *Survey of Current Business* in 1952,[19] an estimating equation prepared by the Office of Business Economics of

---

[19] April 1952, pp. 19–24.

the Department of Commerce for annual new automobile registrations. This equation is:

$$Y = 0.0003239 X_1{}^{2.536} X_2{}^{2.291} X_3{}^{-1.359} 0.932^{X_4} \qquad (1)$$

where Y = new private passenger car registrations per million households[20]

X_1 = disposable personal income per household in 1939 dollars;

X_2 = current annual disposable income per household as a percentage of the preceding year in 1939 dollars;

X_3 = percentage of average retail price of cars to consumer prices measured by consumer price index;

X_4 = average scrappage age in years.

When this equation is fitted to data for 1925 through 1940, $R^2 = 0.98$.

Again, because of the multiplicative form of the equation, the exponents of the independent variables directly show the elasticities if the independent variables are not correlated between themselves. Thus the equation shows that a 1 per cent increase in disposable personal income per household in constant dollars results in a 2.5 per cent

CHART II-4

Annual New Private Passenger Car Registrations for 1925 to 1951, Actual (Solid Line) and Predicted (Broken Line) from Equation:
$$Y = 0.0003239 X_1{}^{2.536} X_2{}^{2.291} X_3{}^{-1.359} 0.932^{X_4}$$

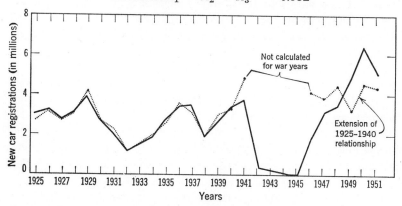

Source: Survey of Current Business (April 1952), p. 20.

[20] Actually this unit is stated in *Survey of Current Business* to be in terms of thousands of households. Correspondence with Mr. L. Jay Atkinson of the Office of Business Economics who did the study revealed that the working papers had been destroyed. However, experimentation quickly discloses a simple error in units.

CHART II-5

Annual New Private Passenger Car Registrations for 1946 to 1958, Actual (Solid Line) and Predicted (Broken Line) from Equation:

$$Y = 0.0003239X_1^{2.536}X_2^{2.291}X_3^{-1.359}0.932^{X_4}$$

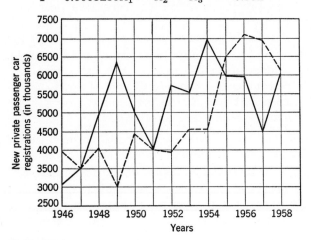

Source: Table II-4.

increase in new cars sold per million households. Likewise, a 1 per cent increase in the ratio of current year's disposable income per household over the prior year's is associated with a 2.3 per cent increase in the number of new cars sold per million households. And a 1 per cent decrease in the price of cars relative to other goods is associated with a 1.4 per cent increase in the number of new cars sold per million households. The factor for change in average scrappage age is quite small quantitatively in the equation.

When the results of substitution for the independent variables in this equation are plotted against the actual new car registrations[21] for the years 1925 to 1940, the fit is good as is shown in Chart II-4.

However, when substitution of the values of the independent variables is made for the later years, 1946 to 1958, the predicting equation does not perform nearly as well as is shown in the following Table II-4 and the accompanying Charts II-5 and II-6.

Besides the predicting equation for new car registrations which we have just presented, the *Survey of Current Business* in 1952 also developed several variations of this equation. These are:

$$Y = 0.0364X_1^{2.51}X_2^{2.33}X_3^{-1.29}0.881^{X_4} \qquad (2)$$

[21] Note that we are using new car sales and registrations interchangeably. They differ slightly.

where Y = new private passenger car registrations per 10 thousand people;

X_1 = disposable personal income per capita in 1939 dollars;

X_2 = percentage current to preceding year of disposable income per capita in 1939 dollars;

X_3 = percentage of average retail price of cars to all consumer prices measured by Consumer Price Index;

X_4 = average scrappage age.

When this equation is fitted to data for 1925 through 1940, $R^2 = 0.98$.

CHART II-6

Annual New Private Passenger Car Registrations for 1946 to 1958, Actual and Predicted from Equation:

$$Y = 0.0003239X_1^{2.536}X_2^{2.291}X_3^{-1.359}0.932^{X_4}$$

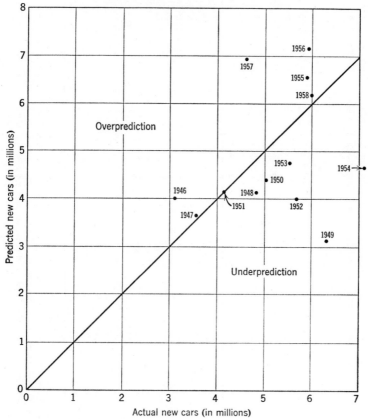

Source: Table II-4.

TABLE II-4

New Private Passenger Car Registrations for 1946–1958, Actual and Predicted from Equation: $Y = 0.0003239 X_1^{2.536} X_2^{2.291} X_3^{-1.359} 0.932^{X_4}$

Year	(1) X_1 = Disposable Personal Income Per Household in 1939 Dollars	(2) X_2 = Current Annual Disposable Income as Per Cent of Preceding Year in 1939 Dollars	(3) X_3 = Ratio of Retail Price Index of Cars to Consumer Price Index	(4) X_4 = Average Scrappage Age in Years	(5) Per Million Households Y-computed	(6) Computed New Car Sales	(7) Actual New Car Sales	(8) Difference (Column 6 minus Column 7)
1945	2782							
1946	2704	0.972	111.3	12.8	103,150	3,940,000	3,177,000	763,000
1947	2530	0.935	102.2	12.3	92,704	3,625,000	3,491,000	134,000
1948	2558	1.011	103.7	13.6	101,950	4,149,000	4,838,000	−689,000
1949	2499	0.976	114.6	14.0	75,150	3,164,000	6,326,000	−3,162,000
1950	2608	1.045	114.4	13.5	101,770	4,437,000	5,060,000	−623,000
1951	2609	1.001	110.9	13.0	92,970	4,156,000	4,158,000	−2,000
1952	2633	1.009	118.3	14.3	86,918	3,955,000	5,739,000	−1,784,000
1953	2710	1.029	118.3	13.8	101,320	4,691,000	5,535,000	−844,000
1954	2695	0.995	115.9	13.2	99,215	4,653,000	7,170,000	−2,517,000
1955	2812	1.044	112.1	12.3	137,530	6,574,000	5,955,000	619,000
1956	2867	1.019	113.4	11.1	146,390	7,144,000	5,982,000	1,162,000
1957	2882	1.005	115.6	11.1	140,010	6,931,000	4,651,000	2,280,000
1958	2813	0.976	116.2	11.1	122,270	6,162,000	6,026,000	136,000

Columns (5)–(8) fall under the heading: New Private Passenger Car Registrations

Sources: Column 1: disposable personal income in 1939 dollars from *Economic Report of President*, 1959, deflated by implicit deflater, personal consumption expenditures; number of households from *Statistical Abstract of U.S.* (each is shown separately in Table II-2). Column 2: computed from column 1. Column 3: note that the percentages in columns 2 and 3 are stated with the latter one hundred times greater—this follows the computations of the Office of Business Economics; source of average retail price of cars and consumer price index: Bureau of Labor Statistics, monthly release, Consumer Price Index. The retail price of car index is based on the standard sedan models of Ford, Chevrolet, and Plymouth, as priced by dealers. Column 4: Average scrappage age is from Automobile Manufacturers Association, *Automobile Facts and Figures* (series discontinued in 1957; value for 1956 projected to 1957 and 1958). Column 6: column 5 multiplied by number of households in millions. Column 7: R. L. Polk and Co.

$$Y = 0.006X_1^{2.46}X_2^{2.28}X_3^{-1.48}0.991^t \qquad (3)$$

where Y, X_1, X_2 and X_3 are the same variables as in equation 1 above and t is the year minus 1933. When this equation is fitted to data for 1925 through 1940, $R^2 = 0.97$

$$Y = 0.000005X_1^{2.45}X_2^{2.47}X_3^{-1.23}0.841^{X_4} \qquad (4)$$

where Y = new private passenger car registrations in thousands.

X_1 = disposable personal income in millions of 1939 dollars.

X_2 = percentage current to preceding year of disposable personal income in millions of 1939 dollars.

X_3 = percentage of average retail price index of cars to consumer prices measured by Consumer Price Index.

X_4 = average scrappage age.

When this equation is fitted to data for 1925 through 1940, $R^2 = 0.97$

$$Y = 50.59 + 0.1001X_1 + 0.0841X_2 - 1.1244X_3 - 6.4374X_4 \qquad (5)$$

where Y, X_1, X_3 and X_4 are the same variables as in equation 1 above and X_2 = change in disposable income per household in 1939 dollars. When this equation is fitted to data for 1925 through 1940, $R^2 = 0.96$.

TABLE II-5

Data to Test Equations (2) Through (5) for New Private Passenger Car Registrations in Addition to Data Available in Tables II-2 and II-4

	(1)	(2)
Year	Population in Millions	Disposable Personal Income in Billions of 1939 Dollars
1945	139.5	104.2
1946	141.0	103.3
1947	143.5	98.9
1948	146.0	104.1
1949	148.6	105.2
1950	151.1	113.7
1951	153.7	116.6
1952	156.4	119.8
1953	159.0	125.5
1954	161.8	126.4
1955	164.6	134.4
1956	167.5	139.9
1957	170.5	142.7
1958	173.4	141.8

Sources: column 1: *Economic Almanac 1960;* column 2: *Economic Report of President, 1960*, deflated by implicit deflator, personal consumption.

These five predicting equations establish several propositions for the period 1925 to 1940 because of the similar values for R^2. First, it appears that it is not material whether per capita or per household figures for disposable personal income are used. In other words the relative movement of the number of households and the population is very similar during the period 1925 to 1940. This appears in comparing equation 1 with 2.

Second, the use of a "time" factor in equation 3 rather than average scrappage age as used in equation 1 makes no appreciable difference in results. This suggests that average scrappage age, which is a rather stable figure, is not a particularly important variable with respect to new car registrations. The so-called time factor is simply an annual increment which might be called a growth or trend factor. Third, the comparison of equation 4 with 1, 2, and 3 suggests to us that disposable personal income, relative car prices and change in disposable personal income over the prior year are the controlling factors as to new car registrations rather than either population or households. This is consistent with the comparison of equations 1 and 2 which suggested that the use of per capita or per household data made no difference.

Equation 5 uses an additive form rather than a multiplicative and uses the absolute change in disposable personal income per household rather than the ratio of the current year's disposable personal income per household to the preceding year's. This appears to yield no significant difference.

It is worth noting that the exponents of the multiplicative equations remain stable in the four equations although there is some difference in the constants.

Comparison of Simple and Complicated Predicting Equations

We are now in a position to approach the question whether a more elaborate predicting equation incorporating additional variables is likely to add significantly to the accuracy of a predicting equation. We are fortunate to have available the General Motors study done by Charles F. Roos and V. von Szelinski in 1938.[22] This study originally started with the concept that total sales of autos are composed of new owner demand and replacement demand, a favorite concept of the Econometric Institute. This group, under the leadership of Roos until his death and now guided by Colin Clark has engaged in extensive work with predicting equations.[23]

In their automobile study, Roos and von Szeliski found it difficult

---

[22] General Motors Corporation, *The Dynamics of Automobile Demand* (1938).
[23] See, for example, Charles Roos, *Dynamics of Economic Growth* (New York: Econometric Institute, 1957).

to determine new and replacement demand for automobiles separately and hence approached the subject through a single predicting equation.

The equation developed by Roos and von Szeliski for new auto sales is

$$S = J^{1.2}P^{-0.65}[0.03C(M - C) + 0.65X]$$

where S = new car sales at retail;
  J = supernumerary income;
  P = index of car prices;
  C = number of cars in use during the year;
  M = computed maximum ownership level;
  X = replacement pressure.

Supernumerary income, a series developed by the Econometric Institute, is disposable personal income after deducting minimum living costs.[24] This is a difficult series to establish empirically unless considerable arbitrariness is permitted. Maximum ownership level is again a computed figure which assumes (a) that at any given time there is a maximum ownership or saturation level which (b) rises from time to time as population (or households or wired homes or some other limiting factor) moves. While the concept may be valid, efforts to determine this level empirically are fraught with dangers in the case of products where multiple ownership exists. Replacement pressure likewise is a computed series and based on the use of a mortality table for consumer durable goods which in turn is applied to prior annual sales figures in order to determine the existing stock of units of that consumer durable good and the number of such units that can be expected to be scrapped during any one year. Such scrappage leads to a presumption of replacement purchasing.[25] Thus we have three of the five variables involved with computed values rather than actual data and in each case, the computation involves considerable arbitrary judgment.

The fit of the Roos-von Szeliski equation to the data for new private passenger car registrations for 1919 to 1938 [26] is shown in Chart II-7.

[24] The Econometric Institute's supernumerary income series from 1925 through 1956 appears in Table 7-1 at page 254 of Milton Spencer, Colin Clark, and Peter Hoguet, *Business and Economic Forecasting* (Homewood, Ill.: Irwin, 1961).

[25] The classical mortality table for consumer durables was devised by B. F. Kimball and is discussed in "A System of Life Tables for Physical Property Based on the Truncated Normal Distribution," *Econometrica*, vol. 15, pp. 342–360 (1947). Table II-7 is based on Kimball.

[26] It is not possible to bring Chart II-7 forward in time to compare the results of the General Motors predicting equation with the Department of Commerce predicting equation on a forecast basis because of the unavailability of the series needed for the General Motors study.

CHART II-7

**Annual New Private Passenger Car Sales for 1919 to 1938,
Actual (Solid Line) and Predicted (Broken Line) from Equation:**
$$S = J^{1.2}P^{0.65}[0.03C(M - C) + 0.65X]$$

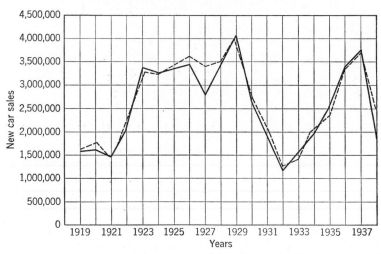

Source: Dynamics of Automobile Demand (General Motors Corporation, 1938), p. 60.

Another comparison between these approaches lies in the price elasticity which the equations show, namely, −0.65 (the exponent of the price index) for Roos-Szeliski compared with the price elasticity shown by the Department of Commerce studies, namely, −1.359 (equation 1), −1.29 (equation 2), −1.48 (equation 3), and −1.23 (equation 4).[27] It is true that the Department of Commerce price elasticity is different, namely, the ratio of the price of autos relative to the price of all consumer goods. A recent and more sophisticated study by Professor Chow[28] establishes the price elasticity for automobiles at from −0.6 to −1.0.

[27] The discrepancy in price elasticity is recognized in Milton Spencer and Louis Siegelman, *Managerial Economics* (Homewood, Ill.: Irwin, 1959) p. 180, note 21, where these authors state that the price elasticity may really be −1.5 (instead of the −.65 shown by Roos-Szeliski) for "statistical reasons" which are unexplained.

[28] Gregory C. Chow, "Statistical Demand Functions for Automobiles and their Use in Forecasting," in Arnold C. Harberger, *The Demand for Durable Goods* (Chicago: University of Chicago Press, 1960) at pp. 141–178. For other automobile demand studies, see Morris Cohen, "How Big is the Automobile Market?" *Business Record* (National Industrial Conference Board) Jan. 1956, pp. 7–12;

The income elasticities for automobiles shown by these studies are as follows: Chow, from 1.4 to 2.0; Roos-Szeliski, 1.2 (using supernumerary income), and the Department of Commerce, 2.536 (equation 1), 2.51 (equation 2), 2.46 (equation 3), and 2.45 (equation 4).

Predicting Equations for Refrigerators

Another example of a predicting equation is furnished in the study of electric refrigerators by the Office of Business Economics of the Department of Commerce published in the *Survey of Current Business* in 1950.[29] In this case the predicting equation developed from 1925-to-1940 data is as appears at the top of page 112.

CHART II-8

Annual Manufacturers' Domestic Sales of Electric Refrigerators for 1927 to 1950, Actual (Solid Line) and Predicted (Broken Line) from Equation:
$$Y = -2812.75 + 34.38X_1 + 35.62X_2 + 2024.27X_3$$

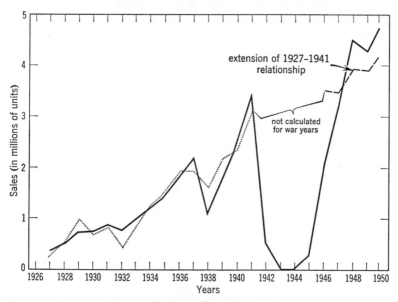

Source: Survey of Current Business, June 1950, p. 8.

Daniel Suits, "The Demand for New Automobiles, in the U.S., 1929–56," *Review of Economics and Statistics,* vol. 40, pp. 273–280 (1958) and Gregory C. Chow, *Demand for Automobiles in the United States, A Study in Consumer Durables* (Amsterdam: North-Holland Publishing Co., 1957).

[29] Department of Commerce: *Survey of Current Business,* June, 1950, pp. 5–10. The conclusion that the price elasticity for refrigerators is between −1.0 and −2.0 is reached in a more sophisticated study by M. L. Burstein, "The Demand

$$Y = -2812.75 + 34.38X_1 + 35.62X_2 + 2024.27X_3$$

where $Y =$ manufacturers domestic sales of electric[30] refrigerators in
thousands;

CHART II-9

**Annual Manufacturers' Domestic Electric Refrigerator Sales for 1946 to
1958, Actual (Solid Line) and Predicted (Broken Line) from Equation:**
$$Y = -2812.75 + 34.38X_1 + 35.62X_2 + 2024.27X_3$$

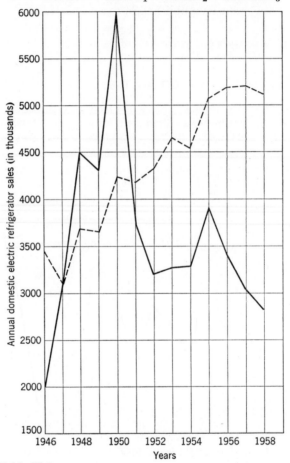

Source: Table II-6.

for Household Refrigerators in the United States," in Arnold Harberger, ed., *The
Demand for Durable Goods* (Chicago: University of Chicago Press, 1960) at
pp. 99–145. Burstein also finds the income elasticity of refrigerators to be between
1 and 2.

[30] The number of gas refrigerators sold has always been less than 1 per cent of
the number of electric. Shifts between gas and electric were not included in the
study.

CHART II-10

Annual Manufacturers' Domestic Electric Refrigerator Sales for 1946 to 1958, Actual and Predicted from Equation:

$$Y = -2812.75 + 34.38X_1 + 35.62X_2 + 2024.27X_3$$

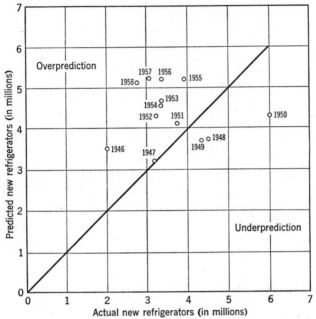

Source: Table II-6.

X_1 = disposable personal income in billions of 1939 dollars;

X_2 = change in disposable personal income from preceding year in billions of 1939 dollars;

X_3 = time in logarithms with 1925 = 1.

For 1925 to 1940, this equation produces $R^2 = 0.98$ with the Chart II-8 showing the results.

When the values of the independent variables for 1946 to 1958 are inserted in the equation, the results are notably poorer as shown in Table II-6 and Charts II-9 and II-10.

The independent variables selected by the Department of Commerce for the refrigerator study were not particularly well chosen. The major defect (which becomes apparent with 1951) is that no recognition is given in the equation to saturation. By 1951 *Electrical Merchandising* estimates that 86 per cent of wired homes had electric refrigerators. While in the case of automobiles significant multiple ownership may make saturation something far in the future, the

TABLE II-6

Annual Domestic Electric Refrigerator Sales for 1946 to 1958, Actual and Predicted from

$$Y_c = -2812.75 + 34.38X_1 + 35.62X_2 + 2024.27X_3$$

Year	(2) Manufacturers' Domestic Sales Electric Refrigerators in Thousands of Units		(3) X_1 = Disposable Income in Billions of 1939 Dollars	(4) X_2 = Change in Disposable Income from Prior Year in Billions of 1939 Dollars	(5) X_3 = Time in Logarithms (1925 = 1)	(6) Difference $Y_c - Y$
	(1) Y-actual	(2) Y_c-estimated				
1945			104.2			
1946	1,997	3,456	103.3	−0.9	1.3424	1459
1947	3,126	3,187	98.9	−4.4	1.3617	61
1948	4,495	3,745	104.1	5.2	1.3802	−750
1949	4,284	3,673	105.2	1.1	1.3979	−611
1950	6,000	4,264	113.7	8.5	1.4150	−1736
1951	3,731	4,197	116.6	2.9	1.4314	466
1952	3,196	4,350	119.8	3.2	1.4472	1164
1953	3,287	4,665	125.5	5.7	1.4624	1378
1954	3,310	4,555	126.4	0.9	1.4771	1245
1955	3,896	5,112	134.4	8.0	1.4914	1216
1956	3,382	5,240	139.9	5.5	1.5051	1858
1957	3,051	5,267	142.7	2.8	1.5182	2216
1958	2,750	5,110	141.8	−0.9	1.5315	2360

Source: column 1: *Electrical Merchandising*, Annual January Statistical Issue; column 3: *Economic Report of the President, 1960* deflated by implicit deflator for personal consumption expenditures, *ibid*; column 4: computed from column 2.

CHART II-11

Survival Pattern for Durable Goods with Average Life of 25-Year Maximum Life

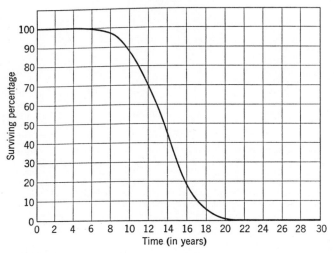

Source: Table II-7.

absence of multiple ownership per household for electric refrigerators makes the current inclusion of saturation more vital.

Slatin of the Econometric Institute in 1958 developed a more complicated predicting equation for electric refrigerators which gives particular recognition to the saturation aspect.[31] Total annual sales are broken down into new-owner sales and replacements.

Replacement Sales

Slatin determined replacement sales by using an assumed maximum life for an electric refrigerator of 25 years. Using the survival table shown in Table II-7 and graphed in Chart II-11, Slatin applies the survival coefficient to each year's sales starting with 1925 to determine (*a*) the number of "drop-outs" (or replacement sales) that will occur in each future year and (*b*) the number of refrigerators in use each

[31] The Slatin study is reported in Milton Spencer and Louis Siegelman, *Managerial Economics* (Homewood, Ill.: Irwin, 1959) at pp. 182 to 186, and appears in greater detail in Milton Spencer, Colin Clark and P. W. Hoguet, *Business and Economic Forecasting* (Homewood, Ill.: Irwin, 1961) pp. 252–279. A full explanation of the Slatin study would require many more pages than are warranted by our purposes. In what follows, we have simplified Slatin's argument (although not omitting essentials) to bring it down to manageable length.

TABLE II-7

Survival Coefficients for Durable Goods of 25-Year Maximum Life

Year	Kimball Survival Coefficient	Year	Kimball Survival Coefficient	Year	Kimball Survival Coefficient
1	1.0000	9	0.9472	17	0.1038
2	1.0000	10	0.8962	18	0.0526
3	0.9999	11	0.8159	19	0.0238
4	0.9997	12	0.7054	20	0.0096
5	0.9989	13	0.5714	21	0.0035
6	0.9965	14	0.4286	22	0.0011
7	0.9904	15	0.2946	23	0.0003
8	0.9762	16	0.1841	24	0.0001
				25	0.0000

Source: Computed by Slatin using Kimball's "System of Life Tables, etc.", *Econometrica*, vol. 15, pp. 342–60 (1947).

Note: The indicated average age of the 25 year life durable is 13.5 years (50 per cent surviving). After the manuscript of this book was completed, the *Chicago Daily News*, July 11, 1961, reported Mr. Herman Lehman, General Manager, Frigidaire Division, General Motors Corp., as stating that the average age of that company's refrigerators had recently gone up from 12 to 14.5 years.

year which is the total of number in use at the start of the year, plus new sales and minus "drop-outs." If actual scrappage figures were available for each year, it would not be necessary to operate from such a table.[32] A check of Slatin and the survival table shown in Table II-7 is available for 1952 from the results of the Survey Research Center of the University of Michigan. Computations based on this 1952 survey are included in Table II-8 for comparison with Kimball's curve. Replacement sales can then be assumed equal to the "drop-outs," or a further refinement can be made to recognize the fact that scrappage probably increases in prosperity and decreases in recession.

New Owner Sales

This leaves the new-owner demand to be determined. To handle this, Slatin assumed that the change in the number of units in use (or the new-owner sales) is dependent on the difference between total use possible less the number in use. In other words, as each year saw a greater percentage of total wired homes equipped with electric refrigerators, the possible new owner sales kept shrinking although at the same time the number of replacement sales increased. Finally,

[32] Because no new refrigerators were made during the war years 1942–45, it was assumed no "drop-outs" occurred, but that all units were repaired and that "drop-outs" began again after the war as if 1942–45 had not been involved.

Another survival computation for refrigerators similar to the Slatin study appears in *Electrical Merchandising*, Sept. 1959, p. 57.

TABLE II-8

Comparison of Aging of Electric Refrigerator Inventory Computed from Kimball's Table Using Survival Coefficients Set Forth in Table II-7 with Aging of Electric Refrigerator Inventory Determined by Survey Research Center of University of Michigan by Survey in 1952

| | (1) | (2) | (3) |
| | | University of Michigan | University of Michigan |
Bought	Slatin-Kimball Table	Survey—Based on Spending Units	Survey—Based on Families
1939 or earlier	14.9%	13.5%	13.6%
1940–44	16.7%	16.4%	16.0%
1945–48	28.5%	30.3%	30.7%
1949–50	28.8%	26.8%	26.7%
1951	11.1%	13.0%	13.1%

Sources: column 1: computed from refrigerator aging, developed by Slatin from Kimball Table, and reported in Milton Spencer, Colin Clark, and P. W. Hoguet, *Business and Economic Forecasting* (Homewood, Ill., Irwin, 1961) pp. 258–261. Columns 2 and 3: computed from data of Survey Research Center, Study 108, Tables DO-5 and DO-9 reporting actual age of refrigerators bought new.

TABLE II-9

Relation of Computed New-Owner Sales of Electric Refrigerators (1935 to 1956) to Wired Homes

	(1)	(2)	(3)	(4)	(5)
	Annual Refrigerator	Computed	New-Owner		Column 3
	Sales in Thousands	Replacements	Purchases	Wired Homes	as Per Cent
Year	of Units	in Thousands	in Thousands	in Millions	of Column 4
1935	1568	68	1500	20.6	7.2%
1940	2600	411	2189	24.6	8.9
1946	2100	898	1202	29.4	4.1
1947	3400	1040	2361	31.2	7.6
1948	4766	1187	3579	33.1	10.8
1949	4450	1350	3100	35.2	8.8
1950	6200	1505	4695	37.2	12.7
1951	4075	1656	2419	39.1	6.2
1952	3570	1777	1793	40.9	4.4
1953	3650	1874	1776	42.4	4.2
1954	3600	1937	1663	43.6	3.8
1955	4200	1990	2210	44.8	4.9
1956	3700	2061	1638	46.1	3.6

Sources: column 1: computed from annual manufacturers' sales (including exports) shown in *Electrical Merchandising;* column 2: computed from column 1 using survival coefficient shown in Table II-7; column 3: column 1 minus column 2; column 4: Edison Electric Institute, *Annual Statistical Report.*

these new owner sales as a percentage of total electric refrigerators in use could be expected to stabilize.

While Slatin uses the ratio of annual new owner sales to total in use as the basis for his work, we will develop a simple model using the ratio of annual new owner sales to total wired houses (as a measure of total possible in use) as shown in Table II-9. We can then compare the results of the complicated Slatin equation with the results of the simple model we will now develop.

Thus, the general shape of the curve showing the new-owner purchases each year as a percentage of the number of total wired homes would be as appears in Chart II-12.

This annual decrease in the ratio of new owners of electric refrigerators as a percentage of total wired homes each year has now leveled at about 4 per cent with the same percentage holding true for many other electric appliances. Note that this increase of 4 per cent is not the ratio of all annual sales to total wired homes at the beginning of

CHART II-12

Ratio of Computed New-Owner Purchases of Electric Refrigerators to Total Wired Homes for 1947 to 1956

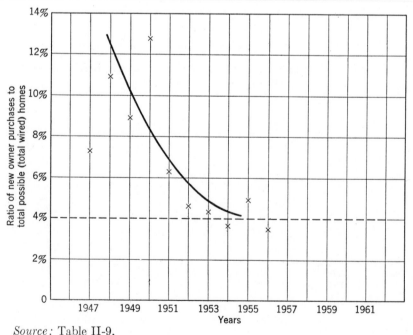

Source: Table II-9.

the year, but excludes replacement purchases which are established from the survival table and thus the ratio is total annual sales less computed replacements as a percentage of total wired homes at the start of the year.

The simple model using annual new owner sales as a percentage of wired homes actually involves two major components:

1. The increase in total wired homes each year;
2. The increase in the number of new owners among the previously wired homes who did not have electric refrigerators.

The annual rate of increase of wired homes during the period 1951 to 1956 as determined from a straight line fitted by semiaverages is 3.2 per cent. If the number of electric refrigerators bought for the annual increment of new wired homes is the same as for all wired homes then about $\frac{4}{5}$ of the 4 per cent factor we are using has this origin and $\frac{1}{5}$ of the 4 per cent originates in new-owner purchases among existing wired homes which did not previously have refrigerators. As the annual rate of increase of wired homes changes, the simple model would be adjusted.

This leaves only the problem of the determination of the "total use possible" since total sales in any year will then be computed replacements plus new owner sales (computed as 4 per cent of total use possible). At any one time this maximum to which the new-owner 4 per cent will be applied is fixed, but it changes as the society and economy change. The simplest model would be to assume that total wired homes represent the maximum. Such a model would assume that the multiple ownership of electric refrigerators by a single home is negligible. The model would also assume that relative price changes (within narrow limits) of electric refrigerators are an unimportant factor and that income changes and credit term changes are also unimportant.

Slatin developed a model which attempts to incorporate price, income and credit term changes as well as the number of wired homes. Thus, for example, because a change of $1.00 in net extension of installment credit excluding automobile credit was found to have three times the impact upon refrigerator sales as does a $1.00 change in supernumerary income, net credit change is weighted three times relative to income in the Slatin formula which appears in Table II-10.

Table II-10 compares the results of the complicated formula by Slatin with the results of the simple model we have been discussing.

Chart II-13 shows the actual sales per year of new electric refrigerators compared with the sales computed by Slatin's predicting equation.

CHART II-13

Annual Manufacturers' Domestic Sales of Electric Refrigerators for 1951–1956; Forecast by Slatin (Broken Line) and Simple (Line of x's) Models, Contrasted with Actual Sales (Solid Line)

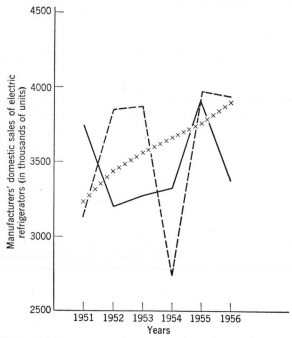

Source: Table II-10.

Comparison of Chart II-13 with Chart II-9 which is based on the Department of Commerce predicting equation establishes two items: (1) the Slatin equation yields markedly better results than the Department of Commerce, particularly after 1950, when saturation becomes the dominant factor; and (2) the Slatin study still leaves a considerable margin of error.

But there are further difficulties about using the Slatin predicting equation which involves these independent variables in predicting new-owner demand (1) wired homes, (2) supernumerary income, (3) net installment credit extension excluding automobile credit, (4) a price index of household furnishings and (5) a trend or time factor. Estimates into the future for (2), (3), and (4) are difficult to establish with any reasonable margin of error. Thus the usefulness of the Slatin predicting equation for forecasting is greatly impaired.

TABLE II-10

Annual Manufacturers' Domestic Sales of Electric Refrigerators for 1951 to 1956: Slatin Forecast from Predicting Equation:

$$S = R + Y\left\{H_w\left[0.0045 + 0.011\left(\frac{1 + 3C/P}{0.10^{0.0271T + 1.035}}\right)\right] - 0.000016Y\right\},$$

Contrasted with Forecast from Simple Model: $S = R + 0.04H_w$

Year	(1) Actual Sales in Thousands	(2) R = Replacement in Thousands	(3) H_w = Wired Homes in Millions	(4) 4% of Wired Homes in Thousands	(5) Simple Model Forecast in Thousands	(6) Slatin Model Forecast in Thousands	(7) Simple Model Difference from Actual in Thousands	(8) Slatin Difference from Actual in Thousands
1951	3731	1656	39.1	1564	3220	3131	−511	−600
1952	3196	1777	40.9	1636	3413	3842	217	646
1953	3287	1874	42.4	1696	3570	3861	283	574
1954	3310	1937	43.6	1744	3681	2742	371	−568
1955	3896	1990	44.8	1792	3782	3982	−114	86
1956	3382	2061	46.1	1844	3905	3922	523	540

Source: Column 1: Electrical Merchandising. Column 2: computed from 25-year survival table shown in Tables II-7 and II-9. Column 3: Edison Electric Institute, Annual Statistical Bulletin. Column 5: Column 2 plus Column 4. Column 6: from Milton Spencer, Colin Clark, and P. W. Hoguet, Business and Economic Forecasting (Homewood, Ill.: Irwin, 1961), pp. 252–279. Column 7: Column 5 minus Column 1. Column 8: Column 6 minus Column 1.

Definition of terms in above equations:

S = total new sales in thousands of units
R = computed replacement sales based on survival table in thousands of units
Y = stock of refrigerators
I = supernumerary income
C = net installment credit extension excluding automobile credit
P = price index of household furnishings
T = trend or time factor

On the other hand, a predicting equation based on the simplified model we have suggested above in which replacement purchases are computed from a survival table and new-owner purchases are computed on the basis of 4 per cent of the maximum ownership which is taken to be the number of wired homes may prove just as accurate after 1950 for "back casting" and much more feasible for forecasting.

It is interesting to note that our simple model outperforms the Slatin model in 5 of the 6 years from 1951 to 1956 (Chart II-13). Note that the 4 per cent of wired homes used as the basis for computing new-owner demand may be expected to drift slowly downward as saturation becomes greater or as the increase in new wired homes declines. Likewise it is a basic assumption of the simple model that the commodity is and will continue to be consumed on a basis of one unit per home.

THE PROBLEM OF WHAT IS MEASURED IN THE CASE OF CONSUMER DURABLES

Although we may be late in raising the point, a consideration of the problem of what is measured or should be measured in the case of analyzing the demand for consumer durables has been delayed until now to take advantage of various questions already raised, such as the new owner demand versus replacement demand.

What the consumer presumably wants is refrigeration *services* rather than a physical object. The Department of Commerce study and the Econometric Institute (Slatin) study both used the physical object as a measure of refrigeration service. In the case of soft goods, such as food, the use of the physical object as a measure of the satisfaction demanded has not been challenged. However, in his study of refrigerators, Burstein[33] has insisted that "an estimate of the rate of consumption of refrigeration services is necessary for each year considered [in a demand study]. This, it must be noted, is definitely not the same problem as estimating the rate of output of new machines [that will be sold]."

Then Burstein sets about determining the amount of "refrigeration service" demanded each year and applies depreciation rates to existing stocks as part of establishing this. Depreciation is not used to establish the number of units retired each year as was done by the Econometric Institute (Slatin) study. The dependent variable in the Burstein predicting equation is thus "per capita consumption of services" determined as we have just outlined but with the additional step of

[33] Burstein, *op. cit* (footnote 29), p. 99.

reduction to a per capita basis by dividing total refrigeration service consumed by population. This "per capita consumption of services" is found to be a function of three variables, namely, real price of refrigerators, real income per capita, and a time or trend variable. For the period 1931 to 1955 (omitting 1942 to 1944), Burstein finds R^2 equal to 0.997.

The Burstein study provides an interesting comparison with the Department of Commerce and Econometric Institute (Slatin) studies. In all cases, these studies show a high R^2 for back-casting. However, Burstein uses refrigerator lives of 4 to 10 years and Slatin uses a life of 25 years. Both agree that replacements constitute the great bulk of the market. The reason these serious differences in the assumed life do not make a sizable difference in the R^2 of the two studies lies in the completely different concepts used; namely in the case of Slatin the actual refrigeration units replaced per year but in the case of Burstein, the "refrigeration service" used per year. In the case of the Burstein study, the predicted "refrigeration service" to be used in future years must then be retranslated into actual units to be purchased just as he had originally translated records of prior actual unit purchases into a figure for "refrigeration service" being consumed in each current year. The test of application of the Burstein method to predictions in *future* years will reveal whether his manipulation artificially produces a high correlation. This refers to our earlier observation that a high R^2 can be achieved in *back casting* by manipulating the individual independent variables until one gets such a result.

THE IDENTIFICATION PROBLEM

In attempting to establish a demand curve for a product, we are confronted with what economists call the identification problem, namely, do the points being developed for a proposed curve truly belong to that curve or to another?

The problem can be illustrated by looking at three basic patterns that may develop when attempting to analyze price-quantity data. Thus Figure II-2a shows a pattern which might develop if we plot the price and quantity data for a product. The pattern suggests that a demand curve is being traced out. Figure II-2b shows data which suggest a supply curve. Figure II-2c shows data suggesting that there are more than one demand curve and/or more than one supply curve involved. How can we be sure in any given case what curve or curves are involved in the data?

An investigation may dispose of the difficulty rather quickly. If,

Figure II-2. Possible patterns for price-quantity data.

by evidence, we can determine, in the case of Figure II-2a for example, that demand has been quite stable relative to supply and that supply has been seriously disturbed, then the data are tracing the demand curve and regression analysis is in order to determine the equation for the demand function. Such is frequently the case for certain agricultural commodities where supply is affected by weather or seasonal patterns. The conclusion is buttressed if there is evidence that the usual demand determinants such as consumers' income, the prices of other goods, the available substitutes, etc. have not changed. In this situation, however, the supply curve cannot be estimated.

Conversely, in the case of Figure II-2b, for example, if the usual supply determinants, such as the prices of the factors of production and technology, have not been changing but demand determinants such as consumer preferences for the product, consumers' income, etc. have been changing, then the data enable us to establish the supply curve by regression analysis. Again, the demand curve cannot be estimated.

This leaves the situation of Figure II-2c, which is not amenable to the procedure we have so far outlined. In the situation shown in Figure II-2c, the establishment of a lead-lag relationship is sometimes fruitful. This is true in the case of some agricultural commodities and other products that have a fixed period of production. By pairing the current year's quantity sold with the preceding year's prices we may be able to develop an estimate of the supply curve.[34] It is to be noted that in this case, the pairing of these current year's prices and the current year's quantities sold may also establish the demand curve. In this case, both demand and supply curves may be developed.

[34] The logic of the relationship of the current year's quantity supplied correlating with last year's (and this year's expected) prices, is examined more fully in Part V, where the "cobweb theorems" are developed under the heading, The Use of Purchase, Loan and Storage Programs to Stabilize Prices. The lag analysis is developed in an illustration in Part IV, under the subheading *Shoe Pricing Analysis: Distributed Lag.* A good example of a lag relationship appears above in Case I-1, Sunburst Corporation, after the text of Part I.

Alternatively, in the case of the situation shown in Figure II-2c, multiple correlation analysis may be able to develop both the demand and supply curves. This would be the case where quantity demanded is a function not only of price of the product but also of other variables such as income and population, and quantity supplied is a function not only of price of the product but of other variables such as the prices of the factors of production. If in this situation, the changes in the variables other than price of the product on the demand side are independent of (not associated with) changes in the variables other than price of the product on the supply side, then both demand and supply curves may be developed from the data. In this case, variables other than those included in the analysis must be (a) insignificant, (b) self-cancelling, or (c) constant during the period whose data are being used as the basis for the analysis.

THE FORMAL RULES FOR IDENTIFICATION*

The preceding presentation of the problem of identification has included some practical proposals for situations that are easier to analyze. Some consideration of the formal rules for identification will furnish the basis for analyzing more involved cases as well as yielding a better understanding of the simpler cases to which rough working rules have been applied.

We will consider only simpler models which are static and made up of linear relationships. Suppose the case of a single commodity A as to which we propose a model as follows:

$$\text{the demand equation, } d = a + bp + m \tag{1}$$
$$\text{the supply equation, } s = c + gp + n \tag{2}$$
$$\text{the identity, or condition of equilibrium, } d = s \tag{3}$$

In this model, d is quantity demanded, s is quantity supplied, p is price, m and n are random errors, and a, b, c, and g are parameters or constants whose values we seek to determine. There are three equations as set forth and three systematic variables (d, s, and p). The model is hence logically complete.

In order to identify a model it is necessary that *each behavioral* equation containing one or more endogenous variables be identified. A behavioral equation is one that describes economic behavior. Thus

---

* The balance of this Part can be omitted at the discretion of the instructor without handicapping the use of the case materials. For a readily available treatment of the identification problem see Lawrence R. Klein, *A Textbook of Econometrics* (Evanston, Ill.: Row, Peterson, 1953), Ch. 3, Sec. 3, pp. 92–100.

a behavioral equation may state a functional relationship, namely, in which one unknown is a function of one or more other variables. Or the behavioral equation may simply state that the variable is constant. Thus the equations 1 and 2 above are behavioral. Equation 3, however, is a definition or statement of equilibrium. An endogenous variable is one that is explained by the model or system since it both determines other variables of the model and is determined by other variables of the model. Hence d, s, p, m, and n are endogenous variables with d, s, and p being systematic and m and n random. Exogenous variables are known or determined outside the model. There are no exogenous variables in the present model.

In what follows, we will speak only of *systematic* endogenous variables when we use the words "endogenous variables."

Rule 1: The necessary condition to identify each behavioral equation having one or more endogenous variables is that the number of variables (exogenous or endogenous) excluded from the equation must be at least one less than the total number of endogenous variables in the model. In the present case, the number of endogenous variables in the model is three (d, s, and p). Equation 1, in order to be identified, must exclude at least two (one less than the total number of endogenous variables) variables either exogenous or endogenous. But equation 1 excludes only one endogenous variable, namely s. Hence equation 1 cannot be identified. The same is true for equation 2. If any behavioral equation in a model cannot be identified, the model cannot be identified.

Rule 2: The necessary and sufficient condition to identify a behavioral equation containing endogenous variables is that it must be possible to construct at least one nonzero determinant of the order of $n - 1$ (where n is the number of behavioral equations containing one or more endogenous variables), such determinant to be constructed from the coefficients of the variables excluded from that equation but contained in the other behavioral equations.

Considering another model will clarify these rules further. Suppose that in addition to equations 1, 2, and 3 above, we have a fourth behavioral equation,

$$y = y_1 \tag{4}$$

in which y is real income. Equation 4 tells us that y has a constant value, namely, y_1 and hence is an exogenous variable.

Further suppose equation 1 is such that demand is partially determined by real income. This can then be written:

$$d = a + bp + ey + m \tag{1a}$$

and the entire model can be recapitulated as follows:

$$d = a + bp + ey + m \qquad (1a)$$
$$s = c + gp + n \qquad (2)$$
$$d = s \qquad (3)$$
$$y = y_1 \qquad (4)$$

There are four systematic variables (d, p, y, and s) and four structural equations. Equations 1a, 2, and 4 are behavioral equations, but only equations 1a and 2 contain endogenous variables.

Rule 1 requires that each behavioral equation, having one or more endogenous variables (of which there are two in this model, equations 1a and 2) must exclude that number of exogenous or endogenous variables which is at least one less than the total number of endogenous variables in the model. Here there are three endogenous variables (d, p, and s), and hence two endogenous or exogenous variables must be excluded from equation 1a in order for the equation to be identified.

Equation 1a excludes only s and, hence, cannot be identified. Hence the model cannot be identified.

Equation 2 excludes d and y and hence this equation meets Rule 1.

To satisfy Rule 2, we must be able to form at least one nonzero second-order determinant from the coefficients of the two variables excluded from equation 2, namely d and y. Since the coefficient of d is 1, we can form such a determinant for equation 2 as long as the other coefficient e is not zero.

If, to the above model, we add a fifth equation such as the wage rate, w, and if the wage rate is constant and exogenous, giving

$$w = w_1 \qquad (5)$$

and if equation 2 depends in part on the wage rate to give

$$s = c + gp + fw + n \qquad (2a)$$

then the equations and the model are identified so long as e and f are not zero.

REDUCTION AND ESTIMATION

We have now established a model that can be identified, namely the preceding model (assuming the coefficients e and f are not zero)

$$d = a + bp + ey + m \qquad (1a)$$
$$s = c + gp + fw + n \qquad (2a)$$
$$d = s \qquad (3)$$
$$y = y_1 \qquad (4)$$
$$w = w_1 \qquad (5)$$

These structural equations are placed into reduced form so that statistical estimation can be undertaken.

To place the equations in reduced form, the endogenous variables are stated in terms of the exogenous variables and the random variables. Specifically, in the above model, equations 4 and 5 are substituted into equations $1a$ and $2a$ respectively. This yields three equations

$$d = a + bp + ey_1 + m \tag{6}$$
$$s = c + gp + fw_1 + n \tag{7}$$
$$d = s \tag{8}$$

If we simply use x to state the quantity sold, we can substitute x for d and x for s, since $d = s$. To proceed to estimating, we use observations of the values of p, y_1, w_1 and x.

We are now in a position to solve for x and p in terms of the exogenous variables, y and w_1, and the random variables, m and n, by substituting equations 6 and 7 into 8 [35] to get

$$p = \frac{(c-a)}{(b-g)} + \frac{f}{(b-g)} w_1 - \frac{e}{(b-g)} y_1 + \frac{(n-m)}{(b-g)} \tag{9}$$

Substituting 9 into 7 [36] to get

$$x = \frac{(ag - cb)}{(g - b)} + \frac{(eg)}{(g - b)} y_1 - \frac{(fb)}{(g - b)} w_1 + \frac{(mg - nb)}{(g - b)} \tag{10}$$

[35] The algebra is as follows: $a + bp + ey + m = c + gp + fw + n$
Transposing:
$$o = (c - a) + (g - b)p - ey + fw + (n - m)$$
$$(b - g)p = (c - a) - ey + fw + (n - m)$$
Dividing by $(b - g)$:
$$p = \frac{(c-a)}{(b-g)} - \frac{e}{(b-g)} y + \frac{f}{(b-g)} w + \frac{(n-m)}{(b-g)}$$

[36] The algebra is as follows. For Eq. 10:
$$x = c + gp + fw + n$$
Substituting 9 into 7,
$$x = c + g\frac{(c-a)}{(b-g)} - \frac{eg}{(b-g)} y + \frac{gf}{(b-g)} w + \frac{g(n-m)}{(b-g)} + fw + n$$
Arranging all terms with $(b - g)$ in denominator,
$$x = \frac{c(b-g) + g(c-a)}{(b-g)} - \frac{eg}{(b-g)} y + \frac{gf}{(b-g)} w + \frac{g(n-m)}{(b-g)} + \frac{(fw+n)(b-g)}{(b-g)}$$
Cancelling terms,
$$x = \frac{cb - \cancel{cg} + \cancel{cg} - ga}{(b-g)} - \frac{ge}{(b-g)} y + \frac{\cancel{gf}}{(b-g)} w + \frac{\cancel{gn} - gm}{(b-g)} + \frac{fwb - \cancel{fwg} + nb - \cancel{ng}}{(b-g)}$$
Changing signs,
$$x = \frac{(ag - cb)}{(g-b)} + \frac{eg}{(g-b)} y - \frac{fb}{(g-b)} w + \frac{(mg - nb)}{(g-b)}$$

Equations 9 and 10 are the reduced form equations of our model and we establish the constants and coefficients by multiple linear regression. Given the estimates of the constants and coefficients we return to the original behavioral equations and can solve for the parameters of any or all of the behavioral equations.

The process just outlined is possible only when the behavioral equations are identified. If the original behavioral equations are not identified, there are not sufficient relationships connecting the original parameters to the reduced-form parameters. When only one nonzero determinant can be formed (according to Rule 2, this occurs when the number of variables excluded is just one less than the total number of endogenous variables) then the model is said to be just identified. But when the excluded variables are more than one less than the total and more than one nonzero determinant can be formed, the model is overidentified and more complicated techniques[37] for solution are needed than those just outlined. To say the model is overidentified means that there are too many connecting relationships among the parameters of the behavioral equations and the parameters of the reduced-form equations.

IDENTIFICATION AS INVOLVED IN THE PRECEDING STUDIES OF THE DEMAND FOR AUTOMOBILES AND REFRIGERATORS

It is now apparent from our discussion of the identification problem that the studies of the demand for automobiles and refrigerators which were presented earlier did not consider the identification aspect. Hence, multiple regressions are not always adequate and the use of two-stage least squares computations may be indicated. To probe more deeply into the indicated problems would carry us beyond the limitations, particularly as to mathematics, which we have imposed upon ourselves.[38]

[37] Cf. C. Hoods and T. C. Koopmans (Eds.), *Studies in Econometric Methods* (New York, Wiley, 1953).

[38] Further development in this area may be pursued in H. Theil, "Estimation of Parameters of Econometric Models," *Bulletin de l'Institut International de Statistique*, Vol. 34, Part 2, pp. 122–29 (1954) which contains many misprints and in Stefan Valavanis, *Econometrics, an Introduction to Maximum Likelihood Methods* (New York: McGraw-Hill, 1959), especially Chapters 4 to 9 inclusive.

CASE II-1. THE SOFT DRINK INDUSTRY*
Soft Goods Demand Analysis

The economic adviser of a large soft-drink manufacturer was asked in 1959 to analyze the demand picture likely to develop in the next decade. He was familiar with studies such as have been prepared by the Econometric Institute in which efforts are made to identify the most significant variables determining demand over periods such as the most recent 20 years of an industry. Such determination is done by multiple correlation analysis. However, he felt that one of the dangers in such an approach was that the assumption of *ceteris paribus* might very well be invalid for those industries involved with heavy rates of growth.

The Basic Data
Accordingly, the economic adviser proposed a broader investigation.

CASE II-1. TABLE I

Comparison of Gross National Product with Bottled Soft-Drink Sales
(1919–1957)

Year	GNP in Billions of Dollars	Soft-Drink Sales in Millions of Dollars	Year	GNP in Billions of Dollars	Soft-Drink Sales in Millions of Dollars
1919	85.3	135.3	1939	91.1	361.7
1920	91.3	NA	1940	100.6	411.7
1921	72.5	NA	1941	125.8	553.9
1922	72.8	NA	1942	159.1	526.2
1923	85.5	153.7	1943	192.5	580.3
1924	85.9	NA	1944	211.4	629.7
1925	90.3	NA	1945	213.6	585.0
1926	96.9	NA	1946	210.7	617.2
1927	95.4	185.6	1947	234.3	745.7
1928	97.2	NA	1948	259.4	835.1
1929	103.8	214.3	1949	251.8	861.0
1930	91.1	NA	1950	284.6	876.5
1931	76.3	172.6	1951	329.0	939.4
1932	58.5	120.7	1952	347.0	1,019.3
1933	56.0	144.8	1953	365.4	1,089.5
1934	65.0	138.2	1954	363.1	1,116.6
1935	72.5	159.9	1955	397.5	1,252.3
1936	82.7	229.8	1956	419.2	1,308.0
1937	90.8	278.6	1957	440.3	1,347.2
1938	85.2	311.7			

Sources: GNP: dates 1919 to 1929: Raymond W. Goldsmith, *A Study of Savings in the United States* (Princeton, N. J.: Princeton University Press, 1956) Vol. III, p. 421; 1930–1957: *Economic Report of the President*, January 1959, Table D-1, page 139. Soft drink sales: American Bottlers of Carbonated Beverages, *Members' Information Bulletin*, June 6, 1958, "Estimated Annual Production-Consumption of Bottled Soft Drinks."
NA = not available.

* With the assistance of Herbert Blutenthal, M.B.A. (Northwestern).

He developed Table I showing the growth of Gross National Product and soft-drink sales from 1919 to 1957. He noted that in the "golden twenties" the soft-drink industry grew at a faster rate than GNP, then in the depression dropped at about the same rate but starting again with 1935 grew at a faster rate except for the World War II period when tight sugar controls restricted growth possibilities.

Table I deals with dollar figures. It likewise contains no adjustment for population nor for the physical quantities of soft drinks represented by the dollars. Bottle sizes vary from 6 to 24 ounces in size. Accordingly, the economist developed Table II.

CASE II-1. TABLE II

U.S. Soft-Drink Bottle Consumption Per Capita (1919–1958)

Year	Annual Per Capita (Bottles)	Year	Annual Per Capita (Bottles)	Year	Annual Per Capita (Bottles)	Year	Annual Per Capita (Bottles)
1919	38.4	1935	37.1	1943	138.6	1951	162.7
1923	41.1	1936	54.9	1944	147.1	1952	174.0
1927	47.6	1937	67.5	1945	132.9	1953	177.5
1929	53.1	1938	75.4	1946	132.3	1954	174.2
1931	38.3	1939	88.6	1947	150.9	1955	184.2
1932	27.1	1940	100.1	1948	164.4	1956	188.9
1933	33.1	1941	133.6	1949	162.0	1957	189.2
1934	31.9	1942	126.2	1950	158.0	1958	189.0*

Source: American Bottlers of Carbonated Beverages, *Members' Information Bulletin,* "Estimated Annual Production-Consumption of Bottled Soft Drinks." Bottles are not of constant size. See Case II-1. Table III.
* estimated.

Sample studies for specific years indicated that the average size of bottle was relatively stable though decreasing somewhat over time as indicated in Table III.

Physical Saturation Limit and Changes in Taste

Noting the sharp increase in per capita consumption from 1919 to 1958 caused the economist to wonder what upper limit there might be to physical consumption of soft drinks. To answer this question, he turned to medical authorities. The results of this inquiry are presented in Table IV.

The economist was amused to find that the more "scientific" field of medicine did not (except in one of these books) indicate the basis for the data and apparently more than one medic had appropriated the same data. Adopting the mode (1200 milliliters) and converting to ounces yields 40.58 ounces as the average beverage intake per capita. The use of this figure would, of course, assume that age distribution

Case II-1. TABLE III

Data on Average Size of Bottle for Soft Drinks (1937–1956)

Year	Size of Bottle	Per Cent of all Bottles	Per Capita Actual Number of Bottles	Per Capita Ounces
1937:	6–7 oz.	64.0%	44	286
	8–9–10	6.3	4	36
	12	14.4	9	108
	16	1.0	1	16
	26–32	14.3	9	261
			67	707
1939:	6–7	57.4	51	332
	8–9–10	4.3	4	36
	12	24.9	22	264
	16	1.0	1	16
	26–32	12.4	11	319
			89	967
1947:	6–7	64.3	97	630
	8–9–10	4.1	6	54
	12	20.9	32	384
	16	0.2	Nil	—
	20–24	1.4	2	44
	28–32	9.1	14	420
			151	1532
1954:	6–7	60.7	105	683
	8–9–10	16.2	28	252
	16–12	15.1	27	324
	20–24	1.2	2	44
	28–32	6.7	12	360
			174	1663
1956:	6–7	60.7	115	745
	8–9–10	16.2	31	275
	12–16	15.2	29	344
	20–24	1.2	2	51
	28–32	6.7	12	378
			189	1793

Source: John J. Riley, *The American Soft Drink Industry* (Washington D.C.: American Bottlers of Carbonated Beverages, 1958), p. 284, Table 10.

CASE II-1. TABLE IV

Average Daily Liquid Intake in Milliliters

Method of Intake	Book I	Book II	Book III	Book IV	Book V	Book VI	Book VII
Beverages	1450	1200	1200	1350	1200	1450	1200
Food	800	1000	1000	900	1000	800	1000
Oxidation	350	300	300	450	300	350	300
Total	2580	2500	2500	2700	2500	2600	2500

Sources: Book I: Bernardo A. Houssay, M.D., *Human Physiology* (New York: McGraw-Hill, 1951), pages 449, 450. Book II: Benjamin Harrow and Abraham Mazur, *Textbook of Biochemistry*, sixth edition (Philadelphia: Saunders, 1954), p. 434. Book III: Harold A. Harper, *Review of Physiological Chemistry*, 4th edition (Los Altos, Calif.: University Medical Publishers, 1953), p. 254. Book IV: William Thorpe, *Biochemistry for Medical Students*, 6th edition (London: Churchill, 1955), page 20. Book V: John F. Fulton, *Textbook of Physiology*, 17th edition (Philadelphia: Saunders, 1955), page 910. Book VI: Sir Charles Lovatt Evans, *Principles of Human Physiology*, 9th edition (Philadelphia: Lea and Febiger, 1945). Book VII: Burnham Walker et al., *Biochemistry and Human Metabolism* (Baltimore: Williams and Wilkens, 1957) page 665.

changes in the population were not particularly significant for this figure.

If all other liquid intake sources are measured on a per capita basis and this total subtracted from 40.58 ounces, the result would be the average water intake per capita (for which no direct data are available). It might then be possible to form a judgment as to the likelihood of further growth in per capita soft-drink consumption on the assumption that soft-drink growth displaces water intake. This conclusion would be enhanced in probability if the beverages competing with soft-drinks were relatively stable in per capita consumption. To examine this theory, Table V was developed.

These data are then converted to liquid measure. Since the only years for which bottle size is available for soft drinks are the years 1937, 1939, 1947, 1954, and 1956 (see Table III), these are the only years in which conversion to liquid measure was undertaken for the other beverages. The conversion ratios used are:

Coffee—1 pound yields 40 cups of 5 ounces[*]
Tea—1 pound yields 200 cups of 5 ounces[†]

[*] V. D. Wickizer, *Tea Under International Regulation*, (Stanford, Calif.: Stanford University Press, 1944), p. 45.
[†] *Ibid.*

Case II-1. TABLE V

Annual Consumption Per Capita in the United States of Liquids and Materials for Liquids

Year	(1) Bottled Soft Drinks (No. of Bottles)	(2) Roasted Coffee (in Pounds)	(3) Tea (in Pounds)	(4) Fluid Milk (in Pounds)	(5) Canned Fruit Juices (in Pounds)	(6) Malt Beverages (in Gallons)	(7) Distilled Spirits (in Wine Gallons)	(8) Wine (in Gallons)
1925	44.1	8.7	0.9	270	0.2			0.03
1926	—	10.2	0.8	270	0.2			—
1927	47.6	10.1	0.7	269	0.3			—
1928	50.5	9.9	0.7	270	0.1	Prohi-	Prohi-	—
1929	53.1	10.1	0.7	272	0.3	bition	bition	—
1930	49.0	10.3	0.7	270	0.3			0.03
1931	38.3	10.8	0.7	268	0.4			—
1932	27.1	10.3	0.7	271	0.4			—
1933	33.1	10.6	0.8	270	0.5			—
1934	31.9	10.2	0.6	258	0.5	7.9	0.46	—
1935	37.1	11.1	0.6	261	2.0	10.3	0.70	0.30
1936	54.9	11.4	0.6	264	2.4	11.8	0.95	—
1937	67.5	11.0	0.7	265	4.4	13.3	1.05	—
1938	75.4	12.3	0.7	263	4.6	12.9	0.98	—
1939	88.6	12.3	0.7	266	5.8	12.3	1.03	—
1940	100.1	12.9	0.7	265	7.1	12.5	1.10	0.66
1941	133.6	13.2	0.8	267	8.4	12.3	1.19	—
1942	126.2	11.3	0.5	290	8.4	14.1	1.42	—
1943	138.6	10.8	0.5	315	7.3	15.8	1.09	—
1944	147.1	13.1	0.5	328	10.2	18.0	1.26	—
1945	132.9	13.6	0.5	335	10.8	18.6	1.44	0.73
1946	132.3	16.6	0.6	323	17.5	18.0	1.65	—
1947	150.9	14.4	0.6	306	15.4	17.9	1.27	—
1948	164.4	15.3	0.6	295	17.2	18.5	1.17	—
1949	162.0	15.5	0.6	296	15.3	17.9	1.14	—
1950	158.0	13.4	0.6	293	13.7	17.2	1.26	0.93
1951	162.7	13.7	0.6	299	14.6	16.8	1.26	0.87
1952	174.0	13.9	0.6	303	13.9	16.8	1.18	0.85
1953	177.5	14.0	0.7	300	13.6	16.6	1.23	0.90
1954	174.2	12.3	0.7	301	13.2	16.5	1.18	0.86
1955	184.2	12.8	0.6	305	13.8	15.9	1.21	0.89
1956	188.9	13.0	0.6	308	14.1	15.9	1.29	0.89
1957	189.2	13.2	0.6	—	—	—	1.25	0.89

Sources: Column 1: Bottled soft drinks: American Bottlers of Carbonated Beverages, *Members' Information Bulletin,* "Estimated Annual Production-Consumption of Bottled Soft Drinks." Column 2: Roasted coffee: United States Department of Agriculture, Bureau of Agricultural Economics, *Consumption of Food in the United States—1909–1952* (Washington D.C.: Sept. 1953), p. 241. Also *Supplement For 1957 to Consumption of Food in the United States 1909–1952.* Above data given on green bean basis. Conversion ratio of 1.2 lbs. of green coffee equals 1.0 lbs. of roasted coffee used in deriving roasted coffee figures. Column 3: Tea: United States Department of Agriculture, Bureau of Agricultural Economics, *Consumption of Food in the United States—1909–1952* (Washington D.C.: Sept. 1953), p. 242. Also *Supplement for 1957 to Consumption of Food in the United States 1909–1952,* p. 23. Column 4: Fluid milk: U.S. Dept. of Agriculture, Agricultural Marketing Service, *Dairy Statistics* (Statistical Bulletin No. 218, Washington D.C.: Oct. 1957), Table 305, page 342. Column 5: Canned fruit juices: United States Department of Agriculture, Bureau of Agricultural Economics, *Consumption of Food in the United States—1909–1952* (Washington D.C.: Sept. 1953), p. 222. Also *Supplement for 1957 to Consumption of Food in the United States—1909–1952,* p. 19. Column 6: Malt beverages: United States Brewers Association, *Brewers Almanac, 1957,* p. 10. Column 7: Distilled spirits: The Distilled Spirits Institute, *Annual Statistical Review 1957,* p. 40. Column 8: Wines: *Statistical Abstract, 1958,* page 797.

Dairy—8.6 pounds of milk yield 1 gallon* (assuming that the food use of milk offsets the exclusion of cream and buttermilk in the calculation)

Fruit Juices—1 pound yields 15 ounces†

Applying these conversion factors to the data in Table V yields Table VI. Table VI indicates that while in 1937–39 the per capita daily intake of water was 2 glasses, this is reduced to 1 glass in 1947–56. Of this (about) 6 ounce shrinkage, soft drinks claim half (from 2 ounces in 1937–39 to 5 in 1956) while the other half was claimed by milk and fruit juices. Or alternatively there has been some shift from coffee and malt beverages to soft drinks, particularly from 1947 to 1956.

The economist concluded that any future per capita increase in soft drinks would have to come from displacing other beverages rather than water as had been the case in the past. This was corroborated in Table II where there had been a noticeable levelling of per capita soft-drink increase in the years 1954 to 1958, and likewise a levelling in dollar sales of soft drinks (Table I) when one corrects for price level changes during these years. Such displacing of beverages other than water would require entirely different promotional costs than water displacement.

The economist likewise concluded that future growth of the soft-drink industry would be heavily a function of population growth alone‡ and that while a straight line fitted through the GNP data of Table I might be appropriate, the correct fit through the soft-drink data of Table I (1917 to 1957) would be a Gompertz curve even though a graph of these data on semi-log paper showed remarkable parallelism to GNP for the period 1917 to 1957.

Relation of Temperature and Income

Pursuing his study further, the economist considered that his isolation of "changes in taste" which he had just completed should be supplemented by an examination of the possible effect of temperature and income upon the demand for soft drinks. To get at temperature he proposed this hypothesis: if temperature is a significant variable,

* U.S. Dept. of Agriculture, *Agricultural Statistics*, 1957, p. vii.

† Assuming fruit juices equivalent to water.

‡ Consumption differences between adults and children appear to be very small whether measured in summer or in winter. This conclusion rests on a sample survey of 1,000 people pre-tested and cross-sectionally balanced on a national basis.

Source: American Bottlers of Carbonated Beverages, *Bottled Soft Drinks, a Survey of Consumer Preferences and Consumption*, 1954.

Case II-1. TABLE VI

Liquid Consumption Per Capita (in Ounces) in the United States

Year	Bottled Soft Drinks	Coffee	Tea	Fluid Milk	Canned Fruit Juices	Malt Beverages	Distilled Spirits	Wines	Total Ounces Consumed Per Capita	Daily Ounces Consumed Per Capita Excluding Water	Daily Water Computed as 40* Ounces Less Other Liquids
				Annual							
1937	707	2200	700	3940	72	1700	134	56†	10209	28	12
1939	967	2460	700	3950	95	1570	132	77†	9951	27	13
1947	1532	2880	600	4560	250	2300	163	102†	12387	34	6
1954	1663	2460	700	4480	211	2110	151	110	11795	32	8
1956	1793	2600	600	4582	225	2080	165	114	12159	34	6

Source: Table V, with conversion ratios stated in text.
* From text following Table IV.
† Estimated from nearest year available in Table V.

then there should be a marked seasonal. Likewise this correlation should be apparent in per capita consumption geographically considered.

A survey in 1957 by American Bottlers of Carbonated Beverages of 551 plants or about 10 per cent of the industry established the following seasonal pattern by bottle sizes as shown in Table VII.

CASE II-1. TABLE VII

Seasonal Distribution and Sales of Bottled Soft Drinks in 1957

Month	6 to 9 Ounces	10 to 12 Ounces	24 Ounces and over
January	6.8%	6.3%	7.0%
February	6.7	6.2	6.6
March	7.1	6.8	7.6
April	8.1	8.1	7.5
May	9.4	9.0	8.8
June	9.5	10.3	9.3
July	11.6	12.1	9.6
August	10.6	10.9	8.9
September	8.2	8.7	8.0
October	7.6	7.7	7.2
November	6.7	6.7	7.4
December	7.7	7.2	12.1

Source: "Bottled Soft Drinks, Sales Distribution—by Months," American Bottlers of Carbonated Beverages, *Members' Information Bulletin, 1957*.

Further evidence of the temperature relationship is found in the breakdown by states in 1956, the only year for which these data are available. The map in Figure I shows the clear influence of temperature bands.

To test temperature relationship for the year 1956, resort was had to the U.S. Weather Bureau's *Climatological Data—National Summary*. To compute an average temperature for each state for the year, the median of available temperatures for the state was selected. Humidity data are not available for the year 1956 by states.

To consider income at the same time, a graphic multiple correlation was undertaken. Disposable income data by states for 1956 were not currently available so per capita income was used. The results of this multiple correlation are shown in Table VIII. The temperature relationship appears clearly. Likewise income appears to be an insignificant

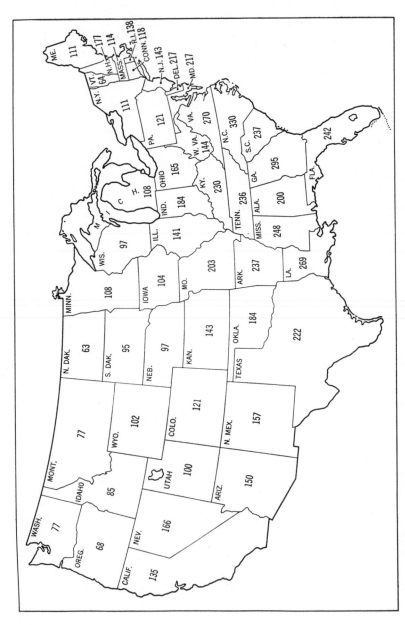

Case II-1. Figure 1. 1956 soft-drink consumption per capita of bottles by states. *Source*: Table VIII.

Multiple Regression of Bottles Consumed, Mean Annual Temperature and Per Capita Income by States in 1956

State	State Number	Y = Bottles Consumed Per Capita	X_1 = Mean Annual Temperature	X_2 = Income Per Capita (in Hundreds of Dollars)	Expected Demand from Regression Line	Actual Demand Less Expected Demand
Alabama	1	200	66°	$13	269	−69
Arizona	2	150	62	17	233	−83
Arkansas	3	237	63	11	242	−5
California	4	135	56	25	178	−43
Colorado	5	121	52	19	142	−21
Connecticut	6	118	50	27	124	−6
Delaware	7	217	54	28	160	+57
Florida	8	242	72	18	324	−82
Georgia	9	295	64	14	251	+44
Idaho	10	85	46	16	87	−2
Illinois	11	141	52	24	142	−1
Indiana	12	184	52	20	142	+42
Iowa	13	104	50	16	123	−19
Kansas	14	143	56	17	178	−35
Kentucky	15	230	56	13	178	+52
Louisiana	16	269	69	15	296	−27
Maine	17	111	41	16	42	+69
Maryland	18	217	54	21	160	+57
Massachusetts	19	114	47	22	96	+18
Michigan	20	108	47	21	96	+12
Minnesota	21	108	41	18	42	+66
Mississippi	22	248	65	10	260	−12
Missouri	23	203	57	19	187	+16
Montana	24	77	44	19	69	+8
Nebraska	25	97	49	16	115	−18
Nevada	26	166	48	24	105	+61
New Hampshire	27	177	35	18	0	+177
New Jersey	28	143	54	24	142	+1
New Mexico	29	157	56	15	178	−21
New York	30	111	48	25	105	+6
North Carolina	31	330	59	13	206	+124
North Dakota	32	63	39	14	23	+40
Ohio	33	165	51	22	133	+32
Oklahoma	34	184	62	16	233	−49
Oregon	35	68	51	19	133	−65
Pennsylvania	36	121	50	20	123	−2
Rhode Island	37	138	50	20	123	+15
South Carolina	38	237	65	12	260	−23
South Dakota	39	95	45	13	78	+17
Tennessee	40	236	60	13	215	+21
Texas	41	222	69	17	296	−74
Utah	42	100	50	16	123	−23
Vermont	43	64	44	16	69	−5
Virginia	44	270	58	16	196	+74
Washington	45	77	49	20	115	−38
West Virginia	46	144	55	15	169	−25
Wisconsin	47	97	46	19	87	+10
Wyoming	48	102	46	19	87	+15

Sources: Bottles consumed per capita: *National Bottler's Gazette,* "The Soft Drinks Industry—A Market Study," 1957, page 2. Mean annual temperature: U.S. Weather Bureau, *Climatological Data— National Summary* (Annual 1956), Vol. 7, No. 13, pages 17–25. Income per capita: U.S. Dept. of Commerce, Office of Business Economics, U.S. Income and Output, a Supplement to the *Survey of Current Business,* Nov., 1958, pages 158–160.

CASE II-1. TABLE IX

Data on the Relation Between Increases in Total Soft-Drink Sales and Increases in Soft-Drink Sales Through Vending Machines (1952–1957)

Year	(1) Total Bottled Soft- Drink Industry Sales	(2) Total Bottled Soft-Drink Sales Through Vending Machines
1952	$1,019,000,000	$300,000,000
1953	1,089,000,000	300,000,000
1954	1,167,000,000	320,000,000
1955	1,252,000,000	380,000,000
1956	1,308,000,000	405,000,000
1957	1,347,000,000	430,000,000

Yearly Increase	Increase in Total Bottled Soft-Drink Sales	Increase in Bottled Soft- Drink Sales Through Vending Machines	Ratio of Vending Machine Increase to Total Industry Bottle Increase
1952–1953	$70,000,000	$ —	—
1953–1954	78,000,000	20,000,000	25.5%
1954–1955	85,000,000	60,000,000	70.5%
1955–1956	56,000,000	25,000,000	45.0%
1956–1957	39,000,000	25,000,000	64.0%

Sources: Column 1: American Bottlers of Carbonated Beverages, *Members' Information Bulletin,* June 6, 1958, "Estimated Annual Production-Consumption of Bottled Soft Drinks." Column 2: National Automatic Merchandising Association, *Directory of Automatic Merchandising* (Chicago), 1954–1959 editions.

factor. Computing R^2 by simple correlation shows temperature explains 77 per cent of the variation between states.*

---

* The *New York Times,* January 9, 1961, p. 125 carried this story: "Over-all sales of the soft drink industry were off 2 to 3 per cent last year because of cooler weather. Lee Talley, President of the Coca-Cola Company said: 'The soft drink industry does not react as violently as do some other businesses. However, the slowdown in general business in recent months plus the persistently unseasonable weather in a number of areas over many months of the past year have undoubtedly been felt by the entire industry.'"

The *Wall Street Journal,* January 10, 1961, p. 5 carried this story: "Canada Dry Corp.'s drop in earnings in the fiscal year ended September 30 resulted mainly from unseasonable weather in North America and Europe, Roy W. Moore, president, said at the annual meeting."

Vending Machine Influence

The economist was aware that in the 1950's there had been a dramatic increase in the use of vending machines in the sale of soft-drinks. Data are available only from 1952 forward. The data are analyzed in Table IX.

If these data were available on a state basis and for a longer period, an examination could be undertaken by multiple correlation to determine the degree to which temperature and vending machine use explain changes in soft-drink consumption. Then examination of the saturation point for vending machine sales could be undertaken.

Price Influence

Price changes are often a significant factor in industry situations. Realizing this, the economist undertook an examination of price elasticity. Using the period 1947–57, an average price per 24-bottle case was established by dividing total sales (Table I) by the number of cases sold. This average price was adjusted by the consumer price index. Quantity was computed as the per capita bottles consumed (Table II) with trend for the eleven years then removed. The results

CASE II-1. TABLE X

Computation of Average Price and Quantity of Soft Drinks (1947–1958)

	(1)	(2)	(3)	(4)	(5)	(6)
			Average			Bottles
	Average	Consumer	Price in	Bottles		Sold
	Price	Price Index	1947–1949	Sold		Trend
Year	Per Case	(1947–1949 = 100)	Dollars	Per Capita	Trend	Removed
1947	$0.827	95.5	$0.87	150.9	3.4	147.5
1948	0.827	102.8	0.80	164.4	6.8	157.6
1949	0.850	101.8	0.83	162.2	10.2	152.0
1950	0.875	102.8	0.85	158.0	13.6	144.4
1951	0.900	111.0	0.82	162.7	17.0	145.7
1952	0.900	113.5	0.80	174.0	20.4	153.6
1953	0.925	114.4	0.81	177.5	23.8	153.7
1954	0.991	114.8	0.86	174.2	27.2	147.0
1955	0.990	114.5	0.87	184.2	30.6	153.6
1956	0.990	116.2	0.85	188.9	34.0	154.9
1957	0.989	120.2	0.82	189.2	37.4	151.8

Source: Column 1: American Bottlers of Carbonated Beverages, *Members' Information Bulletin,* June 6, 1958, "Estimated Annual Production-Consumption of Bottled Soft Drinks." Column 2: *Economic Report of the President,* January, 1959, Table D 39, p. 185. Column 3: column 1 divided by column 2. Column: 4 Case II-1. Table II. Column 6: column 4 minus column 5.

are shown in Table X. The expected inverse relation of changes in price and quantity appears for each year except 1955 and 1957. Price elasticity is then computed as shown in Table XI.

CASE II-1. TABLE XI

Price Elasticity of Demand for Soft Drinks

Years	(1) Per Cent of Change in Quantity	(2) Per Cent of Change in Price	(3) Elasticity
1947–48	+6.9%	−7.5%	−0.92
1948–49	−3.6	+3.7	−0.97
1949–50	−5.0	+2.4	−2.08
1950–51	+0.9	−3.5	−2.57
1951–52	+5.4	−3.1	−1.74
1952–53	nil	+1.9	—
1953–54	−4.4%	+6.2	−0.71
1954–55	+4.5	+0.6	7.5
1955–56	+0.8	−1.7	−0.48
1956–57	−2.0	−3.5	0.57

Sources: Columns 1 and 2: computed from data in Table X. Column 3: column 1 divided by column 2.

In evaluating Tables X and XI, the economist concluded that price elasticity was not a serious factor in the industry. Since incomes appeared to be a negligible factor in soft drinks as already indicated, the economist considered that to the extent any conclusion about price elasticity could be drawn, the elasticity was close to unity.

1. Contrast this analysis and its usefulness with the type of demand analysis presented in studies by the Econometric Institute, Inc. referred to in the text.
2. Prepare a forecast for the industry for 1959 and several succeeding years using the materials developed in this study. Compare the forecast with actual data for these years. What are the origins of the differences?
3. What improvements could be made in this study?

CASE II-2. THE ROOM AIR CONDITIONING INDUSTRY*

Consumer Durable Goods Demand Analysis

Air conditioning as an industry is of recent origin with significant volume starting with the end of World War II and the removal of materials restrictions.

Air conditioning has been classified into four product categories by the industry:

1. Room air conditioners. A self-contained unit capable of serving a single room or small office and marketed through retail outlets at prices from $200 to $400.

2. Other packaged air conditioning. A self-contained unit of larger size (3 tons and up) capable of serving a home, large office, small store or restaurant. These sell at $700 to $900 plus installation costs of about $300.†

3. Components for central systems. A unit serving a large building through ductwork with dispensing units located in the immediate area served. This category includes the central unit and the dispensing units but not the distribution system (ductwork).

4. Automobile air conditioning. This is largely detached from the other types and is characterized by obsolescence with the vehicle.

The sales record of the industry is shown in Table I.

An economist was consulted in late 1958 during the recession of 1957 to 1958. Some industry sources felt that reduced sales were associated with the reduced incomes of the recession and that the Gompertz curve shown by the data for 1946 to 1957 still had a long way to go with only 9.6 per cent of the nation's 48,600,000 residential and rural electric customers equipped with air conditioning at the end of 1957.‡ It is to be noted, however, that since 1946 a total of 1,647,000 units of room type or slightly more than 20 per cent of total factory sales of these units had been for commercial or industrial establishments.§ Sales to this market peaked in 1955 at 27.5 per cent of total

---

* With the assistance of Francis Lynn, M.B.A. (Northwestern).

† Information from Business Research Dept., Carrier Corp.

‡ "Index of Saturation, Jan. 1, 1958," *Electrical Merchandising*, Vol. 90, No. 1, Jan. 1958, p. 307.

§ W. R. Simmons and Associates Research, Inc., "1957 Commercial and Industrial Air Conditioning," a market study sponsored by E. I. du Pont de Nemours and Co.

Case II-2. TABLE I

Air Conditioning Sales in the U.S. 1946–1957

Year	(1) Sales of Room Air Conditioning Units	(2) Sales of Other Packaged Air Conditioning Equipment	(3) Sales of Central Air Conditioning System Components	(4) Automotive Air Conditioning Equipment	(5) Total Sales of Air Conditioning Equipment
1957	$266,788,000	$173,653,000	$59,890,000	$23,361,000	$523,692,000
1956	291,534,000	203,464,000	52,818,000	16,370,000	564,186,000
1955	209,961,000	159,901,000	43,412,000	– – – – –	413,274,000
1954	241,871,000	129,871,000	37,881,000	– – – – –	409,623,000
1953	199,223,000	126,574,000	29,504,000	– – – – –	355,301,000
1952	73,931,000	72,132,000	25,292,000	– – – – –	171,355,000
1951	45,824,000	56,994,000	27,820,000	– – – – –	130,628,000
1950	35,708,000	55,540,000	24,177,000	– – – – –	115,425,000
1949	17,940,000	32,644,000	Unavailable	– – – – –	Incomplete
1948	15,503,000	35,505,000	Unavailable	– – – – –	Incomplete
1947	9,930,000	29,379,000	Unavailable	– – – – –	Incomplete
1946	5,869,000	13,630,000	Unavailable	– – – – –	Incomplete
Total	1,414,082,000	1,087,287,000	Incomplete	39,731,000	Incomplete

Sources: Columns 1, 2, and 4: United States Department of Commerce, Bureau of the Census, *Facts for Industry Series M52A, 1946–1957*, Washington: United States Government Printing Office. Column 3: Estimated from data on the installed value of central air conditioning systems issued by the Air-Conditioning and Refrigeration Institute and a rule-of-thumb in the industry that the factory sale value of the equipment represents about 10 per cent of the total installed values. The remainder is installation costs, duct work and other labor which is done on the structure in which the installation is made. These figures do not reflect any income which the companies in the industry obtain from engineering services and installation work which they might perform as the contractor actually installing the system.

sales and then started a steady decline to only 13.8 per cent in 1957.

On the other hand, the economist found some industry sources* fearful that room-type units had about reached saturation. This group pointed to sales figures for 1953 through 1957 as shown in Table I.

The significance of room-type air conditioners increased from 31 per cent of the total industry in 1950 to 51 per cent in 1957 although other packaged units also increased from 21 per cent of the total industry in 1950 to 33 per cent in 1957. Of the other packaged units, about 45 per cent of sales in 1957 were for residential use.†

At this point, the economist decided to analyze each of the four product types separately.

Room Air Conditioners

Sales of room air conditioners are highly seasonal. Using the data

* "It's More and More a Replacement Market," *Electrical Merchandising,* Vol. 90, No. 1, January 1958, p. 310.

† Claud Wampler. "Air Conditioning Growth Is Just Commencing," *The Commercial and Financial Chronicle,* Vol. 185, April 11, 1957, p. 1697.

for 1953 to 1956, the monthly per cent of the year's sales is as follows*

January	2.5%	May	15.5%	September	2.6%
February	4.5	June	22.5	October	1.6
March	6.8	July	20.9	November	1.6
April	9.5	August	9.9	December	2.1

Industry sources estimate the average life of room types as 7 to 10 years.† Accordingly substantial replacement sales cannot be expected until the 1960's. In 1956, replacements were 1.8 per cent of sales and in 1957, 1.3 per cent.‡

Unit Sales of Room-Type Air Conditioners to Residential and Commercial Users (in Millions), 1946–1951

	Combined		Residential	Commercial
1946	0.02	1952	0.29	0.09
1947	0.05	1953	0.95	0.17
1948	0.08	1954	1.10	0.26
1949	0.09	1955	1.03	0.35
1950	0.20	1956	1.45	0.37
1951	0.24	1957	1.36	0.22
		1958 Estimated Combined: 1.36		

A Gompertz curve fits the combined sales well except for the years 1957 and 1958. The industry had expected sales of 2.25 million units in 1958.§

This raises the question whether saturation might be in the offing or whether some external factor such as weather might be involved.

Weather Factor

The du Pont survey‖ showed only 7.4 per cent of present owners of room types with annual incomes under $3,000. On the other hand, the fifteen states with the largest sales per electric customer in 1955 were as follows:

* "Air Conditioners and Dehumidifiers," *Electrical Merchandising*, Vol. 90, No. 1, January 1958, p. 58.

† Business Research Dept., Carrier Corp., Syracuse, N.Y.

‡ "It's More and More a Replacement Market," op. cit.

§ T. Weber, "Appliance Dealer's Expanding Role in Air Conditioning," *Electrical Merchandising*, Vol. 89, No. 2, Feb. 1957, p. 67ff.

‖ Simmons, *op. cit.*

CASE II-2. TABLE II

Unit Sales of Room Air Conditioning Units Compared to Income in 1955 for Fifteen States with Largest Sales Per Thousand Electricity Customers

State	(1) Unit Sales Per Thousand Electric Customers	(2) Personal Income Per Capita	(3) Ranking by Per Capita Income
Louisiana	101	$1333	39
Texas	96	1614	27
Tennessee	95	1256	42
Missouri	91	1800	19
South Carolina	79	1108	47
Georgia	72	1333	40
Florida	60	1654	25
Kansas	53	1647	26
District of Columbia	52	2324	4
New York	43	2264	7
Arkansas	42	1062	48
Arizona	40	1577	29
Nebraska	39	1540	32
Alabama	38	1181	46
Delaware	35	2513	1

Sources: Column 1: "How Regional Appliance Markets Compare," *Electrical Merchandising*, January, 1956, Volume 88, Number 1, pp. 314–327. Columns 2 and 3: United States Department of Commerce, *Statistical Abstract, 1957*, (Washington: United States Government Printing Office) 1957, Table 370, p. 303.

The economist considered these facts strongly indicative that weather is the most important factor in room-type purchases although income may be a limiting factor.

To measure "weather" the economist adopted the concept of "cooling degree days" * recently developed by the U.S. Weather Bureau. This concept incorporates both temperature and humidity using two formulae:†

$$DI = 0.4(t_d + t_w) + 15$$
or
$$DI = 0.55t_d + 0.2t_{dp} + 17.5$$

* Commonly called the "discomfort index."
† E. C. Thom, "Cooling Degree Days," *Air Conditioning, Heating and Ventilating*, July, 1958, Vol. 55, pp. 66–72.

CASE II-2. TABLE III

Sales of Room Air Conditioners Per Thousand Electricity Customers and Cooling Degree Day Value for Selected Metropolitan Centers, 1955–1957

(1) State / Major Retail Centers	(2) Normal Cooling Degree-Day Value Over Last 5 Years	(3) 1955 Sales Per Thousand Electric Customers	(4) 1955 Cooling Degree-Day Value	(5) 1956 Sales Per Thousand Electric Customers	(6) 1956 Cooling Degree-Day Value	(7) 1957 Sales Per Thousand Electric Customers	(8) 1957 Cooling Degree-Day Value
Alabama — Montgomery	2694	30.8	2709	36.6	2579	38	2755
California — Los Angeles	1026	NA	834	7.1	1075	8	1295
Colorado — Denver	615	10.0	589	16.0	602	2	556
District of Columbia — Washington	1659	70.5	1741	56.3	1482	52	1699
Florida — Tampa	3669	23.5	3522	31.1	3584	33	3803
Georgia — Atlanta	2152	39.7	2174	63.8	2131	74	2168
Illinois — Chicago	1292	32.2	1404	34.0	1192	21	1195
Louisiana — New Orleans	3365	108.2	3488	119.5	3288	170	3417
Massachusetts — Boston	997	27.3	1187	18.6	888	14	1020
Minnesota — Minneapolis-St. Paul	1012	11.8	1201	24.6	923	20	954
Missouri — Kansas City	1946	67.7	1900	50.8	1959	104	1793
New York — New York City	1234	74.2	1375	55.7	1080	59	1270
North Carolina — Raleigh	1927	NA	1947	NA	1832	34	1935
Tennessee — Nashville	2093	132.4	2144	157.2	1991	134	2049
Tennessee — Memphis	2393	108.1	2451	112.1	2309	80	2291
Texas — Houston	3383	141.5	3401	191.8	3314	167	3401
Utah — Salt Lake City	764	2.9	770	2.8	731	4	767

Sources: Columns 2, 4, 6, and 8: Earl C. Thom, "Cooling Degree Days," *Air Conditioning, Heating and Ventilating,* Vol. 55, No. 7, July 1958, pp. 65–72. Columns 3, 5, and 7: "How Regional Appliance Markets Compare," *Electrical Merchandising,* Vols. 88 to 90, No. 1, January 1955, January 1956, and January 1957. NA = not available.

where DI is discomfort index, t_d is dry bulb temperature, t_w is wet bulb temperature and t_{dp} is dew point temperature.

The average Discomfort Index for any day then has the base figure of 60 subtracted from it to arrive at the cooling degree-day value for that date.

The method used to evaluate climatic effect on the potential market involves plotting the sales per thousand electricity customers, against

CASE II-2. CHART I

Annual Room Air Conditioner Sales Per Thousand Electricity Customers and Cooling Degree Days in Selected Cities (1955 to 1957)

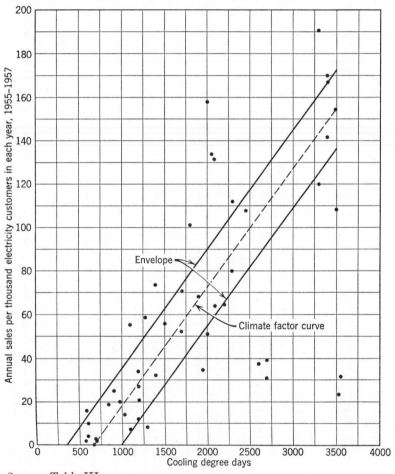

Source: Table III.

CASE II-2. CHART II

Cooling Degree Days and Per Cent of Market Considered to Be Potential

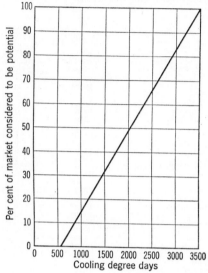

Source: Chart I.

cooling degree-day values for large metropolitan centers for which such information is available, using the 3-year period 1955 to 1957 (Table III).

Plotting the information of Table III on a scatter diagram (Chart I) permits the establishment of an envelope including most points and bisecting this area establishes a linear relation which may be called the climatic propensity to consume air conditioners. This line crosses the zero potential of sales per thousand at 600 cooling degree-day values,* and the total market to be considered as a potential is indicated at 3500 cooling degree-day values.† This linear relation can then be divided into percentages of total market which could be considered as potentials. Chart II shows this percentage scaling which can be termed "climate factor."

Using weather bureau data as to cooling degree-day values for retail centers and applying the climate factor for the centers (Chart II),

---

* A contour weather map indicates only parts of the Rocky Mountain area are thus excluded. See the first reference under Table III.

† A contour weather map indicates only southern Texas and Florida are thus excluded. See *ibid.*

CASE II-2. TABLE IV

Determination of Climate Factor By State and Resulting Percentage of Market Considered to Be Potential

State	Major Retail Center	(2) Cooling Degree-Day Value	(3) Per Cent of Market Considered to be Potential for Retail Center	(4) Per Cent of Market Considered to be Potential for Entire State
Alabama	Birmingham	2500*	0.66	0.66
Arizona	Phoenix	2691	0.73	0.73
Arkansas	Little Rock	2326	0.60	0.60
California	Los Angeles	1026	0.15	0.10‡
	San Francisco	210	N.M.M.†	
Colorado	Denver	615	0.01	0.01
Connecticut	Hartford	1000*	0.14	0.14
Delaware	Wilmington	1500*	0.32	0.32
Dist. of Columbia	Washington	1659	0.37	0.37
Florida	Miami	4603	1.00	1.00‡
	Tampa-St. Petersburg	3669	1.00	
Georgia	Atlanta	2152	0.54	0.54
Idaho	Boise	300*	N.M.M.†	N.M.M.†
Illinois	Chicago	1292	0.25	0.25
Indiana	Indianapolis	1450*	0.30	0.30
Iowa	Des Moines	1600*	0.35	0.35
Kansas	Wichita	1800*	0.42	0.42
Kentucky	Louisville	1500*	0.32	0.32
Louisiana	New Orleans	3365	0.96	0.96
Maine	Portland	600*	0.01	0.01
Maryland	Baltimore	1500*	0.32	0.32
Massachusetts	Boston	997	0.14	0.14
Michigan	Detroit	900*	0.11	0.11
Minnesota	Minneapolis-St. Paul	1012	0.14	0.14
Mississippi	Jackson	2656	0.71	0.71
Missouri	St. Louis	1851	0.44	0.45‡
	Kansas City	1946	0.47	
Montana	Billings	634	0.02	0.02
Nebraska	Omaha	1500*	0.32	0.32
Nevada	Las Vegas	1771	0.41	0.41
New Hampshire	Manchester	800*	0.07	0.07
New Jersey	Newark	1234	0.22	0.22
New Mexico	Albuquerque	1038	0.15	0.15
New York	New York City	1234	0.22	0.20‡
	Albany-Buffalo	850*	0.09	
	Rochester	868	0.10	
North Carolina	Raleigh	1927	0.46	0.46
North Dakota	Fargo	793	0.07	0.07
Ohio	Cleveland	1000*	0.14	0.19‡
	Cincinnati	1324	0.26	
Oklahoma	Oklahoma City	2092	0.52	0.52
Oregon	Portland	300*	N.M.M.†	N.M.M.†
Pennsylvania	Philadelphia	950*	0.13	0.12‡
	Pittsburgh	900*	0.11	
Rhode Island	Providence	1000*	0.14	0.14
South Carolina	Charleston	2700*	0.73	0.73
South Dakota	Sioux Falls	1150*	0.19	0.19
Tennessee	Memphis	2393	0.62	0.58‡
	Nashville	2093	0.52	
Texas	Houston	3383	0.96	0.86‡
	Dallas-Fort Worth	2814	0.77	
	San Antonio	3137	0.87	
Utah	Salt Lake City	764	0.06	0.06
Vermont	Burlington	200*	N.M.M.†	N.M.M.†
Virginia	Richmond	1800*	0.42	0.42
Washington	Seattle	197	N.M.M.†	N.M.M.†
West Virginia	Charleston	1200*	0.21	0.21
Wisconsin	Milwaukee	1150*	0.19	0.19
Wyoming	Cheyenne	600*	0.01	0.01

Sources: Column 1: Gustav E. Larson and Marshall N. Potent, *Selling The United States Market*, Washington: United States Government Printing Office, 1951, pp. 9–11; 106–108. Column 3: determined from Chart II.
* Cooling degree days were estimated from the map published in Thom, *op. cit.*
† N. M. M.: No Measurable Market.
‡ In those states having two or more major retail centers with widely varying cooling degree days, the climate factor for the entire state was determined by averaging the individual city cooling degree days with weighting based on respective population.

Table IV shows the percentage of the entire state's dwellings which may fairly be considered as potential buyers.

This entire procedure assumes (1) that an adequate informational level with respect to air conditioning had been achieved by 1955 to 1957 on the part of all buyers, (2) that weather during this period may fairly be taken as "normal" and (3) that climate is the only operative factor.

Income Factor

Another du Point survey* indicates that only 7.4 per cent of owners in 1955 had annual incomes below $3,000. The last available data on income distributions by states is the 1950 census. To compensate for increases in income from 1949 to 1955, the figure of $2,500 is used as the 1949 equivalent of $3,000 in 1955. Table V is a computation of potential market excluding those with income under $2,500 and applying the climate factor for each state, to arrive at a total potential market of 7.17 million for residences.

Total residential units sold to 1957 were 6.35 million. The du Point study† shows 12.3 per cent of owners of room air conditioners have two units, 2 per cent have three units and 0.5 per cent have four or more units. Thus, approximately 18.5 per cent of the 6.35 million were multiple purchases. An upward adjustment of the potential market of 7.17 million for the 7.4 per cent of low income buyers shows 7.7 million. Adjusting this figure in turn for the 18.5 per cent multiple buyers would show 9.12 million as the potential market. In addition there were 0.61 million central air conditioners‡ for residences sold as of 1956. This contrasts with the 48.6 million frequently used in the industry as the potential market because that is the number of wired homes.

The saturation ratio of 6.35/9.12 or 69.6 per cent (ignoring the central aid conditioners) is high. Some support, however, comes from the prediction by Wampler of Carrier Corp. that the replacement market would reach 2.15 million by 1961.§ Assuming a 4¼ year life this would be consistent.

---

* W. R. Simmons and Associates Research, Inc., "Residential Room Air Conditioning, Use and Preferences," a market study sponsored and published in 1955 by E. I. du Pont de Nemours and Co.

† *Ibid.*, p. 133.

‡ W. R. Simmons and Associates Research, "Central Residential Air Conditioning, Report of 1956 Survey," sponsored and published in 1956 by E. I. du Pont de Nemours and Co.

§ T. Weber, "Appliance Dealers' Expanding Role in Air Conditioning," *op. cit.*, pp. 67, 69.

Case II-2. TABLE V

Determination of Potential Market for Room Air Conditioners

State	(1) Residential Electric Utility Customers in 1958	(2) Family and Unrelated Individuals Per Cent Annual Income over $2500 in 1949	(3) Potential Market as Limited by Income	(4) Fraction of Market Considered to Be Potential Determined by Climate Factor Table IV	(5) Potential Market as Limited by Income and Climate
Alabama	837,000	39.7	332,000	0.66	219,100
Arizona	276,000	52.4	145,000	0.73	106,000
Arkansas	495,000	25.2	125,000	0.60	75,000
California	4,311,000	66.3	2,858,000	0.10	285,800
Colorado	476,500	50.3	240,000	0.01	2,400
Connecticut	715,000	63.4	454,000	0.14	63,600
Delaware	113,000	53.5	605,000	0.32	193,900
Dist. of Columbia	163,000	59.4	97,000	0.37	35,900
Florida	1,306,000	38.7	506,000	1.00	506.000
Georgia	1,011,000	33.6	340,000	0.54	183,700
Idaho	189,500	53.7	102,000	N.M.M.*	N.M.M.*
Illinois	2,742,000	62.1	1,710,000	0.25	427,500
Indiana	1,347,000	56.4	759,000	0.30	227,700
Iowa	805,000	52.1	419,000	0.35	146,500
Kansas	646,000	47.5	307,000	0.42	129,000
Kentucky	789,000	34.5	272,000	0.32	87,000
Louisiana	809,000	36.7	297,000	0.96	285,100
Maine	300,500	43.1	129,000	0.01	1,300
Maryland	761,000	55.7	424,000	0.32	135,800
Massachusetts	1,497,000	58.4	875,000	0.14	122,600
Michigan	2,213,000	63.9	1,412,000	0.11	155,300
Minnesota	947,000	53.4	506,000	0.14	71,000
Mississippi	512,000	20.1	103,000	0.71	73,200
Missouri	1,251,000	44.0	551,000	0.45	248,000
Montana	190,500	53.8	103,000	0.02	2,100
Nebraska	412,000	47.4	195,000	0.32	62,400
Nevada	69,500	57.7	40,000	0.41	16,400
New Hampshire	199,000	47.9	95,000	0.07	6,700
New Jersey	1,714,000	65.5	1,123,000	0.22	247,100
New Mexico	203,000	46.1	94,000	0.15	14,100
New York	4,662,000	60.3	2,811,000	0.20	562,200
North Carolina	1,167,000	35.8	417,000	0.46	191,800
North Dakota	165,000	58.8	97,000	0.07	6,800
Ohio	2,680,000	60.2	1,613,000	0.19	306,500
Oklahoma	680,000	40.8	278,000	0.52	144,500
Oregon	517,000	57.5	297,000	N.M.M.*	N.M.M.*
Pennsylvania	3,079,000	57.1	1,759,000	0.12	211,100
Rhode Island	252,000	53.0	134,000	0.14	18,800
South Carolina	575,000	35.6	205,000	0.73	149,800
South Dakota	183,000	46.5	85,000	0.19	16,200
Tennessee	961,000	34.1	328,000	0.58	190,300
Texas	2,525,000	45.4	1,148,000	0.86	987,300
Utah	220,000	60.0	132,000	0.06	7,900
Vermont	117,500	40.6	48,000	N.M.M.*	N.M.M.*
Virginia	957,000	43.2	413,000	0.42	173,600
Washington	922,000	57.2	470,000	N.M.M.*	N.M.M.*
West Virginia	507,000	46.1	234,000	0.21	49,200
Wisconsin	1,139,000	56.8	647,000	0.19	123,000
Wyoming	91,000	57.2	52,000	0.01	500
Total U.S.	48,600,000	54.3	26,386,000	0.37	7,174,300

Sources: Column 1: Edison Electric Institute, *Statistical Bulletin for the Year 1958*, Table 26. Column 2: United States Department of Commerce, Bureau of the Census, *Census of Population, 1950*, Washington: United States Government Printing Office, 1952, Vol. II, Table 32 of individual states. Column 3: column 1 times column 2. Column 4: Case II-2. Table IV. Column 5: column 3 times column 4.

* N.M.M.: No Measurable Market

The major limitations of this demand study are:

1. The climate factor is limited by the fact that in most cases only one location per state is available to "rate" the state weather-wise.

2. The validity of treating 3,500 cooling degree days as a market potential of 100 per cent when the actual sales in a 3-year period were 150 per thousand (or 400 per thousand, eliminating incomes under $2,500) in the case of the applicable state of Florida.

3. The use of residential electric utility customers interchangeably with families (although in 1958, 99 per cent of families have electric service).*

4. Long-term weather trends indicate somewhat cooler summers beginning before 1960 and reaching into the 1970's.†

5. Future technological changes affecting air conditioning‡ particularly as to product and price cannot be anticipated.

6. Change in income levels and income distribution cannot be anticipated.

With this information, what would be your action if you were part of the management of a room air conditioning manufacturer?

---

* In 1949 there were 35.4 million residential electric customers and in 1958, 48.6 million. Edison Electric Institute, *Statistical Bulletin for the year 1958*, table 26. In 1949 there were 49.4 families and unrelated individuals in the U.S. *Census of Population, 1950,* U.S. Summary, Table 84.

† J. M. Mitchell, "Link Warmer Climate to City Growth," *Heating, Piping and Air Conditioning,* vol. 28, No. 8, August 1956, pp. 92–95.

‡ "New Method of Cooling," *Wall Street Journal,* June 23, 1958, p. 1.

CASE II-3. THE CHEMICAL FERTILIZER INDUSTRY
Demand Analysis—Saturation

Until 1949, the demand for chemical fertilizers had been capable of annual prediction through a formula developed by Mehring:[†]

$$X_0 = 0.03293Y_{-1} + 0.01766Y_0 + 1.159P_{-1} - 18.844$$

where X_0 = fertilizer expenditures in a given year in millions of current dollars

Y_{-1} = cash income of farmers from crops in the previous year plus government payments received in millions of current dollars

Y_0 = cash income of farmers from crops in the given year plus government payments received in millions of current dollars

P_{-1} = the percentage of total cash income of farmers in the previous year remaining after production costs.

The equation was quite accurate both for the United States as a whole and for specific regions. Its accuracy was lower where changes in fertilizer use through improved technology and education were greater (as in the East North Central states). For the period 1943 to 1948 a shortage in production capacity in the fertilizer industry caused some discrepancy between actual fertilizer sales and the sales predicted through the use of this equation. The results of the equation for 1910 to 1951 appear in Table I and Chart I.

It was several years before the change in the close correlation of cash farm income and fertilizer sales which had existed up to 1949 was recognized as something other than random deviations. Then the hunt began for the new determinant or determinants of fertilizer consumption.

The chemical fertilizer industry began in Baltimore about 1850 and particularly in the southeastern part of the United States the use of phosphate spread quickly in the tobacco and cotton areas where the soil had been seriously "mined" for some years. American mining of phosphate began in 1867 but no American production of potash and nitrates (the other two primary chemical fertilizers) began until after World War I. Up to this time imports from Germany and Chili, served as the major sources for potash and nitrates, respectively.

---

[*] With the assistance of John Anderson, M.B.A. (Northwestern).

[†] A. L. Mehring, G. A. Bennett, and J. R. Adams, "Fertilizer Expenditures in Relation to Farm Income in Various States," *Plant Food Journal,* vol. 6, no. 4 (1952).

Case II-3. TABLE I

U.S. Fertilizer Expenditures for 1910 to 1951, Actual and Predicted from Equation*: $X_0 = 0.03293Y_{-1} + 0.01766Y_0 + 1.159P_{-1} - 18.844$

Year	Y Cash Income from Crops and Payments	P Per Cent of Cash Income Remaining after Paying Production Expenses	Expenditures for Fertilizers		
			Actual	X_0 Predicted	Actual as Per Cent of Estimate
	million dollars	*per cent*	*milliod dollars*	*million dollars*	*per cent*
1910	2,950	38	158	. . .	. . .
1911	2,925	35	175	174	101
1912	3,111	35	168	173	97
1913	3,095	35	179	179	100
1914	2,920	32	201	175	115
1915	3,280	34	174	172	101
1916	4,043	37	186	184	101
1917	5,660	43	205	247	83
1918	6,985	44	309	341	91
1919	7,674	42	402	398	101
1920	6,654	28	416	400	104
1921	4,199	16	256	326	78
1922	4,321	26	225	214	105
1923	4,885	25	253	240	105
1924	5,415	26	255	267	96
1925	5,526	32	281	287	98
1926	4,889	29	268	287	93
1927	5,157	30	238	267	89
1928	5,044	29	295	275	107
1929	5,125	31	277	271	102
1930	3,840	22	276	254	109
1931	2,536	12	189	178	106
1932	1,997	20	111	114	97
1933	2,604	30	116	116	100
1934	3,450	33	157	162	97
1935	3,551	35	177	196	90
1936	3,938	35	206	208	99
1937	4,315	33	253	228	111
1938	3,672	29	226	226	100
1939	4,173	29	233	209	111
1940	4,159	27	237	226	105
1941	5,149	34	266	248	107
1942	7,089	40	328	322	102
1943	8,537	43	413	415	99
1944	9,816	43	439	485	90
1945	10,161	41	504	531	95
1946	11,607	42	536	569	94
1947	13,545	43	606	652	93
1948	13,393	38	715	708	101
1949	12,771	34	751	687	109
1950	12,858	31	828	665	124
1951	13,468	32	880	680	129

Sources: Y column: 1910 to 1939, *Agricultural Statistics* (Washington, D. C.: Department of Agriculture, 1942), Table 734; 1940 to 1951, *Farm Income Situation* (Washington, D. C.: Bureau of Agricultural Economics, 1952), Mimeo FIS-134, Table 7. *P* column: 1910 to 1939, *Agricultural Statistics*, Table 735; 1940 to 1951, *Farm Income Situation*, Table 11. "Actual" column: computed from tons of each grade and kind of fertilizer paid for by farmers and its average retail price, from A. L. Mehring, G. A. Bennett, and J. R. Adams, "Fertilizer Expenditures in Relation to Farm Income in Various States," *Plant Food Journal*, vol. 6, no. 4 (1952).

* In the original study by Mehring (see last note of prior page), the coefficient of the Y_{-1} term is 0.3293. Simple experimentation shows this is an error of one decimal place in the coefficient. Thus, the term should be 0.03293.

CASE II-3. CHART I

Fertilizer Expenditures in U.S. for 1910 to 1951, Actual (Solid Line) and
Predicted (Broken Line) from Equation:

$$X_0 = 0.03293Y_{-1} + 0.01766Y_0 + 1.159P_{-1} - 18.844$$

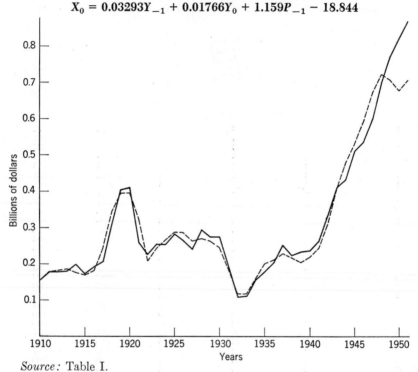

Source: Table I.

The plant nutrients contained in fertilizers are expressed as the
percentage by weight of nutrient (fillers such as sand being added) in
the following order: total nitrogen as N, available soluble phosphate
as P_2O_5 and water soluble potassium oxide as K_2O. Most fertilizers are
sold as "mixed," that is, containing chemical combinations of two or all
three. Some "straight" fertilizers (one chemical only) are sold, especially muriate of potash (60 per cent P_2O), sodium nitrate (16 per
cent N) and normal superphosphate (16 to 20 per cent P_2O_5).* Large
reserves of the basic chemicals used in making all three are available
on the North American continent. Newer methods in nitrogen chemistry have eliminated the older dependence on Chilean nitrates for
nitrogen.

* Further detail in Mirko Lamar, *The World Fertilizer Economy* (Stanford:
Stanford University Press, 1957), and Ursula Ewald, *Recent Developments of the
World Fertilizer Markets* (Kiel: Institut Für Weltwirtschaft an der Universität
Kiel, 1957) English translation by Bande and Grunewald.

CASE II-3. TABLE II

Average Retail Delivered Price Per Ton of Normal and Concentrated
Superphosphate by Regions in 1952

Region	18 Per Cent P_2O_5	20 Per Cent P_2O_5	45 Per Cent P_2O_5
New England	$31.75	$39.60	$ —
Middle Atlantic	30.40	33.90	—
South Atlantic	25.25	28.00	58.50
East North Central	32.25	38.90	70.60
West North Central	38.00	41.25	76.90
East South Central	—	31.20	61.10
West South Central	—	34.05	71.55
Mountain	35.30	—	77.50
Pacific	40.15	42.00	82.75
U.S. Average	30.35	34.20	74.10

Source: A. L. Mehring, J. R. Adams, and R. P. Jacob, *Statistics on Fertilizers and Liming Materials in the United States,* U.S. Dept. of Agriculture Stat. Bull. 191, (1954) Table 60, p. 68.

Table II illustrates some of the aspects of the industry. Prices for normal and concentrated superphosphate by regions are shown. Freight is a large cost, being frequently in the neighborhood of 30 per cent of the delivered selling price. The relatively lower price of concentrated chemicals follows not only from economies of freight but from economies in handling, storage, bagging, etc. The prime deposits of phosphate are in Florida and of potash in New Mexico. Nitrogen is available in the atmosphere for processes now used although earlier processes used Chilean nitrates.

The straight chemicals are typically shipped from the mine where the ore has been highly refined to 1,235 (in 1952) "mixing" plants located close to the market partly to take freight advantages and partly because of the wide variation in soil conditions and in major crops, both of which determine the particular ratio of the three chemicals which is economically desirable to the farmer. When the chemicals are mixed dry, no chemical combination occurs and the industry classifies such a mix as "straight" materials. Mixed materials thus are in liquid form with a chemical combination. From 1955 to 1958 about one-third of the fertilizer tons consumed were straight and two-thirds as mixtures.*

* Walter Scholl, Marion M. Davis, Ester I. Fox, and Anna W. Woodward. *Consumption of Commercial Fertilizers and Primary Plant Nutrients in the United States.* U.S. Dept. of Agriculture, Bull. ARS 41-19-2 (1958).

In 1952 * there were about forty U.S. companies producing phosphate rock with 75 per cent of U.S. production by nine Florida producers. About two hundred plants produced normal superphosphate; twenty-one plants produced concentrated superphosphate, with eight companies accounting for 53% of the superphosphate.

About 90 per cent of the U.S. potash is produced in New Mexico by five firms.

The forty-two plants producing synthetic nitrogen account for 93 per cent of the U.S. output and these plants are reasonably dispersed among twenty-one private firms.

The 1,235 mixing plants (1952) include many which are separately owned and buy from the chemical refiners.

Despite the possibility of oligopolistic pricing at the raw material level, the industry is competitive (partly because of anti-trust action and partly through new entries, especially in nitrogen) and real prices have actually declined in recent years as shown in Table III.

CASE II-3. TABLE III

Price Per Unit of Nutrients F.O.B. Producer of Some Typical Fertilizer Raw Materials

Year	Ammonia Anhydrous		Ammonium Sulphate		18 Per Cent Phosphate		Muriate of Potash	
	Current (1)	Deflated (2)	Current (3)	Deflated (4)	Current (5)	Deflated (6)	Current (7)	Deflated (8)
1943	$1.09	$0.58	$1.42	$0.76			$0.52	$0.28
1944	0.91	0.49	1.42	0.76	$1.38	$0.74	0.52	0.28
1945	0.72	0.38	1.42	0.66			0.52	0.27
1946	0.72	0.33	1.44	0.67			0.51	0.24
1947	0.72	0.28	1.60	0.74			0.43	0.20
1948	0.80	0.29	2.03	0.74			0.40	0.15
1949	0.94	0.39	2.29	0.96			0.40	0.17
1950	0.91	0.37	1.95	0.79	1.48	0.60	0.37	0.15
1951	0.97	0.33	1.97	0.68			0.40	0.14
1952	0.97	0.35	2.09	0.76	1.68	0.61	0.40	0.15

Sources: Mehring et al., USDA Stat. Bull. 191, *op. cit.*, Table I (columns 1 and 3: p. 19; column 5: p. 68; column 6: p. 76). Columns 2, 4, 6, and 8: computed by using USDA index of prices received by farmers.

Table IV sets forth annual data showing (in column 1) the leveling off of fertilizer consumption in tons since the year 1952. However the nutrient consumption (column 6) has continued to grow in tonnage. This is, of course, reconciled by the higher nutrient content per ton (columns 2 to 5). Phosphate usage per ton of fertilizer has been con-

* All of the following data come from sources already cited.

CASE II-3. TABLE IV

Fertilizer and Plant Nutrient Content Data (Excluding Agricultural Lime)

| Year | (1) Fertilizer Consumption in Thousands of Tons | Nutrients as Per Cent of Fertilizer | | | | (6) Nutrients in Thousands of Tons | (7) Gross National Product in Billions of 1954 Dollars | (8) Nutrient in Tons Per Thousand Population | (9) Fertilizer in Tons Per Thousand Population | (10) Expenditure for Fertilizer in Millions |
		(2) N	(3) P_2O_5	(4) K_2O	(5) Total					
1939	7,993	5.0	9.9	5.1	20.0	1,596	$189.3	12.2	61.0	$233
1940	8,656	4.8	10.6	5.0	20.4	1,766	205.8	13.4	65.5	237
1941	9,607	4.8	10.3	4.9	20.0	1,919	238.1	14.4	72.0	266
1942	10,331	3.9	10.9	5.3	20.1	2,076	266.9	15.4	76.6	328
1943	11,734	4.3	10.6	5.5	20.4	2,389	296.7	17.5	85.8	413
1944	13,331	4.8	10.5	4.9	20.2	2,689	317.9	19.4	96.3	439
1945	14,128	4.5	10.2	5.3	20.0	2,832	314.0	20.3	101.0	504
1946	16,166	4.7	10.4	5.3	20.4	3,286	282.5	23.2	114.3	536
1947	17,398	4.8	10.2	5.1	20.1	3,490	282.3	24.2	120.7	606
1948	17,596	4.8	10.5	5.4	20.7	3,641	293.1	24.8	120.0	715
1949	17,928	5.1	10.5	5.9	21.5	3,860	292.7	25.9	120.2	751
1950	19,760	5.7	10.5	6.2	22.4	4,413	318.1	29.1	130.3	828
1951	21,056	6.0	9.9	6.7	22.6	4,769	341.8	30.9	136.4	880
1952	22,797	6.5	9.7	7.1	23.3	5,312	353.5	33.9	145.2	
1953	22,631	7.3	9.8	7.6	24.7	5,577	369.0	35.0	141.8	
1954	22,726	8.6	10.0	8.2	24.8	5,896	363.1	36.3	139.9	
1955	22,194	8.7	10.1	8.4	27.2	6,120	392.7	37.0	134.3	
1956	22,709	9.4	10.1	8.5	29.0	6,055	400.9	36.0	135.0	
1957	22,516	10.1	10.2	8.6	28.9	6,377	408.6	37.3	131.5	
1958	25,143	10.5	10.2	8.7	29.4	6,512	401.0	37.3	144.4	

Sources: Columns 1 to 5: 1939 to 1953: USDA Stat. Bull. 191, *op. cit.* (Table II), p. 105; 1954 to 1958: Walter Scholl, M. M. Davis, Ester I. Fox, and Anna W. Woodard, *Consumption of Commercial Fertilizers and Primary Plant Nutrients in the United States,* U.S. Dept. of Agriculture, Bull. ARS 41-19-2 (1958). Column 9: 1939 to 1953: USDA Stat. Bull. 191, *op. cit.* (Table I), p. 105; 1956 to 1958: Scholl et al., *op. cit.* (Columns 1 to 5, this Table). Column 7: *Survey of Current Business,* July 1959. Columns 8 and 9: computed from columns 1 and 6, using *Current Population Reports,* U.S. Dept. of Commerce, No. 206 (1959). Column 10: computed from USDA, *The Farm Income Situation* (Agriculture Marketing Service, 1958) and Mehring et al., op. cit. (Table II); excludes agricultural Limestone, which runs as high as 20 per cent of the usual fertilizer and lime figures (and as low as 7 per cent).

Note: Blank spaces indicate data not available for some series on a comparable basis.

CASE II-3. TABLE V

All Fertilizers: Consumption and Primary Nutrient Content, by Regions and Territories Years Ending June 30, 1934, 1939, 1946, 1950, 1954, 1958.

	New England in Thousands of Tons	Middle Atlantic in Thousands of Tons	South Atlantic in Thousands of Tons	East North Central in Thousands of Tons	West North Central in Thousands of Tons	East South Central in Thousands of Tons	West South Central in Thousands of Tons	Mountain in Thousands of Tons	Pacific in Thousands of Tons	Territories in Thousands of Tons	Total in Thousands of Tons
1934:											
N	15	28	121	10	1	35	11		19	28	269
P_2O_5	25	85	219	65	9	62	16		13	17	515
K_2O	24	47	109	26	2	25	6	1	5	14	258
Total Fertilizer	283	833	2,749	485	58	687	172	4	183	250	5,707
1939:											
N	16	34	163	18	2	67	22	1	29	33	384
P_2O_5	32	135	262	102	19	89	25	10	22	14	710
K_2O	27	61	169	54	4	39	12		8	24	399
Total Fertilizer	294	1,115	3,492	826	112	1,064	309	29	252	244	7,738
1945:											
N	29	59	231	46	6	113	41	5	67	35	630
P_2O_5	51	210	394	248	81	204	62	29	61	16	1,353
K_2O	47	103	259	157	21	71	23	1	20	25	729
Total Fertilizer	493	1,622	4,653	2,176	462	1,969	620	136	1,070	265	13,466
1950:											
N	24	69	275	95	60	192	95	22	123	50	1,005
P_2O_5	59	246	470	396	193	289	161	39	75	22	1,950
K_2O	46	123	331	299	60	135	50	2	23	35	1,103
Total Fertilizer	505	1,894	5,409	3,434	1,186	2,841	1,288	205	1,215	367	18,344
1954:											
N	25	110	382	261	266	264	182	65	234	58	1,847
P_2O_5	43	234	492	547	338	273	145	59	92	20	2,242
K_2O	43	184	463	594	154	214	85	2	28	39	1,806
Total Fertilizer	417	2,069	6,143	4,823	2,224	3,024	1,395	393	1,875	411	22,773
1958:											
N	31	121	411	338	352	261	261	113	344	51	2,284
P_2O_5	51	224	446	603	359	243	155	79	116	16	2,293
K_2O	47	193	508	628	175	222	81	5	41	35	1,935
Total Fertilizer	438	1,932	5,669	4,678	2,312	2,625	1,341	551	2,613	357	22,516

Sources: Data for the years 1934, 1945, 1950 and 1954 from Mehring et al., *op. cit.* (Table II), Table 107, p. 112. Data for 1958 from Scholl et al., *op. cit.* (Table IV).

stant (column 3), potash is still increasing (column 4) and nitrogen (column 2) has been increasing at a much faster rate than potash.

In per capita terms (columns 8 and 9), fertilizer tonnage has been decreasing and since 1953 nutrient tonnage has been constant for the 6 years from 1953 to 1958. This suggests that the saturation point may have been reached for nutrient sales under present conditions of technology and food preferences.

At the outset of this study the equation was set forth which until 1949 had successfully related fertilizer expenditures in a given year to cash income of farmers in the current and preceding years and to the preceding year's cash income after production costs. Over much of the period down to 1949, United States fertilizer consumption had been dominated by consumption in the South and Southeast as appears in Table V.

Most cash income on southern farms was derived from crops and dealers sold fertilizer on credit. These farmers sought to purchase as much fertilizer as possible because of the severe leaching of the soil. The amount of credit allowed by the dealers was heavily influenced by the payment of the prior year's debts which in turn would depend upon the preceding year's cash income. Since most of these farmers considered the best indicator of farm prices this year was the preceding year's prices, a high correlation would exist between this year's expected income and fertilizer expenditures. This explanation became less satisfactory as fertilizer consumption grew in regions other than the South and as the South shifted away from crops to livestock and other activities and as the Secretary of Agriculture followed the practice of announcing price supports in advance of planting.

A new explanation of fertilizer consumption was offered in 1959 by Dr. R. A. King of North Carolina State College.* In developing his

*J. R. Brake, R. A. King, and W. B. Riggam, "Prediction of Fertilizer Consumption in the U.S.," A. E. Information Series No. 75, North Carolina State College (1960). For a competing explanation, see Zvi Griliches, "The Demand for Fertilizer: an Economic Interpretation of a Technical Change," *Journal of Farm Economics,* vol. 40, pp. 591–606 (1958). Griliches has established a regression equation for nutrient consumption for the same period used by King as: log of total plant nutrient use (units not specified) in any year $= 0.134 - 0.536$ log

$$(0.070)$$

$$\frac{\text{prices paid by farmers per plant nutrient unit}}{\text{index of prices received}} + 0.766 \text{ log total plant nutrient use}$$

$$(0.134)$$

of preceding year.

The numbers in parentheses under the terms of the equation are the standard errors of the coefficients above them. When this equation is fitted to data for 1911 to 1956, R^2 is 0.983.

The Griliches study considers the identification problem.

predicting equation, King considered such factors as: total planted acreage; acreage in major crops; economic position of farmers; availability of fertilizer; price of fertilizer relative to other inputs; recommended fertilization rates; farmers' knowledge and attitude; agricultural changes such as irrigation and hybrids; weather; promotion by fertilizer producers; governmental activities.

It is apparent that many of these factors cannot be quantified. King established the following equation:

$$Y_t = -55 + 1.0662Y_{t-1} - 3.504C + 4.801T - 3.220P + 5.659S$$
$$ (.0142) \qquad (6.403) \quad (1.668) \quad (4.408) \quad (2.053)$$

where Y_t = predicted nutrient consumption in thousands of tons of plant nutrient;

Y_{t-1} = nutrient consumption in prior year in thousands of tons;

C = percentage change in corn acreage planted in millions of acres;

T = percentage change in tobacco acreage planted in millions of acres;

P = percentage change in price of nutrient unit stated as an index number, 1912 = 100;

S = percentage change in cash sales of crops of prior year in billions of current dollars.

The numbers in parentheses indicate the standard deviation of each of the parameters above them. This equation explains 99.3 per cent of the variation in the nutrient consumption from 1911 to 1957. The equation correctly predicts change in direction in 42 of these 46 years. Since 1942 errors have been under 5 per cent in 12 of the 16 years and under 2 per cent in 8 of the 16 years.

It should be remembered that 97 per cent of the variation in annual nutrient consumption can be explained by trend alone. However, trend would never predict a downturn and the predicting equation correctly predicts three of the five changes in direction since 1930.

The disadvantage of the equation is that the lead over actual sales in only a few months. Two of the important determinants, corn and tobacco acreages, are not known until late spring.

Table VI shows the indexes of fertilizer and other input prices. The price of fertilizer has been quite stable in terms of current dollars and in the last decade has been decreasing in terms of constant dollars. On the other hand the indexes of land (measured by interest and taxes) cost and labor cost and machinery cost have doubled. This situation favors substitution of fertilizer for these inputs, a matter which is technologically feasible within limits.

Evidence has already been set forth that the more recent and more

CASE II-3. TABLE VI

Index Numbers of Prices Received for All Products, Prices Paid by Farmers for Specific Production Inputs and All Commodities, and Wholesale Price Indexes for Farm Products and All Commodities

Year	Prices Received All Farm Products (1)	Parity Ratio (2)	Feed (3)	Motor Supplies (4)	Motor Vehicles (5)	Machinery (6)	Building and Fencing Materials (7)
1944	197	108	173	115	211	174	190
1945	207	109	172	115	218	176	195
1946	236	113	200	117	224	182	212
1947	276	115	236	129	260	206	277
1948	287	110	250	144	291	240	308
1949	250	100	206	146	320	270	304
1950	258	101	210	149	320	275	312
1951	302	107	236	156	342	297	346
1952	288	100	251	157	358	308	340
1953	258	92	227	160	355	311	350
1954	249	89	226	162	356	313	350
1955	236	83	210	167	358	313	356
1956	235	82	207	167	381	330	376
1957	242	82	203	172	406	349	388

Year	Fertilizer (8)	All Production Commodities (9)	Interest Per Acre (10)	Taxes Per Acre (11)	Wage Rates Hired Labor (12)	Farm Products (13)	All Commodities (14)
1944	118	173	79	185	318	68.9	67.6
1945	120	176	75	192	359	71.6	68.8
1946	121	191	74	213	387	83.2	78.7
1947	134	224	76	237	419	100.0	96.4
1948	146	250	78	276	442	107.3	104.4
1949	150	238	82	298	430	92.8	99.2
1950	144	246	89	320	425	97.5	103.1
1951	152	273	98	335	470	113.4	114.8
1952	156	274	108	350	503	107.0	111.6
1953	157	253	117	365	513	97.0	110.1
1954	155	252	126	381	510	95.6	110.3
1955	153	248	136	394	516	89.6	110.7
1956	150	249	150	421	536	88.4	114.3
1957	151	258	163	440	558	90.9	117.6

Sources: Agricultural Statistics (United States Department of Agriculture, 1958). Columns 1 and 2 from Table 663, page 466. Columns 3–12 from Table 664, page 467. Columns 13 and 14 from Table 662, page 466.

concentrated fertilizers are more economical (Table II) but as appears in Table V, South Atlantic farmers are resisting this movement (as shown by the much higher ratio of tons of fertilizer to tons of plant nutrient). This is but one illustration of the many imperfections of knowledge on the demand side that plague the fertilizer industry.

What long range forecast can you prepare for the fertilizer industry and what are the most important variables which are assumed constant in your forecast?

part III

Production and cost analysis

PRODUCTION ANALYSIS

Once the demand situation for a product has been analyzed, the likely ranges of production are indicated. The next problem a manager faces is the organization of resources to meet possible production goals. This involves not only the problems of current manufacture and production but the management of inventories. For example, even after the most efficient combination of resources for a given output of goods has been determined, there remain problems of organizing both the inventories of raw materials and the inventories of finished goods so that the total cost of output over a period of time is minimized. Thus analysis may show that a constant rate of production offers savings compared to a rate of production that fluctuates with sales volume as might be true of seasonal variations in the demand for a product.

However, to achieve a constant rate of production in this situation requires a fluctuation at least in the inventories of finished goods. The finished goods inventory fluctuation will be the inverse of the sales fluctuation. As sales go up, finished goods inventory will go down and vice versa. But this carrying of a finished goods inventory in order to maintain a constant rate of production involves an increase in costs compared to the costs of carrying the finished goods that would be carried if the rate of production was permitted to fluctuate with sales. These increased costs of carrying a larger finished goods inventory must be compared with the savings from a constant rather than a fluctuating rate of production in order to establish which method is cheaper. Actually, some intermediate combination may be the cheapest method, namely some variation in the rate of production (but not as large as the variation in sales) and some increase in finished goods inventory (but not enough increase to support a constant rate of production).

The Production Function

Before examining the integration of production with inventory problems, the narrower problem of determining the most efficient combination of resources to achieve output will be examined. If only one combination of resources were possible in production in order to turn out a given output, there would be no need for decision making as to the combination to be used. *The study of the production function is directed to establishing the maximum output that can be achieved with a given set of* resources or inputs and with a given state of technology.

The term "production function" is applied to the relationship between units of output and units of input. The terms "factors of production" and "resources" are used interchangeably with the term "units of input." Thus a production function can be stated in the general form of an equation,

$$Y = f(X_1X_2, \text{etc.}),$$

where Y, the units of output, is a function of the quantity of two or more inputs with X_1 indicating units of labor, for example, and X_2, units of machinery. In the case of a given production function, some factors of production may be assumed as fixed (not varying with output variations). Such factors do not enter into the equation.

A production function may be estimated by least squares curve fitting which will minimize the squares of the vertical deviations of the actual output data from the fitted line when units of output are plotted on the Y-axis and units of a variable input are plotted on the X-axis.[1] In this case certain inputs (such as land or plant) would be considered fixed. Or a production function may be established by a regression equation considering the squares of both the horizontal and vertical deviations of the actual data from the average relationships of output and input.

Table III-1 shows the situation of variation in hours worked per

---

[1] More than one input may be varied with output. In the case of two inputs permitted to vary, the input-output relationship will be a plane in a three dimensional diagram. This can be handled in two dimensions by the use of curves as will be presently explained.

TABLE III-1

Hours Worked and Output in KVA of Transformer Production for One Plant

(1) X = Number of Hours Worked Per Day by Production Employees Working Eight Hours Each Per Day	(2) Number of KVA Per Day Produced by Same Number of Workers on Three Different Days 8 Hours Each Per Day	(3) Y = Average Output for Same Number of Hours Worked (Average of Column 2)	(4) Y/X = Average Output Per Hour	(5) $\Delta Y/\Delta X$ = Marginal Output Per Hour
280	1002 1010 987	1000	3.57	
				3.9
288	1052 1020 1021	1031	3.58	
				4.8
296	1063 1057 1087	1069	3.61	
				6.4
304	1108 1126 1126	1120	3.68	
				5.2
312	1162 1178 1146	1162	3.72	
				3.3
320	1202 1183 1179	1188	3.71	
				5.0
328	1211 1245 1228	1228	3.74	
				2.5
336	1259 1246 1238	1248	3.71	
				2.5
344	1262 1281 1260	1268	3.68	
				2.4
352	1282 1294 1285	1287	3.65	
				−0.6
360	1276 1291 1280	1282	3.56	
				0.6
368	1284 1279 1298	1287	3.50	

CHART III-1

**Transformer Production Function: Output in KVA as a Function of
Production Man Hours Per Day**

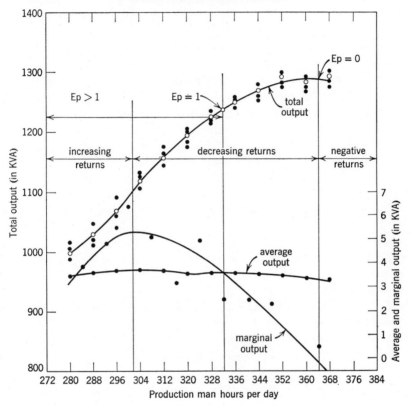

Source: Table III-1.

day by production workers and KVA² of transformer output per day
while holding all the other factors of production constant, such as
machinery, supervision, and plant layout.

The data of Table III-1 are plotted in Chart III-1. This chart clearly
shows that the production function follows the law of diminishing returns or, as it is sometimes called, the law of variable proportions,
which is described in elementary economics books.

² KVA is thousand volt amperes and a measure of size of a transformer. Thus
a 10 KVA transformer can handle double the load possible for a 5 KVA transformer. In the following presentation, it is assumed that labor requirements vary
directly with KVA size.

In Chart III-1, the range from 0 to 300 production man hours per day is the range of increasing marginal returns. The inflexion point of the total output curve (at 300 production man hours per day) lies just above the peak of the marginal output curve. From 300 production man hours per day to 360 is the range of decreasing returns (increase in output at a decreasing rate). The point of unit elasticity of productivity[3] of the total output curve lies at 332 production man hours immediately above the peak of the average output curve (and the marginal output curve passes through this peak). To the left of this point elasticity of productivity is greater than one and to the right less than one. The point of zero elasticity of productivity of the total output curve lies immediately above the point (364 production man hours per day) where the marginal output curve crosses the X-axis for a zero value. Starting with the input point of 364 production man hours per day (the peak of the total output curve) and further increasing input, we have the range of negative returns.

Because of the presence of two flex points in the total curve in Chart III-1 (one at 300 man hours per day and the other at 364) the appropriate curve to fit is a third-degree curve (a curve with an X^3 term which enables the trend computed to change direction twice). A second degree curve with only one change in direction would not show a flex point at 300 units of output. The general form of a third-degree curve is $Y_c = a + bX + cX^2 + dX^3$. A logistic growth curve or a Gompertz growth curve would not be appropriate to the data in Chart III-1 despite the general similarity of the total output curve of Chart III-1 to a growth curve because a growth curve *assumes* cumulative development rising at a geometric rate.

The equation of a third-degree curve fitted to the data in Table III-1 is

$$Y_c = 3816.9 - 46.43X + 0.20X^2 - 0.00026X^3$$

with a standard error of estimate or root mean square of 9.03.[4] and $R^2 = 0.984$. This is the equation of the total output curve. The average

---

[3] Elasticity of productivity is defined as the relative change in output divided by the relative change in input, or for point elasticity and for arc elasticity, respectively:

$$\text{point:} \quad \frac{do/o}{di/i} \qquad\qquad \text{arc:} \quad \frac{(o_1 - o_2)/o_1}{(i_1 - i_2)/i_1}$$

where i is units of input and o units of output

[4] The standard error of estimate or root mean square is the average deviation of the observed values from the fitted line. Thus $RMS = \sqrt{(Y_c - Y)^2/N - M}$, where Y_c are the computed values, Y the actual values, N the numbers of observations and M the number of constants in the regression equation.

output curve is then established by dividing each term of the equation by X, to give

$$\frac{Y_c}{X} = \frac{3816.9}{X} - 46.43 + 0.20X - 0.00026X^2$$

The marginal output curve is derived by differentiating the right hand side of the total output equation to get

$$\frac{dY_c}{dX} = -46.43 + 0.20(2X) - 0.00026(3X^2)$$

This situation offers a convenient opportunity to bring out the need for caution in using computing machinery and in using higher degree equations for extrapolation beyond the range of the actual data. The third-degree curve $Y_c = 3816.9 - 46.43X + 0.20X^2 - 0.00026X^3$ resulted when making the "classical" fit of a third-degree curve on the IBM-650, using library file 6.0.006. This gives a good fit for the range of the data (from $X = 280$ to $X = 368$) since the standard error of estimate (the average deviation of an observed Y from the computed Y) is 9.03 and $R^2 = 0.984$. When the values for Y are determined at intervals of $X = 10$ up to the actual values of X and thereafter for the actual values of X, Table III-2 is established.

TABLE III-2

Y Values Computed at Intervals of $X = 10$ and 8 from the Equation
$Y = 3816.9 - 46.43X + 0.20X^2 - 0.00026X^3$

X	Y_c	X	Y_c	X	Y_c	X	Y_c
0	3816.9	100	929.6	200	534.7	296	1080
10	3372.5	110	803.2	210	573.4	304	1123
20	2966.7	120	700.2	220	620.2	312	1162
30	2598.1	130	619.1	230	673.6	320	1197
40	2265.1	140	558.2	240	732.0	328	1225
50	1966.2	150	516.2	250	793.9	336	1248
60	1699.8	160	491.5	260	857.8	344	1263
70	1464.6	170	482.5	270	922.2	352	1270
80	1258.8	180	487.7	280	985.0	360	1269
90	1081.0	190	505.6	288	1034.0	368	1258

Source: X values for range $X = 280$ to $X = 368$: Table III-1.

The data of Table III-2 are graphed in Chart III-2.

The first flex point indicated by the equation occurs at about $X = 170$, whereas it more probably occurs at an X value of 300 as we

CHART III-2

Observed (x's) and Predicted (o's) Transformer Output from Equation:
$$Y_c = 3816.9 - 46.43X + 0.20X^2 + 0.00026X^3$$

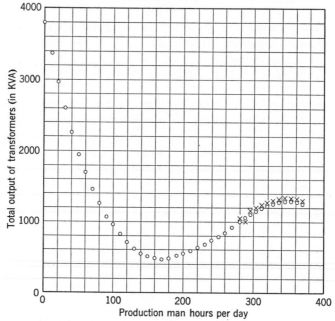

Source: Table III-2.

have already indicated. This may have occurred because of errors of measurement, e.g., the actual Y values, for the range of $X = 336$ to $X = 352$ in Table III-1, are *a priori* inconsistent since the law of diminishing returns specifies that returns increase at an increasing rate and then at a decreasing rate.

The computed values in Table III-2 are meaningless from $X = 0$ up to the beginning of the actual range of values at $X = 280$. What we have done illustrates the danger of extrapolation outside the limits of observed values. This is particularly true the more sensitive the type of curve being fitted. In addition we fitted the curve to only ten observations. The dangers of extrapolation will be reduced as the number of observed values fitted is increased. Lastly we were fortunate in having good *a priori* grounds for rejecting the computed values for the range $X = 0$ to $X = 280$ in the present case.

To check the results, another fit of a third-degree curve was made on the IBM-650 using file 6.0.009, a program that weights each observed value with 1. This resulted in the equation $Y_c = 21840.4 - 214.6X +$ $0.7X^2 - 0.00079X^3$ with a standard error of estimate of 11. When the values of Y are determined at intervals of $X = 10$ to 280 and thereafter at intervals of $X = 8$, Table III-3 is established from $X = 0$ to $X = 368$:

TABLE III-3

Y Values Computed at Intervals of $X = 10$ and 8 from the Equation
$Y = 21840.4 - 214.6X + 0.7X^2 - 0.00079X^3$

X	Y_c	X	Y_c	X	Y_c	X	Y_c
0	21840	100	6808	200	1473	296	1072
10	19766	110	5917	210	1290	304	1113
20	17831	120	5117	220	1152	312	1155
30	16031	130	4405	230	1054	320	1194
40	14361	140	3776	240	991	328	1228
50	12816	150	3225	250	959	336	1256
60	11392	160	2747	260	953	344	1274
70	10084	170	2337	270	968	352	1279
80	8887	180	1992	280	1000	360	1271
90	7797	190	1705	288	1033	368	1245

Source: X values for range $X = 280$ to $X = 368$: Table III-1.

The data of Table III-3 are graphed in Chart III-3.

It is clear that the part of the curve between $X = 0$ and the first flex point at $X = 260$ is again suspect. Likewise the section of the curve from $X = 0$ to $X = 280$ is meaningless although less so as the curve approaches $X = 280$.

Thus while a third-degree curve is the valid fit on *a priori* grounds, the extrapolation of this function beyond the limits of the observations is highly dangerous.

Production Functions, Returns to Scale, and the Isoquant

Up to this point the relation of a single input to output has been considered. This is sometimes called the (single) factor-product relationship. In this case all the other inputs are considered constant. These other factors are considered fixed as in the case of plant.

The next problem is to permit more than one factor to vary. Again we must face the question of returns to scale. If a doubling of all inputs doubles the output, the production function is said to involve constant return or returns proportional to scale. In this situation, the elasticity of productivity is one.

CHART III-3

Observed (x's) and Predicted (o's) Transformer Output from Equation:
$$Y_c = 21840.4 - 214.6X + 0.7X^2 - 0.00079X^3$$

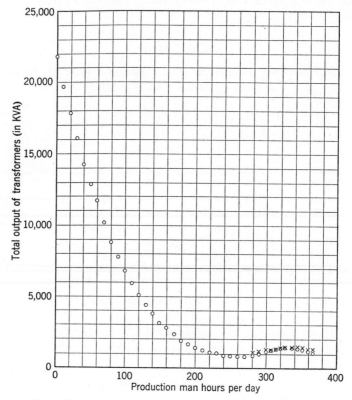

Source: Table III-3.

The other possible situations are either increasing returns to scale (and thus elasticity of productivity is greater than 1) or decreasing returns to scale (and elasticity of productivity is less than 1).

Increasing and decreasing returns to scale stem from two familiar causes: the limitation of management as a factor of production and the "lumpiness" of the factors of production. To the extent that management cannot be increased as efficiently as other factors, there will be an overstraining of management and hence, diminishing returns will set in.

To the extent that factors of production cannot be acquired in the exact quantity required but available units of the factor are more or less than desired, there is "lumpiness" of the factors. In this situation, there will be alternative ranges of increasing and decreasing returns as output expands. Thus returns will be such that the elasticity of productivity is greater and less than one respectively.

This leads to the proposition that if constant returns to scale are assumed, then the sum of the exponents of a logarithmic straight line fitted to the two independent variables will be 1. To illustrate, if the function fitted shows, as did the Cobb-Douglas production function, that output is related to labor and capital in the following manner: $O = 1.01L^{0.75}C^{0.25}$, then the equation *assumes* that a 1 per cent increase in each of capital and labor will result in a 1 per cent increase in output. Because of the logarithmic form, a 1 per cent change in labor input is associated with an 0.75 per cent change in output. A 1 per cent change in capital is associated with an 0.25 per cent change in output. That is, the exponents are directly the elasticities of productivity of the factors of production.

If, however, constant returns to scale is not assumed, the sum of the exponents of the independent variables of a logarithmic straight line fitted to the dependent variable and two independent variables will still continue to be directly the total elasticity of productivity.

Table III-4 sets forth data on transformer production in which

TABLE III-4

Transformer Production Data

N = Number of Men	H = Average Hours Worked Per Day by Each Man	O = Output of KVA
40	8	1000
41	8	1031
42	8	1069
43	8	1120
44	8	1162
40	10	1210
41	10	1258
42	10	1315
43	10	1389
44	10	1453
40	12	1410
41	12	1464
42	12	1529
43	12	1613
44	12	1684

number of men, average hours worked per day by each and output in KVA produced are shown.

Fitting an equation of the form

$$O = aH^bN^c$$

(where O is output in KVA produced, H is average hours worked per day by each man and N is the number of men), to the data in Table III-4 by the graphic method we have shown in Part I above yields the following coefficients:[5]

$$O = 0.196H^{0.880}N^{1.815}$$

The standard error of estimate (or average deviation of an observed value of Y from the computed value of Y) is 12.3 and $R^2 = 0.9965$.

The equation indicates that the relationship of output, number of men and average hours worked is such that a 1 per cent change in number of men produces a 1.8 per cent change in output and a 1 per cent change in hours worked per day by each produces an 0.88 per cent change in output.

From this equation we can derive the isoquants[6] tracing all the combinations of the two factors of production that yield the same output. By setting the equation equal to a single output such as 1200, we then have the equation of an isoquant: $1200 = 0.196H^{0.880}N^{1.815}$. Then substituting any value of H (or N) in the equation we get the associated value of N (or H).

TABLE III-5

Isoquants for Various Outputs Produced by Varying Men and Hours Per Day Developed from the Equation $O = 0.196H^{0.880}N^{1.815}$

$O = 1200$ KVA		$O = 1300$ KVA		$O = 1400$ KVA		$O = 1500$ KVA	
$N =$ Number of Men	$H =$ Daily Hours	$N =$ Number of Men	$H =$ Daily Hours	$N =$ Number of Men	$H =$ Daily Hours	$N =$ Number of Men	$H =$ Daily Hours
38	11.09	38	12.14	38	13.21	38	13.92
40	9.95	40	10.91	40	11.86	40	12.85
42	9.05	42	9.91	42	10.79	42	11.67
44	8.18	44	8.96	44	9.75	44	10.55
46	7.48	46	8.19	46	8.91	46	9.64

[5] When fitted on an IBM-650 computer, using program developed by Northwestern University Computing Center, the equation resulting is $O = 0.192H^{0.884}N^{1.818}$ with a standard error of estimate of 10.8.

[6] An isoquant is defined as the curve passing through the plotted points establishing all the combinations of two factors of production which will produce a given output.

CHART III-4

Isoquants Obtained by Determination of the Various Combinations of Number of Men and Overtime Hours to Achieve a Given Output, Where the Production Function is $O = 0.196H^{0.880}N^{1.815}$

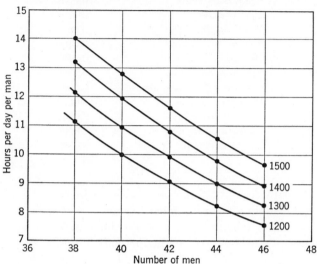

Source: Table III-5.

Similarly, by setting the equation equal to another output, we can get another isoquant.

Thus in Table III-5, isoquants are computed for a number of outputs and these are plotted on Chart III-4.

Isoquants and Factor Prices

The analysis so far has shown the situation regarding the benefits (or losses) in *physical* terms of substituting men for hours (and vice versa) in achieving a given level of production. However this does not establish which is the least cost combination for a particular output. To determine this we need a price for each factor.

Table III-6 shows the fringe benefits paid per hour worked by each man. In addition, all men are paid equally at $2.00 per hour with a 50 per cent premium for overtime.

Overtime costs $1.00 per hour extra whereas it saves $0.83 per hour in fringe benefits.[7]

---

[7] It is assumed that fringe benefits are independent of overtime. Some fringe benefits may not be independent and if they are directly variable with time worked would be excluded from the $0.83 and added to the pay rate in the calculation.

TABLE III-6

Fringe Benefits Per Man Hour Worked Straight Time

Profit sharing	$0.0879
Christmas bonus	0.0057
Rest periods	0.2788
Wash up time	0.0287
Sick leave	0.0109
Holidays	0.0493
Vacation pay	0.1292
Jury duty and funerals	0.0027
Health insurance	0.0512
Welfare program	0.0942
Education program	0.0035
Cafeteria deficit	0.0843

$0.8264, rounded as $0.83

From the data set out, we can establish an isocost line which will show all the combinations of number of men and overtime hours that will cost the same amount. This has been done in Table III-7 for an isocost curve of $1041.44 and again for $999.16, these figures simply being the cost of forty-six men straight time and forty-four men straight time respectively.

The data in Table III-7 have been graphed in Chart III-5. The question now is whether the increase in physical productivity as-

TABLE III-7

Isocost Calculation Showing the Various Combinations of Number of Men and Overtime Hours for Each Man Which Have the Same Total Cost

Daily Total Cost, No Overtime 8 Hours × $2.83/Hour × Number of Men	46 Men $1041.44	44 Men $996.16
2 less men, balance of $ for overtime	$45.28	$45.28
Overtime per man	$\dfrac{\$45.28}{\$3.00} \Big/ 44 = 0.34 \text{ hr.}$	$\dfrac{\$45.28}{\$3.00} \Big/ 42 = 0.36 \text{ hr.}$
4 less men, balance of $ for overtime	$90.56	$90.56
Overtime per man	$\dfrac{\$90.56}{\$3.00} \Big/ 42 = 0.72 \text{ hr.}$	$\dfrac{\$90.56}{\$3.00} \Big/ 40 = 0.75 \text{ hr.}$
6 less men, balance of $ for overtime	$135.84	$135.84
Overtime per man	$\dfrac{\$135.84}{\$3.00} \Big/ 40 = 1.13 \text{ hr.}$	$\dfrac{\$135.84}{\$3.00} \Big/ 38 = 1.19 \text{ hr.}$
8 less men, balance of $ for overtime	$181.12	$181.12
Overtime per man	$\dfrac{\$181.12}{\$3.00} \Big/ 38 = 1.59 \text{ hr.}$	$\dfrac{\$181.12}{\$3.00} \Big/ 36 = 1.68 \text{ hr.}$

CHART III-5

Isocost Curves for Various Combinations of Number of Men and Overtime Hours for Each Man, Which Have the Same Total Cost for All Points on a Given Curve

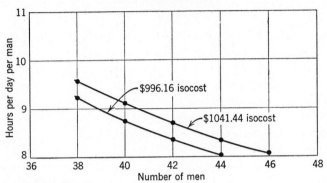

Source: Table III-7.

sociated with overtime hours in the present case (as compared to using added men on straight time hours) is worth the extra premium of $0.17 per hour paid on overtime. In the present case we know from the production function, $O = 0.196H^{0.880}N^{1.815}$ that a 1 per cent increase in the

CHART III-6

Determination of Least-Cost Combination of Number of Men and Overtime Hours to Achieve a Given Output

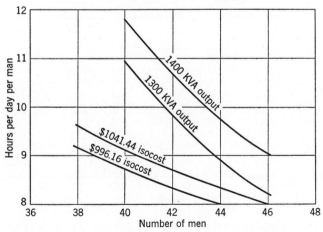

Sources: Charts III-4 and III-5, superimposed on each other.

number of men is associated with a 1.8 per cent increase in a physical output but a 1 per cent increase in overtime is associated with an 0.88 per cent increase in physical output. Hence it is clear that output increases should be brought about by added men rather than overtime hours since overtime is both less productive and more costly than added men.

However, let us follow the technique that would be used if the conditions were reversed, namely, if fringe benefits were well over $1.00 per hour and physical productivity were to decrease as overtime increased. This would be handled by superimposing the isocost curves of Chart III-5 upon the isoquant curves of Chart III-4. We have done this in Chart III-6. The lack of tangency of the two sets of curves indicates that in our actual case expansion will occur along the X axis by adding men on straight time.

Under our reverse assumption (fringe time well over $1.00 per hour), we might have had a situation such as appears in the following Figure III-1.

In such a case, the points of tangency of the isocost and isoquant curves would mark the line of expansion. The points of tangency represent the combinations of number of men and overtime hours on each of the isocost curves for which the *rate* of saving in cost (lower cost of overtime premium compared to fringe benefit) just equals the *rate* of increase in inefficiency by increasing overtime. Notice that under the assumed conditions of Figure III-1, expansion would involve both the increase in overtime and the increase in number of men.

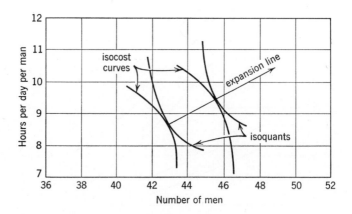

Figure III-1. Determination of least-cost combination of number of men and overtime hours to achieve each given output.

The *Ceteris Paribus* Assumption

Although the following observations are applicable to the preceding materials on forecasting and demand analysis, they have been reserved for this point in order to have a more adequate basis for their appreciation.

Our work has proceeded on the assumption that *all* factors other than those permitted to vary are constant. This is, of course, the famous assumption of *ceteris paribus* which is frequently used by economists (and all scientists, we may add). Thus in the model just examined of the relationship between overtime and added men as alternative factors to be used in increasing or decreasing output (with the least cost combination occurring where the rate of substitution of the factors in physical terms equals the rate of their substitution in the market place), we have assumed that machinery, for example, is constant or that it varies in such a way as to be optimally available as required by the men. Unless this condition is independently verified, we may, in using our data, be measuring not just the change in output associated with changes in the two factors, overtime and added men, but to some extent measuring an effect due in part to the overworking or underavailability of machinery. The behavior of other factors besides machinery must be verified. For example, the adequacy of supervision, of plant layout and of the accessibility of materials must be examined.

The Optimum Size of Lot for Manufacturing and Purchasing

In production analysis, one of the most common problems is the selection of the optimum size of lot to be used in manufacturing or in purchasing raw materials or parts. In the case of manufacturing, increasing the size of the lot to be made spreads the fixed costs of the lot (those costs which do not vary with the size of the lot). These costs are familiarly lumped under the term "set-up" costs. If there are elements in the "set-up" costs which vary with the size of the lot, these variable elements should be eliminated from the analysis. In the case of purchased materials or parts, increasing the size of the lot again spreads the fixed costs of the lot and such costs are familiarly lumped under the term "reorder" costs.

The analysis of a simplified illustrative case will show the techniques employed.[8] Suppose that a manufacturer makes refrigerators for a

---

[8] Further detail is available in such works as: J. F. Magee, *Production Planning and Inventory Control* (New York: McGraw-Hill, 1958) and T. M. Whitin, *The Theory of Inventory Management* (Princeton, N.J.: Princeton University Press, 1953).

mail-order house on a long term contract calling for the delivery of one hundred refrigerators on each of 250 business days in a year. Each refrigerator requires one motor which the manufacturer buys on the outside for $10 each and which he sends his own truck to pick up. The operation of the truck is estimated to cost $100 per trip including the driver's wage and the mileage cost of operation. The truck can make a daily trip for each day's requirements.[9] If the truck picks up several days requirements, then the inventory of the manufacturer will be increased and an increase will occur in the costs of carrying this inventory. Suppose the cost of storing this inventory is $1.00 per motor per year. Suppose further that the manufacturer finds that working capital costs him 10 per cent per year. Then the financing cost of 100 motors carried in inventory is $100 per year (100 times $10 times 10 per cent). Thus the total inventory cost of a daily average inventory of 100 motors is $200 per year,[10] consisting of $100 storage cost and $100 financing cost.

Regardless of the size of shipment the truck handles, the average inventory in the manufacturer's plant will be one half of the truck lot size as long as production is at a uniform rate as Figure III-2 shows. The problem is to determine how often to send the truck (or what is the same thing, what size lot the truck should pick up).

Table III-8 is based on the information we have just set forth and

[9] It is assumed for simplicity that the supplier pays a constant unit price for the motors whether the quantity picked up is 100 motors or some multiple thereof. If unit price varies with the quantity of the pickup, this complicating element can still be introduced into the solution. The quantity discount "break" point will result in a discontinuity of the curve.

[10] To avoid a complication in computing, we are abstracting from including an investment return on the trucking charge of $100. If freight is a major cost, it is worth the effort to do so. The complication, of course, is that the trucking cost curve that results from inclusion of the return on the trucking charge will no longer be linear but curvilinear. Likewise, we have abstracted from the question of how the rate of return to be used on invested money is to be determined. This capital budgeting aspect is reserved for the last part of this book. There is another element that may be important in particular cases. As average in-plant inventory on hand increases, the risk of interruption of the production line due to outages of material is reduced. If a saving can be quantified here, this amount is an offset to the increase in cost following upon the increase in inventory. In particular cases, increase in the size of in-plant inventory (together with its costs) is to be balanced against the reduction in production costs due to reduced outages. If there is considerable variation possible as to this relationship, then this third factor (outages of raw materials or purchased parts) should be incorporated into the two-factor analysis presented in the text. However, typical experience indicates that the degree of variation possible in in-plant inventory is small.

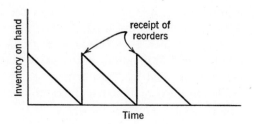

Figure III-2. Inventory on hand between reorder points on the assumption of uniform production rate.

Table III-8

Annual Cost of Trucking and Inventorying Motors by Re-order Size

Trips Per Year	Motors Per Trip	Daily Average Inventory	Annual Inventory Cost	Annual Trucking Cost	Total Cost
250	100	50	$ 100	$25,000	$25,100
50	500	250	500	5,000	5,500
25	1,000	500	1,000	2,500	3,500
12.5	2,000	1,000	2,000	1,250	3,250
5	5,000	2,500	5,000	500	5,500

shows the inventory costs, the trucking costs and the total costs for different numbers of truck trips per year. Chart III-7 is a graph of this

CHART III-7

Determination of Lot Size to Minimize Total Trucking and Inventory Cost

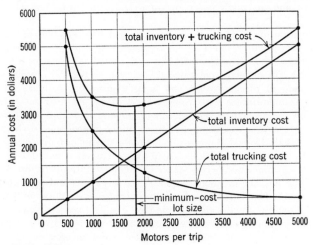

Source: Table III-8.

information. The minimum point of the total cost curve[11] establishes the minimum-cost lot size. In this case that occurs at a shipment of 1,581 motors per truck trip or 15.81 truck trips per year (25,000 motors divided by 1,581 motors per trip) or one every 15.81 days (250 days per year divided by 15.81 trips).

This result can, of course, be established in mathematical terms. The equation[12] is $x = \sqrt{2tu/c}$, where

> x = minimum-cost quantity;
> t = trucking cost or re-order cost;
> u = annual usage in units;
> c = annual cost of inventorying one unit for 1 year.

In the present illustration, t = \$100, u = 25,000 motors and c = \$2. Hence $x = \sqrt{2 \cdot 100 \cdot 25,000/2}.$ = 1,581, the minimum-cost quantity.[13]

It should be emphasized that the price of the finished part or raw material has been assumed constant (other than for quantity discounts). As soon as variation in this price becomes a significant variable, this must enter into consideration. Another way of saying this is that demand must be known in advance—an important assumption.

Optimizing Inventory Under Conditions of Uncertain Demand

The preceding analysis is made on the assumption that the quantity demanded during a period of time is known. The more typical situation,

[11] The fact that the intersection of the total trucking cost curve with the total inventory cost curve might lie just below the minimum point on the total cost curve in the present case is coincidental. The principle is that the minimum point of the total cost curve will lie directly above where the slopes of the two curves (trucking cost and inventory cost) are numerically the same but with opposite signs.

[12] The derivation of the equation is as follows using the symbols in the text and p for the price of a motor and u for the total units used per year. If a quantity x is to be obtained on each order, then u/x is the number of orders per year that must be placed. The average inventory on hand will be $x/2$. The annual total cost of the units and of placing orders and holding inventory will be: $TC = pu + tu/x + xc/2$. Differentiating with respect to x gives: $dTC/dx = -tu/x^2 + c/2$; and setting dTC/dx equal to zero gives $x = \sqrt{2tu/c}$, the minimum point.

[13] This same technique can be applied to a variety of economic problems. Thus, in Edward Smykay, Donald Bowersox, and Frank Mossman, *Physical Distribution Management* (New York: Macmillan, 1961) at p. 123, our Chart III-7 is used to determine the optimum number of plants to minimize total distribution costs. In such a case, the number of plants is placed on the x-axis and total distribution costs on the y-axis. The descending curve (total trucking cost curve in Chart III-7) then traces the total freight cost to produce *a given volume* using a varying number of plants. The ascending curve (total inventory cost curve in Chart III-7) then traces the added costs resulting from increased investment in inventory, building and machinery, etc. as the number of plants increases.

however, involves inventory planning for a demand that is not known, certainly not the exact quantity. What is usually known is some sort of probability distribution as to the quantity that is likely to be demanded. At least there is some expectation as to what the quantity demanded in a time period is likely to be. This, in any event, must be the basis for the decision.

Thus a plant may find that the single quantity which it considers most likely to be shipped in the next year is 1,100 units. There may be very little likelihood that the plant will sell less than 900 units which we assume to be the breakeven volume on this item and little chance it will sell more than 1,300 units. A canvass of the expectations[14] as to sales might produce the following schedule:

Expected Sales	Probability
900 units	0.10
1000 units	0.20
1100 units	0.40
1200 units	0.20
1300 units	0.10
	1.00

[14] Frequently probabilities are available from actual records rather than based on subjective estimates. Thus the study of the hourly sales over a long period may establish the following average daily number of sales per hour:

	Average Number of Sales
First hour	12
Second hour	6
Third hour	3
Fourth hour	1
Fifth hour	2
Sixth hour	5
Seventh hour	7
Eighth hour	13
	49

From this we get the probability table as to hourly sales:

First hour	$12/49 = 0.245$
Second hour	$6/49 = 0.123$
Third hour	$3/49 = 0.061$
Fourth hour	$1/49 = 0.020$
Fifth hour	$2/49 = 0.041$
Sixth hour	$5/49 = 0.102$
Seventh hour	$7/49 = 0.143$
Eighth hour	$13/49 = 0.265$
	1.000

The probabilities in this schedule are so determined as to total 1.00, the customary basis for handling probability.

For simplicity let us assume that the parts required to produce a unit are in a one to one ratio with the finished unit and that a set of these parts needed for one finished unit costs $300. At the end of the year, any "overstock" of these parts has negligible scrap value. A new model using different parts is brought out each year. In addition, experience is that there is no replacement market where parts can be disposed of. The period of production for the parts is so long that once the "model year" has begun it is too late to effect changes in the inventory of parts. For simplicity we abstract from the costs of carrying inventory.

The unit profit on the added 100 units over 900 and up to 1,000 is estimated to be $250 when volume sold is 1,000 units per year, $300 per unit for the added 100 units from 1,000 to 1,100, $350 per unit for the added 100 units from 1,100 to 1,200 and $400 per unit for the added 100 units from 1,200 to 1,300.

This information can be arranged in a table or matrix form.

Possible eventualities as to available sales

Strategy	900	1,000	1,100	1,200	1,300
1. 900 in inventory	0	− $25,000	− $55,000	− $90,000	− $130,000
2. 1,000 in inventory	− $30,000	+ $25,000	− $30,000	− $65,000	− $105,000
3. 1,100 in inventory	− $60,000	+ $25,000 − $30,000	+ $55,000	− $35,000	− $75,000
4. 1,200 in inventory	− $90,000	+ $25,000 − $60,000	+ $55,000 − $30,000	+ $90,000	− $40,000
5. 1,300 in inventory	− $120,000	+ $25,000 − $90,000	+ $55,000 − $60,000	+ $90,000 − $30,000	+ $130,000

A word of explanation of the table is in order. There are five possible strategies as shown at the left, namely, inventories of 900, 1,000, 1,100, 1,200, and 1,300 and five possible eventualities as to available sales, namely, 900, 1,000, 1,100, 1,200, and 1,300 as shown at the top of the table. Each cell shows the net gain or loss of each strategy in the case of each eventuality with reference to the given base point of 900. Thus, if 1,300 are put in inventory (the bottom row of strategies) and only 900 available sales develop, there is a loss on parts of $120,000 (400 unsold at $300 each). And following this row across, if 1,000 sales develop there is a loss of $90,000 on unused parts (300 unsold at $300 each) but a gain of $25,000 in profit on the extra 100 sold over the situation when 900 are sold. Or in the case of 900 in inventory (the top row of strategies) there may be 1,000 sales developing and thus there is a loss of possible profit of $25,000 (row 1, column 2). Thus the minus signs in the cells above the diagonal in the matrix represent the loss of anticipated profits due to inadequacy of inventory, the minus signs in the cells below the diagonal represent losses due to excess inventory, and the plus signs in the cells below the diagonal represent profits due to sales achieved by the added inventory.

We are now in a position to evaluate the five possible strategies by employing the probabilities as to the quantity likely to be demanded which we had established earlier:

Strategy 1:

$$0.1(0) + 0.2(-\$25,000) + 0.4(-\$55,000) + 0.2(-\$90,000) + 0.1(-\$130,000) = -\$58,000$$

Strategy 2:

$$0.1(-\$30,000) + 0.2(\$25,000) + 0.4(-\$30,000) + 0.2(-\$65,000) + 0.1(-\$105,000) = -\$32,500$$

Strategy 3:

$$0.1(-\$60,000) + 0.2(-\$5,000) + 0.4(\$55,000) + 0.2(-\$35,000) + 0.1(-\$75,000) = \$500$$

Strategy 4:

$$0.1(-\$90,000) + 0.2(-\$35,000) + 0.4(\$25,000) + 0.2(\$90,000) + 0.1(-\$40,000) = \$8,000$$

Strategy 5:

$$0.1(-\$120,000) + 0.2(-\$65,000) + 0.4(-\$5,000) + 0.2(\$60,000) + 0.1(\$130,000) = -\$2,000$$

Strategy 4, which suggests placing 1,200 in inventory, is the most profitable decision, given the assumed facts, since strategy 4 maximizes the probable profit.

Notice that we have proceeded in terms of opportunity costs as the economist does, that is, we have charged each strategy with the costs in the form of lost possible profit available if another strategy would have furnished greater profit.

The alert reader will no doubt realize that the problem can be further refined because some point within the 100 unit intervals used is most likely to be the best decision rather than exactly 1,200 in inventory. This would merely involve multiplying the available strategies to reduce the size of the 100 unit interval. If we had used a parallel case of expected sales of 9, 10, 11, 12, and 13 (dropping two zeros) and added two zeros to the unit cost (making this $30,000 instead of $300) and added two zeros to the unit profit (making this $25,000 instead of $250 and so on) we would arrive at strategy 4.

Similarly, to drop the unrealistic assumption of no replacement market, involves merely additional calculations. In this case, a probability as to replacement demands (based on prior experience) is all that is needed. Given these probabilities there are merely additional dollar figures to go into each cell showing the cost of replacement parts not sold and the profit on replacement parts sold and foregone. We are assuming that replacement sales and new owner sales are independent of each other.

In the case of dropping the assumption of no carrying costs of inventory, there are again merely the added costs of carrying which would be inserted in each cell.

Resource Organization and Inventories

At the outset of this Part, we noted that optimum organization of the factors of production was the first step in production analysis and that the next step involves the balancing of savings from a constant (or optimum) rate of production against the costs of carrying a fluctuating inventory (above the minimum required in any event) so as to maintain the constant rate of production. We noted that there would be some intermediate combination of production variations and increase in inventory which avoided the high costs of carrying so large a finished goods inventory as would be needed to achieve a constant rate of production and yet permitted some increase in inventory so as to gain the benefits of a rate of production that was more constant than the rate of sales.

Size of Inventory and Production Costs

The graphic technique can be applied to the present problem of the size of finished inventory and production costs,[15] just as it was used in solving the optimum size of lot discussed in the second preceding section.

Figure III-3 is a graph of the balancing of the costs of increases in inventory against increases in production costs resulting from holding progressively smaller amounts in inventory. There is a size of inventory (OM in Figure III-3) which achieves minimum production costs through complete elimination of interruptions due to missed delivery dates of suppliers, etc. (in the case of raw material inventory) or lost sales, etc. (in the case of finished goods inventory).

As the inventory is progressively reduced below this point, there will be an *increase* in production costs traced by the solid-line curve MN, moving from right to left. Remember, MN traces only the changes in total production costs for a given rate of production. The curve OI

---

[15] The alert reader is by now aware that there is a similar balancing problem (susceptible to the same techniques of solution) at the start of the production process, namely, the balancing of the costs of carrying an increased inventory of raw materials against the savings to be gained in avoiding interruption in production due to failures by suppliers in meeting their delivery dates for such raw materials.

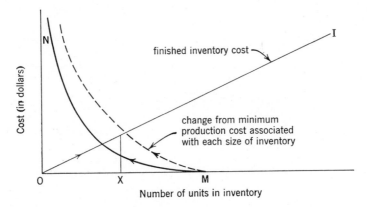

Figure III-3. Costs of increased finished inventory against reduced costs of production associated with such increased finished inventory.

(moving from left to right) traces the increase in cost resulting from increases in inventory. There is a size of inventory (OX) for which the *slopes* of the inventory cost curve and the curve for change in production cost are the same numerically although the signs are opposite. This is the optimum size inventory. Note that the intersection of the two curves has no relevance. It may happen (as in the case of the dotted line curve MN) that the slope of the curve tracing changes in total production cost is greater throughout its length than the slope of the inventory curve. If this is so, then the optimum inventory is OM.

This assumption of linearity in graphically interpolating between actual points may have a particular value where there is difficulty in getting a large number of infinitesimally spaced measurements particularly for the cost curve. Given only a few points on each curve, interpolation may yield an approximation of the true curve whereas establishing the interpolation mathematically would be more difficult.

Size of Inventory and Selling Costs

Figure III-4 is a diagram parallel to Figure III-3 for presentation of the similar problem at the next stage in management, namely, a balancing of the gains in reduced selling costs (such as by increased sales) which follow from the more prompt deliveries possible where a larger inventory of finished goods is carried, against the increased costs of carrying a higher inventory of finished goods.

There is again a size of inventory (OM) which minimizes selling costs and as finished goods inventory is reduced below this level, selling costs increase. Again the optimum inventory is that level at which the

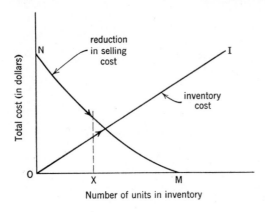

Figure III-4. Costs of increased finished inventory against reduced selling costs associated with such inventory.

slopes of the inventory cost curve (OI) and the curve of increases in selling cost (MN) are equal. If the slope of the selling cost line is less throughout its length than the slope of the inventory cost line, then zero inventory will be the optimum. Conversely, if the slope of the selling cost line is larger than the slope of the inventory cost line throughout its length, the inventory (OM) will be the optimum.

The Best Level When Many Strategic Variables Interact

It is, of course, quite possible that the level of inventory established as optimum from a study of the inventory-production cost situation (Figure III-3) and the inventory-selling cost situation (Figure III-4) may be quite different. This brings out that we have been proceeding by the method of partial equilibrium analysis, namely, by studying two variables while holding all others constant.

We are next confronted by the situation in which all items are considered variable, such as, prices for the goods produced, quantities of the goods produced, size of inventory, costs of all the input factors (including selling costs), etc. Then if as many equations are established as there are variables (with each equation showing the empirical relationship of a number of the variables), the system is determinate[16] and by analysis of the simultaneous equations, values for each of the variables can be determined which will maximize profits. However, each time one of the relationships established by one of the equations is changed, the values of all variables may change.

Further development of the approach just indicated, together with

[16] If certain other conditions are met such as the independence of the equations, that is that none of the equations is a linear combination of any of the others. The reader is referred back to the discussion of the identification problem at the end of Part II where this type of analysis is outlined.

the assistance it can receive from modern electronic computing machines, is just beginning to be seen and lies beyond the scope of mathematics assumed by the present book.

Linear Programming Using the Graphic Method [17]

Economists often employ the marginal analysis approach in allocating scarce resources in order to maximize the attainment of some objective. This marginal approach is shown graphically by indifference or iso curves. The mathematical or linear programming approach is a restatement of this kind of analysis and represents a useful approach for solving certain practical problems.

The central "idea" of linear programming is that in place of the production function (the relation of inputs and outputs) which involves the adding of small increments of a variable input, the more common situation is a process which involves fixed factors which effectively limit the variability of the variable inputs such as labor and materials. Thus a machine is designed for efficient operation over a very narrow range of output variation. Several processes are usually available and the problem thus becomes the selection of the best process for a given output or the most profitable output for given facilities where the facilities are capable of more than one type of product. This will become more apparent as we proceed.

Linear programming makes extensive use of algebraic equations and their manipulation. However, in simple problems, the central ideas of linear programming can be conveyed through the use of the more familiar graphic methods of modern economic analysis.[18] These graphic methods bear a close resemblance to indifference curve analysis.

Single Process for Each Product: Optimum Allocation
of Factors Between Products

To illustrate the use of the graphic method, we will consider the following simple case. A manufacturer has a machine that can be used to make either of two products. If the machine is used to make product 2 it will turn out 15 units per hour but when applied to product 1 it will turn out 20 units per hour. The next step in producing both 1 and 2 is to use a second machine whose capacity will favor product 2:

---

[17] This presentation does not give a full image of linear programming; to do so would require stepping up to a level of mathematics higher than this book assumes.

[18] Cf. Kenneth Boulding and W. Allen Spivey, *Linear Programming and the Theory at the Firm* (New York: Macmillan, 1960) and Robert Dorfman, "Mathematical or Linear Programming," *American Economic Review*, vol. 43, pp. 797–825 (1953). The mathematical approach at a practical level is presented in Abraham Charnes and W. W. Cooper, *Management Models and Industrial Applications of Linear Programming*, 2 vols. (New York: Wiley, 1961).

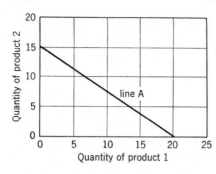

Figure III-5. Constant rate of substitution of a factor in the production of two products.

20 units of product 2 per hour or 10 units of product 1 per hour. Suppose that product 1 yields the company 20 cents per unit gross profit after labor and materials and product 2 yields 15 cents per unit gross profit based on prices offered to the producer. Suppose further that no additional machines can be procured except after a period when the buyer indicates he will no longer be interested in products 1 and 2. Meanwhile the buyer is willing to accept products 1 and 2 in such proportions as the producer finds most profitable.

If we establish the usual coordinates, we can represent the first machine's output by line A in Figure III-5.

Line A indicates that, in one hour, the first machine can be used to produce any combination of units along the line. For example:

15 units of 2 and 0 units of 1 per hour

or 10 units of 2 and 6.6 units of 1 per hour

or 5 units of 2 and 13.3 units of 1 per hour

or 0 units of 2 and 20 units of 1 per hour

Line B in Figure III-7 represents the possibilities of the second machine at full capacity which are 20 units of product 2 or 10 units of product 1.

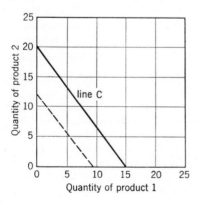

Figure III-6. Iso-net value curve for two products.

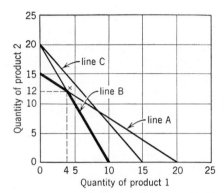

Figure III-7. Use of iso-net value curve and factor curves to determine optimum output of two products.

Line C (in Figures III-6 and III-7) is an iso-net value curve[19] (gross margin after labor and materials) used to represent the relationship of products 1 and 2. Twenty units of 2 at 15 cents each (after labor and materials) are worth as much as 15 units of 1 at 20 cents each.

Any position along line C represents a combination of products 1 and 2 that is equally profitable to the producer. Similarly, any line parallel to line C (such as the dotted line) represents for all points on that line equal profit combinations but at a different amount or level of profit.

Now if we combine our three lines A, B, and C on the same graph we get Figure III-7.

The heavy parts of lines A and B indicate the outer limits of all the combinations of products 1 and 2 which it is possible to produce *using both machines to their maximum capacity*. That is, *any* combination of products 1 and 2 within the area bounded by the heavy parts of lines A and B and by the coordinates is possible. However, the most profitable combination of products 1 and 2 must lie somewhere on the heavy line (the heavy parts of lines A and B).[20] Just where this combination lies depends upon the relative profitability of products 1 and 2. This relative profitability is indicated by the line C in the present case (or by any line parallel to line C). In the present case the line parallel to C and furthest out will touch the heavy line at the point X. The most

---

[19] At various points in this Part, a distinction will be made between an iso-revenue curve which shows equal *sales* figures and an iso-profit or iso-net value curve. The iso-profit curve shows profit and the iso-net value shows the gross profit (sales less cost of goods).

[20] The reason the most profitable combination must lie on this line is that any point "below" or to the "left" always involves less of at least one of the two products.

profitable combination of products 1 and 2 that can be produced as long as the relative profitability of the two products continues is 12 units of product 2 and 4 units of product 1.

Now suppose that the slope of line C shifts (the ratio of profitability of products 1 and 2) so that the slope of line C becomes identical with either of the two segments of the heavy black line. If this happens, then there is a zone of indeterminacy, that is, if the line C is parallel to the left part of the heavy line, then all combinations of products 1 and 2 along this line are equally profitable (and the same for the situation where the line C is parallel to the right part of the heavy line).

Also note that if the slope of the line C becomes less than the slope of the left part of the heavy line, then the most profitable arrangement is to produce only product 2 and none of product 1. Conversely if the slope of line C becomes greater than the slope of the right part of the heavy line, then it is most profitable to produce only product 1 and none of product 2.

Production Rays and Optimizing the Choice of Processes

Thus far we have been assuming that there is only one process that can be used to make each product. If we relax that assumption and deal with the case in which two or more processes can be used to make a product, we can also apply linear programming graphically.

The method of isoquants and isocost curves which was explained earlier on pp. 171 to 178 is appropriate when the factors can be varied infinitesimally. In the case we used, overtime and added men in transformer production illustrated this.

More frequently, however, the inputs can be changed only in terms such as a whole machine. Thus machinery speeds are usually designed for a narrow range of efficient operation. Or, depending on the size of hole to be dug, the choice of efficient earth moving machinery to use is quite limited. This is the situation where linear programming is appropriate.

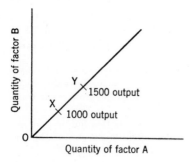

Figure III-8. Production ray assuming fixed factor proportions but not necessarily constant returns to scale.

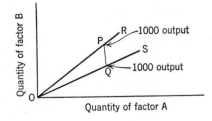

Figure III-9. Production rays for situation where two processes are available.

In a typical case, there may be a small number of different processes available to produce the good in question. Figure III-8 shows a production ray which charts the use of two factors as output is expanded. The straight line form of the ray indicates that the factors are used in fixed proportions, the slope of the line being the ratio of factor B to factor A in the production process. The point X on the ray indicates the quantities of factor A and B needed to make 1,000 units of the product. If the point Y marked 2,000 units, there would be constant returns to scale, the distance on the ray OX being equal to the distance XY. With OY as the point for 1,500 units of output, decreasing returns to scale is indicated between output OX and OY.

If two processes are available to make the product, as in Figure III-9, a straight line can be constructed, as between point P on the OR ray and point Q on the OS ray, to connect the one point on each ray where the output is the same as the output indicated by a point on the other ray. It is immaterial what the returns to scale shown by the two rays may be. It is assumed, however, that the two processes are independent of each other and the factors are available at a constant price.

Each point on this line PQ represents a combination of the two processes which yields the same output as OP units by process OR or OQ units by process OS.[21] Hence this line is an isoquant. It is now a short step to apply the familiar price line indicating the relative prices of the two factors A and B. Thus in Figure III-10, there are three processes (OR, OS, and OT) available to make the product. The two isoquants (1,500 units of output and 1,000 units of output) indicate all the combinations of the three processes that can be used to turn out the respective quantities of output. If the price ratio of factors A and B in the market place is as shown by the line XX, then the point of

---

[21] The formal proof that all points on the line PQ represent combination of processes R and S producing output volume equal to that at points P and Q is found in Robert Dorfman, "Mathematical or Linear Programming," *American Economic Review*, vol. 43, pp. 797–825 (1953) at p. 806, n. 4.

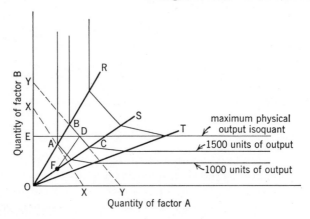

Figure III-10. Use of production rays, isoquants, and price lines to determine optimum process or combination of processes.

tangency A indicates that the most efficient (cheapest) process to use to make 1,000 units is process R exclusively since any other point on the isoquant for 1,000 units of output requires a greater expenditure on the factors A and B.

Similarly, if the price ratio of factors A and B in the market place is shown by the line YY, then the most efficient process to make 1,500 units of output is process R exclusively, process S exclusively or any combination of processes R and S as is indicated respectively by the coinciding of points B and C and of the line BDC with the price line YY.

With a little reflection, it is clear that as long as there is no factor fixed in supply there will always be at least one process by which the entire output can be produced which will be at least as cheap as any other process or combinations of processes. But as soon as one of the factors is fixed in maximum supply as is true of factor B in Figure III-10 when only OE units of it are available,[22] then the optimum program (when the price ratio of factors A and B is as shown by the YY line) is the combination of processes R and S shown by point D. The exact combination of processes R and S is indicated by a line from D parallel to OR, namely, DF.[23] This indicates the use of process

---

[22] It should be noted that if profit is not the object but rather maximum output, then the isoquant which is tangent to EE, the limitation line of factor B, is the optimum and only process T would be used.

[23] A parallel line has the same slope and this in turn means the same ratio of combination of the resources as the line (process) to which it is parallel.

S at the level OF and process R at the level FD.[24] It is clear that at most two processes can be involved in optimum production (even when both factors are in limited supply) and only one will be involved when the factor limitation lines pass through the same *corner* of the isoquant.

This is one of the basic theorems of linear programming: optimum production can be had by using no more processes than the number of factors in limited supply if this number is greater than zero. Which processes will be involved under this rule depends on where the factor limitation lines fall.

It is well to remember the assumptions made as far, namely, that the processes are independent of each other, and that the price of the output (the demand aspect) is constant.[25] If the price of the unit of output varies with the quantity, then isovalue lines replace the isoquant lines.

Reconciling Optimizing of Processes with Optimizing of Factor Allocation Between Products

We are now in a position to show that the answer obtained to the optimum factor allocation between products is consistent with the optimizing of selection of processes.

Referring back to Figure III-7 in which we identified the optimum combination of products 1 and 2 that could be achieved by the use of two machines, we can designate these machines as the two limiting factors. If these machines were not the two limiting factors, then we

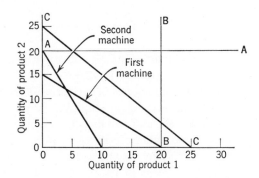

Figure III-11. Figure III-7 reproduced with other factors not effectively limiting production.

[24] For formal proof of this proposition, see the reference in the preceding footnote (21).

[25] That is we have been dealing with a completely elastic demand: the market will take all the units we can product at the same price.

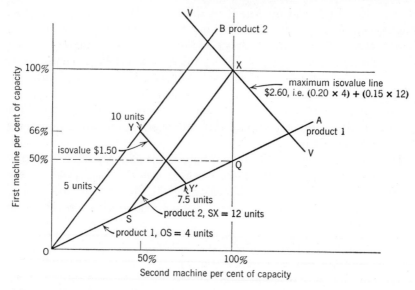

Figure III-12. Optimal process plan for A and B in producing products 1 and 2.

would use whatever two factors were limiting. In any event, we may reproduce Figure III-7 to include other factors as we have done in Figure III-11. There the lines AA and BB indicate fixed factors such as existing power capacity for machinery of the type used by one machine and BB the capacity for the type of power used by the other machine, while CC might indicate plant space capacity. Then factors AA, BB and CC are not limiting. They will not enter into our decision as to selection of processes.

Using the two limiting factors, namely the two machines, we can establish a diagram such as Figure III-12 in which the axes are the percentages of use of the two machines. Then, process rays OA and OB might indicate two different methods of employing the two machines to produce respectively product 1 and product 2. The coordinates for the OA production ray can be taken from the information underlying Figure III-7. Thus at point Q on the OA ray the first machine is at 10 units of product 1 or 50 per cent of its capacity of product 1, and is using 100 per cent of the capacity of machine 2. Other points are similarly established for ray OB, thus for point Y when machine 2 is at 50 per cent of its capacity for product 2, namely 10 units, the capacity of the first machine is 66 per cent used.

As we have already established, these two processes can be worked in combination so long as the capacity of machines 1 and 2 is not exceeded. Thus the line YY' indicates equal profit of various outputs of combinations of products 1 and 2, since the points Y and Y' are equal profit points for combinations of products 1 and 2. Line YY' is an isovalue line for $1.50 since point Y is worth 10 units of product 2 at 15 cents each, and point Y' is 7.5 units of product 1 at 20 cents each. The line VV, parallel to YY', represents the same value relationship of products 1 and 2 as YY' and passes through point X where the two capacity limits intersect. Thus VV gives the highest isovalue line touching the feasible region. A line, XS from X and parallel to OB establishes the point S which splits the optimal program between products 1 and 2.[26]

By principles already indicated in connection with Figure III-10, the length XS represents the gross margin from product 2 in the optimal program (namely $1.80 from 12 units at 15 cents each) and the length SO represents the gross margin from product 1, $0.80 from 4 units at 20 cents each). This establishes the value of VV as $2.60. These two segments show the same relation to each other as the combination of products 1 and 2 indicated by point X in Figure III-7. However the method of Figue III-3 as a method of proceeding is limited to the case of two processes while he method of Figures III-10 and III-12 can handle any number of processes.

Imputing Values to Factors

In traditional marginal analysis, the determinations of prices and outputs are two facets of the same problem of allocating scarce resources. The same duality occurs in linear programming. Hence having already dealt with output determination we now turn to imputing values to the limited resources, in the present case, the two machines. Any nonlimiting facilities, such as plant space, and power facilities such as we have previously indicated in Figure III-11, are, in reality, free goods. This does not mean they are worth nothing, but that it is not worthwhile in the circumstances to increase them nor will any value or cost be imputed to them.

The problem of imputation is: how much is a unit, say 1 hour of the capacity of machine 1, worth to the firm? And how much is such a unit of machine 2 worth?

One item of product 1 uses 5 per cent of the capacity of machine number 1 (see Figure III-5) and 10 per cent of the capacity of machine 2 (see Figure III-7). One item of product 2 uses 6⅔ per cent of the capacity of machine 1 (see Figure III-5) and 5 per cent of the capacity of machine 2 (see Figure III-7).

---

[26] It is clear that a line parallel to OA will establish a converse combination of processes OA and OB.

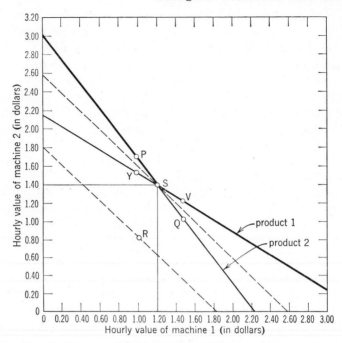

Figure III-13. Implicit value of machines 1 and 2.

If in Figure III-13, we take a possible pair of hourly values for the two machines, such as point R, we would have machine 1 worth \$1.00 and machine 2 worth 80 cents or combined this is \$1.80. Applying the data of the preceding paragraph, the value of 1 unit of product 1 would then be $(0.05 \times \$1.00) + (0.10 \times \$0.80) = \$0.13$. This would be a marginal value since the average is constant. But one item of product 1 is worth 20 cents in the market place as we indicated in the text in discussing Figure III-6. The line that indicates the *total* value of resources used to make product 1 is found by substituting unknowns X and Y for \$1.00 and \$0.80 in the preceding equation:

$$(0.05 \cdot X) + (0.10 \cdot Y) = 0.20$$

Substituting in this equation, if $X = \$1.00$, then $Y = \$1.50$, (point Y) in Figure III-13. If $X = \$1.50$, then $Y = \$1.25$ (point V in Figure III-13). This determines the line marked Product 1, all of whose points are combinations of imputed values which exhaust \$0.20 a unit.

In parallel manner we get the line for Product 2 which is worth \$0.15 an item.

$$(0.066 \cdot X) + (0.05 \cdot Y) = 0.15$$

If $X = \$1.00$, then $Y = \$1.68$ (point P). If $X = \$1.50$, then $Y = \$1.02$ (point Q in Figure III-13). This determines the line marked product 2 all of whose points are combinations of imputed values which exhaust 15 cents a unit.

The intersection of the lines for product 1 and product 2 in Figure III-13 is clearly the only pair of resource values where the marginal resource cost of an added unit of product 1 is equal to the net value of product 1 and similarly for product 2. The heavy line made up of parts of the product 1 line and of the product 2 line is the boundary of a region such that all points on the heavy line or above it give rise to no unimputed surplus. Conversely, each point below the line leaves some unimputed surplus as to at least one product.

Any pair of resource values along the dotted line through R exhausts the same aggregate value of machine 1 and machine 2. Thus the point R determines a combined value of $\$1.00 + 0.80 = \$1.80$ and the dotted line through R is the only line which gives all the combinations of values exhausting a total value of $1.80.

Similarly, the line through S is $2.60. At S in Figure III-13, the total of $2.60 involves an imputed value of machine 1 of $1.20 per hour plus an imputed value of machine 2 of $1.40 per hour. These likewise are the marginal costs of the two machines. This figure of $2.60, the combined value of machines 1 and 2 per hour checks with the amount of $2.60 established in our discussion of Figure III-12.[27]

The Duality Theorem in Linear Programming

In Figure III-7 and again in Figure III-12, we determined the net revenue or value as the highest net value line touched by the possibility boundary, while in Figure III-13, we sought the lowest net value line which touched the boundary. Both answers are the same. This is the duality theorem. We can solve either of the problems, the optimal production program or the valuation of the limiting factors of production, and we have solved the other, which is the dual. Thus one can proceed to solution by working with whichever problem is more convenient.

---

[27] In the present case, the number of limited resources (machines 1 and 2) equals the number of processes (processes A and B). In this case, all resources will have positive imputed values. If the number of limited resources exceeds the number of processes, it is usually true that some of the sources will have imputed values of zero and the number of resources with positive imputed values will equal the number of processes but in special cases the number of resources with positive imputed values may exceed the number of processes. If the number of processes exceeds the number of limited resources, some of the processes will not be used in the optimum program.

It is clear that instead of working graphically as has been done, the same results could have been achieved by the use of equations, with each line represented by an equation and the solution of the system of equations yielding the optimum point (or series of points as in the case of a range where lines coincide).

While this note appears with production illustrations, it is obvious that the logic can be applied to many other types of economic problem.

COST ANALYSIS

Production analysis is narrower in scope than cost analysis. Production analysis frequently is concerned only with direct costs, namely, those that can be easily identified with a particular product. But cost analysis introduces the larger area of overhead costs. Production analysis frequently proceeds in physical terms while cost analysis proceeds in monetary terms. Production analysis typically deals with absolute costs, whereas cost analysis introduces opportunity costs, namely, the opportunity that is foregone when a resource is applied to one use rather than another.

One of the standard approaches to costs in economics is to classify costs into categories since particular problems employ different classifications.

Fixed and Variable Costs

Perhaps the most frequently used classification of costs is fixed and variable. In economic theory, a fixed cost is one that does not vary with output (in the short run), while a variable cost is one that does. In turn, the short run is defined as the period in which some costs are fixed (do not change) and the long run as the period in which all costs can be varied.

The distinction had particular meaning in the nineteenth century and early twentieth century when many factors of production were highly specialized and could not (except at great sacrifice) be changed in their use. Thus buildings were specifically designed for use in a particular industry. If for any reason that industry in that location declined, the building frequently went idle. Today the general purpose building[28] has replaced the old type. If only part of a building needs

---

[28] A general purpose building can be defined as one with a minimum of pillars and inside walls (other than temporary), with general purpose availability of electric outlets, piping, etc., with standard dimensions, lighting, clearances, etc. In short so constructed that a large variety of different businesses can use it with a minimum of alteration between uses by succeeding tenants. Specialized equipment will be cheaper to use if the output variations are smaller and if the risk of premature liquidation is small.

to be specialized, then this part is so located as to give minimum interference with general use of the remainder. The use of standard parts and design for machinery is another illustration. At worst, a machine no longer needed can be "cannibalized," not only for spare parts for its twins, but for parts (such as motors, switches, gears, etc.) for entirely different machines.

It is true that in some industries, such as oil refining, steel production, electric power generation, etc., the significance of fixed costs has not decreased in recent years.

We suggest that the fixed-cost concept has lost much of its significance because fixed costs have become smaller. If this is so, then the classical concept of the long run is gone. Long run may now be better defined as the period required for secondary reactions to occur. Thus if price is cut, the firm may increase output. This is a primary reaction. Additional construction or the entrance of new firms into the industry would be a secondary reaction. For the manager, this raises the question of what changes follow from the decreased importance of fixed costs.

What are the primary uses to which the fixed cost-variable cost concept has been put? The standard graphical presentation is shown in Figure III-14.

The average fixed cost per unit curve (since total fixed cost is constant) is so drawn that the area under it at any point on the curve (volume times fixed cost per unit) is constant. Therefore, it can have no effect on the marginal cost curve which traces the addition to total costs of each additional unit. The vertical distance between the average variable cost per unit curve at any point and the point above it on the average total unit cost curve is exactly the same as the vertical

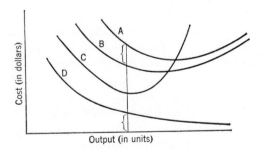

Figure III-14. Average total unit cost (curve A), average unit variable cost (curve B), marginal unit cost (curve C), and average fixed unit cost (curve D), plotted against output per unit of time.

distance between the X axis and a point on the average fixed cost curve directly under our first point. Also, the marginal cost curve must pass through both the ATUC and AVC at the minimum of each.

This is so because at the minimum point of the ATUC and AVC curves, one additional unit will not change the average. The only way this can occur is for the additional unit to have an average value. Since the marginal cost curve traces the cost of the additional units, it must equal the average at this point.

Also, the minimum point of the AVC curve must lie to the left (i.e., at a lower volume of output) of the minimum point of the ATUC curve, and, in turn, the minimum point of the MC curve must lie to the left (i.e., at a lower volume of output) of the minimum point of the AVC curve. The reason why the minimum of the AVC curve lies to the left of the ATUC curve minimum is that the AVC curve reflects variable costs only. Once average variable unit costs are at a minimum, the average total unit cost curve will still decline for a range of output since the decline in average fixed costs per unit will be greater for a short range of output than the increase in average variable costs per unit. When the decline in fixed costs per unit just offsets the increase in variable costs per unit, the average total costs per unit will be at a minimum.

The reason why the MC curve minimum lies to the left of the AVC curve minimum is that, as the AVC curve approaches its minimum, the *rate* of decline decreases and the AVC curve "flattens." The only way for the *rate* of decline of the AVC curve to decrease is for the unit cost of the marginal units to increase. Hence, where the *rate* of change of the AVC curve is at a minimum, the MC curve will be at its minimum, and this is to the left (i.e., at a lower volume of output) of the AVC curve minimum.

The prime reasons for the U shape of short-run[29] average total unit cost curve are the existence of fixed costs and economies of scale. The prime reason for the U shape of the long-run average total unit cost curve is the economies of scale and this in turn rests on the lumpiness of the factors of production and the unique situation of management as a factor of production. Because of the absence of fixed costs in the long-run situation, the long-run cost curves (both average and marginal) are "flatter" than the associated short-run cost curves. (See Figure III-17, further on.)

If fixed costs are no longer as significant in the modern world as they were, then the average (total) unit cost curve loses its curvature

[29] The short run is defined as the period in which some costs are fixed, the long run as the period in which all costs are variable.

and with the loss of curvature there is a vanishing of the ability to distinguish the characteristics of costs of one volume of output compared with other volumes of output. This likewise means that marginal costs are a matter of increased importance since marginal costs are not affected by fixed costs.

Standby, Programmed, and Variable Costs

In place of the classical fixed and variable costs, another set of classifications is proving of increasing usefulness today: standby, programmed, and variable costs.

A standby cost is defined as a cost that would continue or be continued if a plant were temporarily shut down. Thus, standby cost includes only the fixed part of the usual concept of overhead cost.

A programmed cost is one that is postponable and/or so difficult of measurement in its effect (what is received for it) as to be largely discretionary. Examples are research and development, some forms of advertising and employee benefit programs. Thus to say that a programmed cost is discretionary means that the major part of the benefit from the cost is spread over future time periods in a manner that cannot be estimated other than subjectively.

Variable costs are those that vary with output.

In practice, standby costs and variable costs are frequently separated by graphing the totals of the particular cost at different outputs (as in Figure III-15) and after fitting a function (usually a straight line) taking the Y intercept as the standby part.

Of course, if standby cost can be more directly determined (as might be the case, for example, as to personnel), then the Y intercept may be independently determined. Given such a Y intercept, we need fit a function only to the range of the observations without attempting to extrapolate the function outside the range of observations.

It is clear that what is "standby" may vary with the type (or

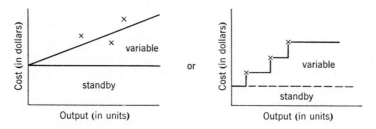

Figure III-15. Total standby and variable costs plotted against output per unit of time.

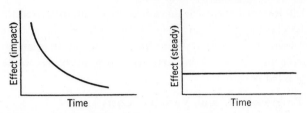

Figure III-16. Impact and steady effects with different patterns over time, but quantitatively identical when discounted over time.

temporariness) of the shutdown. This causes difficulty in precision, but it also is evidence on the question of whether the classical concept of fixed costs is any longer viable.

Because of the great flexibility in the modern economy in the choice of factors of production and in the combinations of factors which can be used to produce a good, the concept of programmed costs has considerable validity. For example, an intense and short-lived advertising campaign may produce the same results over time as a lesser but continuous campaign, as is shown in Figure III-16, which is so drawn that areas under both curves are the same if discounted over time.

Advantages of Standby, Programmed, and Variable Cost Classification Contrasted with Traditional Fixed and Variable Cost Classification

One of the prime purposes of cost analysis is to establish a yardstick so that the actual costs of producing a given volume can be evaluated as to efficiency *after* that particular volume has been produced. The yardstick is also used in planning to estimate the costs of a given volume *before* that volume of production is undertaken, and at a time when the question whether to undertake that particular volume of production is under consideration.

The classification of costs into standby, programmed, and variable[30] is more useful than the classical fixed and variable costs because the classification of accounts used by accountants lends itself more readily to the former. Thus if each account (other than programmed accounts) is broken into two segments, one standby and one variable, as was shown in Figure III-15, it is possible to determine in advance with considerable accuracy what costs will develop for a given volume. And if subsequent production of that volume results in a deviation of the actual costs from the expected costs, the particular account in

---

[30] An actual case employing the use of standby, programmed and variable cost analysis is presented in the Snoeshoes case following Part VI, Capital Budgeting.

which the deviation occurred can be quickly identified and then investigated.

On the other hand, considerable difficulty is experienced in the modern economy in separating costs into fixed and variable by using accounting records. The usual theoretical presentation has in mind that the marginal cost curve (which will be the focal point in deciding whether to undertake a particular production program) is determined solely by the variable cost curve. But if "fixed" costs are subject to alteration (as part of the investigation being carried on to explore the feasibility of a given level of production) then the marginal cost curve must reflect these alterations. The use of the fixed cost concept can thus divert our attention from the costs that are so classified. No managers can afford to let "fixed" costs lie unexamined for any length of time.

Traditional theory would answer that we have a situation in which the scale of operations is subject to rapid change and this should be handled by the same analysis as the traditional short-run and long-run cost curve diagram since all that has happened is that the time interval between the "long run" and the "short run" has been greatly shortened. The traditional presentation of long-run and short-run cost curves is shown in Figure III-17. Each short-run average cost curve is associated with a given scale of plant. The fixed costs for each scale of plant are different from those of every other scale. The long-run cost curve is the envelope of the short-run cost curves.[31]

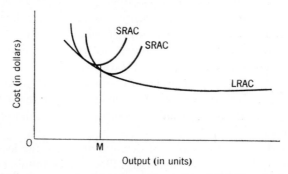

Figure III-17. Long- and short-run cost curves. (SRAC = short-run average cost; LRAC = long-run average cost.)

[31] The most efficient point (for long-run purposes) of the first scale of plant in Figure III-17 is not at the minimum point of the first SRAC curve, but to the left of this. The reason for this can be seen by examining the output OM (in Figure III-17). This output can be produced most efficiently *not* at the low point of the first SRAC curve, but by a somewhat larger scale plant where the second SRAC curve will cut under the first SRAC curve at OM output

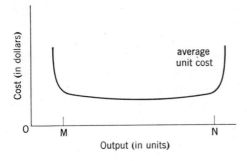

Figure III-18. Average (total) unit cost curve with extended range of constant average unit cost.

Constant Unit Cost as the Typical Situation

In essence, we are arguing that the situation of constant unit costs is the typical condition to be found in the business world. This does not conflict with the U-shaped unit cost curves of traditional theory. Rather, the constant unit cost situation reflects a condition in which the reduction in unit costs that is to be expected from the spreading of fixed costs over more units as volume is increasing appears to be compensated by an increase in variable costs per unit as volume increases. This situation can be shown graphically in Figure III-18.

The actual range of operation of a typical business lies between volume OM and volume ON. No operation for any length of time would occur in the output range from O to M or beyond N. None would because at each end the curve rises too abruptly. At the lower end, the operation would close, at the upper, new plant would be added.

It should be remembered that difficulties in making data measurements are likely to contribute to our inability to detect perceptible curvature in the average unit cost curve for the range between output OM and the output ON in Figure III-18.

It is conceded that in a numerically small number of special cases the traditional, sharply moving U-shaped cost curve is applicable. One category where fixed costs still play such a dominant role is in public utilities.

By comparison with the area of demand analysis, far less empirical work has been done in cost analysis.[32] There are a number of reasons

[32] Among the few studies in cost analysis are Joel Dean, "Statistical Cost Functions of a Hosiery Mill," *Journal of Business,* vol. 14 (1941); Dean, *The Relation of Cost to Output for a Leather Belt Shop* (NBER. Tech. Paper No. 2, 1941); Dean, "Department Store Cost Functions," in Oscar Lange (Ed.), *Studies in Mathematical Economics and Econometries in Memory of Henry Schultz* (University of Chicago Press, 1942); William H. Nicholls, *Labor Productivity Functions in Meat Packing* (University of Chicago Press, 1948); T. D. Yntema Study, TNEC Part 26, Iron and Steel Industry; K. H. Wylie and Mordecai Ezekiel, "The

for this paucity in cost analysis studies. Chief among these reasons has been the data problem. Not only are producers reticent about releasing cost data but the economist cannot use historical data without adjustment when he seeks to establish a long-run cost curve because the long-run curve seeks the alternative possibilities at various levels of output when the producer is free to make all the adjustments necessary to achieve the most favorable combination of the factors of production for a particular scale of output. Actual historical data seldom meet this requirement because production continues while fixed costs are being changed.

Analysis of Costs in the Rayon Industry

One study of considerable interest on the question whether constant costs are typical is found in Markham's *Competition in the Rayon*

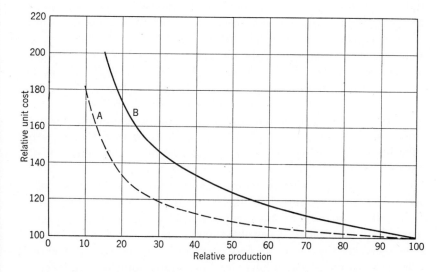

Figure III-19. Variation in unit cost (curve A) with size of plant and (curve B) with per cent of installed capacity operated for optimum plant for output 100. From Jesse W. Markham, *Competition in the Rayon Industry* (Cambridge, Mass.: Harvard University Press, 1952), p. 150.

Cost Curve for Steel Production," *Journal of Political Economy,* vol. 48, 777–821 (1940) and "Cost Functions for the Steel Industry," *Journal of the American Statistical Assn.,* vol. 36, pp. 91–99 (1941); S. H. Walker, H. J. Preston and G. T. Nelson, *An Economic Analysis of Butter—Nonfat Dry Milk Plants,* U. Idaho Agr. Exp. Sta. Res. Bul. No. 20 (June, 1953). Cf. John Johnston, *Statistical Cost Analysis* (New York: McGraw-Hill, 1960).

Industry.[33] For purposes of analyzing cost-price and cost-output questions, he found four areas of cost study are significant: (1) the shape of the short-run cost curve of the firm; (2) the price behavior of the factors of production; (3) the relationship of plant size and technological change to unit costs; and (4) the secular trend in factor prices. The first two relate to the short-run problem and the last two to the long-run problem.

Markham summarizes the results of his cost curve study of the rayon industry in a graph (Figure III-19) showing curve A which traces the relationship of unit costs of plants of a size to minimize cost for successive outputs (the classical long-run cost curve) and curve B which traces the relationship of relative unit cost (Y axis) to the per cent of installed capacity operated (X axis) in the case of a maximum size plant. Both curves were developed on the assumption of constant factor prices for the variable factors (labor and material) and overhead units. The curves were developed by members of the industrial engineering and cost accounting staffs of a large rayon producer operating a number of different size plants.[34] The data are prepared on the basis of 1948 technology and price levels. Because of the very sharp increase in scrap beyond "capacity" output, the rising part of the cost curve has no practical meaning. This scrap shows itself in the form of lower quality yarn as production exceeds capacity. While rayon production has seen no radical change in techniques in the process of production in more than two decades, there have been severe changes in plant construction to accommodate the process.

Curve B is expressed in index form for the maximum size plant operated by this producer and the index of unit cost at each per cent of installed capacity assumes constant factor prices but allows for economical adjustment of variable factors. Hence this curve is directed at establishing the short-run cost curve of economic theory. Curve B reflects a period of curtailment of "moderate duration"—defined as long enough to permit some release of direct labor and some adjustment of overhead. The sharp rise in unit costs as output is curtailed

[33] Jesse W. Markham, *Competition in the Rayon Industry* (Cambridge: Harvard University Press, 1952).

[34] The producer involved declined to permit disclosure of its name. The exact point of view from which the curves were developed is stated as follows: "The relationship which we are submitting to you assumes that periods of curtailment will be sufficiently long to justify a practical contraction of overhead organization. Similarly, in the case of variation due to plant size, we have assumed an overhead organization which would be in agreement with the company's policies and practices."

reflects the high proportion of fixed costs and the relative inflexibility of operations since rayon production is a continuous, 24-hour-a-day operation. At capacity output, fixed costs exclusive of management and supervising salaries amount to 22 per cent of the cost of goods sold and come to 33 per cent including management, supervision and a portion of maintenance. The relative inflexibility of the operation is illustrated by the fact that the spindles and machinery are designed to run at constant speeds (though since this study was made some new developments allow speed variations).

Curve A connects the minimum cost points of a number of short-run plant cost curves for various size plants.[35]

The Markham study offers some evidence for our generalization that constant unit costs represent the typical business condition. It is important that Figure III-19 was developed on the assumption of constant prices for the factors of production. Relatively small variations in the prices of the variable factors (which are $\frac{2}{3}$ of the total unit cost in this case) can offset the economies of scale shown by curve A and the spreading of fixed costs shown by curve B. The relevant (defined as the conditions which have a very high probability of being the actual conditions) ranges of outputs are shown by the far right-hand side of Figure III-19. A 10 per cent decline in the rate of operation is associated with a less than 4 per cent increase in unit costs. A 20 per cent decline in the rate of operation is associated with a less than 8 per cent increase in unit costs. It should be remembered that in testing our hypothesis about constant unit costs we have deliberately chosen a situation extremely unfavorable to our hypothesis, namely, where the minimum feasible scale of operations is large, where flexibility is low, where the ratio of fixed to variable costs is unusually high and where technological change is fast. Despite all these, as soon as we relax the assumption of constant prices for the variable factors of production, constant unit costs can develop.

It should be pointed out that our position with respect to the widespread applicability of constant unit costs abstracts from a major depression such as occurred in the 1930's.

The Use of Production and Cost Analysis

The preceding summary of cost analysis in Markham shows how analysis can be applied in a broader way to get at basic relationships

[35] This is not to be construed as falling victim to the famous Vinerian error of forming the envelope of the long-run cost curve by connecting the minimum points of short-run cost curves as was pointed out earlier, in connection with Figure III-17. Rather, we are connecting the true minimum cost points.

in an industry. There are obvious uses of production and cost analysis in achieving production efficiency in a narrow sense, namely in reducing the unit "cost" of output. The word "cost" has been placed in quotation marks to indicate that the term is being used in the narrow, accounting sense of the costs incurred to bring the unit of output to the end of the production line. In addition, there are allied uses of production and cost analysis to evaluate the performance of the management of the production department. Thus study of the change in the shape of the production function over time may reveal improvement or deterioration in the efficiency of production management. For this purpose, the production function may be studied either in physical terms or in dollar terms or both as has already been indicated.

There are further uses of production and cost analysis which are not so obvious. To illustrate this statement, we again turn to the Markham study of the rayon industry.

Markham found that total unit costs at capacity in the rayon industry roughly break down into one-third labor, one-third material and one-third depreciation, research and other overhead costs.[36] Additional pheonomena observed about the industry are that: (1) product price and output are extremely stable in the short run, but that inventories fluctuate widely; (2) product price changes usually lag about 2 months behind changes in production schedules; and (3) when production cuts bring industry output to about 75 per cent of industry installed capacity, there usually is a price reduction in the industry.

Production and cost analysis aids considerably in understanding these phenomena of the industry and hence in making economic adjustments. The carrying of large inventories is clearly a cost. The problem then is to balance the costs involved in carrying inventories against the savings in unit costs gained by maintaining capacity production. In Figure III-19, it is clear that unit costs begin to rise more sharply in relative amounts as production drops below 75 per cent of installed capacity. Thus as production is curtailed 25 per cent, total unit costs rise 10 per cent, and at 35 per cent reduction in production, total unit costs rise 15 per cent. These are the conditions when the prices of the variable factors (labor and materials) remain constant. Stating the matter another way, curve B indicates that the prices of wages and materials would have to fall 22.5 per cent (remember that wages and materials are two-thirds of total costs) to offset

[36] Confirmed in E. W. K. Schwarz and H. R. Mauersberger, *Rayon and Synthetic Yarn Handbook,* 2nd ed. (New York: Rayon Handbook Co., 1956), p. 29.

the rise in total unit costs that would otherwise occur when production drops from capacity to 65 per cent of capacity. In the very short run (with no time to adjust overhead to the reduction in production to 65 per cent of capacity), the prices of wages and materials would have to drop 33 per cent to maintain total unit costs at their full capacity point.

The demand curve facing individual smaller producers of rayon is highly elastic. Hence, as output is curtailed to the range of 75 per cent of installed capacity, there is great pressure on producers either (a) to cut price or (b) to shut down operations in order to avoid higher total unit cost production. This will be so even when the prices of the variable factors (labor and materials) move downward but do not move downward proportionately more than any decline in the price of rayon. Although Markham was not able to obtain the release of the entire family of short-run cost curves from which curve A was developed, he did gain the information that, for a plant one-half the size of the plant represented by curve B and with its data plotted at 100 for installed capacity, the short-run curve would rise more rapidly (than curve B) as output is contracted.

We can state this another way by saying that the percentage of rise in total unit costs for smaller plants is more than that of larger plants when the same percentage curtailment of installed capacity is put into effect. This difference is a measurement not of the economy of scale in the usual meaning of that term (since both curves were set at a relative cost of 100 for installed capacity) but a measure of the "economy of flexibility." The economy of scale (in its narrower sense) would be measured by the difference (between the two sizes of plants) in total unit costs at installed capacity. This is traced by curve A. What we have described as the "economy of flexibility" is a peculiar advantage of a multiplant producer possessed of different sized plants which enables this producer to allocate the total curtailment of production he faces in an economic way among his several plants.

The analysis just presented aids in understanding an apparently contradictory phenomenon of the rayon industry when inventories are piling up. In this situation, small producers with small plants frequently shade prices but continue at capacity operation to avoid rising total unit costs (which rise more quickly for them than for large plant producers as plant output is curtailed) but large producers with large plants follow the policy (except in severe depression) of curtailment rather than of price cutting.

Thus, cost analysis can lead to an understanding of different pricing, inventory and other practices by different producers in the same industry. Such an understanding may not be achievable in any other way. Clearly such an understanding is vital to the managers of a business.

CASE III-1. WATSON COMPANY
Linear Programming—Graphic Solution—Equations

The Watson Co. is engaged in manufacturing small cranes and mechanical shovels. The manufacturing processes are substantially the same, that is, the company is organized into five departments, each of which is used in the manufacture of cranes and shovels except that separate final assembly lines are used for each of the two products. These departments are: (1) Sheet Metal Stamping, (2) Engine Assembly, (3) Forgings, (4) Foundry, (5) Machining, (6) Final Crane Assembly, and (7) Final Shovel Assembly. Raw materials, labor, and other components are available in virtually unlimited amounts at constant prices in the open market as are purchased parts.

The capacity of each of these departments as presently constituted is, of course, limited. It cannot be changed except by additional investment, and this would require considerable time to implement. The Sheet Metal Stamping Department can turn out sufficient stampings for 40,000 cranes per month or 50,000 shovels per month. Thus stampings for each crane require 0.0025 per cent of monthly capacity and for each shovel, 0.002 per cent of monthly capacity. The variation of combinations possible, for all practical purposes, is such that stampings for another crane can be made by the elimination of stampings for 1.25 shovels. Thus stampings for 30,000 cranes per month and 12,500 shovels or for 20,000 cranes and 25,000 shovels per month can be produced.

The data for the other departments are as follows. Engine Assembly can turn out 45,000 crane engines or 40,000 shovel engines. The Forging Department can turn out forgings for 30,000 cranes or 40,000 shovels. The Foundry Department can turn out castings for 35,000 cranes or 35,000 shovels. The Machining Department can machine parts for 40,000 cranes or 45,000 shovels. The Final Crane Assembly Line can handle 32,000 cranes but only cranes, and the Final Shovel Assembly Line 40,000 shovels but only shovels. All of the foregoing data are monthly figures.

Assume that the sales value of a shovel is $350 greater than the total of all direct costs attributable to its production and that the similar sales value of a crane is $400 over such costs. Further assume that the sales prices for cranes and shovels will not be affected by the number offered by Watson Company to the market and that the company can sell what it can produce.

1. What output yields optimum profit?

2. What output should be undertaken during the period that 50 per cent final crane assembly capacity destroyed by fire is out of production?

3. What output should be undertaken during the period that 75 per cent of final crane assembly capacity destroyed by fire is out of production?

4. What output should be undertaken if the sales values of cranes and shovels are reversed?

5. What would be the answers to questions 1 through 4 if the Watson Co. could find outside suppliers of forgings and foundry parts able to furnish these parts at the same unit price as Watson's cost and without quantity limit?

6. What facility has the most excess capacity if forgings and foundry parts are purchasable outside as indicated in 5? What assumptions are you making in answering this question?

7. How would your evaluation of this situation be affected by the fact that the data may be subject to a margin of error of 5 per cent or more?

8. How would you deal with the situation in which the prices of shovels and cranes would be affected by the number offered for sale?

9. How would you deal with the situation where the number of shovels and cranes that can be sold is limited?

CASE III-2. WISCONSIN CHEESE COMPANY
Linear Programming—Graphic Solution—Inequations*

The Wisconsin Cheese Company was engaged in the marketing of speciality gift boxes of cheese. One of the items to be offered by Wisconsin was a box containing individually wrapped small pieces of Swiss cheese and Cheddar cheese.

The manager of Wisconsin, Mr. Arnold, decided after surveys and other advice that he wanted a 2-pound box with 30 pieces of cheese packed in 35 square inches, with a cheese cost of 72 cents. Swiss cheese cost 48 cents a pound and Cheddar, 24 cents a pound. The marketing experts decided Swiss must be cut into 2-ounce pieces of 1 square inch and Cheddar cheese in 0.8-ounce pieces of 0.7 square inch to attract the feminine eye most successfully. There must be at least five pieces of each type of cheese to get the desired effect.

When Mr. Arnold presented the idea to his production department, he was told it couldn't be done.†

Thereupon Mr. Arnold said maybe what he really meant to say was the box should weigh no less than 2 pounds, cost no more than 72 cents, take no more space than 35 square inches, have at least 30 pieces and any space unused by the cheese could be filled by a very cheap decoration. Other facts the same as before.

Mr. Arnold then challenged them to tell him which combination meeting his specification had the lowest cheese cost, which the lowest shipping weight, and which the fewest pieces and which the most. You are asked to furnish these answers.‡

* An equation is defined as equality on both sides, thus $x + y = 2$, an inequation has either a greater than $>$ sign or a less than $<$ sign and *may* also have an equal sign. Thus there are four types of inequations: $x + y > 2$, $x + y < 2$, $x + \geq 2$, and $x + y \leq 2$.

† The advice to Mr. Arnold was correct. Can you prove it correct?

‡ *Hint:* The solution to equations must be on the lines. The solution to inequations must lie within the area bounded by lines.

CASE III-3. SUNBURST CORPORATION (A)

Cost Analysis—Short-Run Cost Curves

Sunburst corporation was engaged in the manufacture of oil-filled, pole-mounted distribution transformers. These are the familiar "cans" seen on power poles. Sunburst had established a new plant and one of the questions was what the most economical volume might be for this new plant cost-wise. Another question was what extent of variation in monthly unit production costs would be tolerable before questions of inefficiency would arise.

A distribution transformer takes electric power from a high voltage line and steps the voltage down to that desired by the customer. Transmission transformers at points called sub-stations take voltage down from, for example, 132,000 volts to 7,600 volts which is a typical distribution voltage. At this voltage, the electricity goes over wires to a pole near the customer where the electricity enters a distribution transformer. The distribution transformer then steps this voltage down from 7,600 volts to 220 or 110 volts. Distribution transformers come in standard capacity sizes of 1.5KVA, 3KVA, 5KVA, 10KVA, 15KVA, 25KVA, 37.5KVA, 100KVA, 167KVA, 250KVA, 333KVA, and 500-KVA. There are a number of different variations available in each KVA size depending on the voltage on the "high" side (from 7,600 to 220 or from 2,400 to 110), on the protective equipment (against lightning, etc.), the "taps" (variations in "low side" voltage take-offs available), etc.

In a general way the size situation bears some resemblance to milk which can be brought in half-pint, pint, quart, half-gallon, and gallon containers. There is, however, a greater variation in cost per KVA between the KVA in a 3KVA size compared with the cost per KVA in a 50KVA size than there is between the cost per pint of milk in a half-pint container and the cost of milk per pint in a gallon container.

Sunburst did not have separate data available showing "cost of goods manufactured" namely, the cost of labor, materials and factory overhead for the monthly production of units. What Sunburst did have was data showing "cost of goods sold": beginning inventory at cost, plus the cost of units produced in the month, minus the ending inventory at cost. FIFO was the method of inventory valuation used. However more than half and as high as 80 per cent of the units sold each month were actually made in that month. Likewise, the inventory level did not move much from month to month. As appears in Table I,

Sunburst did have data as to the materials content of the cost of goods sold.

There was some variation in the "product mix" from month to month. Thus the percentage of transformers sold in the 5KVA size as a per cent of total sold varied. Likewise, there was a variation in the number sold with protective equipment from month to month. Similarly with other "model" variations offered.

In the manufacture of distribution transformers, largely the same machinery is used to produce the different sizes of units referred to above. A brief description of the process will help explain this. The core of a transformer is electric grade, grain-oriented steel which is wound around a shape which when removed leaves a hole in the center. The number of "winds" and the size of the hole vary with the size of the transformer. This core is then heat-treated to relieve stresses. A copper coil is wound around a similar shape which when removed leaves a hole in the center of the coil. The size of the wire, size of the center shape, number of winds, insulation between layers of winding, etc., vary with the size of the transformer. The core is then slit so that the core and coil can be put together much like two doughnuts can be interlocked if one doughnut is slit to admit the other doughnut so that each doughnut runs through the center hole of the other doughnut. This is a core and coil assembly which is then dipped in varnish and baked dry in ovens. Even the slightest moisture is a great foe of transformer functioning.

The core and coil assembly has terminals to bring the high voltage in and another set to take the low voltage off. The number of turns in the coil and core govern the ratio of the reduction of high to low voltage.

This varnished core and coil are then mounted in a tank or "can" such as one sees on any power pole. The size of this can varies with the size of the core and coil it houses. There are additional mechanisms that are installed for different models, such as a circuit-breaker mechanism or an arrester mechanism. The tank or "can" is then filled with a special transformer oil under vacuum conditions. The oil will dissipate heat to the atmosphere through the walls of the "can" when the transformer is in operation. The transformer cover and porcelain insulators (for the wires in and out) are then secured to the tank.

In a typical transformer plant as many as 3,000 models of different sizes may be built. Sometimes the "run" may be only a few units of the same model and sometimes hundreds of units of the same model.

Tanks are made from hot-rolled sheets using cutters, brake presses, bead rollers (for tank edges), etc. Different size dies are used for the different size tanks.

Elaborate testing of the different sizes and models of the finished product is done but with the same equipment using different instrument settings for different size transformers.

The 10-month period after the plant had passed through its "shakedown" runs yielded the data in Table I.

Case III-3. TABLE I

Output and Cost Record of Sunburst Corporation for 10 Consecutive Months

Month	Number of Units Sold	Average KVA of Each Unit Sold	Cost of Units Sold in Thousands	Material Content in Thousands	Material as Per Cent of Cost of Goods
April	382	16.787	$63.2	$44.7	70.7%
May	311	24.170	61.0	42.4	69.5
June	446	17.148	73.0	52.9	72.5
July	315	15.486	54.9	38.1	69.4
August	268	13.985	41.3	29.3	70.9
September	413	15.588	62.4	44.9	72.0
October	473	18.002	82.6	61.9	74.9
November	434	15.062	66.9	50.8	75.9
December	470	17.702	76.1	54.0	71.0
January	428	14.101	73.5	54.0	73.5

Table I reveals that there is considerable fluctuation in average size among transformers processed during a single month. This is shown by the May production of 311 units with an average size KVA of 24.170, whereas, the following January, 428 units were made with an average size of 14.101 KVA. Another illustration from Table I shows that in August, 268 units were made with an average size of 13.985 KVA, whereas, in January, there were 428 units made with an average size of 14.101 KVA. However, as the last column of Table I shows, the variation in the percentage of material cost of a transformer with the size of transformers is not nearly so great.

Sunburst followed an accounting system which distributed factory overhead according to direct labor costs at a figure approximating 150 per cent of direct labor. Thus the difference between total factory costs and material costs represents a combination of direct labor and overhead in a fixed ratio to each other.

One of the difficulties in the transformer business is that the pricing of the different KVA sizes follows a historical pattern. Thus, when prices for the sizes are once adopted in the industry, the engineering staff of the customer-utilities uses these price ratios in laying out plans for new extensions to existing electric power distribution systems. On the other hand, as technology improves, the betterments do not affect all sizes of KVA in the same proportion as the old costs had been. As a result, some sizes are known to the producer as "juicy" items, in terms of profit, whereas others are called "dogs." This situation continues until there is a realignment of prices for different sizes to reflect the new cost ratios between sizes.

1. What is the optimum volume for this plant?

2. What is a "permissible" variation in the month to month cost of goods sold before you would question the monthly efficiency?

3. What are most likely the principal origins of the variations in the cost of goods sold when volume is constant?

4. If you were asked to increase the accuracy of the computations, what directions would you prepare for the cost accountant?

CASE III-4. SUNBURST CORPORATION (B)*

Cost Analysis—Long-Run Cost Curve

As the business economist for Sunburst Corporation you are pondering how to establish a long-run cost curve for Sunburst.

The record of cost of good sold by Sunburst is set forth in Table I for selected years.

Between 1952–53 and 1953–54, the entire operation was moved from one location to another with radical changes in production methods such as a one floor operation instead of two and the "bringing in" of some parts manufacturing in lieu of the purchase of these parts.

The new facilities were not well adapted, however, and correction of this situation was undertaken in 1954–55.

Sunburst grew rapidly and in 1955–56 additional facilities were constructed and the basic design of the core was changed introducing significant materials savings.

Growth continued rapidly and in 1957–58 additional expansion of facilities was undertaken. This time, however, changes in production methods and product design were not as drastic.

Attention is called to the following statement of Professor John Due:†

It is important to recognize that the long-run average cost schedule does not consist of historical data showing what cost has been in the past with various-sized plants; it shows alternative possibilities at the present time—what cost would be for various levels of output if various-sized plants were built.

Until you read Professor Due's remarks, you had been under the impression that you could take the historical data for Sunburst shown in Table I treating each 11 month period there shown as establishing a short-run cost curve whose envelope would be the long-run cost curve.

Various thoughts pass through your mind as to what the proper course of proceeding may be.

First, it may be that such a thing as a long-run cost curve is an ideological conception of the theoretical economist, one of those empty boxes so often talked about—in short, one of those things that make for good dreaming on a quiet afternoon on the campus after classes are over.

---

* Read the materials in "Sunburst (A)" and then continue.

† John Due, *Intermediate Economic Analysis*, 3rd Edition (Homewood, Ill.: Irwin, 1956), p. 172.

Case III-4. TABLE I

Data on Monthly Cost of Goods Sold, Sunburst Corporation

Month	1952-53			1953-54			1954-55			1956-57			1958-59		
	Units	Average KVA	Costs in Thousands	Units	Average KVA	Costs in Thousands	Units	Average KVA	Costs in Thousands	Units	Average KVA	Costs in Thousands	Units	Average KVA	Costs in Thousands
April	888	6.099	$82.9	796	8.124	$102.3	649	7.300	$ 82.9	1321	10.603	$171.1	1753	12.4	$209.5
May	1001	6.800	92.2	612	7.261	83.0	730	8.400	92.3	1294	12.175	173.7	1572	11.2	193.7
June	774	8.607	120.3	754	8.097	95.0	844	8.599	120.3	1370	9.767	169.6	1475	13.6	205.1
July	1822	7.434	122.9	860	8.944	107.2	1011	7.900	122.9	1263	11.367	170.8	1792	11.3	224.0
August	739	7.805	124.6	757	9.059	98.4	1035	8.325	124.6	1246	9.665	168.5	1656	11.1	199.5
September	1056	6.374	114.2	921	9.360	154.1	970	7.400	114.2	1246	9.518	161.8	1463	12.3	184.8
October	1021	7.231	118.3	667	8.199	81.0	998	9.000	118.3	1447	10.969	233.9	1385	10.5	163.9
November	931	8.952	110.4	753	8.000	94.6	874	9.899	110.4	1299	10.200	169.8	1362	11.4	160.6
December	864	14.442	132.9	715	7.499	89.0	1017	8.900	132.9	970	11.800	133.7	1135	12.0	142.0
January	441	10.757	119.1	570	9.800	78.1	957	10.300	119.1	1597	11.300	220.1	1304	11.8	160.5
February	503	8.483	106.5	511	9.100	70.3	759	10.100	106.5	1838	10.900	231.6	1304	12.4	173.5

Second, it may be that the data in Table I can be dealt with as you originally intended before you came across Professor Due's contention.

Third, it may be that there are some adjustments that can be made to the data in Table I and that this adjusted data could then be dealt with as a good first approximation of what Professor Due would like to have as data if he could ever get it. It seems to you that this adjusted data would be more trustworthy as the basis for a course of action than asking the engineering department to prepare data for different assumed scales of operation at the present time. You believe that if the engineers were to receive such a request from you, they would simply turn to the historical data and start computing from that. In this connection, if you decide to adjust the historical data yourself, you are bothered about just what adjustments you should make of the data.

CASE III-5. SAUKVILLE CANNING COMPANY
Cost Analysis—Demand Shift—Speculation

The Saukville Canning Company was organized in 1920. Saukville is in Ozaukee County just north of Milwaukee County in the heart of the largest pea growing area in the United States. Besides peas, an early crop—picked in June and July, Saukville canned corn, a later crop. In 1939 and 1940, the company also canned tomatoes.

The company had 150 shares of $500 par-value stock issued. Of these 150 shares, 111 were owned in units of 1 and 2 shares each by local growers and business people. The other 39 shares were owned by Mr. Gross who acted as general manager until his death in 1941. The labor for the canning season came largely from the stockholder group.

During 1939, Saukville suffered a net loss of $10,326, and again, in 1940, a loss of $22,728. Exhibit I shows balance sheets, Exhibit II shows income statements from 1939 to 1949. The working capital of $18,000 on hand at the opening of 1940 was wiped out and current liabilities exceeded current assets by $6,000 at the end of the year but Saukville made canning profits of $37,000 in 1942 and $24,000 in 1943, both before income taxes.

In August of 1943, E. C. Roberts became interested in Saukville, mainly because he thought 170,000 cases could be processed in a year with Saukville's equipment. Saukville had been processing only 100,000 cases a year, partly because of inadequate finances. Roberts already operated canning plants at Leroy, Illinois, and Monroe, Ohio. Roberts was also attracted by the fact that pea canning had for many years enjoyed the reputation of being more profitable than the canning of other vegetables.

Climate is the important factor in pea growing. Peas thrive in a cool climate and above all cannot survive a sudden change to hot weather in the ripening season. As little as 24 hours of hot weather will ripen peas to hardness and deprive them of much commercial value. Wisconsin and the Pacific Northwest have the ideal climate.

Roberts operated the plant as lessee for an annual rental of $8,000 from April 1, 1944, making canning profits before income tax of $40,520 for the 9 months ending December 31, 1944 and $24,764 for the calendar year 1945 as shown in Exhibit II. At the same time Roberts bought the mortgage covering Saukville and the 39 shares owned by Gross at his death. This original rental was later revised by Roberts to 8 cents per case for the first 50,000 cases canned, 7 cents per case for the next 50,000 cases and 5 cents per case for cases over 100,000 and a guaranteed minimum of $4,000. The profit and pack history of facilities of the Saukville Canning Co. is shown in Table I.

CASE III-5. TABLE I

Profit and Pack History, Facilities of Saukville Canning Company Under Various Owners

Year	Cases of Pack (24 No. 2 Cans)	Canning Profit Before Income Tax	Year	Cases of Pack (24 No. 2 Cans)	Canning Profit Before Income Tax
1939	75,360	$(11,563)	1944	115,367	$ 40,520
1940	89,700	(23,080)	1945	135,009	24,763
1941	52,475	5,353	1946	87,903	5,696
1942	98,030	37,678	1947	72,345	6,355
1943	110,546	24,262	1948	30,129	(66,445)

While Saukville Canning Co. had used a fiscal year ending March 31 for the years 1941 to 1944 as is widely done in the canning industry, Roberts in contrast used the calendar year ending December 31 as the reporting period in 1944 and 1945 as Saukville had done in 1939 and 1940.

A canning operation such as that here involved would expend about $25,000 for seed and planting costs in March and April.

With the 1940 pack, Saukville had dropped tomatoes as an unprofitable line. Roberts planned to continue the line of peas and corn with a target of 110,000 cases of peas and 60,000 cases of corn. A case consists of 24 cans of the No. 2 size (the familiar store size of 20 ounces).* Peas had tradionally been the profitable crop of the two but frozen peas entered the market and had a sales record as set out in Exhibits VI and VII.

Peas are canned in two types: Alaska and sweet peas. Four grades are used: A (Fancy); B (Extra Standard); C (Standard); and D (Substandard). D grade is not quoted in market records. Peas are also sized by several sizes of sieves. A given pack by a given cannery will, of course, not fall into only one category. There are considerable price differences between the types, grades and sizes of peas as is illustrated in Table II.

Corn is canned in four types: Cream style and whole kernel and white and golden for each. Again four grades are used: A (Fancy); B (Extra Standard); C (Standard); and D (Substandard). Many sizes of can are also packed. Table III gives typical price differentials.

* This size has since been reduced to 17 ounces and is called No. 303.

Case III-5. TABLE II

Price of Canned Peas Per Dozen Cans (No. 2 Size) Central Region F.O.B. Cannery. Ceiling Price 1943

Alaska No. 1 Sieve A	$1.55	Sweet No. 1 Sieve A	$1.55
B	1.40	B	1.40
C	1.25	C	1.25
No. 2 Sieve A	1.45	No. 2 Sieve A	1.55
B	1.30	B	1.40
C	1.15	C	1.25
No. 3 Sieve A	1.35	No. 3 Sieve A	1.45
B	1.20	B	1.30
C	1.10	C	1.15
No. 4 and up A	1.25	No. 4 and up A	1.35
B	1.15	B	1.20
C	1.05	C	1.10
Alaska ungraded A	1.25	No. 5 and up A	1.25
B	1.15	B	1.15
C	1.05	C	1.05
		Sweet ungraded A	1.40
		B	1.20
		C	1.10

Source: *Canning Trade* (1944)

Case III-5. TABLE III

Price of Canned Corn Per Dozen Cans (No. 2 Size) Central Region F.O.B. Cannery, Ceiling Prices 1943

Grade	White Kernel	Cream Style (Except Evergreen and Narrow Grain)	Cream Style: Evergreen and Narrow Grain
Fancy	$1.29	$1.19	$1.09
Extra Standard	1.19	1.09	1.04
Standard	1.09	0.99	—

Source: *Canning Trade* (1944).

Warehouse receipts are used for financing especially by the smaller canneries as soon as the first canning is done in June. When the pack is sold will vary with the condition of the market and the degree of risk the cannery is willing to assume. In short, the canneries can speculate with the pack.

In the present situation, Saukville, for example, had the following inventory on hand December 31, 1940:

Product	Cases of 24 Cans	At Cost	At Market
Peas	34,667.5	$ 46,007.20	$ 57,509.00
Corn	13,111.5	18,356.10	22,945.12
Tomatoes	29,605.0	36,194.24	45,242.80
Other	635.0	508.00	635.00
	77,108.0	$101,065.54	$126,331.92

Thus each year's accounting statement of profits is peculiarly misleading until one adjusts the statement for the profit (or loss) inherent in the inventory. At least this is so if one wants to think in terms of the profits or loss on a given year's crop.

In contrast to 1940, as appears in Exhibit II, Roberts unloaded almost all the 1944 pack before December 31, 1944. In that year Roberts was only able to can 115,637 cases. Then in 1945 Roberts packed 67,639 cases of peas at an average cost of $1.513 a case. He had on hand December 31, 1945, 5,761 of these cases. Roberts packed 67,370 cases of corn at an average cost of $1.872 a case and had on hand December 31, 1945 exactly 30,814 cases.

In 1945, Roberts received ceiling OPA* prices for all sales but with graded variations, the price per case varied from $1.74 to $3.20 for peas. Thus he sold for example:

645 cases Sweets, Fancy No. 4 at $2.48 a case
1431 cases Sweets, Extra Standard No. 4 at $2.30 a case
3686 cases Sweets, Extra Standard No. 5 at $2.18 a case

In 1945, the 59,923 cases of peas sold brought $132,359 and the 33,390 cases of corn sold brought $83,475. Almost all the corn was "fancy whole kernel" and brought $2.50 a case with a few "extra standard."

Roberts violated the OPA price ceiling limits in his 1944 sales and incurred an overcharge liability of $20,129 which came to light during 1945. No income tax liability of Roberts' sole proprietorship is shown. Roberts made no drawings from the business in 1944 but in 1945 took out $19,706.

In connection with the cannery, both Saukville and Roberts operated

---

* These OPA prices refer to prices set by the Office of Price Administration, a government agency with authority to fix maximum prices during World War II. Such prices were commonly called "ceiling prices."

a farm whose net results are reflected in Exhibit II, opposite the heading: "Other Income and Expense." By way of explanation, the U.S. Subsidy appearing on the balance sheet in Exhibit I is handled as a direct offset to the cost of the crop.

The market fluctuations of canned peas and corn F.O.B. cannery over the thirteen year period, 1936 through 1948, are shown in Exhibit III. These prices cover only two specific categories of peas for the central region and one category of corn for that region.

The OPA price period requires some explanation. While the price of a pack once set in a free market tends to hold until the next year, (as shown in Exhibit III), the effect of Pearl Harbor (Dec. 7, 1941) was to start prices up immediately. The crop of peas and corn for 1941 was completely sold out by February of 1942 and no market prices are available for the balance of that year. The Office of Price Administration set the price for the 1942 pack in June of 1942 and for the 1943 pack in March of 1943. There was an area ceiling and a specific ceiling for each cannery. The specific ceiling was computed by starting from a base period allowed price and adding only certain specific increases in costs as allowed. The 1944 pack ceiling was set in September of 1944 and was continued as the ceiling for the 1945 pack.

Roberts was sued by Saukville Canning Company and his lease terminated December 31, 1945. Between October 31 and December 31 of 1945, Roberts sold 2,000 cases of peas and 3,000 cases of corn before garnishment proceedings were begun. The "other assets" includes a garnisheed bank account of $8,467.

The 1945 income statement showing a profit before income taxes of $7,495 should not mislead one. The inventory on hand carries a profit as of December 31, 1945 computed as follows (the pack having been sold but no delivery yet taken by the buyer).

Market value of inventory		$89,959.20
Deduct loading cost	350.00	
Deduct brokerage	3598.37	
Deduct bank charges	100.00	
Deduct labeling	731.50	4,779.87
		$85,179.33
Less auditor's value at cost		66,400.10
Profit on inventory		18,779.23
Profit on shipments made		7,494.91
Total 1945 profit		$26,274.14

In 1946 the Saukville Canning Co. leased its facilities to Saukville Canned Foods, Inc. for the years 1946 and 1947.

Saukville Canned Foods, Inc. was a subsidiary incorporated February 18, 1946 by the Fredonia Canning Co. of Fredonia, Wisconsin for the express purpose of leasing and operating the facilities of Saukville Canning Co. The use of a subsidiary was advisable to insulate the parent from loss operations of the facilities and from possible claims by the lessor Saukville Canning Co. Under the terms of this lease, Saukville Canned Foods, Inc. paid a rental of 10 cents per case packed with a minimum rental of $10,000 per year.

Saukville Canned Foods, Inc. operated at a profit for the years 1946 and 1947 as shown in Exhibit II. From its operations, Saukville Canned Foods, Inc. concluded that the facilities were inadequate to pack more than 100,000 cases a year profitably. During both 1946 and 1947 Saukville Canned Foods, Inc. found it necessary to take about 20 to 25 per cent of the pea crop for which it had contracted to the nearby plant of Fredonia Canning Co. for processing. This was because peak capacity at Saukville was inadequate. In doing this, Fredonia paid Saukville the price Saukville had contracted to pay the farmers and Saukville eliminated the transaction from its operating statement. While the canning machinery on hand could process more than this volume, cooking and other facilities would have to be enlarged to produce an increased volume efficiently. As lessee on a year-to-year basis, Saukville Canned Foods, Inc. was unwilling to make the investment in such enlargements.

To illustrate some of the complexities of the canning business, particularly as it applies to peas, Exhibit IV shows the summaries of costs and selling prices per unit for the years ended March 31 in 1947 and 1948. Exhibit IV also shows a breakdown of the year-end inventory for each of these dates with both market prices and costs shown.

Roberts brought foreclosure on his mortgages and in 1948 again assumed the operation of the Saukville facilities. He decided to do so by incorporating. This would insulate his personal assets from claims arising out of the operation. Thus on March 4, 1948 he incorporated Wisconsin Canned Foods, Inc. and operated the facilities for the 1948 pack. The results of this operation are shown in Exhibits I and II. Roberts had difficulty securing adequate financing to handle packs as large as those of prior years.

In addition, Wisconsin Canned Foods, Inc. on February 17, 1948 entered a lease-purchase agreement for equipment of $26,000 with United Co., and paid $8,000 on this contract in 1948. Wisconsin Canned Foods also borrowed $25,000.

On June 14, 1949, Port Washington State Bank brought foreclosure on the mortgage loan of $25,000 since the interest payment was in default. The Bank also brought foreclosure on its loan of $44,938 dated December 31, 1948 due March 11, 1949 and secured by warehouse receipts and a second mortgage.

Wisconsin Canned Foods, Inc. had decided that liquidation was in order and precipitated a "voluntary" receivership by letting the default in interest occur and failing to negotiate a loan renewal.

The Bank was appointed receiver June 21, 1949 and was authorized to operate for not more than six months. Creditors were directed to file their claims within three months.

On July 2, 1949, the receiver applied for court permission to sell canned corn as follows:

Lot 1,	225 cases at $2.20 per case	$ 990.00
Lot 2,	175 cases at $2.50 per case	875.00
Lot 3,	100 cases at $2.20 per case	1,320.00
Lot 4,	7015 cases at $2.40 per case	33,672.00
	7715	$36,875.00

It is apparent that between the close of the fiscal year, March 31, 1949, when Roberts had sales of $31,093 by disposing of so much of the year's pack as cost him $79,209 (thus having on hand that part of the pack costing $35,219) and the date (June 21, 1949) when the receiver took possession, Roberts had sold some substantial number of cases since the receiver got only 7,715 cases of the total of 30,129 in that year's pack. These receipts Roberts applied to the payment of accounts payable.

The assets of Saukville were finally sold at auction in 1950, and the buildings were bought by Northern Signal Co. On liquidation, the bank was paid in full and general creditors received 26 cents on the dollar.

Why was there trouble in the history of this operation?

(Exhibits I through X follow on pages 230 through 248.)

CASE III-5. EXHIBIT I

Balance Sheets

Saukville Canning Company

	December 31 1939	December 31 1940	March 31 1941	March 31 1942
Cash	$ 221.86	$ 2,117.34	$ 90.34	$ 9,820.34
Receivables	3,973.42	11,398.77	11,861.30	5,715.86
Subsidy U.S. Receivable				
Reserve	(200.00)	(600.00)	(600.00)	(560.65)
Inventories				
Canned Food	88,978.67	101,065.54	47,230.40	1,503.59
Seed	1,174.50	—	6,797.70	20,437.50
Cans, Boxes	3,060.03	1,551.86	3,176.91	10,798.97
Labels	3,045.42	3,462.61	3,462.61	975.34
Miscellaneous	364.28	895.49	32.00	886.15
Total Inventory	96,622.90	106,975.50	60,699.62	34,601.55
Prepaid	1,769.02	1,900.71	2,841.55	1,718.05
Total Current	102,395.22	121,818.29	74,892.81	51,295.15
Lands, Buildings, and Equipment	173,569.07	177,465.84	177,326.59	172,542.17
Reserve	(98,497.17)	(101,618.37)	(102,919.31)	(97,523.79)
Net	75,071.90	75,847.47	74,407.28	75,018.38
Other Assets	68.68	482.00	1,629.65	276.21
Total Assets	$177,535.80	$198,147.76	$150,929.74	$126,589.74
Notes Payable				
Farmers State Bank	—	$ 3,307.00	$ 2,175.00	—
Port Washington State Bank	—	485.00	2,520.00	—
Bank of Sheboygan	$ 61,551.71	26,398.95	15,268.28	—
Individuals	2,500.00	2,200.00	2,700.00	$ 10,300.95
Teutonia State Bank	—	33,812.75	21,706.25	1,669.00
Total Notes Payable	64,051.71	70,568.70	44,369.53	11,969.95
Accounts Payable				
Trade and Others	3,913.94	20,265.86	20,655.91	18,121.16
Growers	11,694.84	32,142.05	4,587.99	—
Income Tax	—	—	—	—
Accrued Liabilities	4,861.22	5,035.20	13,310.38	23,019.35
Total Current	84,521.71	128,011.81	82,924.11	53,110.46
(Deferred Income)	—	—		
Mortgage	80,385.00	80,385.00	80,385.00	80,385.00
Capital Stock Outstanding	75,000.00	75,000.00	75,000.00	75,000.00
Surplus	(62,370.91)	(85,249.05)	(87,379.37)	(81,905.72)
Total Liabilities and Ownership	$177,535.80	$198,147.76	$150,929.74	$126,589.74

EXHIBIT I (*Continued.*)

Balance Sheets

	Saukville Canning Company (*continued*)		E. C. Roberts, doing business as Wisconsin Canned Foods		
	Mar. 31 1943	Mar. 31 1944	Dec. 31 1944	Oct. 31 1945	Dec. 31 1945
Cash	$ 31,710.55	$ 8,206.30	$ 17,949.36	$ 8,414.57	$ 242.00
Receivables	1,817.55	277.64	21,806.52	15,245.24	6,002.13
Subsidy U.S. Receivable			19,344.82	37,773.76	37,772.23
Reserve	(560.65)	(32.89)	—	—	—
Inventories					
Canned Food	—	5,198.01	—	75,042.10	66,400.10
Seed	—	412.30	—		
Cans, Boxes	—	7,335.23	—	6,318.85	7,674.72
Labels	—	1,690.03	—		
Miscellaneous	—	954.40	—		
Total Inventory	17,926.98	15,589.97	14,641.87	81,360.95	74,074.82
Prepaid	—	—	30.00	477.43	760.00
Total Current	50,894.43	24,041.02	73,772.57	143,271.95	118,851.18
Lands, Buildings, and Equipment	169,004.58	165,203.57	4,999.50	8,970.95	8,970.95
Reserve	(98,870.31)	(98,881.06)	552.45	(1,246.43)	1,404.50
Net	70,134.27	66,322.51	4,447.05	7,724.52	7,566.45
Other Assets	1,109.14	1,947.63	1,602.71	4,418.22	9,467.34
Total Assets	$122,137.84	$ 92,311.16	$ 79,840.33	$155,414.69	$135,884.97
Notes Payable					
Farmers State Bank	—	—	—	—	—
Port Washington State Bank	—	—	—	$ 38,418.48	$ 33,758.48
Bank of Sheboygan	—	—	—	—	—
Individuals	$ 1,320.00	—	—	—	—
Teutonia State Bank	—	—	—	—	—
Total Notes Payable	1,320.00	—	—	38,418.48	33,758.48
Accounts Payable					
Trade and Others	5,695.01	$ 2,327.51	$ 14,809.58	8,514.43	11,221.08
Growers	—	—	—	70,679.08	71,303.41
Income Tax	12,169.56	6,943.50	—	—	—
Accrued Liabilities	14,173.72	11,421.10	2,994.21	12,675.20	32,391.53*
Total Current	32,038.29	20,692.11	17,803.79	130,289.19	179,308.52
(Deferred Income)	—	—	—	—	—
Mortgage	77,285.00	47,285.00	—	—	—
Capital Stock Outstanding	75,000.00	75,000.00	—	—	—
Surplus	(62,185.45)	(50,665.95)	32,670.56	25,127.50	16,576.45*
Total Liabilities and Ownership	$122,137.84	$ 92,311.16	$79,840.33	$155,414.69	$135,884.97

* Includes OPA overcharge liability of $20,126.19 on December 31, 1945, which reconciles net worth to canning profit.

(*Continued.*)

EXHIBIT I (*Continued.*)

Balance Sheets

	Saukville Canned Foods, Incorporated		Wisconsin Canned Foods, Incorporated
	March 31, 1947	March 31, 1948	March 31, 1949
Cash	$ 2,778.33	$17,146.37	$ 112.41
Receivables	18,802.56	15,200.20	—
Subsidy U.S. Receivables	—	—	—
Reserve	—	—	—
Inventories			
Canned Food	44,354.24	9,239.28	35,219.70
Seed	12,034.14	—	
Cans, Boxes	2,352.00	3,382.50	11,445.76
Labels	2,500.88	2,357.00	
Miscellaneous	1,365.42	1,120.00	
Total Inventory	84,187.57	45,445.35	46,577.87
Prepaid	2,352.00	—	3,500.00
Total Current	86,539.57	45,445.35	50,277.87
Lands, Buildings, and Equipment	1,281.01	2,967.89	51,477.60
Reserve	248.73	1,242.89	5,040.23
Net	1,032.28	1,725.00	46,437.37
Other Assets	587.26	642.23	3,156.00
Total Assets	$88,159.11	$47,812.58	$99,871.24
Notes Payable			
Farmers State Bank	—	—	—
Port Washington State Bank	$26,927.50	—	$55,510.00
Bank of Sheboygan	—	—	—
Individuals	—	—	1,700.14
Teutonia State Bank	—	—	—
Total Notes Payable	26,927.50	—	57,210.14
Accounts Payable			
Trade and Others	24,555.96	$ 8,761.83	26,460.21
Growers	—	—	8,148.29
Income Tax	1,745.20	2,115.00	—
Accrued Liabilities	4,744.27	193.41	3,660.60
Total Current	57,972.93	11,070.24	95,479.24
(Deferred Income)	—	—	—
Mortgage	—	—	21,250.00
Capital Stock Outstanding	25,000.00	25,000.00	45,000.00
Surplus	5,186.18	11,742.34	(61,858.00)
Total Liabilities and Ownership	$88,159.11	$47,812.58	$99,871.24

EXHIBIT I (*Continued.*)

Balance Sheets

Saukville Canning Company
(One Year After Premises Leased to E. C. Roberts)

	March 31, 1945
Cash	$ 19,974.57
Receivables	325.32
Reserve	(32.89)
Inventories	
Canned Food	
Seed	
Cans, Boxes	
Labels	
Miscellaneous	
Total	3,609.00
Prepaid	—
Total Current	23,876.00
Land, Buildings, and Equipment	165,203.54
Reserve	(105,531.85)
Net	59,671.72
Other Assets	1,680.80
Total Assets	$ 85,238.52
Notes Payable	
Farmers State Bank	
Port Washington State Bank	
Bank of Sheboygan	
Individuals	
Teutonia State Bank	
Total	
Accounts Payable	
Trade and Others	
Growers	
Income Tax	
Accrued Liabilities	
Total Current	15,736.05
(Deferred Income)	5,000.00
Mortgage	47,285.00
Capital Stock	75,000.00
Surplus	(57,782.53)
Total Liabilities and Ownership	$85,238.52

On final liquidation stockholders received 17¢ on dollar.

Profit and Loss Statement

	Year Ended 3/31/45
Rent	$ 8,268.35
Sales	19,581.96
	27,850.31
Book Value of Assets Sold	15,385.82
	12,150.49
Expenses	19,385.82
Loss	7,235.33
Depreciation	$6,640.79

CASE III-5.

Profit and Loss

Saukville Canning Company

	Year Ended December 31, 1939		Year Ended December 31, 1940	
Sales		$182,791.54		$194,335.87
Opening Inventory (Canned)	101,648.05		88,978.67	
Direct Cost	126,568.92		163,731.46	
Factory Overhead	19,409.90		23,100.13	
Total	247,626.87		275,810.16	
Ending Inventory (Canned)	88,978.67		101,065.54	
Cost of Goods		158,648.20		174,744.62
Gross Profit		24,143.34		19,591.25
Selling Expense	19,316.32		26,592.47	
Administrative Expense	9,972.89		9,123.88	
Interest Paid	6,417.44		6,955.37	
Total Expense		35,706.65		42,671.72
Profit Canning Operations		(11,563.31)		(23,080.47)
Other Income*		1,360.78		2,779.88
Other Expenses*		123.75		2,427.55
Profit (or Loss) Before Income Tax		(10,326.28)		(22,728.14)
Income Tax		—		—
Direct Cost Schedule				
Green Peas		$ 13,233.01		$ 28,699.33
Tomatoes		18,853.75		20,954.00
Corn		10,270.07		10,154.36
Pea Labor		4,382.64		8,450.63
Tomato Labor		15,574.98		17,159.20
Corn Labor		4,151.70		4,428.39
Cans		53,006.43		63,146.28
Boxes		4,237.97		7,840.83
Sugar and Salt		2,858.37		2,898.44
		$126,568.92		$163,731.46
Number of Cases Packed		75,360		89,700
Corn		—		—
Peas		—		—

* Other income and expenses include the operations of a farm.

EXHIBIT II

Statements

Saukville Canning Company

	3 Months Ended March 31, 1941		Year Ended March 31, 1942	
Sales		$67,224.13		$195,312.14
Opening Inventory (Canned)	101,065.54		47,230.40	
Direct Cost			90,300.70	
Factory Overhead			17,285.39	
Total			154,816.49	
Ending Inventory (Canned)	47,230.40		1,503.59	
		53,835.14		153,312.90
Gross Profit		13,388.99		41,999.24
Selling Expense	8,921.97		20,637.71	
Administrative Expense	5,176.23		10,261.24	
Interest Paid	1,742.39		5,747.22	
Total Expense		15,840.59		36,646.17
Profit Canning Operations		(2,451.60)		5,353.07
Other Income*		475.92		4,766.56
Other Expenses*		163.04		4,735.33
Profit (or Loss) Before Income Tax		$(2,138.72)		$ 5,384.30
Income Tax				
Direct Cost Schedule				
Green Peas				$ 19,595.29
Tomatoes				—
Corn				14,896.61
Pea Labor				8,162.25
Tomato Labor				—
Corn Labor				6,815.75
Cans				34,671.75
Boxes				2,590.50
Sugar and Salt				3,668.55
				$ 90,300.70
Number of Cases Packed				52,425
Corn				—
Peas				—

* Other income and expenses include the operations of a farm.

(*Continued.*)

EXHIBIT II (*Continued.*)

Profit and Loss Statements

Saukville Canning Company

	Year Ended March 31, 1943		Year Ended March 31, 1944	
Sales		$268,435.31		$254,225.62
Opening Inventory (Canned)	1,503.59		1,336.45	
Direct Cost	164,745.43		161,713.91	
Factory Overhead	28,607.99		33,005.00	
Total	194,857.01		196,055.36	
Ending Inventory (Canned)	1,336.45		3,208.69	
Cost of Goods		193,520.56		192,846.67
Gross Profit		74,914.75		61,378.95
Selling Expense	17,573.08		21,451.42	
Administrative Expense	14,524.49		11,974.41	
Interest Paid	5,139.18		3,690.74	
Total Expense		37,236.75		37,116.57
Profit Canning Operations		37,678.00		24,262.38
Other Income*		527.96		1,829.37
Other Expenses*		4,444.05		7,618.72
Profit (or Loss) Before Income Tax		33,761.91		18,473.03
Income Tax		$ 14,221.35		$ 7,727.30
Direct Cost Schedule				
Green Peas		$ 45,673.32		$ 29,405.79
Tomatoes		—		—
Corn		18,033.75		27,887.55
Pea Labor		16,673.41		17,763.71
Tomato Labor		—		—
Corn Labor		12,111.13		19,051.90
Cans		56,797.45		55,404.65
Boxes		10,495.25		6,628.15
Sugar and Salt		4,961.12		5,572.16
		$164,745.43		$161,713.91
Number of Cases Packed		98,030		110,546
Corn		—		—
Peas		—		—

* Other income and expenses include the operations of a farm.

EXHIBIT II (*Continued.*)

Profit and Loss Statements

E. C. Roberts, Doing Business as Wisconsin Canned Foods

	9 Months Ended December 31, 1944		10 Months Ended October 31, 1945
Sales		$280,312.00	$215,734.84
Opening Inventory (Canned)			261.00
Direct Cost			178,944.78
Factory Overhead	NA		47,732.96†
Total			226,677.74
Ending Inventory (Canned)			73,721.63
Cost of Goods		202,628.96	153,217.11
Gross Profit		77,683.14	62,517.73
Selling Expense	22,604.95		19,654.14
Administrative Expense	13,421.41		14,897.98†
Interest Paid	1,135.96		3,073.70†
Total Expense		37,162.32	37,625.82
Profit Canning Operations		40,520.82	24,891.91
Other Income*		732.92	411.96
Other Expense*		3,813.18	12,857.91
Profit (or Loss) Before Income Tax		$ 37,440.56	$ 12,445.96
Income Tax		—	—
Direct Cost Schedule			
Green Peas			$ 22,725.59
Tomatoes		$61,773.85	—
Corn			35,685.01
Pea Labor			18,280.59
Tomato Labor		37,036.43	—
Corn Labor			19,755.44
Cans		57,126.02	68,542.88
Boxes		7,343.89	8,482.74
Sugar and Salt		4,950.96	5,472.53
		$168,231.15	$178,944.78
Number of Cases Packed		115,367	
Corn		—	—
Peas		—	—

* Other income and expenses include the operations of a farm.

† It is apparent that between October 31 and December 31 there was some reclassification of charges, most likely out of general overhead into factory overhead.

(*Continued*)

EXHIBIT II

Profit and Loss

	E. C. Roberts, Doing Business as Wisconsin Canned Foods (*continued*)	Saukville Canned Foods, Incorporated
	Year Ended December 31, 1945	Year Ended March 31, 1947
Sales	$227,510.26	$208,320.12
Opening Inventory (Canned)	261.00	4,095.00
Direct Cost	179,204.07 †	154,002.60
Factory Overhead	52,707.42 †	51,584.98
Total	232,172.49	209,682.58
Ending Inventory (Canned)	66,400.20	44,354.24
Cost of Goods	165,772.29	165,328.34
Gross Profit	61,737.97	42,991.78
Selling Expense	22,139.94	17,034.68
Administrative Expense	12,452.11 †	17,946.57
Interest Paid	2,381.83 †	2,314.22
Total Expense	36,973.88	37,295.47
Profit Canning Operations	24,763.99	5,696.31
Other Income*	517.30	1,235.07
Other Expense*	17,786.38	—
Profit (or Loss) Before Income Tax	$ 7,494.91	$ 6,931.38
Income Tax	—	—
Direct Cost Schedule		
Green Peas		$45,275.25
Tomatoes	$58,522.13	—
Corn		28,813.73
Pea Labor		15,630.89
Tomato Labor	38,060.79	—
Corn Labor		13,069.40
Cans	68,542.88	42,016.30
Boxes	8,605.74	5,723.92
Sugar and Salt	5,472.53	3,473.11
	$179,204.07	$154,002.60
Number of Cases Packed	135,009	87,903
Corn	67,370	36,644
Peas	67,639	51,259

* Other income and expense included the operations of a farm by E. C. Roberts but not by Saukville Canned Foods, Incorporated.

† It is apparent that between October 31 and December 31 there was some reclassification of charges, most likely out of general overhead into factory overhead.

(*Continued.*)

Statements

	Saukville Canned Foods, Incorporated (*continued*) Year Ended March 31, 1948		Wisconsin Canned Foods, Incorporated Year Ended March 31, 1949	
Sales		$262,167.40		$31,093.61
Opening Inventory (Canned)	44,354.24		—	
Direct Cost	131,494.21		68,954.20	
Factory Overhead	43,118.20		45,475.21	
Total	218,966.65		114,429.41	
Ending Inventory (Canned)	9,239.28		35,219.70	
Cost of Goods		209,727.37		79,209.71
Gross Profit		52,440.03		(48,116.10)
Selling Expense	25,273.70		4,972.73	
Administrative Expense	18,754.25		10,103.21	
Interest Paid	2,057.07		3,253.77	
Total Expense		46,085.02		18,329.71
Profit Canning Operations		6,355.01		(66,445.81)
Other Income‡		624.05		12,893.85§
Other Expense‡		—		6,478.76
Profit (or Loss) Before Income Tax		$ 6,979.06		$(60,030.72)
Income Tax		—		—
Direct Cost Schedule				
Green Peas		$ 27,340.15		$ 10,600.33
Tomatoes		—		—
Corn		23,591.45		20,467.38
Pea Labor		16,970.26		7,726.46
Tomato Labor		—		—
Corn Labor		15,680.91		7,342.95
Cans		37,668.19		18,592.94
Boxes		6,561.00		2,583.12
Sugar and Salt		3,682.25		4,024.87
		$131,494.21		$ 68,954.20
Number of Cases Packed		72,345		30,129
Corn		35,920		13,490
Peas		36,425		16,639

‡ Other income and expense included the operations of a farm by Wisconsin Canned Foods, Incorporated but not by Saukville Canned Foods, Incorporated.

§ Includes gain on sale of real estate of $12,560.95.

CASE III-5.

Spot Prices End of Month F.O.B.

	January			February			March		
Year	Peas A*	Peas S†	Corn‡	Peas A*	Peas S†	Corn‡	Peas A*	Peas S†	Corn‡
1936	$0.70	$1.35	$1.10	$0.70	$1.35	$1.10	$0.70	$1.35	$1.10
1937	1.00	1.35	1.30	1.00	1.30	1.30	0.95	1.27	1.30
1938	0.77	1.17	1.00	0.70	1.17	0.97	0.79	1.12	0.95
1939	0.66	1.10	0.87	0.68	1.10	0.87	0.68	1.10	0.87
1940	0.82	1.25	0.96	0.90	1.15	0.96	0.90	1.15	0.96
1941	0.82	1.12	0.97	0.82	1.12	0.97	0.85	1.12	1.02
1942§	1.10	1.30	1.10	No Quote			No Quote		
1943§							1.05	1.30	1.29
1944–1945									
1946									
1947	1.15	2.10	1.72	1.15	2.10	1.72	1.15	2.10	1.72
1948	0.92	1.60	1.85	0.92	1.60	1.85	0.90	1.60	1.85
1949	1.00	1.70	1.72	1.00	1.70	1.72	1.05	1.70	1.70

	July			August			September		
	Peas A*	Peas S†	Corn‡	Peas A*	Peas S†	Corn‡	Peas A*	Peas S†	Corn‡
1936	$1.02	$1.40	$1.15	$1.07	$1.40	$1.37	$1.05	$1.38	$1.37
1937	0.77	1.15	N.Q.	0.80	1.12	1.05	0.80	1.17	1.02
1938	0.72	1.12	0.90	0.70	1.10	0.87	0.68	1.10	0.90
1939	0.82	1.12	0.97	0.82	1.12	0.91	0.85	1.12	1.00
1940	0.75	1.10	0.96	0.73	1.12	0.96	0.75	1.12	0.96
1941	0.87	1.12	1.15	0.93	1.10	1.15	0.93	1.10	1.10
1942§									
1943§									
1944–1945				1.13	1.54	for 1944–1945 packs[3]			1.38
1946									
1947	1.00	2.00	1.65	1.00	1.57	N.Q.	0.92	1.70	1.67
1948	0.97	1.75	N.Q.	1.12	1.75	1.77	1.12	1.70	1.80
1949	1.02	1.50	1.65	1.02	1.45	1.52	1.05	1.50	1.52

Sources: Canning Trade, 1936 to 1945; Journal of Commerce, October 1945 to April 1948.

* Peas-Alaska type, C grade, no. 4 sieve.

† Peas-Sweet type, A grade, no. 4 sieve.

‡ Corn-Whole kernel yellow type, A grade.

§ Years 1942 through 1945 subject to OPA price controls.

1. OPA price ceilings recognized 4 Regions for corn. Wisconsin was in the unnamed region (III at times, then IV) Region II as to peas and then III.

2. The no quote beginning February 1942 indicates that the market was cleared of the crop and no trading done. This was not true for all canned goods but was true for the central region for corn and peas.

EXHIBIT III

Cannery Per Dozen Cans (No. 2. Size)

	April			May			June	
Peas A*	Peas S†	Corn ‡	Peas A*	Peas S†	Corn ‡	Peas A*	Peas S†	Corn ‡
$0.78	$1.25	$1.10	$0.81	$1.25	$1.15	$0.85	$1.25	$1.15
0.95	1.27	1.30	0.95	1.27	1.30	0.82	1.25	1.20
0.75	1.12	0.90	0.77	1.12	0.90	0.72	1.12	0.90
0.70	1.10	0.87	0.70	1.10	0.87	0.75	1.10	0.92
0.87	1.15	0.96	0.89	1.15	0.96	0.77	1.10	0.96
0.85	1.12	1.15	0.87	1.12	1.10	0.87	1.12	N.Q.

No Quote — (April) No Quote — (May) No Quote — (June)

Ceiling price for 1943 pack announced in March[3]

1.25	2.10	1.55	1.00	2.10	1.55	1.00	2.00	1.60
0.85	N.Q.	1.82	0.85	N.Q.	1.85	0.97	N.Q.	1.85
1.00	1.52	1.72	1.00	1.37	1.60	1.02	N.Q.	1.60

	October			November			December	
Peas A*	Peas S†	Corn ‡	Peas A*	Peas S†	Corn ‡	Peas A*	Peas S†	Corn ‡
$1.05	$1.38	$1.35	$1.02	$1.35	$1.38	$1.00	$1.35	$1.35
0.77	1.17	1.01	0.75	1.17	1.00	0.75	1.17	1.00
0.68	1.10	0.92	0.66	1.10	0.90	0.68	1.10	0.87
0.88	1.25	0.96	0.88	1.25	0.96	0.88	1.25	0.96
0.73	1.12	0.97	0.74	1.12	0.95	0.76	1.12	0.94
0.96	1.15	1.10	1.00	1.15	1.12	1.02	1.15	1.12

for 1944 and 1945 packs announced in September 1944

1.15	1.80	1.70	1.20	1.85	1.95	1.20	2.00	1.95
0.92	1.60	1.85	0.92	1.60	1.85	0.92	1.60	1.85
1.12	1.65	1.70	1.07	1.90	1.72	1.07	1.70	1.72
1.05	1.50	1.52	1.25	1.55	1.45	1.05	1.55	1.40

3. The prices indicated in March 1943 are the prices applicable to the 1943 pack. Similarly the price for the 1944 pack was announced in August 1944 for peas and in September 1944 for corn. The price for the 1945 pack was set as the same as for 1944.

4. The OPA prices shown for 1943, 1944 and 1945 are not necessarily applicable to Saukville Canning Company. They are the ceiling for the area, but the ceiling for a specific cannery was usually under this and computed by specific rules.

5. Starting with 1942 prices are quoted regionally. Previously only nationally. Upon OPA removal of price control in October 1946 prices immediately went up.

CASE III-5. EXHIBIT IV

U.S. Pea and Corn Packs, 1929 to 1948,
Actual Cans All Sizes Converted to Thousands of Cases of 24 No. 303 Cans
(To Convert to No. 2 Can, Divide by 0.82)

Year	U.S. Pea Pack	U.S. Corn Pack	Year	U.S. Pea Pack	U.S. Corn Pack
1929	22,607	21,334	1939	31,610	17,772
1930	26,883	19,144	1940	30,739	18,939
1931	16,209	23,686	1941	35,043	31,853
1932	12,648	11,416	1942	43,012	39,184
1933	15,729	12,435	1943	42,763	35,081
1934	19,205	13,747	1944	38,460	30,609
1935	30,132	26,195	1945	48,372	34,449
1936	20,194	17,838	1946	40,405	37,760
1937	28,630	28,720	1947	28,494	31,829
1938	21,059	24,973	1948	28,630	38,409

Source: National Canners' Association, as reported in *Canners' Almanac*
(Washington: National Canners' Association).

Case III-5. EXHIBIT V

Saukville Canned Foods, Inc.

Year Ended March 31, 1947
Summary

	Peas	Corn
Cases of 24 No. 2 Cans	51,259	36,644
Cost to pack per doz.	$1.140	$1.210
Selling & admin. per doz.	$0.225	$0.225
Total cost to pack & sell	$1.365	$1.435
Average selling price	$1.36	$1.653

Inventory of Canned Goods, March 31, 1947

	No. Cases of 24 No. 2 Cans	Dozen Cans at Market	Total at Market	Lower Cost or Market
Peas: Alaska				
Fancy #1 Sv.	116	$2.25	$ 522.00	$ 262.00
X. Std. #1 Sv.	186	1.85	688.00	420.00
X. Std. #2 Sv.	147	1.75	514.00	332.00
Fancy #3 Sv.	20	1.75	70.00	45.00
X. Std. #3 Sv.	62	1.50	186.00	140.00
Top Std. #3 Sv.	1,280	1.15	2,944.00	2,893.00
Std. #3 Sv.	3,710	1.10	8,162.00	8.162.00
Low Std. #3 Sv.	1,084	0.90	1,951.00	1,951.00
Std. #5 Sv.	285	1.00	570.00	570.00
Total	6,890		15,607.00	14,776.00
Peas: Sweet				
X. Std. #2 Sv.	98	1.70	333.00	221.00
N. Fancy #3 Sv.	281	1.60	899.00	635.00
X. Std. #3 Sv.	160	1.50	480.00	361.00
Std. #3 Sv.	27	1.30	70.00	61.00
N. Fancy #4 Sv.	906	1.45	2,627.00	2,047.00
X. Std. #4 Sv.	594	1.30	1,544.00	1,342.00
Std. #4 Sv.	69	1.20	166.00	156.00
X. Std. #5–6 Sv.	4,796	1.25	11,990.00	10,839.00
Std. #5–6 Sv.	281	1.10	618.00	618.00
Fancy ungraded	1,149	1.60	3,677.00	2,597.00
X. Std. ungraded	294	1.35	794.00	645.00
Total	8,655		23,198.00	19,523.00
Corn				
Fancy	3,970	1.60	12,704.00	—
X. Std.	479	1.40	1,341.00	—
Total	4,449		14,045.00	10,055.00

(*Continued.*)

EXHIBIT V (*Continued.*)

Saukville Canned Foods, Inc.

Year Ended March 31, 1948
Summary

	Peas	Corn
Cases of 24 No. 2 Cans	36,425	35,920
Cost to pack per doz.	$1.189	$1.226
Selling & admin. per doz.	$0.246	$0.246
Total cost to pack & sell	$1.435	$1.472
Average selling price	$1.30	$1.70

Inventory of Canned Goods, March 31, 1948

	No. Cases of 24 No. 2 Cans	Dozen Cans at Market	Total at Market	Dozen Cans at Cost	Lower Cost or Market
Peas: Alaska					
Fancy #1 Sv.	218	$2.40	$1,046.00	$1.20	$ 523.00
Fancy #2 Sv.	165	2.25	743.00	1.20	396.00
N. Fancy #2 Sv.	328	2.00	1,312.00	1.20	787.00
X. Std. #2 Sv.	7	1.65	23.00	1.20	17.00
N. Fancy #3 Sv.	138	1.50	414.00	1.20	331.00
X. Std. #3 Sv.	106	1.20	254.00	1.20	254.00
Std. #3 Sv.	580	0.85	986.00	0.85	986.00
Total	1,542		4,778.00		3,294.00
Peas: Sweet					
Fancy #3 Sv.	281	1.65	927.00	1.20	674.00
X. Std. #3 Sv.	240	1.30	624.00	1.20	576.00
Std. #3 Sv.	66	0.85	112.00	0.85	112.00
Std. #4 Sv.	239	0.80	382.00	0.80	382.00
Fancy #5 Sv.	57	1.15	131.00	1.15	131.00
N. Fancy #5 Sv.	688	1.00	1,376.00	1.00	1,376.00
N. Fancy #6 Sv.	330	1.00	660.00	1.00	663.00
Fancy #6 Sv.	198	1.30	515.00	1.20	475.00
Total	2,099		4,727.00		4,389.00
Corn					
Fancy	600	1.65	1,980.00	1.23	1,476.00
X. Std.	33	1.50	99.00	1.23	81.00
Total	633		2,079.00		1,557.00

CASE III-5. EXHIBIT VI

Frozen Vegetable Production in the United States, 1939 to 1949

	Total U.S. Pack (in Millions of Pounds)			That Part of Total Pack for Retail Sale* (in Millions of Pounds)		
Year	Frozen Peas	Frozen Corn	All Frozen Vegetables	Frozen Peas	Frozen Corn	All Frozen Vegetables
1939	26.6	5.6	72.6			
1940	35.8	7.4	83.3			
1941	44.1	9.6	111.3			
1942	59.0	11.1	152.5	22.4	4.8	57.7
1943	70.3	22.2	207.9	20.8	4.8	66.0
1944	79.1	21.5	237.1	32.7	7.1	103.7
1945	103.8	26.0	308.0	39.2	11.1	137.2
1946	140.6	44.7	450.0	72.0	23.8	254.0
1947	131.8	32.5	346.2	75.2	14.6	200.4
1948	119.0	31.2	446.4	71.7	18.2	284.5
1949	113.3	54.5	563.5	64.6	30.9	363.6

Source: Frozen Food, Fact Book and Directory (New York: National Frozen Food Distributors Association, 1958–1959), p. 45.
* Retail defined as containers of 1 pound or less.

CASE III-5. EXHIBIT VII

Per Capita Consumption, Pounds of Fresh Equivalent in 1949

	Peas	Corn	All Vegetables
Fresh	0.80	7.50	121.1
Canned	8.84	12.19	69.4
Frozen	2.08	0.93	6.7

Source: Statistical and Historical Research Branch, Agricultural Marketing Service, U.S.D.A., as reported in *Canning Trade Almanac* (Washington: National Canners' Association, 1957), p. 347.

CASE III-5. EXHIBIT VIII

Selected Data on Scale of Operations in the Processed Fruit and Vegetable Industry

Year	Number of Firms	Number of Employees	Payroll in Thousands of Dollars	Value Added in Thousands of Dollars	Value of Product in Thousands of Dollars	Value Added Per Employee in Thousands of Dollars	Value Added Per Firm in Thousands of Dollars
Canning, Preserving and Freezing							
1939	3508	NA	NA	$ 319,153	$ 842,238	NA	$104
1947	3825	201,109	$413,041	914,184	2,462,365	$4.5	237
1954	3513	199,235	573,055	1,301,193	3,903,236	6.5	372
1958	1744	202,751	670,588	1,681,842	4,913,364	8.3	965
Canned Fruits and Vegetables Only							
1939	1899	NA	NA	$ 227,399	$ 339,056	NA	$119
1947	2265	135,851	$283,859	608,768	1,031,986	$4.5	267
1954	1758	119,836	354,746	830,019	1,454,300	6.8	472
1958	965*	123,372	424,657	1,109,402	1,890,700	9.0	1149

Source: U.S. Department of Commerce, Bureau of Census, General Statistics for U.S. Table I, reprinted, *Canners' Almanac* (Washington: National Canners' Association, 1960), p. 267.

* Firms with twenty employees and over.

NA = Not available.

CASE III-5. EXHIBIT IX

Sales of Four Largest Canners in Millions of Dollars

	California Packing	H. J. Heinz	Libby, McNeill, and Libby	Stokely-Van Camp	Total Top 4	Per Cent of Industry*
1946	$151.4	$144.2	$127.1	$ 89.0	$ 511.7	
1947	158.9	169.5	145.4	107.0	580.8	23.5%
1948	169.2	174.9	153.6	95.1	592.8	
1949	174.7	170.5	145.3	95.0	585.5	
1950	222.9	189.1	196.4	95.5	703.9	
1951	200.6	206.0	177.1	114.9	698.6	
1952	215.7	219.6	212.1	115.4	762.8	
1953	226.9	220.6	215.4	114.4	773.3	
1954	233.8	234.2	249.6	121.7	839.3	22.9
1955	249.3	262.4	261.9	136.5	910.1	
1956	287.6	278.9	292.5	159.5	1018.5	
1957	325.5	293.8	302.7	159.2	1081.2	
1958	346.4	316.9	296.0	158.4	1117.7	22.7

* Computed as per cent of value of product in Exhibit VIII.
Source: Value Line Investment Survey, January 4, 1960, pp. 1000–1078.

CASE III-5. EXHIBIT X

Beginning Stock, Pack and Ending Stock in Million of Pounds of Canned Vegetables for Pack Years 1936–55

	(1)	(2)	(3)	(4)	(5)	(6)	(7)
						(5) as	(3) as
	Beginning		Total		Ending	Per Cent	Per Cent
	Stock	Pack	Available	Consumed	Stock	of (4)	of (4)
1936	1,378	3,700	5,151	3,588	1,508	42.1	113.6
1937	1,508	4,595	6,168	4,033	2,072	51.4	151.9
1938	2,072	4,212	6,365	4,028	2,272	56.4	158.0
1939	2,272	3,689	6,006	4,325	1,602	37.0	138.9
1940	1,602	4,523	6,127	4,797	1,232	25.7	127.7
1941	1,232	5,769	7,012	5,289	1,452	27.5	132.6
1942	1,452	6,846	8,304	6,768	1,143*	16.9	127.0
1943	4,444*	6,248	10,697	6,007	4,272	71.1	178.5
1944	4,272	6,362	10,636	6,356	4,139	65.1	167.3
1945	4,139	6,552	10,702	6,693	3,822	57.1	159.9
1946	3,822	7,640	11,479	6,687	4,606	68.9	171.7
1947	4,397	6,131	10,547	5,969	4,364	73.1	176.7
1948	4,224	5,767	10,029	5,578	4,325	77.5	179.8
1949	4,333	6,102	10,474	5,718	4,436	77.6	183.2
1950	4,286	5,908	10,274	6,325	3,703	58.5	162.4
1951	4,103	7,806	11,993	6,305	4,913	77.9	190.2
1952	4,540	7,318	11,928	6,366	4,952	77.8	187.4
1953	4,892	7,184	12,140	6,619	5,074	76.7	183.4
1954	5,051	6,660	11,789	6,677	4,760	71.3	176.6
1955	4,790	7,116	12,000	7,054	4,579	64.9	170.1

Source: U.S. Department of Agriculture, Misc. Pub. 691, p. 163, Table 58c. Also in U.S. Department of Agriculture, Agricultural Marketing Service, Handbook 61 (1956), Food Consumption in the United States.

* Change from calendar year to pack year.

Column 3 is column 1 plus column 2 plus imports of 50 to 60 million pounds per year.

Discrepancy of column 5 (which is column 3 minus column 4) arises from military consumption.

part IV
Pricing analysis

Pricing of a product requires that the demand and cost conditions of the product be developed as we have done in the preceding parts.

The solution to the question of what price and volume of production of a particular product will yield the producer the largest profit lies in the principle or necessary condition that output and price will be adjusted until marginal cost equals marginal revenue. Although this principle applies to all markets, the differences between types of market call for separate study of the application of this principle. Also, there are restrictions or constraints on the pricing policies that can be undertaken.

Broadly speaking we can classify the markets a producer might find into the following categories. First, there is the situation of pure competition, defined as a market in which each product seller (or buyer) is so small relative to the total market that his practices have only an infinitesimal effect on the market. Notice that we said "each product seller is so small, etc." Not only is the seller of a finished good a product seller, but so is each seller of a productive service such as a laborer selling his labor. In contrast to the case of pure competition, there is monopolistic (and monopsonistic) competition, defined as a market in which each product seller (or buyer) has a discernible effect on the market by his conduct.

At one extreme of the spectrum of monopolistic (monopsonistic) competition is oligopolistic (oligopsonistic) competition, defined as a market in which there are only a few sellers (buyers) of the product and the seller (buyer) is more acutely aware of the impact of his own conduct on the market and of reactions by his fellow competitors. The case of duopoly (only two sellers) and duopsony (only two buyers) marks the last step in classification before monopoly (only a single seller) and monopsony (only a single buyer). The problems of warfare at one extreme and collusion at the other extreme apply to the range of the spectrum embracing oligopoly (oligopsony), duopoly (duopsony) and monopoly (monopsony). But monopolistic competition is defined to exclude all situations in which there is reaction to one's conduct by competitors. While we speak of a market as if it were defined, all markets in varying degrees overlap with other markets in a number of dimensions, particularly as to time, area and product. The phenomenon of product differentiation, arising from the degrees of distinction recognized by the market place between one

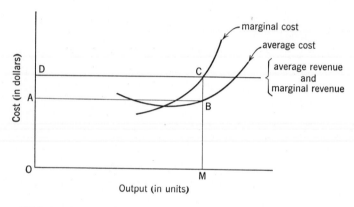

Figure IV-1. Profit maximization under pure competition.

product and its near-substitutes, also obliterates the market concept.

A market is defined in terms of the cross elasticities of demand and supply between one market and another. Thus a firm has a monopoly when the cross elasticity of demand between its product and that of any other producer is zero and a firm is in pure competition when this cross elasticity is infinite.

The degree of freedom which sellers or buyers have in acting with respect to prices is frequently limited by constraints. Most of these restrictions stem from legal and governmental regulation. Thus restraints are imposed by the anti-trust laws and, for example, by labor legislation. Typical restraints will be considered in Part V on Governmental Regulation. The current part on Pricing Analysis is directed primarily to matters of the type of market.

Before going further, we will review the traditional treatment of pricing in the different types of market.

PURE COMPETITION AND MONOPOLY

The graphical presentation in Figure IV-1 is the familar diagram of the adjustment of the individual producer in pure competition. The intersection of the marginal cost curve with the marginal revenue curve determines the volume of output, OM, which yields the largest possible profit,[1] ABCD (or least loss point when the entire average cost curve is above the average revenue curve).

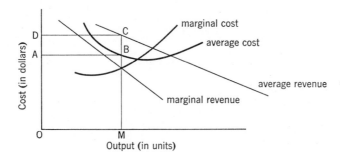

Figure IV-2. Profit maximization under monopoly.

And in the case of monopoly, the familiar diagram for the adjustment of an individual producer is shown in Figure IV-2. Again the intersection of the marginal cost curve with the marginal revenue curve

---

[1] The same result can be established by equations. Thus, suppose price is $50 a unit and the equation of the total cost curve in dollars is $TC = 500 + 0.008x^3 - 0.06x^2 + 4.8x$. Total profit for any output then is $50x$ (total revenue) $- (500 + 0.008x^3 - 0.06x^2 + 4.8x)$. To maximize total profit, differentiate total profit with respect to quantity and set equal to zero. Thus: $dp/dx = 50 - 0.024x^2 + 0.12x - 4.8 = 0$. If we collect the terms, this becomes: $-0.024x^2 + 0.12x + 45.2 = 0$. This is in the form of the general quadratic equation, $ax^2 + bx + c = 0$. Solving for x by using the formula for a general quadratic, $x = (- b \pm \sqrt{b^2 - 4ac})/2a$, we get $x = 40.9$ and -45.9. Since output cannot be negative, we reject -45.9. The two values of x may be the maximum profit output, the minimum profit output, or an inflection point. To check that the output 40.9 is a true maximum, we take the second derivative, $d^2p/dx^2 = -0.048x + 0.12$, and substitute 40.9. The result is negative (-1.7632); hence 40.9 is a maximum. To get the maximum total profit, substitute 40.9 in $50x - (500 + 0.008x^3 - 0.06x^2 + 4.8x)$. This gives the maximum profit $901.73. The same result is achieved by setting marginal cost equal to price. Thus $0.024x^2 - 0.12x + 4.8 = 50$, which is the equation established above.

determines the volume of output, OM, which yields the largest possible profit,[2] ABCD (or least loss where the entire average cost curve is above the average revenue curve).

In turn, the familiar kinked demand curve facing the individual oligopolist is presented as shown in Figure IV-3. In this situation, price increases attempted by one producer are not followed by other producers; hence there is a sharp falloff in volume sold by the price raiser. On the other hand, price cuts by one producer are followed downward by other producers with but scant (and noncompensating) increase in volume sold by the price cutter.

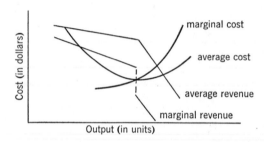

Figure IV-3. Profit maximization under oligopoly.

The diagram is also intended to bring out that costs can change with the resulting change in the marginal cost curve but that price will not change so long as the intersection of the marginal cost curve with the marginal revenue curve occurs within the limits of the dotted portion of the marginal revenue curve in Figure IV-3. This conclusion

---

[2] The same result can be established by equations in a manner parallel to the process set out in the preceding footnote, but with a demand function, say, $x = 2000 - 40y$ with x as quantity demanded and y as price. This can be stated as $y = 50 - 0.025x$, which is the average revenue curve. Since total revenue is price (y) times quantity sold (x), total revenue is $x(50 - 0.025x)$ or $50x - 0.025x^2$. If the total cost function is again (as in the preceding footnote), $TC = 500 + 0.008x^3 - 0.06x^2 + 4.8x$, then total profit is $(50x - 0.025x^2) - (500 + 0.008x^3 - 0.06x^2 + 4.8x)$. Then to maximize profit, differentiate total profit with respect to quantity demanded and set equal to zero. This gives $-0.024x^2 + 0.07x + 45.2$. Solving for x (using the general quadratic form as in the preceding footnote), we get $x = 41.8$ and -44.8. To be sure that 41.8 is a true maximum, we take the second derivative

$$\frac{d^2p}{dx^2} = 0.048x + 0.07 = 0$$

and substitute 41.8. The results are negative (-1.9364) and hence 41.8 is a maximum. To get the maximum total profit, substitute 41.8 in $(50x - 0.025x^2) - (500 + 0.008x^3 - 0.06x^2 + 4.8x)$. This gives the maximum profit of \$866.24.

may be in conflict with empirical evidence such as is presented later in this Part, on p. 264 in the case of shoes. There is a conflict unless it is assumed that there is competition in all cases where pricing is based on costs.

The adjustment of the producer in using the factors of production once the maximum profit output has been established is shown in Figure IV-4 where the isoquant traces all the combinations of factors A and B that the producer can use to produce this optimum profit output in the case of pure competition between the factors. And given the price ratio of factors A and B in the market place (as shown by the

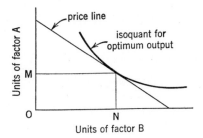

Figure IV-4. Factor adjustment in production under pure competition.

price line in Figure IV-4), the most profitable combination of factors A and B to produce this output is determined, namely, OM units of factor A and ON units of factor B. We should remember that the maximum profit output isoquant which we have taken as given is actually determined simultaneously with the minimum cost combination of factors.

However, traditional theory is seldom presented as dealing with the problem of the choice of products which yields a producer the maximum profit in the multiproduct situation. The complete solution of this problem involves the basic concepts of capital budgeting which are the subject of a separate part later in this book. However, a first approximation can be made at this time without bringing in the complications of capital budgeting.

A producer necessarily involves himself in the employment of capital. Part of that capital may be borrowed, but part of it—the equity—will belong to the producer. On the realistic assumption that a producer's available equity is limited at any one time, the producer is necessarily involved with comparing the return on the investment he has in the manufacture of product A with the return on the investment he has in the manufacture of product B. The principle at work here[3] is that the producer will seek to maximize the profit or return which he receives on the equity that he has available. He will do this by a program such that the marginal rate of return on each alternative investment is equalized.

This rather simple illustration brings out that rate of return on investment is an aspect of pricing analysis which has been neglected in traditional presentations of economic theory. Traditional theory simply rests with the principle that the ratio of the price of each factor (here, capital) divided by the marginal product of that factor in the first use (here, product A) is to be equalized to that same ratio for the same factor in other uses (here, product B).

TARGET PRICING

The consideration of the rate of return aspect in pricing policy has come to be known as "target pricing" with the "target" being a pre-determined return on the investment. This is, for example, the announced pricing policy of General Electric Company—and with the announced goal of a minimum annual return on equity of 20 per cent (after income taxes).[4] The pre-determined "cut-off" rate of return will depend on the risk attitudes of the producer and these attitudes may be conditioned by the available supply of investment opportunities.

We may view the failure (until recently) to develop the rate of return concept as primarily the result of institutional changes in the economy of the twentieth century. Thus the development of great flexibility in modern industry enables producers to add and delete products with a speed unknown even a few decades ago. In fact, producers enter and leave industries within a decade. General purpose buildings, general purpose machinery, flexible distribution organiza-

---

[3] Actually, the producer faces a problem even if there is only one product. Unless the cost curves of the traditional analyses include return on capital (and a return properly weighted for the risk applicable to investment in that particular product), they are not calculated to answer the question of what is the optimum profit output. If the cost curves do not include return, then optimum profit output will usually occur short of the traditional point; that is, it will occur where the marginal rate of profit on the equity has decreased so much that either a switch to another product or cessation is in order since the rate of profit will no longer compensate for risk. The traditional statement includes in costs what are called "opportunity costs," intending thereby to deal with the rate of return in alternative projects. But no operational method for dealing with opportunity costs is made available in traditional theory. Rate of return is the way to make traditional theory operational.

[4] Cf. A. D. H. Kaplan, J. B. Dirlam, and R. F. Lanzillotti, *Pricing in Big Business: A Case Approach* (Washington: Brookings Institute, 1958).

tions, widespread short-term leasing of specialized equipment and high income tax rates with ready markets for resale of rapidly amortized fixed assets so that the loss of switching assets is minimized are but a few of the modern phenomena that have changed the focus of problems for a large part of business.

While marginal revenue and marginal cost continue to be valid and useful concepts, the increase in flexibility and the shortening of the time period that separates long run and short run have increased the significance of variables other than price.

PRICE DISCRIMINATION

Price discrimination is one of the aspects of pricing not yet noted which bears on pricing analysis. Price discrimination is a slippery word. As is said in Alice in Wonderland "Words mean what I choose them to mean." In this same spirit, the term price discrimination is frequently used in different meanings and sometimes in different meanings by the same user at different points in his argument.

One definition, sometimes called first-degree discrimination, refers to charging each buyer the maximum he is willing to pay for each unit. This does not exist as a practice except in auctions where there is no collusion. The term second-degree discrimination is sometimes used to describe the situation in which each buyer is forced to pay a different price but not the maximum he is willing to pay.

The more usual definition of discrimination, frequently called third-degree discrimination, refers to establishing classes of buyers, using the elasticity of demand for each group as the basis for charging a different price to each class. Hence the class of buyers with lower elasticity of demand will be charged higher prices and those with higher elasticity of demand lower prices.

The diagram illustrating the approach to price discrimination taken in traditional theory[5] is shown in Figure IV-5. In this diagram, D_1 shows the demand for the product by the buyers in the class (or for the use) which is more elastic and D_2 shows the demand that is more inelastic. D_{1+2} is the horizontal addition of D_1 and D_2 to show the quantity demanded in both markets combined at each price. MR_1, MR_2 and MR_{1+2} are respectively the marginal revenue curves for D_1, D_2 and D_{1+2}. The intersection of the marginal cost curve with MR_{1+2} determines the *total* output (OM) whose sale will yield the highest *total* profit when sold separately in markets 1 and 2 at the optimum

[5] Another diagrammatic approach is presented in L. W. Weiss, *Economics and American Industry* (New York: Wiley, 1961), p. 191.

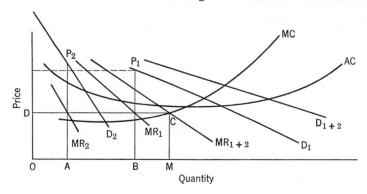

Figure IV-5. Profit maximization by price discrimination in two markets.

prices in those markets. By extending a horizontal line (CD) from the intersection of MC and MR_{1+2} back to the Y axis, this total output is split between the two markets at the point where this horizontal line cuts MR_1, and MR_2, (such a horizontal line measuring equal marginal revenue). This, then, determines OB as the optimum output for market 1 and by going up vertically to the demand curve for this market, the optimum price P_1 is established for the first market. Conversely for market 2, output of OA for that market and price P_2 are established. The horizontal dotted line from P_1 shows that the price is lower in the market whose demand is more elastic (D_1) than the price (P_2) in the market whose demand is less elastic (D_2). The quantity sold in the first market (OB) plus the quantity sold in the second market (OA) exhausts the total quantity (OM).

This solution depends upon the ability of the producer to prevent resale between the markets. This may be done by a number of different devices. For example, potatoes sold for cattle feed (whose demand is more elastic) may be dyed a noninjurious purple to prevent their return to the human market (whose demand is less elastic). Sometimes the product for the two markets may be distinguished in another way such as guarantee or type of finish or model.

This approach to discrimination is frequently said to arise from excess capacity of the producer or from the sharp reductions in marginal cost following upon expanded output.

Such price discrimination encounters difficulties with the Robinson-Patman Act and anti-trust prosecution. The Federal laws permit charging different prices to different buyers (or classes of buyers) only (1) when the costs of serving the buyers differ, and then differences in prices are permitted only to the extent of the cost differences; and (2) to meet in good faith a locally lower price which was not brought about by the producer. The last is the familiar "fight fire with fire" approach.

In examining price discrimination from the viewpoint of target pricing we see a deficiency in the traditional solution which has just been presented. Unless the marginal cost curve is interpreted as derived from an average cost curve which includes the "return to capital," the solution is deficient and even when it includes the return to capital (under the guise of "opportunity costs") this approach at best muddies the waters as was set forth previously in footnote 3.

Although in itself the sound solution, target pricing has been given a great stimulus by the anti-trust laws. Granted that the anti-trust laws limit the freedom with which target pricing may be pursued, the very restriction increases the rewards for careful analysis. A producer who dominates a large part of an industry is presently prevented from pursuing the as yet uncaptured market remaining in the industry by the haunting fear that such growth may precipitate anti-trust proceedings against him. Thus the wise decision may often be for the dominant producer to reserve unto himself the products (and customers) who yield the highest return on his investment and even when customers yield equally profitable average returns on investment, to pursue (or retain) those who involve more stability and less risk. It is true that maximizing the amount of profit produces a maximum amount of return on any given amount of investment. But this is treating the amount of investment as given and also limits the analysis to the particular product and its profits possibilities.

Aside from this added stimulus to target pricing from the anti-trust laws, the traditional diagram is incomplete and in error. The two (or more) classes of buyers constituting the different markets usually involve different risks. These differences in risk may arise from differences in the degree of organization in the classes of buyers, the degree of sophistication in their knowledge of markets and in a hundred other differences. We cannot say *a priori* that the differences in the elasticities of demand of the two groups of buyers are a correct reflection of the differences in risks in serving both groups. Hence capital applied to production for the two markets seeks different returns. The average cost curve cannot reflect these differences since that part of output going to the respective markets is not separately designated when the cost curve is constructed. The reader is referred back to Figure IV-5, the traditional presentation, where only one average cost curve is used.

The traditional diagram is qualified as a solution to the excess capacity situation, namely, an analysis after the investment has been "sunk." However, even this presentation rests upon an institutional assumption which is typically not realistic in modern business. Unless the excess capacity situation is expected to be a short-lived condition, liquidation of that excess capacity (in view of today's flexibility of fixed assets) and re-investment will usually be more profitable. Traditional theory treats the short-run situation as one of "sunk costs," in which case the "sunk costs" are not relevant to decisions since they cannot be undone in any event. Traditional theory presents the adjustment as occurring in the long run, for example, by an individual producer's withdrawal from the industry at the time when replacement of the "sunk costs" is up for consideration. Our point is to deny the usefulness of the classification today when "sunk costs" are not really sunk but can with relatively little loss be converted to other uses. In short, we dispute the concept of inflexibility which underlies the traditional analysis.

TARGET PRICING AND OLIGOPOLY

Oligopoly is defined as the market situation in which there are relatively few sellers of a product. It is more meaningful to define oligopoly[6] as the situation in which sellers are conscious that their pricing activities will induce reactions by competitors as to their pricing.

Traditional theory has spawned the concept of the kinked demand curve as the theoretical apparatus rationalizing the oligopoly situation (Figure IV-3 earlier in this Part). The kinked demand curve (which rests on a priori and not empirical grounds) is taken to represent the situation faced by an individual oligopolist producer. The "break point" in the demand curve represents the proposition that, as an oligopolist cuts his price, his quantity sold will not increase at the expense of his competitors because they will meet the price cut. The only increase in quantity sold will be the oligopolist's proportionate share of the increase in the total quantity sold by all producers because market price has been cut. Correlatively, it is argued that if the oligopolist raises price, he will lose some sales to his competitors because they will not follow the price increase. Thus market price will stay at P (in Figure IV-3). Because of the discontinuity in the marginal revenue curve following from the sharp change in elasticity

---

[6] Oligopoly is sometimes divided into complete and partial. Complete oligopoly is then defined as the joint action of the sellers to maximize the profits of the group of sellers as a whole. The absence of such joint action is then called partial oligopoly.

of the demand curve at the kink point, it is argued that costs will move upward or downward over a significant range without any change in price or quantity of the output. This rests on the ground that the output at which MC intersects the discontinuous MR will not be changed as long as the cost movements do not cause the marginal cost curve to intersect MR outside the discontinuous range.

This elaborate theoretical structure may well be questioned as begging the question. Price leadership—the situation in which price changes in a market are initiated by one producer and quickly followed by the others—exists as a phenomenon in many markets. If the price leader moves so as to reflect cost changes, particularly changes in raw materials and wage rates, there is little doubt that he will be followed. But if the price changes do not reflect cost changes and if the demand curve has not changed, then the "price leader" is frequently not followed.

Thus we are in conflict with the propositions of traditional theory that costs may change but price does not in an oligopoly (within the limits of the discontinuity of the marginal revenue curve) and conversely that the price leader can change prices without costs having changed and other producers will follow because of the kink in the demand curve facing each producer (the price change having raised or lowered the "kink price").

To state that in a partial oligopoly price will not change without a change in costs but in a complete oligopoly the price leader acts in behalf of the others and hence price will be changed is a verbalism.

Target pricing offers a more adequate explanation of the price leadership phenomenon, namely, that the price leader is trying to protect the rate of return on his investment. A simple illustration will show the point. Assume a producer presently sells 50 per cent of the quantity sold in a particular market. Then a producer who sells 5 per cent decides to cut the price. It is more profitable for the large producer to buy out the small than it would be to meet the price cut or even undercut unless the small producer can very quickly be eliminated by an undercut. If the price undercut is to last any length of time, the loss to the price leader of a cut in price (for example, by 10 per cent) on the 50 per cent of the industry's sales he possesses will mean a loss that quickly adds up to the purchase price of acquiring the small producer. The anti-trust act is the principal deterrent discouraging the large producer from pursuing the purchase. The usual reaction of a large producer to the situation is to counter attack with product innovation particularly such as cannot be readily duplicated by the price-cutter. Price leadership in this case is maintained by product differentiation.

It is, of course, a legitimate question why the large producer did not introduce the innovation sooner. Again the rate-of-return approach sheds light. A homely analogy facilitates the argument. Imagine a boxer who feels superior to his opponent in the first round but believes his chances for a knockout in the first round are less than if he waits until the fifth round. If, in the first round, he attempts a knockout but does not succeed, he may believe it will impair his ability to get a knockout in the fifth round, and, furthermore, he may be faced with the greater possibility of losing on points. Therefore, he is worse off in a first-round bid than if he had waited until the fifth round for his bid. The boxer seems well advised to wait until the fifth.

Similarly, the large producer, presently possessed of an innovation, may well seek to minimize the risk to the rate of return on his investment by holding back this innovation. He does this not only because of the competitive situation just discussed but for other reasons as well. For example, he may seek to reduce the risk of not being able to react as quickly as he usually does to the introduction of an innovation by one of his competitors. Of course, there is the counter-risk that, by holding back an innovation, the large producer invites others in. In this discussion, we have been assuming a zero rate of interest when the innovation is withheld for a period.

TARGET PRICING AND THE FULL-COST-VERSUS-MARGINAL-COST QUESTION

There is considerable literature[7] in economics on the question of full-cost pricing versus marginal-cost pricing. Briefly, the issue is whether, given the demand picture for a product, the decision to undertake an order should be based upon costs established by including the allocable share of fixed costs (the so-called full-cost pricing) or whether the decision should employ costs considering only variable costs and any additions to fixed costs (the so-called marginal-cost pricing).

We have already indicated objections to reducing the pricing problem to these terms in the preceding criticisms of traditional analysis. But one point of the traditional handling of marginal-cost pricing versus full-cost pricing should be emphasized: unless the production function is such that for each increase in input factors there is the

---

[7] See, for example, William Fellner, *Competition Among the Few* (New York: Knopf, 1949), A. R. Oxenfeldt, *Industrial Pricing and Market Practices* (Englewood Cliffs, N.J.: Prentice-Hall, 1951). The issue of marginal cost versus full cost is brought out in the Snoeshoes case after Part VI.

same proportionate increase in output,[8] marginal cost pricing may overexhaust or underexhaust the total revenues received by the producer from the sale of his products. This could occur when paying all the units of each type of input at the marginal contribution of the last unit of that input. Totalling the bills for each input could overexhaust or underexhaust total revenue. Overexhaustion would occur when the output is increasing at a less than proportionate rate with increase in input and underexhaustion when the output is increasing at a more than proportionate rate with input.

MECHANICS OF TARGET PRICING

There is available to the public very little material illustrating the mechanics of target pricing with the exception of some materials in public utility rate cases such as are set forth at the end of this Part.

However there is one table showing the pricing mechanics of six representative farm implements introduced in 1956 by International

---

[8] The classic demonstration of the possibility of overexhaustion or underexhaustion of the product when each factor is paid its marginal output appears in E. Schneider, *Theorie der Produktion* (Vienna: Springer, 1934), pp. 19–21.

If price is a function of factors $A, B, C,$ etc., then

$$dP = \left[\left(\frac{\delta P}{\delta A}\right) dA\right] + \left[\left(\frac{\delta P}{\delta B}\right) dB\right] + \left[\left(\frac{\delta P}{\delta C}\right) dC\right] + \cdots \qquad (1)$$

And if we increase each of the factors in a constant proportion φ, then

$$\varphi = \frac{dA}{A} = \frac{dB}{B} = \cdots \qquad (2)$$

If we substitute (2) into (1) and divide by φP,

$$\frac{dP}{\varphi P} = \frac{1}{P}\left[\left(\frac{\delta P}{\delta A}\right) A\right] + \left[\left(\frac{\delta P}{\delta B}\right) B\right] + \left[\left(\frac{\delta P}{\delta C}\right) C\right] + \cdots \qquad (3)$$

But the left hand side of equation 3 is the relative change of product which results when we add an equal relative change in the quantity of all factors and can be called the elasticity of the production function and designated e. Then,

$$Pe = \left[\left(\frac{\delta P}{\delta A}\right) A\right] + \left[\left(\frac{\delta P}{\delta B}\right) B\right] + \left[\left(\frac{\delta P}{\delta C}\right) C\right] + \cdots \qquad (4)$$

When e is greater than 1, there are increasing returns (i.e., decreasing average unit costs), and the product is less than the sum of the respective marginal products of the individual factors times the quantities of the factors. Conversely, if e is less than 1. And, if e equals 1 (constant average unit costs), then payment of the respective marginal products to each factor just exhausts the output. Thus, equation 4 involves no overexhaustion or underexhaustion only for certain values of the variables. For practical purposes, we can identify these values as the minimum point of the U-shaped average cost curve and the entire range of constant costs.

Harvester Company. Table IV-1 shows the target at which the mechanics are aimed, then the introductory information and finally the actual result.

Table IV-1, of course, illustrates the mechanics of pricing towards a target percentage return on sales rather than towards a target percentage return on investment. The adjustment to a return on investment basis would require only the additional establishment of the investment applicable to each product and the knowledge of the inventory turn to be achieved for each product. Return on sales is, of course, linked to return on investment by the inventory turn. Thus: return on the individual sale times inventory turn equals return on in-

TABLE

Price-Cost Analysis, Representative Farm Implements

	Product A			Product B			Product C		
	Target	Intro-ductory	Actual	Target	Intro-ductory	Actual	Target	Intro-ductory	Actual
1. List Price	$592.60	$592.60	$592.60	$455.85	$455.85	$455.85	$687.40	$691.35	$691.35
2. Trade discount 23 per cent	136.30	136.30	136.30	104.85	104.85	104.85	158.10	159.00	159.00
3. Dealer price	456.30	456.30	456.30	351.00	351.00	351.00	529.30	532.35	532.35
4. Cash discount— 2 per cent	9.13	9.13	9.13	7.02	7.02	7.02	10.60	10.65	10.65
5. Net from dealer	447.17	447.17	447.17	343.98	343.98	343.98	518.70	521.70	521.70
6. Sales and administrative expense*	67.08	67.08	67.08	51.60	51.60	51.60	77.81	78.26	78.26
7. Net	380.09	380.09	380.09	292.38	292.38	292.38	440.89	443.44	443.44
8. Manufacturing cost†	270.00	274.97	359.43	214.00	217.42	232.62	380.00	395.33	462.38
9. Profit margin (dollars)	110.09	105.12	20.66	78.38	74.96	59.76	60.89	48.11	−18.94
10. Profit margin as per cent of: *a.* Manufacturing cost	40.8%	38.2%	5.7%	36.6%	34.5%	25.7%	16.0%	12.1%	−4.1%
b. Total unit cost (6) + (8)	32.6	32.5	4.8	29.1	27.9	21.0	13.3	10.2	−3.5
c. Net from dealer	24.6	23.5	4.6	22.3	21.8	17.4	11.7	9.2	−3.6

Source; A. D. H. Kaplan, J. B. Dirlam and R. F. Lanzillotti, *Pricing in Big Business, a Case Approach* (Washington, D. C.: Brookings Institution, 1958), pp. 72f.
* Allocated as normal percentage (15 per cent) of net from dealer.
† Target and introductory prices based on normal manufacturing cost, including plant overhead.

investment. Using R for return, S for sales and I for inventory, we
have said

$$\left(\frac{R}{S}\right)\left(\frac{S}{I}\right) = \frac{R}{I}$$

International Harvester has a profit target of 10 per cent after taxes
as a return on invested capital. This is, on the average, equivalent to 7
per cent on sales since the sales figure averages about 40 per cent
higher than the invested capital figure. As Table IV-1 shows, the individual products deviate from this average of 7 per cent on sales, some
products being priced to yield more and others less. These deviations

IV-1

Introduced in 1956, International Harvester Company

| | Product D | | | Product E | | | Product F | |
Target	Intro-ductory	Actual	Target	Intro-ductory	Actual	Target	Intro-ductory	Actual
$192.50	$208.70	$208.70	$354.55	$354.55	$354.55	$4,607.05	$4,609.10	$4,609.10
44.27	48.00	48.00	81.55	81.55	81.55	1,059.61	1,060.10	1,060.10
148.23	160.70	160.70	273.00	273.00	273.00	3,547.44	3,549.00	3,549.00
2.96	3.23	3.23	5.46	5.46	5.46	70.95	70.98	70.98
145.24	157.47	157.47	267.54	267.54	267.54	3,476.49	3,478.02	3,478.02
21.79	23.62	23.62	40.13	40.13	40.13	521.47	521.70	521.70
123.45	133.85	133.85	227.41	227.41	227.41	2,955.02	2,956.32	2,956.32
96.72	108.24	127.19	170.00	176.52	201.95	2,246.00	2,406.00	2,798.46
26.73	25.61	6.66	57.41	50.89	25.46	709.02	550.32	157.86
27.6%	23.7%	5.2%	33.8%	28.8%	12.6%	31.6%	22.9%	5.6%
22.6	19.4	4.4	27.3	23.5	10.5	25.6	18.8	4.7
18.4	16.3	4.2	21.5	19.0	9.5	20.0	15.8	4.5

were set by International "depending upon such factors as the competitive situation, the intricacy or originality of design, and the estimate of economic worth to the customer." Notice that the quoted language is simply another way of describing elasticity of demand and the principal factors that International considered determinative of that elasticity in the case of each individual product.

There is one additional element in the pricing process which International recognizes: the impact of the particular product upon the "full line" of products that the company offers.

The introductory price is adjusted after initial experience discloses confirmation or deviation of the conditions assumed in establishing the target. Both cost conditions and marketing conditions are checked after this initial experience.

The products reviewed in Table IV-1 show that actual costs of these products were running higher than estimated in each case. In the case of the most favorable of the products in Table IV-1, product B, International expected that the target would be achieved after some additional time in which to overcome the usual difficulties of entering a new product area. In the case of product C, however, the company decided to redesign with two objectives: cost reduction and improved product features which would support a larger volume at the target market price.

If target pricing is to be successful in assuring that actual return will approximate target return, there must be estimates of the elasticities of demand and cost plus knowledge of the conditions of entry which confront new firms. Thus, International, in making its estimates of the costs and profits margins likely to develop as to the products reported in Table IV-1, was making implicit assumptions as to the elasticities of cost and of demand and likewise as to the reactions of competitors. It is not possible from the information in Table IV-1 to identify whether the estimate of elasticity of demand, or of elasticity of cost or of the conditions of entry was primarily responsible for the deviation of actual from target returns. And if the estimates were not formally made, it is more difficult to improve future performance in achieving target returns than if the estimates had been explicit.

SHOE-PRICING ANALYSIS: DISTRIBUTED LAG

The econometric method can be applied to pricing analysis to determine what the basic pattern of price conduct of a firm or industry is. Classical economics, as we have said before, assumes that demand and supply will be adjusted through changes in price. This appears to be a realistic assumption with regard to many consumer nondurable goods in today's economy. However, in some cases of producers' goods the adjustment of quantity demanded and quantity supplied appears to occur through a lengthening of delivery time when quantity demanded increases relative to supply and conversely a shortening of delivery time when quantity demanded decreases relative to supply but with no change in price.

Similarly, the hypothesis can be advanced that price changes for a particular good are a simple reflection of cost changes with the producers adhering closely to a fixed percentage markup. An additional hypothesis can be stated that in such a case producers do not increase prices until finished inventories on hand (manufactured before the increase in costs) are exhausted. Thus if these two hypotheses were true as to a *certain* number of products in the economy, then we would have an explanation why in the 1957–1958 recession *those* prices continued to advance even though the quantity demanded was dropping. Cost increases in the case of these products prior to 1957–1958 were being "passed through" in 1957–1958.

From a microeconomic point of view, the verification of such hypotheses may have significance to the firm. If the hypotheses are true, and if the typical delay between the time of cost increase to the manufacturer and the time of price increase by the manufacturer can be measured, then a purchaser might (if he were a retailer) buy long at the lower price and secure an increase in his profit margin at a later date to the extent he had bought long. Such a purchaser would be assuming that the cost increase was to be permanent, and that the costs of carrying the inventory (such as interest, taxes, warehousing and obsolescence) would not equal the price advantage he would get by buying long.

Just such hypotheses were recently tested with respect to the hide-leather and shoe manufacturing industries by Yance[9] for the period from 1947 to 1956, and the results lend considerable support to the hypotheses. It should be noted that the discussion abstracts from the cost of changing output. The techniques used by Yance are of interest.

Assuming that there is a linear relation between the price of the

---

[9] J. V. Yance, "A Model of Price Flexibility," *American Economic Review*, vol. 50, pp. 401–418 (1960), and W. J. Yordon, Jr.: "A Model of Price Flexibility: Comment" and J. V. Yance, "Reply," both in *American Economic Review*, vol. 51 (1961), pp. 390–394. For another analysis of the hide-leather-shoe sequence see Kalman J. Cohn, *Computer Models of the Shoe, Leather, Hide Sequence* (Englewood Cliffs, N.J.: Prentice-Hall, 1960) and Ruth P. Mack: *Consumption and Business Fluctuations: A Case Study of the Shoe, Leather, Hide Sequence* (New York: National Bureau of Economic Research, 1956).

product (shoes), and the wage rate of that industry and the price of the raw material (leather), it is possible, given the price before a cost increase, to establish a "normal price" which will result from given cost increases on the hypothesis that pricing is set to maintain a constant margin. In equation form, what we are saying is that:

$$PS_t = b + cWM_t + dPL_t \qquad (1)$$

where PS_t is the normal price at a point in time, b is a constant, c is a coefficient applied to WM_t, an index of the average hourly earnings in shoe manufacturing, which timewise is associated with PS_t, and d is a coefficient applied to an index of the price of leather PL_t, which timewise is associated with PS_t.

We then have the matter of the time delay between the time of a cost increase and the following price increase. Defining the difference between the old price and the new normal price after the cost increase as a price gap, Yance tested the hypothesis that the increase in the price of shoes per period of time consequent upon a cost increase would be a constant percentage per period of time of the "unclosed" price gap at the start of each period of time. This percentage Yance established as 19 per cent per month in the case of shoes. This is illustrated in Figure IV-6. In equation form, the price at the end of any month after a cost increase can be expected to be:

$$P_t = P_{t-1} + a(PS - P_{t-1}) \qquad (2)$$

where P_t is the price at the end of any month after a cost increase, P_{t-1} is the price at the end of the previous month, a is the constant percentage of the remaining price gap between the normal price PS and the closing price of the preceding period P_{t-1}.

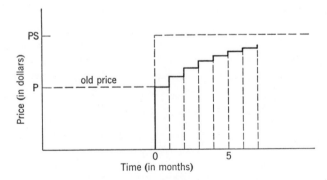

Figure IV-6. Shoe pricing model assuming constant rate per period of adjustment of price to cost increase.

This simple response mechanism has been used by Chenery with respect to the response of investment to demand,[10] by Lintner with respect to the response of dividends to profits and by Nerlove with respect to the response of agricultural supply to prices.[11] Another simple statement of the mechanism appears in a study by Griliches on the demand for fertilizer.[12]

In the case of the price of a commodity, this hypothesis that price change follows cost change is in conflict with the usual presentation of classical economics. In orthodox theory, particularly, after an industry has reached capacity, the hypothesis is that any further increase in quantity demanded will be equilibrated with existing capacity through price adjustment. But our hypothesis is that in the case of durable goods this equilibrating at capacity may rather come through a lengthening of delivery time. Lengthening the delivery period and raising prices are alternatives. The cost of changing the rate of output and the cost of holding inventories will enter the analysis if their relative quantitative amounts are significant.

There is another use to which the proposed model might be put, namely, to measure the degree of price flexibility in an industry. Thus the larger the value of the term a in the equation, $P_t = P_{t-1} + a(PS - P_{t-1})$, the quicker price adjustments take place and the greater the degree of price flexibility in the industry.

To establish a scale for comparing various a values, such as 19 per cent per month with say 40 per cent per month, Yance has shown that a can be translated into the *average* delay in months that a price change occurring at 19 per cent per month or 40 per cent per month requires. This is done by the formula:[13]

$$\text{Average delay in time units} = \left(\frac{1}{a} - 1\right)$$

Thus in the case of an a of 0.19, the average delay in transmitting a cost increase to the expected price increase is 4.3 months. Or in the case of an a of 0.11, 9 months and with an a of 0.5, 1 month.

[10] H. B. Chenery, "Overcapacity and the Acceleration Principle," *Econometrica*, vol. 20, pp. 1–18 (1952).

[11] J. B. Lintner, "Distribution of Incomes of Corporations Among Dividends, Retained Earnings and Taxes," *American Economic Review Proceedings*, vol. 46, pp. 97–113 (1956) and Marc Nerlove, "Estimates of the Elasticities of Supply Selected Agricultural Commodities," *Journal of Farm Economics*, vol. 38, pp. 496–509 (1956).

[12] Zvi Griliches, "The Demand for Fertilizer: An Economic Interpretation of a Technical Change," *Journal of Farm Economics*, vol. 40, pp. 591–606 (1958).

[13] The proof that average delay and a are related as indicated by this formula is set out in the appendix of the Yance reference (footnote 9).

METHOD OF ESTIMATING COEFFICIENTS
AND CONSTANTS

In estimating the coefficients in the first equation above, $PS = b + cWM + dPL$, Yance avoided the process of determining PS from eq. 2 directly. He avoided this method because it assumes successive prices are independent of each other, whereas it is likely there is a high degree of correlation between successive values of prices.

Instead, Yance chose to use differences in the second equation, (where there would be no correlation between successive values of these differences) and then to substitute for PS in the second equation the value of PS as defined by the first equation. Thus the second equation becomes (if we move one term from the right hand side of equation 2 to the left hand side):

$$P_t - P_{t-1} = a(PS - P_{t-1}) \tag{3}$$

and if we substitute the value of PS in equation (1) and write $P_t - P_{t-1}$ as ΔP_t

$$\Delta P_t = a[(b + cWM_t + dPL_t) - P_{t-1}]$$

and multiply out the right-hand side

$$\Delta P_t = ab + acWM_t + adPL_t - aP_{t-1} \tag{4}$$

Then the estimates can be made as follows: the coefficient of P_{t-1} in eq. 4 gives the estimate of a. When this estimate of a is divided into the other terms: ab, $acWM_t$ and $adPL_t$, the estimates of each of the other coefficients (b, c, and d) are obtained.

Yance performed a regression computation[14] for eq. 4 above using data over a period of 10 years, (120 months):

$$\Delta P_t = ab + acWM_t + adPL - aP_{t-1}$$

and obtained these values:

$$\Delta P_t = -1.81 + 12.1WM_t + 0.084PL_t - 0.19P_{t-1}; \; R^2 = 0.41; \; n = 119. \tag{5}$$

The series used in the regression computation are:[15]

ΔP_t = change in price index of shoes from prior month
WM_t = average hourly earnings in shoe manufacturing by months
PL_t = price index of leather by months
P_{t-1} = price index of shoes in preceding month

[14] Note that this relationship can be fitted graphically (additive form) by procedures we have already discussed in Part I.

[15] All series are Bureau of Labor Statistics figures as they appear in National Shoe Manufacturers Association, *Facts and Figures on Footwear*, 13th ed., New York, 1961.

The coefficient of P_{t-1} from the above regression value establishes a as 0.19. If a is 0.19, then the average delay in price response is 4.3 months (by substituting in $\frac{1}{a} - 1$.)

With a as 0.19, we obtain the coefficients (in eq. 5) by dividing each of the terms, $-1.81 + 12.1WM_t$ and $+0.084PL_t$, by the a value of 0.19. The result is the predicting equation: $PS_t = -9.5 + 63.5WM_t + 0.44PL_t$.

With this predicting equation (to determine the expected new or normal price after a cost change), Yance was able to compare the normal price so predicted with the actual prices during the period 1947 to 1956 and thus to show the delay of actual prices graphically. This is shown in Figure IV-7.

The graph in Figure IV-7 is not intended to show goodness of fit, which would involve plotting the model-generated price (*after adjustment for the delayed reaction* of actual price to cost change) and the plotting of actual prices. A graph of goodness of fit would involve shifting the normal price (solid line in Figure IV-7) to the right by four months.

Examination of Figure IV-7 shows that the predicting equation predicts directional changes quite well, working both as to cost increases and cost decreases.

Yance applied the same technique to the leather industry and the

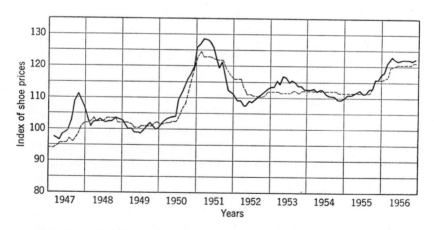

Figure IV-7. Equilibrium (solid line) and actual (broken line) shoe prices. Equation for equilibrium price: $PS_t = -9.5 + 63.5WM_t + 0.44PL_t$. Source for actual prices: United States Wholesale Shoe Price Index, 1947–1949 = 100. From *The American Economic Review,* vol. 50 (June 1960), p. 405.

resulting average time delay (between hide price change or leather labor price change and leather price change) was 1.1 months. The predicting equation in the case of leather prices gave a somewhat better relation to the actual leather prices than is true in the shoe price model. In the case of leather, the time period for the price reaction consequent upon a cost change in short by comparison with a longer period in the case of shoes (1.1 months for leather compared to 4.3 months for shoes). This result is consistent with a proposition that seems to exist in some industries, namely that the nearer to the consumer the industry is, the longer the period for cost changes to be transmitted to price changes. Several possible explanations exist for this phenomenon. Industries closer to the consumer may carry relatively larger inventories of finished stock, thus enabling such industries to delay the price changes while such inventories last. Or, it may be that the closer the industry is to the consumer the less competitive the industry and the more oligopolistic practices exist as would be suggested by "sticky prices." Sufficient evidence is, however, lacking.

PUBLIC-UTILITY PRICING AS AN EXAMPLE OF TARGET PRICING

Regulated industries such as public utilities are a relatively small segment of total business. They are special situations because of the quasi-monopoly status they enjoy and conversely because of the limitations imposed by the regulation of governmental agencies.

However, because of the public records they are required to file and the (recently) frequent rate increase cases in which they have been involved, public utilities furnish excellent sources for data from which to examine the effects of different pricing practices.

There are definite indications today that the basic postulate of utility rate regulation (that profit allowed a utility must be related to the investment and risk) is also the starting point in pricing in much nonregulated business. One logical reason why business often follows this approach to pricing[16] lies in the rapid development of capital budgeting. Under capital budgeting, investment decisions are based upon comparative rates of return. Thus a substantial analogy to utilities in their approach to pricing questions exists if one makes capital budgeting basic to general business decisions.

Two pairs of conflicting principles have received considerable attention in public utility pricing. The first conflict is whether rate of

---

[16] Strict adherence to this principle can raise problems under anti-trust law where tendency to monopoly or restraining trade are questions.

return will be determined on a company-wide basis, that is, the total allowable return determined against the total investment of the public utility or whether each segment of a public utility (such as an individual telephone exchange) is to have its return determined against the investment in that segment, thus making each segment of a public utility in effect a little company by itself. Each segment must then "stand on its own feet." This conflict goes under the label "company-wide versus unit rate making." At the present time, the great preponderance of regulating bodies favors the company-wide approach.

The second conflict is between the *value of service* and the *cost of service* principles. Once the allowed rate of return on the investment of a utility has been determined, under either of the company-wide or unit principles, how should prices be set to produce this rate of return which at this point is actually an allowed *amount* of profit? The value of service principle would base prices on the value of each type of service to each group of customers. This is a vague concept and came into use before much of modern economic analysis had developed.[17] To the extent it can be translated into modern terms, value of service refers to the average revenue (price) which is needed to retain the great bulk of *current* customers. Thus in telephone rates, charges for business phones are consistently higher than charges for the same type of service for a residential subscriber. This is justified by the proposition that the service is worth more to the businessman. The *cost of service* principle would price each service to cover its average cost *at the current volume* plus a profit with the profit dependent on the amount and risk of the investment in that type of service. These two principles have been stated in their "pure" form. Various modifications of the definition of each principle have been made in practice by regulatory agencies.

It should not be thought that the cost of service principle (analogous to pricing under the theory of pure competition) is to be preferred *a priori* to the value of service principle (analogous to pure monopoly

---

[17] The situation we are discussing here is an excellent illustration of one of the objectives of the study of managerial economics: to develop skill in the ability to translate modern economic analysis into terms that are understandable to those who have grown up in the jargon of the market place (or here, the jargon of public utility rate cases, which is ancient and widespread in use). Those who have participated in public utility rate cases understand the crying need for a "translator" who can express the ideas of modern economic analysis in the jargon of the trade. Inability to do this translation job means that the modern economist often is talking to himself and his colleagues. To complain that what is needed is to educate everyone in modern economic analysis is to defer for large areas the date when modern economic analysis may become effective.

pricing). There is respectable authority (Cambridge Professor A. C. Pigou in his *Economics of Welfare*) that monopoly with attendant extensive price discrimination may be socially preferable under given conditions by comparison to pure competition.

Thus in the case of price discrimination under decreasing costs, the society as a whole would be benefitted by a lower per unit cost (as shown in Figure IV-5) and the fact that this industry might not be able to exist under purely competitive conditions because it could not make a profit. But this industry can exist under price discrimination which results in a volume of output greater than pure competition. This is so because one part of the market which is willing to pay a higher price is sold at that higher price, thus enabling the producer to charge the other part (or parts) of the market a lower price (or prices) and still make a better profit than if the producer had to sell *all* the market at the same price. Likewise, it can be shown that a greater consumers' surplus[18] results. In short, the extra profit (compared to a lower monopoly price but with one price for all) from the first market in this sorting out of markets, enables the producer to seek less profit for the remaining units sold in the remaining markets.[19]

With the decision of the *Hope* case[20] by the United States Supreme Court in 1944, it became apparent that regulatory commissions would be free from proceeding on any specific theory in establishing rates. Prior to this decision some state legislatures had enacted laws requiring that regulatory agencies use a specific theory, namely, fair return on fair value because it was thought that the Constitution required this.[21] In the *Hope* case it was recognized that fair return on fair value involves circular reasoning since the value depends on the return allowed. Those states which had felt restricted by the fair return or fair value rule are free (since 1944) to enact other legislation. Reduced to a simple proposition the only rule[22] that a state must observe is that there be a fair balancing of the interests of the customers of the utility against the interests of the investors in the utility. No specific

[18] Consumers' surplus is defined as the excess of the price a consumer is willing to pay for a product over the price he is charged for the product.

[19] In the present discussion we have been assuming the comparability of different individuals as to their satisfactions from given goods. This is another area called "welfare economics," which we do not have the space to explore, that proceeds without this assumption in many cases.

[20] *Federal Power Commission v. Hope Natural Gas Co.*, 320 U.S. 591 (1944).

[21] *Smyth v. Ames*, 169 U.S. 466 (1898), modified in 171 U.S. 361 (1898).

[22] There are, of course, rules of procedure which must be observed. We are speaking here only of the substantive rule of the law. Rules of procedure concern such matters as fair notice of the hearing, opportunity to be heard, etc.

method of doing this is required. Since regulatory agencies are now free to balance the interests of the various groups concerned, pricing the services may involve the use of either or both the value and cost of service principles. Prior to the *Hope* case, many regulatory agencies insisted on cost of service as the only basis for determining rates, unless it could be shown that the value of the service (remember as we have already indicated, this term means a price that the current number of customers are willing to pay) was below cost. In such instances prices were based on the value of this particular service.

It is clear that prices based on value of service may be above or below cost. Under circumstances where the value of service is below cost, prices may be used to accomplish many purposes, such as encouraging a more rapid extension of the service, or promoting the use of new appliances or to encourage substitution of one utility service for another. In most of such programs the prime objective is to increase the load factor[23] and thus eventually to lower average costs and prices to all consumers.

The public utility cases which follow illustrate the methods used by regulatory commissions in determining whether a utility's price is fair and reasonable. Note in these cases that while expenses are carefully scrutinized, the regulatory agency is primarily concerned with the capital invested in property and plant, and the necessary working capital, and with a fair rate of return on this capital investment.

Many firms in other areas use this same basic procedure under certain circumstances. A price leader for example, such as U.S. Steel, General Motors, or Alcoa, is often interested in some target return on investment. Pricing therefore proceeds from costs to ultimate price targets. Another reason why these firms use this approach is to prove to government investigators that prices charged (whether or not these prices actually were based on costs) yield only a fair return on the capital invested. A second use of this kind of procedure is to determine, if and when the value of the service is below cost, whether the production of such services has any indirect value which may promote the overall welfare of the business and thus justify such pricing. For example, the desire to maintain a full line service, or product, or to use idle capacity, or to keep a good labor force intact, or the feeling that eventually the product will be able to bear its full costs and similar possibilities, may cause a firm to continue to pro-

---

[23] Load factor, strictly speaking, is the ratio between the average output to the peak output of a system. However we are using the term in its more popular sense, namely, as the ratio of what the present plant is handling to what it could handle with only small additions at certain points.

duce a product or render a service even though full costs are not currently being covered. While many firms often render services which do not return full costs because they do not know what these costs are, in this study we are concerned only with calculations in which full costs are determined and then because of market conditions the firm or regulatory body knowingly deviates in pricing from those costs having definite objectives in mind.

A third reason for studying public utility pricing is that since agencies that regulate public utilities have set certain standard methods for determining when prices are fair, other regulatory agencies which deal with business find it relatively easy to insist that private industries present similar data in justifying their prices and profits. In such instances if management has a clear conception of the meaning of cost and value of service and their possible uses, prices which otherwise might seem to be unfair or discriminatory may be justified.

The public, moreover, often has the mistaken notion that value of service (the highest price that the great bulk of current users are willing to pay) of every product is about its cost, and that utilities and especially leading industries can always secure a price that is above full cost. There is, for example, the slogan, "charging what the traffic will bear," which originated during the late 1880's and 1890's when trusts were being formed. This slogan carries the implication that the public is being forced to pay exorbitant prices. While it is true that in many instances and times, the value of service (as we have defined that term) is above the average unit cost at the current volume, it is also true that for many products and services, especially in some important areas, value of service is below cost. One need only look at the farm situation to see that the attempt to keep prices at full cost of production *for all those presently in farming* has created great surpluses. Here the value of what is produced, units of output times the unit price that will move the volume produced, is below the cost of production for the volume being produced. There are many other areas in which similar conditions prevail.

A fourth reason for studying public utility pricing and securing a clear understanding of the terms cost versus value of service as those terms are used for pricing purposes relates to the issue of discriminatory pricing. In general the courts have ruled that prices are discriminatory if the net return to the company for the same product or service from various customers is not equal. This general rule is modified in many ways but for the purpose of understanding pricing by firms, we may assume that any deviation from the net return equality standard may bring the company's pricing policy to the attention of regulatory commissions.

Decisions by the court relative to basing points are a case in point. While in theory the idea is F.O.B. mill prices shall prevail, such pricing would run counter to the principle of company-wide rates in public utilities. In the industry sector, common prices often result because of competition. Congress has recognized this point[24] and has qualified full cost as a basis for determining whether or not prices are discriminatory by stating that it is only unlawful to discriminate in price between different purchasers of commodities (*Clayton Act,* Sec. 2) where the effect may be to substantially lessen competition or to tend to create a monopoly in any line of commerce. The law further provides that this does not apply to discrimination "on account of differences in the grade, quality, quantity of the commodity sold," which make only due allowances for differences in the cost of selling or transportation. It further allows price discrimination, "made in good faith to meet competition."

Here then are the broad areas, within which any firm which has some ability to determine market prices is able to adjust its prices between the limits of value of service and cost of service as the terms have been defined. Cost of service is treated as a norm and prices may deviate either above or below full costs depending on the relation of cost and value of service.

With these introductory comments in mind, we shall first analyze certain utility cases to discover procedures used in utility pricing and reasons given for deviating from full cost. Once these principles and reasons are fully understood, we can study pricing in industry. We must realize that, while public utilities generally have a monopoly of one distinct service, they may not be free of the necessity of competing with effective substitutes in all or in many of their uses. It is in these competitive areas that value of the service becomes significant as a pricing policy.

[24] Further elaboration of anti-trust legislation will be found in Part V.

CASE IV-1. COMMUNITY TELEPHONE COMPANY*

Pricing Analysis—Public Utility Pricing

Community Telephone Co. is a small utility operating thirty-one exchanges all within Wisconsin and serving a total of 11,292 stations. In 1948, the company applied for an increase in rates. The company's exchanges are widely scattered but fall into four groups: one near the southern border of Wisconsin (Rock and Walworth counties), one in central Wisconsin, one along the east side of the Mississippi River in the central part of the state, and one in the north central part of the state. At this time, the largest exchange (Black River Falls) had 1,000 stations.

These four groups were amalgamated by purchase with the purchasing company paying $190,059 more than the original cost of the properties in the hands of the original utilities. Beginning in 1941, the Wisconsin Commission ordered this amount amortized by 1961 by an annual write off of $9,503 so that no earnings would be made on the $190,059. The $9,503 is treated as an operating expense.

The financial structure in 1948 showed

1st Mortgage Bonds — 6% due 1949	$525,000
Common Stock	410,700
Recorded surplus	56,039
Total	$991,739

Exhibit I shows the rate base for each exchange. The rate base is the original cost of the plant less accrued depreciation and plus an allocable share of working capital, supplies and materials. In utility rates, the term "working capital" is not used in the usual sense of current assets minus current liabilities but in the sense of the difference in time between payments by customers and payments to suppliers.

In addition, Exhibit I shows by exchanges the operating revenues and operating expenses (including depreciation) and the net income. The principal difference between (a) operating revenues less operating expenses and (b) net income is income taxes. Net income is then shown as a per cent return on the rate base.

Exhibit I then shows the net income after the increase allowed by the Commission and the per cent return. This is on the rate base. Then follows the monthly charge which will yield the increased net income.

*Based on the record in Decision 2-V-2608 by the Wisconsin Public Service Commission. Reported in 34 Public Service Commission of Wisconsin 133 (1949).

The monthly charge shown is for one-party residential service. This is a valid index of other charges which are in a standard ratio to this rate.

Study of Exhibit I shows:

1. The Commission in every instance has ordered rates which will yield 6.5 per cent (with allowance for rounding in the rate) on the rate base of each exchange.

2. Two rates were cut while 24 were raised even though the over-all earnings were raised from $12,300 to $55,735 or from 1.43 per cent to 6.5 per cent.

3. The result of this pricing approach has been that the monthly charge varies from a low of $1.50 in Darien to a high of $3.60 in Glenwood City and Centerville.

4. All of the thirty-one exchanges are very close to each other in population size and in many states the Commission would have applied the same telephone rates throughout. This would assume a value of service approach.

Questions

1. Would this system of pricing be sound for a nonutility business? (Remember that there are different "grades" of service available to a telephone subscriber.) What factors would be determinative?

2. If there were differences in risk of investment at the different exchanges, how should this be handled? (Remember that there are four isolated areas involved here.)

3. The case states that these exchanges are comparable in size, namely from 0-1,000. Can you account for the wide range in income between exchanges? First take gross income and then net income.

4. Compare the rates charged with the rate of return. Any comment?

5. The Commission increased or decreased rates on the basis of present use, that is, it assumed the same use would be made in 1949 and later years as in 1948. Comment.

Exchange	Number of Stations*	Rate Base	Operating Revenue	Operating Expense
Alma Center	396	$ 25,839	$ 9,514	$ 9,147
Arcadia	970	76,409	23,736	25,117
Black River Falls	1863	81,521	39,717	36,948
Blair	472	26,060	11,271	10,360
Boyceville	328	14,331	6,848	5,470
Centerville	256	21,765	5,532	6,578
Clinton	883	43,954	23,949	22,947
Colfax	483	32,874	13,089	11,317
Darien	490	19,829	13,340	9,832
Elk Mound	208	13,504	5,920	5,334
Elmwood	354	19,095	8,558	8,151
Ettrick	416	23,617	9,056	7,790
Fairchild	252	12,717	6,569	5,243
Galesville	777	45,256	18,031	19,291
Glenwood City	635	44,772	14,977	18,237
Hixton	221	10,657	5,133	4,511
Knapp	155	8,177	3,489	3,262
Maiden Rock	169	10,954	4,067	4,415
Melrose	351	25,726	8,294	7,570
Merrillan	154	10,092	3,712	2,771
Osseo	586	29,893	14,326	11,891
Pepin	272	14,055	5,284	4,916
Plum City	201	9,003	3,602	4,147
Prescott	538	24,215	11,344	10,888
Taylor	186	12,721	5,239	4,960
Trempealean	230	10,904	5,623	4,259
Walworth	1623	55,332	42,850	33,439
Wautoma	1028	41,855	23,350	21,971
Westfield	558	46,782	17,012	14,019
Wheeler	104	9,607	3,244	3,264
Whitehall	657	36,581	16,494	16,602
Total (or Average)		$858,097	$383,170	$354,707

* Number of stations as of December 31, 1957. The earlier date of the CASE has little effect on the validity of these data.

Notes:
1. Operating revenue less operating expense gives operating income (not shown).

EXHIBIT I

Company, 1948

Net Operating Income After Tax	Return on Base	Net Income After Commission Increase	Return on Base	Rate One-Party Residential Before Increase	Rate One-Party Residential After Increase
$ (427)	(1.65)%	$ 1,680	6.50%	$1.75	$2.60
(4,417)	(5.78)	4,990	6.53	2.00	3.25
1,761	2.16	5,295	6.50	2.00	2.70
162	0.62	1,692	6.49	2.00	2.65
1,062	7.41	936	6.53	2.00	2.55
(351)	(1.61)	1,305	6.00	2.00	3.60
355	0.81	2,843	6.47	1.75	2.60
1,190	3.62	2,137	6.50	2.00	2.80
3,497	17.64	1,323	6.67	1.75	1.50
327	2.42	877	6.49	2.00	3.00
744	3.90	1,237	6.48	1.50	2.25
(106)	(0.45)	1,535	6.50	2.00	2.70
609	4.79	831	6.53	1.75	1.85
(3,613)	(7.98)	2,964	6.55	2.00	3.20
(3,142)	(7.02)	2,904	6.49	2.25	3.60
141	1.32	689	6.47	1.75	2.30
143	1.75	531	6.49	2.00	3.10
(192)	(1.75)	718	6.55	1.50	2.45
(606)	(2.36)	1,676	6.51	1.75	2.80
658	6.52	657	6.51	1.75	1.95
1,554	5.20	1,946	6.51	2.00	2.30
(82)	(0.60)	909	6.47	1.50	2.45
(365)	(4.05)	584	6.49	1.50	2.55
1,141	4.71	1,573	6.50	1.70	2.05
95	0.75	825	6.49	1.75	2.40
1,242	11.39	706	6.47	2.00	1.95
8,949	16.17	3,594	6.50	2.50	2.40
634	1.51	2,730	6.52	2.25	2.80
2,775	5.93	3,044	6.51	2.00	2.70
(26)	(0.27)	621	6.46	2.00	3.40
(1,410)	(3.85)	2,383	6.51	2.00	2.95
$12,300	1.43%	$55,735	6.50%		

2. Operating income (not shown) less income tax (not shown) gives net operating income.

3. In the case of those exchanges having a negative operating income, there is a reduction of this loss by an income tax *credit*. This makes the column totals tie together with the figures for each exchange.

CASE IV-2. NORTH-WEST TELEPHONE COMPANY*
Price Analysis—Public Utility Pricing

North-West Telephone Co. is a smaller utility operating in south central Wisconsin. It serves a total of nineteen telephone exchanges with a combined total of 17,255 stations in 1947.

Using the actual cost of property when acquired less depreciation, North-West had a 1947 rate base of $804,966. This includes allowance for working capital and materials and supplies. The operating revenues in 1947 totalled $438,029 and operating expenses $406,083. The net income after taxes totalled $22,497 or a return of 2.79 per cent. The utility petitioned for an increase in rates in 1948 to increase the rate of return to 6.7 per cent.

The financial structure of the company in 1948 is:

3% bonds	$225,000
3.5% bonds	70,000
2.75% bonds	138,000
Common Stock and surplus	437,384
	$870,384

Exhibit I shows the rate base for each exchange. This base is the original cost of the plant less accrued depreciation and plus allowance for working capital, supplies and materials. It also shows existing operating revenues and expenses, together with net operating income after taxes and the return which this is on the base of each exchange.

Exhibit I then shows the effect of the rate increase sought by the company at each exchange upon the net operating income after taxes at that exchange together with the rate of return which such income is on the base of each exchange. The increase in net operating revenue sought by the company from the current $22,497 per year to $53,902 comes to 6.7 per cent on the total company base.

The last columns show the monthly rates set by the commission for one-party residential service (other service being in standard ratio to one-party residential). These rates are so set as to yield a return of $51,075 or 6.52 per cent on the total company base and at the same time a deviation of ±0.7 per cent in the rate of return on the base for each exchange will account for all but four of the nineteen exchanges. The range of monthly rates is from a low of $2.10 at Ripon (the

* Based on the record in Decision 2-U-2636 by the Wisconsin Public Service Commission. Reported in 33 P.S.C.W. 347, 76 Public Utility Reports, New Series 23 (1948).

largest exchange) to a high of $3.50 at Tomah (the second largest exchange). Elimination of the losses in return at Trego and Wild Rose would have required rates above the value of the service.

In most states, the commission would have established the over-all rate of return and then permitted the company to set rates at individual exchanges at its discretion. Under this condition, most telephone companies would price the monthly rate by upward steps corresponding to the number of subscribers in the exchange. The proportion of rates to number of subscribers would not be exact but it would follow the value of service principle.

Questions

1. To what extent was the value of service rather than cost of service used in this case?
2. Notice the capital structure of this company. On the basis of a 6.52 per cent return, what is the return on common stock? Does this appear to be a fair return?
3. Notice that while Tomah has a larger rate base than Ripon, operating revenues are higher in Ripon while the rate is lower than Tomah. Does this not show that a low rate brings greater revenue? In other words, does it not appear that a rate of $3.50 per month in Tomah is above the value of the service and should not the Commission have inquired into the difference?
4. Notice that Trego and Wild Rose are being served at a loss. What do you make of this and what would you propose should be done in these villages?
5. If this were a private firm, would you serve all customers at a common rate? If you did, would this be discriminating?

Exchange	Number of Stations	Rate Base	Operating Revenue	Operating Expense	Net Operating Income After Tax
Boyd	221	$ 8,789	$ 4,943	$ 3,885	$ 745
Cadott	404	21,604	10,325	7,565	1,944
Chetek	807	32,564	17,939	20,935	(2,110)
De Forest	924	38,052	20.091	21,511	(1,000)
Delafield	1,055	47,875	23,352	18,535	3,392
Dousman	530	18,663	11,658	10,386	896
Eagle	424	21,134	13,035	11,462	1,108
East Troy	1,483	59,419	35,835	32,462	2,375
Genesee Depot	590	38,073	22,929	21,064	1,314
LaGrange	187	17,379	6,288	3,952	1,645
Mukwonago	1,030	35,812	23,387	22,170	857
Palmyra	607	32,282	16,082	19,911	(697)
Poynette	817	47,225	20,642	22,339	(1,195)
Ripon	3,062	135,984	97,183	78,865	12,900
Spooner	1,387	52,509	30,489	27,948	1,790
Tomah	2,839	148,850	61,418	57,913	2,468
Trego	68	3,273	1,731	2,537	(568)
Wild Rose	350	17,272	8,756	11,860	(2,186)
Wonewoc	470	28,207	11,946	10,783	819
Total (or Average)	17,255	$804,966	$438,029	$406,083	$22,497

Notes:
1. Operating revenue less operating expense gives operating income (not shown).
2. Operating income (not shown) less income tax (not shown) gives net operating income.

EXHIBIT I

Company, 1947

1947 Return on Base	Net Income from Company Proposed Increase	Company- Proposed Return	Net Income Allowed by Com- mission Increase	Commission- Allowed Return	Rate 1-Party Resi- dential Before Increase	1-Party Resi- dential After Increase
8.48%	$ 902	8.60%	$ 623	7.09%	$2.50	$2.40
9.00	2,107	9.75	1,522	7.04	2.50	2.35
(6.48)	1,460	4.48	1,671	5.13	2.25	3.30
(2.63)	2,344	6.16	2,682	7.05	1.50	3.00
7.09	3,652	7.63	3,387	7.07	2.00	2.15
4.80	1,851	9.92	1,347	7.22	2.00	2.40
5.24	1,763	8.34	1,507	7.13	2.00	2.35
4.00	4,950	8.33	4,236	7.13	2.00	2.50
3.45	2,313	6.07	2,701	7.00	2.00	2.60
9.47	1,833	10.55	1,254	7.22	2.00	2.25
2.39	2,869	8.01	2,576	7.19	2.00	2.50
(8.35)	(1,238)	(3.83)	88	0.27	2.00	3.30
(2.53)	2,169	4.59	3,237	6.85	1.50	3.00
9.49	16,016	11.78	9,702	7.13	2.25	2.10
3.41	4,415	8.41	3,721	7.09	2.00	2.50
1.66	6,567	4.41	9,680	6.50	2.50	3.50
(17.35)	(211)	(6.44)	(225)	(6.87)	1.50	2.45
(12.66)	(989)	(5.72)	(626)	(3.62)	2.00	3.30
2.90	1.275	4.52	1,991	7.06	2.25	2.85
2.79	$53,902	6.70	$51,075	6.52		

3. If an exchange has a negative operating income, there is a reduction of this loss by an income tax credit. This makes the column totals tie together with each exchange.

CASE IV-3. WISCONSIN TELEPHONE COMPANY (A)*

Price Analysis—Public Utility Pricing

Wisconsin Telephone Co. is a large utility serving seventy-eight exchanges with some 600,000 stations in 1947. It is a wholly owned subsidiary of American Telephone and Telegraph, financed entirely by common stock. The Commission on November 7, 1947 permitted an interim rate increase to go into effect. This rate increase of $6,359,000 was calculated to allow a return of 4.45 per cent. The interim schedule was subject to possible refunds. One of the reasons for this interim order was the complexity of the case. Another was that between one third and one half of the stations were to be converted from manual to dial operation in the 5 years beginning with 1947. Large savings were expected from conversion. Some experience with dial conversion and its effects would enable the Commission to set rates more accurately and tend to reduce the work of any later proceeding to make adjustments.

This case presented some severe tests for the principle of setting rates to reflect cost differences in the various exchanges. It is obvious that the costs in an exchange converted to dial operation in the 1930's would be radically different from those of one converted in the late 1940's. The extremes in size of exchange and their consequent cost differences are reflected in Table I.

A *Separations Manual* exists for the telephone industry under which interstate business which is subject to regulation by the Federal Communications Commission is separated from intrastate business which is regulated by the states. This manual covers the separation of revenues, expenses and plant. By analogy the manual is used to separate intrastate exchange and intrastate toll business.

The total plant in service allocable to intrastate exchange business as determined under the manual was $104,670,000 at the end of 1948. The segment of depreciation reserve allocable to intrastate business was $42,081,000, of which $11,465,000 was allocable to intrastate toll business. Thus separating intrastate toll from intrastate exchange business by analogous use of the manual gave an intrastate exchange plant net of $74,054,000. The intrastate exchange net income for the

---

*Based on the record in Decision 2-U-2292 by the Wisconsin Public Service Commission. Interim decision in 32 P.S.C.W. 248 (1947) not reported in P.U.R. Final decision in 34 P.S.C.W. 311 (1949), 80 P.U.R. (N.S.) 482 and refund order in 36 P.S.C.W. 113 (1951), 88 P.U.R. (N.S.) 89.

Case IV-3. TABLE I

Expense, Investment, Revenue, and Profit of 78 Exchanges of Wisconsin Telephone Company Classified by Size of Exchange

Number of Exchanges Classified by Number of Stations	Annual Operating Expenses Per Station	Investment Per Station	Company Proposed Revenue Per Station	Profit or Loss Per Station
26 Group A 0–800	$30.34	$107.00	$29.07	$(1.27)
32 Group B 801–2000	32.55	91.00	33.70	1.15
17 Group C 2001–7000	38.37	111.00	41.43	3.06
9 Group D 7001–15,000	41.79	129.00	45.05	3.26
2 Group E 15,001–25,000	55.78	133.00	54.59	(1.19)
1 Madison 32,140	71.79	165.00	63.11	(8.68)
1 Milwaukee 225,229	71.55	215.00	79.29	7.74

year ending December 31, 1948 was $2,402,352 or 3.42 per cent on the net plant (but with no allowance for working capital or supplies).

To allow for dial conversion effects, a pro forma estimate of the next 5 years was established. This estimate makes allowance for working capital and supplies and restoration of plant capacity margins:

Estimated Rate Base Intrastate Exchange

1948	$ 75,494,626
1949	93,384,790
1950	108,449,190
1951	118,205,225
1952	127,337,225
5-year average	104,974,178

Net rate bases for intrastate exchange business were then established for each exchange on a 5-year average basis. These showed that current rates of return varied from a high of 6.37 per cent for the Milwaukee group to a low of −9.94 per cent for Washburn and only 22 of the seventy-seven exchanges showed a profit. The company-wide return would be $4,253,000 on the base of $104,974,000 or 4.05 per cent.

The Commission allowed the company a return of 5.65 per cent on the rate base of $104,974,000 or an increase in net operating income (after taxes) of $1,676,188.

Exhibit I shows the rate base (original cost less accrued depreciation and plus working capital, supplies and materials) for each exchange. Under Wisconsin law, grouping of exchanges is permitted where there

CASE IV-3.

Data Pertinent to Wisconsin Telephone

Exchange	Rate Base 1948–1952 Average	Gross Revenue Present Rates 1948–1952	Net Operating Income After Taxes	Rate of Return Before Increase	Net Operating Income After Allowed Increase	Rate of Return After Increase
Algoma	$ 105,190	$ 36,219	$ (1,515)	(1.44)%	$ 3,488	3.32%
Appelton group	4,740,447	1,289,194	147,633	3.11	281,865	5.95
Ashland	537,473	148,542	(4,352)	(0.81)	16,190	3.01
Baraboo group	287,573	134,021	(2,210)	(0.77)	16,783	5.84
Bayfield	40,267	113,431	(1,093)	(2.71)	958	2.38
Beaver Dam	641,017	175,506	440	0.07	25,759	4.02
Beloit	1,492,493	567,554	(42,320)	(2.84)	24,521	1.64
Berlin	135,483	52,615	(5,869)	(4.33)	2,805	2.07
Burlington	275,229	107,788	1,894	0.69	11,048	4.01
Burnett	32,620	4,752	(754)	(3.33)	(130)	(0.57)
Cedarburg	249,914	67,456	416	0.17	9,440	3.78
Columbus	176,723	55,497	(12,360)	(6.99)	(3,896)	(2.20)
Cornell	59,420	15,261	(552)	(0.93)	1,384	2.33
Darlington group	326,728	52,625	(14,816)	(4.53)	(5,987)	(1.83)
Delavan	277,417	93,850	(6,815)	(2.46)	6,266	2.26
Eau Claire group	2,761,504	843,769	105,669	3.83	184,235	6.67
Ellsworth	167,674	37,198	(9,169)	(5.47)	(3,695)	(2.20)
Evansville	135,349	43,003	(6,715)	(4.96)	311	0.23
Fond du Lac	1,480,758	557,689	11,332	0.76	83,106	5.61
Fort Atkinson	404,692	122,380	(7,225)	(1.79)	9,950	2.46
Genoa City	138,838	26,132	(4,483)	(3.23)	(1,599)	(1.15)
Green Bay group	3,324,438	1,096,264	11,351	0.34	169,520	5.10
Green Lake	79,995	20,192	(1,073)	(1.34)	2,009	2.51
Hartford	180,013	59,018	(4,356)	(2.42)	6,122	3.40
Hartland	134,541	34,068	462	0.34	4,876	3.62
Horicon	105,214	27,020	(2,793)	(2.65)	1,107	1.05
Hortonville	76,615	19,025	(1,047)	(1.37)	1,549	2.02
Hudson	208,521	49,140	(5,787)	(2.78)	2,031	0.97
Hurley	173,017	31,886	(6,146)	(3.55)	1,831	1.06
Janesville	1,493,108	468,246	42,678	2.86	97,528	6.53
Jefferson	151,726	50,983	(6,219)	(4.10)	1,796	1.18
Juneau	101.835	24,269	(2,206)	(2.17)	1,038	1.02
Kenosha	2,664,210	860,666	133,112	5.00	166,210	6.24
Kewaunee	95,527	42,240	(833)	(0.87)	4,716	4.94
Ladysmith	115,716	45,367	(6,440)	(5.57)	1,264	1.09
Lake Geneva group	557,135	121,562	(5,547)	(1.00)	11,387	2.04
Madison	7,325,278	2,175,757	265,028	3.62	490,837	6.70
Manitowoc	1,326,688	408,835	53,928	4.06	82,732	6.24
Marinette	666,715	185,174	2,514	0.38	28,663	4.30

(Continued)

EXHIBIT I

Company Separated by Exchanges

Exchange	Rate Base 1948–1952 Average	Gross Revenue Present Rates 1948–1952	Net Operating Income After Taxes	Rate of Return Before Increase	Net Operating Income After Allowed Increase	Rate of Return After Increase
Mayville	$ 199,674	$ 53,311	$ (11,041)	(5.53)%	$ 2,741	(1.37)%
Mazomanie	71,899	13,798	(2,069)	(2.88)	(164)	(1.23)
Menomonie	414,364	120,369	(24,938)	(6.02)	(7,710)	(1.86)
Merrill	376,415	130,651	(11,528)	(3.06)	6,013	1.60
Milwaukee group	55,120,756	19,557,817	3,512,094	6.37	3,517,183	6.38
New London	169,066	64,765	(7,028)	(4.16)	1,976	1.17
Oconomowoc	355,743	117,343	(5,847)	(1.74)	11,349	3.38
Oconto	162,008	64,765	(9,918)	(6.12)	(321)	(1.20)
Oconto Falls	87,700	21,525	88	0.10	3,073	3.50
Omro	146,559	27,925	(7,064)	(4.82)	(3,241)	(2.21)
Oshkosh	1,677,210	689,689	(78,917)	(4.71)	26,935	1.61
Peshtigo	61,449	21,028	(1,416)	(2.30)·	1,377	2.24
Pewaukee	159,037	46,726	2,777	1.75	9,109	5.73
Port Washington	160,553	66,626	(714)	(0.44)	9,128	5.69
Prentice	24,734	6,047	(1,846)	(7.46)	(429)	(1.73)
Princeton	44,740	15,289	(756)	(0.69)	2,251	5.03
Racine group	4,033,694	1,335,219	151,954	3.77	254,337	6.31
Red Granite	27,245	9,171	(1,831)	(4.92)	(463)	(1.10)
River Falls	236,363	49,611	(6,299)	(2.66)	2,013	0.85
Roberts	21,223	5,044	(1,177)	(5.55)	(379)	(1.79)
Shawano	190,444	73,444	(9,432)	(4.95)	(923)	0.48
Sheboygan group	2,323,218	771,332	119,205	5.13	138,032	5.94
Shullsburg	108,301	18,717	(5,917)	(5.46)	(3,260)	(3.01)
Stanley	71,443	24,330	(1,061)	(1.49)	2,193	3.07
Stevens Point	697,006	233,009	(21,861)	(3.14)	12,385	1.78
Stoughton	208,189	79,422	(4,515)	(2.17)	8,601	4.13
Sturgeon Bay	325,693	113,639	(4,646)	(1.43)	11,952	3.67
Superior	1,394,028	468,512	57,586	4.13	83,027	5.96
Thiensville	129,422	43,777	3,972	3.07	7,383	5.70
Washburn	68,357	22,966	(6,796)	(9.94)	(2,845)	(4.16)
Watertown	495,500	178,041	(7,569)	(1.53)	19,051	3.84
Waukesha	1,041,872	359,827	50,820	4.88	60,163	5.77
Waupaca	153,028	67,084	(4,816)	(3.15)	5,034	3.29
Waupun	196,625	73,337	(6,666)	(3.39)	3,942	2.00
West Bend	453,417	119,192	3,783	0.83	20,199	4.45
Whitewater group	200,457	66,557	(12,273)	(6.12)	(2,486)	(1.24)
Winneconne	52,038	11,801	(806)	(1.55)	943	1.81
Wrightstown	80,048	13,862	(3,508)	(4.38)	(1,560)	(1.95)
Total (or Average)	$104,966,619	$35,329,452	$4,253,803	4.05%	$5,930,991	5.65%

(*Continued*)

EXHIBIT I (*Continued.*)

Monthly One-Party Residential Rate Set by Commission	Areas Included
$2.85	**Waukesha***
3.20	**Manitowoc**
3.30	**Superior**
3.50	Bayfield, Burlington, Burnett, Cornell, Ellsworth, Genoa City, Green Lake, Hartland, Horicon, Hortonville, Juneau, Mazomanie, Oconto Falls, Omro, Peshtigo, Prentice, Princeton, Red Granite, Roberts, Shullsburg, Stanley, Thiensville, Washburn
3.65	**Sheboygan**
3.80	Algoma, Berlin, Cedarburg, Columbus, Darlington, Delavan, Evansville, Hartford, Hudson, Jefferson, **Kenosha,** Kewaunee, Ladysmith, New London, Oconto, Pewaukee, Port Washington, River Falls, Shawano, Stoughton, Wapaca, Waupun, West Bend, Whitewater
4.10	Ashland, Baraboo, Beaver Dam, Eau Claire, Fort Aktinson, **Hurley,** Kaukauna, **Lake Geneva Group,** Marinette, Menomonie, Merrill, **Oconomowoc,** Stevens Point, Sturgeon Bay, Watertown
4.40	Appleton, Beloit, Fond du Lac, Janesville
4.25	**Racine**
4.55	Oshkosh
4.70	Green Bay (De Pere), Madison
5.35	Milwaukee

* Bold-face type indicates exchanges where the Commission approach and the Company approach produced substantially different rates.

is a metropolitan center. Exhibit I shows the current gross revenue, the net operating income after taxes and the rate of return on the rate base for each exchange. The next column sets out the net operating income after taxes allowed by the Commission for each exchange together with the resulting rate of return.

On the third page of Exhibit I are the monthly one-party residential rates for each exchange which yield the allowed net operating income after taxes.

Before these rates were set, the company argued strenuously for rates based upon the value of service principle. The company's arguments are conveniently listed under seven headings:

1. Value of service results in maximum telephone development and keeps in operation many exchanges that might have to be abandoned if cost is the rate basis.

2. Value of service enables the company to improve the quality of service.

3. Value of service avoids discrimination between exchanges by charging the same rates for the same size exchange.

4. Like charges for like service is the most understandable basis for rates as far as customers are concerned.

5. Value of service increases the stability of rates.

6. Value of service is simpler to compute and saves the customer the costs of segregation which he must pay.

7. Value of service increases in proportion to the size of the exchange, particularly the larger number of potential calls.

CASE IV-3. EXHIBIT II

Daily Calling Rate, Available Businesses and Average Tolls to
Adjacent Exchanges Classified by Size of Exchange

Exchange Size, by Number of Stations	Daily Average Calls Per Station	Types of Business Available to Caller	Average Monthly Toll to Adjacent Exchanges
1–900	3.5	100	$0.52
901–2,600	4.1	190	0.39
2,601–8,000	6.7	450	0.14
8,001–28,000	6.9	610	0.08
32,140 (Madison)	7.7	805	0.10
255,229 (Milwaukee)	(Not shown)	1,590	0.02

To support these arguments, the company produced Exhibit II. The data in Exhibit II are not the averages for all exchanges but rather show a typical exchange. The "types of business available to caller" refers to the different types of service which can be reached on the local exchange. The average monthly toll to *adjacent* exchanges is designed to reflect the costs paid to reach parties outside the exchange (but not total toll). It should be pointed out that presumably, the company did not show the Milwaukee calling rate because it did not conform to the pattern. Also Madison includes state government employees and university students, employees and faculty as a large percentage of its population.

In its decision the Commission deviated from the rates sought by the company in eleven of the seventy-eight exchanges. Or to put it another way, cost of service and the company's version of value of service differed in eleven exchanges. Nine of these deviations are shown in bold-face type on the third page of Exhibit I.

These are important deviations however. Racine and Kenosha, neighboring cities of the same size, were ordered to have rates of $4.25 and $3.80 respectively. The company would have set the same rate for both. Waukesha (with depression installed dial), a sizable exchange, has $2.85 whereas tiny Hurley has $4.10 and Waukesha's neighbor, Oconomowoc, of a size between Hurley and Waukesha has $4.10.

After the 1949 decision, the Commission went back to exercise the refund right reserved over the 1947 *interim rate* increase and ordered refunds at all exchanges showing a rate of return over 7 per cent between the date of the interim order of 1947 and the final order of 1949. Refunds were ordered for sixteen of the exchanges. These exchanges are:

Exchange	Rate Base Per Cent Earned 1947–48	Exchange	Rate Base Per Cent Earned 1947–48
Baraboo	8.38	Manitowoc	10.35
Cedarburg	7.91	Milwaukee	7.15
Delavan	10.17	Oconto Falls	7.71
Eau Claire	7.84	Pewaukee	10.35
Hartland	8.20	Superior	9.03
Hurley	7.80	Waukesha	8.52
Kenosha	8.54	West Bend	7.79
Little Chute (in Appleton group)	9.09	Williams Bay (in Lake Geneva group)	10.00

It will be noted that most of those nine exchanges upon whose rates the Commission disagreed with company proposals are in this refund group.

Evaluate the pricing decision of the Commission.

CASE IV-4. WISCONSIN TELEPHONE COMPANY (B)*

Price Analysis—Public Utility Pricing

After the 1949 decision in Wisconsin Telephone Co. (A), substantial wage increases forced the company to apply again for increased intrastate exchange rates on April 27, 1951. This time much opposition to increases in rates split the cities into two camps. One camp headed by Milwaukee fought for the cost of service principle. The other camp headed by Green Bay, Oshkosh, and Fond du Lac fought for value of service. The latter camp consisted of cities where dial conversion was done or to be done at high post-World-War-II prices. The former camp consisted of cities where dial conversion had been done in the depression or, as in the case of Milwaukee, where earnings without any increase were adequate on the exchange rate base.

Exhibit I indicates the degree to which the 1949 rate order was able to pre-determine rates of return. The second column shows the per cent return contemplated after the 1949 rate increase. The third column shows the per cent return as it actually was in 1952. The fourth column shows the difference between the second and third columns. If the Commission's ability to forecast had been perfect, this fourth column would have the same difference figure throughout. The column shows some constancy particularly in view of the difficulties of forecasting in the midst of elaborate dial conversion and the disparity in size of exchanges to say nothing of the effect of the rate increase on telephone use.

To aid in evaluating the difference column, Table I collects the differences in groupings for the seventy-seven exchanges.

The Commission ordered that the monthly rates "insofar as practicable levy like charges for the services in exchanges of comparable size subject to the limitation that neither the service rates nor the rate of return at any one exchange shall be excessive or unjustly or unreasonably high."

This represents something of a shift by the Commission from its earlier position in which the goal was equal rates of return for each exchange let the monthly rates to the subscribers fall where they may. The Commission explained its thinking in this way:

At first blush, it appears that any schedule which results in reasonable profit at some exchanges and losses at others is unlawful and discriminating.

* Based on the record in Decision 2-U-3573 by the Wisconsin Public Service Commission. Final decision in 37 P.S.C.W. 166 (1952).

Case IV-4. EXHIBIT I

Data Pertinent to Wisconsin Telephone Company Separated by Exchanges

Exchange	(1) 1949 One- Party Rate After 1949 Increase	(2) 1952 Per Cent Return Contem- plated in 1949	(3) 1952 Per Cent Return on Rate Base at 1949 Rates	(4) Difference Between Columns 2 and 3	(5) Estimated Per Cent Return on Rate Base After 1952 increase	(6) 1952 Rates After Increase
Algoma	$3.80	3.32%	(2.5)%	(5.82)%	(0.7)%	$4.15
Appleton group	4.40	5.95	4.0	(1.95)	6.7	5.05
Ashland	4.10	3.01	(1.0)	(3.01)	0.7	4.45
Baraboo group	4.10	5.84	2.1	(3.74)	3.8	4.45
Bayfield	3.50	2.38	(4.5)	(6.88)	(0.2)	3.85
Beaver Dam	4.10	4.02	4.5	0.48	5.6	4.45
Beloit	4.40	1.64	(2.7)	(4.43)	(1.0)	4.75
Berlin	3.80	2.07	4.0	1.93	6.8	4.15
Burlington	3.50	4.01	2.2	(1.81)	6.0	4.15
Burnett	3.50	(0.57)	(1.3)	(0.73)	(0.2)	3.85
Cedarburg	3.80	3.78	4.2	0.42	5.7	4.15
Columbus	3.80	(2.20)	(2.8)	(0.60)	(1.1)	4.15
Cornell	3.50	2.33	(0.4)	(2.73)	0.9	3.85
Darlington group	3.80	(1.83)	(1.9)	(0.07)	(1.2)	4.15
Delavan	3.80	2.26	(0.6)	(2.86)	0.8	4.15
Eau Claire group	4.10	6.67	4.2	(2.47)	6.4	4.75
Ellsworth	3.50	(2.20)	(5.7)	(3.50)	(4.3)	3.85
Evansville	3.80	0.23	(0.6)	(0.83)	1.6	4.15
Fond du Lac	4.40	5.61	0.9	(4.71)	2.9	4.75
Fort Atkinson	4.10	2.46	3.5	1.04	5.6	4.45
Genoa City	3.50	(1.15)	1.9	3.05	3.4	3.85
Green Bay group	4.70	5.10	(3.3)	(8.40)	(1.6)	5.05
Green Lake	3.50	2.51	2.0	(0.51)	4.1	3.85
Hartford	3.80	3.40	3.9	0.50	6.1	4.15
Hartland	3.50	3.62	5.4	1.78	7.6	3.85
Horicon	3.50	1.05	3.9	2.85	5.6	3.85
Hortonville	3.50	2.02	(1.7)	(3.72)	0.0	3.85
Hudson	3.80	0.97	(1.8)	(2.77)	(0.3)	4.15
Hurley	4.10	1.06	4.8	3.74	6.6	4.45
Janesville	4.40	6.53	5.0	(1.53)	6.2	4.75
Jefferson	3.80	1.18	3.0	1.82	5.4	4.15
Juneau	3.50	1.02	3.7	2.68	5.3	3.85
Kenosha	3.40	6.24	5.3	(0.94)	6.7	3.70
Kewaunee	3.80	4.94	3.3	(1.64)	5.5	4.15
Ladysmith	3.80	1.09	4.3	3.21	7.2	4.15
Lake Geneva group	4.10	2.04	1.9	(0.14)	2.9	4.45
Madison	4.70	6.70	5.7	(1.00)	6.6	4.85
Manitowoc	3.20	6.24	4.7	(1.54)	7.3	3.85
Marinette	4.10	4.30	4.3	(0.00)	5.6	4.45

(Continued)

EXHIBIT I (*Continued.*)

Exchange	(1) 1949 One-Party Rate After 1949 Increase	(2) 1952 Per Cent Return Contemplated in 1949	(3) 1952 Per Cent Return on Rate Base at 1949 Rates	(4) Difference Between Columns 2 and 3	(5) Estimated Per Cent Return on Rate Base After 1952 Increase	(6) 1952 Rates After Increase
Mayville	$3.80	(1.37)%	1.7 %	3.07 %	3.6 %	$4.15
Mazomanie	3.50	(0.23)	(2.6)	(2.37)	(1.1)	3.85
Menomonie	4.10	(1.86)	(2.8)	(0.94)	(1.2)	4.45
Merrill	4.10	1.60	(1.6)	(3.20)	0.7	4.45
Milwaukee group	5.35	6.38	4.8	(1.52)	6.4	5.85
New London	3.80	1.17	(0.9)	(2.07)	0.9	4.15
Oconomowoc	4.10	3.38	3.1	(0.28)	5.0	4.45
Oconto	3.80	(0.20)	1.7	1.90	4.1	4.15
Oconto Falls	3.50	3.50	1.7	(1.80)	3.4	3.85
Omro	3.50	2.21	(2.7)	(4.91)	(1.4)	3.85
Oshkosh	4.55	1.61	0.0	(1.61)	1.2	4.75
Peshtigo	3.50	2.24	(1.7)	(3.94)	0.8	3.85
Pewaukee	3.80	5.73	5.6	(0.13)	7.1	4.15
Port Washington	3.80	5.69	5.7	0.01	6.4	4.15
Prentice	3.50	(1.73)	(3.9)	(1.17)	(2.2)	3.85
Princeton	3.50	5.03	(1.3)	(6.33)	0.1	3.85
Racine group	4.25	6.31	5.6	(0.71)	6.7	4.50
Red Granite	3.50	(1.10)	(2.7)	(1.60)	(0.9)	3.85
River Falls	3.80	0.85	0.9	0.05	2.0	4.15
Roberts	3.50	(1.79)	(4.5)	(2.71)	(3.4)	3.85
Shawano	3.80	0.48	(1.2)	(1.68)	1.0	4.15
Sheboygan group	3.65	5.94	5.0	(0.94)	6.7	4.10
Shullsburg	3.50	(3.01)	(1.7)	1.31	(0.6)	3.85
Stanley	3.50	3.07	(4.1)	(7.17)	(1.6)	3.85
Stevens Point	4.10	1.78	2.2	0.42	4.0	4.45
Stoughton	3.80	4.13	1.9	(3.13)	3.8	4.15
Sturgeon Bay	4.10	3.67	0.9	(2.77)	2.7	4.45
Superior	3.30	5.96	6.7	0.74	7.7	3.50
Thiensville	3.50	5.70	2.3	(3.40)	4.7	4.15
Washburn	3.50	(4.16)	(5.6)	(0.44)	(3.8)	3.85
Watertown	4.10	3.84	1.7	(2.14)	3.4	4.45
Waukesha	2.85	5.77	4.5	(1.27)	6.9	3.30
Waupaca	3.80	3.29	2.9	(0.39)	5.2	4.15
Waupun	3.80	2.00	3.1	1.10	5.2	4.15
West Bend	3.80	4.45	4.3	(0.15)	(8.3)	4.15
Whitewater group	3.80	(1.24)	(1.0)	0.24	1.0	4.15
Winneconne	3.50	1.81	0.5	(1.31)	2.2	3.85
Wrightstown	3.50	(1.95)	(0.3)	1.65	0.8	4.45
Weighted Average		5.65 %	4.4 %	(1.25)%	5.7 %	

CASE IV-4. TABLE I

Deviations of 1952 Rate of Return by Exchanges from Rate of
Return Contemplated by 1949 Commission Rate Increase
Classified by Intervals of 0.5 and 1.0
(See Column 4 of Exhibit I)

Difference	Number of Exchanges		Difference
Over 3.5%	1	1	Over 3.5%
3.0–3.5	3	5	2.5–3.5
2.5–3.0	2	5	1.5–2.5
2.0–2.5	0	4	0.5–1.5
1.5–2.0	5	15	(0.5)–0.5
1.0–1.5	3	12	(1.5)–(0.5)
0.5–1.0	1	14	(2.5)–(1.5)
0.0–0.5	7	10	(3.5)–(2.5)
(0.5)–0.0	8	4	(4.5)–(3.5)
(1.0)–(0.5)	9	2	(5.5)–(4.5)
(1.5)–(1.0)	3	2	(6.5)–(5.5)
(2.0)–(1.5)	9	2	(7.5)–(6.5)
(2.5)–(2.0)	5	1	Over (7.5)
(3.0)–(2.5)	5		
(3.5)–(3.0)	5		
(4.0)–(3.5)	3		
(4.5)–(4.0)	1		
(5.0)–(4.5)	2		
(5.5)–(5.0)	0		
(6.0)–(5.5)	1		
(6.5)–(6.0)	1		
(7.0)–(6.5)	1		
Over (7.0)	2		

Weighted Average
(1.25)%   (1.25)%

But deviations in net earnings apparent at any one time do not necessarily
present a true picture of what actually transpires over the course of time.
This is particularly true in small exchanges where maintenance and construction programs produce frequent and substantial deviations in net return.

Just as a moving picture records the actual behavior of a moving object, a
true picture of individual exchange operations could be obtained only by a
continuous recording of results of operations. A still picture such as is presented in Exhibit I must be considered and qualified with the knowledge that
earnings at individual exchanges can and do fluctuate from time to time.
Under the circumstances and particularly in view of the limitations of the
data . . . the rates are approved.

Evaluate the decision of the Commission.

CASE IV-5. PACIFIC GAS AND ELECTRIC COMPANY*

Price Analysis—Public Utility Pricing

Pacific Gas and Electric Company in 1951 applied for authority to increase its electric rates so as to receive an estimated 37 million dollars in additional revenue or a 22 per cent increase in revenues. The utility proposed specific rate schedules which would yield such an increase in revenue.

Besides the usual parties appearing in a rate case, namely, the utility, municipalities involved and the experts of the commission, this case saw the California Manufacturers Association and California Farm Bureau Federation take very active parts.

Pacific Gas and Electric Company is the largest utility operating entirely within California and operates in forty-six of the state's fifty-eight counties, furnishing electric, gas, water, and steam-heat service. Pacific serves not only ultimate customers but also serves other utilities which resell Pacific's services. Between 1940 and 1950 the number of electric customers served increased 50 per cent over 1940 to 1,334,000 and the output of electricity increased 100 per cent in this period. Between 1945 and 1951 average hourly rates paid Pacific's employees increased 61 per cent, construction costs increased approximately 68 per cent. Between 1946 and 1950, the capital invested in electric plant increased 92 per cent. Between 1946 and the present case, Pacific sought only one rate increase of 6 per cent effective in 1950. This increase was "across the board" and was not based on a claim to a fair return on Pacific's investment but rather was sought as an interim aid to maintaining Pacific's credit which was vital to facilitating the sale of securities to obtain the funds needed for the extensive 92 per cent capital expansion between 1946 and 1950.

All of these factors, unless offset by other factors, increase costs and reduce the rate of return. In particular, the federal income tax rate increased from 38 per cent in 1949 to 52 per cent in 1952. The rate of return allowed a utility is always determined after income taxes.

Pacific's proposed electric rate schedules were designed to develop a return of 6 per cent on its depreciated cost of fixed assets (plus allow-

* Based on the record in Application No. 32589 filed July 18, 1951 with the California Public Utilities Commission and decided by Decision No. 47832 dated Oct. 15, 1952. Decision reported in part in (1952) 96 P.U.R. (N.S.) 493.

ances for the same return on working capital). The return for 1952 without the rate increase was estimated to be 4.20 per cent on the depreciated cost base of 977 million dollars. The revenues for 1952 by classes of electric service were:

Domestic Service	$ 61,393,000
Commercial & Industrial	96,575,000
Agricultural	29,663,000
Street lighting	2,540,000
Resale	10,433,000
Railway	346,000
Interdepartmental	492,000
Miscellaneous	5,479,000
Total Operating Revenue	$206,921,000

Total operating expenses break-down for 1952 as follows:

Maintenance	$ 11,004,000
Production	
Purchased power	7,528,000
Fuel	31,822,000
Water for power	558,000
Other	7,491,000
Transmission	1,827,000
Distribution	10,552,000
Customers accounting	7,297,000
Sales promotion	1,650,000
Administrative	4,285,000
Pensions, etc.	2,336,000
Uncollectibles	251,000
Total Operating Expense	$ 86,601,000

The existing rate of return then was established by the following computation:

Operating revenues	$206,921,000
Expenses:	
Operating	86,601,000
1952 New Wage Increase	2,626,000
Depreciation	25,120,000
Taxes	51,520,000
Total Expense	$165,867,000
Net revenue for return	41,054,000
Depreciated rate base	976,927,000
Rate of return	4.20%

To support the petitioned 6 per cent return on the rate base, Pacific stated this was the weighted average of its capital structure: 3.27 per cent for bonds, 5.54 per cent for preferred stock and 10.75 per cent for common stock equity. The 10.75 per cent was supported as the 1946 to 1950 average of the thirty-seven electric utilities in the United States with assets over 100 million dollars.

The Commission allowed a rate of return of 5.75 per cent (using an equity return based more on price-earnings ratio than on earnings to book equity) which it held likely to shrink to 5.55 per cent in the immediate future of the next several years based upon continuation of the trend of growth, etc. which had been shrinking the rate of return in the immediately preceding years. This would mean an increase in gross revenues of 33 million dollars was needed to gain this result, compared to the 45 million dollars which Pacific sought.

Pacific made a cost study *including within costs* a 5.61 per cent return on invested capital (see Table I).

CASE IV-5. TABLE I

Cost and Company-Proposed Revenue by Type of Customer

Type of Customer	Cost Per KWH Including Return	Proposed Charge Per KWH
Domestic	2.8183¢	2.9243¢
Small Light and Power	2.0493	3.1915
Large Light and Power		
Transmission	0.9305	0.9865
Distribution	1.2715	1.2610
Agricultural Power	1.8227	1.2625
Resale		
Transmission	1.0501	0.6984
Distribution	1.1166	0.7145
Railway	2.2956	1.4453
Street Lighting	3.9216	4.0838
Interdepartment	1.6270	2.1967

Note: Within the domestic category there are further breakdowns into single family, apartment house, multi-family, heating and cooking, etc.

In cost determination, expenses and return were allocated to three categories: demand costs, commodity costs and customer costs.

Demand costs are those imposed by the type of customer equipment and are influenced more by peak rate of use than volume of use.

Commodity costs are production costs and relate most closely to the kilowatt-hours used by a customer.

Customer costs are those that are largely independent of rates and volume of use and dependent on the number and location of customers.

The segregation between demand and commodity cost is made through the load factor concept. If the load factor (ratio of actual use to what would be used under continuous operation) were 62 per cent, then 62 per cent of the costs would be assigned to commodity costs and 38 per cent to demand costs. In this way, sufficient capacity is assigned to the commodity costs to cover costs when the utility is operating at a 100 per cent load factor.

Customer costs include such services as meter reading for example, as well as the minimum investment needed to connect a customer. For example, the cost of the smallest type transformer to serve a customer is a customer cost and the difference between that type and the type needed to serve the actual needs of the customer is assigned to demand-commodity cost and allocated between them by load factor as already indicated.

The number of customers in the various classes and the use by each is shown in Table II.

CASE IV-5. TABLE II

Customers by Types

Type of Customer	Number of Customers	Annual KWH/Customer	Annual Total KWH by Type (in Thousands)
Residential	1,085,223	2,092	2,270,809
Commercial	226,430	27,705	6,273,344
Agricultural	57,072	42,563	2,429,183
Street Lighting	687	99,792	68,557
Resale	34	45,676,176	1,552,990
Railway	6	4,804,500	28,827
Total (or Average)	1,369,452	9,218	12,623,710
Interdepartmental			26,014

If the rates were set at cost (including 5.6 per cent return) by type of service, the rates of return shown in Table III would result on the investment in each area.

The geographic distribution of customers is shown in Table IV.

It is apparent that some classes of customer would be "subsidizing" other classes if the rates in Table I were adopted. The extent of the "subsidy" can be computed from Table II. Likewise, from Table III

Case IV-5. TABLE III

Area Rates of Return

Area	Rate of Return	Area	Rate of Return
Coast Valleys	6.37%	Sacramento	3.63%
Colgate	5.08	San Francisco	6.09
De Sabla	4.57	San Joaquin	5.91
Drum	3.13	San Luis and Santa Maria	6.40
East Bay	6.22	San Jose	6.37
Humboldt	4.42	Shasta	3.71
North Bay	5.13	Stockton	5.42
Fort Bragg	4.82	System Average	5.61%

Case IV-5. TABLE IV

Geographic Distribution of Customers and Loads

Area	Number of Customers*	Annual KWH Per Customer	Annual Total KWH by Area (in Thousands)
Coast Valleys	41,152	7,774	319,932
Colgate	36,011	7,522	270,886
De Sabla	24,103	9,791	236,001
Drum	18,134	18,120	328,593
East Bay	305,718	9,341	2,855,704
Humboldt	25,591	6,168	157,847
North Bay	112,517	5,856	658,902
Sacramento	33,869	27,823	942,336
San Francisco	279,797	5,076	1,420,267
San Joaquin	254,607	13,053	3,323,558
San Jose	158,325	7,552	1,195,736
Shasta	19,648	11,309	222,200
Stockton	93,203	7,701	717,762
Total (or Average)	1,402,675	9,018	12,649,724

* Varies from Table II because Table II shows averages and Table IV shows year-end customers.

some areas are "subsidizing" others and the amount of the subsidy could be computed if the investment in each area were available. Some idea of the "subsidy" can be gained from Table IV. These statements assume that the cost allocation method above is acceptable and also that the risks associated with each area and type of customer are the same.

The calculations shown in Tables I through IV would yield an increase in revenue of 36.3 million dollars whereas 33 million dollars was authorized under the rate of return allowance. This would leave room for some adjustment in the proposed rate schedules downward.

Besides the area and type differences already noted, rates are varied by zones for residential customers within each area. These zones reflect population density. The greater the density, the lower the costs of service. The variations of zones are shown in Table V (with zone 6 as rural).

Case IV-5. TABLE V

Old and New Zone Rates

	Zones					
Current Rates	1	2	3	4	5	6
Service Charge Per Month	42.00¢	53.00	53.00	53.00	58.00	64.00
1st 40 KWH Per KWH	3.07	3.07	3.39	3.71	3.92	4.66
Next 60 KWH Per KWH	2.23	2.33	2.44	2.54	2.65	3.18
Next 100 KWH Per KWH	1.80	1.91	2.01	2.12	2.12	2.44
Over 200 KWH Per KWH	1.06	1.06	1.06	1.06	1.06	1.17
New Rates						
Service Charge Per Month	50.00¢	60.00	65.00	70.00	75.00	85.00
1st 40 KWH Per KWH	3.80	4.00	4.20	4.40	4.60	5.60
Next 60 KWH Per KWH	2.70	2.80	3.00	3.10	3.20	3.90
Next 100 KWH Per KWH	2.20	2.30	2.40	2.50	2.60	2.90
Over 200 KWH Per KWH	1.20	1.20	1.20	1.20	1.20	1.20

The rates proposed by Pacific in Table I were altered by the Commission as shown in Table VI.

Thus the Commission made the most significant changes to reduce revenues (from the proposed increase by Pacific to the $33 million it would allow) by adjusting the domestic and commercial-industrial rates. In the case of domestic rates, the Commission moved the proposed rate towards cost and in the case of commercial-industrial rates, it moved the proposed rate towards cost (because whatever averaging is used in Table I, the cost cannot be under 2 cents per KWH).

What effect these changes of proposed rates shown in Table IV have on the area rates of return shown in Table II is not set forth by the Commission.

CASE IV-5. TABLE VI

Proposed and Allowed Rate Increases

Type	Sales in Million KWH	Current Revenue in Millions of Dollars	Increase in Millions of Dollars	Per Cent Increase	Cost Per KWH Including Return	Revenue Per KWH After Allowed Increase	Utility's Proposal
Domestic	2,560	$ 61.4	$11.0	17.8%	2.82¢	2.83¢	2.92¢
Commercial	6,759	95.6	13.4	13.9	*	1.63	†
Agricultural	2,785	29.7	5.4	18.2	1.82	1.26	1.26
Street Lighting	77	2.6	0.5	19.9	3.92	3.95	4.08
Resale	1,806	10.4	2.4	23.3	1.08	0.71	0.70
Railway	28	0.3	0.1	19.9	2.30	1.48	1.44
Total (or Average)	14,015	201.0	32.8	16.3			
Interdepartmental	29	0.5	0.1	18.9	1.63	2.02	2.19
Miscellaneous	—	5.5	0.1	1.8	—	—	—
Total (or Average)	14,044	206.9	33.0	15.9			

* No basis available to average from Table I for small and large commercial.
† Again no basis for averaging, but Commission says it cut the proposed increase of 20 per cent for small commercial to 13.9 per cent.

Questions

1. Should or would the type of pricing here set out in detail be applicable to business generally? Assuming the profit motive to be the principle of operation? Suppose a pharmaceutical company followed target pricing?
2. Should or would the approach here set out be altered if gas were highly competitive to electricity?

CASE IV-6. SOUTHERN COUNTIES GAS COMPANY*

Price Analysis—Public Utility Pricing

Southern Counties Gas Company in 1952 applied for authority to increase its gas rates so as to receive an estimated $4.8 millions additional revenue.

Southern's number of customers and sales of gas are classified by type of service in 1952 in Table I.

CASE IV-6. TABLE I

Number of Customers and Sales of Gas by Class of Customer in 1952 by Southern Counties Gas Company

Class of Customer	Number of Customers	Sales in Thousand MCF
Domestic and Commercial	390,905	32,617
Firm Industrial	838	1,802
Interruptible Industrial	338	11,243
Standby Industrial and Steam Generators	8	5,294
Gas Engine	389	844
Wholesale	3	27,365
Total	392,481	79,165

The over-all earnings picture summarized by agreement of the company and the commission for a normalized 1952 is set out in Table II.

Using the actual cost of property when acquired less depreciation, S.C.G. contended for a rate base of $74,882,000 and the commission staff for $71,096,000 or respective rates of return of 4.95 per cent and 5.22 per cent using 1952 earnings. The Commission adopted a rate base of $71,596,000 compromising working capital which was the main difference in rate bases. Rate of return to be allowed was set at 5.95 per cent (or 6.45 per cent currently to cover shrinkage expected in the immediate future due to an annual fall in rate of return of 0.25 per cent resulting from higher replacement costs).

Hence a revenue increase of $1,051,000 was held warranted. In determining how this increased revenue should be achieved, a sharp

* Based on the record in application No. 33341 filed April 23, 1952 with the California Public Utilities Commission and decided by Decision No. 48833 dated July 14, 1953.

CASE IV-6. TABLE II

Computation of Normalized Profit Earned in 1952
by Southern Counties Gas Company

	In Thousands
Operating Revenues	$33,172
Operating Expenses:	
Production	14,899
Transmission	705
Distribution	2,892
Customer Expense	2,040
Sales Promotion	1,086
Administration	1,945
New Wage Contract	104
	23,671
Taxes	4,229
Depreciation	1,563
	29,463
Net for Return	3,709

conflict developed between the utility's expert and the California Manufacturers Association particularly concerning the rate for interruptible gas used for industrial purposes. Specifically CMA contended interruptible gas should not carry a demand charge.

In summary form, the differences between the expert for the utility and CMA are set forth in Table III. Accounting procedures used by gas utilities do not segregate costs to functions so they can be assigned to classes of service as is true of electric accounting procedures. Hence different cost analysis procedures might be adopted. This is the origin of the serious disagreement between the rate of return analysis by classes of service by the utility expert and that of CMA shown in Table III.

The heart of the difference in cost analysis lies in the assignment of costs to demand and commodity functions.* A three-fold classification of costs: demand, commodity and customer costs was agreed upon by SCG and CMA. The difference was in allocation between demand cost and commodity cost. SCG's expert assigned both fixed and variable costs to each function (as is done in electric utilities) but CMA assigned all fixed costs to the demand function and all variable costs to the commodity function (except such fixed and variable costs

---

* See the definitions of demand costs, commodity costs, and customer costs set out in *Pacific Gas and Electric Company*, (Case IV-5), at p. 298.

CASE IV-6. TABLE III

Costs, Revenues, and Rates of Return Developed by Experts for Southern Counties Gas Company and California Manufacturers' Association and Rates Allowed by California Commission

Class	Sales in Thousands of MCF	Average Cost Per MCF at 6.5 Per Cent Return		Pre-Increase Rate of Return		Average Revenue Per MCF		
		SCG*	CMA†	SCG*	CMA†	Before Increase	After Increase Now Allowed	Per Cent Increase in Rate
General	32,617	81.46¢	79.46¢	3.38%	3.59%	64.5¢	69.9¢	8.30%
Gas Engine	844	32.82	35.75	5.51	3.92	31.6	32.8	6.68
Firm Industrial	1,802	33.96	37.32	10.86	7.94	39.9	42.6	3.75
Interruptible Industrial	11,243	18.17	22.35	49.05	10.94	25.5	28.4	11.30
Steam Generation	5,294	16.09	16.51	108.60	35.82	21.3	25.0	16.26
Wholesale San Diego Gas	22,204	22.44	22.53	7.03	6.87	23.1	23.1	none
Pacific Gas and Electric Company	5,161	16.59	16.74	125.00	46.43	22.3	22.3	none
Total (or Average)	79,165	45.83¢	45.83¢	4.48%	4.48%	40.8¢	43.8¢	7.16%

* Calculated by an expert from Southern Counties Gas Company.
† Calculated by an expert from California Manufacturers' Association.

clearly identifiable as customer costs). Another way of putting it is that CMA rejected the load-factor as a basis of allocation. Under the load-factor method, the ratio of average firm use to maximum potential use is established. In this case that ratio was 37 per cent. Then 37 per cent of costs are assigned to commodity function and 63 per cent to demand.

Once the allocation to each of the three functions was made, both the SCG expert and CMA allocated the costs of each function among classes of service in the ratio of peak responsibility, i.e., the estimated participation of each class on the maximum potential peak day. When applied to interruptible service, this means that demand costs can be assigned to interruptible service only to the extent it is not interrupted on the peak day. This, in most cases, would result in no demand costs charged to interruptible service.

To illustrate, if 2.5 per cent of demand cost were assigned to interruptible industrial, the average cost per thousand cubic feet would be 23.86 cents compared to 22.35 cents if no demand costs are so assigned. Similar cost increases of 1.5 cents per thousand cubic feet would be added for each increase of 2.5 per cent of demand costs charged to interruptible industrial.

Interruptible industrial constituted about 15 per cent of the total thousand cubic feet of the utility.

So far, the conflict has been described as between the experts for SCG and CMA. SCG did not commit itself to the reins of its own expert but broadly argued "that practical merchandising and competitive consideration should be controlling (as to rates) and that cost of service is only one of the many factors to be considered in arriving at reasonable rates."

The degree of interruption in interruptible service is shown by the following:

Year	Potential	Curtailment	Sales	Ratio Sales to Potential
1950	12,315,998	528,290	11,787,708	95.7%
1951	12,636,144	1,080,062	11,556,082	91.5
1952	12,320,407	1,947,036	10,373,371	84.2

Based upon the high percentage level of satisfied demand, the Commission refused to find that no demand charge should be made against interruptible service. The Commission decided on an interruptible price of 28.4 cents per thousand cubic feet because this was competitive with fuel oil. By reference to the data in the fourth paragraph preceding this, it is apparent that interruptible gas then carries 10 per cent of the demand cost and, as earlier indicated, interruptible gas is 15 per cent of total gas volume.

The Commission proceeded to argue that even though the division of costs into demand cost, commodity cost and consumer cost or into fixed cost and variable cost is valuable, there are many types of costs that are difficult to fit into these categories. For example, income taxes, depreciation, return, sales promotion, and administrative and general expenses are hard to classify into these categories.

Then the Commission gave attention to the fuel oil clause. For certain industrial uses, gas users can pay a higher rate per heat unit than they would pay for fuel oil; for others, the gas rate must be competitive if gas is to be sold. The fuel clause provides, within certain limits, for a change of ⅙ of 1 cent per thousand cubic feet in the price of gas for each change of 1 cent in industrial fuel oil from a base of 85 cents per barrel. A fuel clause can be used either for competitive rates or to equalize the earnings of the utility between various classes of service. The Commission adopted a so-called "permissive" fuel clause under which changes in fuel oil price permitted the utility to change prices but did not require it to when competitive conditions, for example, permitted it to continue to sell gas at the same price, even though the price of fuel oil dropped. The fuel oil clause was restricted to interruptible gas.

The Commission further provided for six zone rates with the rate differences between zones to reflect customer cost differences following directly from population density.

Likewise the Commission authorized a higher rate for space heating than for other uses on the ground that seasonal peaks resulted in higher plant capacity investment.

The wholesale rate to Pacific Gas and Electric was not adjusted because that contract was to expire in 1953. Likewise the wholesale rate to San Diego Gas & Electric was not adjusted because that rate was subject to Federal Power Commission jurisdiction. Standby industrial was transferred to the firm industrial schedule and limitations on service permitted to the utility to avoid increasing peaks in service.

Questions

1. Assuming that a rate of return approach to pricing is to be used, would a nonutility business present any pricing situations more difficult to deal with than the different classes of service presented in this case?
2. Bearing in mind your answer to the first question, would a rate of return approach to pricing be sound
   a. from the point of view of optimum allocation of the resources of the economy?

   b. from the point of view of maximizing profits to the entrepreneur (bearing in mind that profits must be related to the risks involved)?
   c. from the point of view of promoting competition or monopoly and the interests of the consumer?
3. Is the decision by the Commission sound?

part V

Government regulation

THE RELATIONSHIP OF GOVERNMENTAL REGULATION TO THE PROBLEMS OF MANAGERIAL ECONOMICS

While the American economy may be considered as essentially competitive, the scope of government regulation has greatly increased since the decade of the 1930's. In using the term, competition, we do not imply the concept of pure competition—the situation in which individual sellers and buyers are so small they are unable to affect the price in the market by their individual activities. While the scope of government regulation has greatly increased since 1930, there were many regulatory activities present before that date.

The decisions of the management of a business enterprise inevitably must give consideration to the institutional element of regulation. It has been traditional to approach this problem by first establishing a decision and plan based solely on economic considerations and then making such modifications in the plan as seem required by the restrictions or limitations placed on the situation by government. There is considerable danger in this approach. For example, the analysis may be made in terms of pure competition, and then be "doctored" to consider elements of regulation which are so drastic that they create an essentially different situation.

The essence of scientific method lies in breaking a problem down into its parts, then studying the elements of the problem individually and usually under conditions where many of the elements of the problem are held, or assumed to be, constant. Then a synthesis is undertaken on the basis of the knowledge gained from the detailed study of the individual elements. This synthesis respects the knowledge gained in the analysis and attempts to organize that knowledge into a logically consistent whole.

The major governmental regulations likely to bear upon any particular economic problem of management should be identified first and should be ever present as the analysis proceeds. This does not involve "begging the question" as to what are the major regulations to be considered. As in all scientific investigation, a hypothesis (in this case an assumption that a particular government regulation is a major factor) that is found from the evidence and analysis to be unwarranted is discarded and the investigation starts anew from another hypothesis.

This line of argument is illustrated by some of the considerations that were presented in Part IV. If the anti-trust laws limit a producer to the point where he cannot, under the law, capture more than 50 per cent of the sales in a particular product area without breaking the law, and if breaking the law means incurring legal penalties harsh enough to make it uneconomical to pursue sales in excess of 50 per cent of that product area, how should this institutional element enter into the plan of activities? For a producer to grow as if this restriction did not exist and then to terminate his growth arbitrarily as the 50 per cent point is achieved would only accidentally produce the most profitable plan.

Instead, the producer from the outset might follow a plan designed to do several things, for example (1) pursue that 50 per cent of the sales in this product area which is most profitable from a long-run point of view; (2) pursue that 50 per cent of the product sales which involves the least risk (using the term risk in a broad sense); (3) pursue that 50 per cent of the product sales showing the greatest stability from a cyclical point of view.

It may be argued that this is the plan by which the producer should proceed even if 100 per cent of the sales in a product area were his goal. This, however, is begging the question. The quickest way to achieve 100 per cent sales in a product area is not necessarily to pursue those sales in the order of their profitability. The goal in pursuing 100 per cent of the sales in a product area may very well be to get there as rapidly as possible (whatever the order of profitability of individual sales as they are captured) in order to hasten the day when monopolistic pricing of a 100 per cent controlled market will yield a greater increase in profits that the slower achievement of this point by the niceties of pursuing sales in the order of their current profitability.

Another illustration that comes to mind is the institutional phenomenon of a patent with a 17-year life. The anti-trust laws have circumscribed the ways in which a patent can be employed. Without anticipating materials to be developed later in this Part, we may ask whether expenditures to achieve a vigorous research program should be pursued rather than outlays to develop the strategic position of a patent. The laws limit certain uses to which a patent may be put. The effects of these restrictions are, however, different when the patent is held in an industry where there are thousands of producers, no one of whom significantly affects price, and when the patent holder is a producer in a clearly oligopolistic industry. In fact, it is mainly in the oligopoly area that the restraints on the use of patents apply.

THE AREAS SELECTED FOR STUDY

There are three major areas that will serve conveniently for our consideration of government regulation. These are agriculture, public utilities and the anti-trust laws. The selection is based on a number of considerations. Public utilities[1] are a significant part of the total economy and form the segment of regulation whose history is oldest. For centuries, the common law has been concerned with the regulation of public utilities. This regulation has been particularly directed at controlling the rates (prices) charged by utilities for their services and primarily for the purpose of keeping the profits earned by such enterprises within socially acceptable limits.

Since 1900, it has become increasingly apparent that the attainment of this goal involved controls over such matters as plant construction, standards of service, legitimacy of costs and financing methods and costs. This extension of control has been achieved largely by legislative action in specifying the standards to be applied and the agencies through which control is to be achieved. In essence, a public utility involves the exchange of monopoly and the exclusion of competitors (a limitation sought by utilities) for control over profits and operations (a limitation resisted by utilities). In the present book, this area has been developed through the relatively large number of utility cases included at the end of Part IV and the summary notes which introduce these cases.

The second area selected for examination is agriculture. Again

---

[1] Including all aspects of commercial transportation (railroads, trucks, busses, water carriers, pipelines, air transport, terminals, warehousing, etc.), much of the communication area (telephone, telegraph, radio and television, etc.), much of the power area (electric and gas but not coal or oil directly) and many service areas (such as water, sanitation, etc.)

agriculture represents a major (though decreasing) segment of the total American economy. Another reason for selecting this area has been the fact that agriculture has traditionally been considered as the prime example of pure competition just as utilities have traditionally been classified as the prototype of pure monopoly, that is, a legally created and protected monopoly. Further, this area has seen a rather wide variation in types of regulation attempted. This is in contrast to utilities where the efforts at regulation have followed a single major stream of development.

The third area chosen has been the anti-trust laws. This effort at regulation applies to a larger segment of the economy than the regulation of either utilities or agriculture. The regulation of the anti-trust laws extends not only to the activities of the enterpriser in selling his products but also to the factor markets—the resources employed by the entrepreneur. The most notable exception here is the area of labor as a factor of production. Labor is excepted from the anti-trust laws by the Clayton Act of 1914, but is subjected to regulation by the Wagner Act of 1935 and the Taft-Hartley Law of 1948, in addition to lesser regulatory legislation.

There are additional regulatory activities which are of concern to the manager of an enterprise, which we are excluding in our selection. Perhaps the most significant of these exclusions have been the area of public finance, the collection and expenditure of the revenues of government, the area of labor and the area of international trade regulations. This exclusion can be partially justified on the ground that each of the lesser regulatory activities can be analogized to one of the major areas we are examining.

AGRICULTURAL REGULATION

Many types of governmental regulation are based on non-economic grounds such as political and sociological objectives although sometimes an economic target is likewise specified.[2] Agriculture is a prime example. It would be a mistake to fail to recognize that agricultural regulation has been strongly motivated by efforts to protect "a way of life."

Efforts at agricultural regulations can be classified by the targets at which they have been aimed. The economic programs for regulating agriculture have been directed at these objectives:

[2] To be sure, in all cases of governmental regulation, some attempt is made at developing an economic target or justification.

1. the increasing of the demand for farm products or the cutting of the costs of production of the farmer;

2. the limiting of the supply of farm products through crop limitation and price setting;

3. the maintenance of farmers by relief or gift programs;

4. the support of price levels through purchase, loan and storage programs;

5. the over-all programs of purchase and resale at price differentials such as Agriculture Secretaries Brannan and Benson advocated during the Truman and Eisenhower administrations.

The first of these targets is a goal of many government programs and can directly be classified as economic, at least to the extent that agriculture receives no more than its proportionate share of governmental help. We need not analyze the first target, except to point out abuses and unintended results. Similarly, the third target can be viewed as the responsibility of government when it extends no further than assisting the individual farmer in transition to newer work areas. But the other targets call for examination because of analogous application to business.

Restriction of Supply to Raise Price

The agricultural program to restrict supply in an effort to raise price has been effectuated through the proposal by the Secretary of Agriculture of total acreage controls for specific crops on a national basis together with the assignment of specific acreage quotas to individual farmers. Such a program is diagrammatically shown by Figure V-1.

With existing supply shown by the S_1S_1 curve, the effect of crop regulation is to move the supply curve to the left, say to S_2S_2. The price in the market increases from P_1 to P_2. Assuming that the crop regulation program *can* be carried out so that a lesser quantity of the crop reaches the market, the price in the market will rise. But whether

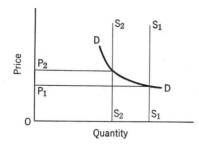

Figure V-1. Supply restriction to raise price.

this price increase is favorable or not depends on the relative elasticities of the demand curve and the supply curve. Assuming that the demand curve for the agricultural product is inelastic, the total revenue following the price increase will be increased as a result of the restriction of supply. If the demand for the agricultural product is elastic, the opposite will result,[3] namely, the restriction of the supply will bring even greater grief to the producers of the product.

This analysis, however, assumes:

1. that the restriction of supply can be enforced (mere control of acreage is not alone the answer, since the farmer can upset the plan by intensified output on the remaining acres);

2. that there is no substitution possible between the product whose supply is controlled and such substitute products as may remain uncontrolled (else the problem being resolved in the situation of the controlled product may be transferred to the market for the substitute products, which may have been in satisfactory adjustment before this transfer);

3. that even if the substitute products are controlled just as the principal product is, the factors of production will not be transferred to producing another product (even though not a substitute product) already in adequate supply;

4. that imports of the regulated product are controlled.

The Use of Purchase, Loan, and Storage Programs to Stabilize Price

The so-called ever-normal granary program is one under which the government purchases (or loans on) crops and stores them for later disposition. This program assumes that the fundamental difficulty is not one of a permanent over-capacity in the product, but, rather, that the problem is the irregularity of year-to-year supply originating with weather and the consequent speculative moves by the farmer-producers. This involves the famous cobweb theorem.

The cobweb theorem involves the situation where (1) the producers assume that the most likely future price is the current price and (2)

[3] This is an application of the principle first applied in the famous dispute whether the use of improved machinery in an industry will result in the displacement of labor within that industry. If the demand for the product of the industry is elastic relative to supply, the introduction of more efficient machinery will result in greater employment within that industry since the labor displaced by the machinery will be more than offset by the increase in the quantity demanded of the product made by that industry. Conversely if the demand for the product of the industry is inelastic relative to supply, then the introduction of labor-saving machinery into that industry will result in net unemployment of labor in that industry.

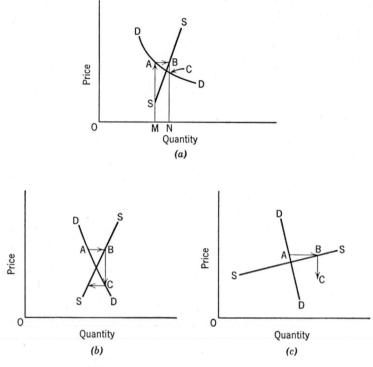

Figure V-2. (*a*) Relatively elastic demand; relatively inelastic supply. (*b*) Demand and supply of same relative elasticity. (*c*) Relatively inelastic demand; relatively elastic supply.

there is a significant gap in harvests (or there are discrete intervals between outputs by various producers) and all harvests occur at about the same time.

In this case, three different situations may exist:

In Figure V-2*a*, we have the situation where in the event of a crop failure, output OM comes to market rather than the equilibrium amount. This output commands price A in the market. Projecting this price to next year, farmers plant output ON, expecting price B, but, when this crop is brought to market, it commands only price C. Projecting this process, it is clear that maladjustments will quickly return to normal. This follows because supply is inelastic relative to demand.

In Figure V-2*b*, we have the situation where the relative elasticities of demand and supply are equal. There may be no return to equilibrium but at least the situation is stable.

In Figure V-2c, we have the situation where demand is inelastic relative to supply. This situation is explosive and unstable. Evidence indicates this is the typical agricultural situation because demand *is* relatively inelastic (see the elasticities for agricultural commodities estimated by Professor Schultz on page 82) and supply elastic due to the relatively free entry to farming.

The ever-normal granary would seem to call for transfer of surpluses from big crop years to fill the shortages of years of crop failure. Diagrammatically this is shown in Figure V-3.

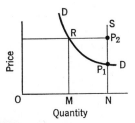

Figure V-3. Purchase (loan) and storage plan.

Because of a bumper crop, output ON comes to market. In a free market this would command price P_1. But if the government purchases the bumper part of the crop (quantity MN), the price will rise to P_2 and quantity OM will move in the free market at that price. What determines (or should determine) the price, P_2, which the government will pay (or loan)? This is where parity prices come in. Price P_2 is set at that level which gives the farmer the same purchasing power per bushel of output sold as he received in a base year when the price was "normal" or "fair." But while this might have been a "normal" price in the base year, there is no presumption that things are now the same as they were in the base year. If conditions are different (such as permanently lower demand for the crop), this program will keep factors of production at work in an area where they are no longer needed and the surpluses will pile up year after year.

The Use of Governmental Purchase from the Producer at a Higher Price and Resale in the Market at a Lower Price in the Same Year

The program proposed during the 1950's calls for government purchase at a higher price and resale into regular trade channels at the market (or lower) price. This is the so-called Brannan, or Benson, Plan. Under this program, the government purchases at a parity price (which was just explained above) and resells at the free market price.

Diagrammatically this is shown in Figure V-4, with the government buying at price P_1 (the parity price) and selling at price P_2.

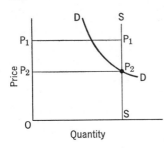

Figure V-4. Purchase at a higher price and resale at a lower price.

This program is merely a variation of the second program. Under the Brannan-Benson Plan, the rectangle $P_1P_1P_2P_2$ in Figure V-4 is the loss to the government, whereas, under the ever-normal granary plan, the rectangle MNP_2R in Figure V-3 is the loss to the government (plus storage charges but minus proceeds of the sale of the excess crop purchased). Thus, whether the ever-normal granary plan or the Brannan-Benson Plan costs the government more will (aside from storage costs and resale proceeds under the ever-normal granary plan) depend on the elasticity of demand for the product. If the demand is inelastic, the Brannan-Benson Plan will cost more; if demand is elastic, the ever-normal granary plan is more expensive to government. But in either case, the basic weaknesses may continue, that is, factors of production will remain at work in areas where the consumers (through their willingness or not to pay prices) do not want the factors at work. This would follow if the government support price is above the equilibrium price.

ANTI-TRUST REGULATION

While agriculture furnishes an example of government regulation in the area of pure competition, and utility regulation gives an example of government regulation in the area of nearly pure monopoly, anti-trust regulation concerns the area in between, the imperfect, monopolistic, or oligopolistic competition, where the producer neither sets the price (monopoly) nor is devoid of influence on price (pure competition) but both affects price by his action and can expect reaction to his price conduct.

Anti-trust regulation must be understood in terms of the policy that lies behind it insofar as that can be identified. European countries have pursued the opposite of an anti-trust policy namely a program of cartels, market shares, etc. and have even made government an instrument of this policy in pursuing nationalistic aims. Historians and political scientists may tell us this has been a necessary part of nationalism, particularly in the nineteenth century.

In the United States, on the other hand, the anti-trust policy seems to stem from the concept of democracy and in part from isolationism and is expressed in the idea of equality of opportunity and freedom of entry for producers together with nondiscrimination for customers. Isolationism may have entered the picture through the earlier American desire to disassociate not only from political "cartels" but also from economic cartels. Broadly speaking, enforcement can come by government suit or under the triple damage provision by persons claiming injury from violation.

The Sherman Act of 1890 begins the legislative history of anti-trust policy in the United States. That act sets forth forbidden practices in two sections: (1) "every contract, combination in the form of trust or otherwise, or conspiracy in restraint of trade or commerce among the several states or with foreign nations" is illegal; and (2) "every person who shall monopolize or attempt to monopolize, or combine or conspire with any other person or persons to monopolize, any part of the trade or commerce among the several states or with foreign nations shall be deemed guilty of a misdemeanor."

Under the impetus of Presidents Theodore Roosevelt and William Howard Taft, some results were achieved in the prevention of the merger of the Northern Pacific Railroad and the Great Northern and in the breaking up into several units of the American Tobacco Company and the Standard Oil Company. But the Supreme Court in 1911 restricted the Sherman Act of 1890 [4] with its famous rule of reason under which only unreasonable restraints of trade were illegal, and mere bigness was not in itself evil or evidence of illegal practices.

To define the area of illegal conduct more specifically and to exclude labor unions from the anti-trust act,[5] the Clayton Act of 1914 was passed. This act attempted to define as illegal four types of activity: (1) exclusive and tying contracts tending to lessen competition; (2) interlocking directorates of companies in the same business or designed to effect control; (3) price discrimination tending to lessen competition; and (4) interlocking stock ownership in competing companies tending to lessen competition.

In 1914, the Federal Trade Commission Act was also passed to sup-

---

[4] It should be noted that according to the common law of today, some restraints of trade are legal. Thus the buyer of a barber shop may exact an enforcible promise from the seller not to compete in the area for a given period of time.

[5] Labor unions had been subjected to the anti-trust law in the famous Danbury Hatters cases, *Loewe v. Lawlor* 208 U.S. 274 (1908) and 235 U.S. 522 (1915).

plement the Sherman Act. The Federal Trade Commission Act made illegal "unfair methods of competition" but suffered from a failure to define what specific conduct was unfair. While the Sherman Act relied upon private citizens and the Department of Justice to claim its benefits for enforcement, the Federal Trade Commission Act was enforced by a federal agency, the Federal Trade Commission.[6] In 1938, the Wheeler-Lea Act added "unfair or deceptive acts or practices" to the scope of the Federal Trade Commission Act.

In 1920, the Webb-Pomerene Act authorized competing firms in the United States to combine for purposes of effective competition in international trade against the cartels encouraged by European law. Thus activities illegal at home became legal abroad.

Little anti-trust prosecution occurred in the 1920's but in the 1930's with the problem of price-cutting generated by the depression, the National Recovery Act Codes were established to deal with the disorganization resulting from cut throat competition. Soon after these came the Robinson-Patman Act of 1936, amending the price discrimination section of the Clayton Act. In essence, price discrimination was defined as charging different prices to different customers unless the differences in price were supported by cost differences. But lowering price in good faith to meet competition was expressly recognized as legal. The Miller-Tydings Act of 1937 legalized resale price maintenance agreements in interstate commerce (under which each purchaser agrees with the seller not to resell below a stated price and to require each subpurchaser to so agree), where the particular state authorized them for intrastate commerce. The McGuire Act of 1952 extended resale price maintenance to apply even to dealers who had not entered written agreements. In 1950, the Kefauver-Celler Antimerger Act plugged a loophole that had existed in the Clayton Act where one business acquired the assets of another (and lessened competition) to avoid the previously banned acquisition of stock.

Business Practices Involved

The principal areas of business practices which have been involved with anti-trust legislation have been:[7] monopoly *per se*, patents, vertical integration and mergers, tying contracts and exclusive deal-

---

[6] The Federal Trade Commission Act also contains provisions preventing false advertising particularly in the food and health areas.

[7] The leading works which expand on our summary presentation are D. F. Pegrum, *Public Regulation of Business* (Homewood, Ill.: Irwin, 1959); Claire Wilcox, *Public Policies Towards Business,* rev. ed. (Homewood, Ill.: Irwin, 1955); and Corwin Edwards, *The Price Discrimination Law* (Washington: Brookings Institute, 1959).

ing, price discrimination, delivered pricing and basing points, and re-sale price maintenance. We summarize the institutional limits placed on business in each of these areas and indicate the economic signifi-cance of such limits.

Monopoly Per Se

By monopoly *per se*, we mean mere bigness or the holding of a high percentage of the total sales in a given product area but without any activities such as can be challenged under the specific practices that we deal with separately. Under the *Standard Oil* case of 1911,[8] the Supreme Court adopted the so-called "rule of reason." Standard Oil controlled about 90 per cent of refined oil production in the United States and all of the important pipelines. A wide assortment of practices such as rail-road rate rebates, espionage, bribery, and price cutting had been used to forge this position. The court found Standard Oil in violation of the Sherman Act and announced that it would apply the test of reasonable-ness to determine whether illegal monopoly and restraint of trade existed. Following this, in the *United States Steel* case,[9] the court dealt with the largest steel producer, who was almost equal in size to all other steel producers combined. In this case, the court indicated, in a four-to-three vote, that mere bigness or unused power for evil was not in it-self a violation of the Sherman Act.

Then in 1945, Judge Learned Hand of the Circuit Court of Appeals established a departure in the *Aluminum Company of America* case[10]

---

[8] *Standard Oil Company of New Jersey v. United States,* 221 U.S. 1 (1911). Contrast the analysis of D. F. Pegrum, *Public Regulation of Business* (Homewood, Ill.: Irwin, 1959), pp. 306f, with J. S. McGee, "Predatory Price Cutting: The Standard Oil (N.J.) Case," *Journal of Law and Economics,* vol. 1, pp. 137–69 (1958).

[9] *United States v. United States Steel Corporation,* 251 U.S. 417 (1920).

[10] *United States v. Aluminum Company of America,* 147 F. (2^d) 416 (1945). De-spite the clarity of Judge Hand's language in the quotation that follows in the text, opinions by nonlawyers exist that "it is apparently no longer true (if it ever was) that one-firm production of some (unspecified) large percentage of any more or less homogeneous product is usually sufficient to prove violation of sec-tion 2 of the Sherman Act." L. S. Keyes, "The Bethlehem-Youngstown Case and the Market Share Criterion," *American Economic Review,* vol. 51 (1961), pp. 643–657. Judge Hand's opinion has been repeatedly cited by the United States Su-preme Court and the only reservation has been whether the Supreme Court will recognize the defense suggested by Hand that the large position of a firm in its industry has been "thrust upon" it. The court so stated in *American Tobacco Co. v. United States,* 328 U.S. 781 (1946) and in *United States v. du Pont de Nemours and Co.,* 357 U.S. 377 (1956). The latter is the "cellophane" decision, in which Du Pont was found to produce 75 per cent of American cellophane but only 18 per cent of the flexible packaging material sales. On the ground that the "market"

which has been substantially followed. This case was referred to the Circuit Court of Appeals by the Supreme Court which was unable to establish a quorum for the case. The Aluminum Company of America was shown to have had a high (though varying) percentage of virgin aluminum production in the United States from 1912 on. For example from 1934 to 1938, it produced an average of more than 90 per cent of all U.S. virgin aluminum. This was held to constitute monopoly. Though no misuse of this position might be shown, the existence of the monopoly was held a violation of the Sherman Act. The only possible defense recognized by the court was whether monopoly had been thrust upon the Aluminum Company. This "passive monopoly" defense was not recognized in the *Aluminum Company* case, because this producer had anticipated all manner of developments and thus prevented competitors from becoming established. The court held that no "specific intent" to establish monopoly need be proven. The effort by the Aluminum Company to defend itself on the ground that it took only fair profits was denied. Judge Hand ruled that 90 per cent of production was enough to constitute monopoly, but "it is doubtful whether 60 to 64 per cent would be enough, and certainly 33 per cent is not."

If a producer is by law limited to no more than say 50 per cent of the output of an industry before he faces the Sherman Act, what should be his plan for further growth? Diversification is an obvious answer. But another alternative might be the realigning of products and other aspects within his own industry so that he maneuvers himself into possession of the most profitable 50 per cent of the business of his industry. The most profitable 50 per cent might be defined in terms of getting the most stable and progressive customers, pursuing the products with the brightest future, and those that require the least specialized production facilities. In short, the producer may pursue that 50 per cent of the industry which offers the highest rate of return on his investment and minimizes the risk. It may very well be that the

---

for cellophane is not just cellophane but all flexible packaging material, the Supreme Court affirmed the finding of the lower court that there was no monopoly by Du Pont. The court expressly relied upon the fact that there is a high cross-elasticity of demand between cellophane and other flexible packaging materials such as glassein and pliofilm.

The 4-to-2 decision that Du Pont violated Section 7 of the amended Clayton Act about intercompany holdings of stock through only 23 per cent ownership of General Motors (*United States v. du Pont de Nemours and Co.*, 353 U.S. 586 (1957)) is not to be confused with Judge Hand's standard in the *Aluminum* case. The influence by ownership of a percentage of another company's stock in vertical integration is not the same question as the percentage a firm needs to have of an industry's market in order to establish a presumption of monopoly.

General Electric Company with its record of 20 per cent per year earned on invested capital, its careful selection of preferred customers and careful culling of products is pursuing this pattern while avoiding charges that it is a monopoly in the electrical field by staying under the "magic" 50 per cent of its industry.

Patents

A patent is a legal monopoly for 17 years granted to an inventor as an incentive to progress and reward for effort. There thus is an apparent conflict between the anti-trust laws which strike down monopoly and the patent laws which grant a monopoly for a "new and useful" development. More than that, patent law permits the inventor (or the one to whom he sells his rights) to refuse to license others. In short, he can insist upon the patent's nonuse. Likewise, as established in the *General Electric* case[11] the patent owner can legally set the price at which the *particular* patented product can be sold. The resolution of this conflict of patent law and anti-trust law will be briefly set forth.

Cross-licensing, or the granting of licenses on *all* patents owned by one party to another in return for a parallel licensing by the other party is in itself legal but becomes illegal when it involves price fixing by the patent owner.[12] The distinction from the *General Electric* case lies in the *grouping* of the patents *and* the price fixing.

Another device that has been upset in the patent field is the use of a patent whose validity is questionable as a tool to require the licensee to adhere to prices. Under a rule of patent law that a licensee cannot question the validity of the patent under which he is licensed, price fixing could be expanded by using questionable patents. The Supreme Court held that the licensee could challenge a patent when he asserted the Sherman Act.[13]

Even though resale price maintenance was legalized by the Miller-Tydings Act, the Supreme Court has held that the patent owner cannot control prices down the line to the ultimate buyer where intermediate buyers do further processing of the product.[14] The patent owner can only set the price on what he sells. However, under the *General Electric* case (above) the patent owner may establish agencies and require the agents (who do no processing) to sell at fixed prices.

Although cross-licensing (without price fixing) is not in itself illegal

---

[11] *United States v. General Electric Company*, 272 U.S. 476 (1926).

[12] *United States v. Line Material Co.*, 333 U.S. 287 (1950).

[13] *Sola Electric Company v. Jefferson Electric Co.*, 317 U.S. 173 (1942).

[14] *United States v. Univis Lens Co.*, 316 U.S. 341 (1942).

under the Sherman Act, such patent pooling can become illegal when it is used as a means of lessening competition. Considerable cross-licensing exists in the automobile industry and this has never been attacked. Thus although pooling in itself is illegal under the Sherman Act, the pooling of patents is legal if it is not done to lessen competition or otherwise serve as a dodge of the anti-trust laws.

Tying contracts by which the patent owner attempts to require that other products be bought from the patent owner[15] or that the licensee not sell other products in connection with the patented item are illegal.

Restrictive licensing by which the patent owner attempts to control the use of a patented article after it is sold or leased and in that effort at control attempts to limit or restrict other non-patented material is illegal. Thus a restriction on a patented movie projector requiring the licensee to rent films from the patent owner is illegal [16] although the patent owner could limit the number of times per year the machine might be used, for example, and the price for each use. To use the price of an article, of which the patented item is a part, as a measure of the amount of royalty to be paid is not, however, an illegal restriction.[17]

The last remaining area is that of acquiring a dominant position with respect to the patents in a particular industry. The classic illustration is United Shoe Machinery Corporation. This producer has been involved in anti-trust litigation since the early days of such statutes and is a famous example of the use of the leasing technique rather than sales to protect its position. In the most recent case involving United Shoe,[18] violation of the anti-trust laws was claimed from the fact that the company had a large number of complementary patents, about four thousand in number, of which 95 per cent were generated by its own research. The company never sold but only leased machinery involving these patents. Some two-thirds of its patents were never put to use. The company never refused to grant licenses of its patents but had not been asked for licenses. The company had not threatened competitors. While each of the company's activities in itself had been legal, the company did hold the dominant position in the industry and supplied from 75 per cent to 85 per cent of the nation's shoe machinery. United Shoe Machinery Corp. was found in violation of the anti-trust

---

[15] *International Salt Company v. United States*, 332 U.S. 392 (1947).

[16] *Motion Picture Patents Company v. Universal Film Manufacturing Company*, 243 U.S. 502 (1917).

[17] *Automatic Radio Manufacturing Company v. Hazeltine Research, Incorporated*, 339 U.S. 827 (1950).

[18] *United States v. United Shoe Machinery Corporation*, 110 F. Supp. 295 (1953).

laws. The position of the company in the industry was enough to establish violation under the rule of the *Aluminum Company* case (just discussed) without going into the question of the patents it held.

We have avoided going into the area of the consequences of anti-trust violation. Fines, triple-damage suits, dissolution, and many other devices are available to deal with violations. This is a legal problem.

The pitfalls in the anti-trust field that may lie in anchoring one's position on patents have been one factor leading many producers to the conclusion that a preferred position is better achieved by a vigorous research program than by patents. In the fast-changing technology of the modern economy, a patent often gives protection to a producer only for the period needed to activate the well-designed research group of a competitor. The research group, often within periods as short as 6 months to a year, circumvents and surpasses the patent. In addition, when a patent is claimed, disclosures must be made to secure the patent and these might be of assistance to competitors in developing new methods for avoidance particularly in the case of process patents.

Vertical Integration and Mergers

Another business practice designed to solidify the position of a producer is vertical integration, the acquisition of all the facilities needed to turn out the finished product. Thus acquisition of sources of raw material and all the intermediate processing steps are the goal of this method of protecting the producer's position from inroads by other finished goods producers or "holdups" by suppliers who may come under the domination of competitors.

Vertical integration, in itself, is not illegal. But if it is used as part of a program which tends to monopoly or tends to lessen competition, it becomes subject to the same rules that apply to monopoly. One of the more recent illustrations of the violation of the anti-trust laws was the *Paramount Pictures* case[19] in which an integrated control of movies from their production through distribution and exhibition was struck down on the ground that trade was restrained and competition lessened. The result was that five interrelated companies were broken down into five disaffiliated producing companies and five disaffiliated theater circuits for exhibition. Actually there was horizontal integration (between the five interrelated companies) as well as vertical integration (each of the five engaged in all activities from producing to exhibiting).

In large part, the standards as to whether a merger will be held legal or illegal under the anti-trust laws are determined by the pre-

[19] *Paramount Pictures, Incorporated v. United States*, 334 U.S. 131 (1948).

vailing rule on the question of monopoly per se and the status of competition in the industry involved. The Celler Antimerger Act of 1950 plugged the last "loophole." But such recent mergers as Nash with Hudson to form American Motors, of Packard with Studebaker, and of Kaiser with Willys were not considered by the enforcement agencies to involve illegal conduct. No doubt this position rested heavily on the idea that such mergers merely encouraged competition in an industry dominated by General Motors, Ford, and Chrysler. On the other hand the Department of Justice opposed the proposed merger of Bethlehem Steel with Youngstown Sheet and Tube and the Federal District Court agreed, as cited in footnote 10.

Tying Contracts and Exclusive Dealing

Tying contracts and exclusive dealing arrangements are not in themselves illegal, but under Section 3 of the Clayton Act they become illegal when they lessen competition or tend to monopoly. The classic case involves International Business Machines.[20] This company leased business machines on the condition that the lessee use only such tabulating cards as were made by International Business Machines. The company had patents on both the machines and the cards, but the machines were such that a lessee could use other cards as well. The court held that IBM could condition the leasing of the machines upon the use of cards of a given specification in order to protect its name, but that the company could not require that the cards be bought from IBM.

In the area of exclusive dealing, the *Standard Oil of California*[21] case stands out as announcing the rule that if a "substantial share of the market" is involved, the inference could be drawn that competition would tend to be lessened, and thus the agreement would be illegal. Standard Oil of California used an exclusive-supply contract with independent dealers in gas and auto accessories. The contract did not require the dealers to buy all their supplies of petroleum products and auto accessories from Standard but only all of such products as the dealer named. Thus the contract was not technically a tying contract but a "full requirements" contract which imposed duties and benefits on Standard and on the dealer. The contracts covered 6.7 per cent of the total business of these products in the California area. The court struck down the arrangement on the basis that a substantial share of the market was involved and the practice tended to lessen competition.

---

[20] *International Business Machines Corporation v. United States,* 298 U.S. 131 (1936).

[21] *Standard Oil of California et al. v. United States,* 337 U.S. 293 (1949).

On the other hand, exclusive dealership arrangements such as prevail in automobile or farm implement selling have not been attacked as illegal.

Price Discrimination

Under the original Section 2 of the Clayton Act, it is illegal to engage in unjustifiable discrimination between purchasers when so doing would tend to lessen competition or to create monopoly.

In the *National Biscuit Company*[22] case, the Circuit Court of Appeals held that there was nothing in the law requiring that a producer's schedule of discounts must reflect cost differences in serving different classes of customers. In the *Nabisco* case, the company refused to accept pooled independent stores as entitled to the same discount that a chain store with the same number and size of outlets would receive. On the other hand, when the *American Can*[23] case reached the Supreme Court, the Department of Justice successfully emphasized that practices which lessened competition among purchasers were as illegal as practices reducing competition among sellers rather than the Federal Trade Commission argument in the *Nabisco* case, which was based on the failure of discounts to follow cost differences.

This difficulty with price discrimination cases resulted in the Robinson-Patman Act amending section 2 of the Clayton Act. The amendment made some half dozen price policies illegal when they injured competitors: (1) selling at unreasonably low prices to destroy competition; (2) charging different prices to different customers where the conditions are the same; (3) paying brokerage where no independent service is performed; (4) giving services, etc. not allowed to others; (5) selling at different prices geographically to eliminate competition; and (6) charging different prices to different buyers where the differences are not supported by cost differences. The burden of proving legality was placed on the suspected company.

One serious problem confronting the economist is that, under the new "cost" test for discrimination, the Federal Trade Commission has refused to recognize marginal cost pricing and has insisted upon average cost pricing.[24]

The reason for this position by the Federal Trade Commission is clear. Once the principle of pricing on the basis of costs is recognized, there is a considerable area for dispute as to which volume of business

---

[22] *National Biscuit Company v. Federal Trade Commission*, 299 F. 733 (1924).

[23] *American Can Company v. United States*, 278 U.S. 245 (1929).

[24] No flat reference can be cited, but there is clear implication that marginal costs will not be used in Federal Trade Commission, *Annual Report*, 1941, p. 26.

is to be considered as marginal. The producer will always contend that the sales on which he has cut price are the marginal sales, while the commission can be expected to maintain that this cutting of price is the very conduct that is illegal. Hence the commission can be expected to contend for average cost pricing and a system of allocating all joint and overhead costs over all sales. The precise defense of marginal cost pricing had been successfully used earlier by Goodyear,[25] in seeking to justify a contract with Sears, Roebuck and Company under which Goodyear supplied all Sears tire requirements at "cost plus 6 per cent," but using a Sears trademark and tread design. The Commission contended this price favored Sears by 12 to 22 per cent even after allowing a price difference based on savings of cost due to quantity and the elimination of some selling expenses. Goodyear argued that this "marginal" business gave it a minimum volume and stability and passed on to Sears all the risks of price declines in labor and raw material costs in addition to credit losses. If the Commission were to recognize marginal cost pricing it would then have a new problem of establishing standards by which to determine which sales are truly marginal and which are really mere price cutting to lessen competition.

Under the Robinson-Patman Act's broadened definition of illegal practices, the Supreme Court in the *Morton Salt* case[26] held illegal a system of discounts such that only five purchasers qualified for the lowest price and some customers were given allowances who were in competition with other customers who did not receive such allowances. The court said the law was designed to protect small buyers by requiring that large buyers get no greater price benefit than cost differences justified. This case has opened the door for extensive scrutiny of price differences not based on cost differences.

The cutting of price in good faith to meet an existing low price has been upheld by the Supreme Court[27] even when there are effects lessening competition. This constitutes one of the main defenses to a price discrimination charge today.

Delivered Pricing and Basing Points

The matter of delivered pricing is illustrated by the situation in

---

[25] *Goodyear Tire and Rubber Company v. Federal Trade Commission*, 92 F (2^d) 677 (1937), reversing 22 F.T.C. 232 (1933).

[26] *Federal Trade Commission v. Morton Salt Company*, 334 U.S. 37 (1948).

[27] *Standard Oil Company v. Federal Trade Commission*, 340 U.S. 231 (1951) and *Federal Trade Commission v. Standard Oil Co.*, 78 S.Ct. 369 (1958). See Norman M. Gold and Richard P. McGrath, "Functional Discounts Under the Robinson-Patman Act: the Standard Oil Case," *Harvard Law Review*, vol. 67, pp. 294f (1954).

which all the buyers in the country (in the case of a single basing point) pay the same price delivered to their door regardless where located. The direct opposite is F.O.B. mill pricing, under which all buyers pay the same price at the mill, and each buyer pays his freight from there.

One form of the problem is the use of a basing point. This is illustrated by the famous "Pittsburgh Plus" of the steel industry. Each buyer paid the price in Pittsburgh plus freight from Pittsburgh regardless of where the steel was made. This was held to be discriminating and an unfair method of competition by the Federal Trade Commission in 1924. U. S. Steel accepted the ruling and switched to a multiple basing-point system.

No further activity by the government occurred until the Robinson-Patman Act provisions on discrimination were passed in 1936. Under this act, the Commission attacked the single basing-point system used for glucose by Corn Products Refining Co. and A. E. Staley Mfg. Co. Although there were a number of separately located producing facilities, the Commission contended that the use of Chicago as a basing point favored Chicago candy manufacturers and was harmful to competition among purchasers. The Supreme Court upheld this position[28] and denied the defense of Staley that it merely followed the use of a basing point by Corn Products in order to meet competition.

By paying no freight on in-bound raw material and no out-bound freight on that part of the finished product sold in the Chicago area, the Chicago candy maker had an advantage, although all candy makers were free to locate in Chicago.

The Commission went further in the *Cement Institute* case and was upheld [29] as to its order that the manufacturers of Portland cement and their association cease colluding to use a multiple basing-point system to reduce competition. The case rests on the collusion. Then the Commission in the *National Lead Company*[30] case sought to stop a "common course" of using a zone-delivered price system, under which one price is charged to all customers in a given area or "zone" regardless of the actual freight differences, and no freight is separately billed. The Supreme Court upheld the Commission's temporary order which was designed to allow new pricing systems to develop, but the Supreme Court clearly said that zone-delivered pricing was not in itself illegal

[28] *Corn Products Refining Company v. Federal Trade Commission*, 324 U.S. 726 (1945), and *Federal Trade Commission v. A. E. Staley Manufacturing Company*, 324 U.S. 746 (1945).

[29] *Federal Trade Commission v. Cement Institute*, 333 U.S. 683 (1948).

[30] *Federal Trade Commission v. National Lead Company*, 352 U.S. 419 (1957).

nor was the absorption of freight as a method of competition. Thus it appears that illegality arises from the pursuit of a common and rigid freight policy (other than F.O.B. mill) which is taken as evidence of an effort to suppress competition.

Resale Price Maintenance

Under resale price maintenance, the producer seeks to control the sale price of his product right down to the retail level. The legalization of this practice by the Miller-Tydings Act of 1937 was a child of the depression. Small retailers saw in retail price maintenance a means of meeting the challenge of the chain store. Labor groups saw in it the answer to the pressure for cutting wages in the depression. Producers saw in it a necessary condition for national advertising campaigns and a preventative against use of the product as a "loss leader" for the promotion of total volume by aggressive retailers. But the practice prevents the passing on to consumers of the economies of mass distribution achievable by large retailers.

Whether as a result of resale price maintenance or not, the rapid rise of the discount house in the 1950's forced many producers to abandon the policy of resale price maintenance in 1958. The discount house offered an independent and effective distribution system of sufficient size to change the distribution of consumer durable goods.

CASE V-1. CANE SUGAR REFINING[*]

Government Regulation

Demand and Retail Prices

Cane sugar refining is an industry involved with considerable government regulation and with an international situation. In addition, it is fully integrated vertically.

The demand for sugar (cane and beet) presents a rather simple situation. Per capita consumption has deviated [†] from 103.3 pounds per person by more than 3 pounds in only one year from 1932 to 1956 as shown in Table I. In 1941 the deviation was 9.5 pounds but this is easily explained as the consequence of hoarding after the Pearl Harbor attack. War years are excluded as distorted by rationing.

Sugar is dealt with in the statistics in terms of "raw value" which is in liquid form of specified condition. Thus 103.3 pounds raw value is equal to 96.3 pounds refined weight. The conversion factor is 1.07.

Hence, it is possible to predict total sugar demand by the formula

$$D_t = \frac{\text{population in millions} \times 103.3}{2 \times 0.99}$$

where D_t is total demand for sugar in thousands of short tons (raw value); 2 is the constant for conversion to short tons; 0.99 is the constant to convert domestic consumption to total demand (1 per cent is exported).

Beet sugar (excluding World War II years) has remained constant at 20 per cent of total sugar demand from 1935 to 1956 with 10 per cent of total sugar being accounted for by direct consumption sugar[‡], imports and sugar from the cane mills of mainland producers. Table II shows these facts.

Thus demand for refined cane sugar can be expressed as

$$D_{rcs} = 0.70 \times D_t$$

where D_{rcs} is demand for refined cane sugar in thousands of short tons (raw value).

---

[*] With the assistance of Bruce Capek, M.B.A. (Northwestern).

[†] Even when syrup is added to the sugar figures, the situation is not particularly changed.

[‡] Defined as refined sugar ready for the consumer.

CASE V-1. TABLE I

Sugar Consumption and Population
United States, 1932–1956

Year	Deliveries* for U.S. Consumption in Thousands of Short Tons, Raw Value	Change in Invisible Inventory† in Thousands of Short Tons, Raw Value	Sugar Consumption‡ in Thousands of Short Tons, Raw Value	Population of U.S., Millions§	Per Capita Consumption in Pounds Raw Value
1932	6,439	NA	6,439	124.9	103.1
1933	6,387	NA	6,387	125.6	101.8
1934	6,332	NA	6,332	126.5	100.2
1935	6,634	NA	6,634	127.4	104.2
1936	6,706	NA	6,706	128.2	104.7
1937	6,671	NA	6,671	129.0	103.3
1938	6,643	153	6,490	130.0	100.0
1939	6,868	40	6,828	131.0	104.2
1940	6,891	160	6,731	132.1	101.9
1941	8,069	524	7,545	133.4	113.0
Rationing, 1942–1947, distorts data					
1948	7,343	−41	7,384	146.6	100.8
1949	7,580	−85	7,665	149.2	101.7
1950	8,279	127	8,152	151.7	107.6
1951	7,737	−158	7,895	154.4	102.4
1952	8,104	−52	8,156	157,0	104.0
1953	8,485	58	8,427	159.6	105.8
1954	8,207	−35	8,242	162.4	101.4
1955	8,399	−49	8,448	165.3	102.2
1956	8,904	81	8,823	168.1	105.0

Sources: Deliveries: *Sugar Statistics and Data*, Statistical Bulletin, U.S. Department of Agriculture, No. 214 (Washington, D.C.: United States Government Printing Office, 1957), Table 1, pp. 1–2. Invisible inventories: *Ibid.*, Table 24, pp. 170–172. Population: *Statistical Abstract of U.S., 1957*, U.S. Department of Commerce, Bureau of Census (Washington, D.C.: United States Government Printing Office, 1957), Table 5, p. 2.

* Deliveries from all sources of all forms of sugar.

† Invisible inventories are those held by wholesalers, retailers, and industry.

‡ Deliveries minus change in invisible inventory. This ignores inventory in individual households which is probably essentially constant except during prewar hoarding. Inventory figures for 1938–1941 are based on deliveries, since prewar inventory figures were collected by sample only.

§ Expressed to nearest 100,000. Includes Armed Forces overseas.

NA = Not available.

CASE V-1. TABLE II

Deliveries of Sugar by Primary Distributors for Domestic Consumption and Export, United States, 1935–1956

Per Cent of Total Sugar Deliveries

	Deliveries by Type		Source of Deliveries by Distributors			
	For U.S.				Importers of Direct	Mainland
	Con-	For	Cane Sugar	Beet Sugar	Con- sumption	Cane Sugar
Year	sumption	Export	Refiners	Processors	Sugar	Mills
1935	98.2	1.8	67.7	21.9	9.1	1.3
1936	99.1	0.9	66.9	20.2	10.6	2.3
1937	99.0	1.0	70.2	18.5	9.1	2.2
1938	99.1	0.9	68.6	21.6	8.4	1.4
1939	98.1	1.9	63.9	25.8	8.2	2.1
1940	97.5	2.5	67.0	22.0	9.8	1.2
1941	99.3	0.7	68.0	24.0	6.9	1.1
	Rationing, 1942–1947, distorts data					
1948	98.8	1.2	69.4	22.3	6.9	1.4
1949	99.3	0.7	72.0	19.5	6.7	1.8
1950	99.4	0.6	71.2	21.0	6.6	1.2
1951	99.0	1.0	70.3	22.2	6.2	1.3
1952	99.7	0.3	72.0	19.2	7.3	1.5
1953	99.7	0.3	71.1	20.6	6.8	1.5
1954	99.8	0.2	69.8	22.0	6.8	1.4
1955	99.2	0.8	71.5	21.4	6.7	0.4
1956	98.4	1.6	70.5	21.9	6.6	1.0

Source: Sugar Statistics and Data, op. cit. (Table I), Table 6, pp. 8–18. Absolute data converted to percentages of total demand.

Pricing in the *cane* sugar industry has been remarkably stable in terms of constant dollars as shown by Table III.

The Refining Process

About 1870, modern centrifugal machines replaced the large "fill houses" where crystallization had taken place and granulators were replaced by drying ovens. The shift to mechanized operations meant the end of family ownership. Large capital requirements led to the corporate form of business and in 1887 the Sugar Refineries Company was formed, and in 1891 this became American Sugar Refining Company, the dominant firm today. The Sugar Trust was quickly formed and after the Sherman Anti-Trust Act of 1893 this was the first trust sued under the new law.

CASE V-1. TABLE III

Actual Sugar Price, Deflated Sugar Price, and Consumer Price Index, by Years, 1932–1956

Year	(1) Refined Cane Sugar Quoted Wholesale Price Per Pound N.Y., with Tax, Annual Average, Cents	(2) Consumer Price Index Base 1947 to 1949	(3) Refined Cane Sugar F.O.B. N.Y., Cents Per Pound in Constant Dollars 1947 to 1949 Base
1932	4.07	58.4	6.98
1933	4.40	55.3	7.95
1934	4.53	57.2	7.94
1935	4.95	58.7	8.42
1936	4.79	59.3	8.08
1937	4.83	61.4	7.87
1938	4.57	60.3	7.60
1939	4.67	59.4	7.86
1940	4.43	59.9	7.40
1941	5.02	62.9	8.00
Rationing, 1942–1947, distorts data			
1948	7.76	102.8	7.56
1949	7.97	101.8	7.83
1950	8.00	102.8	7.79
1951	8.38	111.0	7.55
1952	8.62	113.5	7.60
1953	8.72	114.4	7.62
1954	8.72	114.8	7.60
1955	8.59	114.5	7.50
1956	8.77	116.2	7.48

Sources: Column 1: *Sugar Statistics and Data, op. cit.* (Table I), Table 49, pp. 272–273. Column 2: *Supplement to Survey of Current Business, 1957 Biennial Edition,* U.S. Department of Commerce (Washington, D.C.: United States Government Printing Office, 1957), p. 3. Column 3: column 1 divided by column 2.

The output of the industry increased from 2.8 million tons in 1910 to 5.5 million tons in 1920 largely because of the devastation of European sugar beet fields in World War I. The domestic sugar beet industry grew in the West and this together with low priced imports, mainly from Cuba, caused a decline in the industry in the 1920's. Despite a 2-cents-a-pound tariff in the Hawley-Smoot Act, the drastic drop in

Cuban sugar to less than 1-cent-a-pound (3 cents after tariff) put the industry in desperate shape in the early thirties. The Jones-Costigan Act of 1934 substituted growing and marketing restrictions rather than the tariff as the device to protect the sugar industry. This Act was extended in 1937, 1948, 1953, and 1956 with some amendments, but its basic approach continues and since that time the growth of the industry has been at the same rate as population as was shown in Table I.

The Organization of the Industry

The number of American cane sugar refineries has varied between 18 and 27 from 1909 to 1956 as shown in Table IV.

CASE V-1. TABLE IV

Number of Cane Sugar Refineries, United States, 1909–1956

Year	Number of Establishments*	Year	Number of Establishments*
1909	19	1931	19
1914	18	1933	19
1919	20	1935	18
1921	20	1937	23
1923	20	1939	27
1925	21	1947	25
1927	21	1954	23
1929	21	1956	22

Sources: 1909 to 1947: *U.S. Census of Manufacturers, 1947*, Vol. II, U.S. Bureau of Census (Washington, D.C.: United States Government Printing Office, 1949), Table 1, p. 120. 1954: *U.S. Census of Manufacturers, 1954*, Vol. I, U.S. Bureau of Census (Washington, D.C.: United States Government Printing Office, 1957), p. 204–2. 1956: *Manual of Sugar Companies, 1955/1956* (New York: Farr and Co., 1957), pp. 1–150; 194–203. Turner, *Marketing of Sugar* (Homewood, Ill.: Irwin, 1955), pp. 33–34.

* Establishment is defined by *Census of Manufactures, 1947*, as an individual refinery.

The Sugar Act severely restricts the import of direct consumption sugars (defined as those requiring no further refinement) which compete with the output of domestic refineries.

The 22 cane sugar refineries of 1956 are owned by 17 companies as shown in Table V, and the 4 largest own 10 of the 22 refineries and have 73 per cent of the melting capacity (defined as the quantity of raw sugar that can be dissolved in hot water, the first step in refining).

Case V-1. TABLE V

Composition of Cane Sugar Refining Industry, United States, 1946

Main Company and Subsidiary Companies	Number and Locations of U.S. Cane Sugar Refineries	Daily Melting Capacity Tons of Raw Cane Sugar	Per Cent of Total U.S. Melting Capacity	Data Source
The American Sugar Refining Co.				
Amer. Sugar Ref. Co. of N.Y.	5—Boston, Baltimore, Philadelphia, New York, Chalmette (La.)	8,050	32.6	1
Brooklyn Cooperage Co.				
Sugar Export Corp.				
Central Cunagua, S.A.				
Caonao Warehouses and Agricultural Co.				
The National Sugar Refining Co.	3—Philadelphia, Reserve (La.), New York	5,250	21.2	2
The California-Hawaiian Sugar Refining Corp.	1—Crockett (Calif.)	3,250	13.1	3
United Fruit Co.				
Revere Sugar Refinery	1—Charlestown (Mass.)	1,500	6.1	4
Elders and Fyffes, Ltd.				
United Fruit Sugar Co.				
United Fruit Steamship Co.				
Tropical Radio Telegraph Co.				
Tropical Radio Service Corp.				
Fruit Dispatch Co.				
Numerous other subsidiaries				
The Savannah Sugar Refining Corp.	1—Savannah, Ga.	1,250	5.1	5
Corn Products Refining Co.,				
Refined Sugars and Syrups Div.	1—Yonkers (N.Y.)	1,150	4.6	6
Imperial Sugar Co.	1—Sugar Land (Texas)	1,125	4.5	7
The Cuban-American Sugar Co.				
Cuban-American Sugar Mills Co.				
Cuban-American Mercantile Co.				
Colonial Sugars Co.	1—Gramercy (La.)	875	3.5	8
Compania Electrica del Norte de Oriente				
Compania del Ferrocarril de Puerto Padre				
Suerest Div. of American Molasses	1—Brooklyn	800	3.2	9
The South Coast Corporation	1—Mathews (La.)	530	2.1	10
Henderson Sugar Refinery, Inc.	1—New Orleans	500	2.0	11
Sterling Sugars, Inc.	1—Franklin (La.)	400	1.6	12
Fellsmere Sugar Producers Assn.	1—Fellsmere (Fla.)	N.A.	—	13
Southdown Sugars, Inc.	1—Houma (La.)	N.A.	—	14
Okeelanta Sugar Corp.	1—Okeelanta (Fla.)	N.A.	—	15
J. Aron Co., Inc.	1—Tallieu (La.)	N.A.	—	16

Sources: 1: *Manual of Sugar Companies, 1955–1956* (New York: Farr and Co., 1957), p. 13. 2: *Ibid.,* pp. 95–96. 3: *Ibid.,* p. 194. 4: *Ibid.,* pp. 121–122. 5: *Ibid.,* p. 105. 6: *Ibid.,* p. 198; also, *Annual Report, 1957,* Corn Prod. Ref. Co., p. 6. 7: *Manual of Sugar Companies, 1955–1956, op. cit.,* p. 195. 8: *Ibid.,* pp. 31–32. 9: *Ibid.,* p. 200. 10: *Ibid.,* p. 111. 11: *Ibid.,* p. 195. 12: *Ibid.,* p. 200. 13: Turner, *Marketing of Sugar* (Homewood, Ill.: Irwin, 1955), pp. 33–34. 14. *Ibid.* 15: *Ibid.* 16: *Ibid.*

N.A. = Not available.

The larger companies practice complete vertical integration: growing cane, operating cane mills and even owning the companies that carry on the transportation of cane to the mill and then the refinery. Californian and Hawaiian Sugar Refining Company (not shown in Table V) is an example of "reverse" integration, being owned by 28 Hawaiian sugar producers.

Almost all the cane sugar refineries are located near major United States seaports, on navigable inland waters or accessible by short rail hauls. This follows from the fact that the vast bulk of raw cane sugar is imported. Shipment by boat is in bulk and loading and unloading by conveyors.

The Government's Role

The sugar industry is rigidly regulated by the United States government.

A revenue tariff was placed on sugar from 1789.* This, of course, also acted as protection. Hawaii received this protection by the Reciprocal Treaty of 1875 with the Kingdom of Hawaii. From 1890 to 1894 sugar was duty-free, but the payment of a 2-cents-per-pound bounty to domestic producers continued the protection.

After the Spanish-American War, Puerto Rico and the Philippines received tariff protection, and Cuba received preferred tariff status. The domestic sugar beet industry also grew in the great expansion between 1910 and 1920 to which we have already referred. Recovery of the European sugar beet industry in the 1920's brought an excessive world supply. Other nations with domestic sugar industries then used protective tariffs.

The 2-cent tariff of the Hawley-Smoot Act (exempting the Philippines, Puerto Rico, Hawaii, and the Virgin Islands) beggared Cuba. With the Cuban price at less than 1 cent a pound, domestic sugar was pulled down to 3 cents a pound even after reckoning the tariff.

In this disorganized situation, Congress abandoned the tariff as a control in favor of a marketing quota system. The tariff continued for revenue purposes. An incidental device was a processing tax whose proceeds were directed to relieving growers who were forced to reduce crops as the government sought to watch supply and demand. This was declared unconstitutional in 1936. These quotas are summarized in Table VI for 1934 to 1956.

The basis for the initial quotas was the record of marketings in the period 1925 to 1933 applied against the *expected* United States demand

* Summarized from U.S. Senate Comm. on Finance, *Sugar Act Extension Hearings Report,* 84th Congress 2nd. session, Report 1461.

CASE V-1. TABLE VI

Quotas Under Several United States Sugar Acts, 1934–1956

Year of Sugar Act	Growing Region	Marketing Quota, Short Tons (Raw Value*) Unless Otherwise Indicated		
1934	Domestic Beet	1,550,000 plus 15% demand above 6,452,000		
	Mainland Cane	260,000 plus 15% demand above 6,452,000		
	Hawaii	⌈Average quantity marketed in U.S. during three most repre-		
	Puerto Rico	sentative years during 1925–1933, as determined by Secre-		
	Virgin Islands	tary of Agriculture. To be increased collectively by 70% of		
	Philippines	⌊increase in demand above 6,452,000.		
	Cuba and Foreign			
1937	Domestic Beet	23.19% of total U.S. requirement		
	Mainland Cane	6.29		
	Hawaii	14.04		
	Puerto Rico	11.94		
	Virgin Islands	0.13		
	Philippines	15.41 (952,000 tons minimum guarantee)		
	Cuba	28.60		
	Other Foreign	0.40		
1948 and 1953 Amendment	Domestic Beet	1,800,000	⌈1,800,000	
	Mainland Cane	500,000	500,000	
	Hawaii	1,052,000	1,052,000	
	Puerto Rico	910,000	1,080,000	
	Virgin Islands	6,000	12,000	
	Philippines	952,000 as made	952,000 as made	
	Cuba	98.64% of remainder	96% of remainder	
	Other Foreign	1.36% of remainder	4% of remainder⌋	
1956	Domestic Beet	1,800,000⌉	⌈Plus 55% of	First 165,000 split 51.5%
	Mainland Cane	500,000	amount by	to beet and 48.5% to
	Hawaii	1,052,000	which total	mainland cane. Next
	Puerto Rico	1,080,000	U.S. require-	20,000 to Puerto Rico.
	Virgin Islands	12,000⌋	ment exceeds	Next 3,000 to Virgin Is.
	Philippines	952,000	⌊8,350,000.	Remainder pro-rated.
	Cuba	2,835,840—Plus 29.59% of demand over 8,350,000.		
	Other Foreign	118,160—Plus 15.41% of demand over 8,350,000.		
		8,350,000		

Sources: 1934, 1937, and 1948 (1953): *Sugar Act Extension Hearings*, 84th Congress, 2nd. Session on H.R. 7030, U.S. Senate Committee on Finance (Washington, D.C.: United States Government Printing Office, 1956), p. 42. 1956: Public Law 545, 84th Congress, May 29, 1956, reprinted in *Sugar Reference Book*, Vol. XXV (New York, 1957), pp. 80–81.

* It is the practice of the industry to report production, inventories, deliveries, etc., on a "raw value" basis. This means the weight of the 96 per cent pure sugar, called raw sugar, that is the refiners' raw material. This convention is adopted to avoid confusion arising from the 7 per cent weight loss in refining. Although sugar beets are shipped to the beet processors as beets, they are reported as the equivalent amount of raw cane sugar for uniformity in terminology.

for 1934 of 6.452 million short tons. The actual quantity marketed in 1934 turned out to be 6.574 million short tons.*

The unconstitutionality of the processing tax-subsidy in 1936 threatened to upend the quotas of 1934 unless some form of subsidy assured compliance. The Sugar Act of 1937 adjusted the mainland

* *Sugar Statistics and Data, op. cit.* (Table I), Table 6, p. 200.

cane quota to compensate for mosaic cane disease which had reduced mainland cane production in the base period. A revised (and constitutional) tax-subsidy was enacted in 1937. The 55-45 split between domestic and foreign producers was accepted domestically and abroad.

The quotas were suspended in World War II and Cuban production replaced the lost Philippine production.

After World War II fixed quotas were substituted in the 1948 Act for the percentage quotas of the 1937 Act. Any future growth in production would go 98.64 per cent to Cuba and 1.36 per cent to other foreign countries. In 1951 larger fixed quotas were given Puerto Rico and the Virgin Islands but other areas were held to their absolute quotas of the 1948 Act. As a result, domestic areas in 1953 to 1955 got only 54.2 per cent of the marketings compared to the 55.6 per cent

Case V-1. CHART I

Marketing of Sugar in United States by Source of Supply, 1930–1956*

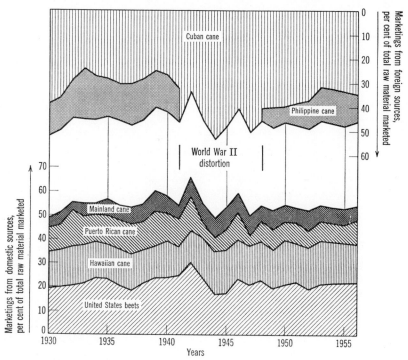

Source: Table VII.

* Virgin Islands and Other Foreign sources omitted since they were less than 1 per cent each.

CASE V-1. TABLE VII

Marketing of Sugar in United States, by Source of Supply, 1930–1956

Percent of Total Marketings For Area

Year	Total Marketings in Thousands of Tons (Raw Value)	Continental United States — Beet	Continental United States — Cane	Hawaii	Puerto Rico	Virgin Islands	Total Domestic	Philippines	Cuba	Other Foreign	Total Foreign
1930	6,683	19.3	3.2	13.0	12.1	0.1	47.7	11.9	39.6	0.8	52.3
1931	6,727	20.0	3.5	14.7	11.8	nil	50.0	13.0	36.6	0.4	50.0
1932	6,203	20.9	2.5	16.6	14.9	0.1	55.0	16.3	28.5	0.2	45.0
1933	6,331	21.6	5.0	15.6	12.5	0.1	54.8	19.7	24.9	0.6	45.2
1934	6,574	23.8	4.1	14.4	12.3	0.1	54.7	16.5	28.3	0.5	45.3
1935	6,277	23.6	5.1	14.8	12.7	nil	56.2	14.6	29.0	0.2	43.8
1936	6,833	20.0	6.0	15.1	13.3	nil	54.4	14.4	30.8	0.4	45.6
1937	6,860	18.1	7.1	14.4	13.1	0.1	52.8	14.5	31.4	1.3	47.2
1938	6,619	21.9	6.8	13.7	12.3	0.1	54.8	14.8	29.4	1.0	45.2
1939	7,466	24.2	7.9	13.0	15.1	0.1	60.3	13.1	25.8	0.8	39.7
1940	6,443	24.0	6.3	14.6	12.4	—	57.3	15.3	27.1	0.3	42.7
1941	8,009	24.4	5.1	11.3	12.4	0.1	53.3	10.7	33.6	2.4	46.7
1942	5,555	30.6	7.3	13.5	15.1	—	66.5	0.4	32.4	0.7	33.5
1943	6,466	23.6	7.1	13.4	9.9	—	54.0	—	44.2	1.8	46.0
1944	6,942	16.6	7.4	11.6	10.7	—	46.3	—	52.2	1.5	53.7
1945	5,997	17.4	6.9	12.4	15.1	0.1	51.9	—	46.6	1.5	48.1
1946	5,657	24.4	7.9	11.2	15.3	0.1	58.9	—	40.3	0.8	41.1
1947	7,759	20.3	4.9	10.9	12.5	—	48.6	—	50.8	0.6	51.4
1948	7,084	23.3	6.4	10.1	14.3	0.1	54.2	3.6	41.3	0.9	45.8
1949	7,588	19.6	7.3	10.1	14.4	0.1	51.5	6.9	40.9	0.7	48.5
1950	8,279	21.1	6.3	13.8	12.8	0.1	54.1	5.7	39.5	0.7	45.9
1951	7,758	22.3	5.9	12.1	12.4	0.1	52.8	9.0	38.0	0.2	47.2
1952	7,991	19.5	7.2	12.2	12.3	0.1	51.3	10.8	37.3	0.6	48.7
1953	8,282	21.1	6.2	13.1	13.5	0.1	54.0	11.3	33.4	1.3	46.0
1954	8,240	21.9	6.1	12.6	13.1	0.1	53.8	11.8	33.0	1.4	46.2
1955	8,396	21.4	6.0	12.5	12.9	0.1	52.9	11.6	34.1	1.4	47.1
1956	8,995	21.8	6.7	12.1	12.6	0.1	53.3	10.9	34.4	1.4	46.7
Weighted average 1934 to 1954 (except 1942–47) to 1/10 of per cent		22.4	6.4	13.2	13.3	0.1	55.4	11.6	32.0	1.0	44.6

Source: Sugar Statistics and Data, op. cit. (Table I), Table 6, pp. 199–200. Converted from actual marketings in thousands of short tons (raw value) to per cent of total marketings marketed by each growing area.

allowed them under the 1937 Act. The 1956 amendment restored domestic participation in growth to the 1937 plan. The results of the quota plan are shown in Table VII and Chart I.

The Secretary of Agriculture determines the "demand" each year, allowing for inventory situations, changes in population, and other demand considerations. When this "demand" is determined, he is directed to provide a supply such that the domestic price is fair (in relation to the Consumer Price Index, current and at the base period) being neither an excessive price nor one failing to maintain the do-

CASE V-1. CHART II

Comparison of Revenue and Payments* Under the Several United States Sugar Acts, 1937–1955. Curve A: Sugar Import Duty and Excise Tax Revenue; Curve B: Payments to Growers Under U.S. Sugar Acts; Shaded Area Between Curves Indicates the Annual Surplus Left in the U.S. Treasury

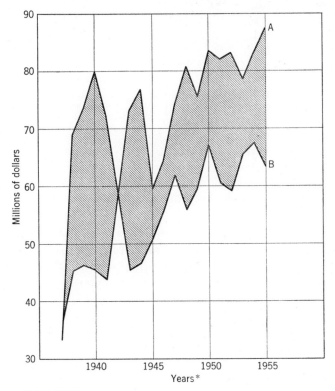

Source: Table VIII.
* Crop years for payments; fiscal years for collections.

Case V-1. TABLE VIII

Comparison of Revenue and Payments Under the Several United States
Sugar Acts, 1937–1955

Year*	Payments to Growers in Thousands of Dollars	Import Duty Plus Excise Tax in Thousands of Dollars
1937	$36,169	$33,249
1938	45,851	68,909
1939	46,414	73,602
1940	45,569	76,695
1941	43,380	72,319
1942	58,023	57,072
1943	45,516	73,887
1944	46,592	76,816
1945	51,144	59,964
1946	55,973	64,267
1947	62,165	74,531
1948	55,770	80,873
1949	59,704	75,279
1950	67,330	83,805
1951	60,537	82,094
1952	59,217	83,136
1953	65,607	78,383
1954	67,557	82,689
1955	63,335	87,700

Source: Sugar Statistics and Data, op. cit. (Table I), Table 62, p. 297.
* Crop years for payments. Fiscal years for collections.

mestic industry. From this total supply he establishes quotas pursuant
to the Act. There are intricate provisions for the allocation of deficits
from any area, but there is an overriding provision that any offshore
area furnishing less than 90 per cent of its quota in any year would
be penalized by a permanent reduction in its quota. The quota system
applies to raw material. Direct consumption sugar (in refined form) is
subject to stricter limitation than the raw material governed by the
quota system. Liquid sugar for this purpose is defined as direct consumption sugar to prevent "leaks" to industrial users who may be
equipped to handle liquid sugar.

Regulation of the area quotas down to the individual growers is
complete. The allocation to individual producers is based on past per-

formance and practice. Thus the Act protects not only the domestic areas but even the marginal producer.

Under the Roosevelt and Truman administrations, the tariff on sugar has gradually been reduced from 2 cents per pound to 0.5 cent per pound. Since the quotas provide protection, the tariff is of the revenue type. This revenue plus the receipts from the 0.535-cent-per-pound tariff on direct consumption sugar provide the funds which Congress appropriates as subsidy at rates from 30 cents per 100 pounds to 80 cents per 100 pounds inversely to the production of the individual producer. Payments are based on what is produced and not on what is not produced.

The results of this tax and subsidy are shown in Table VIII and Chart II. Table IX and Chart III show the "controlled" price of sugar bound for the U.S. market against the free price in the world market for the same Cuban sugar.

CASE V-1. CHART III

Price of Cuban* Raw Sugar for World Market Versus United States Market, 1934–1956. Curve A: Price for U.S. Market; Curve B: Price for World Market; Shaded Area Between Curves Indicates Lower Price to World Market

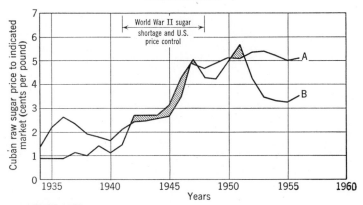

Source: Table IX.
* On board ship at Cuban docks.

Impact of Government Regulation of Raw Sugar Production and Marketing Upon the Cane Refining Industry

While the sugar acts aim at controlling the marketing of raw sugar produced in a number of areas, this legislation indirectly controls the cane sugar refining industry in a number of ways.

First, by virtue of the "freezing" of the ratio of cane sugar to beet

CASE V-1. TABLE IX

Price* of Cuban Raw Sugar for World Market Versus United States Market,
1934–1956

Price in Cents Per Pound for Shipment to:

Year	U.S. Market	World Market
1934	1.37¢	0.91¢
1935	2.21	0.88
1936	2.56	0.88
1937	2.35	1.13
1938	1.90	1.00
1939	1.74	1.43
1940	1.67	1.11
1941	2.09	1.46
1942	2.48	2.69
1943	2.46	2.69
1944	2.59	2.69
1945	2.65	3.14
1946	3.42	4.24
1947	4.97	5.03
1948	4.64	4.23
1949	4.94	4.16
1950	5.09	4.98
1951	5.07	5.67
1952	5.35	4.17
1953	5.43	3.41
1954	5.21	3.26
1955	5.00	3.24
1956	5.10	3.48

Source: Sugar Statistics and Data, op. cit. (Table I), Table 53, pp. 280–283.
* On board ship at Cuban docks.

sugar, the cane sugar refining industry is limited in the percentage of the United States demand for sugar which it can attempt to capture.

Second, with quotas frozen even down to the individual producer of raw sugar, the refineries are largely determined as to the quantity they will process each year.

Third, the Secretary of Agriculture, in effect, sets price through controlling the total supply permitted each year. This in large part controls profits since the spread between the prices of raw sugar and the refined product (the refiners' margin) determines net profits much more than the efficiency of the industry.

CASE V-1. TABLE X

Prices of Raw and Refined Cane Sugar
United States, Annual Averages, 1934–1956

Year	Raw Cane Sugar Duty Paid, New York, Cents Per Pound	Refined Cane Sugar Wholesale,* New York, Cents Per Pound
1934	3.019¢	4.123 ¢
1935	3.231	4.316
1936	3.594	4.691
1937	3.443	4.551
1938	2.936	3.946
1939	2.982	4.037
1940	2.786	3.802
1941	3.378	4.387
1942	3.739	4.913
1943	3.740	4.953
1944	3.743	4.921
1945	3.750	4.855
1946	4.589	5.808
1947	6.217	7.589
1948	5.545	7.042
1949	5.807	7.279
1950	5.932	7.306
1951	6.057	7.673
1952	6.265	7.913
1953	6.287	8.012
1954	6.088	8.014
1955	5.952	7.881
1956	6.086	8.056

Source: Sugar Statistics and Data, op. cit. (Table I), Table 52, pp. 278–279.
* Excludes federal excise tax.

The situation as to the refiners' margin is shown in Table X and Chart IV.

Refining Costs

The facts as to refining costs from 1947 to 1955 are shown in Tables XI and XII. The data are presented on semi-log paper in Chart V to facilitate comparison of rates of change.

CASE V-1. CHART IV

Prices of Raw and Refined Sugar, United States, Annual Averages, 1934 to 1956. Curve A: Refined Cane Sugar, Wholesale,* New York; Curve B: Raw Sugar, Duty Paid, New York

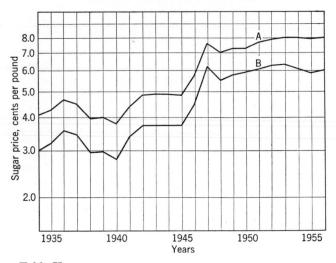

Source: Table X.
* Excluding excise tax.

CASE V-1. CHART V

Cane Sugar Refining Industry Cost—Profit Elements, United States,
1947–1954

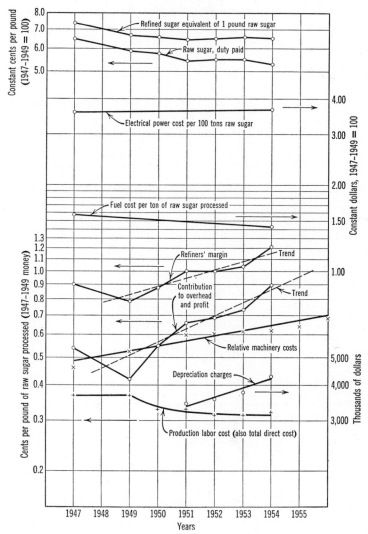

Sources: Table XII for depreciation charges; Table XI for other data.

CASE V-1.

Analysis of Cane Sugar Refining Industry

	(1)	(2)	(3)	(4)	(5)	(6)
Year	Raw Sugar Duty Paid New York Cents Per Pound Deflated	Refined Sugar Cents Per Pound Refined Equivalent New York Deflated	Refiners' Margin Cents Per Pound Raw Sugar Processed	Annual Production Refined Sugar in Thousands of Tons (Raw Value)	Electrical Power Cost Cents Per Pound Raw Sugar Deflated	Fuel Cost Cents Per Pound Raw Sugar Deflated
1947	6.52	7.43	0.91	5,545	0.00002	0.0008
1948	—	—	—	—	—	—
1949	5.91	6.70	0.79	5,515	N.A.	N.A.
1950	5.77	6.65	0.88	5,947	N.A.	N.A.
1951	5.46	6.45	0.99	5,464	N.A.	N.A.
1952	5.52	6.52	1.00	5,872	N.A.	N.A.
1953	5.50	6.54	1.04	6,072	N.A.	N.A.
1954	5.31	6.52	1.21	5,699	0.00002	0.0007

Sources: Column 1: *Sugar Statistics and Data, op. cit.* (Table I), Table 52, p. 279. Deflated using cl. 11. Column 2: *Loc. cit.* Divided by 107 to allow for shrinkage loss in refining. Column 3: Column 2 minus column 1. Column 4: *Sugar Statistics and Data, op. cit.* (Table I), Table 15, pp. 46–56. Column 5: *U.S. Census of Manufacturers, 1954,* Vol. II, U.S. Department of Commerce (Washington, D.C.: U.S. Government Printing Office, 1957), Table 3, p. 20F–7; *U.S. Census of Manufacturers, 1947,* Vol. II, U.S. Department of Commerce, Table 3, p. 123. Converted to unit cost basis by dividing by production in cl. 4. Then statistically deflated using cl. 13. Column 6: *Loc. cit.* Converted to unit cost basis and statistically deflated using cl. 13. Column 7: *U.S. Census of Manufactures, 1954, op. cit.* (this Table),

TABLE XI

Costs, United States, 1947 to 1954

(7)	(8)	(9)	(10)	(11)	(12)	(13)	(14)
Production Labor Cost Cents Per Pound Raw Sugar Deflated	Direct Costs Excluding Raw Sugar Cents Per Pound Deflated	Contribution to Overhead and Profit Cents Per Pound Raw Sugar Deflated	Index Numbers for Deflating to 1947–49 Dollars				Machinery Price Index 1947–1949 = 50
			Labor Cost	Sugar Prices	Fuel Cost	Electrical Power	
0.37	0.37	0.54	94.3	95.5	90.9	98.0	46.2
—	—	—	—	—	—	—	—
0.37	0.37	0.42	103.6	101.8	—	—	53.3
0.33	0.33	0.55	111.9	102.8	—	—	54.3
0.33	0.33	0.66	122.1	111.0	—	—	59.5
0.31	0.31	0.69	128.2	113.5	—	—	60.8
0.31	0.31	0.73	135.3	114.4	—	—	61.5
0.32	0.32	0.89	135.6	114.8	108.1	101.8	62.3

Table 1, p. 20F-3. Converted to unit costs and deflated using columns 4 and 10. Column 8: Total, columns 5, 6, 7 rounded to nearest hundredth of a cent. Column 9: Column 3 minus column 8. Column 10: *Sugar Statistics and Data, op. cit.*, Table 57, p. 292. Column 11: *The Economic Almanac, 1958* (New York: T. Y. Crowell, 1958) p. 71. (Consumer Price Index, 1947–1949 = 100). Column 12: *Supplement to Survey of Current Business, 1957 Biennial Edition*, U.S. Dept. of Commerce (Washington: U.S. Government Printing Office, 1957), p. 29. Column 13: *Loc. cit.* Column 14: *Ibid.*, p. 30. Index expressed with 1947–1949 = 100; however it was halved to facilitate plotting on Figure 6-1 adjacent to "Contribution to Overhead and Profit."

CASE V-1. TABLE XII

Approximation* of Depreciation Charges, United States Cane Sugar Refiners
1951–1954

Cane Sugar Refiner	Melting† Capacity Per Cent of Industry Total	Depreciation Charges in Thousands of Dollars in Indicated Year			
		1951	1952	1953	1954
National Sugar Refining Company	21.2	$ 691	$ 729	$ 759	$ 843
Savannah Sugar Refining Corp.	5.1	211	217	236	275
Totals	26.3	902	946	995	1,118
Approximation for All Refiners	100.0	3,420	3,600	3,780	4,250

Sources: For National Sugar Refining Company: *Manual of Sugar Companies—1955–1956* (New York: Farr and Co., 1957), p. 98; *Manual of Sugar Companies—1953–1954* (New York: Farr and Co., 1954), p. 118. For Savannah Sugar Refining Corporation: *Manual of Sugar Companies—1955–1956, op. cit.* (this Table), p. 108; *Manual of Sugar Companies—1953–1954, op. cit.* (this Table), p. 129.

* Found by adding up reported depreciation charges by companies engaged *only* in refining (omits integrated companies) and dividing by per cent of total melting capacity represented by the companies. These approximations were considered not in the absolute sense but to find the relative change from year to year in recent past.

† From Table V.

Questions

1. Is government regulation of sugar successful?
2. Is such regulation motivated by economic or political considerations?
3. Would you expect that the application of government regulation to agricultural products other than sugar would be more or less difficult (or successful) by comparison with regulation of the sugar industry? Why?

part VI

Capital budgeting

DEFINITION AND TARDY DEVELOPMENT
OF CAPITAL BUDGETING

Capital budgeting or capital management may be defined as the process of determining which investments or allocation of long term funds are to be made by an enterprise.[1] Thus every business is at least *implicitly* engaged in this process. While economists for many years have concerned themselves with the theory of capital and interest[2] and the goal of maximizing the profits of the firm, only recently have they given prime consideration to the problems and processes by which investments and the allocation of funds can be integrated with price theory to achieve the firm's goal. That the theory of capital and interest should continue unrelated for so long a time to the theory of price and the problem of maximizing the profits of the firm requires explanation.[3] Several explanations may be advanced.

---

[1] Capital budgeting can be viewed in a broader sense. How realistic is it to distinguish an outlay for advertising, for example, from an outlay for a machine? Both may involve single period outlays with revenues returned over a number of periods. Both compete for the same funds.

[2] Among the older classics in economics in the area of the theory of capital and interest, three stand out: Eugen von Böhm Bawerk's *Capital and Interest* English translation by William Smart (New York: Brentano, 1890), Irving Fisher, *The Theory of Interest* (New York: Macmillan, 1930), and Knut Wicksell, *Lectures on Political Economy,* English translation by E. Classen (London: Routledge and Kegan Paul, 1934).

[3] The interrelation of price theory and capital theory was finally more fully developed in three works: J. R. Hicks, *Value and Capital* (Oxford: University Press, 1939), Friedrich and Vera Lutz, *The Theory of Investment of The Firm*

351

First, the practical use of the theory of capital budgeting in business applications is heavily dependent upon the availability of sales forecasts which have a livable margin of error. The development of such forecasting techniques has been a matter of recent years.

Second, the maturing of the economy through industrialization has increased the significance of long term capital commitments relative to short term investment.

Third, changes in the economy have made price no longer the dominant variable affecting the quantity of a good that is sold. At least equally significant as variables undergoing change are incomes and income distribution and substitute and new competing products. As has been pointed out earlier in this book, in the nineteenth century, price was the dominant variable and economists concentrated on the study of price.

Fourth, the Great Depression of the 1930's with its attendant overcapacity in many industries delayed new investment and hence the development of capital budgeting. Of course even in the situation where there is excess capacity in some industries (and this tends to be true at some times in all industries but in varying degrees), capital budgeting still has a role to play in examining the question of switching resources from one industry to another. Again at this point we see the significance of our earlier observations about the declining importance of the concept of fixed costs. As standardization and flexibility in the use of capital assets grow, the significance of capital budgeting in examining the alternative opportunities for employment of these capital assets increases.

Fifth, the great increase in income tax rates, which occurred in the decade of the 1940's, continued through the 1950's, and may well extend for many more years, has focused attention on depreciation as a source of funds. This focus became even stronger when the enactments of the Congress recognized various forms of accelerated depreciation such as the rapid depreciation of new facilities certified for defense and the use of double-rate declining balance and sum of the years' digits methods of depreciation. When income tax rates are high, an increase in cash return of capital results from switching tax payments from the present to the future (which is the primary effect of accelerated depreciation) and in the meantime reaping the earning on the deferred tax. This leads to a more careful study of long-term commitments.

(Princeton: Princeton University Press, 1951), Joel Dean, *Capital Budgeting,* (Englewood Cliffs, N.J.: Prentice-Hall, 1951), and the recent Trygve Haavelmo, *A Study in the Theory of Investment* (Chicago: University of Chicago Press, 1960).

Sixth, the dramatic increase of the population in the late 1940's and the decade of the 1950's brought most industries face to face with the problems of economic growth and expansion. The problems were magnified by a rapidly moving price level. If both the population and the price level continue to advance at their recent rates of growth, the positions of the firms within an industry can dramatically change in a relatively short period of time. First, increased activity in the variables makes decision making more difficult. Second, because of the bias introduced into business calculations by the accounting and tax rules that assume a constant price level,[4] the firm is bedeviled in its competitive position by the variety of money costs (in current dollars) shown by competitors. The firm may fully understand that price-level movements invalidate the use of accounting data in the usual manner, but if the firm believes that its competitors do not have such an understanding the firm may be forced to act on the faulty basis of its competitors' thinking. Under conditions of a stable population and a stable price level, the firm is less concerned with this second type of problem.

Lastly, it appears that while economists study the firm in a sense, the classical models were not sufficiently realistic to get at many of the questions we will consider.

THE SCOPE OF CAPITAL BUDGETING

Mr. Claud Wampler of Carrier Corporation recently stated, "There are two ways to go broke running a business: one way is to spend too much, the other is to spend too little."[5] Carrying excess capacity eats into profits. On the other hand, obsolescence and a deficiency in new investment take their toll in rising production costs and competitors quickly pass by the producer whose investment decisions imply a stagnant or shrinking economy at a time when the opposite may be the fact.

The simplest, and perhaps earliest view of the scope of capital budgeting, was that it concerned making replacements at a time when the cost of repair was to be compared with the cost of the replacement together with a reckoning of the greater efficiency of the new machine. However, capital budgeting reaches far beyond the matter of replacements. Capital budgeting concerned itself with such common problems

---

[4] The significance of these accounting and tax rules is considerably reduced by the use of double declining balance or sum of the years' digits depreciation practices.

[5] *Business Week,* September 27, 1958.

as: (1) abandonment of a product line and its equipment through liquidation; (2) abandonment of self-production in favor of purchased parts or vice versa, the so-called make-or-buy question; (3) outright ownership of capital assets versus lease or sale and leaseback; (4) replacement of currently used capital assets by improved and more efficient tools; (5) expansion of existing capital assets in anticipation of increased volume (e.g., switching from a three-shift to a one or two shift operation or vice versa) as in the case of temporarily idle capacity to gain economy in construction; (6) establishment of new product lines; (7) diversification to introduce compensating risks.

In short, capital budgeting is concerned with anything that requires additional investment, including investment in working capital.

OUTLINE OF HOW THE SUBJECT WILL BE DEVELOPED

Before launching into our development, it is well to establish a roadmap for the ground we will cover.[6]

First, the payoff period, the most primitive technique of capital budgeting, will be examined. The payoff period may simply be defined as the period needed to recover the capital of an investment through increased earnings. The cost of capital is not considered.

Second, the discounted cash flow technique will be studied. The *yield method* establishes that rate of return which equalizes the cash outlays and cash income over the years of life of an investment. From this rate of return must be deducted the cost of capital to get the rate of profit. The *net present value method* determines the discounted present value after allowance for an assumed rate for cost of capital which is the rate used in discounting.

Third, we will explore the problem of how long a life should be used in evaluating an investment and how differences in risk between alternative investments should be handled.

Fourth, the problem of early versus long maturity of an investment will be considered.

Fifth, the problem of mutually exclusive and complementary vs. substitutional investments and nonunique solutions will be discussed.

Sixth, the so-called MAPI (Machinery and Allied Products Institute) technique as a short-cut solution will be examined.

Seventh, the problem of establishing the cost of capital and its role in capital budgeting will be considered.

[6] Many of the basic problems of capital budgeting are explored in a collection of essays gathered by Professor Ezra Solomon in book form under the title, *The Management of Corporate Capital* (Glencoe, Ill.: Free Press, 1959).

Eighth, methods of capital budgeting other than pay-off period, discounted cash flow and MAPI will be summarized.

EARLIER BUSINESS PRACTICES: THE PAYOFF PERIOD

One of the earliest concepts developed in business practice to deal with the area of capital budgeting was the payoff period: the period required for a business to get its money back from an investment. The attraction of this concept is its simplicity and conservatism. Simple as it is, the payoff period is frequently incorrectly computed by overlooking income taxes or depreciation. Suppose the installed cost of a new machine is $20,000, but it would save $5,000 per year in operating costs (such as labor, materials, supervision, and depreciation, as shown in the case of new machine I in Table VI-1). On the surface this would indicate the recovery of the investment in 4 years. However, if income taxes are at 50 per cent,[7] it would seem to require 8 years of after-tax earnings to recover the investment. But if the life of the machine is 8 years and straight-line depreciation is used, the payoff period is 4 years since $2,500 per year tax-deductible depreciation will be recovered each year as well as $2,500 in after-tax improved earnings. This, of course, does not reckon the salvage situation on the old machine nor the cost of the capital during the period it is being recovered.[8]

The payoff period, however, does not furnish a rate of return. For example, imagine two new machines costing $20,000 each as in Table VI-1. As in the previous example, the first can be employed with annual savings in operating costs of $5,000 with a machine life of

[7] In succeeding examples, an income tax rate of 50 per cent will be assumed to simplify computation.

[8] In this and the following examples, it is assumed the new machine will have no salvage value. If there is a future salvage value, it would be incorrect to deduct this amount in an undiscounted form from the initial outlay and treat the difference as the new investment. Only the present discounted value of the future salvage amount could be so used as a deduction from the initial outlay.

Also, note that the after-tax earning of the old machine is not included as an earning of the new machine. This is done in recognition of the marginal principle: increments in income are reckoned against increments in investment. The true increment of investment is the installed cost of the new machine minus the present value of the future salvage proceeds (after capital-gains tax, if any) of the new machine. In the usual marginal approach the present salvage value of the old machine less the present value of the future salvage value of the old machine is considered to produce the after-tax earnings of the old machine plus the depreciation charge for the old machine.

TABLE VI-1

Comparison of Annual Operating Costs of Old and New Machines for the Same Number of Units of Output

	Old Machine	New Machine I	New Machine II
Labor	$ 9,000	$3,500	$5,167
Material	2,000	2,000	2,000
Supervision	1,000	1,000	1,000
Depreciation	2,000	2,500	1,333
Total	$14,000	$9,000	$9,500
Saving Before Income Tax		$5,000	$4,500

8 years. The first machine has a payoff period of 4 years after income taxes, and generates a stream of cash of $5,000 per year (after income taxes but with straight-line depreciation added back) for 8 years for a total of $40,000. The second has a payoff period of 5.58 years after income taxes and generates a stream of cash of $3,583 per year (after income taxes but with straight-line depreciation added back) for 15 years for a total of $53,745.

For the first machine, the rate of return equating the $20,000 investment and the stream of $5,000 per year for 8 years is about 20 per cent.[9] For the second machine, the rate of return equating the $20,000 investment and the stream of $3,583 per year for 15 years is 16 per cent.

If money costs more than 16 per cent per year but less than 20 per cent, it is clear that only the first machine is profitable. This brings out two important points. First, the payoff period is exactly what the

[9] Computed as follows on an investment of $20,000:

Present Value at 20% of the Returns of the First Through Eighth Years
(using Gregory's Tables below at pp. 394–407)

Year 1 0.9063 × $5,000 = $4,532	Year 5 0.4072 × $5,000 = $ 2,036
Year 2 0.7421 × $5,000 = $3,711	Year 6 0.3334 × $5,000 = $ 1,667
Year 3 0.6075 × $5,000 = $3,038	Year 7 0.2730 × $5,000 = $ 1,365
Year 4 0.4974 × $5,000 = $2,487	Year 8 0.2235 × $5,000 = $ 1,118
	Present Value of Future Returns: $19,952

This example assumes that the old machine has no remaining depreciation. For a marginal approach, if the old machine has a remaining depreciable balance—say $4,000, then both in determining pre-tax saving and in adding depreciation back to the after-tax saving for each of the first two years of the first new machine's life, we use the differential in depreciation, namely $500, and for the balance of the life we use $2,500 per year as shown in Table VI-1. Computation is similar for the second new machine.

term implies, namely, the period required to get back the principal of the investment and with no discounting of future receipts. However, a shorter payoff period does not in itself mean a higher rate of return on an investment because the length of time over which the machine earns affects the profitability of the investment. In this example, the somewhat smaller annual cash return of the second machine ($3,583 compared to $5,000) is not offset by the fact that the second machine produces the cash stream for a longer period of time (15 years compared to 8 years), because of the *high* rate of return.[10]

The relative profitability of the two machines (which is more correctly[11] shown by comparing 16 per cent to 20 per cent) cannot be approximated by comparing total receipts of $53,745 (which is $3,583 × 15 years) with $40,000 (which is $5,000 × 8 years) or the payoff period ratio of 5.58 years to 4 years.

Even if the annual savings in operating costs were $5,100 for the second machine (which is *greater* than the $5,000 operating savings of the first machine) with the life of fifteen years this does not change the verdict to favoring the second machine. The after-tax cash return in this case is $3,883 per year. The payoff period is 5.15 years and the rate of return is 18 per cent.

These examples have shown that the payoff period is a crude tool to use in making comparisons between investments. But the examples show that when income tax rates are high (thus heightening the significance of the relationship of depreciation and annual operating cost savings) *and* when the investments being compared involve relatively high rates of return (15 per cent and up), the payoff period technique does rough justice when consideration is given to the saving in calculations by using the payoff period. In comparison to other methods we will discuss, it is easy to understand why the payoff period dies such a slow death as a capital budgeting technique.

ALTERNATIVE CURRENT BUSINESS PRACTICES: DISCOUNTED CASH FLOW

In our comments on the payoff-period technique we introduced the concept of a rate of return. Now we will examine that concept in greater detail.

Under the discounted cash flow approach, the rate of return is the discounting rate which makes the expected cash inflow from a new investment equal to the principal of the investment when the invest-

---

[10] At 16 per cent, $1.00 in the fifteenth year is worth only 9.8 cents at present.

[11] We say "more correctly" rather than "correctly" because, for the moment, we are abstracting from the significance of the rate of cost of capital, which will be dealt with later on.

ment is made at a single point in time. When the investment is not made at a single point in time but is expended gradually, both the cash outflow and cash inflow are discounted to a common point in time.

The first step in the discounted cash flow technique is to prepare a year by year schedule of the cash returns (inflow) expected from the investment. This cash inflow consists of the *additions* to cash inflow as a result of making the investment compared to not making the investment. This cash inflow consists of (*a*) the net income from the investment after income taxes plus (*b*) the annual depreciation charge. Depreciation is a so-called "non-cash" cost involving a charge against income and is a deduction for tax purposes.[12] This emphasizes the importance of depreciation. Whether cash is returned to the enterprise through increased earnings after taxes or through depreciation, it is still a return of funds. Thus, the decision of the Congress (as to assets acquired after 1953) allowing the use of various forms of accelerated depreciation (such as the double declining balance or sum of the years' digits methods) is vitally important in that the delay in tax payments increases the rate of return.

Similarly, a year-by-year schedule of cash investments (outflow) is prepared. Care must be taken to schedule as investment those renewals or other expenditures of the project which are not treated as expenses charged in full to a given year's income. In this connection the "start-up" costs incident to getting the project under way are frequently capitalized and made part of the investment. These costs include training of a work force where a branch plant is getting under way, or trial runs to uncover "bugs." If, on the other hand, these costs are deductible for income tax purposes in the year in which incurred, only the cost minus the income tax is an investment. Such deductibility is described as a tax shield.

[12] If a business uses one type of depreciation for its corporate books and a second type for income tax purposes, this second type of depreciation gives the relevant figure for discounting cash flow. Likewise, the net income of the project as computed for income tax purposes is the relevant net income figure. The important element is to determine the cash flow and hence the relevant data are those shown on the income tax return. Of course if the project's true *life* is reflected by the depreciation used for the corporate books rather than the depreciation *life* used for the income tax returns, then this life period but not its depreciation rate should be used. In this case, adjustment must be made for the fact that income taxes will be higher during the last years of the project (where the corporate records deduct a lower depreciation charge in the early years than is taken on the income tax returns) and lower during the early years of the project (where the corporate records deduct a lower depreciation charge in the early years than is taken on the income tax returns).

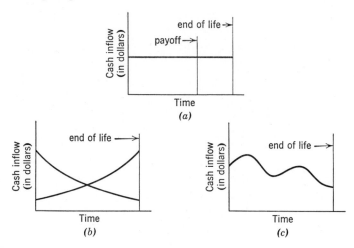

Figure VI-1. Cash inflows with different patterns over time.

The rate of return, to repeat, is that discount rate which makes the expected cash inflow from the project just equal to the investment, namely, to the cash outflow.

It is now apparent that the discounted cash-flow technique deals with two important variables which the payoff period omits from consideration. The first is the life or length of time over which cash will flow in and particularly the length of time beyond the payoff period. The second is the *pattern* of the cash inflow over time. The payoff period technique assumes a uniform cash inflow (as in Figure VI-1a) up to the period of recovery of the invested amount. The discounted cash flow technique is particularly designed to handle patterns such as appear in diagrams (b) and (c) of Figure VI-1, as well as the case of uniform cash inflow and to extend up to the end of the investment and not just up to the payoff point.

The discounted cash-flow method we are describing is also called the "yield method" or the "investors' method" to distinguish it from the "present value" method more aptly termed the "net present value" method.[13]

---

[13] Harold Bierman and Seymour Smidt, in *The Capital Budgeting Decision* (New York: Macmillan, 1960), state on page 34, "there are situations where the yield method may lead to different decisions than those obtained by using the present-value procedure. When the two methods lead to different decisions, the present-value method tends to give better decisions." Unfortunately, this assertion is not supported. Later, on the same page, these authors give a statement which

The yield method seeks that rate of return for discounting cash receipts and outlays which will equate the present value of such receipts and outlays. Thus this rate of return is *before* reckoning the cost of capital. Proposed projects are then ranked by rates of return, but final decision is not to be made on this ranking as we will bring out later in our discussion. On the other hand, the net present value method starts with the cost of capital as given (as a rate) and applies that rate to discounting both cash outlays and cash receipts. The excess of the cash receipts so discounted over the cash outlays so discounted is the "net present value." Proposed projects are then ranked by the size of this net present value." The ranking of projects may be changed by the rate which is assumed for cost of capital.

In Figure VI-1*b*, we illustrate the case of investments which yield successively smaller (1) or greater (2) annual cash inflows. Take first the case of the investment that yields successively smaller cash inflows. It is important to realize that this case illustrates the situation where annual after-tax savings from operating costs may be constant but accelerated depreciation (such as double-declining-balance or sum-of-the-years'-digits methods) is being used. Although the *total* cash recovered may be the same in the case of Figure VI-1*a* and in the case of the descending curve in Figure VI-1*b* (as shown by the fact that the areas under the curves in Figure VI-1*a*, *b*, and *c* may be the same), the rate of return will be higher for the situation depicted by the descending curve in Figure VI-1*b* than for the situation shown in Figure VI-1*a*, because the cash will be recovered sooner. Conversely, the rate of return for the situation reflected by the ascending curve in Figure VI-1*b* will yield a lower rate of return than the situation shown in Figure VI-1*a* even though the *total* cash recovered is the

---

apparently contradicts the first sentence: "It is possible to use the yield method in such a way that it gives the same results as the present-value method."

The second quoted sentence of Bierman and Smidt is the correct one. The first quoted sentence rests on a series of ephemeral points. One is that the yield method would select a project offering a yield of 1,000 per cent on an outlay of a dime rather than 15 per cent yield on an investment of $1,000. Another statement, on page 39, note 3, says, "the yield method implicitly assumes that proceeds are reinvested at the same rate of return as the yield of the investment. The present value method implicitly assumes that the proceeds are reinvested at the cost of capital. . . ." and Bierman and Smidt argue that the latter is the more valid assumption. The problem of whether investments can only be analyzed on the assumption that they continue to perpetuity (which the quotation just cited appears to accept) will be examined later in this part but at present we want to point out that when invested funds are returned to the corporation they may be used to retire debt or distributed to stockholders as liquidation dividends or reemployed in a new investment.

same as shown by the fact that the areas under the curves in Figures VI-1 (*a* and *b*) are the same.

When we come to situations illustrated by Figure VI-1*c*, that is, to irregular patterns of expected cash returns over future years, detailed computations are necessary to determine whether the rate of return to be expected is higher or lower than in the situations illustrated by Figure VI-1 (*a* and *b*). But in general we can observe that present value puts later and earlier flows on a comparable basis.

If we return to the original discussion of the payoff-period technique, it is now apparent that this method treats a dollar recovered in, say, the fourth year, the same as one recovered in the first year. If the payoff period technique is altered to include a discounting of cash inflow over time, then it becomes, in essence, a form of discounted cash flow technique which seeks not a rate of return but a payoff period. Thus, by developing a cumulative cash recovery column in the discounted cash flow technique, this same payoff period can be easily established as part of the rate of return calculation.

THE PROBLEM OF THE HORIZON AND RISK

The discounted cash flow technique focuses attention on the problem of what "horizon" to use in evaluating an investment. What "life" should be assumed for the project? If the rate of return is high, this horizon problem is of smaller practical importance. For example, the present value of $1 received 10 years hence at 30 per cent is 5.0 cents. Thus at 30 per cent the question whether to use a 10- or 15-year life is not as important quantitatively as it would be if the rate of return is 8 per cent in which case the present value of $1 received 10 years hence is 45 cents.

The problem of choosing the "horizon" for an investment quickly directs our attention to the major problem of *risk*.

Even in the case of the payoff-period technique, to make direct comparisons of the payoff periods of two investments assumes that the risks are identical. If the risks are not identical, a crude method of compensating for the differences in risk would be to form a subjective judgment of the relative risks of the projects being compared and to weight the rates of return (or payoff periods) accordingly. Thus if one project is considered twice as risky as another, the rate of return of the first project might be cut in half for purposes of comparison.[14]

---

[14] It should now be apparent that while our discussion of the problems of horizon and risk might *logically* have preceded the discussion of various current

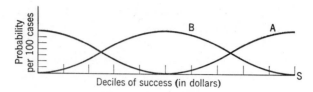

Figure VI-2. Projects with identical present value of returns but different risk patterns.

Risk is a subject on which much further research remains to be done. But some indications of the complexity of analyzing risk can be given. The question is not only one of the risk of failure as a single possible eventuality. Thus one project might have a greater risk of complete failure than another. But if failure can be viewed as a matter of degree, we can establish a distribution of degree of failure as in Figure VI-2.

In Figure VI-2, point S on the X-axis marks the highest possible present value of the expected return of the project. To the left of S on the X-axis are decile points marking percentages of S, the highest present value of the expected return. Probability is measured on the Y-axis with the high points on the curve for project A above complete failure and complete success and with low points between, indicating the small likelihood for partial success. Thus project A has a higher probability of complete failure and also a higher probability of complete success than project B. On the other hand project B has a smaller dispersion and is most likely to be at least partially a success and partially a failure.

Projects A and B both have the same present value of expected return, but each has a different risk pattern. How shall risk be quantified in this situation? Or, in other words, how shall the expected return be weighted (or made comparable) to reflect these risk patterns? In a very simple case, it might be said in everyday language that the risk of project A is half that of project B and, hence, the present value of project B's return should be cut in half to compare with project A. But no such simple summing up of the risk patterns of the two projects shown in Figure VI-2 is possible.

---

business practices since these problems are inherent in all considerations of capital budgeting, the reservation of these difficulties to the present point (after we have established the significance of differences in the points of time at which cash returns are received from an investment) brings them into proper perspective. The same is true of the succeeding problems that we will consider.

One method to deal with this situation is to establish the average probability value of each project and to select the project with the higher value. Thus, suppose that a $10,000 project X has a 25 per cent chance of realizing $10,000 present value of returns, a 25 per cent chance of realizing $15,000 and a 50 per cent chance of realizing $20,000 present value of returns. The average probability is for a $16,250 return. This is computed as 0.5($20,000) + 0.25($15,000) + 0.25($10,000). Project Y, let us suppose, has a 15 per cent chance of realizing $100,000 present value, a 75 per cent chance of yielding $6,000 in present value and a 10 per cent chance of realizing no present value. The average probability is for a $19,500 return. This is computed as 0.15($100,000) + 0.75($6,000) + 0.1(0).[15]

If the utility of money were the same to all people and if it were constant for all amounts of money, project Y would be preferred always and by everybody. But the utility of money to different investors differs and to the same investors differs as between times when he owns different assets. In the case just presented, an investor with limited resources would likely prefer project X despite the fact that its probability value is $16,250 and that of project Y is $19,500. The limited man would forego the $3,500 difference to avoid a 10 per cent chance of no return. A Mellon or a Rockefeller would be likely to prefer project Y, because, over a series of such projects, the result of choosing project Y would be more. This problem of the differing utility of additional amounts of money to different individuals can be handled by what is called the standard-gamble technique which employs ranking. Thus any given individual has six possible returns from the preceding projects X and Y:

Possible Present Values

$100,000	(from Y)
20,000	(from X)
15,000	(from X)
10,000	(from X)
6,000	(from Y)
0	(from Y)

[15] It is important to note that the technique just described can be applied to *any* business decision where there are different probabilities attached to different outcomes. For additional development of this basic concept at an elementary level, see David Miller and Martin Starr: *Executive Decisions and Operations Research* (Englewood Cliffs, N.J.: Prentice-Hall, 1960). This technique belongs to an area called decision theory.

The next step is to establish the point of indifference between each of these possible returns by adjusting the probabilities until the individual can say he is indifferent between each two. Thus we would ask the individual investor whether he preferred $20,000 with complete certainty to a $4/7$ probability of $100,000 (and thus a $3/7$ probability of 0). For comparison, we move the $4/7$ up or down until the individual could say he was indifferent to $20,000 with complete certainty and, let us say, $9/14$ probability of $100,000. We then proceed to the $15,000 outcome for comparison to $20,000 and so on down the ladder. This enables us to establish a table showing indifference probabilities for each possible outcome:

Possible Present Value	Utility to the Individual
$100,000	1 or 1.000
20,000	9/14 or 0.643
15,000	4/7 or 0.571
10,000	3/7 or 0.428
6,000	2/7 or 0.286
0	0 or 0.000

The use of a scale for utility from 0 to 1 is arbitrary but by paralleling the customary range for probability, we can proceed conveniently.

From this utility schedule we can now determine the correct decision between projects X and Y *for this individual* by applying the utility information just gained to the probabilities of each possible outcome for each of projects X and Y.

Project X: $0.643(0.50) + 0.571(0.25) + 0.428(0.25) = 0.5712$
Project Y: $1(0.15) + 0.286(0.75) + 0(0.10) = 0.3645$

Project X is thus the correct decision for this individual since it has the highest average probability when all probabilities are weighted by the individual's utility schedule.

If we think of the corporation as an impersonal body, and *if we assume the utility of additional amounts of money is constant,* we can compare the values of the average probabilities directly (such as the $19,500 for project Y and the $16,250 for project X above).

We also understand that if the decision makers of a corporation let their personal utilities for money enter the calculations, one corporation might prefer project X, another, project Y.

Risk in a business project also involves consideration of the loss picture should a business decide to abandon (or liquidate) an investment in midstream. Because some assets, for example, have ready marketability, they involve significantly smaller risks of loss in liquidation than may be true of the assets involved in another project.

Risk in a business project also involves the time dimension. Risks change during the life of an investment. Two fundamentally different patterns form the extremes here. The first is a project which is anticipating an expected market. By starting early, the rewards are heightened if the expected market development materializes. In this case risk may decrease as the project matures. Compact cars once were an example. At the other pole is the situation, perhaps more typical, where the project starts with a currently low risk. But the further the investment is projected into the future, the greater the degree of risk. Such a situation might be an investment in an electric power distribution system for a suburb. At present individual fuel cells and other phenomena only remotely threaten the future of such investments. But that threat, if it materalizes, is still a number of years away and would affect only the end of the life period of a current investment in an electric power distribution system.

Present business practice establishes the horizon to which a project will be computed largely on the subjective (but informed) evaluations of the situation by management.

SMALL AND LARGE COMPANIES IN CAPITAL BUDGETING

An interesting attack has been made[16] on another aspect of capital budgeting, namely the position of the small company contrasted with the large company when the proposed project represents a larger proportion of the smaller company's total investment fund available. This aspect is in addition to the matter of the utility of money which we have just shown is a necessary element of capital budgeting analysis and typically results in the larger investor being willing to accept a smaller rate of return. The two aspects, namely, the risk of ruin and the utility of money are often intertwined as, indeed, we intertwined them in presenting the utility of money aspect.

The idea of "risk of ruin" is old and simple. The individual gambler whose resources are smaller has a very low probability of surviving ruin against the house whose resources are larger. Or to put it another

[16] David Miller and Martin Starr, *Executive Decisions and Operations Research* (Englewood Cliffs, N.J.: Prentice-Hall, 1960), pp. 366-375.

way, a gambler with larger resources can withstand a longer series of consecutive losses than the gambler whose resources are smaller.

Suppose a gambler with given dollar resources, R, sets out to achieve a dollar figure of winnings, W, by betting a dollar at each turn. Suppose further that he is in a game where the odds of winning and losing are equal. Thus, if we use p to represent the probability of winning and q to represent the probability of losing and set the total probability as equal to 1, we see the chances of winning are $p = 0.5$ and $q = 0.5$. The gambler's chances of ruin when playing against a house with unlimited resources are:

$$\text{Probability of ruin} = 1 - R/(R + W)$$

so that if the gambler has \$1,000 in resources and wants to attain \$2,000 in winnings, betting \$1 per throw, his probability of losing all before attaining the \$2,000 is $1 - 1,000/(1,000 + 2,000)$ or $\frac{2}{3}$. However, if his initial resources are only \$5 and he seeks to win \$2,000 betting \$1 per throw, his chances of ruin have increased from $\frac{2}{3}$ to $399/400$ or $1 - 5/(5 + 2000)$.

If the odds of winning are not even, then with p representing the probability of winning and q (equals $1 - p$) the probability of losing.

$$\text{Probability of ruin} = \frac{(q/p)^R[1 - (q/p)^W]}{1 - (q/p)^{R+W}}$$

If we substitute, for the gambler playing against the house, the true business situation of a company making an infinite series of essential investments each with the same risk of doubling the investment, then the probability of ruin is $(q/p)^R$. If q is greater than p, ruin is certain, namely probability is 1. If $q = p$, the probability of ruin is also 1. But if p is greater than q, it is apparent that the larger R is, the smaller the fraction becomes and the smaller the probability of loss. This is on the assumption that each successive investment has the same probability of success or failure and that each successive investment is of the same size.

If we change the assumptions and let successive investments involve varying amounts of money and at varying risks (but keep p greater than q), we see clearly that the principle still holds; the probability of ruin is always smaller for the one with larger resources as to the same series of investments than it is for the one with the smaller resources. This leads to two corollaries: the risk in the investment must be smaller for the investor with the smaller resources if he is to have the same probability of ruin as an investor with larger resources. Or, the investor with larger resources can undertake a larger investment with the same probability of ruin as the smaller investor undertaking a smaller investment where both investments have the same risk.

These principles can now be put to work. Suppose a company maintains an annual fund of $50,000 for new investment purposes and that the company wants to keep the probability of ruin under 0.1 (or 1 in 10). Suppose there is a proposed investment of $10,000. In order to keep the probability of ruin under 0.1, this project should have a probability of 0.62 of returning $20,000 since $(0.38/0.62)^5$ is approximately 0.1.[17] In this case the return of $20,000 on a $10,000 investment is an even-money bet since $10,000 is laid out whether there is a return or not. If the return is other than $20,000 on this investment, the investment is greater or less than even-money and more complicated mathematics is involved.

On the other hand a company with an annual fund of $200,000 for new investment purposes looking at a $10,000 investment that may return $20,000, could keep its probability of ruin at 0.1 even though the project had only a probability of 0.53 of returning the $20,000 since $(0.47/.53)^{20}$ is approximately 0.1.

Miller and Starr have developed the graph shown in Figure VI-3 which shows the relationship for a fixed probability of ruin of 0.01 between the capital ratio (on the Y-axis) defined as the ratio of the total investment fund available to the proposed investment, and the return ratio (on the X-axis) defined as the ratio of the difference between expected return and the proposed investment to the proposed investment. In this analysis, expected return is, of course, the present value of the future receipts.

The lines on the graph in Figure VI-3 show equal probabilities of success. The lines show that for each probability of success of a venture there is a return ratio below which an infinite amount of capital is needed to maintain the probability of ruin at 0.01. Conversely, for any capital ratio there is a probability of success which requires an infinite return ratio in order to maintain the probability of ruin at 0.01.

Or put in the terms in which it would be used, a project with a 20 per cent chance of success needs a capital ratio of 30 and a return ratio of 7 in order to keep the probability of ruin at 0.01. Or, a project with a 90 per cent chance of success needs a capital ratio of 2.5 and a return ratio of 1 in order to keep the probability of ruin at 0.01.

---

[17] Using q/p^R, with the exponent 5 since there are 5 units of $10,000 in the fund of $50,000. Then that decimal whose fifth power is 0.1 is approximately 0.63. Since $p + q = 1$, we substitute $(1 - q)$ for p in $q/p = 0.63$, and we get $q = 0.38$. Then $p = 0.62$.

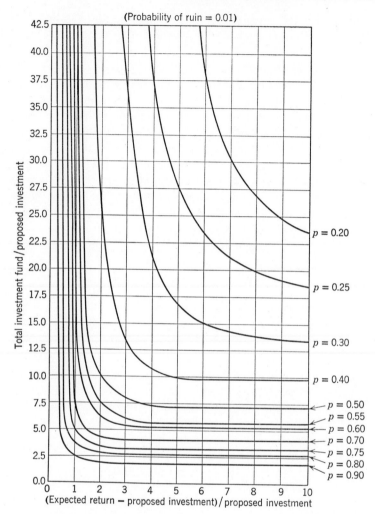

Figure VI-3. Lines of equal probability of success when the probability of ruin is fixed at 0.01 for different capital and return ratios. From David W. Miller and Martin K. Starr, *Executive Decisions and Operations Research* (Englewood Cliffs, N. J.: Prentice-Hall, 1960), p. **373**. (Note: Obvious errors in the labeling of the axes in the original are corrected here.)

As we have already indicated, projects are not likely to have a single probability of success but rather a distribution of probabilities of different degrees of success. But the weighted average of this distribution can be used as a single value.

THE DIFFERENCE BETWEEN EARLY MATURITY
AND LONG MATURITY

Assume there are two projects, each with the same risk (and we mean the same probability pattern of risk in all the aspects just discussed) and the same rate of return as computed under the discounted cash-flow method, and each being the same size as regards funds committed. Project A, however, has a payoff period of 3 years and project B, a payoff period of 4 years. Which project is preferred?[18] There is the temptation to answer quickly that the shorter payoff period is preferred. But what is the basis for this preference? In the case of a few investors such as life insurance companies whose main cash requirements are due to mortality and are highly predictable over time, there is a basis for preference if other things are equal. In this case the preference will usually be for the longer term investment since there will be many more death settlements later than in the first 5 years, for example, rather than in the first 5 years (or even 10 or 15 years).

Among the great majority of investors, however, the basis for preference between two investments, one of longer and one of shorter maturity lies in the expectation of the investor as to what new investment opportunities will develop in the time period between now and the maturity of the longer of the two investments being examined. Unless one's expectations of the future are pessimistic more often than optimistic, we have a sufficient explanation why the typical investor prefers the shorter of two investments, *ceteris paribus*. Or, alternatively, the basis for preference of a longer or shorter maturity could lie in one's expectations as to changes likely to develop in the supply of investible funds or in the balancing of expectations as to investment opportunities and the availability of investment funds.

Casting the same question of early maturity versus long maturity in other language, we are concerned with the liquidity aspect. Liquidity immediately brings to mind the risk of change in the rate of return that can be expected in the future as we indicated by referring to expectations as to future investment opportunities and the future availability of investible funds. There is, however, an additional aspect to liquidity: the effect of the proposed investment commitment upon the liquidity position of the business which is considering the proposal. As the

---

[18] Remember that earlier, in our discussion of payoff period, the use of the shorter period payoff was condoned on the basis that, at high rates of return, the shorter payoff period was a reflection of a *higher rate of return* (as computed by the discounted cash flow method) except in extreme cases.

liquidity of the business considering the investment will be affected
if the investment is made, so will the cost of capital to the business
considering the project. An unbalancing of the liquidity position of
the business so that it has what investors consider an undue number
of long-term investments will cause an unfavorable reaction and drive
up the cost of new capital to that business.

THE MUTUALLY EXCLUSIVE QUESTION: COMPLEMENTARY AND SUBSTITUTIONAL INVESTMENTS AND THE NONUNIQUENESS PROBLEM

Additional complications arise in capital budgeting in some situations. Projects may be mutually exclusive or interdependent.

We have been considering the typical case in which one yield ratio
exists, namely where there is one investment outlay followed by a
series of receipts. There are unusual cases where there may be no one
yield rate or several yield rates. The no-yield—rate case can be illustrated by the example where cash receipts of, say, $600 occur before
the "investment" is made, then at a later time the cash outlay of $500
occurs and still later cash receipts of $21,000 occur. There is no one
yield rate since the investment has a positive present value regardless
of the cost of capital.

The situation of more than one yield rate is illustrated by an
initial investment followed by cash receipts and this in turn followed
by additional cash outlays. The yield rate is that rate which makes
the present value of cash outlays equal to the present value of cash
receipts. In the present case (net outlay, then net receipts, then net
outlay) there are two such yield rates. This is more clearly explained
in Figure VI-4 (*a* and *b*).

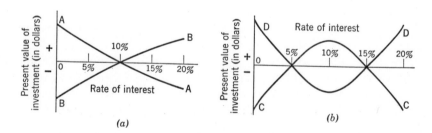

(a)   (b)

Figure VI-4. Present value of net borrower and net lender projects at varying
rates of interest. (Note that the present value of investment in dollars is the
excess of discounted receipts over discounted outlays.)

In Figure VI-4a we have a typical 10 per cent loan agreement (initial outlay followed by successive receipts) as seen in the AA curve from the point of view of the *lender* and in the BB curve from the point of view of the *borrower*. The AA curve shows that the lower the rate of interest assumed by the lender the higher the present value of the investment is to him and the higher the rate of interest assumed the lower the present value of the investment. At an assumed rate of interest of 10 per cent, the investment shows no positive or negative present value. Thus the yield rate (maximum) on this investment is 10 per cent. Curve BB shows the converse from the point of view of a borrower who initially receives funds which he subsequently repays with interest. If the project yields a low rate of return then it has a negative present value. As this rate of return increases, the present value of the investment increases.

In Figure VI-4b, the curve CC illustrates our situation in which the investor is first a net borrower, then a net lender and still later a net borrower. There is a maximum present value on this project which is at a rate of interest of 10 per cent, the point where the curve CC reaches a maximum. But below a market interest rate of 5 per cent and above a market interest rate of 15 per cent, this investment has a negative present value. It may aid us in understanding this curve to remember that if the interest rate is too low, then although the low interest rate is an aid during the period that one is a net borrower, it is a drag when one is a net lender and since the *removal* in terms of time (from the point in time at which present value is reckoned) is different when one is a net lender and a net borrower, changing the rate of interest will change the present value.

Curve DD in Figure VI-4b shows the converse situation in which the investor is first a net lender, then a net borrower and still later a net lender. In this case, the investment is desirable only at interest rates less than 5 per cent or greater than 15 per cent.

We can now apply this principle in an interesting way. Suppose we have the patterns of investment offered by two 3-year projects as shown in Table VI-1.

TABLE VI-1

Comparison of Two Projects: Cash Flows and Yields

Investment	Outlay in First Year	Receipts in Second Year	Receipts in Third Year	Yield
X	$100,000	$100,000	$ 50,000	31.2%
Y	$ 80,000	$ 20,000	$120,000	28.6%

Both of the projects in Table VI-1 are in the typical form: outlay followed by successive receipts. Assuming that investment was uniform over the first year and that receipts came in uniformly over each succeeding year, Gregory's Tables[19] indicate the yields of 31.2 and 28.6 per cent.

Suppose these two projects are mutually exclusive, that is, if one is elected, the other must be foregone, for example whether 6 inch piping will be used in a pipeline or 8 inch. Which one should be chosen? On the surface it would seem that project X should be preferred over Y, since its yield at zero cost of capital is higher (namely 31.2 per cent contrasted with 28.6 per cent). However, which one is to be preferred depends on what the cost of capital is.

If project X is elected, then the incremental position of project X may be shown in Table VI-2.

TABLE VI-2

Incremental Position of Investments in Table VI-1

	Cash		
Investment	Year 1	Year 2	Year 3
X	($100,000)	$100,000	$ 50,000
Y	(80,000)	20,000	115,000
Incremental	(20,000)	80,000	(65,000)

[19] See Gregory's Tables, pages 394–407. Using the Tables, the computation of these yields goes as follows:

Invest-ment	Amount	25 Per Cent Trial Rate		35 Per Cent Trial Rate		Year
		Factor	Factored Amount	Factor	Factored Amount	
X	($100,000)	1.1361	($113,610)	1.1973	($119,730)	1
	100,000	0.8848	88,480	0.8438	84,380	2
	50,000	0.6891	34,455	0.5946	29,730	3
Totals:*			$ 9,325		($ 5,620)	
Y	($ 80,000)	1.1361	($ 90,888)	1.1973	($ 95,784)	1
	20,000	0.8848	17,696	0.8438	16,876	2
	115,000	0.6891	79,246	0.5946	68,379	3
Totals:†			$ 6,054		($ 10,529)	

*Interpolation for investment X: $25 + \dfrac{9325(35 - 25)}{9325 + 5620} = 25 + \dfrac{93250}{14945} = 31.2\%$.

†Interpolation for investment Y: $25 + \dfrac{6054(35 - 25)}{6045 + 10529} = 25 + \dfrac{60540}{16583} = 28.6\%$.

TABLE VI-3

Net Present Value of Incremental Investment in Table VI-2 at Various Rates of Interest

Rate of Interest	Net Present Value	Rate of Interest	Net Present Value
0	−$5,000	50	3,629
10	− 785	60	3,254
12	− 166	70	2,560
20	1,755	80	1,943
30	3,104	90	1,175
40	3,647	100	401

The net present value at the start of year 1 of the incremental investment at various rates of interest is shown in Table VI-3 and Chart VI-1, assuming outlays and proceeds at a uniform rate within each year and using Gregory's tables.

CHART VI-1

Graph of Data of Table VI-3

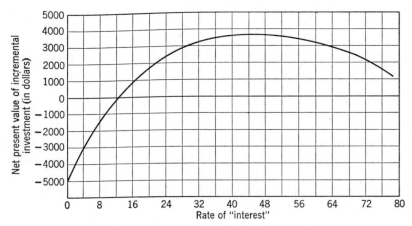

Thus, project Y is preferable to project X as long as the rate used for cost of capital is under about 12 per cent. Then, for the range of a rate of cost of capital of 12 to 100 per cent, project X is preferable. Above a cost of capital of 100 per cent, project Y again becomes preferred. The season for this variation is clear: the alternating pattern of cash receipts and outlays.

It might seem that the point we are making is theoretical, since the rate of "interest" at which Y again becomes preferred is so high: 100 per cent. However, if the flows are altered so that the *difference* in yields is *changed* (from the difference in the present example of 31.2 per cent for project X and 28.6 per cent for project Y shown in Table VI-1), the *range* of cost of capital percentages (in Table VI-3) over which project X is preferred to project Y may be narrowed!

If all the signs of the incremental outlays and receipts in our example were reversed, project X would be preferable to project Y at rates for the cost of capital under 12 per cent and project Y preferred from rates of 12 to 100 per cent.

Another example will clarify the role that the cost of capital plays.

Project	Year	Outlay	Proceeds	Yield	Net Present Value at 10 Per Cent
X	1	$1,000	—	30%	$346.64
	2	—	$ 300.00		
	3	—	1,300.00		
Y	1	1,000	—	35%	299.58
	2	—	1,000.00		
	3	—	472.50		

Project Y appears to be preferable to project X, since Y yields 35 per cent and X, 30 per cent. However, if we assume that the cost of capital is 10 per cent, and *if we assume that funds returned before the end of the year 3 can only be invested at 10 per cent,* then X is preferred to Y since the present value of X at 10 per cent is greater.

This brings out the point that the yield method of computation implies that cash received during the life of the investment is assumed to be reinvested at the project rate. But under the present-value method, cash received during the life of the investment is assumed to be reinvested at the cost of capital rate if that is the rate used to determine the present value. If the reinvestment of the returned funds can bring a rate higher than the cost of capital but less than the project yield, then this higher rate would be used in the present-value determination.

It must be pointed out that both the yield method and the present-value method theoretically assume that the yield rate and the present-value rate will continue in perpetuity, since if, after the end of the life of the investment the funds are employed at rates different from those derived from either the yield method or the present value method, then such changes will affect the computation we are making. This "infinity" aspect can be avoided in the case of the corporation by assuming that funds would be returned to the stockholders (and debt money retired) at the end of the life of the investment. If this is not to be done, the consequences of having surplus funds on hand after the life of the investment must enter into determining the yield or present value of the investment.

In ranking available projects according to their risk-weighted rates of return, how should the problem of interrelated projects be handled? A project whose returns are computed with or without a collateral project may yield different returns. Such a project may involve (a) an increase in returns if a collateral project is adopted or (b) a decrease in returns if the collateral project is adopted. Is it a satisfactory answer to say that the increase or decrease in the returns of the first project (when the second project is introduced) are to be charged to the second project? This would let the mere order in which the projects were undertaken determine their rates of return. In essence this is the same type problem as the joint cost problem of classical economics.

The nonuniqueness question concerns the situation where there is no single answer as to what course of conduct is best. Thus suppose the case of a series of proposed programs involving a discontinuity such that there are available a number of different projects each yielding identical rates of return yet the business cannot adopt them all. Inability to adopt all the projects might be because the cost of capital would increase between the first and the last of the projects. What is the principle for selecting among these projects?

CURRENT BUSINESS PRACTICES: MAPI CHARTS

The use of the discounted cash flow technique involves rather elaborate computations. The cash inflow and outflow for each year of the project are separately computed.[20] To make studies to determine the annual cash inflows and outflows to which discounting will then be applied involves costs not only in the amount of time required to do the studies but in the caliber of the personnel who do the studies. A simpler method employing less time and less skilled personnel has been developed by the Machinery and Allied Products Institute under

[20] One example of such computation appears in footnote 19 in this Part. Other examples appear in the exhibits of the cases after this section.

George Terborgh.[21] This MAPI technique, as it has come to be known, makes some simplifying assumptions and reduces the effort in calculation by using charts.

The MAPI technique in essence establishes a concept called the "next year rate of return." This is the return that will be earned from an investment if it is made now rather than waiting for a year. MAPI is concerned particularly with the replacement of machinery. In this situation the immediate problem is whether to replace the machine now or later. Will replacement (a) pay for itself, (b) yield a return such as the business seeks from its investments and (c) compare favorably with the returns available on other investment opportunities? MAPI assumes that the cost savings of the new machine will follow one of three patterns in the future years of the investment: decrease by a constant amount per annum, decrease at a decreasing rate or decrease at an increasing rate. This will be explained in a moment.

The first factor in using the MAPI technique is to compute the operating advantage of the new machine. This involves a study of direct and indirect labor saving, maintenance saving, tool and supply, scrap, power, space, and other savings.

The second factor is to determine the capital consumption avoided. The old machine may require expenditures to keep it going. This is really new investment. Likewise there will be a drop in salvage value of the old machine in a year. These are offsets to the cost of the new machine if it is purchased.

The third factor is the income tax which must be subtracted from the gains of the first two factors to get at the net gain available to recover the investment in the new machine.

The fourth factor is the determination of the cost of consuming capital. It is here that the MAPI charts are used. These charts are derived by combining (1) the rate at which the new project's earnings will decline (due to increased maintenance, etc.), (2) the service life of the new machinery, (3) the final salvage value of the machinery, (4) the income tax rate, (5) the depreciation system used and (6) the cost of capital to the business (which is taken as the weighted average of the interest paid on borrowed funds, and the after-tax return on equity earned by the business, with the weighting following the debt-equity ratio of the business).

MAPI Chart I, shown here as Chart VI-2, assumes a debt-equity ratio of 25/75, an interest rate of 3 per cent on debt and a 10 per

[21] Machinery and Allied Products Institute, *Business Investment Policy*, (Washington, D.C.: 1959).

CHART VI-2

MAPI Chart Number 1 (Projection Pattern: Standard)

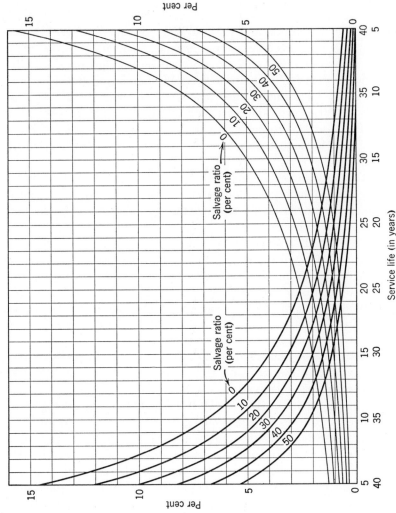

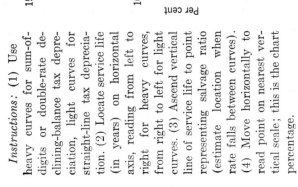

Instructions: (1) Use heavy curves for sum-of-digits or double-rate declining-balance tax depreciation, light curves for straight-line tax depreciation. (2) Locate service life (in years) on horizontal axis, reading from left to right for heavy curves, from right to left for light curves. (3) Ascend vertical line of service life to point representing salvage ratio (estimate location when rate falls between curves). (4) Move horizontally to read point on nearest vertical scale; this is the chart percentage.

Copyright, 1958, Machinery and Allied Products Institute, Washington, D.C. Used by permission.

cent after-tax return on equity. There are two sets of curves: those on the left for double rate declining balance (or sum of the years' digits) depreciation and those at the right for straight line depreciation. The lines trace the salvage ratio as a percentage of the investment. By locating the life of the investment on the horizontal axis (reading from the left for double rate declining balance depreciation and from the right for straight line) one ascends vertically to the applicable salvage ratio curve and from the point on this curve moves horizontally to the nearest vertical axis to get the percentage of the investment that is to be deducted each year as an allowance for the cost of capital consumed.

The fifth factor is to establish net investment. This is the cost of the new machinery (including installation) less the salvage of the old machine and the money that would have been spent in the next year to maintain the old machine.

An example will clarify the computation. Suppose a new machine costs $10,000 and the salvage of the old machine is $500 and the cost to keep the old machinery operating over another five years would be $1,000 or prorated for another year would be $200. A deduction should be made from the $500 salvage figure if there is a capital gains tax on the disposal of the old machine. Assuming there is none, the investment is $8,500.

Assume that the new machine will cut operating costs by $2,000 the first year and that it has a life of 10 years and a salvage of $500 at the end of this time.

The total of operating savings of $2,000 plus the saving of the cost of keeping the old machine going gives $2,200 savings for the first year. At a tax rate of 50 per cent, the after-tax saving is $1,100. This is before the capital-consumption cost. Assuming double-rate declining balance depreciation and supplying the salvage ratio of 5 per cent, MAPI Chart I (Chart VI-2) shows a capital-consumption cost of 6.3 per cent.[22] Applied to $8,500 this is a capital consumption cost of $535 per year. Here is a summary.

---

[22] The 6.3 per cent for capital consumption cost is derived from Chart VI-2 by the following procedure. Since we are using double declining balance depreciation, we read on the X-axis from left to right. The life of the assumed machine is ten years. Hence we move on the X-axis (left to right) to the 10-year point. Follow this line vertically to where the 5 per cent salvage line would be (which we interpolate between the 0 and 10 per cent salvage lines). From this point we proceed horizontally to the left to the Y-axis to get a reading of about 6.3 per cent which is the annual capital consumption.

1. Cost of new machine installed: $10,000
      less salvage of old machine: 500
      less cost of repairing old machine: 1,000
                                              _____
2. Net investment: $ 8,500

3. After-tax saving of new machine
      in next year: 1,100

4. Less capital consumption cost
      (6.3 per cent of net investment):   535
                                              _____
5. Annual return if investment is made: $ 565

6. Annual rate of return on net investment: 6.6%

This 6.6 per cent is termed by MAPI as an "urgency rating" to identify it as an approximation of a rate of return *after* allowing for the cost of capital.

MAPI has developed three general charts reflecting three general patterns of decline in earnings of a new machine over the years of its life. The first is geared to the situation where annual earnings of the new machine will have declined by one-half when the machine reaches the half-way point in its life. The second is geared to a one-third decline in earnings of the new machine by the time the midpoint in life has been reached. The third assumes a two-thirds decline in earnings of the new machine by the time the midpoint in its life has been reached. In our example, we used the first of the three situations, which is the situation assumed by Chart VI-2.

THE COST OF CAPITAL AND THE CUT-OFF RATE

Once the rate of return has been established by the discounted cash flow method, there remains the problem of determining the cost of capital. The rate of return computed under the yield method of discounted cash flow which we have previously examined is the rate of return before deducting the cost of capital. Thus, the rate of return under the discounted cash flow method which we have discussed is equivalent to a situation in which the cost of money is zero. Hence we must now compute the cost of capital and deduct it from the rate of return. MAPI takes the cost of capital into account as part of the computation involved when the chart is used as we have just seen.

Should the cost of capital for a project be reckoned as the actual cost of the particular funds to be applied to the proposed project? The

funds might come from debt sources or from equity. If from debt
sources, the funds carry a lower rate as cost. But then what of the
next project which may come from equity sources since the company
may by then have exhausted its debt limit?[23] This approach would
mean that the mere order in which the projects were adopted would
affect the determination of their profitability. One way of meeting this
difficulty would be to employ a weighted average of the cost of debt
and equity with the weights being established either by the actual or
an ideal debt-equity structure for the business. However, there is something to be said for the first approach, that of using the actual cost
of the funds to be used for the particular project. Such a principle
recognizes that the cost of capital is continuously changing. Interest
rates move up and down and so do equity costs.[24] A compromise approach is possible. At any *one* time all the projects being examined
might be compared by using a weighted average cost of capital. But
between points of time this weighted average cost of capital could
be moved to reflect market changes in the cost of capital.

When the cost of capital is considered, it is the expected or current
cost of capital that is important and not the historical cost. Thus

[23] The debt limit is not a single figure (or ratio to equity) but rather a zone.
As the ratio of debt in the capital structure of a company increases, the interest
rate demanded by the lender increases. This increase in the interest rate tends
to proceed by zones. Thus, for example, the interest rate on debt might be 4 per
cent for the range in which the amount of debt varies from no debt to a debt
equal to 20 per cent of net worth, then 5 per cent for debt for the range where
total debt is equal to an amount that is from 20 to 30 per cent of net worth,
then 6 per cent for debt in the range where total debt is from 30 to 40 per cent
of net worth, and so on. The additional debt for each zone may be subordinated
to prior debt. In this case the rate on the marginal debt would be even higher but
the total amount of interest on the same total debt in either situation (where
all the debt carries the same interest rate and where the prior debt carries a lower
interest rate and the subordinated debt carries a higher rate) would tend to be
the same. The borrower's willingness to set a limit on total debt (whether subordinated or not) affects the rate of interest. These matters are more fully developed in business finance or corporation finance texts. See for example, Bion
Howard and Miller Upton, *Introduction to Business Finance* (New York:
McGraw-Hill, 1952) and Harry Guthmann and Herbert Dougall, *Corporate Financial Policy*, 3d ed. (Englewood Cliffs, N.J.: Prentice-Hall, 1955).

[24] This subject is under current hot debate. It has been argued that the cost
of debt and equity are identical. If this were true, our discussion would be
irrelevant. Cf. Franco Modigliani and M. H. Miller, "The Cost of Capital, Corporation Finance and the Theory of Investment," *American Economic Review*,
vol. 48, pp. 261–97 (1958), and David Durand, "The Cost of Capital in an Imperfect Market: A Reply to Modigliani and Miller," *American Economic Review*,
vol. 49, pp. 639–655 (1959) and "Reply" by Modigliani and Miller, *American
Economic Review*, vol. 49, pp. 655–699 (1959).

with regard to the cost of the debt segment of capital, the relevant interest rate is the cost of new debt and not the average of the cost of existing debt.[25] The average cost of capital refers to the average cost of a capital structure ideally balanced as between the debt component of the structure and the equity component. The cost of the debt component to be averaged with the cost of the equity component is thus not the average of prior debt contracts entered into by the business, but the average of expected future debt contracts.

As yet, we have not explored the matter of the cost of equity. This can be broken down into the cost of "new equity," namely, the sale of new shares of stock, and the cost of retained earnings. The most common basis for determining the cost of new equity is the inverse of the price-earnings ratio, that is, earnings per share divided by market price of a share. This measure is used because new shares can usually be sold for slightly less than the current price-earnings ratio. Largely on the ground that equity is equity and what the new equity costs must be the same rate as is applied to retained earnings, common practice is to use the earnings-price figure if the funds are coming from retained earnings rather than new equity. However, an argument can be made for a distinction between the cost of new equity and that of retained earnings. This argument is that, in the case of a corporation, for the owners to get the earnings out involves at least a capital gains tax of 25 per cent. Hence the cost of retained earnings should be only $\frac{3}{4}$ that of new equity[26] by stockholder subscription.[27] This conflict as to whether the cost of retained earnings should be the expected earnings-price ratio or only $\frac{3}{4}$ of that ratio is actually a conflict as to whether the corporation is the entity whose earnings are to be

[25] The concept of cost of capital as used in capital budgeting is different from that used in public utility rates cases. The difference arises from the difference in objectives: in capital budgeting we are examining the feasibility of a *new* project; in a rate case we are attempting to control profits on *all* the investment commitments, those made and those expected to be made.

[26] This is spelled out as follows: if the expected earnings yield of a business is 12 per cent as shown by the current earnings-price ratio, then a stockholder would find it to his advantage to accept projects earning down to 9 per cent rather than to take money out by selling stock with a maximum capital gains tax of 25 per cent. Do not forget the problem of a tax ultimately to be paid. Of course, if the retained earnings are to be taken out as dividends subject to the regular income tax rate, then the tax rate applicable to each stockholder will be different.

[27] It may be argued that the total of all assets of a business is a source of funds (after deducting currently maturing obligations). This would be on the ground that continuing to hold the present assets rather than liquidating them is itself an investment decision. This would focus attention on comparing proposed projects against existing projects as part of capital budgeting considerations.

maximized or whether the individual stockholder is the one whose earnings should be maximized.

An alternative to the use of the price-earnings ratio to establish the cost of equity is the use of a price-dividend ratio.[28] This approach is directed at maximizing the market value of the equity and has been implemented by Gordon and Shapiro[29] who have employed the concept of the expected rate of profit. This expected rate of profit (R) is approximated by

$$R = D/M + G$$

where D = current dividends per share, M = current market price, and G = expected rate of growth of the dividend.

This can be illustrated by an assumed situation in which a firm is financed entirely by equity (and retained earnings). Assume a firm currently earns $1.00 per share and a share sells for $50 which is a price-earnings ratio of 50, and the firm is paying out 50 per cent of the earnings in dividends. Thus we have a price-dividend ratio of 100. On the assumption of a fixed dividend-payout ratio, the expected rate of profit is then determined by the expected rate of growth of dividends per share. If we assume that the stockholder expects future dividends to increase 10 per cent per year, the following pattern of earnings and dividends per share is expected to develop:

Year	Earnings Per Share	Dividends Per Share	Present Value at 10 Per Cent	Present Value at 11 Per Cent
0	$1.00	$0.50	—	—
1	$1.10	$0.55	$0.50	$0.493
2	$1.21	$0.61	$0.50	$0.490
3	$1.33	$0.67	$0.50	$0.482
4	$1.46	$0.73	$0.50	$0.470
Total			$2.00	$1.935

The market price of a share in the fourth year would be expected to be $100 \times \$0.73$ or $73 if there were to be no change in the price-dividend ratio.

[28] The foundation for this approach is J. B. Williams, *The Theory of Investment Value* (Cambridge, Mass: Harvard University Press, 1938). Williams argues that the value of a firm's equity is the present value of the firm's future dividend payments discounted at a rate appropriate to the uncertainties of the estimate.

[29] M. J. Gordon and Eli Shapiro, "Capital Equipment Analysis: The required Rate of Profit," *Management Science*, vol. 3, pp. 102–110 (1956).

The total of present value of this future price of $73 and the dividends discounted at 10 and 11 per cent would be

	At 10 Per Cent	At 11 Per Cent
Discounted value of $73.00	$48.93	$47.01
Discounted value of dividends	2.00	1.94
Total	$50.93	$48.95

By interpolation, the rate to produce a present value of $50 is about 10.7 per cent.

Hence an investor would demand projects earning 10.7 per cent in order to validate the present market price of $50.

This same result is approximated by the Gordon-Shapiro formula:

$$R = D/M + G$$

since by appropriate substitution in this formula we get:

$$R = 0.50/50.0 + 10\% = 11\%$$

This, then, shifts the question to what rate must capital earn in order to sustain the market price of $50?

While it might seem intuitive that the rate that capital must earn should be 11 per cent (or 10.7 per cent), this 11 per cent is an *average* rate over the life of the proposed project and not the *explicit* rate of the project, namely, that rate which it earns in the first year of the project and which is to be compounded.

Thus Professor Solomon's suggestion[30] that we use the future earnings per share divided by market price of a share is defective in not stating which year's earnings are to be used in making the calculation since the average rate of profit over the life of the proposed project is deceptive as just indicated. What we have been seeking is a marginal return rather than this average return of the project. Digging a bit deeper and assuming we could answer this question, how would the G rate of the Gordon-Shapiro formula be established? Historical dividends per share growth is not the answer since if the company's dividend were currently yielding 1 per cent but its dividends per share have been rising 5 per cent per year, the formula would suggest that projects be accepted that yield 6 per cent

$$R = 0.50/50.0 + 5\% = 6\%$$

[30] Ezra Solomon, "Measuring a Company's Cost of Capital," *Journal of Business,* vol. 28, pp. 240–252 (1955).

In other words, the rate, G, is an unknown and is not to be established by historical evidence but reflects expectations as to the future.

Professor Gordon's evidence[31] indicates that dividend policy (the payout ratio) affects the market price of stocks in such a way as to be a more important factor than retained earnings per share. In this, Professor Gordon supports the classic position of Professors Graham and Dodd,[32] that dividends are entitled to three times the weight given to earnings. The important thing to note is that since the effects of a change in dividend policy on the return of stockholders are not yet established, then the marginal cost of retained earnings is similarly not yet adequately incorporated in theory.

The Borrowing Rate and the Lending Rate

A distinction is taken in the literature of capital budgeting[33] between a "borrowing rate" and a "lending rate." The borrowing rate is that which a given business will have to pay for capital in the market. The lending rate is that which the business would receive if it were to invest its excess funds in the market. The relevant rate for establishing the cost of funds for a project is the borrowing rate. The relevant rate for discounting future cash flows of a project is the lending rate. Thus the lending rate establishes a "cutoff" at which the firm would release funds to the market rather than into its own projects. Because of the peculiar situation in which an industrial company considers itself inept in investing idle cash and hence seeks low yield but safe government bills,[34] the borrowing rate may be above the lending rate and vice versa. If the lending rate is higher, the business would presumably borrow in the market and lend to the market until the gap between the rates closed, as was actually done by some companies in the 1929 era. If the borrowing rate is above the lending rate, the business would cease all borrowing when its internal projects in descending order reached the borrowing rate. It must be remembered that there is no such thing as a single borrowing or lending rate. There are many different "shades" of each depending on the type of security involved:

[31] M. J. Gordon, *The Optimum Dividend Rate* (1959), paper presented at the Sixth Annual International Meeting of the Institute of Management Science at Paris.

[32] Benjamin Graham and D. L. Dodd, *Security Analysis,* 3rd ed. (New York: McGraw-Hill, 1951), p. 586.

[33] Begun by F. and V. Lutz, *The Theory of Investment of the Firm* (Princeton, N.J.: Princeton University Press, 1951), although the seeds of the idea go back as far as Irving Fisher, *The Rate of Interest* (New York: Macmillan, 1907).

[34] Cf. D. P. Jacobs, "The Marketable Security Portfolios of Non-financial Corporations, Investment Practics and Trends," *Journal of Finance,* vol. 15, pp. 341–352 (1960).

debt, preferred equity, common equity, and the myriad subdivisions of each which are closely tied to the risks involved.

Returning to the question of what should be considered the cost of equity, there is a point frequently overlooked in the literature of capital budgeting. If a company presently enjoys exceptional growth prospects, the price-earnings ratio will be high. This means the apparent cost of equity will be low. Since the cost seems low, the company might engage in many projects with a rate of return just above this cost to equity. This would cause the price-earnings ratio to fall drastically and the cost of additional new equity to rise sharply. What we are really saying is that the present price-earnings ratio in the market reflects the expectations of the market place that the future expansion of the business is brighter than the currently proposed project (because after such an investment the ratio of net income to invested capital would fall).

This can currently be illustrated by the price of International Business Machines stock which has a price-earning ratio of over 50. If the market were to become convinced that new money of IBM would go into projects yielding only 2 per cent (which is the cost of capital indicated by the price-earnings ratio of 50), the price-earnings ratio would certainly fall. Thus not only must capital budgeting look to the cost of the funds currently to be used in the project but also the ultimate impact of the project upon the cost of capital in the future.

There is a further consideration as to the cost of capital that needs emphasis. Debt up to a point can enhance the price-earnings ratio of equity. Beyond that point added debt reacts unfavorably on the price-earnings ratio.[35] But even during the range where debt enhances the price-earnings ratio, there are restrictions imposed on the management of a business incident to debt, namely, the maintenance of financial ratios, minimum working capital limits, restrictions on dividends and other restraints reducing the flexibility of the business. These restraints have "opportunity costs" which may involve the foregoing of some projects because they are not possible within the constraints. Such "costs" are, of course, difficult to compute. This has led to the argument that the "safe" cost of capital to use is the cost of equity with no weighting for debt. At the very least, the cost of capital must reflect what the market considers to be a balanced capital structure for the particular firm in its industry. What such a structure is will

[35] This proposition has recently been challenged in the Modigliani and Miller study cited in footnote 24 where evidence is adduced for the position that the debt-equity ratio has no effect on cost of capital because the market has already allowed for this aspect in establishing the price of securities.

vary greatly from industry to industry. This has led to the establishment of ratings by various investment services,[36] particularly for the bonds of particular businesses in particular industries.

The Cut-Off Rate Should Be the Point at Which the Project Rate Equals the Company's Rate of Return on Fixed Assets Plus Net Working Capital [37] or the Cost of Capital, Whichever is Higher

The literature on capital budgeting sometimes states but more often merely implies that projects should be accepted by a company starting with the highest rate of return and continuing down until the last accepted project just earns the cost of capital of the company at the margin. It is our present purpose to examine the soundness of the rule that the cut-off rate should be the cost of capital.

Assume a company has a rate of return of 20 per cent on its total assets. This return is the sum of after-tax profit plus the depreciation charge plus interest on debt and this sum divided by the total assets. Further, assume that the cost of capital of the company is 10 per cent, computing the cost of capital as the weighted average of cost of debt and the cost of equity with the cost of equity computed as the reciprocal of the price-earnings ratio. Assume a proposed project, which under the discounted cash flow method shows an expected rate of return (before cost of capital) of 15 per cent. Assume the project has the same risk as the rest of the company's business. Should the project be accepted?

The project will add a profit over cost of capital and many would accept it on this basis. However, it is submitted that the acceptance of such projects must result in a decline in the price-earnings ratio of the common stock of the company because acceptance will drag down the average rate of earnings.[38] Whether the reduction in price-earnings ratio would result in a change in the price of the stock greater than the change in price which the increase in earnings would cause in the opposite direction depends on the facts of the particular case.

---

[36] E.g., Moody's, Standard and Poor's, and Fitch's.

[37] It must be emphasized that book figures are here assumed equal to market value of the assets. The relevant figure is market value. If (as is almost invariably true today) accounting records understate the market value of assets, then figures from accounting statements such as a balance sheet must be adjusted.

[38] Of course if the present company rate of 20 per cent involves a situation in which there is idle cash in current assets then the acceptance of the project may cause the price-earnings ratio to improve. This merely reflects the substitution at the margin of more profitable employment of some assets for a less profitable employment of those assets. Similarly if the project earns less than the company average but more than another project now in the company's operation, substitution should be made.

Accordingly, it is proposed as a general rule, that the cut-off rate for projects should be the present rate of return on the company's assets provided that rate is above the cost of capital and if the cost of capital is above the present rate of return on the company's assets, then the cost of capital should be cut-off rate. This is not to suggest that the average rate of return should be employed instead of the marginal rate of return but rather that management must recognize that the market place frequently has less information than management. In the present case, where the market place is assumed to be overoptimistic, overexpansion by management can jeopardize the future of the company. If the present rate of return on the company's assets is not satisfactory, a higher, "target" rate can be adopted.

This leaves one refinement, namely, the matter of the definition of what figure should be used for the "assets" of the company against which the sum of after-tax profit plus depreciation charge plus interest should be applied to determine the company's over-all rate of return. It is submitted that fixed assets plus net working capital (where there is no short-term borrowing) or fixed assets plus net working capital plus short-term borrowing should be used. The difference between total assets and the base we propose is, of course, current liabilities other than short-term borrowing. Such current liabilities "finance" an equal amount of assets. The cost of capital of such current liabilities cannot be measurably determined in most cases. Such current liabilities reflect the part of the company's assets being financed by creditors (principally suppliers, wage earners and accrued taxes). Since there is no discount offered by such creditors for *prepayment*,[39] such funds are in effect free of cost within the limits acceptable to such creditors. These limits are set by various ratios adopted particularly by the suppliers. One such limit is the ratio of current assets to current liabilities.

The reduction of total assets by the amount of such current liabilities is particularly appropriate in determining the company's over-all rate of return for purposes of comparison with the project's rate of return since the computation of the project's rate of return typically does not include a consideration of the increase in current assets involved.

Our remarks on the refinement of the asset base of the company for determination of a cut-off rate have had in mind an industrial operation. If the business involved is one, for example merchandising, where the bulk of the assets are current, then the refinement would not be

[39] It is assumed that the company takes all cash discounts and current liabilities contain no discountable items.

applicable since the project would involve measurable cost charges for net working capital.

The Interrelation of the Three Aspects of Capital Budgeting

The alert reader is now aware that there are three interrelated aspects of capital budgeting: (1) what the size of the gross investment is to be; (2) the "mix" or composition of the outlays; and (3) the "mix" or composition of the financing. Each of these three affects the other two and hence all three must be solved simultaneously. We have been examining each of the three in the tradition of neo-classical partial equilibrium analysis, by holding the other two constant.

METHODS OF CAPITAL BUDGETING OTHER THAN PAYOFF PERIOD, DISCOUNTED CASH FLOW, AND MAPI

There are other methods of capital budgeting in addition to the pay-off period, discounted cash flow and MAPI. We can group these methods according to their objectives: rate of return maximization, wealth maximization, and profit maximization. These three standards of measurement will give the same answers when the projects being examined are the same from year to year, and when the projects will continue forever. However, when the earnings streams of the projects vary from year to year or have definite ending dates, the three objectives may give different answers as to the acceptability of specific projects.

The principal criticism of yield maximization, which is illustrated by the discounted cash flow method and MAPI, is that it assumes that the funds made available as recovered from the investment can be reinvested at the same rate of return as these funds earn during the time they are used in the project. This criticism is based on the concept of maximizing the return of the business as a whole. However, such a criticism can be challenged. Yield maximization treats a project as a project. When funds are returned to the treasury of the business they are no longer part of the project. Thus part of the criticism can be met by charging the project with the cost of capital during the period the funds are "idle" less some minimum earning that idle funds might earn in government securities. Since the earnings of governments fluctuate considerably in per cent, the rate to use for governments would be something of a problem. Such an adjustment for "idle" funds would at least make the yields of projects comparable.

Profit maximization as a method of capital budgeting runs into difficulty because profits vary from year to year, and it is not meaningful to speak of maximizing each year's profits when each year's profits depend on the profits of other years. This problem can be dealt with by using a "normal" rate of return for the business to determine the present value of all future profits by discounting. In this way, if the project shows a present value of future profits above zero, the project would be "profitable."

The objective of maximizing the owners' wealth would be the maximizing of the capital gain, namely, the difference between the equity of the owners and their investment. Under this method, the equity of the owners is increased by the project only if discounting the future earnings at the normal rate of the business yields a positive figure. In short the owners' investment is the value of future earnings discounted at the normal rate of the business and only if the project earns a higher rate is there a capital gain.

We have said enough to realize that maximizing profit and maximizing wealth are the same. The essence of the difference between the discounted cash flow technique we described earlier and the concept of maximizing profit (or wealth) is that the latter deals with the difference between the expected earnings of the *business* if the project is accepted compared to the expected earnings of the *business* if the project is not accepted. Thus, in effect, these other methods have the same *goal* we have indicated when we pointed out additional elements which the discounted cash flow technique must consider. One such instance was the discussion of the impact which the project can be expected to have on the price-earnings ratio of the stock.

It should now be apparent that capital budgeting is a subject where further development will occur. We have indicated problems involved for which there are not as yet proposed solutions and certainly, in any event, techniques of measurement remain to be devised for many aspects of capital budgeting such as the matter of risk.

Furthermore, our discussion makes clear that in the current state of knowledge of capital budgeting the models and techniques must be considered as yielding, at best, estimates or shadows of the real thing. The situation is something like that of a river boat pilot in a storm. He is less likely to wind up as a shipwreck if he constantly aims for the channel rather than abandoning all efforts at the helm.

Finally, as between large and small business it is apparent that there are considerable skills required in forecasting sales (the starting point for capital budgeting), in measuring and isolating expected costs and in the computational work involved in capital budgeting. These limit the practical use of capital budgeting to larger projects while MAPI can be used for smaller projects like machinery replacements. It should not be forgotten that large and small businesses are somewhat alike in this respect. Small projects of a large business suffer under the same difficulty as the same projects would in a small business.

NOTE ON HOW TO USE GREGORY'S TABLES IN CAPITAL BUDGETING

This note will explain the manipulation of Gregory's Tables, which are reprinted at the end of this Part. These Tables have been used in the capital budgeting cases included in this Part. This note plus the pertinent cases, can be studied as illustrations of the use of these Tables.

THE USE OF A PARTICULAR POINT IN TIME AS A COMMON REFERENCE POINT

It is customary in much of capital budgeting to use the start of full production as the reference point in time. This is commonly called the "zero point." If another point in time is used, the answer as to the rate of return will not be affected since *at the true rate of return* there is merely a shifting of an equal amount of discounted receipts and expenditures from one year to another. Receipts and expenditures before the zero point are compounded to the zero point. Receipts and expenditures after the zero point are discounted to the zero point.

EXAMPLE OF COMPUTATION *

Assume that the project whose rate of return is to be determined involves:

1. The start of full production January 1, 1959 (zero date).
2. The *expenditure* of $365,000 uniformly over one year for a building commencing January 1, 1957.
3. The *expenditure* of $2,779,000 for machinery uniformly over one half year, starting July 1, 1957.
4. The after-tax *cash savings* (the profit from the investment after tax plus depreciation for the period) from the project (in excess of present production earnings) of $646,213 in the first year of use (starting January 1, 1958) during which year production is uniformly built up to full volume, and thereafter these savings per year are:

1st full year (commencing January 1, 1959)	$1,034,092
2nd full year	987,007
3rd full year	949,340
4th full year	919,205

* Taken from Case VI-2, page 419.

5th full year	895,098
6th full year	875,812
7th full year	860,384
8th full year	848,041
9th full year	838,166
10th full year	830,267

5. Tools are replaced uniformly over the fourth year in the amount of $524,268 and again in the same amount over the eighth year.

6. Agreement that there will be no further earnings after 10 years, and that there is no salvage value at the end of 10 years for the assets.

The method is to assume two trial rates for computation such that one rate is higher than the true rate and one is lower than the true rate. The true rate will be established by interpolation between the results of these two trial rates. The two trial rates chosen are 15 and 30 per cent. Hence these two columns in the table will be used.

If by chance the true rate were selected as a trial rate, the cash outflow discounted at that rate would exactly equal the cash inflow discounted at that rate. If the trial rate is higher than the true rate, the discounted cash inflow at that rate will be smaller than the discounted cash outflow at that rate. Vice versa if the trial rate is lower than the true rate.

The factor applicable to the building expenditure starting January 1, 1957, of $365,000 at the trial rate of 15 per cent, is 1.2535. This is established in the following way. At 15 per cent, the uniform expenditure of $1 over one year before a given date is 1.0789 (as shown in Gregory's Tables (p. 396), part B, from 12 months before to 0). Since this $1 uniformly expended over 1 year is worth $1.0789 (at 15 per cent) at the end of this year and this *entire* amount will be outstanding for another full year before we reach the zero date, this $1.0789 is to be multiplied by the factor of 1.1618 for the second year (as shown in the Tables (p. 396), part A, 12 months before). This product is $1.25346, rounded to 1.2535, which is the factor to use.

The factor applicable to the machinery expenditure of $2,779,000 starting on July 1, 1957 at the trial rate of 15 per cent is 1.2065. This is established in the following way. At 15 per cent, the value of an expenditure of $1 uniformly over 6 months before a given date is 1.0385 (as shown in the Tables (p. 396), part B, from 6 months before to 0). Since this $1 uniformly expended over 6 months is worth $1.0385 at the end of 6 months and this *entire* amount will be outstanding for another full year before we reach the zero date, this $1.0385 is to be multiplied by the factor of 1.1618 for the second year (as shown in the Tables

(p. 396), part A, 12 months before too). This product is $1.20652, rounded to 1.2065, which is the factor to use.

The factor applicable at 15 per cent to the savings from the project in the first year of buildup to full production (from January 1, 1958 to January 1, 1959) on the assumption that the buildup is uniform through the year is 1.0789 (as shown in the Tables (p. 396), part B, 12 months before to 0). Remember the start of *full* production (January 1, 1959) is the zero date.

The factor at 15% to apply to the savings of the project in the first year of full production (after the zero date, January 1, 1959) on the assumption of uniform production through the year is 0.9286 (as shown in the Tables (p. 396), part D, from 0 to 1 year). The factor for the savings at 15 per cent of each succeeding year of full production comes from the same part D of the Tables (p. 396). Likewise for the tool replacements.

We now repeat this entire process, this time using 30 per cent as a trial rate.

We are now in a position to summarize our computations in tabular form, indicating outgoing cash by the use of brackets and incoming cash by the absence of brackets (see Table VI-4).

TABLE VI-4

Summary of Computations Described in This Note

| | | | Calculation to Determine Rate of Return | | | |
| | | | At 15 Per Cent | | At 30 Per Cent | |
			Factor	Amount	Factor	Amount
Construction of building		($365,000)	1,2535	($457,528)	1.5743	($ 574,620)
Machinery		($2,779,000)	1.2065	(3,352,864)	1.4564	(4,047,336)
Partial operation for one year (Zero Date)		$696,213	1.0789	751,144	1.1662	811,923
Full operation	1st year	$1,034,092	0.9286	960,257	0.8640	893,455
	2nd year	$987,007	0.7993	788,914	0.6400	631,684
	3rd year	$949,340	0.6879	653,850	0.4741	450,082
Tool replacement	4th year	($524,268)	0.5921	(310,419)	0.3513	(184,175)
Full operation	4th year	$919,205	0.5921	544,261	0.3513	322,916
	5th year	$895,098	0.5096	456,141	0.2602	232,904
	6th year	$875,812	0.4386	384,131	0.1928	168,856
	7th year	$860,384	0.3775	324,794	0.1428	122,863
Tool replacement	8th year	($524,268)	0.3250	(170,387)	0.1058	(55,468)
Full operation	8th year	$848,041	0.3250	275,613	0.1058	89,723
	9th year	$838,166	0.2797	234,435	0.0784	65,712
	10th year	$830,267	0.2407	199,845	0.0581	48,238
Total				$1,281,387		($1,023,243)

As we have already seen, the net total of $1,281,387 as the sum of the outflows and inflows at the trial rate of 15 per cent, being a posi-

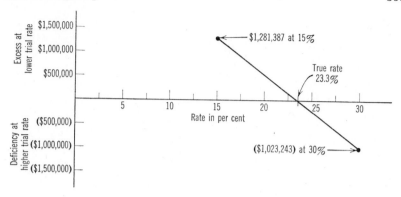

Figure VI-5. Graphic interpolation to establish true rate of return.

tive figure, indicates that the true rate of return is above 15 per cent. Conversely, the net total of ($1,023,243) as the sum of the discounted cash outflows and inflows at the trial rate of 30 per cent, being a negative figure, indicates that the trial rate of return is below 30 per cent. Using the results of the trial rates of 15 and 30 per cent, we can interpolate by formula (straight-line interpolation)

$$15 + \frac{1,281,387(30 - 15)}{1,281,387 + 1,023,243} = 23.3\%$$

This is the lower trial rate plus the quotient of the excess discounted amount at this rate times the difference between the trial rates over the sum of the excess and deficient discounted amounts at the trial rates.

The same result can be obtained graphically as shown in Figure VI-5.

J. C. Gregory's Interest Tables for Determining Rate of Return[36]

DERIVATION OF INTEREST TABLE FACTORS
THERE ARE ONLY TWO FORMULAE USED IN SECTIONS A, B, C, D, AND E

A. IN AN INSTANT.. e^{rt}

WHERE e = 2.71828 (THE WELL KNOWN MATHEMATICAL FACTOR)
         r = ANNUAL RATE OF INTEREST (AS A DECIMAL)
         t = TIME (IN YEARS)

B. UNIFORMLY UNTIL REFERENCE POINT.. $\dfrac{e^{rt}-1}{rt}$

THESE FORMULAE PROVIDE FOR CONTINUOUS COMPOUNDING INSTEAD OF THE CUSTOMARY METHODS OF ANNUAL, SEMI-ANNUAL, OR QUARTERLY COMPOUNDING.

C. IN AN INSTANT AFTER REFERENCE POINT.. RECIPROCAL OF A

EXAMPLE: AT A 10% RATE OF INTEREST
         RECIPROCAL OF 1.1052 (12 MONTHS BEFORE - SECTION A)   = .9048   1 YEAR LATER-SECTION C.
         "   "   1.2214 (2 YEARS   "   "   ")   = .8187   2 YEARS   "   "   "

EACH SUCCEEDING YEAR CAN BE DETERMINED BY USING THE ONE-YEAR FACTOR (.9048) AS A CONSTANT MULTIPLIER OF THE PRECEDING FACTOR AS FOLLOWS:

                    .9048 x .9048 (1 YEAR LATER)   = .8187   2 YEARS LATER
                    .8187 x .9048 (1   "   "   )   = .7408   3   "   "
                    .7408 x .9048 (1   "   "   )   = .6703   4   "   "

D. UNIFORMLY OVER INDIVIDUAL YEARS .... PRODUCT OF B AND C

EXAMPLE: AT A 10% RATE OF INTEREST
    1.0517 (12 MOS.BEFORE TO 0-SECTION B)x .9048(1 YEAR LATER-SECTION C) = .9516 FROM 0 TO 1 YEAR - SECTION D

EACH SUCCEEDING YEAR CAN BE DETERMINED BY USING THE ONE-YEAR FACTOR (.9048) SECTION C AS A CONSTANT MULTIPLIER OF THE PRECEDING FACTOR AS FOLLOWS:

                    .9516 x .9048 (1 YEAR LATER)   = .8611 FROM 1 TO 2 YEARS
                    .8611 x .9048 (1   "   "   )   = .7791 "   2 " 3   "
                    .7791 x .9048 (1   "   "   )   = .7050 "   3 " 4   "

E. UNIFORMLY OVER 5 YEAR PERIODS.. PRODUCT OF B AND C

EXAMPLE: AT A 10% RATE OF INTEREST
    1.2974 (5 YEARS BEFORE TO 0-SECTION B CALCULATED BY FORMULA) x .6065 (5 YEARS LATER-SECTION C)
                                                                 = .7869 FROM 0 TO 5 YRS-SECTION E

.7869 IS ALSO THE AVERAGE OF .9516, .8611, .7791, .7050 AND .6379 SECTION D.
EACH SUCCEEDING 5 YEAR GROUP CAN BE DETERMINED BY USING THE 5-YEAR FACTOR (.6065) SECTION C AS A CONSTANT MULTIPLIER OF THE PRECEDING 5 YEAR FACTOR AS FOLLOWS:

                    .7869 x .6065 (5 YEARS LATER)   = .4773 FROM 5 TO 10 YEARS
                    .4773 x .6065 (5   "   "   )   = .2895 " 10 " 15   "
                    .2895 x .6065 (5   "   "   )   = .1756 " 15 " 20   "

F. DECLINING TO NOTHING AT A CONSTANT RATE

            FORMULA USED IS $\dfrac{2}{rt}\left[1 - \dfrac{1}{rt} + \dfrac{1}{rt}e^{rt}\right]$

[36] Reprinted by permission of the author.

J. C. Gregory's Interest Tables for Determining Rate of Return

CONTINUOUS INTEREST TABLE

COMPOUNDING PERFORMANCE BEFORE REFERENCE POINT WHICH OCCURS:

A. IN AN INSTANT

	1%	2%	3%	4%	5%	6%	7%	8%	9%	10%
1 MONTH BEFORE	1.0008	1.0017	1.0025	1.0033	1.0042	1.0050	1.0059	1.0067	1.0075	1.0084
2 MONTHS	1.0017	1.0033	1.0050	1.0067	1.0084	1.0101	1.0117	1.0134	1.0151	1.0168
3 " "	1.0025	1.0050	1.0075	1.0101	1.0126	1.0151	1.0177	1.0202	1.0228	1.0253
6 MONTHS BEFORE	1.0050	1.0101	1.0151	1.0202	1.0253	1.0305	1.0356	1.0408	1.0460	1.0513
9 " "	1.0075	1.0151	1.0228	1.0305	1.0382	1.0460	1.0539	1.0618	1.0698	1.0779
12 " "	1.0101	1.0202	1.0305	1.0408	1.0513	1.0618	1.0725	1.0833	1.0942	1.1052
1½ YEARS BEFORE	1.0151	1.0305	1.0460	1.0618	1.0779	1.0942	1.1107	1.1275	1.1445	1.1618
2 " "	1.0202	1.0408	1.0618	1.0833	1.1052	1.1275	1.1503	1.1735	1.1972	1.2214
2½ " "	1.0253	1.0513	1.0779	1.1052	1.1331	1.1618	1.1912	1.2214	1.2523	1.2840
3 " "	1.0305	1.0618	1.0942	1.1275	1.1618	1.1972	1.2337	1.2712	1.3100	1.3499

B. UNIFORMLY UNTIL REFERENCE POINT

	1%	2%	3%	4%	5%	6%	7%	8%	9%	10%
FROM 3 MONTHS BEFORE TO 0	1.0013	1.0025	1.0038	1.0050	1.0063	1.0075	1.0088	1.0101	1.0113	1.0126
" 6 " " " 0	1.0025	1.0050	1.0075	1.0101	1.0126	1.0152	1.0177	1.0203	1.0228	1.0254
" 9 " " " 0	1.0038	1.0075	1.0113	1.0152	1.0190	1.0228	1.0267	1.0306	1.0345	1.0385
" 12 " " " 0	1.0050	1.0101	1.0152	1.0203	1.0254	1.0306	1.0358	1.0411	1.0464	1.0517
FROM 2 YEARS BEFORE TO 0	1.0101	1.0203	1.0306	1.0411	1.0517	1.0625	1.0734	1.0844	1.0956	1.1070
" 3 " " " 0	1.0152	1.0306	1.0464	1.0625	1.0789	1.0956	1.1128	1.1302	1.1480	1.1662

DISCOUNTING PERFORMANCE AFTER REFERENCE POINT WHICH OCCURS:

C. IN AN INSTANT

	1%	2%	3%	4%	5%	6%	7%	8%	9%	10%
1 YEAR LATER	.9901	.9802	.9704	.9608	.9512	.9418	.9324	.9231	.9139	.9048
2 YEARS "	.9802	.9608	.9418	.9231	.9048	.8869	.8694	.8521	.8353	.8187
3 " "	.9704	.9418	.9139	.8869	.8607	.8353	.8106	.7866	.7634	.7408
4 " "	.9608	.9231	.8869	.8521	.8187	.7866	.7558	.7261	.6977	.6703
5 " "	.9512	.9048	.8607	.8187	.7788	.7408	.7047	.6703	.6376	.6065
10 YEARS LATER	.9048	.8187	.7408	.6703	.6065	.5488	.4966	.4493	.4066	.3679
15 " "	.8607	.7408	.6376	.5488	.4724	.4066	.3499	.3012	.2592	.2231
20 " "	.8187	.6703	.5488	.4493	.3679	.3012	.2466	.2019	.1653	.1353
25 " "	.7788	.6065	.4724	.3679	.2865	.2231	.1738	.1353	.1054	.0821
30 " "	.7408	.5488	.4066	.3012	.2231	.1653	.1225	.0907	.0672	.0498
35 YEARS LATER	.7047	.4966	.3499	.2466	.1738	.1225	.0863	.0608	.0429	.0302
40 " "	.6703	.4493	.3012	.2019	.1353	.0907	.0608	.0408	.0273	.0183
45 " "	.6376	.4066	.2592	.1653	.1054	.0672	.0429	.0273	.0174	.0111
50 " "	.6065	.3679	.2231	.1353	.0821	.0498	.0302	.0183	.0111	.0067

D. UNIFORMLY OVER INDIVIDUAL YEARS

	1%	2%	3%	4%	5%	6%	7%	8%	9%	10%
FROM 0 TO 1 YEAR	.9950	.9901	.9851	.9803	.9754	.9706	.9658	.9610	.9563	.9516
" 1 " 2 YEARS	.9851	.9705	.9560	.9418	.9278	.9141	.9005	.8872	.8740	.8611
" 2 " 3 "	.9753	.9512	.9278	.9049	.8826	.8608	.8395	.8189	.7988	.7791
" 3 " 4 "	.9656	.9324	.9004	.8694	.8395	.8107	.7829	.7560	.7300	.7050
" 4 " 5 "	.9560	.9140	.8737	.8353	.7986	.7635	.7299	.6979	.6672	.6379
FROM 5 TO 6 YEARS	.9465	.8959	.8479	.8026	.7596	.7190	.6806	.6442	.6098	.5772
" 6 " 7 "	.9371	.8781	.8229	.7711	.7226	.6772	.6346	.5947	.5573	.5223
" 7 " 8 "	.9278	.8607	.7985	.7409	.6874	.6377	.5917	.5490	.5093	.4726
" 8 " 9 "	.9185	.8437	.7749	.7118	.6538	.6006	.5517	.5068	.4655	.4276
" 9 " 10 "	.9094	.8270	.7520	.6839	.6219	.5656	.5144	.4678	.4254	.3869
FROM 10 TO 11 YEARS	.9003	.8106	.7298	.6571	.5916	.5327	.4796	.4318	.3888	.3501
" 11 " 12 "	.8914	.7946	.7082	.6312	.5628	.5016	.4472	.3986	.3553	.3168
" 12 " 13 "	.8825	.7788	.6873	.6065	.5353	.4724	.4169	.3680	.3248	.2866
" 13 " 14 "	.8737	.7634	.6670	.5827	.5092	.4449	.3888	.3397	.2968	.2593
" 14 " 15 "	.8650	.7483	.6473	.5599	.4844	.4190	.3625	.3136	.2713	.2347

E. UNIFORMLY OVER 5 YEAR PERIODS

	1%	2%	3%	4%	5%	6%	7%	8%	9%	10%
FROM 0 TO 5 YEARS	.9754	.9516	.9286	.9063	.8848	.8639	.8438	.8242	.8053	.7869
" 5 " 10 "	.9278	.8611	.7993	.7421	.6891	.6400	.5946	.5525	.5135	.4773
" 10 " 15 "	.8826	.7791	.6879	.6075	.5367	.4741	.4190	.3703	.3274	.2895
" 15 " 20 "	.8395	.7050	.5921	.4974	.4179	.3513	.2953	.2482	.2088	.1756
" 20 " 25 "	.7986	.6379	.5096	.4072	.3255	.2602	.2081	.1664	.1331	.1065
FROM 25 TO 30 YEARS	.7596	.5772	.4386	.3334	.2535	.1928	.1466	.1115	.0849	.0646
" 30 " 35 "	.7226	.5223	.3775	.2730	.1974	.1428	.1033	.0748	.0541	.0392
" 35 " 40 "	.6874	.4726	.3250	.2235	.1538	.1058	.0728	.0501	.0345	.0238
" 40 " 45 "	.6538	.4276	.2797	.1830	.1197	.0784	.0513	.0336	.0220	.0144
" 45 " 50 "	.6219	.3869	.2407	.1498	.0933	.0581	.0362	.0225	.0140	.0087

F. DECLINING TO NOTHING AT CONSTANT RATE

	1%	2%	3%	4%	5%	6%	7%	8%	9%	10%
FROM 0 TO 5 YEARS	.9832	.9675	.9518	.9365	.9216	.9071	.8929	.8790	.8655	.8522
" 0 " 10 "	.9675	.9365	.9071	.8790	.8522	.8267	.8024	.7792	.7570	.7358
" 0 " 15 "	.9518	.9071	.8655	.8267	.7906	.7570	.7255	.6961	.6686	.6428
" 0 " 20 "	.9365	.8790	.8267	.7792	.7358	.6961	.6598	.6265	.5959	.5677
" 0 " 25 "	.9216	.8522	.7906	.7358	.6867	.6428	.6033	.5677	.5355	.5063
FROM 0 TO 30 YEARS	.9071	.8267	.7570	.6961	.6428	.5959	.5544	.5176	.4848	.4555
" 0 " 35 "	.8929	.8024	.7255	.6598	.6083	.5544	.5119	.4747	.4420	.4131

J. C. Gregory's Interest Tables for Determining Rate of Return

COMPOUNDING PERFORMANCE BEFORE REFERENCE POINT WHICH OCCURS:

CONTINUOUS INTEREST TABLE

A. IN AN INSTANT

	11%	12%	13%	14%	15%	16%	17%	18%	19%	20%
1 MONTH BEFORE	1.0092	1.0101	1.0109	1.0117	1.0126	1.0134	1.0143	1.0151	1.0160	1.0168
2 MONTHS "	1.0185	1.0202	1.0219	1.0236	1.0253	1.0270	1.0287	1.0305	1.0322	1.0339
3 "	1.0279	1.0305	1.0330	1.0356	1.0382	1.0408	1.0434	1.0460	1.0486	1.0513
6 MONTHS BEFORE	1.0565	1.0618	1.0672	1.0725	1.0779	1.0833	1.0887	1.0942	1.0997	1.1052
9 "	1.0860	1.0942	1.1024	1.1107	1.1191	1.1275	1.1360	1.1445	1.1532	1.1618
12 "	1.1163	1.1275	1.1388	1.1503	1.1618	1.1735	1.1853	1.1972	1.2092	1.2214
1½ YEARS BEFORE	1.1794	1.1972	1.2153	1.2337	1.2523	1.2712	1.2905	1.3100	1.3298	1.3499
2 "	1.2461	1.2712	1.2969	1.3231	1.3499	1.3771	1.4049	1.4333	1.4623	1.4918
2½ "	1.3165	1.3499	1.3840	1.4191	1.4550	1.4918	1.5296	1.5683	1.6080	1.6487
3 "	1.3910	1.4333	1.4770	1.5220	1.5683	1.6161	1.6653	1.7160	1.7683	1.8221

B. UNIFORMLY UNTIL REFERENCE POINT

	11%	12%	13%	14%	15%	16%	17%	18%	19%	20%
FROM 3 MONTHS BEFORE TO 0	1.0139	1.0152	1.0164	1.0177	1.0190	1.0203	1.0216	1.0228	1.0241	1.0254
" 6 " " 0	1.0280	1.0306	1.0332	1.0358	1.0385	1.0411	1.0437	1.0464	1.0490	1.0517
" 9 " " 0	1.0424	1.0463	1.0504	1.0544	1.0584	1.0624	1.0666	1.0706	1.0748	1.0789
" 12 " " 0	1.0571	1.0625	1.0679	1.0734	1.0789	1.0844	1.0900	1.0956	1.1013	1.1070
FROM 2 YEARS BEFORE TO 0	1.1185	1.1302	1.1420	1.1540	1.1662	1.1785	1.1910	1.2037	1.2165	1.2296
" 3 " " 0	1.1848	1.2037	1.2230	1.2426	1.2629	1.2835	1.3045	1.3259	1.3478	1.3702

DISCOUNTING PERFORMANCE AFTER REFERENCE POINT WHICH OCCURS:

C. IN AN INSTANT

	11%	12%	13%	14%	15%	16%	17%	18%	19%	20%
1 YEAR LATER	.8958	.8869	.8781	.8694	.8607	.8521	.8437	.8353	.8270	.8187
2 YEARS "	.8025	.7866	.7711	.7558	.7408	.7261	.7118	.6977	.6839	.6703
3 "	.7189	.6977	.6771	.6570	.6376	.6188	.6005	.5827	.5655	.5488
4 "	.6440	.6188	.5945	.5712	.5488	.5273	.5066	.4868	.4677	.4493
5 "	.5770	.5488	.5220	.4966	.4724	.4493	.4274	.4065	.3867	.3679
10 YEARS LATER	.3329	.3012	.2725	.2466	.2231	.2019	.1827	.1653	.1496	.1353
15 "	.1921	.1653	.1423	.1225	.1054	.0907	.0781	.0672	.0578	.0498
20 "	.1108	.0907	.0743	.0608	.0498	.0408	.0334	.0273	.0224	.0183
25 "	.0639	.0498	.0388	.0302	.0235	.0183	.0143	.0111	.0087	.0067
30 "	.0369	.0273	.0202	.0150	.0111	.0082	.0061	.0045	.0033	.0025
35 YEARS LATER	.0213	.0150	.0106	.0074	.0052	.0037	.0026	.0018	.0013	.0009
40 "	.0123	.0082	.0055	.0037	.0025	.0017	.0011	.0007	.0005	.0003
45 "	.0071	.0045	.0029	.0018	.0012	.0007	.0005	.0003	.0002	.0001
50 "	.0041	.0025	.0015	.0009	.0006	.0003	.0002	.0001	.0001	.0000

D. UNIFORMLY OVER INDIVIDUAL YEARS

	11%	12%	13%	14%	15%	16%	17%	18%	19%	20%
FROM 0 TO 1 YEAR	.9470	.9423	.9377	.9332	.9286	.9241	.9196	.9152	.9107	.9063
" 1 " 2 YEARS	.8483	.8358	.8234	.8112	.7993	.7875	.7759	.7644	.7531	.7421
" 2 " 3 "	.7600	.7413	.7230	.7053	.6879	.6710	.6546	.6385	.6228	.6075
" 3 " 4 "	.6808	.6574	.6349	.6131	.5921	.5718	.5522	.5333	.5150	.4974
" 4 " 5 "	.6099	.5831	.5575	.5330	.5096	.4873	.4659	.4455	.4259	.4072
FROM 5 TO 6 YEARS	.5463	.5172	.4895	.4634	.4386	.4152	.3931	.3721	.3522	.3334
" 6 " 7 "	.4894	.4588	.4299	.4029	.3775	.3538	.3316	.3108	.2913	.2730
" 7 " 8 "	.4385	.4069	.3775	.3502	.3250	.3015	.2798	.2596	.2409	.2235
" 8 " 9 "	.3928	.3609	.3314	.3045	.2797	.2569	.2360	.2168	.1992	.1830
" 9 " 10 "	.3519	.3201	.2910	.2647	.2407	.2189	.1991	.1811	.1647	.1498
FROM 10 TO 11 YEARS	.3152	.2839	.2556	.2301	.2072	.1866	.1680	.1513	.1362	.1227
" 11 " 12 "	.2824	.2518	.2244	.2000	.1783	.1590	.1417	.1264	.1126	.1004
" 12 " 13 "	.2530	.2233	.1970	.1739	.1535	.1355	.1196	.1055	.0932	.0822
" 13 " 14 "	.2266	.1981	.1730	.1512	.1321	.1154	.1009	.0882	.0770	.0673
" 14 " 15 "	.2030	.1757	.1519	.1314	.1137	.0984	.0851	.0736	.0637	.0551

E. UNIFORMLY OVER 5 YEAR PERIODS

	11%	12%	13%	14%	15%	16%	17%	18%	19%	20%
FROM 0 TO 5 YEARS	.7692	.7520	.7353	.7192	.7035	.6883	.6736	.6594	.6455	.6321
" 5 " 10 "	.4438	.4127	.3839	.3571	.3323	.3093	.2879	.2681	.2497	.2325
" 10 " 15 "	.2560	.2265	.2004	.1773	.1570	.1390	.1231	.1090	.0966	.0855
" 15 " 20 "	.1477	.1243	.1046	.0881	.0742	.0624	.0526	.0443	.0373	.0315
" 20 " 25 "	.0852	.0682	.0546	.0437	.0350	.0281	.0225	.0180	.0144	.0116
FROM 25 TO 30 YEARS	.0492	.0374	.0285	.0217	.0165	.0126	.0096	.0073	.0056	.0043
" 30 " 35 "	.0284	.0205	.0149	.0108	.0078	.0057	.0041	.0030	.0022	.0016
" 35 " 40 "	.0164	.0113	.0078	.0054	.0037	.0025	.0018	.0012	.0008	.0006
" 40 " 45 "	.0094	.0062	.0041	.0027	.0017	.0011	.0008	.0005	.0003	.0002
" 45 " 50 "	.0054	.0034	.0021	.0013	.0008	.0005	.0003	.0002	.0001	.0001

F. DECLINING TO NOTHING AT CONSTANT RATE

	11%	12%	13%	14%	15%	16%	17%	18%	19%	20%
FROM 0 TO 5 YEARS	.8393	.8267	.8144	.8024	.7906	.7792	.7679	.7570	.7462	7358
" 0 TO 10 "	.7155	.6961	.6776	.6598	.6428	.6265	.6109	.5959	.5814	.5677
" 0 TO 15 "	.6186	.5959	.5745	.5544	.5355	.5176	.5008	.4848	.4698	.4555
" 0 TO 20 "	.5417	.5176	.4953	.4747	.4555	.4376	.4210	.4055	.3909	.3773
" 0 TO 25 "	.4797	.4555	.4334	.4131	.3945	.3773	.3614	.3468	.3332	.3205
FROM 0 TO 30 YEARS	.4292	.4055	.3840	.3645	.3468	.3306	.3157	.3020	.2895	.2779
" 0 " 35 "	.3874	.3645	.3440	.3254	.3088	.2936	.2798	.2672	.2556	.2449

J. C. Gregory's Interest Tables for Determining Rate of Return

COMPOUNDING PERFORMANCE BEFORE
REFERENCE POINT WHICH OCCURS:

CONTINUOUS INTEREST TABLE

	21%	22%	23%	24%	25%	26%	27%	28%	29%	30%
A. IN AN INSTANT										
1 MONTH BEFORE	1.0177	1.0185	1.0194	1.0202	1.0211	1.0219	1.0228	1.0236	1.0245	1.0253
2 MONTHS "	1.0356	1.0373	1.0391	1.0408	1.0425	1.0443	1.0460	1.0478	1.0495	1.0513
3 " "	1.0539	1.0565	1.0592	1.0618	1.0645	1.0672	1.0698	1.0725	1.0752	1.0779
6 MONTHS BEFORE	1.1107	1.1163	1.1219	1.1275	1.1331	1.1388	1.1445	1.1503	1.1560	1.1618
9 " "	1.1706	1.1794	1.1883	1.1972	1.2062	1.2153	1.2245	1.2337	1.2430	1.2523
12 " "	1.2337	1.2461	1.2586	1.2712	1.2840	1.2969	1.3100	1.3231	1.3364	1.3499
1½ YEARS BEFORE	1.3703	1.3910	1.4120	1.4333	1.4550	1.4770	1.4993	1.5220	1.5450	1.5683
2 " "	1.5220	1.5527	1.5841	1.6161	1.6487	1.6820	1.7160	1.7507	1.7860	1.8221
2½ " "	1.6905	1.7333	1.7771	1.8221	1.8682	1.9155	1.9640	2.0138	2.0647	2.1170
3 " "	1.8776	1.9348	1.9937	2.0544	2.1170	2.1815	2.2479	2.3164	2.3869	2.4596
B. UNIFORMLY UNTIL REFERENCE POINT										
FROM 3 MONTHS BEFORE TO 0	1.0267	1.0280	1.0293	1.0306	1.0319	1.0332	1.0345	1.0358	1.0371	1.0385
" 6 " " " 0	1.0544	1.0571	1.0598	1.0625	1.0652	1.0679	1.0706	1.0734	1.0761	1.0789
" 9 " " " 0	1.0831	1.0872	1.0914	1.0957	1.0999	1.1042	1.1084	1.1128	1.1171	1.1214
" 12 " " " 0	1.1128	1.1185	1.1244	1.1302	1.1361	1.1420	1.1480	1.1540	1.1601	1.1662
FROM 2 YEARS BEFORE TO 0	1.2428	1.2562	1.2697	1.2835	1.2974	1.3116	1.3259	1.3405	1.3552	1.3702
" 3 " " " 0	1.3930	1.4164	1.4402	1.4645	1.4893	1.5147	1.5406	1.5671	1.5942	1.6218

DISCOUNTING PERFORMANCE AFTER
REFERENCE POINT WHICH OCCURS:

	21%	22%	23%	24%	25%	26%	27%	28%	29%	30%
C. IN AN INSTANT										
1 YEAR LATER	.8106	.8025	.7945	.7866	.7788	.7711	.7634	.7558	.7483	.7408
2 YEARS "	.6570	.6440	.6313	.6188	.6065	.5945	.5827	.5712	.5599	.5488
3 " "	.5326	.5169	.5016	.4868	.4724	.4584	.4449	.4317	.4190	.4066
4 " "	.4317	.4148	.3985	.3829	.3679	.3535	.3396	.3263	.3135	.3012
5 " "	.3499	.3329	.3166	.3012	.2865	.2725	.2592	.2466	.2346	.2231
10 YEARS LATER	.1225	.1108	.1003	.0907	.0821	.0743	.0672	.0608	.0550	.0498
15 " "	.0429	.0369	.0317	.0273	.0235	.0202	.0174	.0150	.0129	.0111
20 " "	.0150	.0123	.0101	.0082	.0067	.0055	.0045	.0037	.0030	.0025
25 " "	.0052	.0041	.0032	.0025	.0019	.0015	.0012	.0009	.0007	.0006
30 " "	.0018	.0014	.0010	.0007	.0006	.0004	.0003	.0002	.0002	.0001
35 YEARS LATER	.0006	.0005	.0003	.0002	.0002	.0001	.0001	.0001	—	—
40 " "	.0002	.0002	.0001	.0001	—	—	—	—	—	—
45 " "	.0001	.0001	—	—	—	—	—	—	—	—
50 " "	—	—	—	—	—	—	—	—	—	—
D. UNIFORMLY OVER INDIVIDUAL YEARS										
FROM 0 TO 1 YEAR	.9020	.8976	.8933	.8890	.8848	.8806	.8764	.8722	.8681	.8640
" 1 " 2 YEARS	.7311	.7204	.7098	.6993	.6891	.6790	.6690	.6592	.6495	.6400
" 2 " 3 "	.5926	.5781	.5639	.5501	.5367	.5235	.5107	.4982	.4860	.4741
" 3 " 4 "	.4804	.4639	.4481	.4327	.4179	.4037	.3899	.3765	.3637	.3513
" 4 " 5 "	.3894	.3723	.3560	.3404	.3255	.3112	.2976	.2846	.2721	.2602
FROM 5 TO 6 YEARS	.3156	.2988	.2829	.2678	.2535	.2400	.2272	.2151	.2036	.1928
" 6 " 7 "	.2558	.2398	.2247	.2106	.1974	.1850	.1734	.1626	.1524	.1428
" 7 " 8 "	.2074	.1924	.1786	.1657	.1538	.1427	.1324	.1229	.1140	.1058
" 8 " 9 "	.1681	.1544	.1419	.1303	.1197	.1100	.1011	.0929	.0853	.0784
" 9 " 10 "	.1363	.1239	.1127	.1025	.0933	.0848	.0772	.0702	.0638	.0581
FROM 10 TO 11 YEARS	.1105	.0995	.0896	.0807	.0726	.0654	.0589	.0530	.0478	.0430
" 11 " 12 "	.0895	.0798	.0711	.0634	.0566	.0504	.0450	.0401	.0357	.0319
" 12 " 13 "	.0726	.0641	.0565	.0499	.0441	.0389	.0343	.0303	.0267	.0236
" 13 " 14 "	.0588	.0514	.0449	.0393	.0343	.0300	.0262	.0229	.0200	.0175
" 14 " 15 "	.0477	.0413	.0357	.0309	.0267	.0231	.0200	.0173	.0150	.0130
E. UNIFORMLY OVER 5 YEAR PERIODS										
FROM 0 TO 5 YEARS	.6191	.6065	.5942	.5823	.5708	.5596	.5487	.5381	.5279	.5179
" 5 " 10 "	.2166	.2019	.1882	.1754	.1635	.1525	.1422	.1327	.1238	.1156
" 10 " 15 "	.0758	.0672	.0596	.0528	.0469	.0416	.0369	.0327	.0290	.0258
" 15 " 20 "	.0265	.0224	.0189	.0159	.0134	.0113	.0096	.0081	.0068	.0058
" 20 " 25 "	.0093	.0074	.0060	.0048	.0038	.0031	.0025	.0020	.0016	.0013
FROM 25 TO 30 YEARS	.0032	.0025	.0019	.0014	.0011	.0008	.0006	.0005	.0004	.0003
" 30 " 35 "	.0011	.0008	.0006	.0004	.0003	.0002	.0002	.0001	.0001	.0001
" 35 " 40 "	.0004	.0003	.0002	.0001	.0001	.0001	—	—	—	—
" 40 " 45 "	.0001	.0001	.0001	—	—	—	—	—	—	—
" 45 " 50 "	.0000	—	—	—	—	—	—	—	—	—
F. DECLINING TO NOTHING AT CONSTANT RATE										
FROM 0 TO 5 YEARS	.7255	.7155	.7057	.6961	.6867	.6776	.6686	.6598	.6512	.6428
" 0 " 10 "	.5544	.5417	.5294	.5176	.5063	.4953	.4848	.4747	.4649	.4555
" 0 " 15 "	.4420	.4292	.4170	.4055	.3945	.3840	.3740	.3645	.3554	.3468
" 0 " 20 "	.3645	.3525	.3412	.3306	.3205	.3111	.3020	.2936	.2856	.2779
" 0 " 25 "	.3088	.2978	.2875	.2779	.2689	.2604	.2525	.2449	.2378	.2311
FROM 0 TO 30 YEARS	.2672	.2572	.2479	.2392	.2311	.2235	.2166	.2098	.2036	.1975
" 0 " 35 "	.2351	.2260	.2177	.2098	.2026	.1957	.1893	.1834	.1776	.1723

J. C. Gregory's Interest Tables for Determining Rate of Return

CONTINUOUS INTEREST TABLE

COMPOUNDING PERFORMANCE BEFORE REFERENCE POINT WHICH OCCURS:

A. IN AN INSTANT

	31%	32%	33%	34%	35%	36%	37%	38%	39%	40%
1 MONTH BEFORE	1.0262	1.0270	1.0279	1.0287	1.0296	1.0305	1.0313	1.0322	1.0330	1.0339
2 MONTHS "	1.0530	1.0548	1.0565	1.0583	1.0601	1.0618	1.0636	1.0654	1.0672	1.0689
3 " "	1.0806	1.0833	1.0860	1.0887	1.0914	1.0942	1.0969	1.0997	1.1024	1.1052
6 MONTHS BEFORE	1.1677	1.1735	1.1794	1.1853	1.1912	1.1972	1.2032	1.2092	1.2153	1.2214
9 " "	1.2618	1.2712	1.2808	1.2905	1.3002	1.3100	1.3198	1.3298	1.3398	1.3499
12 " "	1.3634	1.3771	1.3910	1.4049	1.4191	1.4333	1.4477	1.4623	1.4770	1.4918
1½ YEARS BEFORE	1.5920	1.6161	1.6405	1.6653	1.6905	1.7160	1.7419	1.7683	1.7950	1.8221
2 " "	1.8589	1.8965	1.9348	1.9739	2.0138	2.0544	2.0959	2.1383	2.1815	2.2255
2½ " "	2.1706	2.2255	2.2819	2.3396	2.3989	2.4596	2.5219	2.5857	2.6512	2.7183
3 " "	2.5345	2.6117	2.6912	2.7732	2.8577	2.9447	3.0344	3.1268	3.2220	3.3201

B. UNIFORMLY UNTIL REFERENCE POINT

	31%	32%	33%	34%	35%	36%	37%	38%	39%	40%
FROM 3 MONTHS BEFORE TO 0	1.0398	1.0411	1.0424	1.0437	1.0451	1.0464	1.0477	1.0490	1.0504	1.0517
" 6 " " " 0	1.0817	1.0844	1.0872	1.0900	1.0928	1.0957	1.0985	1.1013	1.1042	1.1070
" 9 " " " 0	1.1258	1.1302	1.1346	1.1391	1.1435	1.1480	1.1525	1.1571	1.1616	1.1662
" 12 " " " 0	1.1723	1.1785	1.1848	1.1910	1.1973	1.2037	1.2101	1.2165	1.2230	1.2296
FROM 2 YEARS BEFORE TO 0	1.3854	1.4008	1.4164	1.4322	1.4482	1.4645	1.4810	1.4977	1.5147	1.5319
" 3 " " " 0	1.6500	1.6789	1.7083	1.7384	1.7692	1.8006	1.8328	1.8656	1.8991	1.9334

DISCOUNTING PERFORMANCE AFTER REFERENCE POINT WHICH OCCURS:

C. IN AN INSTANT

	31%	32%	33%	34%	35%	36%	37%	38%	39%	40%
1 YEAR LATER	.7334	.7261	.7189	.7118	.7047	.6977	.6907	.6839	.6771	.6703
2 YEARS "	.5379	.5273	.5169	.5066	.4966	.4868	.4771	.4677	.4584	.4493
3 " "	.3946	.3829	.3716	.3606	.3499	.3396	.3296	.3198	.3104	.3012
4 " "	.2894	.2780	.2671	.2567	.2466	.2369	.2276	.2187	.2101	.2019
5 " "	.2122	.2019	.1921	.1827	.1738	.1653	.1572	.1496	.1423	.1353
10 YEARS LATER	.0450	.0408	.0369	.0334	.0302	.0273	.0247	.0224	.0202	.0183
15 " "	.0096	.0082	.0071	.0061	.0052	.0045	.0039	.0033	.0029	.0025
20 " "	.0020	.0017	.0014	.0011	.0009	.0007	.0006	.0005	.0004	.0003
25 " "	.0004	.0003	.0003	.0002	.0002	.0001	.0001	.0001	.0001	—
30 " "	.0001	.0001	.0001	—	—	—	—	—	—	—
35 YEARS LATER	—	—	—	—	—	—	—	—	—	—
40 " "	—	—	—	—	—	—	—	—	—	—
45 " "	—	—	—	—	—	—	—	—	—	—
50 " "	—	—	—	—	—	—	—	—	—	—

D. UNIFORMLY OVER INDIVIDUAL YEARS

	31%	32%	33%	34%	35%	36%	37%	38%	39%	40%
FROM 0 TO 1 YEAR	.8598	.8558	.8517	.8477	.8438	.8398	.8359	.8319	.8281	.8242
" 1 " 2 YEARS	.6307	.6214	.6123	.6034	.5946	.5859	.5774	.5689	.5606	.5525
" 2 " 3 "	.4626	.4512	.4402	.4295	.4190	.4088	.3988	.3891	.3796	.3703
" 3 " 4 "	.3393	.3277	.3165	.3057	.2953	.2852	.2755	.2661	.2570	.2482
" 4 " 5 "	.2488	.2379	.2275	.2176	.2081	.1990	.1903	.1820	.1740	.1664
FROM 5 TO 6 YEARS	.1825	.1728	.1636	.1549	.1466	.1388	.1314	.1244	.1178	.1115
" 6 " 7 "	.1339	.1255	.1176	.1102	.1033	.0968	.0908	.0851	.0798	.0748
" 7 " 8 "	.0982	.0911	.0845	.0785	.0728	.0676	.0627	.0582	.0540	.0501
" 8 " 9 "	.0720	.0662	.0608	.0558	.0513	.0471	.0433	.0398	.0366	.0336
" 9 " 10 "	.0528	.0480	.0437	.0397	.0362	.0329	.0299	.0272	.0248	.0225
FROM 10 TO 11 YEARS	.0387	.0349	.0314	.0283	.0255	.0229	.0207	.0186	.0168	.0151
" 11 " 12 "	.0284	.0253	.0226	.0201	.0180	.0160	.0143	.0127	.0113	.0101
" 12 " 13 "	.0208	.0184	.0162	.0143	.0127	.0112	.0099	.0087	.0077	.0068
" 13 " 14 "	.0159	.0134	.0117	.0102	.0089	.0078	.0068	.0060	.0052	.0045
" 14 " 15 "	.0112	.0097	.0084	.0073	.0063	.0054	.0047	.0041	.0035	.0030

E. UNIFORMLY OVER 5 YEAR PERIODS

	31%	32%	33%	34%	35%	36%	37%	38%	39%	40%
FROM 0 TO 5 YEARS	.5082	.4988	.4897	.4808	.4721	.4637	.4555	.4476	.4399	.4323
" 5 " 10 "	.1079	.1007	.0940	.0878	.0820	.0767	.0716	.0670	.0626	.0585
" 10 " 15 "	.0229	.0203	.0181	.0160	.0143	.0127	.0113	.0100	.0089	.0079
" 15 " 20 "	.0049	.0041	.0035	.0029	.0025	.0021	.0018	.0015	.0013	.0011
" 20 " 25 "	.0010	.0008	.0007	.0005	.0004	.0003	.0003	.0002	.0002	.0001
FROM 25 TO 30 YEARS	.0002	.0002	.0001	.0001	.0001	.0001	—	—	—	—
" 30 " 35 "	—	—	—	—	—	—	—	—	—	—
" 35 " 40 "	—	—	—	—	—	—	—	—	—	—
" 40 " 45 "	—	—	—	—	—	—	—	—	—	—
" 45 " 50 "	—	—	—	—	—	—	—	—	—	—

F. DECLINING TO NOTHING AT CONSTANT RATE

	31%	32%	33%	34%	35%	36%	37%	38%	39%	40%
FROM 0 TO 5 YEARS	.6345	.6265	.6186	.6109	.6033	.5959	.5886	.5814	.5745	.5677
" 0 " 10 "	.4464	.4376	.4292	.4210	.4131	.4055	.3981	.3909	.3840	.3773
" 0 " 15 "	.3385	.3306	.3230	.3157	.3088	.3020	.2957	.2895	.2836	.2779
" 0 " 20 "	.2707	.2637	.2572	.2509	.2449	.2392	.2337	.2285	.2235	.2188
" 0 " 25 "	.2248	.2188	.2132	.2076	.2026	.1975	.1930	.1884	.1842	.1800
FROM 0 TO 30 YEARS	.1920	.1867	.1817	.1769	.1723	.1680	.1640	.1601	.1563	.1528
" 0 " 35 "	.1673	.1627	.1582	.1540	.1499	.1462	.1425	.1391	.1358	.1327

J. C. Gregory's Interest Tables for Determining Rate of Return

COMPOUNDING PERFORMANCE BEFORE REFERENCE POINT WHICH OCCURS:

CONTINUOUS INTEREST TABLE

	41%	42%	43%	44%	45%	46%	47%	48%	49%	50%
A. IN AN INSTANT										
1 MONTH BEFORE	1.0348	1.0356	1.0365	1.0373	1.0382	1.0390	1.0399	1.0408	1.0417	1.0425
2 MONTHS BEFORE	1.0707	1.0725	1.0743	1.0761	1.0779	1.0797	1.0815	1.0833	1.0851	1.0869
3 " "	1.1079	1.1107	1.1135	1.1163	1.1191	1.1219	1.1247	1.1275	1.1303	1.1331
6 MONTHS BEFORE	1.2275	1.2337	1.2399	1.2461	1.2523	1.2586	1.2649	1.2712	1.2776	1.2840
9 " "	1.3600	1.3703	1.3806	1.3910	1.4014	1.4120	1.4226	1.4333	1.4441	1.4450
12 " "	1.5068	1.5220	1.5373	1.5527	1.5683	1.5841	1.6000	1.6161	1.6323	1.64
1½ YEARS BEFORE	1.8497	1.8776	1.9060	1.9348	1.9640	1.9937	2.0238	2.0544	2.0855	2.1170
2 " "	2.2705	2.3164	2.3632	2.4109	2.4596	2.5093	2.5600	2.6117	2.6645	2.7183
2¼ " "	2.7871	2.8577	2.9300	3.0042	3.0802	3.1582	3.2381	3.3201	3.4042	3.4903
3 " "	3.4212	3.5254	3.6328	3.7434	3.8574	3.9749	4.0960	4.2207	4.3492	4.4817
B. UNIFORMLY UNTIL REFERENCE POINT										
FROM 3 MONTHS BEFORE TO 0	1.0531	1.0544	1.0557	1.0571	1.0584	1.0598	1.0611	1.0625	1.0638	1.0652
" 6 " " " 0	1.1099	1.1128	1.1156	1.1185	1.1214	1.1244	1.1273	1.1302	1.1331	1.1361
" 9 " " " 0	1.1708	1.1754	1.1801	1.1848	1.1895	1.1942	1.1989	1.2037	1.2085	1.2133
" 12 " " " 0	1.2361	1.2428	1.2494	1.2562	1.2629	1.2697	1.2766	1.2835	1.2904	1.2974
FROM 2 YEARS BEFORE TO 0	1.5494	1.5671	1.5851	1.6033	1.6218	1.6403	1.6596	1.6789	1.6984	1.7183
" 3 " " " 0	1.9685	2.0043	2.0409	2.0784	2.1166	2.1557	2.1957	2.2366	2.2784	2.3211

DISCOUNTING PERFORMANCE AFTER REFERENCE POINT WHICH OCCURS:

	41%	42%	43%	44%	45%	46%	47%	48%	49%	50%
C. IN AN INSTANT										
1 YEAR LATER	.6637	.6570	.6505	.6440	.6376	.6313	.6250	.6188	.6126	.6065
2 YEARS "	.4404	.4317	.4232	.4148	.4066	.3985	.3906	.3829	.3753	.3679
3 " "	.2923	.2837	.2753	.2671	.2592	.2516	.2441	.2369	.2299	.2231
4 " "	.1940	.1864	.1791	.1720	.1653	.1588	.1526	.1466	.1409	.1353
5 " "	.1287	.1225	.1165	.1108	.1054	.1003	.0954	.0907	.0863	.0821
10 YEARS LATER	.0166	.0150	.0136	.0123	.0111	.0101	.0091	.0082	.0074	.0067
15 " "	.0021	.0018	.0016	.0014	.0012	.0010	.0009	.0007	.0006	.0006
20 " "	.0003	.0002	.0002	.0002	.0001	.0001	.0001	.0001	.0001	—
25 " "	—	—	—	—	—	—	—	—	—	—
30 " "	—	—	—	—	—	—	—	—	—	—
35 YEARS LATER	—	—	—	—	—	—	—	—	—	—
40 " "	—	—	—	—	—	—	—	—	—	—
45 " "	—	—	—	—	—	—	—	—	—	—
50 " "	—	—	—	—	—	—	—	—	—	—
D. UNIFORMLY OVER INDIVIDUAL YEARS										
FROM 0 TO 1 YEAR	.8204	.8166	.8128	.8090	.8053	.8016	.7979	.7942	.7906	.7869
" 1 " 2 YEARS	.5444	.5365	.5287	.5210	.5135	.5060	.4987	.4914	.4843	.4773
" 2 " 3 "	.3613	.3525	.3439	.3357	.3274	.3194	.3117	.3041	.2967	.2895
" 3 " 4 "	.2398	.2316	.2237	.2162	.2088	.2017	.1948	.1882	.1818	.1756
" 4 " 5 "	.1591	.1522	.1455	.1392	.1331	.1273	.1217	.1164	.1114	.1065
FROM 5 TO 6 YEARS	.1056	.1000	.0947	.0897	.0849	.0804	.0762	.0720	.0682	.0646
" 6 " 7 "	.0701	.0657	.0616	.0577	.0541	.0507	.0476	.0446	.0418	.0392
" 7 " 8 "	.0465	.0432	.0401	.0372	.0345	.0320	.0298	.0276	.0256	.0238
" 8 " 9 "	.0309	.0284	.0260	.0240	.0220	.0202	.0186	.0171	.0157	.0144
" 9 " 10 "	.0205	.0186	.0170	.0154	.0140	.0128	.0116	.0106	.0096	.0087
FROM 10 TO 11 YEARS	.0136	.0122	.0110	.0099	.0089	.0081	.0073	.0065	.0059	.0053
" 11 " 12 "	.0090	.0080	.0072	.0064	.0057	.0051	.0045	.0040	.0036	.0032
" 12 " 13 "	.0060	.0053	.0047	.0041	.0036	.0032	.0028	.0025	.0022	.0020
" 13 " 14 "	.0040	.0035	.0030	.0027	.0023	.0020	.0018	.0015	.0014	.0012
" 14 " 15 "	.0026	.0023	.0020	.0017	.0015	.0013	.0011	.0010	.0008	.0007
E. UNIFORMLY OVER 5 YEAR PERIODS										
FROM 0 TO 5 YEARS	.4250	4179	.4109	.4042	.3976	.3912	.3849	.3789	.3729	.3672
" 5 " 10 "	.0547	.0512	.0479	.0448	.0419	.0392	.0367	.0344	.0322	.0301
" 10 " 15 "	.0070	.0063	.0056	.0050	.0044	.0039	.0035	.0031	.0028	.0025
" 15 " 20 "	.0009	.0008	.0007	.0006	.0005	.0004	.0003	.0003	.0002	.0002
" 20 " 25 "	.0001	.0001	.0001	.0001	—	—	—	—	—	—
FROM 25 TO 30 YEARS	—	—	—	—	—	—	—	—	—	—
" 30 " 35 "	—	—	—	—	—	—	—	—	—	—
" 35 " 40 "	—	—	—	—	—	—	—	—	—	—
" 40 " 45 "	—	—	—	—	—	—	—	—	—	—
" 45 " 50 "	—	—	—	—	—	—	—	—	—	—
F. DECLINING TO NOTHING AT CONSTANT RATE										
FROM 0 TO 5 YEARS	.5610	.5544	.5480	.5417	.5355	.5294	.5234	.5176	.5119	.5063
" 0 " 10 "	.3708	.3645	.3584	.3525	.3468	.3412	.3358	.3306	.3254	.3205
" 0 " 15 "	.2724	.2672	.2621	.2572	.2525	.2479	.2434	.2392	.2351	.2311
" 0 " 20 "	.2143	.2098	.2056	.2016	.1975	.1939	.1902	.1867	.1834	.1800
" 0 " 25 "	.1761	.1723	.1687	.1653	.1620	.1588	.1557	.1528	.1499	.1472
FROM 0 TO 30 YEARS	.1494	.1462	.1430	.1401	.1372	.1345	.1318	.1292	.1268	.1244
" 0 " 35 "	.1297	.1268	.1240	.1214	.1189	.1165	.1142	.1120	.1198	.1078

J. C. Gregory's Interest Tables for Determining Rate of Return

CONTINUOUS INTEREST TABLE

COMPOUNDING PERFORMANCE BEFORE REFERENCE POINT WHICH OCCURS:

	51%	52%	53%	54%	55%	56%	57%	58%	59%	60%
A. IN AN INSTANT										
1 MONTH BEFORE	1.0434	1.0443	1.0452	1.0460	1.0469	1.0478	1.0486	1.0495	1.0504	1.0513
2 MONTHS BEFORE	1.0887	1.0905	1.0924	1.0942	1.0960	1.0978	1.0997	1.1015	1.1033	1.1052
3 " "	1.1360	1.1388	1.1417	1.1417	1.1445	1.1474	1.1503	1.1532	1.1560	1.1589	1.1618
6 MONTHS BEFORE	1.2905	1.2969	1.3034	1.3100	1.3165	1.3231	1.3298	1.3364	1.3431	1.3499
9 " "	1.4659	1.4770	1.4881	1.4993	1.5106	1.5220	1.5334	1.5450	1.5566	1.5683
12 " "	1.6653	1.6820	1.6989	1.7160	1.7333	1.7507	1.7683	1.7860	1.8040	1.8221
1½ YEARS BEFORE	2.1490	2.1815	2.2144	2.2479	2.2819	2.3164	2.3515	2.3869	2.4230	2.4596
2 " "	2.7732	2.8292	2.8864	2.9447	3.0042	3.0649	3.1269	3.1899	3.2544	3.3201
2½ " "	3.5787	3.6693	3.7622	3.8574	3.9551	4.0552	4.1580	4.2631	4.3710	4.4817
3 " "	4.6182	4.7588	4.9037	5.0531	5.2070	5.3656	5.5292	5.6973	5.8709	6.0496
B. UNIFORMLY UNTIL REFERENCE POINT										
FROM 3 MONTHS BEFORE TO 0	1.0665	1.0679	1.0693	1.0706	1.0720	1.0734	1.0748	1.0761	1.0775	1.0789
" 6 " " " 0	1.1391	1.1420	1.1450	1.1480	1.1510	1.1540	1.1571	1.1601	1.1631	1.1662
" 9 " " " 0	1.2182	1.2230	1.2279	1.2328	1.2378	1.2428	1.2478	1.2528	1.2578	1.2629
" 12 " " " 0	1.3045	1.3116	1.3187	1.3259	1.3332	1.3405	1.3478	1.3552	1.3627	1.3702
FROM 2 YEARS BEFORE TO 0	1.7384	1.7589	1.7796	1.8006	1.8220	1.8436	1.8656	1.8879	1.9105	1.9334
" 3 " " " 0	2.3648	2.4095	2.4552	2.5019	2.5497	2.5986	2.6485	2.6996	2.7519	2.8054

DISCOUNTING PERFORMANCE AFTER REFERENCE POINT WHICH OCCURS:

	51%	52%	53%	54%	55%	56%	57%	58%	59%	60%
C. IN AN INSTANT										
1 YEAR LATER	.6005	.5945	.5886	.5827	.5770	.5712	.5655	.5599	.5543	.5488
2 YEARS "	.3606	.3535	.3465	.3396	.3329	.3263	.3198	.3135	.3073	.3012
3 " "	.2165	.2101	.2039	.1979	.1921	.1864	.1809	.1755	.1703	.1653
4 " "	.1300	.1249	.1200	.1153	.1108	.1065	.1023	.0983	.0944	.0907
5 " "	.0781	.0743	.0706	.0672	.0639	.0608	.0578	.0550	.0523	.0498
10 YEARS LATER	.0061	.0055	.0050	.0045	.0041	.0037	.0033	.0030	.0027	.0025
15 " "	.0005	.0004	.0004	.0003	.0003	.0002	.0002	.0002	.0001	.0001
20 " "	—	—	—	—	—	—	—	—	—	—
25 " "	—	—	—	—	—	—	—	—	—	—
30 " "	—	—	—	—	—	—	—	—	—	—
35 YEARS LATER	—	—	—	—	—	—	—	—	—	—
40 " "	—	—	—	—	—	—	—	—	—	—
45 " "	—	—	—	—	—	—	—	—	—	—
50 " "	—	—	—	—	—	—	—	—	—	—
D. UNIFORMLY OVER INDIVIDUAL YEARS										
FROM 0 TO 1 YEAR	.7833	.7798	.7762	.7727	.7692	.7657	.7622	.7588	.7554	.7520
" 1 " 2 YEARS	.4704	.4636	.4569	.4503	.4438	.4374	.4311	.4248	.4187	.4127
" 2 " 3 "	.2825	.2756	.2689	.2624	.2560	.2498	.2438	.2379	.2321	.2265
" 3 " 4 "	.1696	.1639	.1583	.1529	.1477	.1427	.1379	.1332	.1287	.1243
" 4 " 5 "	.1019	.0974	.0932	.0891	.0852	.0815	.0780	.0746	.0713	.0682
FROM 5 TO 6 YEARS	.0612	.0579	.0548	.0519	.0492	.0466	.0441	.0418	.0395	.0374
" 6 " 7 "	.0367	.0344	.0323	.0303	.0284	.0266	.0249	.0234	.0219	.0205
" 7 " 8 "	.0221	.0205	.0190	.0176	.0164	.0152	.0141	.0131	.0121	.0113
" 8 " 9 "	.0132	.0122	.0112	.0103	.0094	.0087	.0080	.0073	.0067	.0062
" 9 " 10 "	.0080	.0072	.0066	.0060	.0054	.0050	.0045	.0041	.0037	.0034
FROM 10 TO 11 YEARS	.0048	.0043	.0039	.0035	.0031	.0028	.0026	.0023	.0021	.0019
" 11 " 12 "	.0029	.0026	.0023	.0020	.0018	.0016	.0014	.0013	.0011	.0010
" 12 " 13 "	.0017	.0015	.0013	.0012	.0010	.0009	.0008	.0007	.0006	.0006
" 13 " 14 "	.0010	.0009	.0008	.0007	.0006	.0005	.0005	.0004	.0004	.0003
" 14 " 15 "	.0006	.0005	.0005	.0004	.0004	.0003	.0003	.0002	.0002	.0002
E. UNIFORMLY OVER 5 YEAR PERIODS										
FROM 0 TO 5 YEARS	.3615	.3561	.3507	.3455	.3404	.3354	.3306	.3259	.3212	.3167
" 5 " 10 "	.0282	.0264	.0248	.0232	.0217	.0204	.0191	.0179	.0168	.0158
" 10 " 15 "	.0022	.0020	.0018	.0016	.0014	.0012	.0011	.0010	.0009	.0008
" 15 " 20 "	.0002	.0001	.0001	.0001	.0001	.0001	.0001	.0001	—	—
" 20 " 25 "	—	—	—	—	—	—	—	—	—	—
FROM 25 TO 30 YEARS	—	—	—	—	—	—	—	—	—	—
" 30 " 35 "	—	—	—	—	—	—	—	—	—	—
" 35 " 40 "	—	—	—	—	—	—	—	—	—	—
" 40 " 45 "	—	—	—	—	—	—	—	—	—	—
" 45 " 50 "	—	—	—	—	—	—	—	—	—	—
F. DECLINING TO NOTHING AT CONSTANT RATE										
FROM 0 TO 5 YEARS	.5008	.4953	.4900	.4848	.4797	.4747	.4698	.4649	.4602	.4555
" 0 " 10 "	.3157	.3111	.3065	.3020	.2978	.2936	.2895	.2856	.2817	.2779
" 0 " 15 "	.2273	.2235	.2200	.2166	.2132	.2098	.2066	.2036	.2006	.1975
" 0 " 20 "	.1769	.1738	.1709	.1680	.1653	.1627	.1601	.1576	.1551	.1528
" 0 " 25 "	.1446	.1420	.1396	.1372	.1349	.1327	.1305	.1284	.1264	.1244
FROM 0 TO 30 YEARS	.1221	.1200	.1179	.1158	.1139	.1120	.1101	.1084	.1066	.1049
" 0 " 35 "	.1057	.1039	.1020	.1002	.0985	.0968	.0952	.0937	.0921	.0907

J. C. Gregory's Interest Tables for Determining Rate of Return

COMPOUNDING PERFORMANCE BEFORE REFERENCE POINT WHICH OCCURS:		CONTINUOUS INTEREST TABLE								
	61%	62%	63%	64%	65%	66%	67%	68%	69%	70%
A. IN AN INSTANT										
1 MONTH BEFORE	1.0521	1.0530	1.0539	1.0548	1.0557	1.0565	1.0574	1.0583	1.0592	1.0601
2 MONTHS "	1.1070	1.1089	1.1107	1.1126	1.1144	1.1163	1.1181	1.1200	1.1219	1.1237
3 " "	1.1647	1.1677	1.1677	1.1706	1.1735	1.1764	1.1794	1.1823	1.1853	1.1883	1.1912
6 MONTHS BEFORE	1.3566	1.3634	1.3703	1.3771	1.3840	1.3910	1.3979	1.4049	1.4120	1.4191
9 " "	1.5801	1.5920	1.6040	1.6161	1.6282	1.6405	1.6528	1.6653	1.6778	1.6905
12 " "	1.8404	1.8589	1.8776	1.8965	1.9155	1.9348	1.9542	1.9739	1.9937	2.0138
1½ YEARS BEFORE	2.4968	2.5345	2.5728	2.6117	2.6512	2.6912	2.7319	2.7732	2.8151	2.8577
2 " "	3.3872	3.4556	3.5254	3.5966	3.6693	3.7434	3.8190	3.8962	3.9749	4.0552
2½ " "	4.5951	4.7115	4.8307	4.9530	5.0784	5.2070	5.3388	5.4739	5.6125	5.7546
3 " "	6.2339	6.4237	6.6194	6.8210	7.0287	7.2427	7.4633	7.6906	7.9248	8.1662
B. UNIFORMLY UNTIL REFERENCE POINT										
FROM 3 MONTHS BEFORE TO 0	1.0803	1.0817	1.0831	1.0844	1.0858	1.0872	1.0886	1.0900	1.0914	1.0928
" 6 " " 0	1.1693	1.1723	1.1754	1.1785	1.1816	1.1848	1.1879	1.1910	1.1942	1.1973
" 9 " " 0	1.2680	1.2731	1.2783	1.2835	1.2887	1.2939	1.2992	1.3045	1.3098	1.3152
" 12 " " 0	1.3778	1.3854	1.3930	1.4008	1.4085	1.4164	1.4242	1.4322	1.4402	1.4482
FROM 2 YEARS BEFORE TO 0	1.9567	1.9803	2.0043	2.0286	2.0533	2.0783	2.1038	2.1295	2.1557	2.1823
" 3 " " " 0	2.8601	2.9160	2.9732	3.0318	3.0916	3.1529	3.2156	3.2797	3.3453	3.4125
DISCOUNTING PERFORMANCE AFTER REFERENCE POINT WHICH OCCURS:										
C. IN AN INSTANT										
1 YEAR LATER	.5434	.5379	.5326	.5273	.5220	.5169	.5117	.5066	.5016	.4966
2 YEARS "	.2952	.2894	.2837	.2780	.2725	.2671	.2618	.2567	.2516	.2466
3 " "	.1604	.1557	.1511	.1466	.1423	.1381	.1340	.1300	.1262	.1225
4 " "	.0872	.0837	.0805	.0773	.0743	.0714	.0686	.0659	.0633	.0608
5 " "	.0474	.0450	.0429	.0408	.0388	.0369	.0351	.0334	.0317	.0302
10 YEARS LATER	.0022	.0020	.0018	.0017	.0015	.0014	.0012	.0011	.0010	.0009
15 " "	.0001	.0001	.0001	.0001	.0001	.0001	—	—	.0010	—
20 " "	—	—	—	—	—	—	—	—.	—	—
25 " "	—	—	—	—	—	—	—	—	—	—
30 " "	—	—	—	—	—	—	—	—	—	—
35 YEARS LATER	—	—	—	—	—	—	—	—	—	—
40 " "	—	—	—	—	—	—	—	—	—	—
45 " "	—	—	—	—	—	—	—	—	—	—
50 " "	—	—	—	—	—	—	—	—	—	—
D. UNIFORMLY OVER INDIVIDUAL YEARS										
FROM 0 TO 1 YEAR	.7486	.7452	.7419	.7386	.7353	.7320	.7288	.7256	.7224	.7192
" 1 " 2 YEARS	.4068	.4009	.3951	.3895	.3839	.3784	.3729	.3676	.3623	.3571
" 2 " 3 "	.2210	.2157	.2104	.2054	.2004	.1956	.1908	.1862	.1817	.1773
" 3 " 4 "	.1201	.1160	.1121	.1083	.1046	.1011	.0977	.0943	.0912	.0881
" 4 " 5 "	.0652	.0624	.0597	.0571	.0546	.0522	.0500	.0478	.0457	.0437
FROM 5 TO 6 YEARS	.0355	.0336	.0318	.0301	.0285	.0270	.0256	.0242	.0229	.0217
" 6 " 7 "	.0193	.0181	.0169	.0159	.0149	.0140	.0131	.0123	.0115	.0108
" 7 " 8 "	.0105	.0097	.0090	.0084	.0078	.0072	.0067	.0062	.0058	.0054
" 8 " 9 "	.0057	.0052	.0048	.0044	.0041	.0037	.0034	.0031	.0029	.0027
" 9 " 10 "	.0031	.0028	.0026	.0023	.0021	.0019	.0018	.0016	.0015	.0013
FROM 10 TO 11 YEARS	.0017	.0015	.0014	.0012	.0011	.0010	.0009	.0008	.0007	.0007
" 11 " 12 "	.0009	.0008	.0007	.0006	.0006	.0005	.0005	.0004	.0004	.0003
" 12 " 13 "	.0005	.0004	.0004	.0003	.0003	.0003	.0003	.0002	.0002	.0002
" 13 " 14 "	.0003	.0002	.0002	.0002	.0002	.0001	.0001	.0001	.0001	.0001
" 14 " 15 "	.0001	.0001	.0001	.0001	.0001	.0001	.0001	.0001	—	.0001
E. UNIFORMLY OVER 5 YEAR PERIODS										
FROM 0 TO 5 YEARS	.3123	.3080	.3039	.2998	.2958	.2919	.2880	.2843	.2807	.2771
" 5 " 10 "	.0148	.0139	.0130	.0122	.0115	.0108	.0101	.0095	.0089	.0084
" 10 " 15 "	.0007	.0006	.0006	.0005	.0004	.0004	.0004	.0003	.0003	.0003
" 15 " 20 "	—	—	—	—	—	—	—	—	—	—
" 20 " 25 "	—	—	—	—	—	—	—	—	—	—
FROM 25 TO 30 YEARS	—	—	—	—	—	—	—	—	—	—
" 30 " 35 "	—	—	—	—	—	—	—	—	—	—
" 35 " 40 "	—	—	—	—	—	—	—	—	—	—
" 40 " 45 "	—	—	—	—	—	—	—	—	—	—
" 45 " 50 "	—	—	—	—	—	—	—	—	—	—
F. DECLINING TO NOTHING AT CONSTANT RATE										
FROM 0 TO 5 YEARS	.4509	.4464	.4420	.4376	.4334	.4292	.4251	.4210	.4170	.4131
" 0 " 10 "	.2742	.2707	.2672	.2637	.2604	.2572	.2540	.2509	.2479	.2449
" 0 " 15 "	.1948	.1920	.1893	.1867	.1842	.1817	.1792	.1769	.1746	.1723
" 0 " 20 "	.1505	.1483	.1462	.1441	.1420	.1401	.1382	.1363	.1345	.1327
" 0 " 25 "	.1225	.1207	.1189	.1172	.1155	.1139	.1123	.1107	.1092	.1078
FROM 0 TO 30 YEARS	.1033	.1018	.1002	.0987	.0973	.0959	.0946	.0932	.0919	.0907
" 0 " 35 "	.0893	.0879	.0866	.0854	.0841	.0828	.0817	.0806	.0795	.0784

J. C. Gregory's Interest Tables for Determining Rate of Return

COMPOUNDING PERFORMANCE BEFORE REFERENCE POINT WHICH OCCURS:

CONTINUOUS INTEREST TABLE

	71%	72%	73%	74%	75%	76%	77%	78%	79%	80%
A. IN AN INSTANT										
1 MONTH BEFORE	1.0610	1.0618	1.0627	1.0636	1.0645	1.0654	1.0663	1.0672	1.0680	1.0689
2 MONTHS "	1.1256	1.1275	1.1294	1.1313	1.1331	1.1350	1.1369	1.1388	1.1407	1.1426
3 " "	1.1942	1.1972	1.2002	1.2032	1.2062	1.2093	1.2123	1.2153	1.2184	1.2214
6 MONTHS BEFORE	1.4262	1.4333	1.4405	1.4477	1.4550	1.4623	1.4696	1.4770	1.4844	1.4918
9 " "	1.7032	1.7160	1.7289	1.7419	1.7551	1.7683	1.7816	1.7950	1.8085	1.8221
12 " "	2.0340	2.0544	2.0751	2.0959	2.1170	2.1383	2.1598	2.1815	2.2034	2.2255
1½ YEARS BEFORE	2.9008	2.9447	2.9892	3.0344	3.0802	3.1268	3.1740	3.2220	3.2707	3.3201
2 " "	4.1371	4.2207	4.3060	4.3929	4.4817	4.5722	4.6646	4.7588	4.8550	4.9530
2½ " "	5.9003	6.0497	6.2028	6.3598	6.5208	6.6859	6.8551	7.0287	7.2066	7.3891
3 " "	8.4149	8.6711	8.9352	9.2073	9.4877	9.7767	10.0744	10.3812	10.6974	11.0232
B. UNIFORMLY UNTIL REFERENCE POINT										
FROM 3 MONTHS BEFORE TO 0	1.0942	1.0957	1.0971	1.0985	1.0999	1.1013	1.1027	1.1042	1.1056	1.1070
" 6 " " " 0	1.2005	1.2037	1.2069	1.2101	1.2133	1.2165	1.2198	1.2230	1.2263	1.2296
" 9 " " " 0	1.3205	1.3259	1.3314	1.3368	1.3423	1.3478	1.3534	1.3590	1.3646	1.3702
" 12 " " " 0	1.4563	1.4645	1.4727	1.4810	1.4893	1.4977	1.5062	1.5147	1.5233	1.5319
FROM 2 YEARS BEFORE TO 0	2.2092	2.2366	2.2644	2.2925	2.3211	2.3501	2.3796	2.4095	2.4399	2.4707
" 3 " " " 0	3.4812	3.5515	3.6234	3.6970	3.7723	3.8494	3.9283	4.0091	4.0917	4.1763

DISCOUNTING PERFORMANCE AFTER REFERENCE POINT WHICH OCCURS:

	71%	72%	73%	74%	75%	76%	77%	78%	79%	80%
C. IN AN INSTANT										
1 YEAR LATER	.4916	.4868	.4819	.4771	.4724	.4677	.4630	.4584	.4538	.4493
2 YEARS "	.2417	.2369	.2322	.2276	.2231	.2187	.2144	.2101	.2060	.2019
3 " "	.1188	.1153	.1119	.1086	.1054	.1023	.0993	.0963	.0935	.0907
4 " "	.0584	.0561	.0539	.0518	.0498	.0478	.0460	.0442	.0424	.0408
5 " "	.0287	.0273	.0260	.0247	.0235	.0224	.0213	.0202	.0193	.0183
10 YEARS LATER	.0008	.0007	.0007	.0006	.0006	.0005	.0005	.0004	.0004	.0003
15 " "	—	—	—	—	—	—	—	—	—	—
20 " "	—	—	—	—	—	—	—	—	—	—
25 " "	—	—	—	—	—	—	—	—	—	—
30 " "	—	—	—	—	—	—	—	—	—	—
35 " "	—	—	—	—	—	—	—	—	—	—
40 " "	—	—	—	—	—	—	—	—	—	—
45 " "	—	—	—	—	—	—	—	—	—	—
50 " "	—	—	—	—	—	—	—	—	—	—
D. UNIFORMLY OVER INDIVIDUAL YEARS										
FROM 0 TO 1 YEAR	.7160	.7128	.7097	.7066	.7035	.7004	.6974	.6944	.6913	.6883
" 1 " 2 YEARS	.3520	.3470	.3420	.3371	.3323	.3276	.3229	.3183	.3138	.3093
" 2 " 3 "	.1731	.1689	.1648	.1608	.1570	.1532	.1495	.1459	.1424	.1390
" 3 " 4 "	.0851	.0822	.0794	.0767	.0741	.0716	.0692	.0669	.0646	.0624
" 4 " 5 "	.0418	.0400	.0383	.0366	.0350	.0335	.0321	.0307	.0293	.0281
FROM 5 TO 6 YEARS	.0206	.0195	.0184	.0175	.0165	.0157	.0148	.0141	.0133	.0126
" 6 " 7 "	.0101	.0095	.0089	.0083	.0078	.0073	.0069	.0064	.0060	.0057
" 7 " 8 "	.0050	.0046	.0043	.0040	.0037	.0034	.0032	.0030	.0027	.0025
" 8 " 9 "	.0024	.0022	.0021	.0019	.0017	.0016	.0015	.0014	.0012	.0011
" 9 " 10 "	.0012	.0011	.0010	.0009	.0008	.0007	.0007	.0006	.0006	.0005
FROM 10 TO 11 YEARS	.0006	.0005	.0005	.0004	.0004	.0004	.0003	.0003	.0003	.0002
" 11 " 12 "	.0003	.0003	.0002	.0002	.0002	.0002	.0002	.0001	.0001	.0001
" 12 " 13 "	.0001	.0001	.0001	.0001	.0001	.0001	.0001	.0001	.0001	—
" 13 " 14 "	.0001	.0001	.0001	—	—	—	—	—	—	—
" 14 " 15 "	—	—	—	—	—	—	—	—	—	—
E. UNIFORMLY OVER 5 YEAR PERIODS										
FROM 0 TO 5 YEARS	.2736	.2702	.2669	.2636	.2604	.2573	.2542	.2512	.2483	.2454
" 5 " 10 "	.0079	.0074	.0069	.0065	.0061	.0058	.0054	.0051	.0048	.0045
" 10 " 15 "	.0002	.0002	.0002	.0002	.0001	.0001	.0001	.0001	.0001	.0001
" 15 " 20 "	—	—	—	—	—	—	—	—	—	—
" 20 " 25 "	—	—	—	—	—	—	—	—	—	—
FROM 25 TO 30 YEARS	—	—	—	—	—	—	—	—	—	—
" 30 " 35 "	—	—	—	—	—	—	—	—	—	—
" 35 " 40 "	—	—	—	—	—	—	—	—	—	—
" 40 " 45 "	—	—	—	—	—	—	—	—	—	—
" 45 " 50 "	—	—	—	—	—	—	—	—	—	—
F. DECLINING TO NOTHING AT CONSTANT RATE										
FROM 0 TO 5 YEARS	.4092	.4055	.4017	.3981	.3945	.3909	.3874	.3840	.3806	.3773
" 0 " 10 "	.2420	.2392	.2364	.2337	.2311	.2285	.2260	.2235	.2212	.2188
" 0 " 15 "	.1701	.1680	.1660	.1640	.1620	.1601	.1582	.1563	.1545	.1528
" 0 " 20 "	.1309	.1292	.1276	.1260	.1244	.1229	.1214	.1200	.1186	.1172
" 0 " 25 "	.1063	.1049	.1036	.1023	.1010	.0997	.0985	.0973	.0961	.0950
FROM 0 TO 30 YEARS	.0895	.0883	.0872	.0861	.0850	.0839	.0828	.0818	.0809	.0800
" 0 " 35 "	.0773	.0763	.0754	.0745	.0736	.0728	.0719	.0711	.0702	.0693

J. C. Gregory's Interest Tables for Determining Rate of Return

COMPOUNDING PERFORMANCE BEFORE REFERENCE POINT WHICH OCCURS:	81%	82%	83%	84%	85%	86%	87%	88%	89%	90%
A. IN AN INSTANT										
1 MONTH BEFORE	1.0698	1.0707	1.0716	1.0725	1.0734	1.0743	1.0752	1.0761	1.0770	1.0779
2 MONTHS "	1.1445	1.1464	1.1484	1.1503	1.1522	1.1541	1.1560	1.1580	1.1599	1.1618
3 " "	1.2245	1.2275	1.2306	1.2337	1.2368	1.2399	1.2430	1.2461	1.2492	1.2523
6 MONTHS BEFORE	1.4993	1.5068	1.5144	1.5220	1.5296	1.5373	1.5450	1.5527	1.5605	1.5683
9 " "	1.8358	1.8497	1.8636	1.8776	1.8917	1.9060	1.9203	1.9348	1.9494	1.9640
12 " "	2.2479	2.2705	2.2933	2.3164	2.3396	2.3632	2.3869	2 4109	2.4351	2.4596
1½ YEARS BEFORE	3.3703	3.4212	3.4729	3.5254	3.5787	3.6328	3.6877	3.7434	3.8000	3.8574
2 " "	5.0531	5.1552	5.2593	5.3656	5.4739	5.5845	5.6973	5.8124	5.9299	6.0496
2½ " "	7.5761	7.7679	7.9645	8.1662	8.3729	8.5849	8.8022	9.0250	9.2535	9.4877
3 " "	11.3589	11.7048	12.0613	12.4286	12.8071	13.1971	13.5990	14.0132	14.4400	14.8797
B. UNIFORMLY UNTIL REFERENCE POINT										
FROM 3 MONTHS BEFORE TO 0	1.1084	1.1099	1.1113	1.1128	1.1142	1.1156	1.1171	1.1185	1.1200	1.1214
" 6 " " " 0	1.2328	1.2361	1.2394	1.2428	1.2461	1.2494	1.2528	1.2562	1.2595	1.2629
" 9 " " " 0	1.3759	1.3816	1.3873	1.3930	1.3988	1.4046	1.4105	1.4164	1.4223	1.4282
" 12 " " " 0	1.5406	1.5494	1.5582	1.5671	1.5761	1.5851	1.5942	1.6033	1.6125	1.6218
FROM 2 YEARS BEFORE TO 0	2.5019	2.5336	2.5658	2.5986	2.6317	2.6654	2.6996	2.7343	2.7696	2.8054
" 3 " " " 0	4.2630	4.3516	4.4423	4.5352	4.6302	4.7276	4.8272	4.9292	5.0337	5.1406

DISCOUNTING PERFORMANCE AFTER REFERENCE POINT WHICH OCCURS:

	81%	82%	83%	84%	85%	86%	87%	88%	89%	90%
C. IN AN INSTANT										
1 YEAR LATER	.4449	.4404	.4360	.4317	.4274	.4232	.4190	.4148	.4107	.4066
2 YEARS "	.1979	.1940	.1901	.1864	.1827	.1791	.1755	.1720	.1686	.1653
3 " "	.0880	.0854	.0829	.0805	.0781	.0758	.0735	.0714	.0693	.0672
4 " "	.0392	.0376	.0362	.0347	.0334	.0321	.0308	.0296	.0284	.0273
5 " "	.0174	.0166	.0158	.0150	.0143	.0136	.0129	.0123	.0117	.0111
10 YEARS LATER	.0003	.0003	.0002	.0002	.0002	.0002	.0002	.0002	.0001	.0001
15 " "	—	—	—	—	—	—	—	—	—	—
20 " "	—	—	—	—	—	—	—	—	—	—
25 " "	—	—	—	—	—	—	—	—	—	—
30 " "	—	—	—	—	—	—	—	—	—	—
35 YEARS LATER	—	—	—	—	—	—	—	—	—	—
40 " "	—	—	—	—	—	—	—	—	—	—
45 " "	—	—	—	—	—	—	—	—	—	—
50 " "	—	—	—	—	—	—	—	—	—	—
D. UNIFORMLY OVER INDIVIDUAL YEARS										
FROM 0 TO 1 YEAR	.6854	.6824	.6795	.6765	.6736	.6707	.6679	.6650	.6622	.6594
" 1 " 2 YEARS	.3049	.3006	.2963	.2921	.2879	.2838	.2798	.2758	.2719	.2681
" 2 " 3 "	.1356	.1324	.1292	.1261	.1231	.1201	.1172	.1144	.1117	.1090
" 3 " 4 "	.0603	.0583	.0563	.0544	.0526	.0508	.0491	.0475	.0459	.0443
" 4 " 5 "	.0268	.0257	.0246	.0235	.0225	.0215	.0206	.0197	.0188	.0180
FROM 5 TO 6 YEARS	.0119	.0113	.0107	.0101	.0096	.0091	.0086	.0082	.0077	.0073
" 6 " 7 "	.0053	.0050	.0047	.0044	.0041	.0039	.0036	.0034	.0032	.0030
" 7 " 8 "	.0024	.0022	.0020	.0019	.0018	.0016	.0015	.0014	.0013	.0012
" 8 " 9 "	.0011	.0010	.0009	.0008	.0008	.0007	.0006	.0006	.0005	.0005
" 9 " 10 "	.0005	.0004	.0004	.0004	.0003	.0003	.0003	.0002	.0002	.0002
FROM 10 TO 11 YEARS	.0002	.0002	.0002	.0002	.0001	.0001	.0001	.0001	.0001	.0001
" 11 " 12 "	.0001	.0001	.0001	.0001	.0001	.0001	—	—	—	—
" 12 " 13 "	—	—	—	—	—	—	—	—	—	—
" 13 " 14 "	—	—	—	—	—	—	—	—	—	—
" 14 " 15 "	—	—	—	—	—	—	—	—	—	—
E. UNIFORMLY OVER 5 YEAR PERIODS										
FROM 0 TO 5 YEARS	.2426	.2399	.2372	.2345	.2319	.2294	.2269	.2245	.2221	.2198
" 5 " 10 "	.0042	.0040	.0037	.0035	.0033	.0031	.0029	.0028	.0026	.0024
" 10 " 15 "	.0001	.0001	.0001	.0001	—	—	—	—	—	—
" 15 " 20 "	—	—	—	—	—	—	—	—	—	—
" 20 " 25 "	—	—	—	—	—	—	—	—	—	—
FROM 25 TO 30 YEARS	—	—	—	—	—	—	—	—	—	—
" 30 " 35 "	—	—	—	—	—	—	—	—	—	—
" 35 " 40 "	—	—	—	—	—	—	—	—	—	—
" 40 " 45 "	—	—	—	—	—	—	—	—	—	—
" 45 " 50 "	—	—	—	—	—	—	—	—	—	—
F. DECLINING TO NOTHING AT CONSTANT RATE										
FROM 0 TO 5 YEARS	.3740	.3708	.3676	.3645	.3614	.3584	.3554	.3525	.3496	.3468
" 0 " 10 "	.2166	.2143	.2121	.2098	.2076	.2056	.2036	.2016	.1995	.1975
" 0 " 15 "	.1511	.1494	.1477	.1462	.1446	.1430	.1415	.1401	.1386	.1372
" 0 " 20 "	.1158	.1145	.1133	.1120	.1107	.1195	.1084	.1072	.1060	.1049
" 0 " 25 "	.0939	.0928	.0917	.0907	.0897	.0887	.0877	.0868	.0859	.0850
FROM 0 TO 30 YEARS	.0790	.0781	.0772	.0763	.0755	.0747	.0740	.0733	.0725	.0718
" 0 " 35 "	.0685	.0676	.0667	.0659	.0650	.0642	.0635	.0628	.0622	.0615

J. C. Gregory's Interest Tables for Determining Rate of Return

COMPOUNDING PERFORMANCE BEFORE REFERENCE POINT WHICH OCCURS:

CONTINUOUS INTEREST TABLE

A. IN AN INSTANT

	91%	92%	93%	94%	95%	96%	97%	98%	99%	100%
1 MONTH BEFORE	1.0788	1.0797	1.0806	1.0815	1.0824	1.0833	1.0842	1.0851	1.0860	1.0869
2 MONTHS "	1.1638	1.1657	1.1677	1.1696	1.1716	1.1735	1.1755	1.1774	1.1794	1.1814
3 " "	1.2555	1.2586	1.2618	1.2649	1.2681	1.2712	1.2744	1.2776	1.2808	1.2840
6 MONTHS BEFORE	1.5762	1.5841	1.5920	1.6000	1.6080	1.6161	1.6242	1.6323	1.6405	1.6487
9 " "	1.9788	1.9937	2.0087	2.0238	2.0391	2.0544	2.0699	2.0855	2.1012	2.1170
12 " "	2.4843	2.5093	2.5345	2.5600	2.5857	2.6117	2.6379	2.6645	2.6912	2.7183
1½ YEARS BEFORE	3.9157	3.9749	4.0350	4.0960	4.1579	4.2207	4.2845	4.3492	4.4150	4.4817
2 " "	6.1719	6.2965	6.4237	6.5535	6.6859	6.8210	6.9588	7.0993	7.2427	7.3891
2½ " "	9.7279	9.9742	10.2267	10.4856	10.7510	11.0232	11.3022	11.5883	11.8817	12.1825
3 " "	15.3329	15.7998	16.2810	16.7769	17.2878	17.8143	18.3568	18.9158	19.4919	20.0855

B. UNIFORMLY UNTIL REFERENCE POINT

	91%	92%	93%	94%	95%	96%	97%	98%	99%	100%
FROM 3 MONTHS BEFORE TO 0	1.1229	1.1244	1.1258	1.1273	1.1287	1.1302	1.1317	1.1331	1.1346	1.1361
" 6 " " " 0	1.2663	1.2697	1.2731	1.2766	1.2800	1.2835	1.2870	1.2904	1.2939	1.2974
" 9 " " " 0	1.4342	1.4402	1.4462	1.4523	1.4584	1.4645	1.4707	1.4768	1.4831	1.4893
" 12 " " " 0	1.6311	1.6403	1.6500	1.6596	1.6692	1.6789	1.6886	1.6984	1.7083	1.7183
FROM 2 YEARS BEFORE TO 0	2.8417	2.8786	2.9160	2.9540	2.9926	3.0318	3.0715	3.1119	3.1529	3.1945
" 3 " " " 0	5.2501	5.3623	5.4771	5.5946	5.7150	5.8383	5.9645	6.0938	6.2262	6.3619

DISCOUNTING PERFORMANCE AFTER REFERENCE POINT WHICH OCCURS:

C. IN AN INSTANT

	91%	92%	93%	94%	95%	96%	97%	98%	99%	100%
1 YEAR LATER	.4025	.3985	.3946	.3906	.3867	.3829	.3791	.3753	.3716	.3679
2 YEARS "	.1620	.1588	.1557	.1526	.1496	.1466	.1437	.1409	.1381	.1353
3 " "	.0652	.0633	.0614	.0596	.0578	.0561	.0545	.0529	.0513	.0498
4 " "	.0263	.0252	.0242	.0233	.0224	.0215	.0207	.0198	.0191	.0183
5 " "	.0106	.0101	.0096	.0091	.0087	.0082	.0078	.0074	.0071	.0067
10 YEARS LATER	.0001	.0001	.0001	.0001	.0001	.0001	.0001	.0001	.0001	—
15 " "	—	—	—	—	—	—	—	—	—	—
20 " "	—	—	—	—	—	—	—	—	—	—
25 " "	—	—	—	—	—	—	—	—	—	—
30 " "	—	—	—	—	—	—	—	—	—	—
35 YEARS LATER	—	—	—	—	—	—	—	—	—	—
40 " "	—	—	—	—	—	—	—	—	—	—
45 " "	—	—	—	—	—	—	—	—	—	—
50 " "	—	—	—	—	—	—	—	—	—	—

D. UNIFORMLY OVER INDIVIDUAL YEARS

	91%	92%	93%	94%	95%	96%	97%	98%	99%	100%
FROM 0 TO 1 YEAR	.6566	.6537	.6510	.6483	.6455	.6428	.6401	.6374	.6348	.6321
" 1 " 2 YEARS	.2643	.2605	.2569	.2532	.2497	.2461	.2427	.2392	.2359	.2325
" 2 " 3 "	.1064	.1038	.1013	.0989	.0966	.0942	.0920	.0898	.0876	.0855
" 3 " 4 "	.0428	.0414	.0400	.0386	.0373	.0361	.0349	.0337	.0326	.0315
" 4 " 5 "	.0172	.0165	.0158	.0151	.0144	.0138	.0132	.0126	.0121	.0116
FROM 5 TO 6 YEARS	.0069	.0066	.0062	.0059	.0056	.0053	.0050	.0047	.0045	.0043
" 6 " 7 "	.0028	.0026	.0025	.0023	.0022	.0020	.0019	.0018	.0017	.0016
" 7 " 8 "	.0011	.0010	.0010	.0009	.0008	.0008	.0007	.0007	.0006	.0006
" 8 " 9 "	.0005	.0004	.0004	.0004	.0003	.0003	.0003	.0003	.0002	.0002
" 9 " 10 "	.0002	.0002	.0002	.0001	.0001	.0001	.0001	.0001	.0001	.0001
FROM 10 TO 11 YEARS	.0001	.0001	.0001	.0001	—	—	—	—	—	—
" 11 " 12 "	—	—	—	—	—	—	—	—	—	—
" 12 " 13 "	—	—	—	—	—	—	—	—	—	—
" 13 " 14 "	—	—	—	—	—	—	—	—	—	—
" 14 " 15 "	—	—	—	—	—	—	—	—	—	—

E. UNIFORMLY OVER 5 YEAR PERIODS

	91%	92%	93%	94%	95%	96%	97%	98%	99%	100%
FROM 0 TO 5 YEARS	.2175	.2152	.2130	.2108	.2087	.2066	.2045	.2027	.2006	.1987
" 5 " 10 "	.0023	.0022	.0020	.0019	.0018	.0017	.0016	.0015	.0014	.0013
" 10 " 15 "	—	—	—	—	—	—	—	—	—	—
" 15 " 20 "	—	—	—	—	—	—	—	—	—	—
" 20 " 25 "	—	—	—	—	—	—	—	—	—	—
FROM 25 TO 30 YEARS	—	—	—	—	—	—	—	—	—	—
" 30 " 35 "	—	—	—	—	—	—	—	—	—	—
" 35 " 40 "	—	—	—	—	—	—	—	—	—	—
" 40 " 45 "	—	—	—	—	—	—	—	—	—	—
" 45 " 50 "	—	—	—	—	—	—	—	—	—	—

F. DECLINING TO NOTHING AT CONSTANT RATE

	91%	92%	93%	94%	95%	96%	97%	98%	99%	100%
FROM 0 TO 5 YEARS	.3440	.3412	.3385	.3358	.3332	.3306	.3281	.3254	.3230	.3205
" 0 " 10 "	.1957	.1939	.1920	.1902	.1884	.1867	.1850	.1834	.1817	.1800
" 0 " 15 "	.1358	.1345	.1331	.1318	.1305	.1292	.1280	.1268	.1256	.1244
" 0 " 20 "	.1039	.1028	.1018	.1007	.0997	.0987	.0978	.0968	.0959	.0950
" 0 " 25 "	.0841	.0832	.0823	.0815	.0808	.0800	.0792	.0784	.0777	.0769
FROM 0 TO 30 YEARS	.0711	.0703	.0696	.0688	.0681	.0674	.0666	.0659	.0651	.0644
" 0 " 35 "	.0608	.0602	.0595	.0589	.0583	.0577	.0572	.0566	.0561	.0555

J. C. Gregory's Interest Tables for Determining Rate of Return

USE OF INTEREST TABLES
FOR DETERMINING RATE OF RETURN

PRELIMINARY BASIC DATA

The material, to which the interest factors are to be applied, consists of the schedule of all disbursements and receipts involved in the project and is known as the Time Table. The net addition of all cash and equivalent transactions indicated in the Time Table will be the profit to be realized from the project at no interest.

ZERO POINT SELECTION

The choice of the time to which all cash transactions will be referred has no bearing upon the result and may be made either arbitrarily or for some reason of convenience. It can be the date of the first expenditure, the last receipt, or any intervening point. In the average case the date of starting profitable operations is most expedient.

SUB-DIVISIONS OF INTEREST TABLE

In order to accommodate Time Table items which may be prior or subsequent to the selected zero point, or which may represent transactions in either a lump sum or spread over a period, the following tables are provided. All of these tables have been based on continuous compounding which avoids the arbitrary selection of some time period and provides flexibility for accurate extension beyond the recorded scope of the derived factors.

A - Prior and Instantaneous items will be subject to compounding from the date of the transaction to the zero point.

B - Prior and Continuous items are assumed to occur at a constant rate during the specified period and will be subject to compounding to the zero point.

C - Subsequent and Instantaneous items will be subject to discounting back to the zero point from the date of the foreseen transaction.

D - Subsequent and Continuous One Year items are assumed to be spread uniformly through any designated year and will be subject to discounting back to the zero point.

E - Subsequent and Continuous Five Year groupings have been added for use when the longer period can be considered as involving a fairly constant rate of cash receipts.

F - Subsequent and Diminishing items are those which decline from a maximum in the first operating year to zero at the end of the project life, by arithmetic progression. This table entails the minimum effort when that particular pattern of project receipts is presented.

INITIAL TRIAL RATE

A glance at the figures in the Time Table will provide an approximate idea as to the rate which should be applied for the first trial. In most cases it will be found that the average annual net receipt during the first half of the project's operating life, divided by the gross outlay required will give a reasonable starting point.

APPLICATION OF INTEREST FACTORS

With the Zero Point selected and a trial rate indicated the figures in the Time Table should be extended by the appropriate factors from the interest tables. The column headed by the trial rate will contain all the necessary factors for the usual problem. Each item in the Time Table should be scrutinized to determine which of the six sub-divisions of the interest table is needed and which line should be used. The extensions can then be made one by one, being careful to treat all expenditures as negative and all receipts as positive. The net of the extended figures will be zero if the trial rate is correct, but if this net is a positive figure the trial rate is too low, and vice versa. A second trial rate can then be used and another net of extended figures procured. This will generally permit the determination of the final rate of return by interpolation without further calculation unless an unusual degree of accuracy is required.

FLEXIBILITY FOR EXTENSION

A clear understanding of the basic content of each of the tables will make it possible to select a factor for almost any condition which may be presented, without resorting to the derivation formula. A few examples will indicate how readily these extensions can be made:

Instantaneous Outlay 4 Years before Zero Point, @ 5%

(Table A) 1 Yr. @ 20%	1.2214
(A) 2 Yrs. @ 10%	1.2214
(A) 1 Yr. @ 5% x (A) 3 Yrs.@ 5% 1.0513 x 1.1618	1.2214
(A) 2 Yrs.@ 5% x (A) 2 Yrs.@ 5% 1.1052 x 1.1052	1.2214
(C) 4 Yrs. @ 5% Reciprocal 1/.8187	1.2214

Spread $1\frac{1}{2}$ Years to Zero Point, @ 8%

(B) 3 Yrs. @ 4%	1.0625
(B) 1 Yr. @ 12%	1.0625
(B) 1/2 Yr. @ 24%	1.0625

Spread 3 Yrs. to 2 Yrs. before Zero Point, @ 10%

    (B) 1 Yr. @ 10% x(A) 2 Yrs.@ 10% 1.0517x 1.2214   1.2845

Instantaneous Receipt 8 Years after Zero Point, @ 5%

    (C) 1 Yr. @ 40%   .6703

    (C) 4 Yrs. @ 10%   .6703

    (C) 40 Yrs. @ 1%   .6703

    (C) 5 Yrs. @ 5% x (C) 3 Yrs. @ 5% .7788 x .8607   .6703

Spread 19 Yrs. to 20 Yrs. after Zero Point, @ 5%

    (D) 14 Yrs. to 15 Yrs.@ 5% x(C) 5Yrs.@5% .4844x.7788   .3772

    (D) 4 Yrs. to 5 Yrs.@5% x (C) 15 Yrs.@5% .7986x.4724   .3772

Example

The following example may serve to illustrate the solution of Rate of Return for a hypothetical project.

Years after Zero Point	Amount Received (same as extension at 0%)	Inter-est Table	Calculation at			
			(R) = 5%		(R') = 10%	
			Factors	Value at Zero point	Factors	Value at Zero point
-3	(-150)	A	1.1618	(-174.3)	1.3499	(-202.5)
-3 to -2	(-50)	B & A	1.0254x1.1052	(-56.7)	1.0517x1.2214	(-64.2)
-2 to 0	(-70)	B	1.0517	(-73.6)	1.1070	(-77.5)
0 - 1	30	D	.9754	29.3	.9516	28.5
1 - 2	40	D	.9278	37.1	.8611	34.4
2 - 3	50	D	.8826	44.1	.7791	39.0
3 - 4	40	D	.8395	33.6	.7050	28.2
4 - 5	30	D	.7986	24.0	.6379	19.1
5	(-20)	C	.7788	(-15.6)	.6065	(-12.1)
5 - 10 (constant)	50	E	.6891	103.4	.4773	71.6
10 - 20 (declining)	50	C & F	.6065 x .8522	77.5	.3679 x .7358	40.6
Net Receipt	200			(V) 28.8		(V')(-94.9)

For interpolating between 5% and 10%, it will be noted that in that 5% interval the net receipt decreased from plus 28.8 to minus 94.9, or 123.7, for an average decrease of 24.7 for each percent. At 24.7 for each percent, it is apparent that the 28.8 shown at 5% would decline to 0 in 28.8/24.7, or 1.2 more percent, for a final evaluation of 6.2%. If careful attention is given to signs the following simple formula can be used for either interpolation or extrapolation:

Rate of Return is $R + \dfrac{V(R' - R)}{V - V'}$ $5 + \dfrac{28.8 (10 - 5)}{28.8 + 94.9}$ or 6.2

CASE VI-1. X-ACT EQUIPMENT COMPANY

Capital Budgeting—Make or Buy

In 1957 the Executive Committee of the Board of Directors of X-Act were interested in a report presented by the president relative to the advantages of making rather than buying certain parts used in the manufacturing of its products.

The president had presented the general thinking of his staff on this subject and had outlined in broad terms the investment or capital budgeting approach to such problems.

Pursuant to the discussion the president was requested to present a detailed report showing the advantages of a make policy over a buy policy. The financial officer was directed by the president to enlist such assistance as he needed and to report back.

REPORT OF FINANCIAL OFFICER

SUBJECT: Analysis of Proposal to Make Parts 1, 2, 3, 4, and 5

This department has been asked to determine the relative advantages of making rather than buying certain parts and to show in terms of the investment needed, the rate which such investment can earn.

The parts when purchased are now completely finished. The proposal suggests buying material in the form of bar stock and making and finishing the parts.

Findings

The tables and other data attached to this report projected over 10 years show the following:

1. An initial investment of $237,768 in new machinery and $27,000 in floor space or a total new investment of $264,768 will be necessary if the parts are made. This investment must be increased over the period to $341,400.

2. An average cash return of 26 per cent, after taxes, may be expected over the 10-year period.

3. The payoff period is about 4 years.

4. The annual cash inflow after taxes will vary from $21,000 to $107,000.

Recommendation

The conclusions are very favorable to a make versus buy decision on the basis of a 10-year projection.

Factors to Consider

1. The fact that the returns are so favorable raises certain questions: (a) why other manufacturers are buying rather than making parts; (b) why present makers have to charge the prices they do.

2. Is there any chance that our major supplier who now sells us the major share of his output will not be willing to lower prices if confronted with the possibility that we may make our parts?

3. The estimates of savings are based on production claims by makers of the machinery we must purchase. These may be too optimistic, hence we should take this into account.

4. There is a possibility that we can purchase a plant to make these parts from one of our suppliers. Will it be cheaper to buy a plant than to enlarge our own?

5. The data have been related to what appears to be a reasonable growth factor. This rate should be considered. We may grow more or less rapidly than the projection.

6. Favorable as the returns are, we cannot say that it gives us the most for our money. How much savings we lose by passing up another project in favor of this one should be considered.

7. We have assumed that manufacturing costs will not rise appreciably during the next 10 years, or that if they do, product prices will move in proportion.

8. We assume that we will have no labor difficulties even though our labor rate is lower than it is in the large cities. If wages increase for us we assume that they will also increase for our supplier and competitors.

9. We assume that the standards which are set and which gives us considerable leeway in machine tools will not change. If, however, they should be tightened we would lose a considerable part of our profit advantage through having to purchase more machines.

10. Since the future cannot be predicted accurately this high return may simply reflect uncertainty.

11. Taking all of the uncertainties into account the fact that we will have all of the investment returned to us in four years means that we are taking a chance on four years only. That is, we would not receive any return on our investment if we stopped making in 4 years. However, it would be expected that in such a possibility, we could sell the machinery and thus secure some return.

Data on Which Conclusions Are Based

Case VI-1. EXHIBIT I

Estimated Capital Investment Requirements—10-Year Projection

Immediate Requirements in 1958

Item		Cost
3 automatic screw machines		$114,922
1 centerless grinder		32,710
2 internal grinders		48,720
1 hone		26,383
1 furnace (part time)		8,333
1 furnace (part time)		6,000
7 tool cabinets		700
Total machine cost		$237,768
Rounding this figure		$238,000
Floor space is estimated at 200 sq. ft. per machine (including furnaces) at $15 per sq. ft.—1800 sq. ft.		27,000
Total investment needed in 1958		$265,000
Projected additional investment in 1961		
1 automatic screw machine	$40,000*	
floor space	3,200†	43,200
Projected additional investment 1962		
1 hone	30,000*	
floor space	3,200†	33,200
Grand Total of New Investment Required Over the 10-Year Period:		$341,400

* An increase in the cost of machines is assumed.
† An increase in cost of floor space is assumed.

Case VI-1. EXHIBIT II

Comparison of Unit Costs and Savings as Calculated by Factory Methods

Item	Part 1	Part 2	Part 3	Part 4	Part 5
Cost to purchase finished	$0.3510	$0.2775	$0.3125	$0.6580	$0.2688
Estimated cost to make:					
Material unit	0.1100	0.0400	0.0600	0.1100	0.0500
Labor unit	0.0356	0.0270	0.0346	0.0356	0.0346
Overhead	0.0456	0.0346	0.0443	0.0456	0.0443
Depreciation (considered on an annual basis in exhibit III)	—	—	—	—	—
Total unit cost before depreciation	$0.1912	$0.1016	$0.1389	$0.1912	$0.1289
Unit savings before depreciation	0.1598	0.1759	0.1736	0.4596	0.1399
Savings as a per cent of purchase price (before depreciation)	45%	63%	55%	69%	52%

CASE VI-1. EXHIBIT III

Total Savings Before Depreciation from Making Rather Than Buying—1959

Part	Quantity Needed	Unit Purchase Price	Total Purchase Cost	Unit Cost to Make	Total Make Cost	Annual Savings Total
1	144,000	$0.3510	$ 50,544	$0.1912	$27,532	$ 23,012
2	288,000	0.2775	79,920	0.1016	29,260	50,660
3	96,000	0.3125	30,000	0.1389	13,334	16,666
4	7,200	0.6580	4,737	0.1912	1,376	3,361
5	216,000	0.2688	58,060	0.1289	27,842	30,218
Total			$223,261		$99,344	$123,917

Total Savings After Depreciation—1959 from Making Rather Than Buying

Depreciation on a 10-year basis using the double declining balance method*
for 1959 = $31,372. $123,917 − $31,372 = $92,545 profit before taxes.

After taxes of $48,123 (at 52 per cent), the net profit is $44,422, or a return of
14 per cent for the first full year of operation.

---

* The double declining balance method of depreciation uses double the rate
of straight line depreciation and applies this rate to the undepreciated balance
at the start of each year. Thus an asset with 10 years of estimated life will,
under this method, have a depreciation of 20 per cent of 100 per cent the first
year, 20 per cent of 80 per cent the second, etc. No salvage figure is used in this
method.

Case VI-1.

Cash Savings of Make Over Buy

(1)	(2)	(3)	(4)	(5)	(6)	(7)
Year	Index of Volume Require- ments	Purchase Costs	Make Costs Before Depre- ciation	Gross Savings Before Depre- ciation	Depre- ciation Double Declining Method	Book Savings Before Tax
1958*	21*	$ 47,389	$ 21,057	$ 26,332	$16,749	$ 9,583
1959	100	223,261†	99,344†	123,917†	31,372†	92,545
1960	130	290,239	129,147	161,092	27,302	133,790
1961	144	321,496	143,056	178,440	26,540	151,900
1962	151	337,124	150,009	187,115	27,983	159,132
1963	157	350,520	155,970	194,550	26,476	168,074
1964	157	350,520	155,970	194,550	23,049	171,501
1965	157	350.520	155,970	194,550	20,108	174,442
1966	157	350,520	155,970	194,550	17,513	177,037
1967	157	350,520	155,970	194,550	16,717	177,833

* 6 months.
† From Exhibit III.

EXHIBIT IV

and Cash Flow Over 10-Year Period

(8)	(9)	(10)	(11)	(12)	(13)	(14)
		Add Back Depre-	Cumu-	Cumu-	Per Cent of Invest- ment	
	Book Savings	ciation (6)	lative Cash	lative Cash	Re- covered	Cumu-
Tax:	After	Plus	Paid	Received	End of	lative
52%	Tax	(9)	Out	See (10)	Year	Years
$ 4,983	$ 4,600	$ 21,349	$265,000‡	$ 21,349	8.1%	½
48,123	44,442	75,794	265,000	97,143	36.7	1½
69,570	64,220	91,522	265,000	188,665	71.1	2½
78,988	72,912	99,452	308,200§	288,117	93.4	3½
82,748	76,384	104,367	341,400¶	392,484	115.0	4½
87,398	80,676	107,152	341,400	499,636	146.3	5½
89,180	83,321	105,370	341,400	605,006	177.2	6½
90,709	83,733	103,841	341,400	708,847	207.6	7½
92,509	84,978	102,491	341,400	811,338	237.6	8½
92,473	85,360	102,077	341,400	913,415	267.5	9½

‡ Figure rounded from $264,768, Exhibit 1.

§ 1961—Necessary to purchase another machine and provide floor space—$43,200, from Exhibit I.

¶ 1962—Necessary to purchase one more hone and provide floor space—$33,200, from Exhibit I.

CASE VI-1. EXHIBIT V

Capital Equipment Analysis—Manufacture of Parts 1, 2, 3, 4 and 5— Return on Investment Calculation

Explanation of Outlay and Savings	Cash Outlay*	Cash Savings After Tax†	15% Rate of Return		30% Rate of Return	
			Discount Factor‡	Amount	Discount Factor	Amount
Approve project 7-1-57		From column 10 of Exhibit IV				
Order machinery to be delivered at end of longest lead time or nine months from 7-1-57						
Receive all machinery 4-1-58	$238,000		(1.1191)	($266,346)	(1.2523)	($298,047)
Provide floor space 4-1-58	27,000		(1.1191)	(30,216)	(1.2523)	(33,812)
Begin production 5-1-58 Begin to get savings 6-1-58 at an increasing rate so that full unit savings are attained by 12-31-58						
Savings: 1958 (½ at ½ rate)		$ 21,349	1.0385	22,170	1.0789	23,033
Savings: 1959 (Full year at full rate)		75,794	0.9286	70,382	0.8640	65,486
Savings: 1960		91,522	0.7993	78,153	0.6400	58,574
Savings: 1961		99.452	0.6879	68,413	0.4741	47,150
Buy 1 more screw machine 1961	40,000		(0.6376)	(25,504)	(0.4066)	(16,264)
Provide floor space	3,200		(0.6376)	(2,040)	(0.4066)	(13,011)
Savings: 1962		104,367	0.5921	61,796	0.3513	36,664
Buy 1 more hone 1962	30,000		(0.5488)	(16,464)	(0.3012)	(9,036)
Provide floor space	3,200		(0.5488)	(1,756)	(0.3012)	(964)
Savings: 1963		107,152	0.5096	54,604	0.2602	27,880
Savings: 1964		105,370	0.4386	46,215	0.1928	20,315
Savings: 1965		103,841	0.3775	39,200	0.1428	14,828
Savings: 1966		102,491	0.3250	33,310	0.1058	10,844
Savings: 1967		102,077	0.2797	28,550	0.0784	8,003
Totals for 10 years						
Cash Outlay	$341,400					
Cash Savings		$913,415				
Totals				$155,467		($58,357)

Calculation of Final Result:

$$15\% + \frac{155.467(30 - 15)}{155,467 + 58,357} = 15\% + \frac{2,332,005}{213,824} = 15\% + 10.9\% = 25.9\% \text{ Return on Investment}$$

* From Exhibit I.
† From Exhibit IV, column 10.
‡ For the explanation of the discount factor, see the Gregory Tables, pp. 394–407.

CASE VI-1. EXHIBIT VI

Manufacture of Parts 1, 2, 3, 4, and 5: Calculations of Overhead Excluding Depreciation

I. Controlling Items Calculated to Average Rate Experienced by the Departments That Produce Parts 1, 2, 3, 4, and 5 (Average Rate for first 5 months of 1957: 75 per cent of direct labor)
  A. Salaries:
     1. factory supervision
     2. waiting and lost machine time
     3. wash tank
     4. janitors
     5. set-up
     6. material handling
     7. rework
     8. personnel training
     9. service stores
     10. production office
     11. tool cribs
     12. process inspection
     13. overtime premiums
     14. finished process inspection
     15. other wages
     16. maintenance
        a. buildings
        b. miscellaneous equipment
        c. tools
        d. moving machinery and equipment
  B. Supplies:
     1. Maintenance
        a. machinery
        b. miscellaneous equipment
        c. gauges
     2. operating supplies
  C. Other:
     1. factory scrap
     2. factory experimental
     3. traveling

II. Other Items Calculated at Their Average Plant-Wide Relation to Direct Labor (Rate: 53 per cent of direct labor).
  A. Salaries:
     1. factory executive offices
     2. night idle time
     3. tool design
     4. time study
     5. building construction
     6. engineers and firemen
     7. watchmen
     8. production design
     9. production testing
     10. engineering
     11. drafting
     12. medical
     13. vacation pay
     14. emergency absence
     15. statistical quality control
     16. material control—process
     17. safety
     18. holiday pay
     19. sick leave
     20. jury duty
     21. union duty
     22. maintenance of gauges
  B. Supplies:
     1. heat treat
     2. shoes and glasses
  C. Other:
     1. taxes
     2. insurance
     3. inventory control

III. Typical Items Considered Not Pertinent or of No Difference in Make Versus Buy (Zero Rate).
  A. Salaries:
     1. clerical—production departments
     2. receiving
     3. main stock room
     4. overstock storage
     5. service shipping
     6. application engineering
     7. over-all quality inspection
     8. traffic
     9. pilot center
     10. purchasing
     11. office methods
     12. supplies and other:
        a. crating and shipping
        b. fuel oil
        c. vendor scrap
        d. pattern scrap
        e. gas
        f. freight
  B. All departments not otherwise mentioned.

CASE VI-1. EXHIBIT VII

1956 Condensed Balance Sheet
(in Millions)

Current Assets	$15.7	Current Liabilities	$ 6.4
Other Assets	1.5	Long-term Loan at 5.5%	4.5
Plant and Equipment net	6.4	Capital* and Surplus	13.2
Prepaid and Deferred	0.5		
	$24.1		$24.1

1956 Income Statement
(in Millions)

Net Sales	$52.9
Cost of Goods	37.9
Gross Profit	15.0
Sales, General	8.9
Profit on Sales	6.1
Income Taxes	3.2
Net Profit	2.9
Depreciation	1.3

* The price-earnings ratio for the stock of X-Act varied between 7.4 and 13.4 during the year.

CASE VI-2. ARRO-TRU COMPANY
Capital Budgeting—Make, Buy, or Buy the Maker

In April, 1956, the Arro-Tru Co. was considering the question of "bringing in" the production of a major component for its product in the heavy-goods field. A careful study revealed that: manufacturing this component in the currently required quantities of 100 per day would call for an investment of $2,360,833 to cover the needed machinery and 18,800 square feet of floor space. Careful estimates of operating savings at the current volume indicated that there were possible annual savings of $1,373,400 before taxes or a payout period of 1.72 years.

A revised report in July of 1956 indicated total investment would be $2,915,460 and the payout period 2.02 years for a contemplated enlarged output of 170 per day. As the program of investigation proceeded, questions were raised about increases in indirect costs that would be incurred such as added building services (increase in utilities, special air lines, etc.), effects on inventory to be carried, the possibility of incorporating some used equipment instead of new, lead time in procuring equipment, set-up time and time to bring to full production.

The particular component involved was produced in several models. As a result of more detailed investigation, the effect of the product mix on the proposed program was brought to light in August, 1956. On model 1 of the component, the saving of making over buying was computed as $53.15 each but on model 2 only $21.31 compared to the vendor's prices.

The summary of savings for different volumes and mixes is shown in Table I. Production schedule 3 in Table I shows an annual rate of return of the investment of 23 per cent as calculated in Exhibit I by the discounted cash flow method. Exhibit I also shows an annual rate of profit before the cost of capital of 11.6 per cent as calculated and an annual rate of urgency of 27.0 per cent (profit after assumed cost of capital) as calculated.

Table II is a revision of Table I and allows for somewhat higher costs in connection with production schedule 3 in Table I. This revision is based on the assumption that higher skilled labor would be needed to make the component than for the rest of the product. Table II also takes into consideration the fact that income taxes on cost saving cannot be used to repay the investment.

Case VI-2. TABLE I

Investment, Savings, and Pay-Out Period of Alternate Production Schedules

Production Schedules	Investment	Cost Savings Per Year Before Taxes	Pay-Out Period
1. Model 1 (64 per day) Model 2 (36 per day)	$2,360,833*	$1,373,400†	1.72 years
2. Model 1 (75 per day) Model 2 (95 per day)	$2,915,459	$1,442,568	2.02 years
3. Model 1 (105 per day) Model 2 (65 per day)	$3,143,513	$1,742,475	1.80 years

* For a method of determining investment, see Case VI-1, Exhibit I, and Case VI-3, Exhibit III.

† For methods of determining cost savings, see Case VI-1, Exhibits II, III, and IV; and Case VI-3, Exhibits II, IV, and V.

Case VI-2. TABLE II

Revision of Production Schedule 3 in Table I

Production Schedules	Cost Savings	Pay-Out Period Before Taxes	Pay-Out Period After Taxes
1. Revised from Table I (100 per day)	$792,606	3.97 years	4.63 years
3. Revised from Table I (170 per day)	$1,345,160	2.34 years	3.33 years

In addition, these factors were developed by further investigation (of which only 2 and 4 below are included in the revised cost savings calculations presented in Table II):

1. Reduction in direct material commitments $3,191,000.

2. Increased payroll of 133 men at $558,600 per yr.

3. Reduction of inventory of $540,565 or about 50 per cent of present inventory of this component.

4. Reduced freight $50,000.

5. Better quality control of the component.

The company was currently producing 100 units of its product per day but was committed to expansion of its facilities to produce 170 units per day.

Other considerations bearing on the program included these facts:

1. The indicated very large savings raise the question why there was not a rush of people to get into such a lucrative business.

2. The estimates of machinery time used in the calculations are based on estimates supplied by machine tool manufacturers which have been partially discounted, since at times machining time has run 25 to 35 per cent higher than machine tool vendors' estimates.

3. Most of the machinery has a very special purpose and would not be adaptable to other types of manufacture if required production does not equal the capacity of the facilities.

4. If machining time estimates are low, not only will operating costs be higher, but additional machinery would have to be purchased to meet the assumed volume.

5. Not all factors can be anticipated, and prior experience indicates estimates of savings tend to be high, and estimates of investment low.

6. Manufacture of this component is highly specialized and it will take time to train operators, develop techniques, etc., so that full volume production and savings cannot be expected at the start.

7. The 50 per cent reduction in inventory of this component calculated to result indicates that present lead times may be out of line or the estimates of savings by the proposal overly optimistic.

In the midst of these calculations, the current major supplier of the component offered to sell his facilities for $1,500,000. The supplier was meeting most of the current volume of the component needed by Arro-Tru, although Arro-Tru also made some purchases at a higher price from a second supplier for the express purpose of maintaining a second source of supply. In addition, 50 per cent of the supplier's dollar sales were to customers other than Arro-Tru. Book net worth of the supplier was $760,000 and his current earnings were $180,000 per year. The supplier was considered to be operating in an inefficient manner by modern industrial standards.

The volume performance of Arro-Tru as a measure of the stability of the likely use to be made of the supplier's facilities is shown in Table III. Exhibit II shows the balance sheets and Exhibit III shows income statements of Arro-Tru for 1956 and 1957.

Rate of Return Calculation on
(Discounted Cash Flow Method

Assumed zero point is 2 years after start
of construction.
Depreciation double declining balance.

Explanation of Investment and Savings	Amount Paid Out	Savings Before Tax	Less 52% Income Tax	Savings After Tax
Construction of building; payments spread over one year	$ 365,000			
Purchase of machines, tools, fixtures; payments spread over the 6 months preceding start of production (overlap last 6 months of building construction)	2,779,000			
Cash savings; build up to full amount at full volume by end of first year of production		$ 250,610	$130,317	$120,293
(Savings from then on are assumed to be the full amount at full volume throughout the year.)				
First year of full savings at full volume		1,190,324	618,968	571,356
Second year of full savings at full volume		1,280,872	666,053	614,819
Third year of full savings at full volume		1,353,308	703,720	649,588
Short-life tools, etc., replaced in fourth year	524,268			
Fourth year of full savings		1,411,260	733,855	677,405
Fifth year of full savings		1,457,620	757,962	699,658
Sixth year of full savings		1,494,708	777,248	717,460
Seventh year of full savings		1,524,378	793,676	731,702
Tools replaced again in eighth year	524,268			
Eighth year of full savings		1,548,114	805,019	743,095
Ninth year of full savings		1,567,104	814,894	752,210
Tenth year of savings		1,582,294	822,793	759,501
Net savings after 10 years of full savings				$7,037,087
Interpolation and final result				

EXHIBIT I

Project to Make Component A
Based on 170 Units Per Day)

Add Back Depreciation Deducted For Taxes	Cash Savings After Tax	Calculation to Determine Discounted Cash Rate of Return			
		15% Trial Rate		30% Trial Rate	
		Factor*	Amount	Factor*	Amount
		1.2535	$ (457,528)	1.5743	$ (574,620)
		1.2065	(3,352,864)	1.4564	(4,047,336)
$ 575,920	$ 696,213	1.0789	751,144	1.1662	811,923
462,736	1,034,092	0.9286	960,257	0.8640	893,455
372,188	987,007	0.7993	788,914	0.6400	631,684
299,752	949,340	0.6879	653,050	0.4741	450,082
		0.5921	(310,419)	0.3513	(184,175)
241,800	919,205	0.5921	544,261	0.3513	322,916
195,440	895,098	0.5096	456,141	0.2602	232,904
158,352	875,812	0.4386	384,131	0.1928	168,856
128,682	860,384	0.3775	324,794	0.1428	122,863
		0.3250	(170,387)	0.1058	(55,468)
104,946	848,041	0.3250	275,613	0.1058	89,723
85,956	838,166	0.2797	234,435	0.0784	65,712
70,766	830,267	0.2407	199,845	0.0581	48,238
$2,696,538	$9,733,625		$1,281,387		($1,023,243)

$$15 + \frac{1,281,387(30-15)}{1,281,387 + 1,023,243} = 15 + \frac{19,220,805}{2,304,630} = 15 + 8.34 = 23.3\% \text{ Rate of Return}$$

* For the table of "factors" see J. C. Gregory Tables, pp. 394–407.

EXHIBIT I ⟨*Continued.*⟩

Discounted Profit Method Based on 170 Units Per Day	Machinery and Allied Products Institute Method Based on 170 Units Per Day

Discounted Profit Method Based on 170 Units Per Day

Calculation to Determine Exact Rate

	10% Trial Rate		15% Trial Rate
			Amount (from
Factor	Amount		Previous Page)
1.1623	$ (424,239)		$ (457,528)
1.1328	(3,148,051)		(3,352,864)
1.0254	123,348		129,784
0.9516	543,702		530,561
0.8611	529,420		491,425
0.7791	506,094		446,852
0.7050	(369,609)		(310,409)
0.7050	477,571		401,092
0.6379	446,312		356,546
0.5772	414,118		314,678
0.5223	382,168		276,217
0.4726	(247,769)		(170,387)
0.4726	341,187		241,506
0.4276	321,645		210,393
0.3869	293,851		182,812
0.3869†	(−30,357)†		(−18,865)†
	$4,389,416§		$3,581,866§
	($4,159,311¶)		($4,101,946¶)

Interpolation and final result:

$$4{,}389{,}416 - 807{,}550 \,\frac{x}{5} = 4{,}158{,}311 - 57{,}365 \,\frac{x}{5}$$

$$X = 1.6\%$$
$$10 + 1.6 = 11.6\%.$$

Machinery and Allied Products Institute Method Based on 170 Units Per Day

Installed cost (See Table I.)	$3,144,000
Disposal value†	78,462
Net investment	3,065,538

Next year advantage

First full year operating advantage (before depreciation and income tax)	1,653,060
After income tax but including depreciation	1,034,092
MAPI Chart allowance‡ 6.7% of net investment	205,355
Amount available for return on investment	828,737
MAPI urgency rating (828.7/3065) = 27.0% (Yield after 25% debt at 3% and 75% equity earning at 10%)	

† Realized salvage assumed equal to undepreciated balance at end of 10 years to compare with alternate methods. Undepreciated balance is slightly understated due to omission of 4th (and last) year balance of renewal of $524,268.

‡ Using MAPI Chart 1, p. 377, 10 year life and salvage equal to undepreciated balance of $78,462 or 2.5% for a chart percentage of 6.7%.

§ Profit total of figures not in parentheses.

¶ Investment total of figures in parentheses.

CASE VI-2. TABLE III

Arro-Tru Sales Record 1959 to 1957

Year	Sales In Millions	Year	Sales In Millions
1950	$53.7	1954	$ 75.6
1951	$77.1	1955	$100.8
1952	$71.4	1956	$133.6
1953	$72.4	1957	$140.4

CASE VI-2. EXHIBIT II

Arro-Tru Condensed Balance Sheets in Millions

	1956	1957
Current Assets	$39.7	$45.1
Investments and Other Assets	3.8	8.1
Plant and Equipment (Net)	16.1	24.5
Prepaid and Deferred	1.2	1.3
Total assets	$60.8	$79.0
Current Liabilities	16.2	17.7
Long-Term Borrowings	11.4 at 5.5%	23.0 at 4.5%
Capital* and Surplus	33.2	38.3
Total Liabilities and Net Worth	$60.8	$79.0

* The price-earnings ratio during 1957 varied between 8.3 and 15.5.

CASE VI-2. EXHIBIT III

Arro-Tru Income Statements in Millions

	1956	1957
Net Sales	$133.6	$140.4
Cost of Goods	95.7	100.7
Gross Profit	37.9	39.7
Sales, General, Research	22.9	26.4
Profit on Sales	15.0	13.3
Federal Income Taxes	7.9	6.9
Net Profit	7.1	6.4
Depreciation	3.2	2.9

Table IV gives a picture of the return earned by Arro-Tru and four other companies in the same industry, on net worth plus borrowings:

Case VI-2. TABLE IV

Percentage Earned on Net Worth Plus Borrowings by Arro-Tru and Four Competitors

Year	Arro-Tru	Company A	Company B	Company C	Company D
1953	7.0	21.0	9.6	23.9	5.8
1954	11.8	24.3	11.3	31.3	6.6
1955	16.8	29.0	15.0	33.2	8.3
1956	18.1	18.0	20.2	33.2	14.8
1957	12.7	9.6	11.3	24.0	11.1

For comparison purposes, the per cent earned on sales of the same companies is set forth in Table V.

Case VI-2. TABLE V

Percentage Earned on Sales by Arro-Tru and Four Competitors

Year	Arro-Tru	Company A	Company B	Company C	Company D
1953	2.9	6.0	4.7	8.0	3.3
1954	4.9	8.2	6.3	10.3	4.6
1955	5.6	9.6	6.6	11.4	5.4
1956	5.3	7.8	8.1	10.3	7.8
1957	4.6	7.7	6.1	10.0	7.1

A preliminary study of the financial aspects of the supplier yielded the information in Table VI.

Case VI-2. TABLE VI

Sales and Pre-Tax Earnings on Sales of Arro-Tru Supplier

Year	Sales in Millions	Profit Before Tax as Per Cent of Sales
1955	$1.8	10.2
1956	$2.6	15.6
1957 (first 9 months)	$2.1	14.6

If the supplier were purchased, Arro-Tru expected to place additional business in that facility to raise the total annual sales volume to 3 million dollars. Applying a before-tax earning of 14.5 per cent to the 3 million dollars would yield an annual profit before tax of $435,000. The saving on the additional business to be transferred would be an estimated $92,000 per year or the difference between the present purchase price that a second supplier of the same parts quotes and the purchase price available from the supplier up for sale. In addition, the elimination of certain duplicated inspections would save about $30,000 per year and freight savings of $5,000 per year were also contemplated if the supplier were purchased. Certain floor space savings would also result for Arro-Tru for which no dollar computations were readily available. All these calculations are on the assumption of 170 units per day of the component.

Arro-Tru would acquire considerable know-how in the field of this component if it were to purchase the supplier. In addition executives paid $80,000 per year would withdraw from the supplier.

CASE VI-3. ARCTIC MANUFACTURING COMPANY
Capital Budgeting—Make or Buy

Arctic Manufacturing Co. was engaged in the manufacture of motors. For some years the company had purchased an attachment for its motors. The current price for this attachment was $203. In 1958 the company president decided to investigate the profitability of manufacturing this part rather than purchasing it and instructed Ross Jones, the finance officer, to make a study of the matter and prepare a documented report for the consideration of management. That report is set forth below. The balance sheet and income statement of Arctic appear in Exhibit VI.

In pursuing these studies, the finance officer was in the habit of employing *Interest Tables for Determining Rate of Return on Profit Projects** prepared by J. C. Gregory as issued by the Atlantic Refining Company. This table was used in preparing Exhibit I.

Arctic expected to have unused space available through 1964 as a result of the enlargement of its facilities. This enlargement was pursued under a program which sought economies in construction costs by building somewhat in advance of use or need and likewise economies in operating costs by having completed units of maximum efficiency once they were fully occupied.

As a member of management, you are asked to evaluate the report and in particular to indicate what additional matters, if any, should be investigated before the decision to make or buy is made.

REPORT
SUBJECT: Analysis of Proposal to Make Attachment A
Purpose

As requested by the President, we have analyzed the proposal to make attachment A. This report shows the financial effects of such a decision in terms of return on investment and cash recovery and includes our recommendation for further review by management. Money to cover the investment contemplated can be borrowed at 4 per cent.

Results and Recommendations

Our analysis indicates that an unusually high return on investment—49 per cent—would be earned on the project as it is set out in this report. Changes in assumed motor and attachment A sales volumes, and approval of other projects would considerably affect the return on this project.

Accordingly it is recommended that management review this report and, if changes in various factors are believed to be desirable, that we revise the

* As set forth below, pp. 394-407.

Case VI-3. EXHIBIT I

Attachment A Manufacture Project Timetable and Return on Investment Calculation

Timetable	Cash Outlay	Cash Savings After Tax*	15% Trial Rate of Return		30% Trial Rate of Return	
			Discount Factor	Amount	Discount Factor	Amount
8-1-58 Assume project to make Attachment A is approved						
8-1-58 to 11-30-58 Prepare drawings; order patterns, castings, tooling; prepare routing sheets	$ 10,000		(1.0385)	$(10,385)	(1.0789)	$(10,789)
9-1-58 to 12-31-58 Receive and pay for patterns, tools, machinery, and equipment	60,690		(1.0385)	(63,307)	(1.0789)	(65,769)
12-1-58 to 2-28-59 Machine, assemble and test pre-production units in Research Lab	5,000		(1.0190)	(5,095)	(1.0385)	(5,192)
3-1-59 Begin production			Assumed zero date for return calculations			
3-1-59 to 12-31-59 Allowing for break-in time and gradual increase in production and efficiency, take equivalent of 8 months production and savings only for 1959		$ 98,169	0.9286	91,159	0.8640	84,818
12-31-59 Purchase additional machinery (See Exhibit C)	$ 60,000		(0.8607)	(51,642)	(0.7408)	(44,448)
1960 Annual savings		$139,579	0.7993	111,565	0.6400	89,331
12-31-60 Purchase additional machinery (See Exhibit C)	75,000		(0.7408)	(55,560)	(0.5488)	(41,160)
1961 Annual savings		151,138	0.6879	103,968	0.4741	71,655
12-31-61 Purchase additional machinery (See Exhibit C)	80,000		(0.6376)	(51,008)	(0.4066)	(32,528)
1962 Annual savings		159,517	0.5921	94,450	0.3513	56,038
1963 Annual savings		160,168	0.5096	81,622	0.2602	41,676
1964 Annual savings		158,663	0.4386	69,589	0.1928	30,590
Total for 1958 to 1964:	$290,690	$867,234		$315,360		$174,222

Calculation of Return on Investment by extrapolation of trial rates:

$$15\% + \frac{315,360(0.30 - 0.15)}{315,360 - 174,222} = 15\% + \frac{47,304}{141,381} = 15\% + 33.458\% = 48.458\%$$

* But with depreciation added back.

analysis to see what effect those new assumptions produce in terms of return on investment.

Why Return on Investment Is So High

The 49 per cent is a measure of the return on the investment expenditures which would be made as a result of the decision to manufacture attachment

A. This is a much different return from what we would get by measuring return against total assets used for attachment A manufacture.

In other words, this analysis considers only those changes in investment and operating costs which occur as the result of a decision to make attachment A. Costs which remain the same whether we make or buy attachment A are not brought into the calculations because no matter which alternative we follow those costs are unaffected. Thus the costs used in this report are not those we would use in a pricing study. Rather, this analysis answers the question: What would be the net effect on total company profits of this decision.

Other reasons for such a high return, pertinent more to the attachment A situation itself than to the use of any one return on investment technique, are as follows:

1. Surplus Capacity. Much surplus capacity would be used—floor space, machinery, staff functions, and related facilities. The fact that Attachment A is a new product—different from the mere addition of a new model to an existing motor series—does not mean our surplus facilities cannot be well utilized on attachment A.

   However, if this program is deferred until higher motor volumes or other projects use up the now existing excess capacity, then a much lower rate of return would result. Thus, the longer we wait, the higher the required investment expenditures become and consequently, the less attractive is the proposal.

2. Fast Depreciation. Most of the initial cash outlay is for expense and short life patterns, tools, etc. In comparison with a project such as attachment B which has a higher ratio of long life machinery, the attachment A proposal shows a higher rate of return and cash recovery.

3. Limited Expenditures. No additional expenditures are anticipated after the third year of production. With low usage—15 attachments a day— patterns and tooling are likely to last longer than usual. However, in the area of machinery, any fast increase in motor production or any kind of higher priority demand for now surplus capacity might mean more cash payments for machinery for attachment A. Of course the higher the investment, the lower the rate of return.

4. Staggered Cash Outlay. The method used in this analysis discounts future cash outlay and savings. Thus the longer we can put off additional expenditures after we begin to get savings, the higher the return. With attachment B though, we needed virtually all the equipment just to begin production; with attachment A we can begin to get savings with only a third of the ultimate investment.

5. Brief Break-In Time. In comparison with other projects, we can begin to get savings from efficient production more quickly after starting production.

Other Factors:

It might be well to emphasize the following:

1. That this project does not include the manufacture of attachment A other than the 1 and 2 motor models.

2. That a change in assumed attachment A usage would have a significant

effect on profitability of the project. Further, attachment A usage as a per cent of motors which could use them has declined drastically in the last two or three years, making any optimistic forecast somewhat volatile.

3. That although we can use the general purpose attachment A machinery on other jobs, if we decide to go back to Excello for the attachment which we now purchase after making attachment A for a while, we will have lost our ability to hold Excello's price down. As long as Excello doesn't know our future usage and as long as we have the alternative of making attachment A, Excello should be inclined to hold prices down.

4. That the more we indicate to Excello that we are breaking away from them, the less likely they will be to keep the prices down on the remaining purchased parts.

5. That if we give high priority to research to make drawings, we lose the benefits of projects displaced by the attachment A workload.

6. That we face customer resistance if we substitute attachment A without passing on some form of benefit in improved performance or lower cost. We are not providing for improved design and if we lower our price, we lower the return on investment.

7. That we don't have prints or experience in making attachment A and that our estimates of tooling and machining costs should be regarded accordingly.

9. That most of the preceding factors could reduce the indicated 49 per cent return considerably.

Exhibits I, II, III, and IV show the calculations behind the 49 per cent return.

Ross Jones,
Finance Department

Case VI-3. EXHIBIT II

Unit Volume Assumptions as to Manufacture of Attachment A

	1958	1959	1960	1961	1962	1963	1964
Annual motor sales (total)	22,208	27,280	31,300	36,625	41,275	45,425	50,150
Annual 1 and 2 motor sales	18,580	21,750	21,775	23,000	24,500	25,825	26,150
Annual attachment A usage for 1 and 2 motors	3,190	3,390	3,330	3,370	3,470	3,530	3,500
Working days	242	254	253	253	253	254	254
Total motors per day	92	107	124	145	163	178	197
1 and 2 motors per day	76	86	86	91	90	102	103
Attachment A for 1 and 2 motors per day	14	14	14	14	14	14	14
Breaking points for additional machinery requirements, i.e., the point at which unused present capacity will be exhausted by growth in motor production		113 motors per day	130 motors per day	153 motors per day			

Case VI-3. EXHIBIT III

Capital Equipment Expenditures for Manufacture of Attachment A

1958: Initial Requirements to Begin Production	
Multiple spindle drill press, standard	$14,000
Fixtures	21,490
Patterns and dies	10,000
Checking fixtures and test equipment	8,800
Assembly fixtures and gravity conveyor	3,400
Material handling equipment	3,000
Total for 1958	$60,690

1959: Additional Requirements for Production at 113 Motors Per Day Level	
Machine tool A	$40,000
Special drill	20,000
Total for 1959	$60,000

1960: Additional Requirements for Production at 130 Motors Per Day Level	
Grinder unit A	$35,000
Copy lathe	40,000
Total for 1960	$75,000

1961: Additional Requirements for Production at 153 Motors Per Day Level	
Set of Warner and Swasey units	$60,000
Grinder unit A	20,000
Total for 1961	$80,000

Summary of Capital Expenditures, 1958 to 1961	
1958	$ 60,690
1959	60,000
1960	75,000
1961	80,000
	$275,690

Footnotes for Case VI-3 EXHIBIT IV page 433.

* No increase in purchase costs, wage rates or material costs on basis of simplifying assumption that our costs and vendor costs would change correspondingly.

† Based on present average rates in departments which would run attachment A.

‡ Based on double-declining balance method used by the company for income tax purposes. The company's books, however, record depreciation on a straight-line basis. See note to Exhibit VI for a fuller explanation.

CASE VI-3. EXHIBIT IV

Calculation of After-Tax Cash Savings in Manufacture of Attachment A

	1959	1960	1961	1962	1963	1964
Assumed volume of attachment A in units	3,400	3,300	3,400	3,500	3,500	3,500
IF PURCHASED	(All succeeding figures are in dollars)					
Unit purchase cost* (Rounded figure)	$203.00	$203.00	$203.00	$203.00	$203.00	$203.00
Total annual purchase cost	690,200	669,900	690,200	710,500	710,500	710,500
IF MADE						
Unit material cost	60.42	60.42	60.42	60.42	60.42	60.42
Unit labor cost at $2.30 per hour†	25.39	25.39	25.39	25.39	25.39	25.39
Annual material and labor costs	291,754	283,173	291,754	300,335	300,335	300,335
Annual plant overhead excluding depreciation	100,000	100,000	100,000	100,000	100,000	100,000
Depreciation‡	26,179	17,712	24,393	25,072	21,708	18,814
Total annual manufacturing costs	417,933	400,885	416,147	425,407	422,043	419,149
Warranty expenses in excess of Excello's experience	20,000	15,000	10,000	5,000	0	0
Total annual costs if made	437,933	415,885	426,147	430,407	422,043	419,149
Book savings before tax if made	252,267	254,015	264,053	280,093	288,457	291,351
Tax at 52 per cent of book savings	131,179	132,148	137,308	145,648	149,997	151,502
Book savings after tax if made	121,088	121,867	126,745	134,445	138,460	139,849
Add back non-cash tax reduction for depreciation	26,179	17,712	24,393	25,072	21,708	18,814
Cash savings after tax if made	147,267	139,579	151,138	159,517	160,168	158,663

See foot of page 432 for footnote references.

CASE VI-3. EXHIBIT V

Estimate of Plant Overhead

Incorporated in the Rate of Return Calculation of Exhibit I

In estimating plant overhead and general administrative expense, we followed the technique of considering only incremental costs. We therefore analyzed each classification or account of plant overhead to see which would be changed over the years from 1958 to 1964 as a result of a decision to make attachment A.

Special Provision

In addition to the ordinary expenses listed below, a provision of $20,000 per year was made to cover creeping overhead. This provision recognizes that deciding to make attachment A will cause expenditures to be made which cannot be traced back to the attachment A project at the time they will be made. For example, we now have adequate floor space, electrical capacity, staff sections, management time, etc. Using up the now-surplus capacity will require gradual increases. Thus rather than charge attachment A with an immediate cost of floor space utilized, we spread the cost over later years.

Factory Supervision

By increasing shop employment by some twenty-two direct labor people, it is anticipated that somewhere in the shop this will result in an additional foreman. Thus $7,500 was included.

Night Idle Time

To minimize investment costs, it is planned to use surplus machine time. Most likely any surplus hours available are on the night shifts and an amount of $4,140 was estimated for this item.

Related Services

By adding roughly $8,000 direct labor monthly to the shop, the following increases are anticipated:

Janitors	$ 2,000
Material Handling	4,000
Tool Crib	4,000
Maintenance	4,000
Process Inspection	4,000
	$18,000

Fringe Benefits

Our experience has been that fringe benefits run approximately 15% of direct labor costs. An amount of $14,000 has been included.

Taxes and Insurance

Social security, unemployment, and property taxes and property and liability insurance total an approximate $14,000 per year based on the people and assets assumed in this proposal.

General Expenses

Operating supplies are estimated at $8,000 per year. Factory scrap is esti-
mated at $3,000 per year. Both of these are based on experience in Depart-
ment 241 where most of the attachment A machining would be done.

Vendor scrap is estimated at $1,000 per year.

Utility costs are estimated to increase $1,000 per year.

A lump sum of about $9,000 is included for numerous items which will
definitely increase but which are too small to estimate individually. Safety
shoes, glasses, first aid, employment, labor accounting, payroll, casting yard,
inventory handling and carrying costs, and time study reviews are some of
the more obvious examples of this category.

Summary

Special Provision	$ 20,000
Supervision	7,500
Night Idle Time	4,140
Related Services	18,000
Fringe Benefits	14,000
Taxes and Insurance	14,000
General and Administrative	22,360
Total	$100,000

Case VI-3. EXHIBIT VI

Arctic Manufacturing Company Condensed Balance Sheet
December 31, 1957, in Millions

Cash	$ 3.35	Payables	$ 3.43
Receivables	11.28	Accrued	4.14
Inventories	13.97	Income Taxes	3.67
Total Current	$28.60	Total Current	$11.24
Investments	5.16	Term Loan 5.5%	8.00
Plant and Equipment	23.30	Bonds 4.5%	6.13
Depreciation Reserve	(7.71)	Reserve Taxes*	0.45
Prepaid and Deferred	0.83	Capital and Surplus†	24.36
	$50.18		$50.18

Operating Statement for Year Ended December 31, 1957, in Millions

Net Sales	$88.95
Cost of Goods	63.92
Gross Profit	25.03
Sales and General	16.24
Profit on Sales	8.79
Income Taxes	4.71
Net Profit	$ 4.08
Depreciation	1.86*

* The company uses the double-declining method for income tax purposes but keeps its corporate books on a straight-line basis. Hence the deduction for tax purposes exceeds the amount shown in this balance sheet and the company is making provision with this reserve for future depreciation on its records which will not be allowed for tax purposes at such time. This provision in reserve is made at the 52 per cent rate of income tax.

† The price-earnings ratio of Arctic stock averaged about 12 during 1957.

CASE VI-4. MELLO, INCORPORATED

Capital Budgeting—Make or Buy

In October of 1956, Mello, Inc. was examining its program for profitable opportunities for internal investment. One likely project suggested was the purchase of shafts in blank form after heat treating and centerless grinding rather than the purchase of the machined part. Mello would then perform the machining of the blanks.

To undertake such a program, Mello would have to buy five machines for a total of $103,975, and incidental tools of $2,000. Added floor space requirements would total 1,000 square feet. Mello considered its building life to be 30 years and its cost of construction $16 per square foot. The machines would have a life of 15 years and the tools a life of 4 years.

In addition, eight and a half hours per day of surplus time from other machines available in the plant would be needed. While this one project would not be enough to call for any immediate purchase of such machines, the demand for surplus machine time and the similar demand for additional power and other services were significant factors in the overall cost of expanding plant output. Thus it was recognized that the project's real investment would be something larger than the cash outlay of $121,975.

The current balance sheet and income statement of Mello are shown in Exhibit I.

The following schedule was developed by the cost department:

		Model 1 Shaft		Model 2 Shaft
Cost to Buy		$5.25		$4.98
Cost to Make				
Material	$1.666		$1.666	
Labor	0.422		0.450	
Factory Overhead	1.021		1.089	
Total		3.11		3.21
Saving by Making		$2.14		$1.77

The effect of this saving on an annual basis is shown in Exhibit II. This gives effect to the product mix expected to develop between Models 1 and 2.

Some additional information bears on the proposal. This would be

Case VI-4. EXHIBIT I

Balance Sheet Dec. 31, 1955 in Millions

Cash	$ 2.43	Payables	$ 3.68
Receivables	8.38	Accrued	3.41
Inventories	8.55	Income Taxes*	—
Total Current	19.36	Total Current	7.09
Investments	1.52	Notes Payable at 3.5%	5.28
Plant and Equipment	13.42		
Depreciation	(5.47)	Capital and Surplus	17.01
Prepaid and Deferred	0.55		
Total	$29.38	Total	$29.38

* Income taxes fully funded.
Price–earnings ratio 1955, high 9.1, low 5.7.

Income Statement for Year 1955 in Millions

Net Sales	$64.80
Cost of Goods	45.70
Gross Profit	19.10
Sales and General	11.40
Profit on Sales	7.70
Income Tax	4.10
Net Income	3.60
Depreciation	1.70

the first experience of Mello with machining shafts. A higher than average labor rate is assumed in order to cover the matter of lack of experience in this area. The proposal could be considered partially as "researching" because success in the program might well lead to the introduction of other machining operations on parts presently purchased and involving similar machining.

The calculation of depreciation shown in Exhibit II is on a straight line basis. Actually Mello reports in its financial statements on this basis but for income tax purposes uses the double declining balance method which results in depreciation charges significantly larger than straight line. Exhibit III shows the rate of return calculations using Gregory's tables and assuming the double declining balance method on the ground that this reflects the true cash savings. Exhibit III was prepared on the ground that payout period must be rejected as a method because (1) it does not give a realistic picture of cash re-

Case VI-4. EXHIBIT II

Annual Calculations of "Buy" Versus "Make"

		Daily Volume of 100 Units		Daily Volume of 150 Units
Cost to Buy		$154,260		$230,772
Cost to Make:				
Material	$49,980		$74,770	
Labor	12,996		19,441	
Factory Overhead	12,866		19,246	
Excluding Depreciation		$ 75,842		$113,457
Gross Savings		$ 78,418		$117,315
Straight line depreciation		6,192		7,964
Net Savings before tax		$ 72,226		$109,351
Net Savings after tax		$ 34,668		$ 52,488
Before tax payout in years		1.44*		0.97
After tax payout in years		2.99†		2.02

* Computed as investment of $121,975 (shown in Exhibit III) divided by gross savings of $78,418 plus depreciation of $6,192.

† Computed as investment of $121,975 divided by after-tax savings of $34,668 plus depreciation of $6,192.

covery; and (2) it tells the story on short-run liquidity but this doesn't insure long-run profits.

In the preparation of the unit cost information shown on p. 437, factory overhead is at 242 per cent of direct labor, the over-all experience of Mello. But in Exhibits II and III, the rate used is 99 per cent of direct labor on the ground that only the overhead added by the proposal should be considered, i.e., expenses which stay the same whether the proposal is accepted or not are excluded.

In the preparation of Exhibit III, the finance officer of Mello argued that the indicated 38.3 per cent rate of return sums up in one concise rating:

1. the estimated life of the project
2. the timing, duration and amount of savings
3. the impact of income tax on savings
4. the time lag between cash layout and cash receipt
5. a figure directly comparable with the same type of figure for other proposals which would not be true for payout figures

CASE VI-4.

Rate of Return

Explanation of Payments and Savings	Cash Payments	Book Savings Before Tax	Tax at 52% of Book Savings
Purchase and make machinery and tooling.			
Payments spread over three month period starting one year before reference point, which is start of production.	$105,975		
Provide floor space when machinery comes in, uniformly over 1year before reference point.	16,000		
Receive cash savings during first year of production at an increasing rate, to average out to one half of a normal year's savings.			
Savings first year (half of average)		$ 50,674	$26,350
Savings second year		102,550	53,326
Savings third year		104,722	54,455
Savings fourth year		106,406	55,331
Replace short life tools in 4th year	2,000		
Savings fifth year		107,392	55,844
Savings sixth year		108,446	56,392
Savings seventh year		109,851	57,122
Savings eighth year		110,856	57,645
Replace short life tools in 8th year	2,000		
Savings ninth year		111,263	57,856
Savings tenth year		111,181	57,814
Net Savings After Ten Years of Production			

EXHIBIT III

Calculation

Book Savings After Tax	Depre- ciation Deducted For Tax	Cash Savings After Tax	Rate Calculation			
			15% Trial Rate		30% Trial Rate	
			Factor	Amount	Factor	Amount
			(1.1404)*	$(120,854)	(1.3005)	$(137,820)
			(1.1618)	(18,589)	(1.3499)	(21,598)
$24,324	$ 7,964	$ 32,288	1.0789	34,836	1.1662	37,654
49,224	14,727	63,951	0.9286	59,385	0.8640	55,254
50,267	12,555	62,822	0.7993	50,213	0.6400	40,206
51,075	10,871	61,946	0.6879	42,613	0.4741	29,369
			(0.6879)	(1,376)	(0.4741)	(948)
51,548	9,885	61,433	0.5921	36,374	0.3513	21,581
52,054	8,831	60,885	0.5096	31,026	0.2602	15,842
52,729	7,426	60,155	0.4386	26,384	0.1928	11,598
53,211	6,421	59,632	0.3775	22,511	0.1428	8,515
			(0.3775)	(755)	(0.1428)	(286)
53,407	6,014	59,421	0.3250	19,312	0.1058	6,287
53,367	6,096	59,463	0.2797	16,632	0.0784	4,662
		$581,996		$197,712		$ 70,316

Calculation of Final Result

$$15 + \frac{197,712(30 - 15)}{197,712 - 70,316} = 15 + \frac{2,965,680}{127,396} = 15 + 23.3 = 38.3\% \text{ Rate of Return}$$

* Uniformly over 3 months = 1.0190. Fully outstanding over 9 months = 1.1191. Product = 1.1404.

Exhibit II uses straight line depreciation, the method employed by Mello in its financial statements but Exhibit III uses the double declining balance method which Mello employed for tax purposes. This was done on the ground that after-tax savings are the relevant figure in determining rate of return on an investment.

CASE VI-5. SNOESHOES, INCORPORATED
Capital Budgeting—Branch Plant

In 1959, Snoeshoes, Inc. had before its management the matter of examining the rate of return of its new branch plant. This examination was directed to a hind-sight check on the wisdom of such a branch plant. This in turn would be relevant to the question of future branch plants. Snoeshoes used an April 1 fiscal year.

Snoeshoes was engaged in the manufacture of industrial goods. Its main plant was in Nottingham, Tennessee where the business had begun 10 years earlier. Snoeshoes sold nationally and was recognized as one of the larger companies in its product line although not one of the top four in size. In 1957 Snoeshoes decided to build a branch plant at Tularosa, California with the idea that a branch plant in and of itself would add materially to Snoeshoes' sales in that area.

The branch plant began full production on October 1, 1958, exactly one year after construction of the building had begun. Installment of equipment had begun April 1, 1958, as had production. The 6-month period of equipment installation also involved some production which could be characterized as half-scale.

In considering rate of return, Snoeshoes invited Hopp, Stamp, and Yump to submit its calculations of rate of return (Schedules I through X, at the end of this Case). The financial officer disagreed with some computations and prepared his own analysis (Exhibit I, which appears after Schedule X).

Hopp, Stamp, and Yump are certified public accountants with offices in more than twenty of the largest cities of the country. They argued that a marginal approach should be taken. That is, the branch plant should be viewed as responsible for an estimated addition to sales. Only this addition should be considered as the source of return on the investment. At least this would be true until the facilities at Nottingham were fully utilized thus forcing Snoeshoes to expand facilities. When pressed by Hopp, Stamp, and Yump, management stated that present facilities in Tennessee might reach a 2 shift capacity in 1963 at about $8.5 million a year sales but that storage space at Nottingham costing $50,000 would have to be added in 1961 if the Tularosa plant were to be deferred until 1963 rather than built in 1958 as it was. The finance officer argued that this approach involved needless speculation as to when the additional facilities would have to be built. He advocated that the rate of return on Tularosa should be computed on the

443

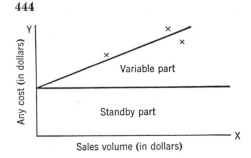

Case VI-5. Figure I. Separation of a cost account into variable part and standby part.

assumption that *all* the sales shipped from Tularosa should be considered as the source of return on the investment.

Both computers agreed upon the estimated *total* sales to be shipped from the Tularosa plant in the next 10 years and both accepted the company's estimate of *total* sales by the company over the next 10 years.

Both computers used the same profit contribution figure for the Tularosa plant, namely, 29.45 per cent. Snoeshoes used a standard cost system and broke costs down into programmed, standby, and variable costs. Profit contribution is defined as sales less variable costs. Programmed costs are those which are largely independent of volume and subject to considerable discretion; for example, advertising and research. Standby costs are those which would be sustained even if a plant were shut down temporarily. In practice standby costs are typically determined as the Y intercept in Figure I with the cost line fitted through observed points and extrapolated to the Y axis.

Both computers had the same data available as to fixed asset costs of the Tularosa plant (land, buildings, machinery, etc.). Both computers used the same depreciation time for individual depreciable assets and the same depreciation method, namely, the double declining balance method. Both computers used a 10-year period to determine rate of return.

Hopp, Stamp, and Yump insisted that it was necessary to consider residual values at the end of 10 years to determine the rate of return and likewise that straight line depreciation should be used for determining residual value (on the ground that straight line balances would better approximate the market value of the residuals) even though the double declining balance method had been used for purposes of determining profits in the 10-year projection.

The finance officer attacked this shift of depreciation methods as arbitrary and inconsistent, and particularly that there was no evidence that a straight line undepreciated balance was better evidence of market value. But the finance officer further attacked the entire concept of using residuals in computing a rate of return. His position was that the 10-year period (or whatever period may be used in capital budgeting or rate of return questions) is determined as the horizon beyond which risk will not permit assuming the investment to have predictable value. He contended that since earnings beyond the 10-year period were omitted from Hopp, Stamp, and Yump's calculations, then undepreciated balances must also be omitted. His rate of return result was 12 per cent.

However, in order to furnish a figure comparable to that of Hopp, Stamp, and Yump, the financial officer computed a rate of return allowing for residuals. His answer was 18.1 per cent. The answer of Hopp, Stamp, and Yump was 12 per cent using a low estimate of additional sales resulting in the Tularosa area due to location of a plant there or 16 per cent using a high estimate of such additional sales.

Another critical difference between the two computers was that the financial officer allocated part of company-wide overhead to the Tularosa plant in the ratio of the sales shipped from the Tularosa plant to total company sales in any period. These company-wide overheads (such as research, executive salaries, etc.) he established at 7.2 per cent of total company sales by study of the company's past experience. Hopp, Stamp, and Yump, with its "marginal approach" omitted such overhead entirely in its computation. The finance officer attacked this as amateur economics on the ground that even if these expenditures would not change whether there was a plant at Tularosa or not (a point which he did not concede), there were what economists call "opportunity costs." The very existence of the Tularosa plant, for example, tied up executive time and took their attention from activities they otherwise would be productively engaged in. Ultimately, he argued there would be an addition to these overheads if not by the first branch plant, then surely by the second and third. And should all of this increase, if it came with the second plant, be charged to that plant? And if not, then should one at that time recompute the rate of return of the first plant?

In addition, the "marginal" approach involved the assumption that the production function was homogeneous.

This conflict on the marginal approach also extended to the working capital question. The financial officer argued that the Tularosa plant should be charged with the working capital required to run it. This figure for the tenth year of the Tularosa plant he established as $579,100. He had carefully examined Snoeshoes' recent history and found that working capital varied in direct proportion to sales. The finance officer used net working capital (current assets minus current liabilities) as his definition of working capital for rate of return questions.

On the other hand, Hopp, Stamp, and Yump used a working capital definition of current assets. They further recognized as working capital to be used for rate of return questions only the addition to working capital associated with the additional sales which would result in the Tularosa area because of the location of a plant there. This amount they set at $60,000 to $62,000.

Both computers used interest costs (on both long- and short-term money) as expenses before the rate of return arrived at. Interest was at 5.5 per cent and the ratio of short- and long-term debt to equity was 42 per cent.

To highlight his dispute of the "marginal" method of Hopp, Stamp, and Yump, the finance officer pointed out that the accountants used 29.45 per cent, the profit contribution of the Tularosa plant on the actual *total* sales from that plant. The finance officer argued that if the accountants were to stay consistent in their use of marginalism they must evolve a separate profit contribution rate for the "additional" sales from the Tularosa operation being so located and a separate profit contribution rate for the sales if not so located. He pointed out that the Nottingham profit contribution rate was 33 per cent and argued the accountants should have used this for those sales from the Tularosa area which they assumed would have developed in the Tularosa area in the absence of the Tularosa plant.

The dispute as to the marginal approach also appeared in the programmed and standby expenses. Hopp, Stamp, and Yump recognized (Schedule VI) only the *additional* standby costs at Tularosa through the year 1963 arising from building the plant in 1958. This was $120,000 per year. The finance officer, on the other hand, charged the full standby and programmed costs of Tularosa for each of the ten years. This was $206,000 per year.

The financial officer and Hopp, Stamp, and Yump both used J. C. Gregory's tables for discounting and interpolated where necessary.

Hopp, Stamp, and Yump assumed that when any funds were returned to Snoeshoes, Inc. from the Tularosa plant they should be assumed to continue to earn the company's actual earning rate of 12 per cent in 1957. The finance officer disputed that the company's rate of return was 12 per cent on investment, arguing that this was the rate Snoeshoes, Inc., earned on total assets (which it was) but that this was not a "rate of return" which applies to an investment concept and in any event that it was not part of a rate of return calculation to assume that money returned was necessarily reinvested and particularly not to assume it would be reinvested at the company's going rate of return. The company-wide return on net fixed assets plus net working capital was 20 per cent.

This dispute is brought out more clearly by explaining the two calculations. The finance officer discounts all future expenditures and cash receipts back to the zero date at two assumed trial rates of return (10 and 20 per cent) and then interpolates to get that rate of return which makes discounted future expenditures just equal to discounted future cash receipts. The zero date is the start of full production. (October 1, 1958)

Hopp, Stamp, and Yump, on the other hand, discounted all future expenditures to their zero date (which is the start of partial production, March 31, 1958) at the average earning rate of Snoeshoes, 12 per cent. They then considered, all cash receipts as earning 12 per cent to the horizon date 10 years later (March 31, 1968). Their rate of return then was that rate which equated (*a*) the cash receipts thus compounded at 12 per cent to March 31, 1968, with (*b*) the expenditures discounted back to March 31, 1958, at 12 per cent.

The objection of the finance officer to this manner of proceeding was that while the method of Hopp, Stamp, and Yump would always produce a lower rate of return than the finance officer's method when the project was one that earned more than the average rate of return of the company, the accountants' method would artificially inflate the project's rate of return when the project earned less than the average of the company.

In reply, Hopp, Stamp, and Yump retorted that the finance officer was assuming in his calculation that when funds were returned by the investment, they continued to earn the project rate. This the finance officer denied, stating that when funds were returned to the company's treasury by the project, they were then eliminated in the calculation.

Note that in making the comparison, it was necessary for the finance officer to use the midpoints of years for sales and cost figures to preserve comparability since he used October 1, 1958 as the base date of reckoning rate of return. The conflict of thinking further extended to Hopp, Stamp, and Yump's insistence (Schedules VIII and IX) that since 43 per cent of the dollar volume of parts used at Tularosa were made at Nottingham, this called for an adjustment although the parts moved from one plant to another at a price covering labor, materials and the variable part of factory overhead.

The finance officer argued that basically Hopp, Stamp, and Yump were doing everything in a roundabout way instead of using direct methods and that such roundabout calculations would introduce new errors each time. He illustrated his point in this way: Hopp, Stamp, and Yump speculated as to when Tularosa would have to be built anyway (1963) but then found themselves guessing as to additional storage space ($50,000) that would be needed at Nottingham in 1961 if Tularosa were built in 1963. Would Snoeshoes build or rent if this were the case? Instead, the finance officer pointed out he did no speculating. Because Tularosa was built in 1958, and all its sales, etc., were reckoned against it, the Nottingham plant now, as a matter of fact, had ample released space for years beyond 1961.

Case VI-5. SCHEDULE I
Sales Forecasts in Millions

Year Ending March 31	Low Estimate			High Estimate			Long-Range Planned Sales	Total Company Expected Sales Without Tularosa Plant	
	Sales Without Plant	Sales Because of Plant	Total Sales	Sales Without Plant	Sales Because of Plant	Total Sales		Low Estimate	High Estimate
1959	$0.85	$0.25	$1.10	$0.650	$0.450	$1.10	$ 5.1	$4.85	$4.650
1960	0.89	0.41	1.30	0.675	0.625	1.30	6.1	5.69	5.475
1961	0.93	0.57	1.50	0.700	0.800	1.50	7.4	6.83	6.600
1962	0.97	0.78	1.75	0.725	1.025	1.75	8.5	7.72	7.475
1963	1.00	1.00	2.00	0.750	1.250	2.00	10.3	9.30	9.050 (Additional facilities required)
1964	1.07	1.13	2.20	0.800	1.400	2.20	12.2		
1965	1.14	1.26	2.40	0.875	1.525	2.40	14.4		
1966	1.21	1.34	2.55	0.950	1.600	2.55	17.0		
1967	1.28	1.42	2.70	1.025	1.675	2.70	20.0		

Case VI-5. SCHEDULE II

Present Value of Investment in Property, Plant and Equipment Because Tularosa Plant Was Acquired, Beginning 1958

Asset	Present Value at March 31, 1958
Tools	$ 4,521
Machinery and equipment	51,495
Patterns and dies	4,637
Furniture and fixtures	16,532
Automotive equipment	11,538
Building	121,948
Building equipment	13,262
Land improvements	4,315
Land	14,780
Reinvestment in tools after 8 years discounted to present value at 12%	1,731
Reinvestment in patterns and dies after 3 years, 6 years and 9 years discounted to present value at 12%	7,067
Investment in storage space at Nottingham as of March 31, 1963 discounted to present value at 12%	27,440
Less residual value of assets at the end of 10 years discounted to present value at 12% (per schedule below)	(49,429)
Present value of investment in property, plant and equipment if Tularosa plant is acquired March 31, 1958	$229,837

Asset	Undepreciated Value After 10 Years (Straight Line)
Tools	$ 3,391
Patterns and dies	3,091
Machinery and equipment	17,165
Building	91,461
Building equipment	6,631
Land improvements	2,589
Land	14,780
Storage space at Nottingham	25,000
Residual value	$164,108
Present value at 12 per cent	$ 49,429

CASE VI-5. SCHEDULE III

Present Value of Investment in Property, Plant and Equipment if Facilities Are Acquired as Needed in 1963

Asset	Present Value at March 31, 1958
Tools	$ 2,481
Machinery and equipment	28,260
Patterns and dies	2,545
Furniture and fixtures	9,073
Automotive equipment	6,332
Building	66,925
Building equipment	7,278
Land improvements	2,368
Land	8,111
Storage space at Nottingham acquired March 31, 1961 discounted to March 31, 1958 at 12%	39,330
Reinvestment patterns and dies after 3 years discounted to March 31, 1958 at 12%	1,776
Less residual value of assets at the end of 10 years discounted to March 31, 1958 at 12 per cent (per schedule below)	(67,470)
Present value of investment in property, plant and equipment if facilities are acquired as needed	$107,009

Asset	Undepreciated Value After 10 Years (Straight Line)
Tools	$ 1,695
Patterns and dies	1,545
Machinery and equipment	34,347
Furniture and fixtures	8,266
Automotive equipment	5,769
Building	106,704
Building equipment	9,947
Land improvements	3,452
Land	14,780
Storage space at Nottingham	37,500
Total residual	$224,005
Present value at 12%	$ 67,470

Case VI-5. SCHEDULE IV

Net Incremental Investment in Working Capital (All Figures in Thousands)

	Year Ending March 31	Plant Built March 31, 1958		Plant Built as Facilities Are Needed		Difference	
		Low*	High†	Low*	High†	Low*	High†
Cash	Initially	$ 35	$ 35			$ 35	$ 35
	1960						
	1961						
	1962						
	1963			$ 35	$ 35	$(35)	$(35)
	1964						
	1965						
	1966						
	1967						
	1968						
	Residuals	$ 35	$ 35	$ 35	$ 35	0	0
Accounts Receivable	Initially	$ 25	$ 45			$ 25	$ 45
	1960	16	18			16	18
	1961	16	18			16	18
	1962	21	22			21	22
	1963	22	22	$ 25	$ 45	(3)	(23)
	1964	13	15	16	18	(3)	(3)
	1965	13	13	16	18	(3)	(5)
	1966	8	7	21	22	(13)	(15)
	1967	8	8	22	22	(14)	(14)
	1968	8	7	13	15	(5)	(8)
	Residuals	$150	$175	$113	$140	$ 37	$ 35
Finished Goods Inventory	Initially	$ 23	$ 23			$ 23	$ 23
	1960	3	3			3	3
	1961	3	3			3	3
	1962	2	2			2	2
	1963	3	3	$ 23	$ 23	(20)	(20)
	1964	2	2	3	3	(1)	(1)
	1965	3	3	3	3		
	1966	3	3	2	2	1	1
	1967	3	3	3	3		
	1968	3	3	2	2	1	1
	Residuals	$ 48	$ 48	$ 36	$ 36	$ 12	$ 12
Work in Process Inventory	Initially	$ 5	$ 5			$ 5	$ 5
	1960	1	1			1	1
	1961	1	1			1	1
	1962						
	1963	1	1	$ 5	$ 5	(4)	(4)
	1964			1	1	(1)	(1)
	1965	1	1	1	1		
	1966						
	1967	1	1	1	1		
	1968	1	1			1	1
	Residuals	$ 11	$ 11	$ 8	$ 8	$ 3	$ 3

* Low estimate (1959 sales contribution $250,000).
† High estimate (1959 sales contribution $450,000).

SCHEDULE IV (*Continued.*)

Raw Materials Inventory						
Initially	$ 20	$ 20			$ 20	$ 20
1960	2	2			2	2
1961	3	3			3	3
1962	2	2			2	2
1963	3	3	$ 20	$ 20	(17)	(17)
1964	2	2	2	2		
1965	3	3	3	3		
1966	2	2	2	2		
1967	3	3	3	3		
1968	2	2	2	2		
Residuals	$ 42	$ 42	$ 32	$ 32	$ 10	$ 10

Summary

Year Ending March 31	Total Difference		Present Value at 12%	
	Low*	High†	Low*	High†
Initially	$ 108	$ 128	$ 108	$ 128
1960	22	24	18	20
1961	23	25	17	18
1962	25	26	16	17
1963	(79)	(99)	(46)	(57)
1964	(5)	(5)	(3)	(2)
1965	(3)	(5)	(1)	(2)
1966	(12)	(14)	(5)	(5)
1967	(14)	(14)	(5)	(5)
1968	(3)	(6)	(1)	(2)
Residuals	$62	$60	$98	$107
Present value of incremental investment in working capital			$ 98	$ 107
Less difference in residuals at the end of 10 years	$ 62	$ 60	18	18
Present value of net increment investment in working capital			$ 80	$ 89

* Low estimate (1959 sales contribution $250,000).
† High estimate (1959 sales contribution $450,000).

Case VI-5. SCHEDULE V

Expensed Items to Be Treated as Investment

A. If Tularosa Plant Is Acquired
   March 31, 1958

Moving expense		$20,048
Startup costs	$29,019	
Less shipment of inventory	6,600	22,419
Per diem for training and administration		3,300
		$46,127
Less income taxes avoided		23,987

Present value of expensed items to be treated as investment if Tularosa plant is acquired March 31, 1958 $22,140

B. If Tularosa Plant Is Acquired as
   Facilities Are Needed

Expenses to be treated as investment, net of tax effect, as determined above, incurred March 31, 1963 $22,140

Discount factor at 12%   0.5488

Present value at March 31, 1958 of expensed items to be treated as investment if Tularosa plant is acquired as facilities are needed $12,150

CASE VI-5. SCHEDULE VI

Additional Annual Standby Costs*—Tularosa Plant

Additional production and maintenance standby expense	$ 26,000
Additional commercial standby not including sales standby expense	82,570
Additional office sales standby expense	11,360
Additional annual standby costs at the Tularosa plant*	$119,930

* Not including depreciation.

Case VI-5. SCHEDULE VII

Incremental Depreciation

Year Ending March 31,

	1959	1960	1961	1962	1963	1964	1965	1966	1967	1968
Actual Tularosa depreciation	$10,797	$20,943	$19,544	$18,065	$16,613	$15,186	$13,782	$12,399	$11,537	$10,771
Storage space—Nottingham	–0–	–0–	–0–	–0–	–0–	2,380	4,645	4,405	4,165	3,960
Total depreciation with Tularosa plant	$10,797	$20,943	$19,544	$18,065	$16,613	$17,566	$18,427	$16,804	$15,702	$14,731
Less depreciation expense if Tularosa plant were built at March 31, 1963:										
Storage space at Nottingham				(2,380)	(4,645)	(4,405)	(4,165)	(3,930)	(3,690)	(3,450)
Plant facilities built in 1963						(10,797)	(20,943)	(19,544)	(18,065)	(16,613)
Incremental depreciation —Tularosa plant	$10,797	$20,943	$19,544	$15,685	$11,968	$ 2,364	($6,681)	($6,670)	($6,053)	($5,332)

CASE VI-5. SCHEDULE VIII

Future Value of Incremental Cash Flow Resulting from Tularosa Plant—Low Estimate (All Figures in Thousands)*

	1959	1960	1961	1962	1963	1964	1965	1966	1967	1968	Total
Additional sales because Tularosa plant was built before facilities were required	$250	$410	$570	$780	$1,000	$1,130	$1,260	$1,340	$1,420	$1,500	
Less additional sales if Tularosa plant were built when facilities were required						(250)	(410)	(570)	(780)	(1,000)	
Incremental sales because Tularosa plant was built before facilities were required	$250	$410	$570	$780	$1,000	$880	$850	$770	$640	$500	
Profit contribution on incremental sales	$74	$121	$168	$230	$295	$260	$251	$227	$189	$147	
Less: Additional standby expenses as a result of acquiring the Tularosa plant at March 31, 1958	(120)	(120)	(120)	(120)	(120)						
Portion of profit contribution attributable to Nottingham facilities						($112)	(108)	(98)	(81)	(63)	
Incremental depreciation tax shield	(11)	(21)	(20)	(16)	(12)	(2)	7	7	6	5	
Incremental profit before taxes	$(57)	$(20)	$28	$94	$163	$146	$150	$136	$114	$89	
Less income taxes	30	10	14	49	84	76	78	71	59	(46)	
Incremental profit after taxes	$(27)	$(10)	$14	$45	$78	$70	$72	$65	$55	$43	
Incremental cash flow from depreciation	11	21	19	16	12	2	(7)	(7)	(6)	(5)	
Incremental cash flow	$(16)	$11	$33	$61	$90	$72	$65	$58	$49	$38	
Compounding factor at 12%	2.945	2.612	2.316	2.054	1.822	1.616	1.433	1.271	1.127	1.000	
Incremental cash flow compounded to March 31, 1968 at 12%	$(49)	$30	$77	$125	$164	$117	$93	$75	$55	$38	$725

* Figures may appear not to add correctly, but this is because they have been rounded off.

Case VI-5. SCHEDULE IX

Future Value of Incremental Cash Flow Resulting from Tularosa Plant— High Estimate (All Figures in Thousands)*

	1959	1960	1961	1962	1963	1964	1965	1966	1967	1968	Total
Additional sales because Tularosa plant was built before facilities were required	$ 450	$ 625	$ 800	$1,025	$1,250	$1,400	$1,525	$1,600	$1,675	$1,750	
Less additional sales if Tularosa plant were built when facilities were required						450	625	800	1,025	1,250	
Incremental sales because Tularosa plant was built before facilities were required	$ 450	$ 625	$ 800	$1,025	$1,250	$ 950	$ 900	$ 800	$ 650	$ 500	
Profit contribution on incremental sales	$ 133	$ 185	$ 236	$ 302	$ 369	$ 280	$ 265	$ 236	$ 191	$ 147	
Less: Additional standby expenses as a result of having the Tularosa plant	($ 120)	($ 120)	($ 120)	($ 120)	($ 120)						
Portion of profit contribution attributable to Nottingham facilities	($ 11)	($ 21)	($ 20)	($ 16)	($ 12)	($ 121)	($ 114)	($ 101)	($ 82)	($ 63)	
Incremental depreciation tax shield						($ 2)	$ 7	$ 7	$ 6	$ 5	
Incremental profit before taxes	$ 2	$ 44	$ 96	$ 166	$ 236	$ 157	$ 158	$ 141	$ 115	$ 89	
Less income taxes	($ 1)	($ 22)	($ 50)	($ 86)	($ 123)	($ 81)	($ 82)	($ 73)	($ 60)	($ 46)	
Incremental profit after taxes	$ 1	$ 20	$ 46	$ 80	$ 113	$ 76	$ 76	$ 68	$ 55	$ 43	
Incremental cash flow from depreciation	$ 11	$ 21	$ 20	$ 16	$ 12	$ 2	($ 7)	($ 7)	($ 6)	($ 5)	
Incremental cash flow	$ 12	$ 41	$ 66	$ 96	$ 125	$ 78	$ 69	$ 61	$ 49	$ 38	
Compounding factor at 12%	2.945	2.612	2.316	2.054	1.822	1.616	1.433	1.271	1.127	1.000	
Incremental cash flow compounded to March 31, 1968 at 12%	$ 34	$ 109	$ 152	$ 196	$ 229	$ 125	$ 99	$ 78	$ 56	$ 38	$1,118

* Figures may appear not to add correctly, but this is because they have been rounded off.

Case VI-5. SCHEDULE X

Return on Investment—Tularosa Plant

	Condition of Low Estimate of Sales Resulting from Tularosa Plant	Condition of High Estimate of Sales Resulting from Tularosa Plant
Present value of investment in property, plant and equipment if Tularosa plant is acquired March 31, 1958, per Schedule II	$229,837	$ 229,837
Less present value of investment in property, plant and equipment if facilities are acquired as needed, per Schedule III	107,009	107,009
Incremental investment in property, plant and equipment	$122,828	$ 122,828
Present value of expensed items to be treated as investment if Tularosa plant is acquired March 31, 1958, per Schedule V	$ 22,140	$ 22,140
Less present value of expensed items to be treated as investment if facilities are acquired as needed, per Schedule V	$ 12,150	$ 12,150
Incremental investment in expensed terms	9,990	9,990
Incremental investment in working capital, per Schedule IV	80,276	89,499
Incremental investment due to acquiring the Tularosa plant in 1958	$213,094	$ 222,317
Future value of incremental cash flow resulting from Tularosa plant as of March 31, 1968, per Schedules VIII and IX	$724,986	$1,117,950
Future value of incremental cash flow divided by present value of incremental investment	3.4022	5.0286
Return on investment—Tularosa plant	12.24%	16.15%

CASE VI-5.

Finance Officer's Computation of

Zero date: Oct. 1, 1958,
the start of full
production

	(1) Amount Paid Out: Fixed Assets and Working Capital in Millions of Dollars*	(2) Branch Sales in Millions	(3) Total Company Sales in Millions	(4) Branch Profit Contribution at 29.45% of Sales
Construction of building, started Oct. 1, 1957 and spread out over 1 year	($154,305) x			
Starting costs (uniformly 6 months prior to zero date)	(22,140)			
Machines and equipment (uniformly over 6 months prior to zero date)	(88,723) x			
1st half-year operation	(112,500) o	$0.550	$2.55	$161,975
1st full year	(137,500) o	1.200	5.60	353,400
2nd full year	(33,500) o	1.400	6.75	412,300
2½-year pattern and die replacement	(4,637) x			
3rd full year	(50,400) o	1.625	7.95	478,562
4th full year	(41,200) o	1.875	9.40	552,187
5th full year	(50,200) o	2.100	11.25	618,450
5½-year pattern and die replacement	(4,637) x			
6th full year	(49,600) o	2.300	13.30	677,350
7th full year	(19,800) o	2.475	15.70	728,887
7½-year tool replacement	(4,521) x			
8th full year	(49,300) o	2.625	18.50	773,062
8½-year pattern and die replacement	(4,637) x			
9th full year		2.775	21.50	817,238
½ full year	(35,100) o	1.425	11.50	419,662
Fixed asset total	(261,460)			
Working capital total	(579,100)			
Total Outlay	($830,560)			

* Key to column 1: x = fixed asset expenditure; o = working capital increase.

EXHIBIT I

Rate of Return for Tularosa Plant

(5)	(6)	(7)	(8)	(9)	(10)
Less Company-Wide Overhead Allocation: 7.2% of Sales	Tularosa Programmed and Standby Expenses	Profit Before Tax	Profit After Tax At 52%	Add Back Depreciation	Cash Inflow
$ 38,556	$103,000	$ 20,419	$ 9,801	$ 5,398	$ 15,199
92,232	206,000	55,168	26,480	15,870	42,351
106,560	206,000	99,740	47,875	20,243	68,118
122,400	206,000	150,162	72,078	18,804	90,882
140,904	206,000	205,283	98,563	17,339	115,875
158,112	206,000	254,338	122,082	15,899	137,981
176,256	206,000	295,094	141,645	14,484	156,129
183,600	206,000	229,287	162,858	12,970	175,828
201,600	206,000	365,462	175,421	11,848	187,269
198,720	206,000	412,518	198,009	11,169	209,178
99,360	103,000	217,302	104,305	5,400	109,705
				$149,424	

(*Continued.*)

EXHIBIT I (*Continued.*)

	(11)	(12)	(13)	(14)	(15)	(16)
	10 Per Cent Trial Rate			20 Per Cent Trial Rate		
	Factor	Amount: Column 10 × Factor	Amount: Column 1 × Factor	Factor	Amount: Column 10 × Factor	Amount: Column 1 × Factor
Construction of building, started Oct. 1, 1957 and spread out over 1 year	1.0517		($166,282)	1.1090		($171,124)
Starting costs (uniformly 6 months prior to zero date)	1.0254		(22,702)	1.0517		(23,285)
Machines and equipment (uniformly over 6 months prior to zero date)	1.0254		(90,977)	1.0517		(93,310)
1st half-year operation	1.0254	$ 15,588	(115,357)	1.0517	$ 15,985	(118,316)
1st full year	0.9516	40,301	(130,245)	0.9063	38,383	(124,616)
2nd full year	0.8611	58,656	(28,847)	0.7421	50,550	(24,860)
2½-year pattern and die replacement	0.7791		(3,613)	0.6075	2,817	
3rd full year	0.7791	70,806	(39,267)	0.6075	55,211	(30,618)
4th full year	0.7050	81,692	(29,046)	0.4974	57,636	(20,493)
5th full year	0.6379	88,018	(32,023)	0.4072	56,186	(20,441)
5½-year pattern and die replacement	0.5772		(2,676)	0.3334		(1,546)
6th full year	0.5772	90,118	(28,629)	0.3334	52,053	(16,537)
7th full year	0.5223	91,835	(10,341)	0.2730	48,001	(5,405)
7½-year tool replacement	0.4726		(2,137)	0.2235		(1,010)
8th full year	0.4726	88,503	(23,299)	0.2235	41,855	(11,019)
8½-year pattern and die replacement	0.4276		(1,983)	0.1830		(849)
9th full year	0.4276	89,445		0.1830	38,280	
½ full year	0.4072	44,672	(14,293)	0.1664	18,255	(5,840)
Total		$759,634	($737,717)		$475,212	($668,961)
Net discounted value (excluding residuals)			$ 21,917			($193,749)

Residuals after 9½ years:
Fixed assets: $261,460
Less depreciation: 149,424

Residual: $112,036
Ending working
  capital: $579,100

| Total residuals: | $691,136 | 0.3869 | | $267,400 | 0.1498 | $103,532 |
| Net discounted value (including residuals) | | | | $289,317 | | ($ 90,217) |

Interpolation before residual: $10 + \dfrac{21,917 (20 - 10)}{21,917 + 193,749} = 10 + \dfrac{219,170}{215,666} = 10 + 1 = 11\%$

Interpolation after residuals computed above: $10 + \dfrac{289,317 (20 - 10)}{289,317 + 90,217} = 10 + \dfrac{2,893,170}{379,536} = 10 + 7.6 = 17.6\%.$

CASE VI-6. WISCONSIN TELEPHONE COMPANY (A)
Preliminary Note on Public Utility Rate Regulation

This note presents the broad outlines of public utility rate regulations for those not familiar with the institutional phenomenon.

A public utility receives protection from the state as a monopoly; that is, the entry of other entrepreneurs into the same business in the same area is controlled by the state. In return, the public utility consents to serve all comers at the established rates and submits to rate control by the state. Rate control is directed to a control of the profits of the public utility and control over the rates charged to various classes of customers, particularly to avoid or minimize discrimination between classes of customers. Standards of service are also under state control.

The leading case on rate regulation had been *Smyth v. Ames* decided by the U.S. Supreme Court in 1898, under the constitutional limitation on deprivation of property without due process of law. The formula developed by this case was that a public utility is entitled to such rates as will yield a fair return on the fair value of its property devoted to public service. Since value depends upon return, this formula involved circular reasoning. In practice, however, this came to mean the examination of the assets of the utility and setting a value upon them. This is the rate base. Then a rate of return was established and applied against this rate base to determine what profit the public utility would be permitted a chance to earn. There was, of course, no guarantee that this profit could be achieved under the circumstances. The rate of return was usually determined by examining the returns being earned by other public utilities operating under similar conditions.

Then in 1944 in the *Hope* case, the U.S. Supreme Court adopted a new set of principles. A public utility was now to have such rates as represented a fair balancing of the interests of the investor in the securities of that utility against the interests of the customers of that utility (in lower rates and better service). The court very clearly ruled that the specific formula of *Smyth v. Ames* was not mandatory. Other formulae might be developed. Under this rule, the so-called "cost of capital" approach received a strong impetus. The cost of capital theory of rate regulation involves an examination of the right hand side of the balance sheet as opposed to the formula of *Smyth v. Ames,* which involves concentration on the left hand side of the balance sheet. The cost of capital theory seeks to determine what profit is needed by the

utility to maintain its securities and to continue to be able to attract
new capital when it is needed. Specifically this involves determining
the weighted average of returns needed for bonds, preferred stock
and common stock. In the case of the common stock component of
this average, consideration centers on yields, price-earnings ratios and
pay-out ratios. In the Wisconsin cases which follow, the application
of this cost of capital approach is illustrated.

Some states still adhere to the *Smyth v. Ames* thinking. In such
states, three categories have developed. The first is the "original cost"
school which starts with the depreciated book value of the assets as
the rate base. The second is the "reproduction cost" school which in
various ways seeks to determine as the rate base, the present cost of
reproducing the depreciated property at current costs. The third is
the "fair value" school which uses an average of the original cost rate
base and the reproduction cost rate base, using various weighting
systems.

Because it happens that in public utilities current assets are small in
relation to fixed assets and the difference between current assets and
current liabilities is smaller than in other businesses, the shift from
the asset side of the balance sheet as a rate base to the liability side
of the balance sheet as a rate base is not as drastic a step as might
appear at first blush.

The following references will be of assistance:

1. From the regulating commission's viewpoint: J. C. Bonbright,
"Public Utility Rate Control in a Period of Price Inflation," *Land
Economics*, vol. 27, no. 1, February 1951, p. 16.

2. From the utility's viewpoint: Walter Morton, "Rate of Return
and Value of Money in Public Utilities," *Land Economics*, vol. 28, no.
2, May 1952, p. 91.

3. Examining both of these and contributing further: E. W. Clemens,
"Some Aspects of the Rate of Return Problem," *Land Economics*, vol.
30, no. 1, February 1954, p. 32; Lionel Thatcher, "Cost of Capital
Techniques Employed in Determining the Rate of Return for Public
Utilities," *Land Economics*, vol. 30, no. 2, May 1954, p. 85; and
Fred P. Morrissey, "A Reconsideration of Cost of Capital and Reason-
able Rate of Return," *Land Economics*, vol. 31, no. 3, August 1955,
p. 229.

4. As to the disparity in the theory of rate control among the states:
E. E. Nemmers, "The Hope Case—Pandora's Box," *Illinois Law Review* (now *Northwestern Law Quarterly*), vol. 45, no. 4, September
1950, p. 460.

THE CASE *—CAPITAL BUDGETING—COST OF CAPITAL

The Wisconsin Telephone Co. is the largest telephone utility operating in Wisconsin. It is financed solely with common stock and is a wholly owned subsidiary of American Telephone and Telegraph Company. Wisconsin Telephone Company applied September 18, 1947, to the Wisconsin Public Service Commission for an increase in intrastate exchange rates. The post-World War II inflation had increased costs and reduced exchange earnings. An interim increase, subject to later refund orders, was granted while the involved matter of detailed investigation was carried on. The final decision was reached July 18, 1949.

In Wisconsin, rates for utilities are set on the cost of capital theory. This result can be expressed then as a return on depreciated original cost of plant actually in use, plus any allowance for working capital, supplies and materials.

The *total* condensed balance sheet for 1948 appears in Exhibit I. An income statement showing intrastate exchange operations only is also shown in Exhibit I. Intrastate plant and operations must be separated from interstate since the latter are subject to Federal Communications Commission regulation. Further, intrastate plant and operations must be separated into toll and exchange since the petition for rate increases relates only to exchange rates. When this is done, the book figures for net plant of intrastate exchange operations in 1948 is:

Plant in service	$104,670,000
Depreciation	30,616,000
Net Plant	$ 74,054,000

Separation is made on the use principle pursuant to a detailed manual adopted by regulatory bodies throughout the country.

Thus the net operating income of $2,402,000 from intrastate exchange operations is a return of 3.24 per cent on the net plant of $74,-054,000.

The utility was in the midst of converting one-half of its plant to dial operations. This change was expected to be achieved in five years and to involve substantial savings over manual operations.

Hence the Commission sought to set rates against the estimated

---

* Based on the record in Decision 2-U-2292 by the Wisconsin Public Service Commission. Interim decision in 32 P.S.C.W. 248 (1947) not reported in P.U.R. Final decision in 34 P.S.C.W. 311 (1949), 80 P.U.R. (N.S.) 482 and refund decision in 36 P.S.C.W. 113 (1951), 88 P.U.R. (N.S.) 89.

Additional data of the situation appear in Case IV-3, p. 284.

CASE VI-6. EXHIBIT I

Total Balance Sheet for Wisconsin Telephone Company June 30, 1948 (in Thousands)

Assets		Liabilities	
Telephone plant in service	$126,292	Common stock at par	$ 87,000
Telephone plant in		Surplus	5,455
construction	12,864	Total	$ 92,455
Property held for future		Depreciation	47,031
use	122	Current accrued	10,359
Other physical property	41	Deferred credits	37
Materials and supplies	3,475	Total	$149,882
Other investments	1		
Cash	1,786		
Other current (mostly			
receivables)	4,509		
Prepaid and deferred	792		
Total	$149,882		

Income Statement Year Ended December 31, 1948 as Estimated for Intrastate Exchange Operations (in Thousands)

Operating Revenues		Operating Expenses	
Local service	$30,258	Traffic	6,706
Toll service	—	Maintenance	9,673
Miscellaneous	1,997	Commercial	3,001
Less: bad debts	(50)	Accounting	617
Total	$32,205	Depreciation	3,007
		General	1,264
		Rent	206
		Pensions	1,346
		Social Security	327
		License contract	302
		Gross Revenue Tax	1,816
		Other operating taxes	28
		Total	$28,298

Operating Income		3,907
Income taxes		1,505
Net Operating Income		$ 2,402

situation as it would develop during the five years. This would reduce future rate proceedings.

Wisconsin Telephone Co. presented its computations as to intrastate rate base in Table I, which shows the combined toll and exchange data for intrastate rate base.

CASE VI-6. TABLE I

Estimated Wisconsin Intrastate Rate Base (in Thousands) Proposed by the Utility* and Intrastate Exchange Rate Base Allowed by the Commission

	1948	1949	1950	1951	1952
Telephone Plant					
Intrastate Toll	$ 29,818	33,837	37,520	42,069	45,139
All Exchanges	104,671	123,089	136,765	148,317	160,379
Total Intrastate	$134,489	156,926	174,285	190,386	205,518
Materials	2,812	2,345	1,878	1,880	1,883
Working Capital	1,636	1,635	1,647	1,667	1,707
Total	$138,937	160,906	177,810	193,933	209,108
Depreciation	42,081	40,363	41,006	43,212	46,851
Net Intrastate					
Rate Base	$ 96,856	120,543	136,804	150,721	162,257
Intrastate *Exchange*					
Base as *allowed* by					
Commission	$ 75,495	95,385	108,449	118,205	127,337

* Left-hand side of the Balance Sheet.

"Working capital" in rate cases is a term used otherwise than in the sense of current assets less current liabilities. It is, in this case, an estimate of the amount sufficient to cover expenses for 8 days in the case of exchange service and 36 days in toll service, these being the times elapsed between rendition of service and collection of the revenues. Against this is computed a credit for time between cost incurred and expense paid. Delay in income tax payment alone wipes out the working capital claim in the present case. The Commission rejected any allowance for working capital. The other differences between the company's proposed base (other than that one is for total intrastate plant and the other for intrastate exchange plant only) arise from differences in allocating book net plant between interstate, intrastate, toll and exchange.

Current costs and service rates showed 59 of the 77 exchanges of the utility operating at a loss but the overall earning of $4,253,725 for all

CASE VI-6. TABLE II

Computations Establishing the Company's Claim to a 6.75 Per Cent Return on the Rate Base

		In Thousands
1. Total Bell System capital*		$6,276,679
2. Deduct investment in certain non-consolidated companies		88,525
3. Balance of Bell System Capital		$6,188,154
4. Annual earnings needed at 6.75 per cent		417,000
5. Deduct		
License contract revenues	$23,582	
Western Electric income†	23,772	
Other income	4,748	
Total	$52,102	
Less A. T. and T. license contract expenses (other than long lines)	30,667	
Net Deduction		21,435
6. Annual earnings needed by Bell from telephone operations		395,565
7. Portion needed from Wisconsin intrastate in proportion of rate bases of total Bell and Wisconsin intrastate of 1.56 per cent		6,182
8. Tax savings‡ due to interest deductions of Bell as allocated to Wisconsin (at 1.56 per cent above)		381
9. Earnings needed from Wisconsin intrastate		5,801
10. Less earnings for disallowed intrastate rate base (mostly interest during construction and this is disallowed from a rate base in Wisconsin)		518
11. Operating income needed from Wisconsin intrastate operations		5,283
12. Per cent return on an assumed rate base of $78,036,000 as of 6/30/48 ($5,283,000/78,036,000)		6.77%

* The calculation establishing this figure is shown in Table III.

† Western Electric is the manufacturer of telephone equipment and is wholly owned by A. T. and T. The investment in Western Electric and income received from Western Electric are excluded in determining a rate base and income.

‡ This tax savings computation follows from the fact that Wisconsin Telephone Co. is financed 100 per cent by common stock whereas if it had the Bell System average of bonds in its capital structure, the earnings needed to cover bond interest would be a deduction for income taxes.

the company's operations showed a 4.05 per cent return because of (1) the profitability of the large exchanges such as Milwaukee and (2) the relative profitability of toll service.

The Comany's Position as to Rate Base and Rate of Return

The company contended for an allowable rate of return of 6.77 per cent on the intrastate exchange rate base. This rate of return was arrived at in the following manner on the ground that the true owner of Wisconsin Telephone Company is American Telephone and Telegraph Company.

In connection with the following calculations, American Telephone and Telegraph Company "licenses" its subsidiaries to use patents, services, etc., at a royalty of 1 per cent of annual revenues. In the computation shown in Table II, the contract rate for the license is ignored and the revenues from the license and the expenses of furnishing the licenses service are shown.

The 6.75 per cent (rounding of 6.77 per cent) earnings requirement of Bell System capital used above is established in the following manner. The utility argued that a reasonable capital structure for Bell is one third fixed charge capital, and two thirds common stock at the following rates:

One third fixed charge capital at   2.93% (cost)
Two thirds common capital stock at <u>8.67%</u>
Average   6.75%

The 2.93 per cent is the actual average of interest on outstanding debt of the Bell System. The utility cited the 1920–1947 average debt of 33.8 per cent for Bell. The Commission, however, would accept neither this debt-equity ratio nor the 8.67 per cent return on equity.

The Commission's Reasoning as to Rate of Return
Needed by Bell System as a Whole

On June 30, 1948, Bell System capital was 49 per cent fixed charge and 51 per cent common capital, established as shown in Table III. As listed in Table III, the 10-year convertible debentures are convertible at 140, the 15-year convertible debentures are convertible at 150. If all were presently convertible, the debt-common ratio would be 39.2 per cent debt and 60.8 per cent common.

Table IV shows relevant financial averages of A. T. and T. for 1920–1947, as submitted to the Commission. In Table IV, it is apparent that earnings declined so the $9-dividend was barely covered. Yet market price increased in recent years so that the yield dropped. From this the Commission concluded that 7.5 (and not 8.67)

CASE VI-6. TABLE III

Bell System's Division Between Debt and Equity on June 30, 1948

	In Thousands	Per Cent of Total
Common Stock A. T. and T. at par	$2,270,446	
Premiums	437,359	
Surplus	345,363	
	$3,053,168	
Common Stocks of subsidiaries held by public at par	96,614	
Applicable Surplus	4,551	
Total Common Capital—Bell System	$3,154,333	50.3%
Employees stock plan installments	47,818	0.7%
Fixed charge capital, A. T. and T.		
10 year convertible debentures, 1957	244,139	
15 year convertible debentures, 1961	279,485	
Other debentures	1,090,000	
	$1,613,624	
Debt of associated companies	1,443,000	
Preferred Stock of associated companies	17,904	
Total fixed charge capital	$3,074,528	49.0%
Total Bell System capital (as used in preceding calculation)	$6,276,679	100.0%

CASE VI-6. TABLE IV

Various Financial Averages for American Telephone and Telegraph Company

	1920–1947	1936–1940	1943–1947
Average investment per share	$137.22	$132.19	$134.30
Average market price per share	149.98	160.63	166.34
Average earnings per share	10.59	9.88	9.04
Per cent earned on average investment	7.72%	7.4 %	6.7 %
Per cent earned on market price	7.06%	6.2 %	5.4 %
Per cent dividends of market price	6.00%	5.6 %	5.4 %
Per cent dividends of earnings	85.00%	91.0 %	99.0 %

per cent was sufficient to maintain the equity investment and attract capital. It would have done so on the average for the preceding 10 years (as shown above in per cent earned on average investment from 1936 to 1947).

Assuming the convertible debentures are converted and applying this 7.5 per cent allowed by the Commission on equity, the return needed would be computed as follows:

CASE VI-6. TABLE V

Computation Showing Rate of Return Allowed by Commission

	Amount of Capital	Return	
		Amount	Per Cent
Common capital, including minority interest and employees	$3,963,173,000	$297,238,000	7.50%
Fixed-charge capital	2,550,904,000	75,648,000	2.97%
Total (or average)	$6,514,077,000	$372,886,000	5.72%

Using the actual A. T. and T. capitalization June 30, 1948 (with convertible debentures unconverted), and the return of 5.72 per cent on total capital structure (as just computed) would yield actual current earnings of 8.5 per cent on A. T. and T. common capital or $11.43 per share as appears in Table VI.

CASE VI-6. TABLE VI

Translation of Allowance of 5.72 Per Cent on Rate Base to $11.43 Per Common Share

	In Thousands
5.72 per cent on $6,276,679,000*	$359,026
Deduct fixed charges	90,003
Balance	$269,023
Deduct interest on employees installments at 2.0 per cent	961
Common stock earnings	$268,062
Earned on common capital (including minority interest) of $3,154,333,000	8.5%
Earnings per share A. T. and T. common (22,704,464 shares)	$11.43

* From Table III. Conversion rights would raise this to $6,514,077,000.

The Commission's Reasoning as to Rate Base

The Wisconsin rate base of $104,974,178 for intrastate exchange (the 5-year average of 1948–1952 allowed figures shown in Table I) represents 1.44 per cent of the total Bell System base for intrastate exchange. This percentage the Municipalities Defense Committee contended for. However, 1.56 per cent is the percentage if net total intrastate plant is computed against the parallel Bell System figure. In short, Wisconsin has relatively more intrastate toll plant than the system average. This the utility contended for.

The Commission elected to use a percentage of 1.454 per cent. This was used as the percentage of total *capital* (not rate base) devoted to Wisconsin intrastate operations. The Commission contended this was more logical since the total Bell System capital return requirement had been used to establish the return requirement on that part of the capital in Wisconsin. This 1.454 per cent was computed as shown in Table VII. The Commission rounded this up to 1.5 per cent on the

Case VI-6. TABLE VII

Computations Establishing Wisconsin's Percentage of Bell System Capital

	In Thousands
Total Bell System capital 6/30/48	$6,276,679
Less investment in nonconsolidated companies	88,525
Less investment in Western Electric	304,775
Bell System telephone capital	$5,883,379
Wisconsin capital 6/30/48	$ 92,455
Intrastate portion, 92.5 per cent (based on proportion of net intrastate Wisconsin plant of $73,299,000 to total Wisconsin plant $79,261,000)	$ 85,521
Per cent Wisconsin intrastate capital to Bell System capital	1.454%

ground that the current rate of increase in invested capital of the Bell System in Wisconsin exceeds that of the average of the Bell System as a whole.

The Commission's Adjustment of Rate of Return Needed by Bell System as a Whole to Recapture Profit of License Contract

The Commission then made certain adjustments to the allowed 5.72 per cent return on invested capital (determined in Table V) for the Bell System in order to arrive at the rate of return to be allowed in Wisconsin. These adjustments appear in Table VIII. The calculation in

CASE VI-6. TABLE VIII

Final Adjustments to Return Allowed Bell System

	In Thousands
5.72% on Bell System capital of $6,188,154,000 which is total capital less investment in non-consolidated companies	$353,962
Deduct license contract revenues	23,582
Deduct Western Electric Co. earnings computed at 7.8% (average of 1916–1947) on Western's investment of $304,775,000 on 6/30/48	23,772
Deduct other income	4,748
Credit A. T. and T. general expenses less that part billed to Long Lines	30,667
Total return required by Bell System for telephone operations	$332,527

Table VIII eliminates the intrasystem profit on the license contract by allowing only the applicable actual expenditures made by the parent company for the benefit of the subsidiaries.

Final Return Allowance Based on Preceding Findings of Commission

The Wisconsin portion of the Bell System telephone earnings requirement of $322,527,000 was computed by the commission as $4,637,000 which is arrived at as shown in Table IX. This 5.42 per cent allowed

CASE VI-6. TABLE IX

Final Adjustment of Rate of Return Allowed Wisconsin Telephone Company

	In Thousands
Bell System telephone earnings needed	$332,527
1.5 per cent portion allocable to Wisconsin intrastate before adjustment for income taxes	5,003
Income tax saving allocated to Wisconsin intrastate operations*	366
Net return needed from Wisconsin intrastate	$ 4,637
Per cent on Wisconsin intrastate capital of $85,521,000 on 6/30/48	5.42%

* The income tax saving follows the theory advanced by the Commission that since the Wisconsin Company has no debt capital, the Wisconsin Company is to be credited with a share of the tax savings gained by the debt financing of the Bell System as if Wisconsin had the same debt-equity ratio as the Bell System.

rate of return on Wisconsin intrastate capital (right hand side of balance sheet) was then converted to an allowance of 5.51 per cent on the intrastate *exchange* rate base (left hand side of balance sheet) of $75,495,000 which the Commission had allowed as shown in Table I above. No method of conversion was indicated. On a pro forma basis this 5.51 per cent would rise to 5.65 per cent within 2 years because of the savings in dial conversion.

The Issues

After the decision of the Wisconsin Public Service Commission, three professors were examining the impact of the case particularly with regard to its effect on the finances of the company and examining what the company might present in its next rate case. This next proceeding was certain to develop since wage increases were clearly on the horizon and these would drive down the profit of the company unless rates could again be raised.

The professorial group consisted of Professor Abercrombie, of the finance department, Professor Putnam, of the economics department and Professor Iola, of the law school.

Professor Abercrombie began by saying that the rate case had two basic questions: what the rate base should be and what the rate of return should be. As to rate base, the company had contended for an intrastate *exchange* rate base of $78,036,000 in terms of the right hand side of the balance sheet. The Commission had recognized a rate base for *total* intrastate (both exchange and toll) of $85,521,000 in terms of the right hand side of the balance sheet.

Professor Abercrombie continued that he did not see how it was possible to determine the way the commission split its allowed *total* intrastate capital of $85,521,000 into the intrastate exchange and intrastate toll components. Hence it would not be possible to determine exactly how much the company's figure of $78,036,000 (for intrastate *exchange*) had been whittled down.

Professor Iola stated that there did not seem to be sufficient legal basis to argue with the rate base decision. Under the Supreme Court's rule in the *Hope* case, if the end result, that is, the return on capital allowed by the decision of the Commission, were adequate to maintain the company's credit, then all legal objections to the decision would be at an end. He thought it much wiser to concentrate on rate of return.

Here Professor Putnam pointed out that the company contended for 6.77 (rounded to 6.75) per cent on its rate base and the commission allowed a rate of return of 5.42 per cent on its rate base.

Professor Putnam said the heart of the rate of return dispute centered on two points: the company contended for a capital structure with one-third debt and two-thirds common while the commission used 49.7 per cent debt and 50.3 per cent common. The other dispute was as to the earning to be allowed on the common, the company contended for 8.67 per cent and the Commission allowed 7.5 per cent.

Professor Putnam pointed out that the company had advanced the one-third debt and two-thirds common structure on the three fold basis that (1) this was the average ratio that had existed in the Bell System for many years; (2) this was close to the present ratio of 39.2 per cent debt and 60.8 per cent common *if* all the convertible debentures were converted; and (3) the telephone business could not on the average carry the 40 per cent debt which characterized electric utilities, for example, because the telephone business was subject to greater cyclical fluctuation than the electric power industry.

On the other hand, the Commission had used the actual debt-equity ratio as it presently stood for the company, being unwilling to treat convertible debentures as having been converted. Presumably the Commission would in future cases recognize new percentages of debt and common to the extent that the convertible debentures had then been converted. In short the Commission was claiming for telephone users the benefits of the convertible debentures so long as they remained unconverted.

Professor Abercrombie noted that with reference to the 7.5 per cent return figure the Commission had applied the average earning on the book value of its equity that Bell had earned from 1920 to 1947. The company's contention for 8.67 per cent on equity, had been arrived at in the following way. The Wisconsin commission had recently been allowing other telephone companies 6.5 to 6.8 per cent on total capital. Bell debt cost 2.97 per cent and taking the average allowable on all Bell capital as 6.77 per cent, it would require 8.67 per cent on equity to achieve the 6.77 per cent figure.

Professor Putnam said that one way to present the rate of return question in the next case would be to argue for the current cost of debt. Instead of using the actual interest requirement of 2.97 per cent, the current cost of bonds should be used. This was higher. If the Commission wanted to use the current cost of equity it must stay consistent and use the current cost of debt.

Professor Abercrombie said the Commission could take the position that debt and equity were different since the bondholder bargained for a fixed return over a fixed period and the stockholder bargained for current earnings.

Further, Professor Abercrombie said it seemed clear that the Commission was not going to allow Bell as much over-all as the 6.5 to 6.8 per cent it allowed smaller Wisconsin telephone companies. This, no doubt, followed the argument that a bigger company could get money cheaper and the telephone user was entitled to this benefit.

Professor Iola pointed out that in the *Southwestern Bell* case in the 1920's, Mr. Justice Brandeis had argued that a more efficient utility was entitled to a better than average earning. On this basis Bell might argue that it should be allowed at least part of the difference between the cost of capital of the smaller utility and the actual cost of capital of Bell.

Professor Putnam said that a much stronger argument could be made that inflation was corroding the stockholders' investment and that some adjustment should be made such as was the contention of Professor Walter Morton of the University of Wisconsin, namely, by a measure of the annual corrosive effects of inflation. This annual amount could be reduced to a percentage of the stock and included as a separate component of the rate of return.

On the other hand, Professor Putnam said, Professor Bonbright of Columbia University had been arguing that even if there was corrosion of utility common stocks, the investing public still liked them and poured forth its funds for new utility issues. Professor Bonbright's position was substantially that justice was not involved. The only question was to determine what rate of return was necessary to continue to draw forth the funds utilities needed.

CASE VI-7. WISCONSIN TELEPHONE COMPANY (B)*

Capital Budgeting—Cost of Capital

After the decision (Case VI-6) of July 18, 1949, by the Wisconsin Public Service Commission allowing the Wisconsin Telephone Co. an earning of 5.5 per cent on the intrastate exchange rate base, costs continued to rise rapidly. In particular, wages moved up sharply. As a result, earnings dropped to 4.4 per cent on the intra-state exchange rate base in 1952. Anticipating the delay involved in a rate case, the utility had filed a petition for an increase on April 27, 1951. During the course of the case, the Company presented its Balance Sheet and Income Statement as of December 31, 1951. This appears in Exhibit I. The final decision was reached April 9, 1952. A rate base of 121 million dollars was established in a manner similar to that in the preceding Wisconsin Telephone case.

The utility contended for a 7.5 per cent return on a rate base giving equal weight to original cost and current cost. The then current cost index was 140 per cent of original cost. Thus this would be equal to a 9 per cent return on the original cost base of 121 million dollars above. To get this amount would require rates yielding an annual 21.8 per cent return before income taxes. The Commission pointed out that this would be almost double the before-tax return to other telephone utilities in the state.

Outline of Conclusions of Experts

Jackson Martindell, a financial consultant, testified for the utility that its current cost of capital was between 7.5 and 8 per cent. He assumed a capital structure of one-third debt and two-thirds equity. Using a cost of debt of 3.25 per cent and a cost of equity of 10 per cent, he arrived at an average of 7.75 per cent. Martindell arrived at the 3.25 per cent figure for debt on the basis of utility bond issues during 1949, 1950, and 1951 to May 31. The 3.25 per cent he established as the current cost of debt. Equity cost was based on electric utility stock offerings of more than $10,000,000 each during the same 1949, 1950, and 1951 period using the earnings-issue-price ratios of 9.5 per cent in 1949, 10.4 per cent in 1950 and 10.3 per cent for 1951.

Milo Snyder, investment banker and securities dealer, testified for

---

* If Case VI-6 has not been used, the Preliminary Note on Public Utility Rate Regulation appearing before that case should be read.

Based on the record in Decision 2-U-3573 by the Wisconsin Public Service Commission. Final decision in 37 P.S.C.W. 166 (1952).

Additional data of the situation appear in Case IV-4, p. 292.

CASE VI-7. EXHIBIT I

Balance Sheet December 31, 1951 (in Thousands)

Assets		Liabilities	
Telephone plant	$186,555	Common stock	$122,000
Construction in progress	666	Advance	1,100
Miscellaneous	52	Customers deposits	1,419
Cash	2,727	Payables	6,600
Receivables	6,677	Taxes	11,681
Materials	1,633	Depreciation	49,644
Prepaid and Deferred	1,310	Deferred credits	58
Total	$199,620	Accruals	1,604
		Surplus	5,514
		Total	$199,620

Total Income Statement for Year Ended December 31, 1951 (in Thousands)

Operating Revenues		Operating Expenses	
Local	$36,935	Maintenance	$12,442
Toll	20,233	Depreciation	5,473
Miscellaneous	3,207	Traffic	10,744
Total	$60,375	Commercial	5,006
		Rent	620
		Miscellaneous	7,158
		Income Taxes	6,693
		Other Taxes	5,250
		Total	$53,386

Operating Income	6,989
Non-operating income (net)	108
	$ 7,097
Fixed charges	52
Net Income	$ 7,045

the utility to a current cost of capital to the utility of 7.5 per cent. His estimate used current debt cost of 3.25 per cent, current equity cost of 10 per cent and a debt-equity structure in the ratio of 37–63.

Snyder testified pessimistically about A. T. and T. as an investment and that his firm advised clients against the stock. Specifically, he criticized the issuance of convertible debentures by A. T. and T. and argued their success was due to the fact that the small and less informed investor was oversold on telephone stock.

Both Martindell and Snyder were of the opinion that the record number of A. T. and T. stockholders was an unhappy condition in that it indicated large and informed buyers were not buying. In the face of the large annual new capital requirements of A. T. and T., this boded no good.

Snyder testified that his firm would not recommend A. T. and T. as an investment until the pay-out ratio was down to 65 per cent while the dividend remained at $9.

Dr. James C. Bonbright, professor at Columbia University, appeared for the staff of the Wisconsin Public Service Commission and testified as to the cost of capital to the Bell System. Lack of time prevented him from studying the local peculiarities of the Wisconsin Telephone Company. Bonbright concluded the over-all cost of capital to the Bell System was 6.25 per cent, using a capital structure of 45 per cent debt and 55 per cent common equity. He took the cost of debt capital as 3 per cent, the approximate actual cost of Bell System debt. The cost of equity was estimated first, at 8.71 per cent or the earnings necessary to maintain the $9 dividend with a 75 per cent pay-out ratio, and second, at 8.89 per cent, the earnings ratio indicated by a dividend yield of 6 per cent, with 10 per cent allowance for under-pricing and a 75 per cent dividend pay-out. Weighting this with 3 per cent debt requires average earnings of 6.14 and 6.24 per cent, respectively.

Bonbright stated that he placed greater reliance on his first method (accepting the established dividend) rather than the second, which involves the bothersome problem of underpricing and also some conjecture as to what average market yield should be used.

Asel Colbert, Chief of the Accounts and Finance Department of the Commission, testified that a 5.50 per cent return would be reasonable after crediting to Wisconsin its share of the federal income tax savings due to the interest expense of A. T. and T. Company and the fact that Wisconsin Telephone Co. is financed 100 per cent by common stock, all held by A. T. and T. Without this tax adjustment the return would be 5.85 per cent.

The 5.85 per cent for Bell *telephone* activities stems from a 6 per cent return requirement for all Bell activities. The 6 per cent represents the weighted average of the actual cost of Bell debt of 2.93 per cent, the actual 6 per cent on preferred stock capital and 7.77 per cent on common stock equity assuming the conversion of all convertible debentures (with the resultant 37–63 ratio of debt to common equity and with the small amount of preferred actually outstanding).

A 7.7 per cent return for common equity would result if one assumes the $9 dividend and an 85 per cent dividend pay-out ratio or an earning

of $10.60 per share or 7.62 per cent on book value. The 7.7 per cent
equity return would produce a Bell System weighted average return
of 5.9 per cent. If 5.9 per cent is rounded to 6 per cent, this would give
common earnings of $10.82 per share or 7.77 per cent on book value
and a pay-out of 83.2 per cent.

From a 6 per cent figure just indicated, Colbert deducted the average
earnings on the Western Electric Company investment of A. T. and T.,
the net income from the license contract and miscellaneous activities
to arrive at 5.88 per cent needed for the telephone business.

The Commission's Analysis of the Experts' Conclusions and Methods

The Commission accepted the Bonbright-Colbert debt cost figure of
3 per cent on the ground that the relevant cost was the actual interest
payments to be covered and not what the cost would be if the bonds
were now to be sold.

On the cost of equity capital, Martindell had justified the use of
electric utilities as "the best available data on direct offers of common
stock in recent periods." Snyder argued that equity capital to utilities
had cost at least 10 per cent in terms of prospective earnings. Martindell passed by the fact that A. T. and T. had procured 40 per cent
of its equity between January 1, 1946, and October 31, 1951, and had
raised more than half of this amount during 1950 and 1951. The Commission pointed out that Martindell's 10 per cent was based on electric
utilities with 49.62 per cent debt, 17.67 per cent preferred stock and
32.71 per cent common stock with a weighted cost of 5.66 per cent using
10 per cent for equity, 4.5 per cent for preferred and 3.2 per cent for
debt. However, the Commission pointed out that the Martindell comparison was rather fair as indicated by Table I, if one uses 8.08 per
cent as the cost of equity for a telephone utility.

But the question is whether a 10 per cent cost of equity can be
applied to a telephone company with an assumed 33–67 debt-equity
ratio. If so, then a telephone company with thin equity would find
its equity cost more than 10 per cent. But General Telephone Corporation with only 24 per cent equity (lower than the thirteen electric
utilities) in 1951 issued new common at an earnings-issue-price basis
of 11.3 per cent.

The Commission pointed out that while Bonbright used a 75 per cent
pay-out ratio, he also used a 55 per cent common equity rate while
Colbert used an 85 per cent pay-out ratio with a 63 per cent common
equity ratio. This reduced the significance of the differences in pay-
out ratios used. These the Commission claimed were normal relationships, citing an exhibit of electric utilities showing a dividend pay-out
average of 76 per cent for utilities with 55 per cent common equity

CASE VI-7. TABLE I

Debt-Equity Ratios and Costs of Capital for Thirteen Electric Utilities

		Cost of Capital	
	Security Ratio	Per Cent	Weighted
13 Electric Utilities 12/31/50			
Common Stock	32.70%	10.00%	3.27%
Preferred Stock	17.67%	4.50	0.80
Total Stock	50.38%	8.08	4.07
Debt	49.62%	3.20	1.59
	100.00%	—	5.66
Bell System 3/31/51			
Total Stock	51.63%	8.08	4.17
Debt	48.37%	2.97	1.44
	100.00%	—	5.61

while the pay-out average was 83 per cent for utilities with 63 per cent common equity.

Martindell advocated increasing either the rate base or the rate of return to compensate the utility investor for inflation. Bonbright, in response, pointed to the successful issuance of large amounts of new utility stocks after inflation was apparent as an indication that there was no drying up of the source of utility capital because of its failure to furnish an inflation hedge. Any "escalator clause" for utility investors as an inflation protection would itself be inflationary and create discrimination against other fixed-income groups in the economy.

The Commission accepted Colbert's reasoning that if an inflation clause were put in utility common stocks, this investment would be higher-grade than bonds or preferred stocks during a period of rising prices and hence it would carry a low return. The Commission concluded that "if in the face of alternative investment opportunities, the allowed rate of return attracts the necessary utility capital, then it has made full allowance for the factor of inflation."

The Commission allowed 6.1 per cent for the entire Bell System capital. This is 6 per cent for the telephone capital or 5.7 per cent for Wisconsin after giving effect to the income tax saving allocation.

The Issues

The same professors who had met to discuss Case VI-6 met again to discuss this second Wisconsin Telephone Co. case decision. These were Abercrombie of finance, Putnam of economics, and Iola of the law school. By this time each of the professors had already been contacted by utilities and commissions in different parts of the country to serve as expert witnesses since the number of rate cases had swelled and there was a heavy demand for experts to testify in these cases.

Professor Abercrombie opened by stating he was preparing to testify for utilities. He felt there were questions which had not yet been considered in these rate cases. For one thing, what about the future? Every business involves risk. If there is inadequate compensation for risk, then the business must somehow seek to reduce the risk. In the utility business one can reduce risk by reducing replacements and holding the lid on expansion of both plant and service. This may be to the disadvantage of society. It also raises injustices between past, present, and future utility users. Instead of current users paying current costs and past users past costs, the decision of the Wisconsin Commission let current users have the benefit of debt contracts, favorable to the current consumers but negotiated in past years. In the failure to allow some increase in return as a compensation for the inadequacy of present depreciation charges to permit generating the funds needed for replacements in the future, the commission was simply making sure that vast new issues would be required in the future (a) to fill the gap created by inadequacy of the depreciation reserve to provide replacements; and (b) to provide for the great growth in the future following on the "baby boom" that started after World War II. The returns needed to support such issues would be higher than if future issues were smaller.

Professor Putnam said he was going to testify for the commissions. Against Abercrombie's argument he cited the fact that improved technology had always closed the gap that bothered Abercrombie. When it came time for replacement, the funds would not be there to replace what was worn out but, on the other hand, a more efficient replacement would be available. Efficiency in the utility business was increasing just about as fast as the price level.

Professor Abercrombie suggested that such statements ought to be quantified with specific figures.

Professor Putnam said he would offer some. About 75 per cent of the plant dollars on the Wisconsin Telephone Company balance sheet of December 31, 1951 (Exhibit I) were invested in the post-World War II years. Depreciation on that plant was about right then in terms of the price level.

Professor Abercrombie said that it seemed to him this thing must be answerable in terms of the type of computation of weighted cost of capital used by the Commission in the second Wisconsin Telephone Co. case.

Professor Iola said that the law seemed to be that the Commission should allow a rate of return that took some account of the prospective effect of the rate decision and did not stop the clock at a particular instant to see if the rate of return was proper at that point in time.

Professor Abercrombie then jumped on the argument used in the second Wisconsin Telephone Co. case by Professor Bonbright, that the ability of the utilities to get money in 1949 to 1951 from investors who apparently did not realize the effects of inflation proved that it was not necessary to make an allowance for inflation in the determination of rate of return. This approach was bound to lead to disaster. Investors would eventually become "sour" on utility common stocks and would demand an unduly high rate of return. Future rate payers would suffer. Abercrombie concurred in the judgment of Snyder that telephone (and other utility) stocks had been "oversold" to small investors.

Professor Putnam countered that pension funds, profit-sharing trusts and similar funds had been piling up rapidly since World War II. Corporations were turning more and more to financing through retained earnings rather than new issues. The supply of funds seeking investment had simply gotten way ahead of investment opportunities. In addition, the investor was favoring equity more and more rather than debt securities. Hence the yield of stocks would go down and their price-earnings ratios higher and higher. The pendulum was simply swinging in favor of the utility rate payer as a result of all this. No doubt at some time in the future the pendulum would swing the other way and the utility rate payer would be hard hit. Putnam said he expected that in the immediate future the rate on new utility debt would rise sharply. Certainly this was indicated by his analysis of the bond situation.

appendix 1

List of cases and pages on

which they appear

485

appendix 2

List of economic series available in this book and pages on which they appear

INDEX

DATE DUE

M.